Eckard Rolf (Hrsg.)

Pragmatik

Linguistische Berichte
Sonderheft 8/1997

Eckard Rolf (Hrsg.)

Pragmatik

Implikaturen und Sprechakte

Springer Fachmedien Wiesbaden GmbH

Linguistische Berichte
Forschung   Information   Diskussion

Herausgeber
Günther Grewendorf (Universität Frankfurt)
Arnim von Stechow (Universität Tübingen)

Beirat
Hans Altmann (München), Ria de Bleser (Aachen), Manfred Bierwisch (Berlin),
Rainer Dietrich (Berlin), Norbert Dittmar (Berlin), Sascha W. Felix (Passau),
Hubert Haider (Stuttgart), Joachim Jacobs (Wuppertal), Wolfgang Klein (Nijmegen),
Manfred Krifka (Austin), Klaus Mattheier (Heidelberg), Uwe Mönnich (Tübingen),
Frans Plank (Konstanz), Dieter Wunderlich (Düsseldorf), Theo Vennemann (München)

Redaktion
Günther Grewendorf (Universität Frankfurt), Herwig Krenn (Universität Bochum),
Klaus Müllner (Kelkheim), Arnim von Stechow (Universität Tübingen)

Alle *redaktionellen* Zuschriften und Sendungen erbitten wir nur an die verantwortliche Redaktion der Linguistischen Berichte, z. Hd.: Professor Günther Grewendorf, Johann Wolfgang Goethe-Universität Frankfurt, Institut für Deutsche Sprache und Literatur II, Gräfstr. 76, D-60486 Frankfurt am Main.

Mitteilungen, die für das LB-Info bestimmt sind, schicken Sie bitte immer an die Teilredaktion LB-Info, zu Händen von Prof. Dr. Herwig Krenn, Romanisches Seminar der Ruhr-Universität Bochum bzw. Herrn Klaus Müllner, Postfach 21 51, D-65779 Kelkheim.

Die Linguistischen Berichte erscheinen sechsmal im Jahr. Jahrgangsumfang ca. 480 S.

Jährlich erscheint ein Sonderheft, das je nach Umfang berechnet und den Abonnenten bei Bezug im Jahr des Erscheinens mit einem Nachlaß gegen Rechnung geliefert wird.

Bezugsbedingungen

Jahresabonnement (1997)	DM 154,– / öS 1124,– / sFr 137,–
Studentenabonnement (1997)	DM 88,– / öS 642,– / sFr 80,–
Zweijahresabonnement (1997/98)	DM 277,– / öS 2022,– / sFr 246,–
Jahresabonnement priv. (1997)	DM 88,– / öS 642,– / sFr 80,–x
Zweijahresabonnement priv. (1997/98)	DM 158,– / öS 1153,– / sFr 141,–x
Einzelheftpreis	DM 27,– / öS 197,– / sFr 25,–
	jeweils zuzüglich Versandkosten

Alle Bezugspreise und Versandkosten unterliegen der Preisbindung.

Jede Verwertung außerhalb der engen Grenzen des Urheberrechtsgesetzes ist ohne Zustimmung des Verlags unzulässig und strafbar. Das gilt insbesondere für Vervielfältigungen, Übersetzungen, Mikroverfilmungen und die Einspeicherung und Verarbeitung in elektronischen Systemen.

© 1997 Springer Fachmedien Wiesbaden
Ursprünglich erschienen bei Westdeutscher Verlag GmbH, Opladen 1997

ISSN 0935-9249
ISBN 978-3-531-13105-4   ISBN 978-3-663-11116-0 (eBook)
DOI 10.1007/978-3-663-11116-0

Inhalt

Eckard Rolf (Münster)
Einleitung 7

Tanja Autenrieth (Tübingen)
Tautologien sind Tautologien 12

Kent Bach (San Fransisco)
The Semantics-Pragmatics Distinction: What It Is and Why It Matters 33

Thomas Becker (München)
Was wir von Aristoteles über die Bedeutung deutscher Wörter lernen können:
Über konversationelle Implikaturen und Wortsemantik 51

Graham H. Bird (Manchester)
Explicature, Impliciture, and Implicature 72

Diane Blakemore (Southampton)
On Non-Truth Conditional Meaning 92

Robyn Carston (London)
Enrichment and Loosening: Complementary Processes in Deriving the Proposition Expressed? 103

Steven Davis (Burnaby)
Conversation and Norms 128

Jörg Hagemann (Hamburg) / *Eckard Rolf* (Münster)
Nicht-zentrale Sprechakte 145

Robert M. Harnish (Tucson)
Performatives and Standardization: A Progress Report 161

Josef Klein (Koblenz)
Kategorien der Unterhaltsamkeit. Grundlagen einer Theorie der Unterhaltung mit
kritischem Rückgriff auf Grice 176

Frank Liedtke (Düsseldorf)
Gesagt - getan: Über illokutionäre Indikatoren 189

Georg Meggle (Leipzig) / *Maria Ulkan* (München)
Informatives and/or Directives? (A New Start in Speech Act Classification) . . . 214

Jörg Meibauer (Tübingen)
Modulare Pragmatik und die Maximen der Modalität 226

Beatrice Primus (Stuttgart)
Maximen in Interaktion: Faktoren der Informativitätsverstärkung 257

Anne Reboul / Jacques Moeschler (Genf)
Reduction and Contextualization in Pragmatics and Discourse Analysis 283

Eckard Rolf (Münster)
Der 'Gricesche Konversationszirkel' 296

Savas L. Tsohatzidis (Thessaloniki)
Why Gricean Democracy Is Worse than Either Russellian or Strawsonian
Monarchy 312

Daniel Vanderveken (Québec)
Formal Pragmatics of Non Literal Meaning 324

Mitarbeiter dieses Sonderheftes 342

Einleitung*

Was unter 'Pragmatik' verstanden werden könnte, muß hier nicht eigens erläutert werden: es kann den einschlägigen Monographien, Anthologien und Einführungen ohne Mühe entnommen werden (s. z. B. Blakemore 1992, Davis 1991, Gazdar 1979, Green 1989, Grundy 1995, Levinson 1983, Mey 1993, Segerdahl 1996, Yule 1996). Wie der Untertitel des vorliegenden Sonderheftes verrät, werden zwei der fünf Teilgebiete behandelt, die Levinson dem Bereich der Pragmatik subsumiert: Deixis, Präsuppositionen und Gesprächsstrukturen bleiben außen vor, fokussiert werden Konversations-Implikaturen und Sprechakte. Die Konzentration auf diese Teilgebiete geschieht nicht ohne Grund, denn gerade die Implikaturen und die Sprechakte haben die Aufmerksamkeit in den vergangenen Jahren erneut auf sich zu lenken gewußt. Letzteres mag sich den posthum erschienenen *Studies in the Way of Words* (Grice 1989) verdanken, ebenso den Arbeiten Horns (1988, 1989), Hirschbergs (1991), einem von Tsohatzidis (1994) herausgegebenen Aufsatzband sowie den Monographien zur Illokutionslogik (s. Searle & Vanderveken 1985; Vanderveken 1990, 1991). Vornehmlich durch die Sprechakttheorie und die Theorie der Konversations-Implikaturen ist der Weg zu einer *systematischen* Pragmatik frei geworden: "It was partly the work of the speech act theorists (Austin and Searle in particular), but especially the work of Paul Grice, that opened up the prospect of a systematic pragmatics." (Levinson 1995: 91)

Der K.u.K.-Zusammenhang, das Gricesche Konstrukt, bestehend aus Kooperationsprinzip und Konversationsmaximen, gehört zum *Hintergrund der Bedeutung* im Sinne Searles (vgl. Searle 1980 und 1983: 141ff.). Überhaupt besteht zwischen den Überlegungen Searles und denjenigen von Grice von Anfang an eine gewisse Nähe. Es sind Thesen Searles, mit denen sich Grice bei dem, was er 1967 in seiner Vorlesung in Harvard vorträgt, in nicht unerheblichem Maße auseinandersetzt (vgl. Rolf 1995).

Die - insgesamt elf - Griceschen Konversationsmaximen (um von anderen hier schweigen zu dürfen) haben noch nicht überall die ihnen gebührende Beachtung gefunden - obwohl zutreffen könnte, was Heringer behauptet, wenn er sagt:

> Eine der größten linguistischen Entdeckungen dieses Jahrhunderts sind nach meiner Meinung die Griceschen Maximen. Und ich denke, daß hier wirklich die Redeweise 'Entdeckungen' angebracht ist, wo sonst in der Darstellung linguistischer Theorien eher der Ausdruck 'Erfindungen' zu wählen wäre. Die Griceschen Maximen haben uns das Funktionieren menschlicher Kommunikation besser verstehen lassen, sie haben die kommunikative Analyse entscheidend verbessert, sie haben auch den Grund gelegt für eine Ethik der Kommunikation. Es ist verblüffend, daß es so lange dauerte, bis sie entdeckt wurden. (Heringer 1994: 40f.)

Den Griceschen Maximen (oder vereinfachten Versionen derselben) kann hinsichtlich der menschlichen Kommunikation so etwas wie Allgegenwärtigkeit attestiert werden. Die Maximen werden nicht nur dann 'aufgerufen', wenn gegen sie flagrant verstoßen wird, den Kommunikationspartnern dienen sie als Orientierungsgrößen auch dann, wenn Äußerungen gemacht worden sind, die als normal, unauffällig, unmarkiert einzustufen sind. Man könnte die Griceschen Maximen, wie Levinson (1995: 96) vorschlägt, als *Standardheuristiken* betrachten, als Systeme von Annahmen, auf die zurückgegriffen wird, um den Informationsgehalt von Äußerungen anzureichern - was in einer vorhersagbaren Weise geschehen kann, es sei denn, es wird explizit angezeigt, daß die entsprechenden Annahmen im gerade vorliegenden Fall nicht zutreffen. Solche Standardheuristiken können die Aufmerksamkeit auf das jeweils Nicht-Gesagte lenken - und auf diese Weise metasprachliche Information in den Blick bringen, sie können aber z. B. auch Informationen herausfiltern, die sich auf stereotype Eigenschaften der jeweils thematisierten Domäne beziehen. Zusammen mit den Heuristiken und dem semantischen Gehalt der jeweiligen Äußerung stellen diese - metasprachlichen und Weltstruktur-bezogenen - Informationen eine Prämissenmenge bereit, die Folgerungen ergibt, aufgrund derer Infomationen in Äußerungen hineingelesen werden können (vgl. Levinson 1995: 97ff.).

Die Beiträge dieses Sonderheftes befassen sich schwerpunktmäßig (A) mit Fragen aus dem Kontext der Theorie der Konversations-Implikaturen oder (B) mit Fragen sprechakttheoretischer Art; (C) es gibt auch Beiträge, in denen auf beide Theoriekomplexe gleichermaßen Bezug genommen wird.

Dem Bereich A sind die Artikel von Tanja Autenrieth, Kent Bach, Thomas Becker, Graham H. Bird, Diane Blakemore, Robyn Carston, Steven Davis, Josef Klein, Jörg Meibauer, Beatrice Primus, Eckard Rolf und Savas L. Tsohatzidis zuzurechnen, dem Bereich B gehören die Beiträge von Robert M. Harnish, Frank Liedtke und Georg Meggle / Maria Ulkan an, am ehesten in den Bereich C gehören die Beiträge von Daniel Vanderveken und Jörg Hagemann / Eckard Rolf; der Artikel von Anne Reboul / Jacques Moeschler ist allgemeinerer und grundsätzlicherer Art.

Tanja Autenrieth unterzieht mit den Tautologien eine Äußerungsart einer eingehenden Untersuchung, die oftmals mit der ersten Griceschen Konversationsmaxime in Verbindung gebracht wird (vgl. Levinson 1983, 110f.). Autenrieth versucht zu erkunden, inwiefern die kontextuelle Unangemessenheit bestimmter Typen tautologischer Sätze bereits auf deren semantischen Gehalt zurückgeführt werden kann.

Kent Bach widmet sich der sogenannten Semantik/Pragmatik-Schnittstelle. Er unterscheidet zwischen semantischer und pragmatischer Information. Die erstere ist sprachlichen Ausdrücken (Sätzen und deren Konstituenten) zu entnehmen, die letztere deren Äußerungen. Semantische Information ist in dem verschlüsselt, was geäußert wird, pragmatische Information wird durch den Akt der Äußerung erzeugt. Die Interpretation eines Satzes ist grundsätzlich von der Interpretation einer Äußerung zu unterscheiden: die erstere ist Ausdruck einer speziellen Sprachkompetenz, die letztere Ausdruck einer allgemeinen kommunikativen Rationalität.

Thomas Becker untersucht die Implikationsverhältnisse subkonträrer und subalterner Sätze. Er zeigt zum einen auf, inwiefern Sätze, die Ausdrücke enthalten, die im Südwesten

(I) beziehungsweise Südosten (O) des logischen Quadrats anzusiedeln sind, einander wechselseitig konversationell implizieren; anhand solcher Differenzpaare wie 'und/oder', 'müssen/können' und 'weil/wenn' wird zudem demonstriert, inwiefern die Wahl der einen Ausdrucksalternative die signifikante Nicht-Wahl der jeweils anderen ist.

Graham H. Bird widmet sich einer Differenzierung, mit deren Hilfe das Gebiet zwischen dem Gesagten und dem konversationell Implizierten genauer erfaßt werden soll. Bird unterscheidet zwischen (i) dem, was ein Sprecher tatsächlich gesagt hat - im Unterschied zu dem, was er eigentlich nicht gesagt hat; (ii) dem, was der Sprecher wörtlich gemeint hat - im Unterschied zu dem, was er im übertragenen Sinne gemeint hat; und (iii) dem, was der Sprecher tatsächlich gemeint hat - im Unterschied zu dem, was er eigentlich nicht gemeint hat.

Diane Blakemore versucht den Begriff des konventional Implizierten zu vermeiden. Zu diesem Zweck unterscheidet sie eine konzeptionelle von einer prozeduralen Bedeutung. Diese Differenz soll nicht konfundiert werden mit der Differenz wahrheitsfunktional/nichtwahrheitsfunktional. Blakemore bezieht sich auf Grices - im Hinblick auf Sätze, die z. B. solche Ausdrücke wie 'confidentially' enthalten, getroffene - Unterscheidung zwischen untergeordneten und übergeordneten Sprechakten. Ein Sprechakt der letzteren Art 'kommentiert' den untergeordneten Sprechakt in einer bestimmten Weise. Ausdrücke wie 'confidentially' haben keinen Einfluß auf die Wahrheitsbedingungen der sie beherbergenden 'Gast'-Sätze, sind deshalb auch nicht zu deren konzeptioneller Bedeutung zu rechnen, sondern, als Kommentare, zur prozeduralen Bedeutung.

Robyn Carston befaßt sich mit zwei Möglichkeiten, die wörtliche Bedeutung hinter sich zu lassen: (i) Anreicherung ('enrichment'), (ii) Lockerung ('loosening'). Carston legt dar, daß diese beiden Interpretationsverfahren (a) unterschiedliche kognitive Effekte haben, daß sie (b) in einem (scheinbar) asymmetrischen Verhältnis zueinander stehen und daß (c) die Anreicherung in bestimmten Fällen gleichzusetzen ist mit der negierten Lockerung.

Steven Davis legt dar, daß der K.u.K.-Zusammenhang unter anderem auch im Sinne einer Spezifikation *praktischer* oder *moralischer* Normen aufgefaßt werden kann. Davis reformuliert die erste Gricesche Qualitätsmaxime als 'Maxime der Aufrichtigkeit': "Don't be insincere in your linguistic interventions." Dies soll keine instrumentelle Maxime sein, sondern eine Maxime des 'Hintergrunds'.

Jörg Hagemann und *Eckard Rolf* beziehen sich auf eine Erscheinung, die bisher wenig beachtet worden ist: nicht-zentrale Sprechakte. Es werden Überlegungen vorgetragen, die darzulegen versuchen, wie Sprechakte dieses Typs in sprechakttheoretischer beziehungsweise illokutionslogischer Hinsicht einzuschätzen sind.

Robert M. Harnish befaßt sich mit zwei alternativen Erklärungsmodellen für das Phänomen der 'Standardisierung': Danach beruht die Performativität performativer Äußerungen (i) entweder auf der kontextuellen Unangemessenheit ihrer konstativen Interpretation oder (ii) auf dem Umstand, *daß* der geäußerte Satz *geäußert* wird. Dem zweiten Erklärungsmodell zufolge muß nicht, was ein Vorteil sein könnte, angenommen werden, daß performative Äußerungen konstativ sind.

Josef Klein formuliert Maximen der Unterhaltungskommunikation, die von der (bloßen) Informationskommunikation unterschieden wird. Während das Ziel der Informationskommunikation in der Erweiterung des Wissens oder der Vermittlung von Erkenntnissen gesehen wird, soll die Unterhaltungskommunikation auf Entspannung abzielen. *Abwechslung, Unbeschwertheit, Interessantheit* und *Eingängigkeit* stellen die Dimensionen dar, denen die einzelnen Maximen der Unterhaltungskommunikation subsumiert werden.

Frank Liedtke vertritt die Auffassung, daß illokutionäre Indikatoren die illokutionäre Kraft einer Äußerung *indizieren*, daß sie die illokutionäre Kraft aber nicht *konstituieren* oder *modifizieren*. Liedtke unterscheidet zwei Verwendungsweisen für illokutionäre Indikatoren: (i) den resultativen Modus und (ii) den instrumentalen Modus. Für den instrumentalen Verwendungsmodus wird eine Definiton des Indikatorbegriffs vorgeschlagen.

Georg Meggle und *Maria Ulkan* versuchen die Informationshandlungen als die grundlegenden kommunikativen Akte auszuweisen. Aufforderungshandlungen können dann als spezielle Informationshandlungen bestimmt werden. Jede Aufforderungshandlung ist *auch* eine Informationshandlung, jede Informationshandlung ist *auch* eine Aufforderung. Den Informationshandlungen sollen, nach Meggle / Ulkan, alle anderen Sprechakttypen subsumiert werden können.

Jörg Meibauer diskutiert Möglichkeiten einer Reduktion der Griceschen Modalitätsmaximen und zeigt Vorteile einer solchen Reduktion auf (z. B. soll der Verarbeitungsaufwand von Äußerungen verringert sein).

Beatrice Primus versucht darzulegen, daß es Implikaturen gibt, denen eine Maximen-*Interaktion* zugrunde liegt. Unterschieden werden Implikaturen, die auf einer Interaktion der ersten Griceschen Quantitätsmaxime beruhen (i) mit einer der Qualitätsmaximen (qq-Implikaturen), (ii) mit einer 'Höflichkeitsmaxime' (qh-Implikaturen) und (iii) der Relationsmaxime (qr-Implikaturen).

Anne Reboul und *Jacques Moeschler* vertreten, ausgehend von bestimmten Definitionen für die Größen 'Diskurs' und 'Äußerung', die These, daß ein Diskurs reduzierbar ist auf die Äußerungen, aus denen er besteht und auf die Beziehungen, die zwischen diesen Äußerungen existieren.

Eckard Rolf setzt sich mit einem von Levinson gegen Grice erhoben Zirkularitäts-Vorwurf auseinander. Diesem Vorwurf zufolge spielt das Gesagte bei Grice nicht nur eine aktive, Implikatur-bestimmende Rolle, sondern auch eine passive: das Gesagte wird zugleich durch Implikaturen bestimmt. Es wird darzulegen versucht, inwiefern Levinsons Vorwurf unberechtigt ist.

Savas L. Tsohatzidis versucht darzulegen, daß der Disput zwischen Russell und Strawson hinsichtlich der Wahrheit beziehungsweise Unbestimmtheit von Sätzen mit Referenzfehlschlägen unter alleiniger Bezugnahme auf den Griceschen Annullierbarkeitstest nicht gelöst werden kann.

Daniel Vanderveken befaßt sich mit den Möglichkeiten nicht-wörtlich zu verstehender Sprechakte. Er geht davon aus, daß nicht-wörtliche Sprechakte annullierbar und nichtabtrennbar sind. Vanderveken legt dar, daß ein nicht-wörtlicher Sprechakt im Falle einer Maximenausbeutung mit dem sogenannten 'primären' Sprechakt gleichzusetzen ist, im Falle der Ingebrauchnahme einer Konversationsmaxime ist ein nicht-wörtlich zu verstehender Sprechakt gleichzusetzen mit dem sogenannten 'sekundären' Sprechakt.

Literatur

Blakemore, D. (1992): Understanding Utterances. An Introduction to Pragmatics. Oxford: Blackwell.
Davis, S., ed. (1991): Pragmatics. A Reader. Oxford: Oxford University Press.
Gazdar, G. (1979): Pragmatics. Implicature, Presupposition, and Logical Form. New York: Academic Press.
Green, G.M. (1989): Pragmatics and Natural Language Understanding. Hillsdale, New Jersey: Lawrence Erlbaum.
Grice, P. (1989): Studies in the Way of Words. Cambridge, Mass.: Harvard University Press.
Grundy, P. (1995): Doing Pragmatics. London: Edward Arnold.
Heringer, H.J. (1994): "Gricesche Maximen und interkulturelle Kommunikation". Sprache und Literatur 74, 40-49.
Hirschberg, J. (1991): A Theory of Scalar Implicature. New York: Garland.
Horn, L.R. (1988): "Pragmatic Theory". In: F.J. Newmeyer, ed.: Linguistics: The Cambridge Survey. Vol. I: Linguistic Theory: Foundations. Cambridge: Cambridge University Press, 113-145.
Horn, L.R. (1989): A Natural History of Negation. Chicago: The University of Chicago Press.
Levinson, S.C. (1983): Pragmatics. Cambridge: Cambridge University Press.
Levinson, S.C. (1995): "Three levels of meaning". In: F.R. Palmer, ed.: Grammar and meaning. Essays in honour of SIR JOHN LYONS. Cambridge: Cambridge University Press, 90-115.
Mey, J.L. (1993): Pragmatics. An Introduction. Oxford: Blackwell.
Rolf, E. (1995): "Zur Grammatikalisierung konversationeller Implikaturen". In: F. Liedtke, ed.: Implikaturen. Grammatische und pragmatische Analysen. Tübingen: Niemeyer, 87-102.
Searle, J.R. (1980): "The Background of Meaning". In: J.R. Searle & F. Kiefer & M. Bierwisch, eds.: Speech Act Theory and Pragmatics. Dordrecht: Reidel, 221-232.
Searle, J.R. (1983): Intentionality. An essay in the philosophy of mind. Cambridge: Cambridge University Press.
Searle, J.R. & D. Vanderveken (1985): Foundations of illocutionary logic. Cambridge: Cambridge University Press.
Segerdahl, P. (1996): Language Use. A Philosophical Investigation into the Basic Notions of Pragmatics. New York: St. Martin's Press.
Tsohatzidis, S.L. (1994): Foundations of speech act theory. Philosophical and linguistic perspectives. London: Routledge.
Vanderveken, D. (1990): Meaning and Speech Acts. Vol. I: Principles of Language Use. Cambridge: Cambridge University Press.
Vanderveken, D. (1991): Meaning and Speech Acts. Vol. II: Formal Semantics of Success and Satisfaction. Cambridge: Cambridge University Press.
Yule, G. (1996): Pragmatics. Oxford: Oxford University Press.

Eckard Rolf
(Gastherausgeber)

Münster, September 1997

---

* Für die Unterstützung und Hilfe bei der Erstellung dieses Sonderheftes bin ich der Ruhr-Universität Bochum, der Westfälischen Wilhelms-Universität Münster sowie Susanne Höfer-Lutz und Jörg Hagemann zu großem Dank verpflichtet.

Tautologien sind Tautologien

Tanja Autenrieth, Tübingen

1 Einleitung

Das linguistische Interesse an tautologischen Sätzen wie "Ein Kind ist ein Kind." oder "Entweder es klappt, oder es klappt nicht." geht v.a. auf Grice (1975) zurück. Er greift das Thema in *Logic and Conversation* auf, wobei er annimmt, daß solche Sätze bezüglich ihres semantischen Gehalts nicht informativ sind und ihre Bedeutung somit aufgrund eines Verstoßes gegen die erste Quantitätsmaxime, d.h. ausschließlich auf der kommunikativen Ebene zustandekommt.

In neuerer Zeit wurden einige Ansätze als Alternativen zu dieser Analyse vorgestellt. Dabei wird u.a. die Auffassung vertreten, daß die Bedeutung tautologischer Sätze völlig unabhängig von pragmatischen Interpretationsmechanismen zu erklären ist (Wierzbicka 1987, 1988).

Dem stehen einige "moderat pragmatische" Ansätze (Farghal 1992, Fraser 1988, Okamoto 1993) sowie ein erweiterter, neben der Quantitätsmaxime auch die Relevanzmaxime miteinbeziehender Gricescher Ansatz (Ward & Hirschberg 1990) gegenüber.

In der vorliegenden Arbeit soll im Rahmen eines modularen Ansatzes gezeigt werden, daß die Gricesche Implikaturtheorie für die Analyse der Bedeutung tautologischer Sätze nutzbringend ist, den tautologischen Sätzen aber mehr semantischer Gehalt zugeschrieben werden muß, als dies von Grice angenommen wird. Dabei spielen sowohl die syntaktische Struktur tautologischer Sätze als auch Bedeutungseinheiten im Lexikon und eine Theorie der Alltagskenntnis eine wichtige Rolle.

Im Zentrum der Betrachtungen stehen nominale Tautologien[1]. Es soll gezeigt werden, daß v.a. die grammatische Struktur des Gleichsetzungsnominativs in Verbindung mit der lexikalischen Bedeutung der jeweiligen Substantive den semantischen Gehalt der nominalen Tautologien, d.h. die Ebene der sprachlich determinierten Bedeutung im Sinne von Bierwisch (1979, 1982, 1983, 1987), determiniert. Der wichtigste Punkt ist dabei, daß innerhalb der syntaktischen Struktur des Gleichsetzungsnominativs die prädikative Lesart der jeweils zweiten NP bei tautologischen Konstruktionen obligatorisch ist, so daß die Basis für eine Äußerungsbedeutung entsteht, die die Zuweisung einer durch die Alltagskenntnis zu bestimmenden Menge von Eigenschaften zum Inhalt hat. Hieraus ist schließlich auch der kommunikative Sinn solcher Äußerungen ableitbar.

1.1 Das Phänomen

Sog. Tautologien treten in unterschiedlicher syntaktischer Form auf, der eine jeweils entsprechende logische Form zugeordnet werden kann. Die folgende Typologie soll die Bandbreite der Konstruktionsmöglichkeiten tautologischer Sätze veranschaulichen. Sie ist an Fritz (1981) sowie Ward & Hirschberg (1990) orientiert:

a. Disjunktive [p v ¬ p]:
(1)   Entweder er ist zu Hause, oder er ist nicht zu Hause.

b. Konditionalsätze [p→ p]:
(2)   Wenn er zu Hause ist, dann ist er zu Hause.

c. Äquative:
1. nominale Äquative [a = a]:
(3)   Krieg ist Krieg.
(4)   Ein Kind ist ein Kind.
(5)   Kinder sind (halt) Kinder.
(6)   Die Uni ist (halt) die Uni.
(7)   Deine Kinder sind (halt) deine Kinder.

2. adjektivische/adverbiale Äquative [a = a]:
(8)   Gesagt ist gesagt.
(9)   Heute ist heute.

d. Subordinationstautologien [p ← p]²:
(10)   Es ist so, weil es so ist.
(11)   Es ist soweit, wenn es soweit ist.

e. Relativsätze [p ← p]³:
(12)   Was ich will, das will ich.
(13)   Ich sage, was ich sage.

Allen diesen Sätzen ist gemeinsam, daß sie aufgrund ihrer logischen Form in allen möglichen Welten notwendigerweise wahr sind. Dies macht es unmöglich, tautologischen Sätzen im Rahmen der traditionellen Wahrheitsbedingungensemantik semantischen Gehalt zuzuordnen.

Das gleiche Problem tritt bei kontradiktorischen Sätzen wie (14) auf, die aufgrund ihrer logischen Form notwendigerweise falsch sind. Denn auch in diesen Fällen ist es mit der üblichen Herangehensweise nicht möglich, eine wahrheitsrelevante Bedeutung und somit semantischen Gehalt festzumachen.

(14)   Er ist dafür und er ist nicht dafür.
         [p ∧ ¬ p]

Gesondert zu behandeln sind Fälle wie die unter (15) aufgelisteten, die einen hohen Grad an Usualisierung aufweisen. Sie können den Typen (a) - (e) zugeordnet werden:

(15)   - Dienst ist Dienst und Schnaps ist Schnaps.
        - Wer hat, der hat.
        - Doof bleibt doof.
        - Was sein muß, muß sein.
        - Was zuviel ist, ist zuviel.
        - Sicher ist sicher.
        etc.

Zu den Tautologien werden von Levinson (1983: 125) auch Sätze wie (16) und (17) gezählt. Sie unterscheiden sich allerdings in einem wichtigen Punkt von den bisher behandelten Fällen. Der tautologische Effekt entsteht nicht wie sonst durch die Verwendung von identischem Wortmaterial im zweiten Teil der Struktur. Statt dessen wird im Prädikatsteil eine Definition bzw. semantische Entsprechung der jeweiligen NP geliefert.

(16)   Ein Quadrat hat vier Seiten.
(17)   Ein Rappe ist ein schwarzes Pferd.

Auch diese Sätze sind notwendigerweise wahre Aussagen. Es handelt sich jedoch im Gegensatz zu den anderen Typen um analytische und nicht um logische Wahrheiten. In bestimmten Kontexten sind solche Sätze eindeutig informativ, nämlich dann, wenn der Hörer - z.B. ein kleines Kind - nicht über die nötigen Kenntnisse verfügt, um die Aussage als notwendigerweise wahr analysieren zu können. Interessanterweise sind die analytischen Tautologietypen nicht immer in gleicher Weise verwendbar wie die logischen. Ich werde auf diesen Punkt in Abschnitt 3.3. eingehen.

1.2 Der Gricesche Ansatz

Die auf Grice (1975) zurückgehende Analyse basiert auf der an der klassischen Wahrheitsbedingungensemantik orientierten Annahme, daß tautologische Sätze, da sie aufgrund ihrer logischen Form notwendigerweise wahr sind, auch semantisch "uninformativ" sein müssen. Für Grice ist deshalb die Bedeutung solcher Äußerungen ausschließlich auf konversationelle Implikaturen, die aufgrund eines Verstoßes gegen die erste Quantitätsmaxime zustandekommen, zurückführbar. Der eklatante Verstoß gegen diese Maxime durch die 'Uninformativität' der tautologischen Sätze muß, wie Levinson (1983: 111) feststellt, durch eine "informative Inferenz" ausgeglichen werden, wenn von der Aufrechterhaltung des Kooperationsprinzips ausgegangen werden soll.

So gibt Levinson (1983: 111) im Anschluß an Grice für Sätze wie

(18)   War is war.
(19)   Either John will come or he won't.
(20)   If he does it he does it.

folgende kommunikative Bedeutungen an:

(18') Terrible things always happen in war, that's its nature and it's no good lamenting that particular disaster.
(19') Calm down there's no point in worrying about whether he's going to come because there's nothing we can do about it.
(20') It's no concern of ours.

Levinson selbst weist aber auch auf Schwachpunkte dieser Analyse hin:
1. Sie ist insofern unbefriedigend, als nicht klar wird, wie die entsprechenden Implikaturen *genau* zustandekommen. Levinson (1983: 111) nimmt an, daß hier auch die Relevanzmaxime eine wichtige Rolle spielt.
2. Geht man davon aus, daß Implikaturen allein aus der (im klassischen Sinn) wahrheitsrelevanten Bedeutung von Sätzen abgeleitet werden, so kann nicht erklärt werden, warum z.B.) (18) - (20) trotz gleicher Wahrheitsbedingungen so offensichtlich unterschiedliche Implikaturen haben wie die von Levinson skizzierten. Er vermutet deshalb (1983: 125), daß auch die inhärente Struktur der semantischen Repräsentation durch eine gewisse "sensitivity to logical form" wesentlich für die Interpretation ist, ohne aber genauer auszuführen, wie man sich solche Einflüsse in bezug auf die Tautologien vorzustellen hat.
Es lassen sich noch weitere Argumente finden, die gegen die Auffassung sprechen, daß tautologische Konstruktionen semantisch nicht informativ seien. Ein wichtiger Punkt, der gegen diese Annahme spricht, ist, daß tautologische Äquative unter bestimmten Umständen negierbar sind (vgl. hierzu auch unten):

(21)   Mehrheit ist nicht Mehrheit. (DIE ZEIT vom 30.11.1995)

Außerdem ist auf einer solchen Basis auch schwer erklärbar, weshalb und, obwohl ebenfalls tautologisch in dem Sinn, daß die Aussagen notwendigerweise wahr sind, allenfalls komisch wirken, nicht aber die sinnvollen kommunikativen Effekte wie die üblichen tautologischen Konstruktionen hervorrufen können:

(22)   *Angeklagter:* Zu meiner Verteidigung will ich nochmals betonen, daß ich zwischen meinem ersten und meinem zweiten Unfall keine weiteren Unfälle gebaut habe.[4]
(23)   Unerlaubtes Parken nicht gestattet. (Aufschrift auf einem Schild in der Tübinger Altstadt).

Es stellt sich also die Frage, ob ein rein wahrheitsfunktionaler Zugriff im Fall tautologischer Sätze sinnvoll ist bzw. wieviel Raum der Pragmatik beim Zustandekommen der Bedeutung dieser Konstruktionen gegeben werden muß.

Betrachten wir zunächst einige der neueren Ansätze zur Erklärung des Phänomens.

2 Die neuere Diskussion

Wierzbicka (1987) bezeichnet die Gricesche Analyse als 'radikal pragmatisch' und will dieser eine "radikal semantische" gegenüberstellen. Ihrer Auffassung nach kommt die Bedeutung tautologischer Äußerungen wie "Boys will be boys." nicht durch universalwirkende Interpretationsmechanismen zustande, sondern ist einzelsprachlich festgelegt. Als Begründung für diese Haltung führt sie an, daß eine wörtliche Übertragung solcher Sätze in andere Sprachen nicht generell möglich ist bzw., wenn sie möglich ist, häufig mit dem Verlust von Implikaturen einhergeht. Außerdem würden bestimmte tautologische Äußerungen in anderen Sprachen in veränderter kommunikativer Bedeutung verwendet werden (1987: 96). Ward & Hirschberg (1990: 509) weisen jedoch auf die grundsätzliche Problematik wörtlicher Übersetzungen hin, denn auch in vielen anderen Fällen entstehen bei wörtlicher Übersetzung Bedeutungsverluste bzw. -veränderungen, oder es treten veränderte Implikaturen auf, deren Status als solche dennoch nicht angreifbar ist.[5] Außerdem tauchen zahlreiche der tautologischen Konstruktionen in identischer Form und Verwendung durchaus in unterschiedlichen Sprachen auf. So entspricht das französische

(24)   Si je me fâche, je me fâche.

dem englischen

(25)   When I get angry, I get angry.

in jeder Hinsicht.

Zahlreiche weitere Beispiele für derartige Eins-zu-Eins-Entsprechungen finden sich in Ward & Hirschberg (1990: 509f.).

Man kann Wierzbicka allerdings insofern recht geben, als ihre Beobachtungen in bezug auf usualisierte Fälle wie z.B. den in (16) für das Deutsche angeführten richtig sind. Ich halte es jedoch für problematisch, sich auf solche Fälle zu konzentrieren und daraus Verallgemeinerungen für das Zustandekommen der Bedeutung von tautologischen Äußerungen abzuleiten. Im Zentrum der Bedeutungsanalyse muß die produktive Seite des 'tautologischen Musters' stehen, die frei von Idiosynkrasien ist und weitreichendere Schlüsse über das Verhältnis von semantischem Gehalt und durch pragmatische Mechanismen zustandekommenden Bedeutungselementen erlaubt.

Schließlich versucht Wierzbicka (1987: 103f.), mit Hilfe einer semantischen Metasprache einzelsprachliche Bedeutungen, die sie mit verschiedenen syntaktischen Typen verknüpft, beschreibbar zu machen. Sie unterscheidet beispielsweise tautologische Äußerungen, die

a) "a sober attitude toward human activities" (ebd.) ausdrücken und mit der syntaktischen Form
$$N_{abstr} \text{ is } N_{abstr}$$
verbunden sind, so z.B. (hier nochmals wiederholt):

(18)   War is war.

b) "tolerance for human nature" (ebd.) einfordern und dem syntaktischen Typus
$$N_{humpl} \text{ is } N_{humpl}$$
enstprechen, vgl.:

(26)   Children are children.

sowie

c) "tautologies of obligation" (ebd.), die als syntaktische Basis
     (ART) N is (ART) N
aufweisen, vgl.:

(27)   A father is a father.

Auf der Basis der von ihr entwickelten semantischen Metasprache lassen sich dann z.B. für Wierzbickas Typ (a) folgende Bedeutungen wiedergeben (Wierzbicka 1987: 105):

(A)   Everyone knows that, when people do things of this kind (X), they have to cause some bad things to happen to other people.
(B)   I assume that I don't have to say what things.
(C)   When one perceives that such bad things happen, one should not cause oneself to feel something bad because of that.
(D)   One should understand that it cannot be different [cannot be changed?].

Diese Bedeutungsangabe entspricht jedoch sowohl in ihrer (meta-) sprachlichen Form als auch inhaltlich im wesentlichen derjenigen, die Levinson (1983: 111) für tautologische Sätze wie "War is war." angibt (vgl. oben). Der einzige Unterschied ist, daß Wierzbicka ausschließt, daß beim Zustandekommen dieser Bedeutungen (auch) pragmatische Mechanismen wirksam werden.

In einer Replik auf Wierzbicka zeigt Fraser (1988: 218), daß sich leicht Beispiele finden lassen, die von Wierzbickas Typologie nicht adäquat erfaßt werden können. So müßte z.B.

(28)   Love is love.

aufgrund seiner syntaktischen Struktur zu Wierzbickas Typ (a) gezählt werden und somit das Bedeutungselement 'everyone knows that, when people do things of this kind, they have to cause some bad things to happen to other people' enthalten, was im allgemeinen wohl eher nicht zutreffend ist.

Das zeigt, daß derartige positive oder negative Bewertungen nicht auf die grammatische Struktur des jeweiligen tautologischen Satzes zurückzuführen sind, sondern auf der Basis der spezifischen Bedeutung des verwendeten Nomens zustandekommen. Daß sie pragmatischer Natur sind, veranschaulichen Fälle wie die folgenden, in denen ein und derselbe tautologische Satz völlig unterschiedliche Bewertungen zum Ausdruck bringen kann:

(29)   A: Diese Farbqualität! Wirklich ganz was anderes als ein einfaches Foto.
          B: Dias sind halt Dias.

(30)   A: Ewig diese Sortiererei und dann muß man jedesmal extra die Leinwand aufstellen...
          B: Dias sind halt Dias.

Der semantische Gehalt von tautologischen Sätzen besteht aber für Wierzbicka gerade im Ausdruck einer je nach Tautologietyp spezifizierten "attitude". Deshalb widerspricht sie auch der traditionellen Annahme, tautologische Sätze seien notwendigerweise wahr, da Einstellungen weder wahr noch falsch sein könnten. Es sollte jedoch m.E. nicht in Frage gestellt werden, daß es möglich ist, tautologische Sätze im Sinne der traditionellen wahrheitsfunktionalen Semantik zu analysieren. Betrachtet man die logische Form dieser Sätze, so handelt es sich unbestreitbar um notwendigerweise wahre Aussagen. Wie erklärungsrelevant eine solche Art der Betrachtung ist und welche anderen Faktoren den semantischen Gehalt bestimmen können, ist eine andere, unabhängig davon zu stellende Frage.

Im Gegensatz zu Wierzbicka greifen Ward & Hirschberg (1990) bei ihrer Analyse wieder auf rein pragmatische Erklärungsmuster zurück. Sie verändern den Griceschen Ansatz jedoch dahingehend, daß sie die Interpretation tautologischer Konstruktionen nicht nur auf der Basis der ersten Quantitäts-, sondern auch der Relationsmaxime erklären. So gehen sie beispielsweise davon aus (1990: 513), daß durch Äußerungen der Form 'a is a' ausgedrückt wird, daß alle alternativen Äußerungen der Form 'a is b' (wobei 'b' entweder eine bestimmte Eigenschaft von 'a' oder eine andere Entsprechung von 'a' ist) oder der Form 'some a is b' (wobei 'b' Eigenschaften oder Entsprechungen einer Untereinheit von 'a' identifiziert) nicht relevant sind, da sie vom Sprecher bewußt nicht gewählt wurden. Analog dazu gilt:

(a)   für Disjunktive; p v ¬ p: alternative Disjunktive wie p v q sind nicht relevant.
(b)   für Konditionale; if p then p: Alternativen wie 'if p then q' sind nicht relevant.
(c)   für andere Typen: Alternativen zu 'when p, p', 'p because p', 'what p, p' etc. wie z.B. 'when p, q' sind nicht relevant.

Die jeweiligen Alternativen sind entweder vorher explizit im Kontext geäußert worden oder aus dem Kontext ableitbar. Vgl. folgendes Beispiel (Ward & Hirschberg 1990: 518):

(31)　*X:*　On the one hand, you realize that your work isn't bad, because there is a lot of worse work out there. But on the other hand, you realize that *it's not bad because it's not bad.*

Nach Ward und Hirschberg wird in (31) die Auffassung als irrelevant zurückgewiesen, daß jemandes Arbeit deshalb nicht schlecht ist, weil die Arbeit anderer Leute schlimmer ist. Diese Erklärung erscheint mir jedoch nicht völlig befriedigend, denn allein der Ausschluß alternativer Äußerungen als nicht relevant kann noch nicht die Relevanz der jeweils aktuellen Äußerungen erklären. Insbesondere dann nicht, wenn diese Äußerungen als 'uninformativ' gelten (vgl. dazu die Kritik von Okamoto 1993: 464). Dennoch zeigen Ward und Hirschberg v.a. durch die Hinzunahme der Relationsmaxime und die Tatsache, daß die als irrelevant ausgeschlossenen Alternativen sich auf Eigenschaften des in der Tautologie verwendeten Begriffs beziehen, wichtige neue Aspekte für die Bedeutungsbeschreibung tautologischer Äußerungen auf. Mit dem zweiten Punkt werde ich mich in Abschnitt 3.2, mit dem ersten in 3.3 näher auseinandersetzen.

3 Äquative

Die nominalen Äquative sind ein besonders geeignetes Beispiel, um zu zeigen, inwiefern andersartige zum semantischen Gehalt gehörende Informationen als die im klassischen Sinn wahrheitsfunktional erfaßbaren für die Interpretation eine Rolle spielen können. Deshalb werde ich mich bei den folgenden Überlegungen auf diesen Tautologietyp konzentrieren. Levinsons Vermutung, daß nicht nur der wahrheitsrelevante 'Inhalt', sondern auch die aus der syntaktischen Form resultierende inhärente Struktur der logischen Form für die Interpretation tautologischer Sätze eine Rolle spielt, scheint hier bestätigt. Dies soll im folgenden anhand der Variation von Numerus und Determinierergebrauch illustriert werden.

3.1 Einfluß von Determinierergebrauch und Numerus der Nps

Es soll hier nicht so weit gegangen werden, aufgrund von syntaktischen Spezifizierungen die gesamte Bedeutung tautologischer Äußerungen als semantischen Gehalt zu definieren bzw. letzteren je nach Determinierer, Numerus und ± abstraktem Nomen festzulegen, wie Wierzbicka das tut. Statt dessen sollen die unterschiedlichen syntaktischen Strukturen als Faktoren angesehen werden, die in eine sprachlich determinierte Bedeutung im Sinne von Bierwisch (1979, 1982, 1983, 1987) eingehen. Das bedeutet, daß durch die Differenzierungen von Determinierer und Numerus jeweils unterschiedliche sprachlich determinierte Bedeutungen entstehen, die in Verbindung mit dem Kontext entsprechend unterschiedliche Äußerungsbedeutungen und unterschiedliche kommunikative Bedeutungen ergeben. Für eine solche Sicht der Dinge sprechen Minimalpaare wie die folgenden:

(32)   A: Die Kinder haben mal wieder das ganze Haus auf den Kopf gestellt.
        B: (a)   Kinder sind eben Kinder.
              (b)   Deine Kinder sind eben deine Kinder.
              (c)   Die Kinder sind eben die Kinder.

(32a) und (32b) scheinen geradezu gegensätzliche Implikaturen zu erzeugen, die folgendermaßen skizziert werden können: In (a) verweist der Sprecher auf das Verhalten, das aufgrund der Eigenschaften von Kindern im allgemeinen grundsätzlich von allen Kindern zu erwarten ist. Deshalb kann (a) als Toleranzforderung interpretiert werden. In (b) dagegen gibt der Sprecher als Begründung für das Verhalten der Kinder, von denen die Rede ist, die Tatsache an, daß es sich um A's Kinder handelt. Dies ermöglicht z.B. die Implikatur, daß B A unzureichende Erziehung seiner Kinder vorwirft.

Auch (c) kann als Toleranzforderung verstanden werden, hier erfolgt jedoch weder ein Verweis auf das Verhalten von Kindern im allgemeinen, noch darauf, daß es sich um A's Kinder handelt, sondern schlicht auf die Eigenschaften der Kinder, von denen gerade die Rede ist. Vgl. hierzu auch folgende Beispiele:

(33)[6]   Das Ehepaar Herr und Frau A schauen fern. Der Film wird unterbrochen für eine Werbung für Bier. [Ein Mann spricht]: Meine Frau steht schon seit Wochen in der Küche und bereitet das Essen für Weihnachten vor. Ich bin für die Getränke zuständig, und ich werde Veltins Bier kaufen.

      (a)   *Herr A (grinsend)*: Der Mann ist eben der Mann.[7]
      (b)   *Frau A (kopfschüttelnd)*: Männer sind eben Männer.

(34)   A: Läßt du dir etwa vom Stellvertreter deines Chefs etwas sagen?
        B: (a)   Chef ist Chef.
              (b)   Der Chef ist der Chef.

Allein die Variation in Numerus und Artikelgebrauch ermöglicht auch hier völlig verschiedene Implikaturen: In (33a) und (33b) werden beinahe konträre Ansichten über das Anrecht von Männern auf traditionelles Rollenverhalten vertreten. (34a) würde normalerweise als affirmative, (34b) dagegen als negative Antwort aufgefaßt werden.[8]

Da in (32) - (34) aber nicht kontextuelle Faktoren für die Bedeutungsveränderungen auf der kommunikativen Ebene verantwortlich sein können, müssen diese Unterschiede auf Variationen in der sprachlich determinierten Bedeutung zurückgeführt werden.

Ein sehr starker Unangemessenheitseffekt, der ebenfalls auf den Einfluß von Numerus und Determiniergebrauch zurückzuführen zu sein scheint, tritt in (35) auf:

(35) A: Die Kinder haben wieder das ganze Haus verwüstet.
B: *Kind ist Kind.

Dies ist nicht etwa dadurch erklärbar, daß der Numerus der NP in der Äußerung von B nicht mit dem Numerus der NP in der vorhergehenden Äußerung übereinstimmt. (36) und (37) sind völlig unproblematisch, ohne daß eine solche Bedingung erfüllt wäre:

(36) A: Unser Kind hat das gesamte Haus verwüstet.
B: Kinder sind halt Kinder.

(37) A: Peter kauft nur Bücher mit Goldschnitt.
B: So ein Spinner. Buch ist (doch) Buch.

Es handelt sich bei (35) und (37) um den in mehrfacher Hinsicht besonderen Fall der zählbaren Nomina im Singular ohne Artikel oder Quantifizierer. Sie treten nur in spezifischen Umgebungen wie z.B. Koordination, PPs oder typischerweise in prädikativer Funktion auf.

Die besonderen Bedeutungseffekte, die mit dem Gebrauch dieser Nomina innerhalb tautologischer Äquative einhergehen, lassen sich sehr deutlich am Unterschied zwischen (35) und (37) veranschaulichen: Im Gegensatz zu (35) enthält der Kontext von (37) einen indirekten Vergleich, und zwar den zwischen Büchern mit Goldschnitt und anderen Büchern.[9] Genau auf diesen Vergleich wird aber mit der tautologischen Äußerung Bezug genommen. D.h., durch die Verwendung des tautologischen Satzes "Buch ist (doch) Buch."[10] wird implikatiert, daß "ein Buch wie das andere"[11] ist, es wird also eine Komparation zum Ausdruck gebracht. Im Kontext von (35) liegt aber keine solche Komparation vor, da hier von typischen Eigenschaften von Kindern die Rede ist, ohne daß dabei ein Vergleich zu anderen Kindern mit anderen Eigenschaften thematisiert wäre. Dies erklärt hier die Unangemessenheit der Verwendung dieses Tautologietyps.

Die Richtigkeit einer solchen Analyse wird auch durch folgendes Phänomen bestätigt: Es scheint gerade zu diesem Tautologietypus eine offensichtlich nicht-tautologische Variante mit Vergleichspartikel zu geben, die (insbesondere negiert) relativ häufig auftritt:

(38) (a) Pizza ist (nicht) gleich Pizza.
(b) Zahncreme ist (nicht) gleich Zahncreme.
(c) Auto ist (nicht) gleich Auto.

Es handelt sich dabei meiner Meinung nach um ein und dieselbe Struktur wie bei den 'rein tautologischen' Fällen. In den Varianten mit Vergleichspartikel wird aber die sonst implikatierte Komparation Teil der explizierten Äußerungsbedeutung.

Aus syntaktischer[12] (und wahrheitsfunktionaler) Sicht ist interessant, daß direkte Verneinung innerhalb tautologischer Sätze ohne weitere kontextuelle Bedingungen nur bei diesem Tautologietypus und nur in dieser Bedeutungsvariante möglich zu sein scheint:

(39) (a) ?Kinder sind nicht Kinder. Kind ist nicht Kind.
     (b) ?Mehrheiten sind nicht Mehrheiten. Mehrheit ist nicht Mehrheit.
     (c) ?Pizzas sind nicht Pizzas. Pizza ist nicht Pizza.

Damit auch die anderen Tautologietypen direkt negierbar sind, müssen weitere kontextuelle Faktoren hinzukommen:

(40) (a) Kinder sind nicht Kinder, wenn sie nicht öfter mal zu laut sind.
     (b) Ein Sommersemester ist kein Sommersemester ohne mindestens einen Freibadbesuch.
     (c) Peter wäre nicht (mehr) Peter ohne seine Lederjacke.

Auch die Art der Negierbarkeit ist also offensichtlich von Determinierer, Numerus und lexikalischer Bedeutung der jeweiligen NP abhängig.

Wie die Ausführungen dieses Abschnitts gezeigt haben, können lexikalische Informationen relevante Veränderungen in der semantischen Struktur der jeweiligen tautologischen Sätze verursachen. Eine Analyse unter rein wahrheitsrelevanten Aspekten wird diesen Unterschieden aber nicht gerecht.

3.2 Die Struktur des Gleichsetzungsnominativs

3.2.1 Prädikative Verwendung der zweiten NP in tautologischen Äquativen

Die Variation des Determinierers und des Numerus als Faktoren, die in die grammatisch determinierte Bedeutung eingehen, genügen allerdings noch nicht, um zu erklären, auf welcher semantischen Basis die unterschiedlichen kommunikativen Effekte tautologischer Äußerungen zustandekommen. Ich möchte deshalb nochmals auf den bereits im Zusammenhang mit dem Ansatz von Ward & Hirschberg (1990) angesprochenen Punkt zurückkommen, daß auch die Zuweisung von Prädikaten ein Element der Bedeutung tautologischer Sätze ausmacht.[13]

Auch hierbei ist die syntaktische Struktur der nominalen Äquative die wesentliche Ausgangsbasis. Dies wird klar, wenn man sich vor Augen führt, daß die nominalen Äquative stets die Form des Gleichsetzungsnominativs haben.

(41) (a) Frau Maiers Mann ist Arzt.
     (b) Arzt ist Arzt.

(42) (a) Berlin ist die Hauptstadt von Deutschland.
     (b) Berlin ist Berlin.

Bei Gleichsetzungsnominativen können jedoch grundsätzlich zwei verschiedene Typen auftreten. Vgl. (43) und (44):

(43) (a) Der Abendstern ist die Venus.
(b) Der Morgenstern ist die Venus.
(c) Der Abendstern ist der Morgenstern.

(44) Der Morgenstern ist ein heller Stern.

Während in (43) die Identifizierung der Referenten zweier NPs vorliegt, ist die NP *ein heller Stern* in (44) nicht-referentiell und dient dazu, dem Referenten der NP *der Morgenstern*, bestimmte Eigenschaften zuzuordnen.

Es soll gezeigt werden, daß die jeweils zweite NP tautologischer Äquative obligatorisch als nicht-referentielles Prädikativ gebraucht ist. D.h., die nominalen Äquative entsprechen grundsätzlich dem semantischen Typus von (44), nicht aber dem von (43). Dafür sprechen folgende Argumente:

1. Symptomatisch für nicht-referentiellen, prädikativen Gebrauch von NPs im Rahmen des Gleichsetzungsnominativs ist, wie schon erwähnt (vgl. auch Steinitz 1980: 252), der artikellose Gebrauch der Substantive im Singular wie oben in (41) oder z.B. auch in (45) und (46):

(45) Peter ist Bayer.
(46) Max ist Physiker.

Genau dieses Phänomen kann aber auch bei tautologischen Äquativen auftreten, wie z.B. (47) zeigt:

(47) Bei Peter ist das Wochenende Wochenende.

Hier wird das übliche Schema insofern aufgebrochen, als nicht wie sonst beide NPs exakt parallel konstruiert sind. Der typische "tautologische" Bedeutungseffekt bleibt aber erhalten, so daß (47) durchaus als Argument für prädikativen Status der zweiten NP tautologischer Äquative gewertet werden kann.

2. In Fällen, in denen ein Referent direkt erfragt wird, sind tautologische Äquative als Antworten unmöglich. Wenn dagegen Eigenschaften erfragt werden, gibt es eine solche Beschränkung nicht:

(48) *A*: Wer von den Leuten hier im Raum ist dein Vater?
B: *Oh, mein Vater ist mein Vater...

(49) *A*: Was ist dein Vater für ein Mensch?
B: Oh, mein Vater ist mein Vater...

3. Eine weitere Beobachtung geht auf Reis (1982: 12) zurück. Sie stellt fest, daß beim Gleichsetzungsnominativ selbst bei so eindeutig anaphorischer Situation wie den tautologischen Äquativen keine Reflexivierung eintritt:

(50)   Dienst ist Dienst.   *Dienst ist sich(/er/er selbst).
       Chomsky ist eben Chomsky.   *Chomsky ist eben sich (/er/er selbst).

Da eine wesentliche Bedingung für Reflexivierung Koreferenz ist, spricht alles dafür, das Unterbleiben von Reflexivierung in diesen Fällen durch das Fehlen von Referenz zu erklären. Der Gleichsetzungsnominativ in dieser Verwendung hat damit also eindeutig prädikative Funktion.

   4. Doron (1983) beschreibt einige Tests zur Unterscheidung von referentiellem und prädikativem Gebrauch von NPs. Leider sind die meisten davon für unsere Zwecke unbrauchbar, da sie auf Phänomenen wie eindeutigem Anaphernbezug bei nicht-identischen NPs beruhen. Eine Ausnahme bildet aber folgender Test von Doron (1983: 148): Im Englischen können nicht-restriktive Relativsätze (RSe) mit *who* nur in Verbindung mit referierenden Prädikaten auftreten:

(51)   (a) John is Mr. Smith, who I was telling you about.
       (b) ?John is a man, who I was telling you about.

Wie (52) veranschaulicht, gilt dasselbe auch für deutsche nicht-restriktive RSe mit Personenbezug[14]:

(52)   (a) Der Mann dort drüben ist Herr Schmidt, über den ich ja schon mit dir gesprochen habe.
       (b) *Herr Schmidt ist ein Mann, über den ich ja schon mit dir gesprochen habe.

Dieser Test ist durchaus auf den Fall der tautologischen Äquative übertragbar und bestätigt ebenfalls die Annahme, daß hier prädikativer Gebrauch vorliegt:

(53)   (a) *Mein Vater ist eben mein Vater, der ja früher Soldat war.
       (b) *Die Kinder sind halt die Kinder, mit denen du ja morgen in den Zoo gehen willst.

Bei nicht-persönlichem Bezug des weiterführenden RS scheint im Deutschen identisches Verhalten vorzuliegen:

(54)   Berlin ist die Hauptstadt Deutschlands, über die du ja schon so viel weißt.
(55)   ?Berlin ist ein einziges Chaos, über das du ja schon so viel weißt.

und entsprechend:

(56)   ?Krieg ist Krieg, über den du ja schon so viel weißt.

5. Interessant sind hinsichtlich der Frage nach dem prädikativen Status der zweiten NP außerdem einige den nominalen Äquativen verwandte Fälle wie die folgenden:

(57) Was macht den Mann zum Mann?
(58) Laß Arbeit Arbeit sein.
(59) Peter möchte eine Frau heiraten, die eine Frau ist.

Ähnlich wie bei den tautologischen Sätzen ist hier das doppelte Auftreten einer NP das wesentliche Element der Strukturen, wobei jedoch viel offensichtlicher als bei den tautologischen Fällen diese zweite identische NP dazu dient, auf ganz bestimmte Eigenschaften zu verweisen. Die mit einem Satz wie (57) ausgedrückte Frage entspricht in etwa der Paraphrase in (61) nicht aber der in (60):

(60) Welches Ereignis führt dazu, daß eine Person x zum Mann wird?
(61) Welches sind die typischen Eigenschaften, die eine Person x als Mann kennzeichnen?

Ebenso geht es in (58) um typische Eigenschaften, die mit dem Begriff Arbeit unausweichlich verbunden sind (oder sein sollen) bzw. in (59) um diejenigen Eigenschaften, die eine Frau besitzen muß, um den stereotypen Vorstellungen mancher Männer von Frauen zu entsprechen.

Alles in allem liegen also gute Gründe vor, um von prädikativem, nicht-referentiellem Status der jeweils zweiten NP in tautologischen Äquativen auszugehen.

3.2.2 Konsequenzen aus dem prädikativen Status

Im folgenden möchte ich zeigen, welche Konsequenzen aus dem prädikativen Status der zweiten NP für die semantische Beschreibung tautologischer Gleichsetzungsnominative entstehen. Wichtig ist vor allem, auf welche Art von Eigenschaften die prädikativen Substantive verweisen.

Anhand der folgenden Beispiele soll dieser Frage näher nachgegangen werden.

(62) *Vater*: Warum ist denn gerade Black Beauty dein Lieblingspferd?
 Tochter: (a) Ein Rappe ist eben ein Rappe...
 (b) *Ein Rappe ist eben ein schwarzes Pferd...

(63) *A*: Peters kariertes Sporthemd paßt nun aber wirklich nicht zu seiner gestreiften Hose.
 B: (a) Ein Junggeselle ist halt ein Junggeselle...
 (b) *Ein Junggeselle ist halt ein unverheirateter Mann...

Es handelt sich bei (62b) und (63b) um Fälle, die, wie bereits in Abschnitt 1 angesprochen, nicht logische sondern analytische Wahrheiten ausdrücken. Ganz offensichtlich verhalten sie sich anders als die übrigen nominalen Äquative. Der Unterschied zwischen Tautologien, die auf logischen und auf analytischen Wahrheiten beruhen, dürfte sich aber, wie ja auch schon von Levinson (1983) selbstverständlich vorausgesetzt, nicht auf die kommunikative Verwendbarkeit auswirken. Die erste Quantitätsmaxime wird in genau gleicher Weise verletzt, außer es liegt eine der oben beschriebenen 'Lernsituationen' vor, was aber hier nicht der Fall ist.

Auf der Basis der obigen Ausführungen läßt sich die Unangemessenheit der (b)-Varianten aber einfach erklären. Mit Begriffen wie 'Rappe' oder 'Junggeselle' verweist der Sprecher auf Eigenschaften, die mit solchen wie 'schwarzes Pferd' oder 'unverheirateter Mann' nicht so offensichtlich verknüpft werden. Es handelt sich um bestimmte, auf dem Weltwissen im weitesten Sinne beruhende stereotype Vorstellungen wie 'rassig', 'temperamentvoll', 'edel' in bezug auf 'Rappe' oder etwa 'schrullig', 'eigenbrötlerisch', 'versponnen' für 'Junggeselle'. Gerade solche Eigenschaften sind es aber, auf die es in (62) und (63) ankommt, während Eigenschaften wie [UNVERHEIRATETE ERWACHSENE MÄNNLICHE PERSON] oder [SCHWARZES PFERD] nur eine Teilmenge der Prädikate bilden, die durch die entsprechenden Strukturen in (62) und (63) zugewiesen werden können.

In diesen Zusammenhang passen auch die folgenden in Bierwisch (1979: 139) diskutierten Beispiele:

(64)   Fridolin gibt sich als Junggeselle aus, obwohl er seit drei Jahren verheiratet ist.
(65)   Professor Rumpelstilz ist der typischste Junggeselle, den ich kenne.

Während in (64) die wörtliche Bedeutung identisch mit der üblichen Analyse [UNVERHEIRATETE ERWACHSENE MÄNNLICHE PERSON] ist, müßten in (65) "Kenntnisse über stereotype Vorstellungen von der Lebensweise unverheirateter Männer" (ebd.) in die wörtliche Bedeutung eingehen. Bierwisch spricht hier von einer konzeptuellen Verschiebung, was m.E. aber nicht ganz einsichtig ist und von ihm auch nicht näher begründet wird. Naheliegender erscheint es mir, solche Fälle in Verbindung mit dem in Bierwisch (1983: 96ff.) beschriebenen Typ von Zusammenspiel semantischer und konzeptueller Strukturen zu sehen, den er am Beispiel von Begriffen wie 'Löwe' illustriert. Anhand eines Schemas von Begriffsbestimmung durch Angabe von Genus proximum und Differentia specifica, kann 'Löwe' analysiert werden als 'ein Tier, das...'. Dabei ist 'ein Tier' das Genus proximum, für die Differentia specifica, die Löwen von anderen Tieren wie Leoparden, Tigern oder Pantern unterscheiden, stehen zunächst nur die drei Punkte. Es ist offensichtlich, daß in derselben Weise auch 'Junggeselle' analysierbar ist, als 'ein Mensch, der...', wobei die Differentia specifica diejenigen Eigenschaften ausmachen, die Junggesellen von anderen Menschen unterscheiden.

Eine zentrale Frage ist nun, welche Art von Spezifizierungen an die Stelle der drei Punkte treten. Für Bierwisch handelt es sich dabei um eine Menge von Eigenschaften, die zusammen die 'Alltagstheorie über Löwenhaftigkeit' ausmachen (ebenso denkbar: die 'Alltagstheorie über Junggesellenhaftigkeit'). Sie kann durch ein System von Propositionen $P_1, P_2, P_3, ...P_n$ wiedergegeben werden, wobei mindestens einige dieser P_i die Form

$$\forall x\, [P_i(x)]$$

haben müssen.

Genau um diese Art von 'Sachkenntnissen', die nicht identisch mit der lexikalischen Kenntnis sind (ein Zuwachs an biologischen Kenntnissen über Löwen verändert nicht den Gebrauch des Lexems "Löwe"), geht es aber in tautologischen Äußerungen.

Da es sich bei diesen Sach- oder Alltagskenntnissen nun aber um konzeptuelle Einheiten handelt, kann man davon ausgehen, daß durch Anreicherung mit konzeptuellen Informationen der "Alltagstheorie" für einen tautologischen Satz eine Äußerungsbedeutung zustandekommt, die in etwa durch (66) wiedergegeben werden kann:

(66) $\lambda P \lambda Q [Q(x) \rightarrow P(x)]$ Löwe, P_i

Durch Lamda-Konversion ergibt sich dann:

(67) $\forall x [\text{Löwe}(x) \rightarrow P_i(x)]$

(67) kann folgendermaßen paraphrasiert werden:

(68)   Für alle Löwen gelten alle in der Alltagskenntnis vorhandenen "Gesetzesaussagen"[15] über die Eigenschaften von Löwen (in gleicher Weise).

Bei dieser Analyse gehe ich davon aus, daß die Generalisierung zur Allaussage aufgrund des generischen Status der NPs zustandekommt[16]. Deutlich wird dabei auch, daß die erste der beiden NPs einen anderen semantischen Status besitzt als die zweite und allein der Begriffs- bzw. Extensionsbestimmung dient. Ausschlaggebend für das Abrufen der entsprechenden Alltagskenntnisse ist die lexikalische Bedeutung der verwendeten Substantive.

In derselben Art und Weise kann auch ein tautologischer Satz über Junggesellen analysiert werden:

Für einen Satz wie (69) ergibt sich (70) und durch Lambda-Konversion (71):

(69)   Junggesellen sind eben Junggesellen.

(70) $\lambda P \lambda Q [Q(x) \rightarrow P(x)]$ Junggeselle, P_i

(71) $\forall x [\text{Junggeselle}(x) \rightarrow P_i(x)]$

Das bedeutet:

(72)   Für alle Junggesellen gelten alle in der Alltagskenntnis vorhandenen "Gesetzesaussagen" über die Eigenschaften von Junggesellen (in gleicher Weise).

Auf den ersten Blick können Aussagen wie die in (66) - (72) skizzierten zwar trivial erscheinen, es handelt sich aber in keinem Fall um "Tautologien" im logischen Sinn.

Im nächsten Abschnitt möchte ich zeigen, daß Äußerungsbedeutungen dieses Typs die Grundlage für die typischen kommunikativen Verwendungen tautologischer Sätze bilden.

3.3 Der kommunikative Sinn tautologischer Äußerungen

Für das Zustandekommen des kommunikativen Sinns tautologischer Äußerungen ist in erster Linie eine weitere Spezifizierung der Eigenschaften, auf die die prädikative NP der Gleichsetzungsnominative verweist, notwendig.

Auf dieser Ebene sind nun kommunikative Prinzipien von Bedeutung, und ein Rückgriff auf die Gricesche Relationsmaxime ist für die Analyse sehr sinnvoll.

Zur Veranschaulichung sollen nochmals Beispiele betrachtet werden, in denen ein und derselbe tautologische Satz mit unterschiedlichen Bedeutungseffekten in unterschiedlichen Kontexten verwendet wird.

(73)   *A*:   Willst du tatsächlich mit dieser Rostlaube durch ganz Europa fahren?
        B: Warum nicht? Ein Auto ist ein Auto.

(74)   *A*:   Es stimmt nicht, daß ich unnötig die Umwelt verpeste. Mein Auto hat einen Katalysator.
        B: Ach komm, ein Auto ist ein Auto.

In (73) und (74) sind jeweils unterschiedliche Teilmengen der Eigenschaften, die Autos aufgrund der Alltagskenntnis zugeschrieben werden, relevant. Ihre Relevanz resultiert in beiden Fällen aus der Tatsache, daß es gerade diese Eigenschaften sind, die vom Sprecher der Vorgängeräußerung für spezifische Elemente der Extension von 'Auto' - nämlich der konkreten Objekte, von denen im Kontext die Rede ist - hinterfragt werden. In (73) handelt es sich dabei um die Eigenschaft von Autos, als Transportmittel für weite Strecken geeignet zu sein. Indem B auf A's Frage mit dem tautolgischen Gleichsetzungsnominativ reagiert, behauptet er, daß diese Eigenschaft zur Menge P_i der Eigenschaften gehört, die allen Autos gleichermaßen eigen sind, somit also auch für das Auto, von dem im Kontext die Rede ist ('Rostlaube'). Auf der Sprechaktebene kann dadurch ein Widerspruch ausgedrückt werden.

In der gleichen Weise kann auch (74) analysiert werden. In diesem Kontext sind jedoch andere Eigenschaften von Autos relevant. A versucht mit seiner Äußerung, die Behauptung abzumildern, alle Autos müßten notwendigerweise eine Gefahr für die Umwelt darstellen. Er postuliert, daß zumindest das im Kontext thematisierte Auto von der Gruppe der umweltgefährdenden Exemplare auszuschließen ist. Auch in diesem Fall wird auf der illokutionären Ebene ein Widerspruch ausgedrückt. Die Aussage, daß alle aus der Alltagskenntnis resultierenden Annahmen über Autos für alle Autos (gleichermaßen) gelten, kann im vorliegenden Kontext nur dann relevant sein und dem Kooperationsprinzip genügen, wenn 'Umweltschädlichkeit' zur Menge dieser Eigenschaften gezählt wird. Die Menge P_i der aufgrund der Alltagskenntnis zuzuweisenden Eigenschaften liegt also nicht von vornherein fest. Dies ist ein wesentlicher Aspekt für den 'informativen' Behauptungscharakter tautologischer Äußerungen. B macht somit durch den Gebrauch des tautologischen Satzes deutlich, daß seiner Auffassung nach Umweltschädlichkeit eine Eigenschaft ist, die gemäß der 'Gesetzesaussagen' über Autos auch A's Auto besitzt.

Auch kommunikative Effekte anderer typischer Verwendungen sind auf der oben beschriebenen semantischen Grundlage leicht rekonstruierbar.

Eine häufig beschriebene Art der Verwendung der Äquative ist die als "tautologies of obligation" (Vgl. Wierzbicka (1987), Farghal (1992), Okamoto (1993)), die (75) veranschaulicht:

(75) A: Die arme Petra muß, bevor sie auszieht, die gesamte Wohnung renovieren.
      B: Ein Vertrag ist halt ein Vertrag.

Aufgrund der Verwendung des Modalverbs 'müssen' in der Äußerung von A ist das Element der Verpflichtung bereits im Kontext vorhanden. Es ist also offensichtlich, daß der tautologische Satz nur dann kooperativ eingesetzt ist, wenn die relevante Eigenschaft aus der Menge der alltagstheoretische festgelegten Annahmen über Verträge die der gegenseitigen Verpflichtung ist.

Indem B äußert, daß diese Eigenschaften ausnahmslos für alle Verträge gelten, kann er auf der kommunikativen Ebene zum Ausdruck bringen, daß ein betroffener Vertragspartner zwar zu bedauern ist, es aber keinen Grund zu lamentieren gibt, da der eingetretene Zustand aufgrund der aus der Gegenseitigkeit von Verträgen erwachsenden Pflichten ohnehin unvermeidlich ist. Dies beinhaltet den häufig in der Literatur erwähnten "fatalistischen" Effekt tautologischer Sätze, der sich z.B. auch in Levinsons Umschreibung der kommunikativen Bedeutung von "War is war." niederschlägt.

Diese fatalistische Bedeutungsvariante ist es im übrigen auch, die im Deutschen typischerweise mit der Verwendung der MPn *halt/eben* einhergeht. Das Merkmal <EVIDENT>, das Thurmair (1989) für die Bedeutung dieser Partikeln u.a. angibt, macht deutlich, daß die Verwendung von *halt* oder *eben* dazu dienen kann, diesen spezifischen kommunikativen Effekt tautologischer Äußerungen zu verstärken. Fehlt der "fatalistische" Bedeutungseffekt, können auch die MPn nicht auftreten:

(76) A: Die arme Petra muß, bevor sie auszieht, die gesamte Wohnung renovieren.
      B: Ein Vertrag ist eben ein Vertrag.

(77) A: Ich habe von Frau Maier nur einen handgeschriebenen Vertrag.
      B: Macht nichts. Ein Vertrag ist (*eben) ein Vertrag.

4 Schluß

In dieser Arbeit wurde anhand der nominalen Äquative zu zeigen versucht, daß die klassische wahrheitsfunktionale Analyse sog. 'Tautologien' als semantische Basis für das Zustandekommen des kommunikativen Sinns solcher Sätze unzureichend ist.

Unter Rückgriff auf Bierwischs 2-Ebenen-Semantik konnte dargelegt werden, inwiefern die grammatische Struktur tautologischer Gleichsetzungsnominative die semantische Struktur dieser Sätze determiniert. Dabei wird die jeweils zweite NP als prädikativ analysiert. So erhält man eine Struktur, in der die beiden formal identischen NPs unterschiedlichen semantischen Status haben. Es ergibt sich dadurch eine 'informative' semantische Basis der tautologischen Äquative. Diese ermöglicht es, durch den Verweis auf Eigenschaften, die die Alltagskenntnis auf der Ebene der Äußerungsbedeutung den entsprechenden Begriffen zuschreibt, typische kommunikative Effekte solcher Sätze mit Hilfe der Griceschen Relationsmaxime zu rekonstruieren.

Es bleibt zu klären, inwiefern ähnliche Strukturen für die anderen Tautologietypen auszumachen sind und ob auch diesen eine 'informative' semantische Basis zugrundeliegt. Prinzipiell scheint mir dies möglich zu sein.

Anmerkungen

1 Obwohl es mein Anliegen ist, in der vorliegenden Arbeit zu zeigen, daß die gemeinhin als Tautologien bezeichneten Phänomene nicht "echte" Tautologien im Sinne der Logik sind, verwende ich aus Gründen der Einfachheit den herkömmlichen Begriff.
2 Mit Hilfe der Aussagenlogik, auf die hier in Analogie zu den anderen Fällen zurückgegriffen werden soll, ist bei diesen Typen nur eine annäherungsweise Formalisierung möglich. Auf Behelfe wie z.B. "p because p" bei Ward & Hirschberg (1990) möchte ich verzichten.
3 Hier gilt bezüglich der Formalisierung dasselbe wie bei den Subordinationstautologien.
4 Für das Aufspüren dieses Beispiels danke ich Marga Reis.
5 Vgl. z.B. die problematische wörtliche Übersetzung des französischen Satzes (i) "Je vais chercher le dictionnaire." ins Deutsche als (ii) "Ich gehe das Wörterbuch suchen.". Hier sind völlig unterschiedliche Implikaturen ableitbar (z.B. aus (i): *Der Sprecher weiß nicht, wo das Wörterbuch ist*, aus (ii) dagegen *Der Sprecher weiß, wo das Wörterbuch ist.*), die aber dennoch unbestreitbar aufgrund pragmatischer Mechanismen inferiert werden, da sie auf der Grundlage veränderten propositionalen Gehalts zustandekommen. Der veränderte propositionale Gehalt und die entsprechend unterschiedlichen Implikaturen sind dabei auf eine inkorrekte *wörtliche* Übersetzung zurückzuführen, der jedoch auch ein korrektes ebenso *wörtliches*, i.S. von "einer der wörtlichen, d.h. nicht übertragenen Bedeutung entsprechendes", Pendant gegenübersteht, nämlich (iii) "Ich hole das Wörterbuch.", bei dem solche Probleme nicht auftreten.
6 Für dieses Beispiel danke ich Andreas Gerster, Stephanie Schirken und Nicola Becker.
7 Die NP *der Mann* weist hier eine abhängig generische Lesart auf. Vgl. Chur (1993: 160) bzw. Dahl (1988: 89), der für einen Satz wie "Der Mann ist (normalerweise) physisch stärker als die Frau." folgende Interpretation angibt: "For any occasion x of type T, the man in x is physically stronger than the woman in x."
8 In bezug auf (33) könnte allerdings bestritten werden, daß es sich tatsächlich um ein Minimalpaar handelt, da die Sprecherrolle variiert. Daß dies jedoch nicht ausschlaggebend für die

unterschiedlichen Bedeutungseffekte sein kann, zeigt ein Austausch der Sprecherrollen (im Kontext von (33)):
(a') *Herr A (kopfschüttelnd)*: Männer sind eben Männer.
(b') *Frau A (grinsend)*: Der Mann ist eben der Mann.
Die Bedeutungsunterschiede bleiben dieselben. Es tritt allerdings ein zusätzlicher (ironischer) Effekt auf, da die Sprecher sich - gerade aufgrund dieser Bedeutungen - konträr zu ihrer eigenen Geschlechtszugehörigkeit verhalten.

9   Dieser Vergleichskontext entsteht innerhalb der Äußerung von A durch die Verwendung der Gradpartikel *nur* und die Fokussierung der Bezugskonstituente *Bücher mit Goldschnitt*. Alle Alternativen zu *Bücher mit Goldschnitt* werden dadurch (auf der wahrheitsfunktionalen Ebene) ausgeschlossen und sind somit, da indirekt im Diskurs thematisiert, Teil des Kontextes.

10 Hier liegt der einzig mögliche Fall der Verwendung einer anderen Modalpartikel als *halt/ eben* in nominalen Tautologien vor.

11 Zur näheren Erläuterung solcher Bedeutungseffekte s.u. Abschnitt 3.3.

12 Chur (1993: 231) geht bezüglich der zählbaren artikellosen Substantive im Singular davon aus, daß ein solches "einzelnes Nomen in prädikativer Funktion [...] einen offensichtlichen Verstoß gegen die Struktur einer NP" (ebd.) darstellt, da eine derartige Verwendung "normalerweise nicht erlaubt" sei. Sie nimmt deshalb an, daß hier gar keine NP vorliegt. Gerade die Verwendung in tautologischen Äquativen ist evtl. ein Argument für eine solche Auffassung, da hier einerseits die spezifischen Bedeutungseffekte, die oben beschrieben wurden, auftreten und andererseits die Negation mit *nicht* anstatt *kein* vorliegt, was möglicherweise für eine kategoriale Einstufung als Adjektiv spricht. Dies kann allerdings nur in bezug auf die zweite der beiden Nps eindeutig konstatiert werden.

13 Vgl. diesbezüglich auch Escandell-Vidal (1990: 7): "In the sentence NP1=NP1
    (i) NP1 NP1 is a qualitative intensification of NP1 (to be read as 'NP1 with its prototypical features') [...]."
    Hier von prototypischen Eigenschaften auszugehen, erscheint mir jedoch als zu starke Einschränkung. Wie weiter unten noch deutlich werden soll, handelt es sich eher um Stereotype.

14 Die nomenbezogenen RSe werden durch die Verwendung von Modalpartikeln wie *ja* eindeutig als nicht-restriktiv gekennzeichnet. Vgl. Brandt (1990: 41), Thurmair (1989: 81f.).

15 Vgl. Bierwisch (1983: 97).

16 Generischer Gebrauch ist bei den nominalen Äquativen ein häufig auftretendes Phänomen. Dennoch ist Generizität nicht grundsätzlich mit diesen Strukturen verbunden. Es gibt ebenso zahlreiche Beispiele mit nicht-generischen NPs, wie z.B. in den bereits oben angeführten Fällen "Mein Vater ist eben mein Vater." oder "Die Kinder sind eben die Kinder." Dabei handelt es sich jedoch, soweit ich es übersehen kann, grundsätzlich um Bezeichnungen für Personen, also eindeutige Identifizierungen.

Literatur

Bierwisch, M. (1979): "Wörtliche Bedeutung - Eine pragmatische Gretchenfrage". In: G. Grewendorf, ed.: Sprechakttheorie und Semantik. Frankfurt/Main: Suhrkamp, 119-148.

Bierwisch, M. (1982): "Formal and Lexical Semantics". Linguistische Berichte 80, 3-17.

Bierwisch, M. (1983): "Semantische und konzeptuelle Repräsentationen lexikalischer Einheiten". In: R. Ruzicka & W. Motsch, eds.: Untersuchungen zur Semantik. Berlin: Akademie-Verlag, 61-99.

Bierwisch, M. (1987): "Linguistik als kognitive Wissenschaft. Erläuterungen zu einem Forschungsprogramm". Zeitschrift für Germanistik 6, 645-667.

Brandt, M. (1990): Weiterführende Nebensätze. Zu ihrer Syntax, Semantik und Pragmatik. Stockholm: Almquist & Wiksell.
Chur, J. (1993): Generische Nominalphrasen im Deutschen. Eine Untersuchung zu Referenz und Semantik. Tübingen: Narr.
Dahl, Ö. (1988): "Inherited genericity". In: M. Krifka, ed.: Genericity in natural language. Proceedings of the 1988 Tübingen conference. Tübingen: SNS-Bericht 47, 85-94.
Doron, E. (1988): "The semantics of predicate nominals". Linguistics 26, 281-301.
Escandell-Vidal, V. (1990): Nominal tautologies in Spanish. Paper presented at the 1990 International Conference on Pragmatics, Barcelona, Spain.
Farghal, M. (1992): "Colloquial Jordanian Arabic tautologies". Journal of Pragmatics 17, 215-220.
Fraser, B. (1988): "Motor oil is motor oil. An account of English nominal tautologies". Journal of Pragmatics 12, 215-220.
Fritz, G. (1981): "Zur Verwendung tautologischer Sätze in der Umgangssprache". Wirkendes Wort: Deutsche Sprache in Forschung und Lehre 6, 398-415.
Gibbs, R.W. jr. & N.S. McCarrel (1990): "Why boys will be boys and girls will be girls: Understanding colloquial tautologies". Journal of Psycholinguistic Research 19/2, 125-145.
Grice, H.P. (1975): "Logic and Conversation". In: P. Cole & J. Morgan, eds.: Speech Acts. New York: Academic Press, 41-58.
Heidolph, K.E. & W. Flämig & W. Motsch (1981): Grundzüge einer deutschen Grammatik. Berlin: Akademie-Verlag.
Heim, I. (1991): "Artikel und Definitheit". In: A.v. Stechow & D. Wunderlich, eds.: Semantik. Ein internationales Handbuch der zeitgenössischen Forschung. Berlin/New York: de Gruyter, 487-535.
Levinson, St.C. (1983): Pragmatics. Cambridge: Cambridge University Press.
Leys, O. (1973a): "Bemerkungen zum Reflexivpronomen". Linguistische Studien IV. Festgabe für Paul Grebe zum 65. Geburtstag. Düsseldorf: Schwann, 152-157.
Leys, O. (1973b): "Das Reflexivpronomen: eine Variante des Personalpronomens". Leuvense Bijdragen 62, 251-266.
Okamoto, S. (1993): "Nominal repetitive constructions in Japanese: the 'tautology' controversy revisited". Journal of Pragmatics 20, 433-466.
Putnam, H. (1975): "The meaning of meaning". In: K. Gunderson, ed.: Language, mind, and knowledge. Minneapolis: University of Minnesota Press, 131-193.
Reis, M. (1982): Reflexivierung im Deutschen. Präsentiert auf der "Journée annuelle des linguistes de l'association des germanistes de l'enseignement supérieur (AGES)". Nancy, 12. Dez. 1981.
Schwarz, M. & J. Chur (1993): Semantik. Ein Arbeitsbuch. Tübingen: Narr.
Steinitz, R. (1980): "Das Prädikat". In: E. Heidolph e.a., eds.: Grundzüge einer deutschen Grammatik. Berlin: Akademie-Verlag, 247-254 (Kap. 2.2.4).
Thurmair, M. (1989): Modalpartikeln und ihre Kombinationen. Tübingen: Niemeyer.
Ward, G.L. & J. Hirschberg (1990): "A pragmatic analysis of tautological utterances". Journal of Pragmatics 15, 507-520.
Wierzbicka, A. (1987): "Boys will be boys: 'radical pragmatics' vs. 'radical semantics'". Language 63, 95-114.
Wierzbicka, A. (1988): "Boys will be boys. A rejoinder to Bruce Fraser". Journal of Pragmatics 12, 221-224.

The Semantics-Pragmatics Distinction: What It Is and Why It Matters

Kent Bach, San Francisco

The distinction between semantics and pragmatics is easier to apply than to explain. Explaining it is complicated by the fact that many conflicting formulations have been proposed over the past sixty years. This might suggest that there is no one way of drawing the distinction and that how to draw it is merely a terminological question, a matter of arbitrary stipulation. In my view, though, these diverse formulations, despite their conflicts, all shed light on the distinction as it is commonly applied, in both linguistics and philosophy. Although it is generally clear what is at issue when people apply the distinction to specific linguistic phenomena, what is less clear, in some cases anyway, is whether a given phenomenon is semantic or pragmatic, or both. Fortunately, there are other phenomena that are uncontroversially semantic or, as the case may be, uncontroversially pragmatic. Their example will help us get clear on what the semantics-pragmatics distinction is.

1 Rationale

Perhaps the main reason for introducing the semantics-pragmatics distinction is to provide a framework for explaining the variety of ways in which what a speaker conveys can fail to be fully determined by the (conventional) linguistic meaning of the sentence he utters:

- indexicality
- ambiguity
- vagueness (and open-texture)
- semantic underdetermination
- implicitness
- implicature
- nonliteralness
- non-truth-conditional content
- illocutionary force

The null hypothesis is that there is always some pragmatic explanation for how, in any given case, sentence meaning can underdetermine what the speaker means. For example, the null hypothesis about controversial claims of ambiguity (on tests for ambiguity see Atlas 1989: ch. 2) is that diverse uses of an expression are best explained not by different pieces of linguistic information (several conventional meanings) but by one piece of linguistic information combined with extralinguistic information. As Green has written:

> The possibility of accounting for meaning properties and syntactic distributions of uses of linguistic expressions in terms of conversational inferences rather than semantic entailments or grammatical ill-formedness was welcomed by many linguists as a means of avoiding redundant analyses on the one hand and analyses which postulate rampant ambiguity on the other. (Green 1989: 106)

However, it is merely the null hypothesis that a given linguistic phenomenon has a pragmatic explanation. Particular phenomena and specific constructions obviously have to assessed on a case-by-case basis.

Another reason for invoking the semantics-pragmatics distinction is to shed light on a number of other distinctions:

- type vs. token
- sentence vs. utterance
- meaning vs. use
- context-invariant vs. context-sensitive meaning
- linguistic vs. speaker's meaning
- literal vs. nonliteral use
- saying vs. implying
- content vs. force

Contrary to many of the formulations that have appeared since Morris's initial formulation in 1938 (see the Appendix), the semantics-pragmatics distinction does not coincide with any of these other distinctions. Even so, it should respect them.

Properly formulated, it should take into account the wide range of items that have been described as semantic or pragmatic or both:

- phenomena: ambiguities, implications, presuppositions
- anomalies: paradoxes, contradictions, nonsense
- meanings: contents, interpretations
- knowledge: information, intuitions, processes
- rules and principles
- explanations

It would require a detailed lexicographic analysis of the terms 'semantic' and 'pragmatic' to do full justice to their various applications. However, these should be kept in mind in the following discussion, which will emphasize the semantics-pragmatics distinction as it reflects the difference between linguistic and extralinguistic information available to language users.

Three disclaimers: (1) I will not use the term 'pragmatics' so broadly as to apply to the full range of phenomena falling under the heading of language use. That would take us too far afield, into such areas as social psychology, sociolinguistics, cultural anthropology, and rhetoric. I will restrict the discussion to those aspects of use that are directly related to acts of communication, and not even include perlocutionary acts and collateral speech acts (Bach & Harnish 1979: 81-103). For it is in the context of communication that the question arises of where to draw the line between semantics and pragmatics. (2) Unless otherwise indicated, I will be treating sentences as the primary linguistic unit with respect to which the semantics-pragmatics distinction applies. This does not do justice to the fact that phrases can often be used as complete utterances nor to the alleged fact that there are certain intersentential semantic phenomena (for examples see Prince 1988). (3) I am not assuming any particular framework for semantics, formal or otherwise. I do assume that the meaning of a sentence depends entirely on the meanings of its constituents and its syntactic structure, but I am taking no position on whether sentence semantics should rely on the notion of truth conditions or propositions (however conceived). I will speak indifferently of a sentence's truth condition, its truth-conditional content, and the proposition it expresses.

2 Philosophical Background

The semantics-pragmatics distinction has long been methodologically important in both linguistic and philosophy. It was implicit in philosophy a half century ago in discussions of pragmatic paradoxes and contextual implication (for a survey see Hungerland 1960), a forerunner of Grice's notion of conversational implicature. It has often been invoked for corrective purposes. It was invoked by Strawson (1950), albeit implicitly, when he argued that Russell in his theory of descriptions had confused (linguistic) meaning and reference. Reference, Strawson contended, is something that speakers do, not words. Here Strawson anticipated the distinction between linguistic meaning and speaker's meaning, which, along with the related distinction between what is said and what is implicated, became widely influential as the result of the work of Grice (collected in Grice 1989). Ironically, it was also Strawson (1952) who proposed a semantic account of presupposition. This was thought to make further trouble for Russell until presupposition came to be seen as a pragmatic phenomenon (Stalnaker 1974, Grice 1981/1989: ch. 17). Treating it as semantic led linguists down a blind alley for many years, searching for a solution to the "projection problem", a problem that does not arise when presupposition is seen as pragmatic.

In the sixties, invoking the semantics-pragmatics distinction enabled philosophers to stem the excesses of ordinary language philosophy practiced by Austin and his followers. Their "linguistic botanizing" and rampant appeals to "what we would say" were overly ambitious in their attempt to get philosophical mileage out of subtle features of ordinary usage. Later Austin implicitly acknowledged the semantics-pragmatics distinction by contrasting locutionary and illocutionary acts (1960: 93-101). Grice (1961/1989: ch. 15, and 1967/1989: ch. 2), by applying the notion of conversational implicature and wielding his "modified" Occam's Razor, and Searle (1969: ch. 6), with his exposure of the "assertion" and the "speech act" fallacies, challenged proposed analyses of various epistemological, logical, and ethical terms, such as 'looks,' 'knows,' 'or,' and 'good.' Philosophers' extravagant claims of semantic ambiguity were later decried by Kripke as "the lazy man's approach in philosophy" (Kripke 1977: 268). Kripke illustrated how to avoid this by invoking the distinction between semantic reference and speaker's reference to show that the difference between reference and attributive uses of definite descriptions, which had been thought to undermine Russell's theory of descriptions, is merely pragmatic (see also Bach 1987a: chs. 5 & 6, and Neale 1990). Philosophers have since made similar moves on other important topics:

- contrastive explanations
- counterfactual conditionals
- domains of discourse
- illocutionary standardization
- indefinite descriptions
- logical form
- propositional attitude ascriptions
- relative terms
- similarity sentences
- speech act modifiers

3 Linguistic Background

In linguistics the category of pragmatics has served mainly as a bin for disposing of phenomena that would otherwise be the business of semantics (as part of grammar) to explain. Relegating such phenomena to pragmatics freed linguistic theory, already becoming more and more complex, of numerous additional complications. A notable exception to this strategy was the systematic attempt by generative semanticists, in their campaign to undermine the autonomy of syntax, to empty the "pragmatic wastebasket, " so-called by Bar-Hillel, who wisely advised linguists "to first bring some order into the contents of this wastebasket" (1971: 401). Many defied his advice and included everything but the kitchen sink in semantics. The performative hypothesis was the most prominent example (for a brief history see Sadock 1988). Historically, generative semantics is best remembered for generating the "linguistics wars" which have been chronicled in detail by Harris (1993).

In a more positive vein, the distinction between semantics and pragmatics has served to separate strictly linguistic facts about utterances from those that involve the actions, intentions, and inferences of language users (speaker-hearers). However, there are some linguistic phenomena that seem to straddle the semantics-pragmatics boundary:

- adjectival modification
- ambiguity vs. polysemy

- anaphora
- compounds and noun-noun pairs
- interpretation of quantificational phrases
- nominalizations

And there are many linguistic phenomena which might seem at first glance to be pragmatic but, because of their syntactic basis, are arguably semantic. Space limitations prevent detailed discussion, but here are a few examples:

- constraints on anaphoric reference (c-command violations)
- empty categories
- implicit arguments
- implicit quantification over events
- thematic roles and complementation
- obligatory adjuncts with certain accomplishment verbs
- lexical alternations
- factive verbs
- negative polarity items
- connotations
- it-clefts, wh-clefts, preposing, inversion, topicalization and other devices of information packaging
- discourse modifiers and speech act adverbials

Most of these are syntactico-semantic phenomena that seem to explain certain cooccurrence and interpretational regularities. For example, implicit quantification over events helps explain the semantics of verbs, tense, and aspect, and the roles of adverbs (for a detailed account see Parsons 1990). The last three items on the list above involve semantic properties concerning use, not truth conditions. These properties are not pragmatic just because they pertain to use, for they are linguistically marked.

4   Formulations

The semantics-pragmatics distinction has been formulated in various ways, generally without recognition that the different versions do not coincide. Historically, formulations have fallen into three main types, depending on which other distinction the semantics-pragmatics distinction was thought to coincide with:

- linguistic (conventional) meaning vs. use
- truth-conditional vs. non-truth-conditional meaning
- context independence vs. context dependence

The Appendix collects a variety of formulations that rely on one or another of these distinctions. Here we will briefly review the three types and identify their shortcomings.

For purposes of clarifying the semantics-pragmatics distinction, the distinction between (linguistic) meaning and use is misleading at best. It neglects the case of expressions whose literal meaning is related to use. In addition to the obvious fact that features of illocutionary force can be linguistically encoded, notably by mood (Harnish 1994), there is the interesting case of expressions that are used to perform second-order or what Grice called "noncentral" speech acts (1989: 122). These are acts of commenting on the force, the point, or the role in the discourse of one's utterance. Grice's examples were limited to adverbs like 'however' and 'moreover,' but the list may be easily expanded to include such speech act adverbials as:

(1)   after all, anyway, at any rate, besides, be that as it may, by the way, first of all, finally, frankly, furthermore, if you want my opinion, in conclusion, indeed, in other words, now that you mention it, on the other hand, otherwise, speaking for myself, strictly speaking, to begin with, to oversimplify, to put it mildly

With these it seems that the only way to specify their semantic contribution (when they occur initially or are otherwise set off) is to specify how they are to be used (see Bach 1994a: 148-149). Note that performatives do *not* fall in this category (Bach & Harnish 1979: 10 and 1992).

Speech act adverbials also illustrate that an expression's semantics can consist in non-truth-conditional meaning. Semantic presupposition would illustrate this too if there were such a thing, but Stalnaker (1974) and Grice (1981/1989: ch. 17) have made compelling cases that there is not. Even so, it may be granted that those linguistic devices, such as it-clefts and wh-clefts, which have been thought to encode semantic presupposition, do have some non-truth-conditional function. Like such devices as preposing, inversion, and topicalization, they serve to organize the presentation of information and to redirect focus.

Another example of non-truth-conditional meaning is provided by directly referential expressions, such as indexicals and demonstratives. As Kaplan (1989) has pointed out, if I say, "You are here," it is not part of the truth condition of what I say that I am speaking to you at a certain place. The truth-conditional content of this sentence, relative to the context, is that the person being spoken to is where the speaker is, but this is a singular proposition involving that person and that place. It would be true even if the speaker were silent or not even there. What Kaplan calls the "character" of the terms 'you' and 'here' determines their contribution to the content (relative to the context) of the sentence being uttered, but character is not part of that content.

Now the notion of context is often invoked to explain how pragmatics complements semantics. It is a platitude that a sentence's linguistic meaning generally does not determine what is said in its utterance and that the gap between linguistic meaning and what is said is filled by something called "context." The intuitive idea behind this platitude is that there are different things that a speaker can mean, even when using his words in a thoroughly literal way (even that he is speaking literally is a matter of context - there is no such thing as Katz's "null context" (1977: 14) but only informationally impoverished contexts). What one says in uttering the words can vary, so what fixes what one says cannot be facts about the words alone but must also include facts about the circumstances in which one is using them; those facts comprise the "context of utterance."

It turns out, however, that context plays a role in semantics as well as pragmatics. As we saw above, with indexicals and demonstratives (and tense also), in these cases it is on the semantic side of the ledger that content varies with context. So the distinction between context invariance and context dependence does not provide the basis for drawing the semantics-pragmatics distinction. Confusion on this point, at least prior to Kaplan's work, may have been caused by the use of the term 'pragmatics,' by such philosophers as Bar-Hillel (1954) and Montague (1974), to mean indexical semantics. Also, confusion has been caused by the fact that the limited notion of context relevant to the way in which the reference of terms like 'you' and 'here' is sensitive to context is rarely distinguished from the very broad notion of context that is relevant to pragmatics. Let me explain.

There are two sorts of contextual information, one much more restricted in scope and limited in role than the other. Information that plays the limited role of combining with linguistic information to determine content (in the sense of fixing it) is restricted to a short list of variables, such as the identity of the speaker and the hearer and the time and place of an utterance. Contextual information in the broad sense is anything that the hearer is to take into account to determine (in the sense of ascertain) the speaker's communicative intention. It is often said that what a speaker means "depends on context," is "determined by context" or is "a matter of context," but this is not narrow context in the semantically relevant sense discussed above. When it is said that "Context makes it clear that ...," what is meant is that there are items of information that the hearer can reasonably suppose the speaker to have intended him to take into account to determine what the speaker means. In this broad, pragmatic sense, which is also relevant to whether the speech act is being performed successfully and felicitiously, context does not literally determine content. So not just any sort of context variability is semantic. The variability must be provided for by lexical meaning and sentence grammar.

An important complication here is that there are many (indicative) sentences that do not express complete propositions even relative to a context. Though syntactically complete, they are semantically incomplete (Bach 1994a, 1994b). Here are some straightforward examples (given as the grammatical member of a minimal pair):

(2) Fred finished/*completed yesterday.
(3) Sam ate/*devoured earlier.
(4) Jack tried/*attempted again later.

In each case, even though the verb lacks the complement that a similar verb requires, the sentence is syntactically complete. But the sentence is not semantically complete and the hearer must infer some completing material, e.g., 'the job,' 'lunch,' and 'to call Jill,' to understand the speaker. A pragmatic process of completion is required to arrive at a full proposition, at something with a determinate truth condition. These cases are also counterexamples to the truth-conditional conception of semantics. There is no theoretical basis for denying their semantic incompleteness by inventing hidden syntactic slots that must be filled in order for a complete proposition to be expressed. Rather, we must just acknowledge the fact that some sentences are semantically incomplete (and not just in need semantic values, as with indexicals) and that understanding utterances of them requires pragmatic supplementation.

There is the case of sentences which, strictly and literally, express an unrestricted proposition but are typically used to convey something more specific:

(5) I haven't taken a bath [today].
(6) Nobody [important] goes there any more because it is too crowded.
(7) Abe didn't have sex and [thereby] get infected; he got infected and [then] had sex.

It is sometimes argued that because such sentences are standardly used without the bracketed material but such material is understood anyway, this material enters into what is said by the utterance, into its explicit content (Sperber and Wilson 1986, Récanati 1989). However, this material is not uttered and does not correspond to anything in the syntactic structure of the uttered sentence (even as an empty category in the sense of GB theory). So it is not explicit. It is not implied by what is said but that does not make it explicit either - it is implicit in what said. Such utterances are understood by way of a pragmatic process of expansion. Expansion, like completion, is a process required for the recognition of what I call "conversational implicitures," as opposed to Gricean implicatures (Bach 1994a, 1994b).

We have seen that the various traditional ways of formulating the semantics-pragmatics distinction either leave something out or draw the line at the wrong place. This is similar to what Levinson (1983: 3-35) concluded in his survey of actual and possible formulations, although he ended up opting for the truth-conditional conception of semantics (he did so only provisionally and for historical rather than theoretical reasons). We need a better formulation. Otherwise, we will be left with what Horn (1988: 114) calls the "disjunctive attitude," supposing, if only by default, that any phenomenon that is "too ill-behaved and variable to be treated coherently within the syntactic component, [...] [not] quite arbitrary enough for the lexicon or quite phonological enough for the phonology [...] must be pragmatic."

5 A Better Formulation

What we need is a formulation of the semantics-pragmatics distinction that takes the above distinctions into account but does not rely on them too heavily. It needs to accommodate the following facts, that:

- only literal contents are semantically relevant
- some expressions, as a matter of meaning, are context-sensitive
- narrow context is relevant to semantics, broad context to pragmatics
- non-truth-conditional, use-related information can be linguistically encoded
- rules for using expressions do not determine their actual use

These facts can all be accommodated on the supposition that semantic information pertains to linguistic expressions (sentences and their constituents), whereas pragmatic information pertains to utterances and facts surrounding them. Semantic information about sentences is part of sentence grammar, and it includes information about expressions whose meanings are relevant to use rather than to truth conditions. Linguistically encoded information can pertain to how the present utterance relates to the previous, to the topic of the present utterance, or to what the speaker is doing. That there are these sorts of linguistically encoded information shows that the business of sentence semantics cannot be confined to giving the proposition it expresses. Sentences can do more than express propositions. Also, as we have seen, there are sentences which do less than express propositions, because they are semantically incomplete.

Pragmatic information concerns facts relevant to making sense of a speaker's utterance of a sentence (or other expression). The hearer thereby seeks to identify the speaker's intention in making the utterance. In effect the hearer seeks to explain the fact that the speaker said what he said, in the way he said it. Because the intention is communicative, the hearer's task of identifying it is driven partly by the assumption that the speaker intends him to do this. The speaker succeeds in communicating if the hearer identifies his intention in this way, for communicative intentions are intentions whose "fulfillment consists in their recognition" (Bach & Harnish 1979: 15). Pragmatics is concerned with whatever information is relevant, over and above the linguistic properties of a sentence, to understanding its utterance.

Consider some examples involving pronouns. There is no semantic basis for interpreting the pronouns one way in

(8)   Ann told Betty that she wanted to borrow her car.

and the opposite way in

(9)   Ann told Betty that she could not borrow her car.

The hearer relies on extralinguistic information to interpret one utterance one way and the other in the opposite way. The so-called "E-type" pronoun in

(10)   Most philosophers who have written a book think it is brilliant.

is interpreted as going proxy for the description 'the book he wrote,' and the "pronoun of laziness" in

(11)   John carried his luggage but everyone else checked it in.

is also interpreted descriptively - 'it' is not taken as being used to refer to John's luggage (see Bach 1987a: 258-261, and Neale 1990: 180-191). In none of these cases is there any semantic requirement that the pronoun be interpreted in a certain way. The explanation for the preferred interpretation is pragmatic.

As part of linguistics and philosophy of language, pragmatics does not provide detailed explanations of how interpretation works in actual practice. This is a problem for cognitive and social psychology. For this reason it seems futile for linguists to seek a formal pragmatics. The task of explaining how utterances change context, for example, or how they exploit context, is not a job for linguistic theory by itself. The task is impossible without introducing general considerations about human reasoning and rational communication. Similarly, it is unreasonable to complain that theories like Grice's account of conversational implicature provide no algorithm for conversational inference, so that, when applied to particular cases they simply pull implicatures out of a hat (see Sperber & Wilson 1986, Kempson 1988, Davies 1996). This is not just a problem for Grice's theory.

At any rate, whereas semantic information is grammatically associated with the linguistic material uttered, pragmatic information arises only in relation to the act of uttering that material. (In fact, a stony silence can impart pragmatic information and thereby communicate something.) Whereas semantic information is encoded in what is uttered, pragmatic information is generated by the act of uttering it. No sentence encodes the fact that it is being uttered. Even the sentence 'I am speaking' is not analytic. The act of producing the utterance exploits the information encoded but by its very performance creates new information. That information, combined with the information encoded, provides the basis for the hearer's identification of the speaker's communicative intention. Contextual information is relevant to the hearer's inference only insofar as it can reasonably be taken as intended to be taken into account, and that requires the supposition that the speaker is producing the utterance with the intention that it be taken into account. In contrast, the encoded information provides the input to the hearer's inference in any context.

6 Challenges

I foresee three main challenges to the semantics-pragmatics distinction, at least as it has been drawn here. They would contend that our formulation rests on one or another false assumption, (1) that semantics is autonomous from pragmatics, (2) that literal meaning is a viable notion, and (3) that communication involves Gricean reflexive intentions. In reply, I will suggest that each challenge identifies certain empirical complications for the application of the semantics-pragmatics distinction but does not undermine the distinction itself. For this reason, defending those assumptions against these challenges will help clarify the distinction.

6.1 Semantic Autonomy

Occasionally it is claimed that pragmatics somehow impinges on semantics. Consider, for example, that words are often used in creative ways that depart from any of their conventional meanings, e.g., using nouns as verbs (Clark 1992: chs. 10 & 11) or cases of metonymy or deferred reference. Utterances of sentences like

(12) Chicago always votes Democrat.
(13) Philosophy has a tenure-track opening.
(14) John was so thirsty he drank three mugs.

depart from their literal meanings, although people generally don't think of such uses as not quite literal. In such cases the sentence possesses no meaning other than its usual conventional meaning(s) - it just is not being used in accordance with its meaning(s).
Whereas the difference between

(15) Josh played his favorite violin yesterday.

and

(16) Josh played his favorite concerto yesterday.

seems to have a clearly semantic basis (in terms of the different thematic roles of 'concerto' and 'violin'), the autonomy of semantics relative to pramatics might be challenged on account of examples like the following:

(17) John finished the newspaper/the letter/the meal.
(18) Jack enjoyed the food/the movie/the day.
(19) Jill wants a soda/a salad/a fork/a car.

What ordinarily counts as finishing a newspaper, a letter, or a meal varies from one case to another. Typically, you finish reading a newspaper, finish reading or writing a letter, and finish cooking or eating a meal. It seems to be a matter of semantics that verbs like 'start' and 'finish' are understood as having a verb (in gerundive form) in its complement, but it is a pragmatic matter which verb that is. The situation is similar with 'enjoy' and 'want' in the other examples above. Taken by themselves, these sentences are semantically incomplete in the sense described earlier. This does not mean, however, that the pragmatic processes required for understanding utterances of them somehow impinges upon their semantics. Nor is this shown, as Récanati (1989, 1995) has argued, by the fact that the completion is accomplished before the entire sentence is processed. The semantics-pragmatics distinction is concerned with the information available to the hearer, not with its real-time, online processing, which, it may be granted, is far from sequential.
Gazdar (1979: 164-168) argues against the autonomy of semantics by means of examples of other sorts. One of his examples is:

(20) To have a child and get married is worse than getting married and having a child.

Since the alternatives here are semantically equivalent, given the logical conjunction reading of 'and,' how can we explain the force of an utterance of this sentence? Gazdar thinks that the correct pragmatic explanation has semantic import. However, as we saw earlier with a similar example, the proper pragmatic explanation appeals to the process of expansion, which has no semantic repercussions. It requires merely the supposition that the sentence is not being used with its strict, conventional meaning. On the expansion story, this follows from the fact that its utterance would normally be understood as including two implicit occurrences of the word 'then.'

Gazdar also argues the meaning of this permission sentence,

(21) Inmates may smoke or drink.

is stronger than the combined meaning of the disjunction of permissions,

(22) Inmates may smoke or inmates may drink.

and offers an account of its semantics that involves pragmatic considerations. However, this example may be disposed of in Gricean fashion. For if the utterance of 'Inmates may smoke or drink' is a permission, presumably it is a permission that can be complied with. The inmates can only be expected to interpret it in such a way that they can determine what they are permitted to do. If its import were either to permit smoking or to permit drinking without specifying which, there would be no way for an inmate to know how to comply with it.

6.2 Literal Meaning

In formulating the semantics-pragmatics distinction, I have made no attempt to characterize the job of semantics. But as we have seen, there is more for a semantic theory of a language to do than to give a compositional account of the truth conditions of or the proposition expressed by each sentence, as a function of its syntactic structure and the semantic values of its constituents. But it would seem that the semantics-pragmatics distinction as formulated presupposes a well-defined level of lexical semantics and a viable distinction between literal and nonliteral meaning. There are several possible reasons for doubting that there is such a level.

I am not referring here to general skepticism about linguistic meaning, based on behaviorism about language use. Nor am I referring to doubts about linguistic meaning based on the familiar observation that most words are impossible to define, at least in terms of singly necessary and jointly sufficient conditions of application, and are vague or open-textured. These platitudes show not that Wittgenstein and Quine were right about linguistic meaning but only that it is not what philosophers used to think it to be. The two arguments I want to consider claim that the notion of literal meaning required by the semantics-pragmatics distinction cannot do justice to the general context-dependence of language.

One such argument is based on polysemy, as exemplified by the adjectives 'sad,' 'long,' and 'dangerous' as they occur in the following phrases:

(23) sad person/sad face/sad day/sad music
(24) long stick/long movie/long book
(25) dangerous drug/dangerous game/dangerous road

The import of these adjectives varies with the noun they modify, but they do not seem to be cases of ambiguity, of linguistic coincidence (or else they would not have similarly-behaving counterparts in other languages). The argument is that since this variation in import is not due to ambiguity, it must have a pragmatic explanation. However, there is an alternative possibility, namely that polysemy involves what Pustejovsky (1995) calls "co-compositionality": what varies from case to case is not a term's semantic properties but how those properties interact with those of the term it is construction with. I do not endorse Pustejovsky's ambitious theory of how this works, but certainly it is an improvement over what he calls "sense enumeration lexicons" (1995: 29). The relevant point here is that the phenomenon seems too systematic to be relegated to pragmatics. It does not justify the claim that pragmatics impinges on semantics.

The other argument relies on the observation that natural language is context-sensitive through and through. Contrary to the Gricean picture, it is argued, understanding an utterance is not just a matter of knowing the conventional meaning of what is uttered and, as necessary, resolving ambiguities, determining references, and distinguishing what is implicated from what is said. From this it is inferred that, even leaving aside disambiguation and reference fixing, there is often a pragmatic element in what is said, which, therefore, is not determined by the semantics of what is uttered. The general context-dependence of "interpretations" of utterances is supposed to show that what is said is not a purely semantic matter (Kempson 1988, Récanati 1989, 1996).

The trouble with these arguments is that they run roughshod over a number of straightforward distinctions. Ignoring Austin's distinction between locutionary and illocutionary acts (1960: 92-101), they fail to distinguish what is said from what is stated. They fail to distinguish what is said, in the strict and literal sense tied to the syntactic form of the sentence, with what is directly communicated in uttering the sentence, which may include elements that are not associated with anything in the sentence. They fail to distinguish context in the narrow sense described earlier, which is relevant to the interpretation of the sentence uttered, from context in the broad sense, which is relevant to the interpretation of its utterance, i.e., to identifying the speaker's overall communicative intention.

It is trivially true that in the broad sense of context every utterance is context-sensitive. After all, it is never part of the meaning of a sentence that on a particular occasion of use it is being used to communicate. That is something the hearer presumes from the fact that the speaker is uttering the sentence. This "communicative presumption," as Bach and Harnish (1979: 7) call it, comes into play even if what the speaker means does not extend beyond or depart in any way from the meaning of the sentence he utters. For it is never part of what a sentence encodes that it has to be used literally - the hearer must infer (even if only by default) that it is being used literally. The utterance does not carry its literalness on its sleeve. It might contain the word 'literally,' but even that word can be used nonliterally.

6.3   Gricean Intentions

Our formulation of the semantics-pragmatics distinction relies heavily on a Gricean conception of communicative intentions, for it takes as key to the pragmatic side the idea that in any communication situation extralinguistic information comes into play because, and only because, such information is intended, or taken by the hearer as intended, to be taken into account. So another way of challenging our formulation of the semantics-pragmatics distinction would be to challenge the Gricean view of communication.

Such a challenge has been mounted by Sperber & Wilson (1986) with their so-called relevance theory (in relevance theory 'relevance' does not mean relevance). The "principle of relevance" states that, as a matter of general cognitive fact, people seek to maximize contextual effects at a minimum of processing cost. Apart from not explaining how to measure contextual effects and processing costs, how to make them commensurate with each other, or why there is always a unique way satisfying the principle (Bach and Harnish 1987), relevance theory ignores the fundamental fact that the hearer is to recognize the speaker's intention partly on the basis that he is so intended. Instead, relevance theory seems to assume that in the context of communication everyone is an applied relevance theorist. That is, people are supposed to gear their utterances to their listeners' inherent propensity to discover maximize contextual effects at a minimum of processing cost.

Contrary to Sperber and Wilson's complaint that Grice's account requires the hearer to know what the speaker's intention is in order to identify it (1986: 28-31 and 256-257), there is nothing paradoxical about the reflexivity of communicative intentions (Bach 1987b). For all that this reflexivity involves is that the hearer is to take into account the fact that he is intended to identify the speaker's intention, whatever that intention is. That is, the hearer may presume that the speaker's intention is identifiable under the circumstances. This leaves open, of course, the question of how the hearer, even when armed with that presumption, manages to figure out the speaker's intention. The basic shortcoming of relevance theory is that it provides no place for this presumption. It replaces the distinctive feature of rational communication with an a priori generalization about human cognitive processes.

Relevance theory does not do justice to the fact that whereas semantic information is associated with the sentence uttered, pragmatic information is tied to the fact that the speaker is uttering it. Any contextual information, whether about the immediate situation (including what has been said previously), the conversants' relationship, or their background knowledge, is relevant (in the ordinary sense of 'relevant') to the interpretation of the utterance only because it is intended, or can reasonably be taken as intended, to be taken into account. That is why, for example, the pragmatic paradoxes philosophers discussed a half century ago arise only because the speaker actually utters the seemingly paradox sentence, e.g.,

(26) It is raining but I don't believe it.
(27) I am not speaking.
(28) I am lying.

This fact was also essential to the notion of contextual implication that predated Grice's notion of conversational implicature. It is essential to understanding why presupposition is a pragmatic phenomenon, something done by speakers not by their words, and why implicatures "are carried not by what is said but only by the saying of what is said, or by 'putting it that way'" (Grice 1967/1989: 39).

7   Conclusion: Benefits

There is nothing new in our formulation of the semantics-pragmatics distinction. It is relies on the familiar distinctions between sentences and utterances and between linguistic (grammatical) and extralinguistic information. What is new, if anything, is the way in which it accommodates various other distinctions without attempting to reduce the semantics-pragmatics distinction to any of these. The present formulation has aimed to:

1. simplify the task of semantic theory by identifying a principled reason which, when applicable, justifies not addressing certain phenomena that might otherwise seem the business of semantics to explain,
2. keep open the option that certain seemingly pragmatic phenomena might be correlated with or constrained by syntactic features in such a way as merit classification as semantic,
3. avoid burdening semantics with the false assumption that every (indicative) sentence expresses a proposition (even relative to a context) and does nothing else,
4. accommodate the fact that contextual parameters and speech act information can be linguistically encoded, but without equating context in the broad sense relevant to communication with context in the narrow sense relevant to providing values for the contextual parameters that determine or at least constrain the force of literal utterances,
5. respect intuitions about what is and what is not semantic without always accepting them at face value (sometimes intuitions are better accounted for not by explaining them but by explaining them away), and
6. justify and preserve the distinction between interpretation of a sentence and interpretation of an utterance and thereby the distinction between narrow linguistic competence and general communicative rationality.

These broad features of our account do not determine on which side of the semantics-pragmatics boundary particular linguistic phenomena fall. Whether a given phenomenon has a semantic or a pragmatic explanation or, as is often the case, some combination of both, must be settled on a case-by-case basis. Obviously it is one thing to formulate the semantics-pragmatics distinction and another thing to apply it.

8 Appendix: A Chronology of Formulations

Morris (1938):
  Semantics deals with the relation of signs to [...] objects which they may or do denote. Pragmatics concerns the relation of signs to their interpreters. (1938, 1971: 35, 43)

Stalnaker (1972):
  Syntax studies sentences, semantics studies propositions. Pragmatics is the study of linguistic acts and the contexts in which they are performed. There are two major types of problems to be solved within pragmatics: first, to define interesting types of speech acts and speech products; second, to characterize the features of the speech context which help determine which proposition is expressed by a given sentence. [...] It is a semantic problem to specify the rules for matching up sentences of a natural language with the propositions that they express. In most cases, however, the rules will not match sentences directly with propositions, but will match sentences with propositions relative to features of the context in which the sentence is used. These contextual features are part of the subject matter of pragmatics. (p. 383)

Katz (1977):
  [I] draw the theoretical line between semantic interpretation and pragmatic interpretation by taking the semantic component to properly represent only those aspects of the meaning of the sentence that an ideal speaker-hearer of the language would know in an anonymous letter situation, [...] [where there is] no clue whatever about the motive, circumstances of transmission, or any other factor relevant to understanding the sentence on the basis of its context of utterance. (p. 14)

Gazdar (1979):
  PRAGMATICS = MEANING - TRUTH CONDITIONS (p. 2)
  What we need in addition is some function that tells us about the meaning of utterances. [...] The domain of this pragmatic function is the set of utterances, which are pairs of sentences and contexts, so that for each utterance, our function will return as a value a new context - the context as changed by the sentence uttered [...] . And we can treat the meaning of the utterance as the difference between the original context and the context arrived at by utterance the sentence. [This applies to only] a restricted subset of pragmatic aspects of meaning. (pp. 4f.)

Kempson (1988):
  Semantics provides a complete account of sentence meaning for the language, [by] recursively specifying the truth conditions of the sentences of the language. [...]

Pragmatics provides an account of how sentences are used in utterances to convey information in context. (p. 139)

The Oxford Companion to Philosophy (Fotion 1995):
Pragmatics is the study of language which focuses attention on the users and the context of language use rather than on reference, truth, or grammar. (p. 709)

The Cambridge Dictionary of Philosophy (Lycan 1995):
Pragmatics studies the use of language in context, and the context-dependence of various aspects of linguistic interpretation. [...] [Its branches include the theory of how] one and the same sentence can express different meanings or propositions from context to context, owing to ambiguity or indexicality or both, [...] speech act theory, and the theory of conversational implicature. (p. 588)

The Blackwell Companion to Philosophy (Davies 1996):
The distinction between semantics and pragmatics is, roughly, the distinction between the significance conventionally or literally attached to words, and thence to whole sentences, and the further significance that can be worked out, by more general principles, using contextual information. (p. 124)

References

Atlas, J. (1989): Philosophy Without Ambiguity. Oxford: Oxford University Press.
Austin, J. (1962): How To Do Things With Words. Oxford: Oxford University Press.
Bach, K. (1987a): Thought and Reference. Oxford: Oxford University Press.
Bach, K. (1987b): "On communicative intentions". Mind & Language 2, 141-154.
Bach, K. (1994a): "Conversational impliciture". Mind & Language 9, 124-162.
Bach, K. (1994b): "Semantic slack: What is Said and More". In: S.L. Tsohatzidis, ed.: Foundations of Speech Act Theory. London: Routledge, 267-291.
Bach, K. & R. Harnish (1979): Linguistic Communication and Speech Acts. Cambridge, Mass: The MIT Press.
Bach, K. & R. Harnish (1987): "Relevant questions". Brain and Behavioral Sciences 10, 711-712.
Bach, K. & R. Harnish (1992): "How performatives really work: a reply to Searle". Linguistics and Philosophy 15, 93-110.
Bar-Hillel, Y. (1954): "Indexical expressions". Mind 63, 359-379.
Bar-Hillel, Y. (1971): "Out of the pragmatic wastebasket". Linguistic Inquiry 2, 401-407.
Clark, H. (1992): Arenas of Language Use. Chicago: University of Chicago Press.
Davies, M. (1995): "Philosophy of language". In: N. Bunnin & E. Tsui-James, eds.: The Blackwell Companion to Philosophy. Oxford: Blackwell, 90-139.
Fotion, N. (1995): "Pragmatics". In: T. Honderich, ed.: The Oxford Companion to Philosophy. Oxford: Oxford University Press, 709.
Gazdar, G. (1979): Pragmatics: Implicature, Presupposition, and Logical Form. London: Academic Press.
Green, G. (1989): Pragmatics and Natural Language Understanding. Hillsdale, NJ: Lawrence Erlbaum Associates.
Grice, P. (1989): Studies in the Way of Words. Cambridge, Mass.: Harvard University Press.
Harnish, R. (1994): "Mood, meaning, and speech acts". In: S.L. Tsohatzidis, ed.: Foundations of Speech Act Theory. London: Routledge, 407-459.
Harris, R. (1993): The Linguistics Wars. Oxford: Oxford University Press.

Horn, L. (1988): "Pragmatic theory". In: F. Newmeyer, ed.: Linguistics: The Cambridge Survey, Vol. I. Cambridge: Cambridge University Press, 113-145.
Hungerland, I. (1960): "Contextual implication". Inquiry 3, 211-258.
Kaplan, D. (1989): "Demonstratives". In: J. Almog & J. Perry & H. Wettstein, eds.: Themes from Kaplan. Oxford: Oxford University Press, 481-563.
Katz, J. (1977): Propositional Structure and Illocutionary Force. New York: Crowell.
Kempson, R. (1988): "Grammar and conversational principles". In: F. Newmeyer, ed.: Linguistics: The Cambridge Survey, Vol. II. Cambridge: Cambridge University Press, 139-163.
Kripke, S. (1977): "Speaker's reference and semantic reference". Midwest Studies in Philosophy 2, 255-296.
Levinson, S. (1983): Pragmatics. Cambridge: Cambridge University Press.
Lycan, W. (1995): "Philosophy of language". In: R. Audi, ed.: The Cambridge Dictionary of Philosophy. Cambridge: Cambridge University Press, 586-589.
Montague, R. (1974): Pragmatics. In: R. Thomason, ed.: Formal Philosophy. New Haven: Yale University Press.
Morris, C. (1938, 1971): "Foundations of the theory of signs". In: C. Morris: Writings on the Theory of Signs. The Hague: Mouton, 17-74.
Neale, S. (1990): Descriptions. Cambridge, Mass.: The MIT Press.
Parsons, T. (1990): Events in the Semantics of English. Cambridge, Mass.: The MIT Press.
Prince, E. (1988): "Discourse analysis". In: F. Newmeyer, ed.: Linguistics: The Cambridge Survey, Vol. II. Cambridge, Eng.: Cambridge University Press, 164-182.
Pustejovsky, J. (1995): The Generative Lexicon. Cambridge, Mass.: The MIT Press.
Récanati, F. (1989): "The pragmatics of what is said". Mind & Language 4, 295-329.
Récanati, F. (1995): "The alleged priority of literal interpretation". Cognitive Science 19, 207-232.
Récanati, F. (1996): "Domains of discourse". Linguistics and Philosophy 19, 445-475.
Sadock, J. (1988): "Speech act distinctions in grammar". In: F. Newmeyer, ed.: Linguistics: The Cambridge Survey, Vol II. Cambridge, Eng.: Cambridge University Press, 183-197.
Searle, J.R. (1969): Speech Acts. Cambridge, Eng.: Cambridge University Press.
Sperber, D. & D. Wilson (1986): Relevance. Cambridge, Mass.: Harvard University Press.
Stalnaker, R. (1972): "Pragmatics". In: G. Harman & D. Davidson, eds.: Semantics of Natural Language. Dordrecht: Reidel, 380-397.
Stalnaker, R. (1974): "Pragmatic Presuppositions". In: M. Munitz & P. Unger, eds.: Semantics and Philosophy. New York: New York University Press, 197-213.
Strawson, P. (1950): "On referring". Mind 59, 320-344.
Strawson, P. (1952): Introduction to Logical Theory. London: Methuen.

Was wir von Aristoteles über die Bedeutung deutscher Wörter lernen können: Über konversationelle Implikaturen und Wortsemantik*

Thomas Becker, München

1 Das logische Quadrat des Aristoteles

Aristoteles unterscheidet in seinen "Kategorien" mehrere Arten von Oppositionen, darunter die "Kontrarietät" von der "Kontradiktion", z. B.:[1]

(1) Konträr (enantíon): *gut/schlecht, jeder Mensch ist weiß/kein Mensch ist weiß* (Kat. 12a, De int. 17b);
kontradiktorisch (antíphasis): *Sokrates ist krank/Sokrates ist nicht krank* (Kat. 13b).

Diesen beiden Arten von Gegensätzen entsprechen zwei verschiedene Arten von sprachlicher Negation, die konträre und die kontradiktorische Negation. Von einem kontradiktorischen Satzpaar gilt, daß immer genau ein Satz wahr ist und der andere falsch - *tertium non datur*. Sokrates ist entweder krank oder nicht. Wenn es Sokrates nicht gibt, dann ist der Satz *Sokrates ist nicht krank* für Aristoteles wahr: "Denn wenn er nicht ist, ist es falsch, daß er krank ist, und wahr, daß er nicht krank ist" (Kat. 13b). Der Satz *Sokrates ist nicht krank* ist für Aristoteles nämlich keine Aussage über Sokrates, daß er nicht-krank, also gesund ist, es ist vielmehr die Aussage, daß das Prädikat 'krank' dem Subjekt 'Sokrates' nicht zugesprochen werden kann, und dafür ist die Nicht-Existenz des Subjekts ein hinreichender Grund.

Dieses *tertium non datur* gilt nicht für die konträre Negation: Nicht alles ist gut oder schlecht, vieles ist mittelmäßig. Es ist auch nicht so, daß entweder "jeder Mensch weiß ist", oder "kein Mensch weiß ist", vielmehr sind manche so und manche so. Zu konträren Sätzen gibt es ein "Mittleres" (Kat. 12a, Met. 10, 1057a). Konträre Sätze können gleichzeitig falsch sein. Der kontradiktorische Gegensatz dagegen hat nach Aristoteles kein Mittleres (Kat. 13b, Met. 10, 1057a).

---

*   Für wertvolle Hinweise bedanke ich mich bei Beatrice Primus.

Es gibt also mindestens zwei Arten von Negation. Weil nun die beiden Arten von Negation verschieden sind, so gelangt man durch die kontradiktorische Negation eines Satzes zu einem anderen Satz als durch die konträre Negation. Wenn man einen konträr negierten Satz noch einmal kontradiktorisch negiert, kommt man nicht an den Ausgangspunkt zurück, sondern an eine andere Stelle. So wird durch die beiden Arten der Negation ein Quadrat von vier Sätzen aufgespannt, die in bestimmten Beziehungen zueinander stehen, vgl. Fig. 1:[2]

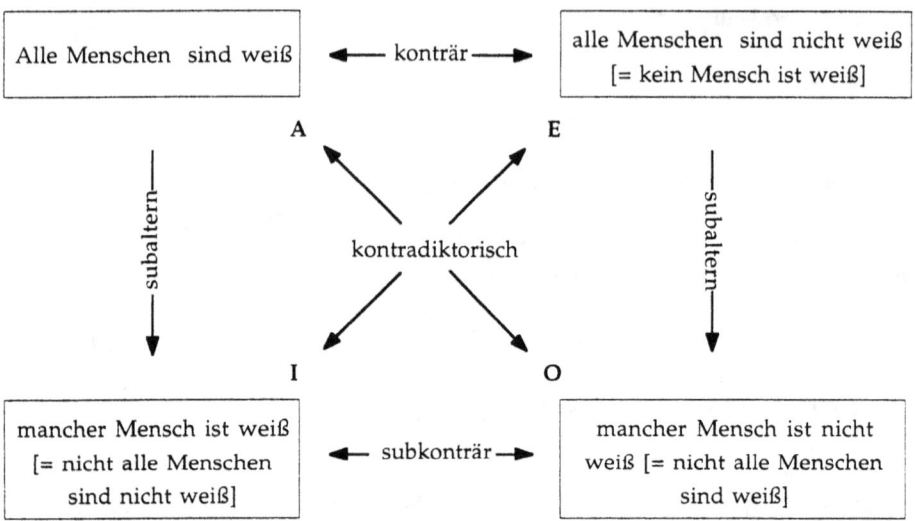

Fig. 1: **Das logische Quadrat des Aristoteles:**

Kontradiktorische Sätze können nach der klassischen Logik nicht gleichzeitig falsch sein, d. h. es muß immer einer von beiden wahr sein, der andere falsch. Konträre Sätze können hingegen gleichzeitig falsch sein, nämlich wenn das "Tertium" gegeben ist, in dem Beispiel der Graphik in Fig. 1, wenn manche Menschen weiß sind, andere nicht. Mit Aristoteles' Worten (An. pr., 63b):

> Ich lasse aber dem sprachlichen Ausdruck nach sich vier Arten von Sätzen entgegengesetzt sein: jedem und keinem zukommen, jedem und nicht jedem, einem und keinem, einem und einem nicht, in Wirklichkeit aber nur drei. Denn einem und einem nicht ist sich nur im Worte entgegengesetzt. Hiervon sind mir konträr entgegengesetzt die allgemeinen Aussagen: jedem und keinem zukommen: wie: jede Wissenschaft ist sittlich gut oder ist eine Tugend und: keine ist es; die anderen gelten mir als kontradiktorisch entgegengesetzt.

Subkonträre Sätze sind kompatibel, "nur im Worte entgegengesetzt", sie "können [...] gleichzeitig wahr sein" (De int. 17b). Die Negation führt dann zu einem inkompatiblen

Satz, wenn sie weiten Skopus hat, d. h. außerhalb des Quantors steht, wie bei der kontradiktorischen Negation:

(2) Weiter Skopus der Negation:
Alle Menschen sind weiß / Nicht alle Menschen sind weiß:
$\forall x[M(x) \Rightarrow W(x)] / \neg \forall x[M(x) \Rightarrow W(x)]$;
Mancher Mensch ist weiß / Nicht mancher (=kein) Mensch ist weiß:
$\exists x[M(x) \wedge W(x)] / \neg \exists x[M(x) \wedge W(x)]$

Bei der inneren Negation (mit engem Skopus bezüglich des Quantors) hängt es von der Stärke des Quantors ab, ob der negierte Satz zum ursprünglichen inkompatibel ist (vgl. Löbner 1990: 92ff., Horn 1989: 237):

(3) Enger Skopus der Negation:
Alle Menschen sind weiß / Alle Menschen sind nicht weiß:
$\forall x[M(x) \Rightarrow W(x)] / \forall x[M(x) \Rightarrow \neg W(x)]$;
Mancher Mensch ist weiß/ Mancher Mensch ist nicht weiß:
$\exists x[M(x) \wedge W(x)] / \exists x[M(x) \wedge \neg W(x)]$

Die innere Negation führt bei dem schwachen Existenzquantor nicht zu einem inkompatiblen Satz. Der stärkste schwache Quantor ist "die Hälfte der", vgl. Tab. 1:[3]

Tab. 1: Starke und schwache Operatoren		
Ausgangssatz:	Innere Negation davon:	
Alle Menschen sind weiß	Alle Menschen sind nicht weiß	inkompatibel[4]
Die meisten Menschen sind weiß	Die meisten Menschen sind nicht weiß	inkompatibel
Die Hälfte der Menschen ist weiß	Die Hälfte der Menschen ist nicht weiß	kompatibel
Viele Menschen sind weiß	Viele Menschen sind nicht weiß	kompatibel
Mancher Mensch ist weiß	Mancher Mensch ist nicht weiß	kompatibel

Die Darstellung in Tab. 1 ist allerdings nicht korrekt; sie enthält einen Fehler, der vielen unterläuft, z. B. Aristoteles selbst. *Alle Menschen sind weiß* und *Alle Menschen sind nicht weiß* sind nicht inkompatibel. Aristoteles' System ist nur dann konsistent, wenn man fordert, daß jedes Prädikat mindestens auf ein Objekt zutrifft. Diese Forderung ist jedoch zu stark, denn von einem Einhorn möchte man doch wenigstens sagen können, daß es nicht existiert. Der Satz *Manches Einhorn ist nicht weiß* ist falsch, weil es keine Einhörner gibt; der dazu kontradiktorische Satz *Alle Einhörner sind weiß* ist somit wahr.[5] Weil *Manches Einhorn ist weiß* falsch ist, ist *Alle Einhörner sind nicht weiß* bzw. *Kein Einhorn ist weiß* wahr. Für Einhörner sind der affirmative und der negative Allsatz gleichzeitig wahr, somit nicht inkompatibel. Nach Aristoteles aber "können diese Sätze nicht zugleich wahr sein" (De int. 17b). An den Einhörnern erkennt man auch, daß aus dem All-Satz der Existenzsatz nicht folgt, denn der All-Satz ist für Einhörner wahr, der Existenzsatz falsch. Für Aristoteles gilt jedoch die Folgerung: "Wenn A jedem B zukommt, kommt auch B irgendeinem A zu" (An. pr. 25a).[6] Diese Komplikation der leeren Allsätze stört ein wenig die Symmetrie des logischen Quadrats.

Zurück zum subkonträren Satzpaar *Mancher Mensch ist weiß/Mancher Mensch ist nicht weiß*. Die Intuition kann einen dazu verleiten, diese Sätze für bedeutungsgleich zu halten, wobei der eine aus dem anderen folgt und umgekehrt. Aristoteles äußert sich m. W. nicht zu diesem Satzpaar, aber zu dem entsprechenden subkonträren im modalen logischen Quadrat, vgl. Fig. 2:[7]

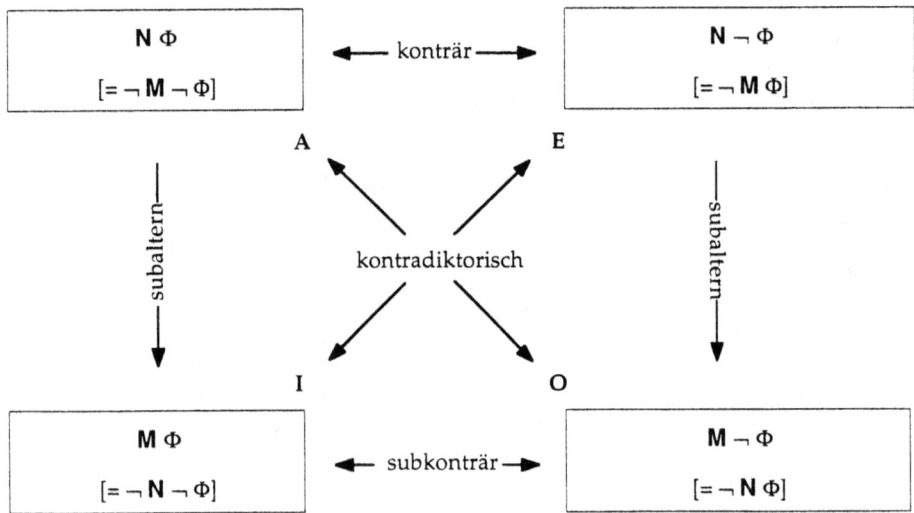

Fig. 2: **Das logische Quadrat für modale Operatoren:**

Das modale subkonträre Satzpaar ist nach Aristoteles äquivalent (De int. 21b):

> Deshalb möchten sich auch die Bestimmungen vermögend zu sein und vermögend nicht zu sein gegenseitig zu folgen scheinen: ein und dasselbe ist vermögend zu sein und nicht zu sein.

Diese Äquivalenz ist vertretbar, wenn man unter "möglich" soviel versteht wie "kontingent", also "weder notwendig noch unmöglich". Sie führt aber zu einem Widerspruch, wenn man annimmt, "möglich, daß Φ" folge aus "notwendig, daß Φ".[8] Diese Folgerungsbeziehung beweist Aristoteles jedoch (De int.22b):

> Denn was notwendig ist, ist vermögend zu sein [= möglich]. Denn sonst würde die Negation folgen, da man alles entweder bejahen oder verneinen muß. Es würde mithin, wenn es nicht vermögend wäre zu sein, unmöglich sein, so daß, was notwendig ist, unmöglich wäre, was doch ungereimt ist.

Die Formulierung "sonst würde die Negation folgen" ist etwas verwirrend, was die Überzeugungskraft des Beweises schmälert (vgl. dazu Weidemann 1994: 433ff.). Mit etwas gutem Willen kann man ihn so interpretieren: Jeder Satz, der notwendig wahr ist, ist möglicherweise wahr. Andernfalls gäbe es einen Satz, der notwendig wahr ist und nicht möglicherweise wahr, also einen Satz, der notwendigerweise wahr ist und notwendigerweise nicht wahr ist (wegen der Äquivalenz von "nicht möglich" und "notwendig nicht", vgl. Fig. 2). Das ist der Beweis der Folgerung von der linken oberen Ecke des Quadrats ("A" im logischen Quadrat) auf die linke untere (I). Nun behauptet Aristoteles (ohne Beweis), daß auch aus I der subkonträre Satz O folgt, also insgesamt aus A seine Kontradiktion O (ibid.):

> Nun folgt aber auf vermögend zu sein: nicht unvermögend zu sein, hierauf aber: nicht notwendig seiend; mithin ergibt sich, daß das notwendig Seiende nicht notwendig ist, was ungereimt ist.

Aristoteles löst diesen Widerspruch auf, indem er zwei Bedeutungen von "möglich" ansetzt (De int.23a):

> Einige Vermögen aber sind homonym. [...] So folgt auf das notwendig Seiende das Vermögen zu sein, jedoch nicht jedes solche Vermögen.

Der mit "kontingent" übersetzte Begriff (endechómenon) ist nach De int. 22a mit "möglich" äquivalent:

> Auf vermögend zu sein (dynatón eînai) folgt kontingent sein nach Seite des Seins (endéchesthai eînai), und dieses ist mit jenem konvertibel.

Er verwendet ihn aber auch in der modernen Bedeutung 'nicht notwendig und nicht notwendig nicht' (An. pr. 32a):

> Es lassen sich aber alle kontingenten Sätze (propositiones de contingenti) umkehren [...], wie z.B. der Satz: es ist kontingent (vermögend) zu sein, mit dem Satz: es ist kontingent (vermögend) nicht zu sein, vertauscht werden kann.

Auch "kontingent" bleibt mehrdeutig (An. pr. 25a):

> Bei den kontingenten (eine Möglichkeit aussprechenden) Sätzen muß man unterscheiden, da man von kontingent in vielfachem Sinne spricht. Denn wir nennen in gleicher Weise das Notwendige kontingent, das nicht Notwendige und das Mögliche.

Diese Mehrdeutigkeit des Begriffs "möglich" ist zwar eine Unsauberkeit der Aristotelischen Modallogik, sie entspricht aber dem Gebrauch dieses Wortes. Wenn wir in einem Satz das Wort *möglicherweise* gebrauchen, schließen wir normalerweise aus, daß der Satz notwendigerweise wahr ist, manchmal jedoch nicht. Dieser uneinheitliche Gebrauch betrifft nicht nur Sätze mit dem Wort *möglicherweise*, sondern alle partikulär affirmativen Sätze (I). Wenn jemand sagt: *Manche Teilnehmer haben die Klausur bestanden*, so versteht man den Satz so, daß nicht alle Teilnehmer die Klausur bestanden haben. Trotzdem ist der Satz nicht falsch, wenn alle Teilnehmer bestanden haben.

Ein drittes Beispiel ist der Gebrauch von *oder*. Die aussagenlogischen Junktoren *und* und *oder* lassen sich in einem logischen Quadrat anordnen, vgl. Fig. 3:

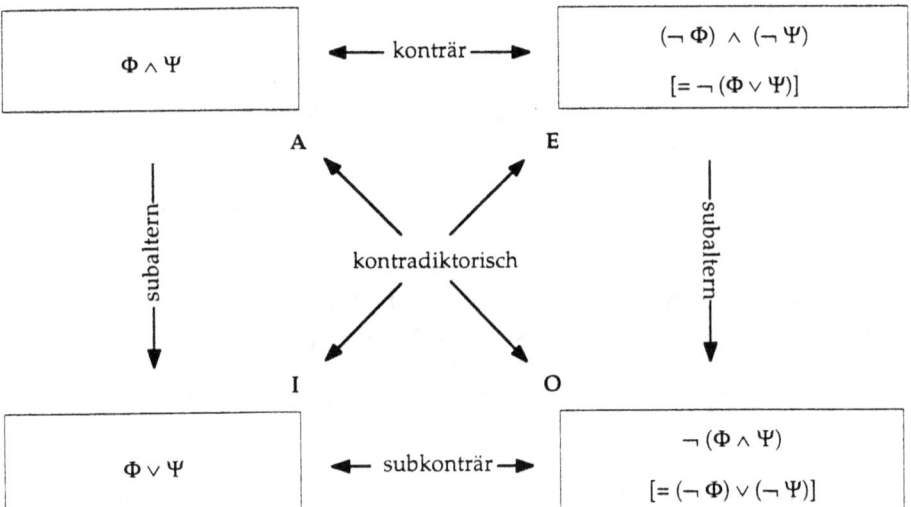

Fig. 3: **Das logische Quadrat für "und" und "oder":**

Die aussagenlogische Formel "Φ / Ψ" ist auch dann wahr, wenn sowohl Φ als auch Ψ wahr sind. Das wird häufig als Abweichung vom allgemeinen Sprachgebrauch angesehen, der in Duden GWb (s. v. *oder*) verzeichnet ist: "drückt aus, daß von zwei od. mehreren Möglichkeiten jeweils nur eine als Tatsache feststehen kann". Diese Bedeutung wird auch das exklusive *oder* genannt, das den Fall "$\Phi \wedge \Psi$" ausschließt. Wenn jemand sagt, daß er nach Frankreich oder Italien fährt, dann wird er so verstanden, daß er nicht in beide Länder zu fahren beabsichtigt. Die aussagenlogische Bedeutung, das "inklusive *oder"*, ist in Duden GWb nicht verzeichnet, obwohl wir das Wort manchmal auch so verstehen. Im deutschen Strafgesetzbuch steht sinngemäß, daß derjenige mit Freiheitsstrafe nicht unter 2 Jahren bestraft wird, der Geld fälscht oder gefälschtes Geld in den Verkehr bringt (§146 StGB). Wer beides tut, kann sich vor Gericht nicht darauf berufen, daß er nicht A *oder* B gemacht hat, sondern A *und* B.

Die Aufdeckung der Systematik hinter diesen drei vermeintlichen Ambiguitäten verdanken wir Horn (1972)[9], der zeigte, daß in allen Fällen die inklusive (die universelle Affirmation A einschließende) Variante als Bedeutung dieser Ausdrücke angenommen werden kann. Die Negation der universellen Affirmation (O) ist nicht Bestandteil der Bedeutung, sondern wird in manchen (nicht allen!) Fällen durch eine "konversationelle Implikatur" erschlossen[10]; das sind Schlüsse, die nicht aus dem Gesagten allein gezogen werden, sondern aus dem Gesagten und weiteren Prämissen, und zwar zusätzlicher situativer Information. Zu diesen zusätzlichen Prämissen gehört die Annahme, daß der Sprecher der Äußerung kooperativ ist, d. h. bestimmte Maximen der Konversation einhält (Grice 1975: 45ff.). Zu diesen Maximen gehört die Regel ("Quantity 1"): "Make your contribution as informative as is required (for the current purposes of the exchange)". Situationsabhängig ist auch (wie in der Maxime ausgedrückt) der Grad der erforderlichen Informativität. Diese Prämissen ergeben sich aus der Beurteilung der Situation durch den Hörer, der dabei erlernte Normalitätsannahmen zugrundelegt, die so elementar sind, daß man sich ihrer normalerweise nicht bewußt ist und daß es einen erheblichen Aufwand kostet, sich über sie hinwegzusetzen. Sie sind wohl nicht so elementar wie die Normalitätsannahmen der Gestaltwahrnehmung[11], aber durchaus mit ihnen vergleichbar. Betrachten wir z. B. den folgenden Dialog:

(4) A: Können deine Töchter Fremdsprachen?
     B: Paula spricht Französisch.

Die Information, daß Paula eine Tochter von B ist und Französisch für Paula eine Fremdsprache ist, ist in der Antwort von B nicht "gesagt", sondern wird (neben vielen anderen Informationen) aus dem situativen Kontext erschlossen, z. B. aus der Annahme, daß die Äußerung von B relevant ist, daß er die Frage beantwortet und nicht etwa einfach das Thema wechselt. Es ist eine besonders hinterhältige Art der Täuschung, durch die Äußerung eines wahren Satzes und die Ausnutzung von solchen Normalitätsannahmen in die Irre zu führen, gerade weil die Rolle der Normalitätsannahmen den Hörern meistens nicht bewußt ist.

Die Bedeutung der partikularen Affirmation (I) schließt die Negation der universellen Affirmation (O) nicht ein, vielmehr ist sie konversationell impliziert. Wer den Satz äußert: *Manche Teilnehmer haben die Klausur bestanden* und weiß, daß alle bestanden haben, verletzt die genannte Maxime der Quantität und macht seine Aussage nicht so informativ wie erforderlich. Die konversationelle Implikatur der partikularen Sätze ist wechselseitig: "manche nicht" impliziert auch "manche doch" etc. Mit der Hornschen Beschreibung der Operatoren des logischen Quadrats läßt sich sowohl der exklusive als auch der inklusive Gebrauch dieser Wörter auf einheitliche Weise erklären.

Der nichtssagende Begriff "subkonträr" läßt sich jetzt inhaltlich füllen:

(5) Zwei subkonträre Sätze
  (a) unterscheiden sich durch die innere Negation (der Bereich der Negation liegt innerhalb des Bereichs des logischen Operators);
  (b) sie implizieren sich gegenseitig konversationell.

Auch der Begriff "subaltern" läßt sich präziser fassen, wenn man "(sub-)konträre Negation" mit innerer Negation gleichsetzt.[12] Für die bisher betrachteten Operatoren gilt, daß sie zueinander dual sind, d. h. daß der eine durch die innere und äußere Negation aus dem anderen definierbar ist und daß die innere Negation des einen mit der äußeren des anderen äquivalent ist, vgl. (6):

(6) Dualitätsgesetze in Quantoren-, Aussagen- und Modallogik:
  Gesetze der Quantorennegation:
  (a) $\neg \forall x[Px] \Leftrightarrow \exists x [\neg Px]$
  (b) $\neg \exists x[Px] \Leftrightarrow \forall x [\neg Px]$
  De Morgansche Gesetze der Aussagenlogik:
  (a) $\neg(\Phi \wedge \Psi) \Leftrightarrow \neg \Phi \vee \neg \Psi$
  (b) $\neg(\Phi \vee \Psi) \Leftrightarrow \neg \Phi \wedge \neg \Psi$
  Dualitätsgesetze der modalen Aussagenlogik:
  (a) $\neg N\Phi \Leftrightarrow M \neg \Phi$
  (b) $\neg M\Phi \Leftrightarrow N \neg \Phi$
  Allgemein:
  F und f seien dual, α' sei das Komplement von α:
  $[f(x_1, \ldots x_n)]' = F(x_1', \ldots x_n')$

Wenn man (sub-)konträre Negation mit innerer Negation gleichsetzt, ist ein Satz zu einem anderen subaltern, wenn er aus ihm durch Ersetzung eines starken Operators durch dessen schwachen dualen Operator entsteht.

Das logische Quadrat läßt sich nach diesen Modifikationen wie in Fig. 4 darstellen:

Fig. 4: **Das logische Quadrat des Aristoteles** (revidierte Version):

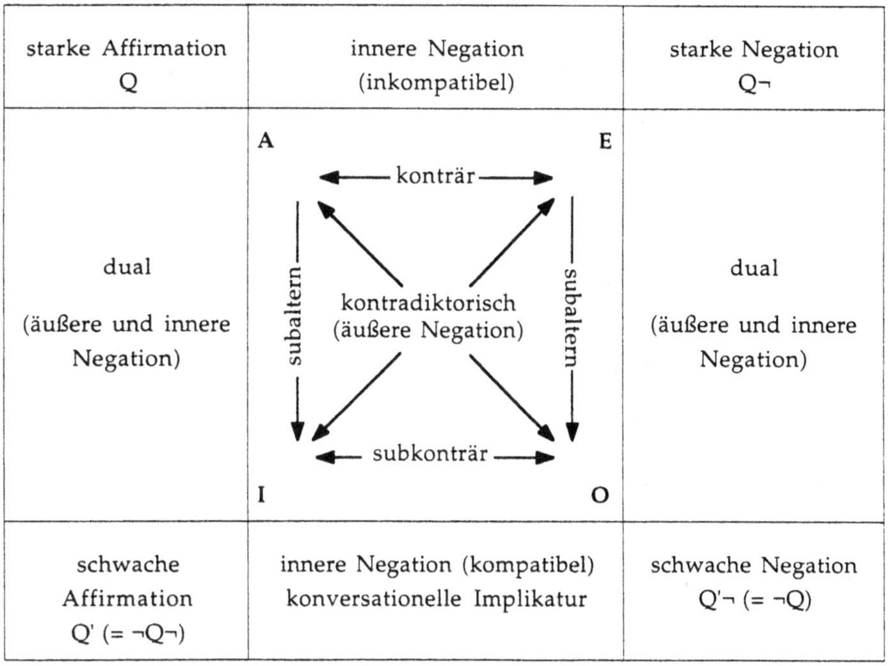

starke Affirmation Q	innere Negation (inkompatibel)	starke Negation Q¬
dual (äußere und innere Negation)	A ←— konträr —→ E subaltern ↕ kontradiktorisch (äußere Negation) ↕ subaltern I ←— subkonträr —→ O	dual (äußere und innere Negation)
schwache Affirmation Q' (= ¬Q¬)	innere Negation (kompatibel) konversationelle Implikatur	schwache Negation Q'¬ (= ¬Q)

In dieser Form ist das logische Quadrat ein nützliches Werkzeug, ein heuristisches Mittel, mit dem man die Erkenntnisse, die die Logiker im Laufe der Jahrhunderte über einige logische Operatoren gewonnen haben, auf andere natürlichsprachliche Wörter übertragen kann.

2 Weitere duale Operatoren

Nach Löbner (1990) gibt es in den natürlichen Sprachen weit mehr duale Operatoren als die in der formalen Logik üblicherweise beschriebenen. Ein Teil der von ihm beschriebenen und noch einige weitere (§ 3) sollen im folgenden daraufhin untersucht werden, ob ihre Bedeutung in der gleichen Weise präzisiert werden kann wie bei den logischen Operatoren, d. h. ob ein Teil der mutmaßlichen Bedeutung in die Pragmatik ausgelagert werden kann.[13]

Betrachten wir zunächst einige Dualitätsgruppen, die sich unmittelbar an All- und Existenzquantor anschließen, die gewissermaßen angereicherte Quantoren sind. Bereits die bisher betrachteten Operatoren bauen auf den Quantoren auf: "Notwendig, daß Φ" wird in der Mögliche-Welten-Semantik verstanden als 'Φ ist in allen möglichen Welten wahr', entsprechend "möglich": in 'einer Welt wahr'. Die Verknüpfung mit *und* bedeutet, daß alle verknüpften Sätze wahr sind, bei *oder* ist mindestens einer der Sätze wahr.

Ebenso lassen sich die folgenden Wörter paraphrasieren: *überall* bedeutet 'an allen Orten' und *immer* 'zu allen Zeiten':[14]

überall	nirgends
mancherorts	nicht überall

immer	nie
manchmal	nicht immer

'Nirgends' ist soviel wie 'überall nicht', 'nie' soviel wie 'immer nicht', wobei der Bereich der Negation innerhalb dessen der Adverbien ist. 'Nicht nirgends' ist 'mancherorts', 'nicht nie' ist 'manchmal'; hier ist der Bereich der Negation außerhalb.

Wenn jemand sagt, daß es "mancherorts Coca-Cola gibt", dann sagt er, daß es nicht nirgends Coca-Cola gibt. Wenn wir ihn so verstehen, daß es nicht überall Coca-Cola gibt, so ist dies eine konversationelle Implikatur. Seine Äußerung ist nicht falsch, wenn sich herausstellen sollte, daß es überall Coca-Cola gibt; wenn er gewußt hat, daß es überall Coca-Cola gibt, dann hat er den Hörer getäuscht, aber nichts Falsches gesagt.

Für das Wort *manchmal* gibt Duden GWb an erster Stelle die Grundbedeutung an: "nicht regelmäßig". Diese Angabe ist etwas unvorsichtig, wie das logische Quadrat lehrt, obwohl sie wohl selten in die Irre führt. Ein Adverbial "manchmal, wenn nicht sogar regelmäßig" ist nicht widersprüchlich und muß nicht als Korrektur interpretiert werden.

Daß 'einer von beiden' nicht bedeutet 'einer von beiden nicht' sondern dies konversationell impliziert, zeigt der Vergleich mit *und/oder*:

A und B	weder A noch B
A oder B	nicht A oder nicht B

beide	keiner von beiden
einer von beiden	einer von beiden nicht

Einige Modalverben bilden Dualitätsgruppen:

müssen	nicht können
können	nicht müssen, nicht brauchen

müssen	nicht dürfen
dürfen	nicht müssen, nicht brauchen zu

Wer etwas nicht tun darf, der muß es nicht-tun. Wenn jemand von sich behauptet, daß er etwas tun darf, so schließen wir daraus, daß er es nicht tun muß, aber dies gehört nicht zur Bedeutung von *dürfen*.

Es gibt noch weitere Verben, die mit Zwang und Erlaubnis zu tun haben und Dualitätsgruppen bilden, zumindest in den Verwendungen, in denen die Valenzrahmen zusammenpassen:

zwingen, zu tun	hindern, zu tun

fordern	ablehnen/ verwehren

tun lassen	erlassen/ freistellen	akzeptieren/ gewähren	verzichten (können)
befehlen	verbieten	sich drängen	sich weigern
erlauben	nicht befehlen	bereit sein	sich nicht drängen

Ein Verb, das gerade von Politikern gerne für pragmatische Täuschungen verwendet wird, ist *bereit sein, etwas zu tun*. Sie sind häufig "bereit, das schwere Amt zu übernehmen" und wollen mit dieser Äußerung davon ablenken, wie sehr sie sich danach gedrängt haben.

Dual zueinander sind auch *zu* und *genug*, deren Zusammenhang auch daran erkennbar ist, daß beide den "Dativus judicantis" regieren (Eisenberg 1994: 299):

Das ist mir *zu* groß	Das ist mir *nicht* groß *genug*
Das ist mir groß *genug*	Das ist mir *nicht zu* groß

Für das Wort *genug* in *groß genug* gibt das Duden GWb als Grundbedeutung an: "in zufriedenstellendem Maß", was soviel bedeutet wie 'auch nicht zu groß'. Das stimmt natürlich auch nicht ganz. Ein 10-Liter-Eimer Himbeereis ist sicher genug für drei Sechsjährige, aber das Maß ist nicht zufriedenstellend sondern sogar wieder beunruhigend. Die meisten, die von einer Sache genug haben, haben von ihr eher zuviel bekommen.

Ein Dualitätspaar sind auch die Wörter *nur* (in quantitativer Verwendung) und *auch*:[15] Die konträre oder innere Negation des Satzes: *Er liest nur Krimis* ist der Satz: *Er liest nur Nicht-Krimis*. Wenn man diesen Satz kontradiktorisch negiert, kommt man zu dem Satz: *Er liest nicht nur Nicht-Krimis*. 'Nicht nur Nicht-Krimis' ist soviel wie 'auch Krimis'.

Er liest *nur* Krimis: Alles, was er liest, ist Krimi	Er liest *nur* Nicht-Krimis: Alles, was er liest, ist Nicht-Krimi
Er liest *auch* Krimis: Manches, was er liest, ist Krimi	Er liest *auch* Nicht-Krimis: Manches, was er liest, ist Nicht-Krimi

Man kann die Wörter *nur* und *auch* mit den Wörtern *alle* und *manche* umschreiben: Wenn jemand nur Krimis liest, so ist alles was er liest, Krimi. Wenn man entsprechend den Satz: *Er liest auch Krimis* mit dem Wort *manche* paraphrasiert, kommt man zu der Bedeutung: 'Manches, was er liest ist Krimi'. Diese Paraphrase ist auf den ersten Blick völlig unangemessen, denn sie bedeutet soviel wie *Er liest Krimis*, als ob das Wort *auch* überhaupt nichts bedeutete. Was das Wort *auch* aber leistet, ist der Bezug auf die Alternativen: *Auch Krimis* bedeutet scheinbar soviel wie 'auch etwas anderes, auch Nicht-

Krimis'. Das logische Quadrat aber lehrt, daß dieser Alternativenbezug eine konversationelle Implikatur ist. Wenn *nur* und *auch* dual zueinander sind, so bedeutet das Wort *auch* überhaupt nichts. Es löst aber erstens eine Implikatur aus, und es hat zweitens einen bestimmten Fokus: *liest Krímis* löst *Auch ér* eine andere Implikatur aus als *Er liest auch Krímis*. Fokus und Implikatur hängen eng zusammen: Die Leistung der Partikel, nämlich der Alternativenbezug, ist nichts anderes als die explizite Rücknahme der Implikatur, die durch den Fokus ausgelöst wird (zu dieser Fokusimplikatur vgl. Primus i. V.):

(7) Er liest Krímis ⇒konv. Impl. Er liest nur Krimis
     Ér liest Krimis ⇒konv. Impl. Nur er liest Krimis

Daß das Wort *auch* überhaupt nichts bedeutet, ist ein überraschendes Ergebnis. Die Feuerprobe für diese Analyse ist das Kriterium der Aufhebbarkeit. Wenn "auch nicht-Krimis" eine Implikatur ist, so ist sie aufhebbar. Wenn das nicht der Fall wäre, so wäre die Antwort in dem folgenden Dialog widersprüchlich:

(8) A: Lest ihr Eierköpfe eigentlich auch Krimis?
     B: Ja, wir lesen alle auch Krimis, manche von uns sogar nur Krimis.

Das logische Quadrat erklärt auch den Gebrauch der Litotes (Horn 1989: 303ff.). Das antonymbildende Adjektivpräfix *un-* negiert nicht kontradiktorisch, sondern konträr; zwischen *schön* und *unschön* gibt es ein "Mittleres". Die beiden Negationen in dem Ausdruck *nicht unschön* heben sich somit nicht auf, sondern bilden das Duale des Ausgangsworts, also einen schwächeren Ausdruck:

schön	unschön
nicht unschön	nicht schön

Dieser schwächere Ausdruck *nicht unschön* bezeichnet scheinbar das Mittlere zwischen *schön* und *unschön*: 'nicht unschön, aber auch nicht schön'. Wenn die kontradiktorische Negation *nicht* das Komplement bildet, wie sonst überall auch, so müßte jedoch die Bedeutung von *nicht unschön* den Fall *schön* mit einschließen, vgl. Fig. 5:

Fig. 5: **Komplementarität der Negation:**

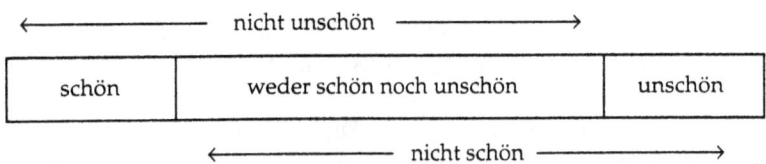

Diese scheinbare Bedeutungskomponente 'auch nicht schön' ist eine konversationelle Implikatur, was auch der Aufhebbarkeitstest zeigt: "Dieses Bild ist nicht unschön, es ist sogar schön!"[16]

3 Eine Verallgemeinerung des logischen Quadrats

Der Begriff der Kontrarietät bedarf ebenfalls einer Präzisierung. Er wird auch in einer allgemeineren Weise verwendet, ohne die Bedeutungskomponente der Gegensätzlichkeit: "Zwei Aussagen sind konträr, wenn nur eine von beiden wahr, beide jedoch falsch sein können: [...] Inas Vogel singt/ist gestorben"[17]. Ein solcher Begriff ist durchaus sinnvoll, aber es ist nicht der Aristotelische, denn Aristoteles verwendet nicht nur die Bezeichnung *enantíos* 'entgegengesetzt', sondern macht auch an einigen Stellen explizit, daß die Gegensätzlichkeit zur Kontrarietät gehört, z. B. Kat. 6a: "man bestimmt als konträr, was in derselben Gattung am weitesten voneinander absteht".[18]

Betrachten wir in dem allgemeinen Fall von einem Paar zweier Sätze, bei denen es ein Mittleres gibt, die Sätze in den oberen Feldern des nicht-aristotelischen Quadrats in Fig. 6:

Fig. 6: **Das Quadrat für A ⊂ B:**

(A ist echte Teilmenge von B, α' ist das Komplement von α)

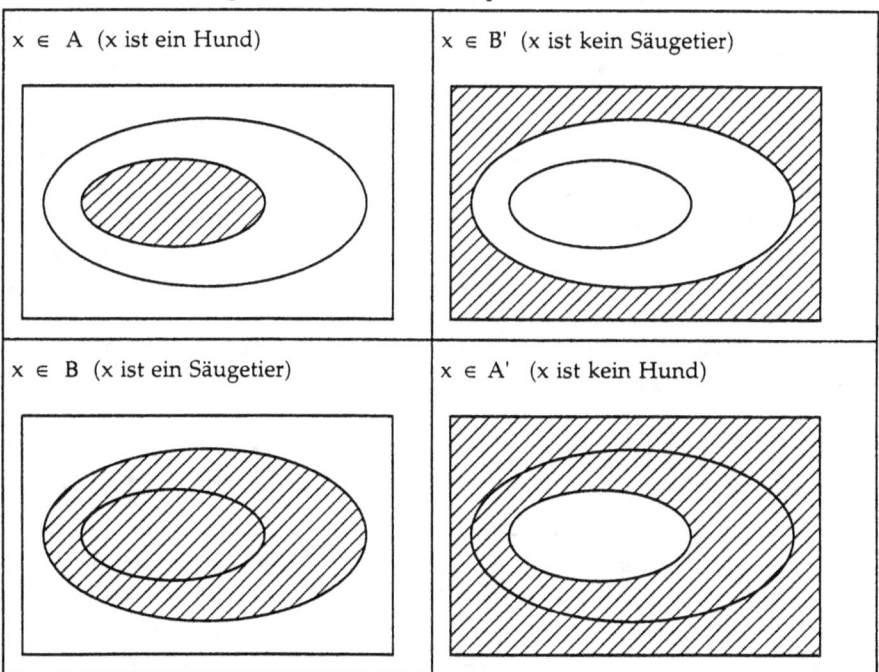

Zwischen diesen Sätzen gibt es ein "Mittleres", vgl. Fig. 7:

Fig. 7: **Das "Mittlere" von A und B'**
(= die Differenz B\A)

x ∉ A ∧ x ∉ B'
(x ist ein Säugetier, aber kein Hund)

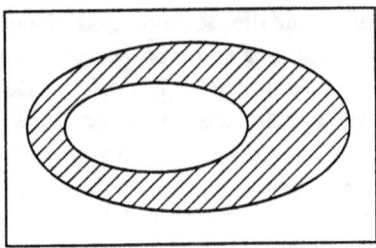

Daß dieses Quadrat so aussieht wie ein Aristotelisches und den Eindruck einer polaren Kontrarietät erweckt, liegt an den besonderen Gegebenheiten[19] der graphischen Darstellung: Es gibt nur zwei Mengen, so daß die beiden Sätze als "ganz innen" und "ganz außen" interpretiert werden können. Eine solche Interpretation ist im allgemeinen Fall nicht möglich, etwa mit den Beispielen *Hund* und *Säugetier*. Die konversationelle Implikatur von I nach O gilt hier nicht: Aus 'x ist ein Säugetier' folgt nicht konversationell: 'x ist kein Hund'. Die Folgerungsbeziehung von A nach I und die Existenz eines "Mittleren" zwischen A und E sind kein hinreichender Grund für die Auslösung einer konversationellen Implikatur.[20] Das liegt daran, daß die Hyponymierelation zu allgemein ist; die Wahl des Wortes *Säugetier* durch den Sprecher wird vom Hörer im allgemeinen nicht als signifikante Nicht-Wahl des Wortes *Hund* verstanden. Schon weil es Katzen gibt, bilden *Hund* und *Säugetier* keine Skala.[21] Die Verwandschaft dualer Wörter ist dagegen hinreichend für die Auslösung einer Implikatur. Für die Implikatur genügt aber der Umstand, daß es nur ein prominentes Hyponym gibt, wie bei der Implikatur von "x ist Rechteck" auf "x ist kein Quadrat". In diesem Fall hat das Wort *Rechteck* durch die Implikatur die zweite, pragmatische Verwendungsbedeutung "ungleichseitiges Rechteck" angenommen, ist somit zu sich selbst hyponym, also ein "Autohyponym" (Horn 1984a: 32, 1984b: 145).

Ein vieldiskutierter Fall, der auf diese Weise erklärt werden kann, ist die Autohyponymie bei Personenbezeichnungen, bei denen auch eine movierte Form geläufig ist:

x ist Rentnerin	x ist kein Rentner
x ist Rentner	x ist keine Rentnerin

Hier wird die Implikatur ausgelöst (von "x ist Rentner" auf "x ist keine Rentnerin"), weil der paradigmatische Zusammenhang eng genug ist und keine weiteren prominenten Hyponyme stören. Auf diese Weise ist zu *Rentner* das Autohyponym "männlicher Rentner" entstanden. Je geläufiger die movierte Form ist, desto zwingender ist die Implikatur:

(10) (a) Sie suchen einen Gutachter für diese Aufgabe.
 (b) Sie suchen einen Rentner für diese Aufgabe.
 (c) Sie suchen einen Kindergärtner für diese Aufgabe.

Bei (c) ist die Implikatur "keine weibliche Person" am stärksten; dies belegt (neben der Aufhebbarkeit), daß es sich um eine pragmatische Folgerung handelt und nicht um Wortsemantik. Es ist auch zu erwarten, daß die Implikaturen um so zwingender werden, je mehr sich die Verwendung der movierten Formen durchsetzt.

Daß Autohyponyme auch bei Verben zu finden sind, zeigt das Paar *gehen* und *laufen*. In (10) bzw. (11) sind die Bedeutungsangaben von *laufen* in Duden GWb und Grimm DWb auszugsweise wiedergegeben:

(11) Duden GWb: *laufen*
 (a) "sich in aufrechter Haltung auf den Füßen in schnellerem Tempo so fortbewegen, daß sich jeweils schrittweise für einen kurzen Augenblick beide Sohlen vom Boden lösen";
 (b) (ugs.) 'gehen'.

(12) Grimm DWb: *laufen*
 "im eigentlichsten sinne, von einer schnellen gleichmäszigen fortbewegung [...], während *gehen* die gemessenere, *springen* die satzweise ausdrückt[22], obschon die Grenzen nicht immer scharf gezogen werden. denn das intensivere *laufen* verwandelt sich oft in einen bloszen derberen ausdruck für *gehen* [...]: sogar *langsam laufen* für *langsam gehen*"

Die Grundbedeutung von *gehen* nach Duden BWb ist in (12) auszugsweise wiedergegeben:

(13) Duden GWb: *gehen*
 sich in aufrechter Haltung auf den Füßen schrittweise fortbewegen

Das Abgrenzungskriterium von *gehen* und *laufen* ist in (11a) präzise wiedergegeben: auch beim schnellen Gehen lösen sich nie beide Sohlen vom Boden, der "Laufschritt" oder Sprung ist ausgeschlossen. Langsames Laufen ist dagegen möglich, in dieser Bedeutung wird *laufen* jedoch als umgangssprachlich charakterisiert. Dieser Gebrauch von *laufen* läßt sich pragmatisch erklären. Die Bedeutung von *gehen* ist etwa 'laufen ohne zu springen', wobei 'gehen' ganz in 'laufen' enthalten ist, vgl. Fig. 8:

Fig. 8: **Das Quadrat für** *gehen* ⊂ *laufen*:

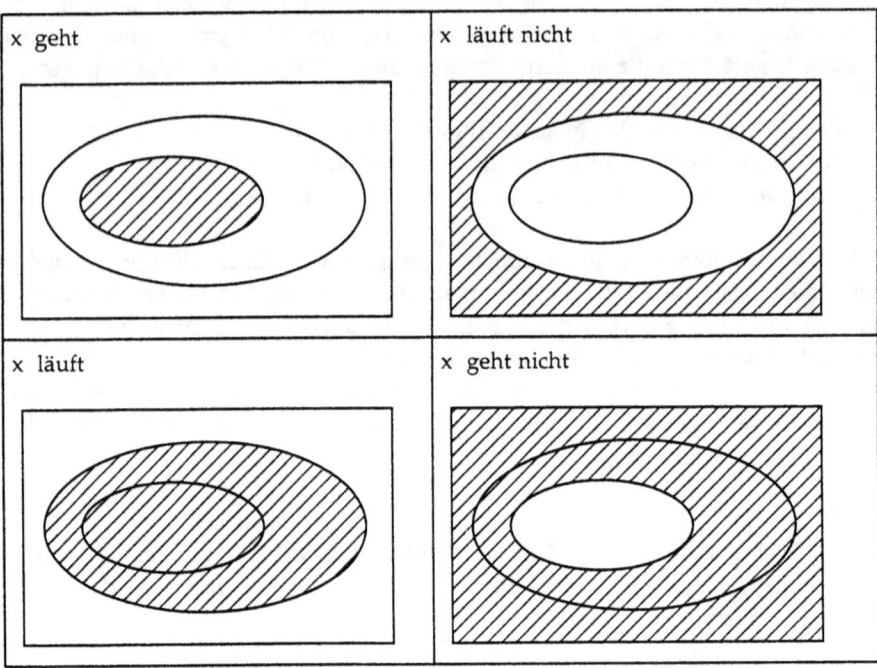

Die Verwendung von *laufen* wird wegen der engen Beziehung zu *gehen* als signifikante Nicht-Verwendung von *gehen* interpretiert. Die "Signifikanz" der Nicht-Verwendung von *gehen* ist eine konversationelle Implikatur, durch die das Autohyponym "laufen, ohne zu gehen" entsteht, vgl. Fig. 9:

Fig. 9: **Das Autohyponym von** *laufen*:
x läuft, aber geht nicht

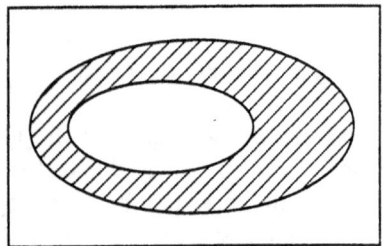

Die Verwendung von *laufen* in der Bedeutung 'gehen' ist weniger sorgfältiger Sprachgebrauch und weniger präzise (zumal *gehen* das häufigere Wort ist), wodurch sie umgangssprachlichen Charakter annimmt.

Ein noch subtileres Beispiel für Autohyponymie ist die Konjunktion *wenn* in *Wenn er Geld hat, kauft er sich ein Auto*. Dieser konditionale Satz ist auch dann wahr, wenn beide Teilsätze wahr sind, obwohl mit seiner Äußerung auch die Nicht-Faktizität der Sätze ausgedrückt werden kann. *Wenn*-Sätze sind nach Hartung (1964: 352) hypothetisch, aber irgendwie auch nicht:

> Hypothetische *wenn*-Sätze können in entsprechende *weil*-Sätze umgeformt werden. Dabei geht der hypothetische Charakter der Aussage verloren [...]. Die *wenn*-Sätze beschränken sich jedoch nicht auf hypothetische Sätze.

In dem kausalen Satz *Weil er Geld hat, kauft er sich ein Auto* wird dieselbe Konditionalität ausgedrückt und zusätzlich die Faktizität der beiden Sätze.[23] Die Konjunktion *weil* ist somit hyponym zu *wenn*, vgl. Fig. 10:

Fig. 10: **Das Quadrat für *weil* ⊂ *wenn*:**

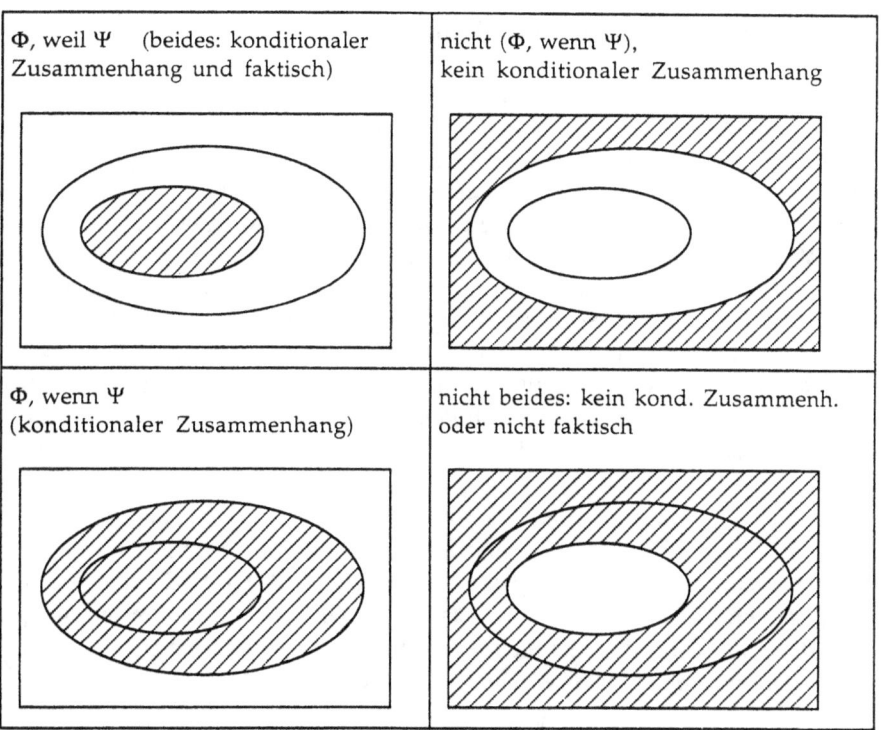

Die Obermenge ist die Menge der Paare von Sachverhalten, die in einer konditionalen Relation stehen ("Φ, wenn Ψ"); die Teilmenge ist die Menge der Paare von Sachverhalten, die obendrein der Fall sind ("Φ, weil Ψ" = "Φ, wenn Ψ, und Φ und Ψ"). Die Nicht-Faktizität ergibt sich als konversationelle Implikatur: Aus dem Feld I = "konditionaler Zusammenhang" folgt O = "kein konditionaler Zusammenhang oder nicht faktisch"; zusammen mit I ergibt das: "nicht faktisch". Durch diese Implikatur ergibt sich als Autohyponym zum konditionalen *wenn* das hypothetisch-konditionale *wenn*. An diesem Beispiel zeigt sich die Nützlichkeit des logischen Quadrats: ohne seine Hilfe ist das Vorliegen der Implikatur nicht so leicht erkennbar.

Die Paare *Rentnerin/Rentner*, *gehen/laufen* und *weil/wenn* sind zwar nicht Dualitätspaare im strengen Sinn, aber sie sind Formulierungsalternativen, die untereinander enger verwandt sind als die übrigen Begriffe der jeweiligen Wortfelder. Wenn die übrigen Alternativen ausgeblendet werden, bilden sie so etwas wie ein "lokales Dualitätspaar". Notwendig für die Auslösung einer Implikatur ist somit neben der Hyponymie nur eine enge paradigmatische Alternativenbeziehung, die eine dritte prominente Alternative ausschließt, so daß die Wahl der einen eine signifikante Nicht-Wahl der anderen darstellt: Die Zweisamkeit ist entscheidend.[24]

4 Resümee und Schlußbemerkung

Die Semantik dualer Operatoren wie *alle/manche*, *und/oder* etc. läßt sich nach L. Horn dadurch präzisieren, daß man die konversationellen Implikaturen subkonträrer Paare aus ihrer Bedeutung herausnimmt. Dadurch kann die Semantik der Operatoren einheitlich beschrieben werden und trotzdem die uneinheitliche Gebrauchsbedeutung erfaßt werden. Diese Präzisierung kann auch auf die weiteren dualen Operatoren übertragen werden, die nach S. Löbner in den natürlichen Sprachen zahlreich vorhanden sind (*immer/manchmal* etc.). Diese Präzisierung der Bedeutung kann ferner bei solchen hyponymen Ausdrücken angewendet werden, die zwar nicht im strengen Sinne dual sind, aber durch die Ausblendung weiterer Kohyponyme zu "lokalen Dualitätsgruppen" werden können, wobei die Wahl der einen Formulierungsalternative eine signifikante Nicht-Wahl der anderen ist. Dies wurde an den Beispielen *Rentnerin/Rentner*, *gehen/laufen* und *weil/wenn* gezeigt. Das logische Quadrat des Aristoteles erweist sich dabei als nützliches heuristisches Hilfsmittel.

Gegen den Titel dieses Aufsatzes könnte man vielleicht einwenden, daß die Lehren über deutsche Wörter nicht aus den Schriften des Aristoteles gezogen wurden, sondern hauptsächlich aus den jüngsten Ergänzungen durch H. P. Grice, Laurence Horn und Sebastian Löbner. Ein solcher Einwand wäre nicht überzeugend; denn wenn die genannten Gelehrten (und deren Lehrer) nichts von Aristoteles gelernt hätten, so könnten wir wohl auch von ihnen nicht viel über deutsche Wörter lernen.

Anmerkungen

1 Die folgenden Aristotelischen Schriften wurden herangezogen: Kategorien (Kat.), De interpretatione/Lehre vom Satz (De int.), Metaphysik (Met.), Analytica priora/Erste Analytik (An. pr.), Topik (Top.); Übersetzungen nach den Ausgaben der "Philosophischen Bibliothek", Felix Meiner Verlag, Hamburg.

2 Die lateinischen Bezeichnungen der Beziehungen gehen auf Boethius zurück (vgl. Migne 1891: 321), die graphische Darstellung mindestens auf Apuleius (vgl. Sullivan 1967, Londey/ Johanson 1987). Die vier Ecken des Quadrats wurden im Mittelalter mit den vier ersten Vokalbuchstaben "durchnumeriert", wobei den affirmativen Ecken die beiden ersten Vokale von *affirmo* entsprechen, den negativen die von *nego*.

3 Von Winston Churchill erzählt man die Anekdote, daß er einmal behauptet hat: "Die Hälfte des Kabinetts sind Esel". Als das heulende und schnaubende Parlament ihn nötigen will, diese Behauptung zurückzuziehen, "dementiert" er mit den Worten: "Die Hälfte des Kabinetts sind keine Esel".

4 Zum Problem der "leeren Allsätze" s. u.

5 Daß man sich dagegen sträubt, diesen Satz als wahr anzuerkennen, läßt sich damit erklären, daß mit ihm kaum je relevante Information transportiert wird. Bei komplexen Prädikaten sträubt man sich weniger: Der Satz "Alle, die immerhin den Anfangsbuchstaben richtig geraten haben, bekommen einen Trostpreis" gilt auch (und gerade dann), wenn es keiner geschafft hat.

6 Wegen der Konvertibilität der Existenzsätze kommt dann auch A irgendeinem B zu: "Wenn A einem B zukommt, muß auch B einem A zukommen" (ibid.). Vgl. auch Top. 109a: "haben wir gezeigt, daß etwas allem zukommt, so haben wir auch gezeigt, daß es einigem zukommt".

7 M Φ =: 'es ist möglich, daß Φ', N Φ =: 'es ist notwendig, daß Φ'.

8 Vgl. hierzu Horn (1973, 1990).

9 Vgl. Horn (1973: 207, 1989: 212). Zur dazu kritischen Literatur vgl. Horn (1989: 250). Diese Form des "Bedeutungsminimalismus" fordern u. a. Ziff (1960: 44), Grice (1978: 118f.), Posner (1979: 369ff.).

10 Vgl. dazu genauer Grice (1975), Gazdar (1979: Kap. 3), Levinson (1983: Kap. 3), Hirschberg (1991). Zu den Vorläufern von Grice vgl. Horn (1990).

11 Etwa die Annahme, daß eine Kugel, die hinter einem Hindernis verschwindet und die, die auf der anderen Seite herauskommt, identisch sind, vgl. Rock (1984).

12 Weiter unten wird untersucht, ob man "konträre Negation" nicht doch allgemeiner fassen kann.

13 Löbner (1990) entdeckte die weiteren natürlichsprachlichen Dualitätsgruppen, hat sie aber nicht unter diesem Gesichtspunkt untersucht.

14 Die Anordnung der Begriffe in den Kästchen entspricht der im logischen Quadrat.

15 Die folgende Analyse ist nur tentativ, weil wichtige Probleme ausgeklammert werden, z. B. die Möglichkeit der Reduktion der zwei Typen quantitativ und skalar auf eine (Jacobs 1983: 164), und die Verallgemeinerung der hier vorgeschlagenen Quantifikationsanalyse auf alle Verwendungen.

16 Die Litotes *nicht unschön* hat zwar normalerweise nicht die Bedeutung 'ausgesprochen schön', doch kann zu bestimmten Zeiten diese Konvention entstehen, z. B. zur Zeit des Humanismus, beschrieben von Erasmus von Rotterdam. Dies ist eine R-Implikatur ganz im Sinne der Theorie von Horn, vgl. Horn (1989: 304).

17 Metzler Lexikon Sprache, hg. v. Helmut Glück, Stuttgart 1993, s. v. *Kontrarität* [sic].

18 Vgl. auch De int. 23b, Met. 1055a (an mehreren Stellen).
19 Die Relevanz dieser Besonderheit wird unten noch ausführlicher dargestellt.
20 Dies wird von einigen als Problem der skalaren Implikaturen angesehen, vgl. Levinson (1987: 121, Fn 3). Entsprechend kann man nicht aus "A" auf "¬B" (für beliebiges B ≠ A) folgern, trotz (A ∧ B) => A.
21 Wenn die Menge der Alternativen lokal auf *Hund* und *Säugetier* eingeschränkt ist, etwa durch den Kontext, kann die Implikatur ausgelöst werden: *War es ein Hund? Es war ein Säugetier.* Vgl. dazu Matsumoto (1995: 29). *Hund* und *Säugetier* bilden dann eine lokale Dualitätsgruppe, s. u.
22 Die Bedeutung von *springen* war auch zu Grimms Zeiten sehr vielfältig (vgl. Grimm DWb s. v.), daß es nicht als weiteres Hyponym die konversationelle Implikatur stört.
23 Zu dem problematischen Zusammenhang von Konditionalität und Kausalität vgl. Sæbø (1991: 626).
24 In einer mehr-als-zweistelligen Skala (z. B. *manchmal* < *oft* < *meistens* < *immer*) wird der stärkere Nachbar konversationell ausgeschlossen ('manchmal' => "nicht oft"), der Ausschluß der übrigen folgt logisch aus der Implikatur. Zum Alternativenbezug im allgemeinen vgl. auch Matsumoto (1995).

Literatur

Aristoteles: Siehe Fußnote 1.
Duden GWb: Duden. Das große Wörterbuch der deutschen Sprache in acht Bänden. 2., völlig neu bearbeitete und stark erweiterte Auflage. Hg. und bearbeitet vom Wissenschaftlichen Rat und den Mitarbeitern der Dudenredaktion unter der Leitung von Günther Drosdowski. Mannheim: Dudenverlag.
Eisenberg, P. (1994): Grundriß der deutschen Grammatik. 3., überarbeitete Auflage. Stuttgart: Metzler.
Gazdar, G. (1979). Pragmatics: implicature, presupposition and logical form. New York: Academic Press.
Grice, H.P. (1975). "Logic and conversation". In: P. Cole & J. Morgan, eds.: Syntax and semantics. Bd. 3: Speech acts. New York: Academic Press, 41-58.
Grice, H.P. (1978): "Further notes on logic and conversation". In: P. Cole, ed.: Syntax and Semantics. Bd. 9: Pragmatics. New York: Academic Press, 113-127.
Grimm DWb: Deutsches Wörterbuch von Jacob und Wilhelm Grimm. 16 Bände. Leipzig: Hirzel. 1854-1960. Quellenverzeichnis 1971. Nachdruck München 1984: dtv.
Hartung, W. (1964): "Die bedingenden Konjunktionen der deutschen Gegenwartssprache". Beiträge zur Geschichte der deutschen Sprache und Literatur (Halle) 86, 350-387.
Hirschberg, J. (1991): A theory of scalar implicature. New York: Garland.
Horn, L.R. (1972): On the semantic properties of logical operators in English. Diss. Univ. of California, Los Angeles: Univ. Microfilms Internat., Ann Arbor, Mich.
Horn, L.R. (1973): "Greek Grice: a brief survey of proto-conversational rules in the history of logic". In: C. Corum & T.C. Smith-Stark & A. Weiser: Papers from the 9th Regional Meeting of the Chicago Linguistic Society. Chicago: Chicago Linguistic Society, 205-214.

Horn, L.R. (1984a): "Toward a new taxonomy for pragmatic inference: Q-based and R-based implicature". In: D. Schiffrin, ed.: Meaning, form, and use in context: linguistic applications. Washington, D. C.: Georgetown University Press, 11-42.

Horn, L.R. (1984b): "In defense of privative ambiguity". In: Proceedings of the 10th Annual Meeting of the Berkeley Linguistics Society, 141-156.

Horn, L.R. (1989). A natural history of negation. Chicago: University of Chicago Press.

Horn, L.R. (1990): "Hamburgers and truth: why Gricean explanation is Gricean". In: K. Hall, J.P. Koenig, M. Meacham, S. Reinmann & L.A. Sutton, eds.: Proceedings of the 16th annual meeting of the Berkeley Linguistics Society. Parasession on the legacy of Grice. Berkeley: Berkeley Linguistics Society, 454-471.

Jacobs, J. (1983): Fokus und Skalen. Zur Syntax und Semantik der Gradpartikeln im Deutschen. Tübingen: Niemeyer.

Levinson, S.C. (1983): Pragmatics. Cambridge: Cambridge University Press. Deutsche Übersetzung: Pragmatik. Tübingen (1990): Niemeyer.

Levinson, S.C. (1987): "Minimization and conversational inference". In: J. Verschueren & M. Bertuccelli-Papi, eds.: The pragmatic perspective. Selected papers from the 1985 International Pragmatics Conference. Amsterdam: Benjamins, 61-129.

Löbner, S. (1990): Wahr neben falsch. Duale Operatoren als die Quantoren natürlicher Sprache. Tübingen: Niemeyer.

Londey , D. & C. Johanson (1987): The logic of Apuleius. Including a complete Latin text and English translation of the Peri Hermeneias of Apuleius of Madaura. Leiden: Brill.

Matsumoto, Y. (1995). "The conversational condition on Horn scales". Linguistics and Philosophy 18, 21-60.

Migne, J.P., ed.: (1891): Patrologia Latina. Bd. 64: Manlii Severini Boetii opera omnia. Tomus posterior. Paris: Migne.

Posner, R. (1979): "Bedeutung und Gebrauch der Satzverknüpfer in den natürlichen Sprachen". In: G. Grewendorf, ed.: Sprechakttheorie und Semantik. Frankfurt/Main: Suhrkamp, 345-385.

Primus, B. (1997): Eine fokustheoretische Rekonstruktion konversationeller Quantitätsimplikaturen. In diesem Band.

Rock, I. (1984): Perception. New York: Scientific American Library.

Sæbø, K. (1991): "Causal and purposive clauses". In: A.v. Stechow & D. Wunderlich, eds.: Semantik. Ein internationales Handbuch der zeitgenössischen Forschung. Berlin: de Gruyter, 623-631.

Sullivan, M.W. (1967): Apuleian Logic. The nature, sources, and influence of Apuleius's Peri Hermeneias. Amsterdam: North Holland.

Weidemann, H. (1994): Aristoteles: Peri Hermeneias. Übersetzt und erläutert von Hermann Weidemann. Berlin: Akademie Verlag (Lizenzausgabe der Wissenschaftlichen Buchgesellschaft, Darmstadt).

Ziff, P. (1960): Semantic analysis. Ithaca, NY: Cornell University Press. Cornell Paperbacks 1967.

Explicature, Impliciture, and Implicature

Graham H. Bird, Manchester

Pragmatics relies for its very existence, and its distinction from other branches of linguistic theory, on an intuitive contrast between the strict semantic content of some utterance and what is communicated or understood beyond that. In recent work of Robyn Carston (1988), François Récanati (1991), and Kent Bach (1994a: 1994b) that intuitive contrast has been examined more closely with the aim of improving on Grice's original distinction between what is said and what is implicated in some utterance. These commentators disagree at various points, but they all accept that Grice's contrast, at least if it is regarded as exhaustive, is over-simple; and all seek to remedy that weakness with a more subtle classification. Carston, for example, deploys initially a Principle of Functional Independence (PFI) to classify as 'explicatures' items, such as temporal or causal aspects of conjunction, which Grice treated as implicatures. Both Récanati and Bach accept that specific conclusion but question the grounds on which she based it. Kent Bach, however, disputes other 'inflationary' tendencies which lead Récanati to include in 'explicature' what Récanati calls 'strengthening' and 'saturation', and Kent Bach calls 'sentence non-literality' and 'semantic under-determination'. The two types of case are recognised by both Récanati and Bach, but classified differently. For Bach they are *neither* explicatures, part of what was said, *nor* Gricean implicatures, and so deserve a special classification as 'implicitures'.

These debates represent the best current attempts to refine Grice's theory, and to offer a needed insight into the line of demarcation between semantics and pragmatics. My aim is to review the debate, to evaluate some of the disagreements, and also to widen the scope of the discussion. For the specific issues are quite narrowly focussed on Grice's original account, and there are more general background issues which deserve comment. For those reasons I want first, in section 1, to comment summarily on some of those background issues before considering, in section 2, some more specific issues which arise in its shadow. In section 3 I try to draw these threads together, and arrive at some conclusions.

1 Background Issues

1.1 Theory and Practice

Almost all the contributors accept that a truth-condition theory, of some sort, has some role to play in formal semantics and in the semantics of natural language (NL), and all accept that a pragmatic theory will extend beyond such accounts. It is not necessary here to consider different varieties of formal truth condition theory, whether of a Tarski-Davidson or 'possible worlds' type, but it is important to notice that semantic theories of NL may be more or less demanding. A more demanding theory will take into account determinate reference and disambiguation, which may be available only in a particular context of utterance. A theory for some NL which aims to provide a recursive account of truth conditions for every well formed sentence in that NL will be of the more demanding type, since without those features of determinate reference and disambiguation it will not be possible to identify conditions which make *every* sentence true. A less demanding theory of what Carston calls 'linguistic sense' might provide only a general template for such truth conditions without fully determining them in every case. She speaks (1988: 178) of this as "translations of linguistic forms into logical forms, partially articulated conceptual representations which are the output of a grammar" and says (1988: 175) that "while linguistic sense makes a crucial contribution to truth conditions it almost never supplies a truth evaluable propositional form." A propositional form, for her, is "a well-formed formula which (a) undergoes formal logical (truth-preserving) operations determined by its structure, and (b) is semantically complete in that it is capable of being true or false". She then paints the following picture of the inter-relations between these theoretical items (1988: 178):

> Natural language semantics is autonomous and provides the input to pragmatics, which plays a major role in determining the explicature of an utterance as well as determining implicatures, both of which are distinct and complete propositional forms and the domain for truth-conditional semantics.

For the present I shall not consider the plausibility of these structures, but only comment on some general ambiguities and dangers in them. It is important to distinguish the relevant formal theories from the psychological processing which realises them in individual speaker/hearers (S/Hs). It is true that ideally we should hope for formal theories which match the psychological processing which S/Hs undergo, but it would be a mistake simply to identify these. A formal theory which does not match exactly such processing may still have value in elucidating aspects of the structure of some NL; and the requirements of theory may not be the same as those for psychological processing[1]. It is natural, for example, to require for theory a certain order of priority, as well as simplicity and determinacy, but these requirements may not be matched by the processes which S/Hs carry out in understanding and interpreting utterances.

  The discussion assumes, for example, a certain priority for semantics over pragmatics. The latter is *defined* in terms of those aspects of interpretation which go beyond semantic features of utterance. But the analytic claim that pragmatic interpretation is in that way dependent upon a given, independently identifiable, semantic content does not entitle us to postulate a parallel temporal priority in processing. The analytic priority is a requirement of theory which cannot be assumed to be, and almost certainly is not, generally matched by any temporal priority in processing. It is as unplausible to suppose that in hearing some utterance we first process it semantically and then subsequently consider its additional pragmatic interpretation as to suppose that we first hear acoustic, or phonetic, items before grasping the syntax or semantics of what is said. For the most part we understand utterances immediately and as S/Hs are not equipped to distinguish the aspects which figure in semantic or pragmatic theory. There seem to be two distinguishable stances, that of the theorist and that of S/Hs, which cannot be assumed to be the same[2]

It may be thought that the danger of identifying the two stances, and of *assuming* processes which match theory, is not serious, and yet I shall suggest that in some of the discussion of familiar cases such as temporal/causal 'and' such dangers do not seem always avoided. Someone who might be tempted to claim, for example, that temporal interpretations of 'and' must be included in what was said, in 'explicature', because Hs immediately so interpret the utterance is at least close to committing this mistake. It was no part of Grice's view that such temporal/causal aspects belong to implicature because they are not immediately imputed to the utterance. His view assigned them to that category as part of an overall theory of language, in which the truth-functional aspects of conjunction could form a core set of truth conditions for 'and'. Given that semantics provides such a basic account of conjunction a further theory, of implicature, was required to explain the additional non-truth-functional aspects of our interpretation. These theories need say nothing about processing, and in particular do not need to be committed to any temporal priorities in such processing to match the priorities between the various theories. Similar points can be made about simplicity and determinacy[3]. The requirements for simplicity or determinacy in theory may not be requirements for S/Hs in discourse.

1.2 Sentences, and Utterances; Meaning and Interpretation

Different types of linguistic theory will focus not only on different features of language but also on different units. In line with what was suggested above the differences in these units will tend to reflect those theoretical features rather than discriminations made by S/Hs. What was called above 'linguistic sense', for example, will be attached naturally to *sentences* and their sub-sentential components, while a pragmatic theory will attach its features typically to *utterances* of sentences. It is in those terms that Carston (1988) distinguished 'linguistic semantics', which has to do with the linguistic sense of sentences, from truth-conditional semantics which requires determinate references of a sort available only in utterances of context-sensitive sentences. If we use the terms 'meaning' or 'sense' for properties of sentences in linguistic semantics, then we can use the term 'interpretation' for pragmatic features of utterance. We can further speak of 'utterance interpretation' as the characteristic operation of S/Hs with which pragmatics deals. I want to outline three points about utterance interpretation.

First it seems both unrealistic and ill-advised to deal with utterance interpretation by means of single utterances. It may be that grammar and some formal semantics can properly focus on single sentences, because such theories will concentrate on the compositional structure of the sentence, in order either to licence it as well formed or to show how its meaning is a function of the meanings of its components[4]. But utterances, and utterance interpretation, cannot adequately be dealt with in such a way, utterance by utterance. The interpretation of an utterance in context will typically depend upon what has preceded it in conversation, and what succeeds it, and this is acknowledged by the development in Grice (1989) and Sperber & Wilson (1986) of fragments of conversational exchange where Ss and Hs interact. It is, therefore, puzzling to find Kent Bach (1994a: 124), in his contributions to the debate, confining his official interest to single sentence utterances. He says:

> People use larger chunks of language than sentences of course, but from the point of view of grammar the sentence is the basic unit. Our discussion will not take up pragmatic phenomena that involve multi-sentence utterances.

This restriction might be understood simply to exclude cases where S utters more than one sentence, but it might also be read as excluding any prior stimulus to the utterance or any subsequent response to it. That latter restriction seems ill motivated for utterance interpretation. Equally the reference to grammar seems misleading, for the reasons given already, since utterance interpretation occurs essentially in a conversational context where more than one sentence, and more than one S, is involved, and where there is interaction between S and H. Grammar can reasonably be confined to single sentences and the internal structure of its components; utterance interpretation, which essentially involves conversational exchanges and interaction between Ss and Hs, cannot be so confined.

That interaction between Ss and Hs, and the reciprocating nature of their relationship, serves also to draw attention to a further feature of utterance interpretation which I shall label "speaker/hearer (S/H) parity". If this implies only that both Ss and Hs have a role in the conduct of conversation, then it will seem both uninteresting and uncontroversial. Yet it is worth making explicit in order to correct a distortion which attaches to Grice's 'intentional' account of communication and meaning. In that account all the emphasis is placed on S's intentions, and on the ideal of 'transparency' or 'openness' with which communication is effected through H's recognition of S's intentions, including S's intention that his intentions be recognised. Yet if conversation has the interactive character suggested above we might expect Hs to have as much importance as Ss, and H's responses to have as much importance as S's intentions. Since this aspect of Grice's theory has become so deeply entrenched, I will be able only to outline some of the considerations which can be used to counter an over-emphasis on S, and S's intentions[5]. It is not my aim to *reject* an important, even essential, role for S's intentions, but only to *add* to it in such a way as to give H parity of status.

For those reasons it is not necessary for me to deny the evident intentional features of such verbs as 'communicate' or 'mean'. Plainly if we speak of an engine 'communicating' motion to the wheels of a car, we use the verb in a non-intentional, causal, sense to be contrasted with intentional linguistic communication. And the same intentionality can be associated even more clearly with such a verb as 'mean'. In this way such verbs as 'communicate' and 'mean' are essentially S-words, and it was this feature on which Grice placed such emphasis. But to correct an over-emphasis on that side we might also note that other verbs, such as 'understand', or 'interpret', are characteristically H-words. If it is S who produces token utterances with a communicative intention, it is H who listens to, and interprets, what is said. Hs, of course, in turn become Ss, but their responses then reflect precisely the understanding they have of the original utterance. It is not that Hs are purely passive 'receivers', or 'decoders', of S's intentions, mere sounding boards with no more active role to play. It is a measure of the interactive character of such exercises, in which H plays not merely a passive, but an active and substantial role, that they should be given parity with their interlocutors. It may still be thought that H's role is, if not totally passive, at least subsidiary, not least because Hs actually communicate only when they adopt the role of Ss. I have suggested already that this under-states their role, just because their role as Ss itself depends upon their interpretation of their interlocutor's utterances. But more can be said of this by indicating three ways in which H's understanding may actually go beyond S's intentions.

(a) What S actually says may be correctly interpreted by H but incorrectly understood by S. In that case H's interpretation will not match S's intentions, but it will be H who is right and S wrong. Such situations can arise for both semantic and pragmatic features.

(b) H's inferences from what S said may not have been envisaged by S even though they are adequately licenced as part of what S communicated. Here there is no question of correctness or incorrectness; it is simply that S fails to see some legitimate consequences of what S says. This circumstance, too, may arise both semantically and pragmatically. In the latter case it may be marked by S's subsequent avowals, such as "I didn't mean to be tactless, inconsiderate etc.", or "I was merely stating a fact; not complaining" etc.

(c) The future of a conversational exchange may be determined just as much by H's inferences, or interpretation, as S's intentions. One way in which this typically arises, which I say more about later, has to do with the 'hypothesis-forming-and-testing' character of conversation. H may wish to pursue S's initial utterance by querying, or clarifying, some aspect of what S said. Flexibility of this kind is not merely an add-on extra in conversation but rather an essential aspect of it. To eliminate that aspect, as I indicate later, is to replace conversation with bare communication. It is also to echo Récanati's claim about the 'free' rather than 'controlled' nature of utterance interpretation.

These claims indicate two further comments; one to do with the criteria for 'what is said', and a second to do with Kent Bach's classification of 'sentence non-literality'. For so far there is no good reason to expect that there will be no one single criterion to identify 'what is said' and differentiate it from other aspects of utterance interpretation. Instead we can expect a range of equally legitimate criteria, which focus on different aspects of the utterance. It would be possible, though in this context perhaps not significant, to identify what is said in terms of phonetic, or even acoustic, criteria. But we may, as Kent Bach's (1994a,b) discussion suggests, focus instead on the actual words uttered and their determinate order in order to identify, without additional interpretation, what was said. That criterion will evidently be close to Grice's account of what is said in terms of a correspondence to 'the elements of (the sentence), their order and their syntactic character' (1994b: 270). If, on the other side, we allow paraphrases to count as part of what is said, then we involve additional criteria and get closer to Carston's, and Sperber and Wilson's, account of explicature. To arrive exactly at that notion, however, we have to add into what is said items which do not simply correspond to elements of the sentence uttered but are typically understood as part of what S intended to communicate. There is a tendency to assume that we have to choose among these different criteria only one which is correct, as if they are all in competition, but it seems better to treat them as alternative, but compatible, accounts which arise from their divergent emphases on different, abstracted, factors in the communicative process. Such a liberal policy does not mean that nothing can be ruled out. Evidently some inferences which H may draw from S's utterance could not possibly be included in what S actually said or even meant. The policy does, however, relieve us from the responsibility of rejecting all but one of the alternative criteria.

The second point follows directly from that last observation. Kent Bach coins the notion of 'sentence non-literality' to cover cases where the actual meaning of the uttered sentence is not the common interpretation. Such an utterance as

(1)   Everyone went to Paris

is commonly interpreted as

(1)   (a)   Everyone (in the group) went to Paris.

Bach criticises Récanati's inflationary wish to include the common interpretation (1a) in what is said on the ground that it would be an error to infer from the fact that (1) contains no words used figuratively to the conclusion that what is literally said is (1a). To be valid the inference, according to Bach, would require an additional premiss, namely that the only non-literal uses of *sentences* have to contain some figurative *word*. Bach rejects that premiss, since he believes that (1) is non-literal, or figurative, not at the level of the individual *words* but at that of the *sentence* as a whole. Sentence non-literality then enables us to *separate* the non-literal interpretation, (1a), from what was said, (1). For Bach the non-literal interpretation belongs to the 'impliciture' of the utterance and not to its explicature, and in such cases the impliciture expresses something instead of, not as well as, what was said.

Whether or not Récanati made the questioned assumptions, I want to suggest that Bach's own strategy is at least not obligatory. For his classification is in danger of confusing two quite different contrasts, namely one between what was, and was not, *actually* said, and another between what was, or was not, *literally* meant. We might, consequently, construct a different scheme in line with these contrasts of the following kind:

I. What was *actually* said by S (that is, (1)) as opposed to what was *not* actually said by S (that is, (1a)).
II. What was *literally* meant, as opposed to what was *figuratively* meant, by S if applicable. (In this case nothing was figuratively meant. If S had said "He is a pig", then we could distinguish the literal and the figurative meaning of what S said.)
III. What was *actually* meant by S (that is (1a)) as opposed to what was *not* actually meant by S (that is, (1))[6].

If we adopt this scheme then there is no need to coin the notion of sentence non-literality to cover cases (1) and (1a). Indeed the notion then appears as a hybrid result of a cross classification between what was, or was not, actually said and what was, or was not, literally meant. It seems independently implausible to classify (1a) as *figurative*, even though it is clear that the common interpretation is at odds with what was *actually* said, namely (1). Bach seems to have arrived at this view partly because he holds that (1) is already a complete proposition, so that the common interpretation has to be represented as 'saying something and meaning something else instead' (fleshing out) rather than as 'saying something and meaning something else as well' (filling in). I shall later question such a contrast. If there are grounds for disputing Récanati's inflationary tendencies, then there are also grounds for disputing Bach's alternative classification of the phenomena.

1.3 Strategies and Principles of Utterance Interpretation

As I suggested earlier we might call the techniques Ss use in utterance interpretation 'strategies' and the theoretical accounts of the process 'principles'. While ideally strategies and principles should match there is room for theoretical principles which either do not, or do not exactly, or are not known to, match the strategies which S/Hs deploy. Just as we might formulate objective principles for chess governing 'best play' in certain types of position, which are not used by chess players but are used by computers, so we might formulate general principles governing semantic or pragmatic features of language which tell us something of the structure of language, or language use, even though the principles are not acknowledged by S/Hs. Whatever the status of the principles offered by all the contributors it is clear that there are many, and that they are rarely subject to empirical test[7]. There is an inevitable reliance on linguistic intuitions which may even be built in to some principle such as Récanati's Principle of Availability (PA).

Despite the multiplicity of current principles I want to add one which seems to have utility in connection with S/H strategies, and is directly relevant to the more detailed issues discussed here[8]. I want to claim that in conversation S/Hs naturally follow a 'hypothesis-forming-and-testing' (HFT) strategy, and that this forms an essential part of conversational conduct. Such a principle has probably wider implications, too, since it seems likely that all cognitive activities are governed by such a principle. Perceptual interpretation, for example, undoubtedly has as an integral part some procedure for forming and testing hypotheses about what is perceived, and the same will hold for the best response to adopt in the face of such interpretation. Advocacy of any such general principle, however, deserves to be modest, and I make three points about this principle to limit its scope and to indicate its particular importance for the current issues. First HFT is not intended to be an unique solution to the problem of utterance (or cognitive) interpretation; nor is it intended to be incompatible with other such principles (e.g. Grice's Cooperative principle (CP), Sperber and Wilson's Principle of Relevance (PR) and others discussed by Récanati). HFT is not proposed as the fundamental, over-riding, principle governing utterance interpretation, but only as one among a whole range of strategies[9].

HFT nevertheless has direct relevance to the present issues. It echoes what has been suggested earlier of the interactive nature of conversation, and of the notion of S/H parity. For, crudely, part of the interaction between Ss and Hs involves their reciprocal grasp of what has been said so far and what needs to be further said. Each will form hypotheses about the other's utterances, their significance, plausibility, basis, and truth. They will act as what Brandom (1994) calls 'deontic scorekeepers' where part of the normative character of the operation has to do with the proper evidence for the utterance and the proper response to be made to it. Although I illustrate this with reference to 'cognitive', or 'alethic', cases there is no difficulty in applying it also to other kinds of case such as the evaluative, or expressive. In all these contexts *both* S and H typically register hypotheses about what has been said and what should be added. Both share exactly the same posture in this respect and so exemplify what was earlier called 'S/H parity'.

HFT also has direct relevance to the pragmatic phenomena at issue here. For they typically rest on the existence of 'gaps' between what was actually said, or literally meant, and some further message recovered over and above that minimal account. These gaps, however, clearly reflect the scope for forming hypotheses and then, if necessary, testing them. All the linguistic phenomena noted in the discussion arise from unclarities, or queries, in the interpretation of what was originally uttered. Utterance interpretation seems closely involved in hypothesising and testing just because the additional items are *not* explicit and may be diversely interpreted. For these reasons it is surely correct to see such gaps, and the attempts to remedy them, not as faults in conversation but as essential to it[10]. If utterances, per impossibile, were always so complete and so lucid as to stand in no need of further exploration, then this would prevent conversation, or eliminate one essential feature of it. Instead there would be packets of 'complete' information to be communicated in turn by S and by H, but with no evident link between one utterance and another. There would be communication, but no conversation; and the impossibility of such a scenario serves also to underline the endemic flexibility in conversation. Though Récanati may not have had this in mind these points echo what he suggested about the 'free' rather than 'controlled' nature of such conversation[11].

To see the phenomena in this light is to rectify one misunderstanding. To emphasise the 'incompleteness', the 'gaps', in conversation may suggest an ideal of completeness which is not only at odds with the very nature of conversation, but impossible to attain in any case. We might say that such an emphasis puts the default position in the wrong place. It is not that our conversation is, unfortunately, irremediably loose and incomplete;

still less that our aim should be to eliminate these gaps in our utterances. Rather our utterances are endemically incomplete and have that character as an essential part of what it is to exchange ideas in conversation[12]. The default position is one of 'incompleteness', not the unattainable ideal of 'completeness'. However, even if we effect such a correction, it does not help directly to explain how we might classify the various types of incompleteness in conversation which generate the contested cases of explicature, impliciture, and implicature. All that it does is to put that whole issue into a proper perspective[13]. Whether that helps to clarify any of the detailed issues will be considered in 2.

2   More Specific Issues

I want to examine two representative issues in this section: One has to do with the criteria, and arguments, for including temporal (and other) aspects of conjunction in what S said, and the second concerns the notions of 'completeness' and 'incompleteness' in utterance. The first issue is a familiar case, in which Grice classified the temporal aspect of 'and' as an implicature, but which both Récanati and Carston classify as an explicature. The second raises a central question about the basis for the classifications of explicature, impliciture, and implicature in terms of gaps in utterance.

2.1   Temporal 'and' Again

One of the central arguments used by both Récanati and Robyn Carston[14] for including temporal features of 'and' in explicature derives from an early argument of Jonathan Cohen's. I shall be concerned not with Cohen's own view but with the use made of his material by the two more recent commentators. For both, in different ways, accept Cohen's central point as the basis for attributing such features to explicature, but they disagree about the arguments on which that conclusion should be based. Récanati, for example, rejects Carston's use of a 'Principle of Functional Independence' (PFI) to arrive at the conclusion, and instead appeals directly to a 'Scope' Principle (SP). That latter principle is designed to draw a distinction between those Gricean implicatures which do, and those which do not, "fall within the scope of logical operators". Récanati believes that only the latter can be regarded as genuine implicatures, and that the former should instead be classified as part of what is said, that is, as explicatures. I consider first Récanati's position and then Carston's.

Récanati outlines Cohen's position in the following way: Where we understand conjoined propositions reporting events to include reference to their temporal order, even though that order is not explicitly marked, we may apply logical operations to those propositions. Intuitively, and in context, we distinguish

(2)   They got married and had a child

from

(3)   They had a child and got married

in terms of the opposed imputed ordering of the two events. Cohen pointed out that the same differential understanding may apply to more complex cases involving logical operations, such as

(4)   If they got married and had a child, then the parents in law will be pleased; but if they had a child and got married, then the parents in law will not be pleased.

Of these more complex cases Récanati says that a Gricean account is 'problematic', 'for it is unclear how it can be applied extending it to these complex cases is hardly a credible move'.

Récanati, like Carston, accepts that Cohen's own conclusion, which attributes the temporal features to a semantic account of 'and', is both unplausible and only optional. It is unplausible in multiplying semantic accounts of 'and' for all the numerous different aspects, causal, inferential and others, which can be associated with the connective. And it is not obligatory, since Carston's alternative conclusion is available, in which these features are pragmatically determined aspects of what is said rather than part of the 'linguistic sense' of the sentences. Récanati's own view is that SP yields the same results as his preferred 'Availability Principle' (AP), but he adds the provisos that 'the issue is not so simple' and that the 'criterion could still be tested and weakened in various ways'[15].

I want to note three anxieties about such a line of argument. First, as presented, the argument rests on the distinction between the 'simple' cases ((2) and (3)) and the more complex one (4); and yet it is hard to see why that distinction is relevant. For if it is natural to interpret (4) as attributing a determinate temporal order to the two conjoined events, it is just as natural to interpret (2) or (3) in the same way. The principal difference between them lies not in their naturalness, nor, except accidentally, in the contrast between their respective simplicity and complexity, but in the different motives we might have for imputing that temporal order. In the case of (4) the evident motive is to avoid the attribution of inconsistency to S, or to what S said, whereas in the case of (2) or (3) it is rather to eliminate indeterminacy in interpretation. In neither case, however, are we compelled to follow such motives. We may leave (2) and (3) indeterminate, or apply the HFT strategy to clarify the issue; and we may choose to ascribe inconsistency to S in the case of (4). We might distinguish the strength of the motives in these two cases, and regard the latter as owing its strength to the force of logic. But the criterion spoke of items 'falling within the scope of logical operators' and that could be met even if no such evident inconsistency arises. If, for example, we take just one of the hypotheticals and consider

(5)   If they got married and had a child, then the parents in law will be pleased

there is no pressure from a possible inconsistency, and the relation between antecedent and consequent demonstrates the same indeterminacy as the simpler cases (2) and (3).

It is also unclear, second, whether such cases as (4) or (5) are genuine criticisms of Grice's account. Grice had no need to deny that faced with any of these utterances in context we will naturally impute a determinate order to the conjuncts. Indeed his notion of a 'conventional implicature' seemed designed to acknowledge cases where there is a strong preference to impute some such interpretation rather than simply to leave the options open or, under HFT, to test them. That such implicatures were treated as non-cancellable was an indication of that preference. He would have agreed that we *do* so interpret these utterances, but wanted then to go on to ask: How do we, as theorists, assign these features to different branches of linguistic theory? His answer was that in the truth-functional characterisation of '&' in propositional logic we have a basic, core, account of its truth conditions which can be allocated to semantic theory, while the additional non-truth-functional aspects can be assigned to pragmatic interpretation. Grice was not required to suppose that the interpretative features could not themselves be given a truth evaluation; clearly whether the conjoined events occurred in one order rather than another can be determined as true or false. To think otherwise would be to confuse truth-evaluability with truth-functionality. Nor was he required to suppose that such an assignment to different branches of liguistic theory corresponded to a temporal order in the processing of such utterances. Even if there is a logical priority attached to semantic content over pragmatic interpretation, on the ground that without the former there would be nothing for the latter to interpret, it does not follow that there is a corresponding processing order in which Hs first identify semantic content and then look for a pragmatic interpretation. And it would be quite unrealistic to suppose that such procedures always do take place. When we hear (2) or (5) we immediately recognise the relevance of temporal order, whether or not we then take the step of making it determinate. Understood in the way I have indicated Grice's distinction between a semantic core and a pragmatic addition was at the level of theory and not at the level of processing.

These points indicate also a weakness in Kent Bach's discussion. For he claims that Grice's separation of semantic and pragmatic aspects in such cases, and especially for 'conventional implicatures', was 'arbitrary'. For Bach it rested on nothing more than a wish to preserve a truth-functional account of conjunction. He, therefore, rejects Grice's idea of conventional implicature and is prepared to include *those* features in explicature, and seems tempted to treat temporal 'and' in a similar way. But if what I have suggested is correct, then the charge of arbitrariness is too strong. It is not entirely arbitrary to think of truth-functional 'and' as a central core common to all propositional uses of the term; it is not entirely arbitrary to think of such a core as providing a truth-conditional account of conjunction; and it is not entirely arbitrary to allocate that account to a semantic theory and the additional features to a pragmatic theory. Grice's account is certainly not obligatory, and his grounds for holding it are not decisive; but these weaknesses fall some way short of arbitrariness[16]

The third anxiety concerns the criterion of 'falling within the scope of logical operators'. I have suggested already that the use of this phrase in the argument separating the simple from the complex cases is liable to mislead. But the criterion itself remains unclear. It may be used, as was noted above, to show that we may perform logical operations on utterances pragmatically interpreted; but it may also be used to indicate the relation which holds between an uttered content and its implicature. Grice himself raised the question of the effect which negation, or denial, may have in this context. He rejected the idea that utterances entail their implicatures because he recognised that the falsity of the implicature did not demonstrate the falsity of the utterance. MTT simply did not apply to such relations. Where an *implicature* turns out to be false, although the utterance might be misleading, it would be strictly wrong to regard S as having *said* something false. He seems to have recognised that such an issue could not be settled merely by consulting our intuitions, for they pull us in conflicting directions. It is hard to think that these claims hold any *less* for temporal conjunction than for other cases of implicature. If I am led by S's utterance of (2) into thinking that the order of events was that of the conjuncts, and this turns out to be false, then while I may think that S misled me, he may reply that he never actually *said* that they *were* so ordered. In this respect Récanati's distinction, governed by SP, between genuine and other implicatures is open to question. It responds to two different conceptions of 'falling within the scope of logical operators' and it is not clear that either constitutes an objection to Grice's own view.

It is also true that to deny the utterance may be to deny the implicature; or that we may wish to deny the implicature by denying the utterance. If S utters (2) and I demur on the ground not that the events never occurred but that they happened in another order, then my attitude can be expressed, at least initially, by a denial of (2). Just as the assertion of (2) without the intention of determining a specific order for the events, and without any cancellation clause such as 'but not necessarily in that order', is misleading; so the bare denial of (2) as a means of denying the order is similarly misleading. In both cases there is scope for further exploration of the position under HFT. Nevertheless this is another way in which implicatures can 'fall within the scope of logical operators'. We might say that this third way defines a notion of 'pragmatic denial', which does not operate with exactly the same standard propositional logic as ordinary negation. In this third way, however, Grice's own position seems to be confirmed rather than rejected. Until Récanati's use of SP to separate genuine implicatures from explicatures can resolve these problems the case really is not made out. He was, after all, quite right to say that the matter is not 'so simple'.

2.2   Gaps and Completeness

It was noted earlier that the very idea of pragmatics rests on a distinction between a given semantic content and an additional interpretation. That characterisation does not by itself invoke the idea of a gap, or incompleteness, in utterance, for we may additionally interpret, or draw inferences from, an uttered content which contains no overt gaps. The notion of incompleteness is, however, central to the range of cases discussed in this context, and it is important to know what it amounts to and how far it ranges. In the discussion an utterance is variously said to be 'complete' iff it is truth-evaluable, or iff it contains no syntactic, semantic, or pragmatic gaps, or iff it has a semantic analysis. Evidently only the first of these avoids the danger of circularity, and it is in some such terms that both Bach and Récanati separate their two cases of expansion and strengthening, or sentence non-literality and semantic under-determination. I want to argue that the criterion does not adequately serve to distinguish the two types of case, and also that the criterion itself is inadequate.

For both Bach and Récanati the utterance of

(1)   Everyone went to Paris

has to be distinguished from utterance of

(6)   Steel is (not) strong enough.

Both need to be interpreted pragmatically, so that (1) is understood as

(1)   (a) Everyone (in the group) went to Paris

while (6) is understood as

(6)   (a) Steel is (not) strong enough (for this task).

But (1) is already a complete proposition while (6) is only a 'proposition radical'. Hence, for Bach, when S utters (1) he means something else instead, namely (1a), while when S utters (6) he means something else as well. (1) requires 'fleshing out' while (6) requires 'filling in'. Bach's view is that (1a) and (6a) count as 'implicitures', that is, neither explicatures nor implicatures; Récanati classifies them both as explicatures in accordance with his PA.

The assumed distinction between (1) and (6) can, however, be questioned. (1), for example, is unspecific in the domain of quantificaion and in its temporal references[17]. If we were to formulate it as a truth-evaluable, complete, proposition we would have to specify the domain not only with respect to persons but also to persons at some time or at any time. (1) might claim only that all persons living at t went to Paris, or, more adventurously, that all persons who have ever lived, went to Paris. Beyond that we would also have to specify whether the event of going to Paris is to be located at some specific time or whether (1) signifies that everyone who has ever lived went to Paris at some time or other. We certainly expect the claim that every person who has ever lived went to Paris at some particular time is false; our expectation of the falsity of the claims that every person who has ever lived went to Paris at some time or other, or that every person living at some specific time went to Paris at some time or other, is rather less strong. The point is, however, that (1) is interpretable in these different ways, which determine different truth conditions for the utterance.

These points are not confined to this example but hold generally for others. Utterance of

(7)   I have had breakfast

will typically be interpreted as

(7)   (a) I have had breakfast (today).

The suggestion is that (7a) is arrived at because the complete proposition (7) is obviously false or inapposite, since it expresses the claim

(7)   (b) I have had breakfast (in the past).

But it is at least open to us to say, by contrast, that (7) no more expresses (7b) than (7a). (7) by itself is unspecific with regard to either interpretation, or to put it differently, both (7a) and (7b) are possible interpretations of (7). There is no more reason to treat (7) as expressing (7b) than (7a), even though in some appropriate context our preference for one or other account will be more marked. Moreover the fact that in some cases those preferences will be apparent in the proposition itself does not count against these claims. Unlike (7) we will expect to interpret

(8)   I have eaten caviare

not as

(8)   (a) I have eaten caviare (today)

but as

(8)   (b) I have eaten caviare (in the past).

Such a case, however, still offers only an indeterminate utterance interpretable in different ways, one of which in context is likely to be strongly preferred.
    In all these cases it is open to Hs to deploy HFT in order to check which of the alternative interpretations is the more appropriate. In all of them, however, the claim that the original utterances are complete and truth-evaluable seems wrong. (1), (7), and (8) are no more truth-evaluable, as they stand, than (6) with which they are contrasted. If (6) achieves only the status of 'proposition radical', then (1), (7), and (8) seem to be in the same condition. Such a conclusion reinforces the earlier query about Bach's category of 'sentence non-literality'. One motive for introducing it was the belief that the uttered sentences express complete propositions quite different from the preferred interpretations. If S could not have meant literally what the original utterance expressed, then it may seem natural to say that S meant something else non-literally. However, if there is no significant difference between the two types of case, and if the preferred interpretations trade on incompleteness in both types of case, then that motive lapses.

On the other side of the equation, that is in the examples of filling in, there is also some additional complexity. It is possible to regard (6) as expressing a complete proposition rather than a proposition radical. This can best be seen by considering a different utterance with the same form, such as

(9)   Chairmen of privatised Utilities have enough money.

The natural interpretation here is not that such Chairmen have enough money to buy some unspecified good such as a Scottish estate, but rather that their salaries are already quite high enough, and should not be increased. A parallel interpretation could be provided for (6) in some contexts which would not require further specification of a particular task. It is worth noting in this case that although there is no need to envisage a completion of the form 'enough for what?', there is still room for further elaboration. For the claim, as interpreted, raises at once the question of the standard by which those salaries are judged high enough already. If we treat this as a further 'gap' in the utterance, then evidently it is a gap of a different kind. It is salient in terms of the pursuit of the conversation, but it is not directly relevant to the truth-evaluability of the utterance. Such gaps seem highly significant in pragmatic interpretation, but they go beyond the kinds of incompleteness considered in the discussion so far. That particular example does not, of course, provide a case of sentence non-literality any more than (1) does. Like the other cases there is a preferred reading for (9), but there still remain alternative interpretations of the utterance.

The discussion shows that the category distinction, which both Bach and Récanati accept, between the two kinds of case is insecure, so that we may treat both as incomplete, as requiring filling in rather than fleshing out. It does not yet show whether we should classify these cases as explicatures, following Récanati, or as implicitures, following Bach. In the concluding section I want to put that question into the wider context of the previous discussion.

3   Conclusion

The discussion does not yield a decisive conclusion about these issues and the classification of the problem cases, but it offers some guidance. It is easy to be sympathetic to Kent Bach's central claim that in none of these cases is the additional material *explicitly* stated by S. There evidently is a sense for 'what S said' in which the required natural completions are not actually present in the words which S utters. The motive which leads us to talk of 'incomplete' utterances in such cases leads also to a recognition that the utterance itself is *not* entirely explicit at these points. What is true is that normal S/Hs recognise such gaps and take steps to accommodate their understanding, and their responses, to them. So any argument which assimilates the two types of case and regards them both as resulting from gaps in utterance also strengthens the resistance to treating them as explicatures, as what S *explicitly* said. Equally the claim that Récanati's argument for including temporal features of 'and' in explicature is not itself decisive gives us some reason to exclude even those features from explicature. That is so, as I suggested, even in the light of the claim that S/Hs in context may immediately interpret such conjunctions in terms of a determinate temporal order. It is also true that we may construct other notions of 'what S said' which include these contested items. Trivially, if we define what S said by reference to the standard way in which H will interpret such utterances then these items will appear in *that* account of explicature. But such a move is unsatisfactory both because it achieves its result only trivially, and also because in bulding into what is said items which demonstrably belong to pragmatic interpretation we blur the very distinction, between semantic and pragmatic features, which the discussion seeks to clarify.

If we have reason to exclude these cases from explicature do we also have reason to separate them from Gricean implicature? The general view which regards a simple, exhaustive, division between what S said and what S implicated as too undiscriminating is obviously correct. That may motivate construction of midway positions, such as Kent Bach's implicitures, which are neither explicatures nor Gricean implicatures. It motivated also Sperber and Wilson's original conception of explicature, even though it then comes to be located uneasily somewhere between explicit semantic content and implicature. More neutrally what can be clearly seen is that some of these extra items are closer to the original utterance than others. One test for this would be whether the items are naturally expressed in less than propositional form, and so require reference to the original content to be significant. Kent Bach (1994: 284-287) gives a host of such examples. This will cover all the add-on phrases, which themselves may have different roles, which complete utterances where, for example, the referential phrases are unspecific. Another test, different from this in its requirement that the items should all be full propositional forms, would be Carston's 'logical independence' test. I have not argued against such a test and its appeal to PFI here, but I believe that it is open to strong objections. The required completions for cases like (7) and (8) will be different again, but they too seem intuitively closer to the original content than the standard Gricean implicates.

What this begins to suggest is a range of cases more or less closely linked to the original content. A rough order would start with determinate reference and disambiguation, bring in the various types of add-on phrase, and then move on to Grice's 'conventional implicatures' if we accept them at all. From there we can map such cases as temporal/causal 'ands', and on to the more standard Gricean implicates which themselves may not be all of exactly the same type. I would want, however, to extend the catalogue further still to include other gaps in utterance, like that noted for (9), which have some link with the original utterance but exemplify the essential conversational invitation to pursue any items left incomplete at the point of S's utterance. In this way the notion of 'incompleteness' becomes considerably extended, but in the light of the earlier discussion that extended account seems to be needed if we are to give an adequate account of conversation and utterance interpretation[18]

These comments point in the direction of a radical conclusion. Kent Bach (1994a: 124) rightly pointed to the need for a catalogue "of ways in which what is communicated in an utterance can go beyond sentence meaning". But these comments suggest a much more complicated, and discriminating, catalogue of such cases than any so far proposed. The proposals made so far may indeed capture some of the aspects of the central phenomenon, without, however, either capturing them all or relating them all to each other. For the suggestion is not only that the noted phenomena might all be included in some way in the catalogue, but also that the catalogue should be extended to cover an even wider range of cases. It would have to cover all the linguistically significant dimensions of incompleteness which an utterance in its context exemplifies. It would not, then, be simply a question of debating whether we should accept Grice's dual, or Kent Bach's triple, classification scheme; nor would it profitably be simply a question of devising some new category located somewhere between the existing Gricean pair. Both 'explicature' and 'impliciture' usefully draw attention to that wider range of cases, but they understate both its extent and the detailed differences within the range. If the account I have given of these divergent cases within that umbrella is plausible, then the catalogue of which Bach spoke is going to be much larger than the dual or triple schemes so far offered.

Notes

1 Philosophers debated these issues extensively with respect to formal semantic theories following Dummett (1975). Among the contributors were Evans (1985) and Davies (1986, 1987). It is, however, hard to believe that such a theory must reflect exactly the competence which Ss exhibit, and there is room, therefore, for some divergence between theory and practice even in that context.
2 Vanderveken's (1990/91) account of speech acts is a good example of a formal presentation of part of a pragmatic theory.
3 Grice's (1989) references to 'calculability' of implicatures, and Sperber & Wilson's (1986: 254) belief that the Principle of Relevance can provide 'rich and precise non-demonstrative inferences', make claims for determinacy in utterance interpretation which may be unrealistic. There is good reason, as I suggest later (see notes 11 and 18), to think that utterance interpretation essentially lacks determinate precision of these kinds.
4 Theorists like Quine (1960), who stress the 'holistic' character of language, would want to qualify this claim.
5 Stendhal in the novel *Le Rouge et Le Noir* quotes from R.P. Malagrida in the heading to Chapter XXII: La parole a été donnée à l'homme pour cacher la pensée. Though Grice's emphasis on transparency and openness is not strictly rejected by such a claim it can serve as a useful corrective.
6 The classification scheme could be made more complete, and more complex, by explicitly distinguishing between what the sentence uttered means and what S means in uttering it. But the simpler scheme clarifies the central point more directly.
7 Sperber & Wilson (1994: 257, 259-260) recognise the need for experimental work in pragmatics, and suggest in their Postface that more empirical work needs to be done in relation to their Principle of Relevance. Some such experimental work will deal with the psychological processing which S/Hs undertake, but it would be a mistake to think that no other kind of theory is possible. Perhaps any current tendency to accept such a view is an over-reaction to the Fregean rejection of 'psychologism' in semantics. Psychological theory cannot be dispensed with in these contexts, but something between the extremes of a total rejection of psychology and a total rejection of anything else seems the best option.
8 I had tentatively canvassed this idea in Bird (1979).

9   Such a principle raises the still controversial question about its application to non-linguistic creatures. But I have no qualms about ascribing the relevant 'sub-doxastic' states to animals which exhibit the proper complexity in non-linguistic behaviour. See, for a review of some evidence, Whiten (1991).

10 Although neither Sperber & Wilson (1986) nor Kent Bach (1994b) succumb to the simple idea that gaps in utterance are simply a fault their references to "semantic slack" or "loose talk" gesture towards such a belief.

11 Récanati (1991: 99) says: "I will simply assume (1) that context-dependence extends far beyond reference assignment, and (2) that it is generally 'free' rather than 'controlled' in the sense that the linguistic meaning of a context-sensitive expression constrains its possible semantic values but does not consist in a 'rule' or 'function' taking us from context to semantic value". Although Récanati offers no specific examples of such freedom it deserves to cover all the cases of 'incompleteness' which will be considered later. In particular it suggests, as I indicate in note 18, a greater flexibility in choosing between quantifiers or name variables as a means of closing some incomplete utterance than would be legitimate in a formal logical account.

12 Kent Bach (1994b: 279) notes this aspect incidentally in saying: "Then they are in a position to appreciate the difference between what is said, for example, with (9), 'I have had breakfast', and with (9-R), 'I have had breakfast today'. They can then understand the point of the question 'Do you mean today?' and the non-redundancy of using the word 'today' as in (9-R)". Bach uses this to query Récanati's appeal to S/H intuitions, under his Principle of Availability, by suggesting that some acquaintance with Grice's views might alter the intuitive response. My suggestion is rather that, under HFT, S/Hs do not need to be acquainted with Grice in order to appreciate these points: S/Hs readily understand where such gaps occur and the possibility of pursuing them in further exchanges.

13 We lack, and need, ideas about the formal techniques which implement any hypothesis-forming and testing strategy. Kent Bach (1994a: 155) is right to indicate such a lack in relation to the characterisation of 'salience' in this context. William James spoke of the need for a 'logic of science' in the nineteenth century and philosophers such as Popper and others have since then attempted to remedy this lack. See, for a recent discussion, Stich (1993).

14 I have not been able to include an examination of Carston's (1988) argument from her Principle of Functional Independence (PFI) for the inclusion of temporal features in the explicature of conjunctions. The argument is complex, and interesting, but I believe that it is open to a number of objections which prevent it from being valid. Récanati (1991) attempts to refute PFI by reference to counter-examples, and this results in disagreement over what constitutes a genuine counter-example. To show that the argument is invalid, however, avoids that inconclusiveness and also serves to explain why disagreement arises over the suggested counter-examples.

15 It is not usually made clear how restricted are the conjunctive utterances which we immediately interpret in a temporally ordered way. Of course there is a restriction to events, and also to events where the alternative temporal orders are distinct and salient. In many other cases, even where events are at issue, there is a real question whether the events are temporally ordered as before and after at all. If I say "I lived in London and went to school in Brighton", for example, the temporal orderings are more complex, and may need to be checked to become determinate.

16 Kent Bach (1994b) makes the claim in relation to Grice's 'conventional implicatures', and I have not discussed the grounds on which he rejects that classification. I have, however, queried one of his reasons, namely the 'arbitrariness' of Grice's appeal to truth-functionality. Another of his reasons for the rejection issues also in some unclarity, once he introduces the idea

of 'illocutionary adverbials' into Grice's discussion of 'non-central speech acts'. For on one page (1994b: 277) he says that for non-central speech acts "the problematic element does not enter into what is said"; while on another (1994b: 277-278) he says that "what is said should be determined by the meanings of the elements of the sentence and their syntactic structure - as adjusted for any needed disambiguation or indexical reference-fixing as well as for any elements being used to make running commentary on the utterance". If the elements used to make running commentaries correspond to the non-central speech acts, as they seem to, then it is not clear where they are located.

17 Kent Bach (1994a: 133) notes that typically spatio-temporal location will need to be determined in order to achieve a complete proposition; but it is just those elements which are missing in (1).

18 A possible example of Récanati's notion of 'free' rather than 'controlled' aspects of utterance interpretation arises from these cases of incompleteness. For it is always possible to achieve the closure of such utterances by using a quantifier or some so far unspecified name variable even in cases which are not directly referential. We might note in the case of (N), for example, that steel is strong enough for some task or other, or for a particular so far unspecified task, and may not choose between these. Conversation can be, and often is, carried on without that degree of precision, and this makes it impossible to achieve for utterance interpretation the level of determinacy that we might expect in the context of semantics or logic.

References

Bach, K. (1994a): "Conversational Impliciture". Mind and Language 9, 124-162.
Bach, K. (1994b): "Semantic Slack: What is Said and More". In: S.L.Tsohatzidis, ed.: Foundations of Speech Act Theory. London: Routledge, 267-291.
Bird, G.H. (1979): "Speech Acts and Conversation". Philosophical Quarterly 29, 142-152.
Bird, G.H. (1994): "Relevance Theory and Speech Acts". In: S.L.Tsohatzidis, ed.: Foundations of Speech Act Theory. London: Routledge, 292-312.
Brandom, R. (1994): Making It Explicit. Cambridge, Mass.: Harvard University Press.
Carston, R. (1988): "Implicature, Explicature, and Truth-Conditional Semantics". In: R. Kempson, ed.: Mental Representations. Cambridge: Cambridge University Press, 151-183.
Cohen, L.J. (1971): "Some Remarks on Grice's Views About the Logical Particles of Natural Language". In: Y. Bar-Hillel, ed.: Pragmatics of Natural Language. Dordrecht: Reidel, 50-68.
Davies, M. (1986): "Tacit Knowledge and the Structure of Thought". In: C. Travis, ed.: Meaning and Interpretation. Oxford: Blackwell, 127-159.
Davies, M. (1987): "Tacit Knowledge and Semantic Theory". Mind XCVI, 441-462.
Dummett, M. (1975): "What is a Theory of Meaning?". In: S. Guttenplan, ed.: Mind and Language. Oxford: Blackwell, 97-139.
Evans, G. (1985): "Semantic Theory and Tacit Knowledge". In: G. Evans: Collected Papers. Oxford: Oxford University Press, 322-342.
Grice, P. (1989): Studies in the Way of Words. Cambridge, Mass.: Harvard University Press.
Quine, W.V.O. (1960): Word and Object. Cambridge, Mass.: The MIT Press.
Récanati, F. (1991): "The Pragmatics of What is Said". In: S. Davis, ed.: Pragmatics: A Reader. Oxford: Oxford University Press, 97-120.
Récanati, F. (1993): Direct Reference: From Language to Thought. Oxford: Blackwell.
Smith, B. (1992): "Understanding Language". Proceedings of the Aristotelian Society XCII, 109-141.
Sperber, D. & D. Wilson (1986): Relevance: Communication and Cognition. Oxford: Blackwell.

Sperber, D. & D. Wilson (1994): Relevance: Communication and Cognition. 2nd. edition. Oxford: Blackwell.
Stich, S. (1993): "Naturalizing Epistemology, Quine, Simon, and Prospects for Pragmatism". In: C. Hookway & D. Peterson, eds.: Philosophy and Cognitive Science. Cambridge: Cambridge University Press, 1-17.
Vanderveken, D. (1990-1991): Meaning and Speech Acts. Vols. I and II. Cambridge: Cambridge University Press.
Whiten, A., ed. (1991): Natural Theories of Mind. Oxford: Blackwell.

On Non-Truth Conditional Meaning

Diane Blakemore, Southampton

1 Introduction

For some time now semanticists have been concerned with a range of phenomena which suggest that linguistic meaning cannot be defined in terms of truth conditions. Some phenomena have become more notorious than others, and different writers have their different favourites. For example, speech act theorists have tended to focus their attention on illocutionary adverbials like the one in (1) and attitudinal adverbials such as the one in (2) (see Bach & Harnish 1979, Urmson 1963). Those working in Gricean pragmatics have been more interested in a range of so-called 'little' words which include the ones in (3 - 5) (see Grice 1989, Karttunen & Peters 1975). And in discourse theory and theories of text representation, where the interest in non-truth conditionality is perhaps more incidental, the focus is on so-called discourse connectives like the ones in (4 - 6) and particles like the one in (7) (see Knott & Dale 1994, Fraser 1990, Schiffrin 1987).

(1) *Confidentially*, she is going to leave.
(2) *Unfortunately*, she is going to leave.
(3) She's *even* going to leave.
(4) I thought she was happy] *but* she's going to leave.
(5) She hasn't got anything to do] *so* she's going to leave.
(6) [She wants some time alone] *In other words*, she's going to leave.
(7) She's going to leave, *huh*.

Given the range of non-truth conditional phenomena and the theoretical differences between the various people who have studied them, it is not really surprising that no single theory of non-truth-conditional meaning has emerged. But then again, it is not clear that we should want a unitary account of all the different phenomena which have been identified as examples of non-truth-conditional meaning: perhaps the only thing that the expressions in (1-7) have in common is that they don't contribute to the truth conditions of the utterances that contain them.

My own interest in non-truth-conditional meaning began with an attempt to use Sperber & Wilson's (1986) relevance theoretic approach to utterance understanding to provide a more explanatory account of the phenomena Grice analysed as conventional implicatures, and was restricted to a sub-set of the expressions classified as discourse markers or connectives (*but, so, after all, moreover* and *too*). It was tempting to think that my analysis of these expressions as semantic constraints on relevance might extend to all non-truth conditional phenomena, or, at the very least all so-called discourse connectives. However, my attempt to provide a re-assessment of conventional implicature led to a different semantic distinction - the distinction between conceptual and procedural meaning - which it turns out, is *not* co-extensive with the distinction between truth conditional and non-truth conditional meaning. Non-truth conditional meaning cannot be identified with procedural meaning.

My aim in this paper is to explain why this is the case. However, at the same time I want to demonstrate that the distinction between conceptual and procedural meaning is important in an account of the relationship between linguistic form and pragmatic interpretation.

2   Procedural Meaning

Karttunen (1974) and Karttunen & Peters (1975) linked Grice's notion of conventional implicature to the notion of pragmatic presupposition (see Stalnaker 1974). For example, Karttunen describes *too* as a rhetorical device whose presence or absence does not have any bearing on the proposition the sentence containing it expresses, but rather relates the sentence to a particular kind of conversational context. If the appropriate context is not available, then the utterance is not false but inappropriate.

But why should there be such words? The Gricean explanation for *conversational* implicature lies in the fact that the very act of communicating creates expectations (of informativeness, truthfulness, relevance and so on). One might think that conventional implicatures, because they are conventional, should have a very different kind of explanation. However, my argument in my 1987 book was that the existence of expressions that impose constraints on contexts follows from the nature of the processes involved in utterance interpretation and the principle which governs those processes. In particular, their existence can be explained in terms of Sperber & Wilson's (1986) claim that utterance interpretation involves not only linguistic decoding but also inferential processes which are constrained by the Principle of Relevance.

The assumption that an utterance is consistent with the Principle of Relevance is based on the hearer's recognition that it is an act of ostensive communication - that is, an act of deliberate, overt communication in which the speaker not only intends to convey a particular message but is also actively helping the hearer recognize this. From the speaker's point of view, it is simply not worth engaging in such an act unless the audience pays attention to it. But equally, from the hearer's point of view it is not worth paying attention to an act of communication unless there is information worth processing - or in other words, unless it is relevant. This means that a speaker who requests the hearer's attention, for example by producing an utterance, communicates his assumption that his utterance is relevant.

Relevance is defined in terms of *contextual effect* and *processing effort*. Contextual effects are simply the ways in which a new piece of information may interact with contextual assumptions to yield an improvement to the hearer's overall representation of the world. These are not confined to new assumptions derived from combining the new information with contextual assumptions, but may also include increased evidence for existing assumptions or even the elimination of existing assumptions. Processing effort is a function not only of the linguistic complexity of the utterance itself, but also of the cost of accessing and using contextual assumptions in the derivation of contextual effects.

Sperber and Wilson argue that the presumption of relevance carried by every act of ostensive communication has two aspects: first, it creates a presumption that the information it communicates interacts with the context for derivation of adequate *contextual effects*; and second, it creates a presumption that no gratuitous processing effort is required for the recovery of effects. Taken together, these presumptions define a level of *optimal relevance*. And the principle of relevance is simply the thesis that every act of ostensive communication communicates a presumption of its own optimal relevance.

For Grice, the role of the maxims is restricted to the recovery of implicatures. Indeed, what a speaker implicates is distinguished from what a speaker says by the fact that its recovery depends on the assumption that the maxims are being followed. However, for Sperber and Wilson the inferential phase of communication is not restricted to the recovery of implicit content. It also plays a role in the identification of explicit content or *explicatures*.

This point has been underlined by Robyn Carston (1988, 1993, forthcoming) who has shown how inferential enrichment processes constrained by the principle of relevance bridge the gap between the linguistically decoded logical form of an utterance and its explicit content. This means that linguistic meaning plays a role in the recovery of explicit content only in the sense that it encodes constituents of the representations which undergo inferential enrichment processes.

Now, while these representations are not fully propositional, they are nevertheless conceptual in the sense that, in contrast with other representations assigned to utterances in the course of their interpretation (for example, phonological and syntactic ones), they can act as the input to logical inference rules and can enter into contradiction and entailment relations. For example, the logical form of (8a) which I have represented in (8b) entails (9a) and is contradictory with (9b).

(8)   (a)   She gave it to him.
        (b)   Some female gave some object to some male.

(9)   (a)   Someone gave something to someone.
        (b)   No-one has ever been given anything.

This would suggest that the role of linguistic decoding as an input to the inferential phase of utterance interpretation is to encode constituents of conceptual representations.

However, there is more to utterance interpretation than the recovery of explicatures. On the assumption that an utterance is consistent with the Principle of Relevance, a hearer is entitled to expect that she can combine its explicatures with contextual assumptions for the derivation of contextual effects, or in other words, that its explicit content can be taken as input to inferential computations which yield contextual effects. But this suggests that there is another way in which linguistic decoding may act as input to the inferential phase of utterance interpretation. For surely, since the hearer is expected not just to construct conceptual representations but also to perform computations over them in the derivation of contextual effects, linguistic meaning may encode not just constituents of conceptual representations but also instructions or procedures for manipulating them in inferences. Indeed, if these inferences are constrained by the Principle of Relevance, then this is just what we might expect. For such constraints would have the advantage of guiding the hearer towards the intended contextual effects for a minimum cost in processing.

Consider, for example, the sequence in (10) (adapted from Hobbs 1979):

(10) (a) Tom can open Bill's safe.
 (b) He knows the combination.

Although the interpretation of the first segment provides a highly accessible context for the interpretation of the second, it does not guarantee a unique interpretation. The assumption that the proposition expressed by the first segment of (10) is a part of the context for the interpretation of the second is consistent with either the interpretation in which (b) is relevant as evidence for the proposition that Tom can open Bill's safe or with the interpretation in which (b) is relevant as an implication of the proposition that Tom can open Bill's safe.

This would suggest that an expression which guided the hearer towards either of these interpretations is a constraint on the role that the proposition it introduces plays in the inferences performed in the course of establishing its relevance. Thus according to this analysis, the role of *so* in a sequence like (11) is not to contribute to the proposition expressed by the utterance it prefaces, but to constrain the inferential computations that proposition enters into - or, in other words, its relevance.

(11) (a) Tom can open Bill's safe.
 (b) So he knows the combination.

More specifically, *so* encodes the procedural information in (12).

(12) Process the proposition expressed by (11b) as a conclusion.

Since this constraint can be satisfied only if the hearer supplies a further contextual premise - for example, the one in (13) - the use of *so* might be regarded as a constraint on the hearer's choice of context for the interpretation of the utterance that contains it.

(13) If someone can open Bill's safe, then they must know the combination of numbers which unlocks it.

Indeed, it might be argued that we should regard these linguistically encoded constraints not as constraints on contextual effects, but as constraints on contexts. I have vacillated between the two positions in my own work. However, as we shall see in the final section of this paper, there is at least one phenomenon which seems to be evidence for the analysis of expressions like *so* and *still* as constraints on contextual effects.

As I have said, my (1987) analysis of expressions like *so* was intended as a re-analysis of the expressions Grice (1989) called *conventional implicatures*. Clearly, the term *conventional* was intended to distinguish these semantically encoded aspects of meaning from those aspects of interpretation which Grice explained in terms of pragmatically determined inference. Nevertheless, he chose to call them implicatures, and implicatures are propositions with their own truth conditions and truth values. Accordingly, it is not surprising that when he discusses the notion further in his 'Retrospective Epilogue' (Grice 1989) he analyses them in conceptual terms.

The basic idea underlying Grice's analysis of expressions like *so* is that the speaker of an utterance such as (11) is performing two speech acts, a "lower-order" or "ground-floor" speech act and a "higher-order" speech act in which the speaker is "commenting in a certain way on the lower-order act" (1989: 362). Thus the speaker of an utterance of the form in (14) might be regarded as performing a higher order act which communicates with the information in (15).[1]

(14) P. So Q
(15) Q is a consequence of P.

(15) expresses in conceptual terms what I have argued should be expressed as a procedural constraint on inferences. If Grice is right, then similar conceptual accounts can be given for other expressions which I have argued should be analysed in procedural terms, for example, utterance initial *well* in (16), utterance initial *still* in (17) and utterance initial *anyway* in (18).

(16) She sounded altogether stricken, terrified. Oh I can't explain it. - *Well*, what do you expect? the doctor asked. She's not yet twenty is she?
 (from Agatha Christie *Ordeal by Innocence* cited by Carlson (1984))

(17) A: It'll be a lot of work and it's a 12 hour plane journey.
 B: *Still*, Tokyo's a great place.

(18) (continuation of (17))
 A: Yeah, I've always wanted to go there. I wonder how much time I'll get to see anything. There must be a free afternoon. Or I could stay an extra day, I suppose...
 B: *Anyway*, I think you should go.

The question is, who is right - or perhaps even does it matter? My main concern in the rest of this paper is to explain why it does.

In the first place, it seems that there is something suspicious about the idea that a phenomenon could be at once conventional - that is, linguistically encoded - and an implicature - that is, propositional. To accept the notion of a conventional implicature is to accept that a single expression can encode something propositional. My suspicion does not derive from a belief that only sentences can be used to express propositions. Dummett's view that "a sentence [...] is the smallest unit of language with which a linguistic act can be accomplished" (Dummett 1973:194) cannot be maintained. Speakers can and do use single words and phrases to express propositions. For example, a speaker may use (19) to communicate the proposition in (20).

(19) Coffee.
(20) I want coffee.

However, (20) is not *encoded* by (19). It is constructed from (19) by inferential enrichment processes constrained by the principle of relevance. In a different context the concept encoded by *coffee* might be interpreted as a constituent of quite a different proposition, say (21) or (22).

(21) You need to buy coffee.
(22) The bushes you can see are coffee bushes.

This might suggest that a conceptual account of expressions like *so*, *well*, *anyway*, and *still* would be acceptable if it treated them as encoding not propositional representations, but concepts which are constituents of a propositional representations which are recovered by enrichment processes in accordance with the principle of relevance.

However, if these expressions encode concepts, what are they? As Wilson & Sperber have pointed out, "discourse connectives are notoriously difficult to pin down in conceptual terms" (1993: 16). It is well known just how difficult it is for native speakers to explain the meanings of expressions like *well*, *doch*, or *en effet* to non-native speakers. Moreover, if expressions like *so*, *well* and *afterall* do encode concepts, then why are they restricted to higher-order speech acts? It is true that there is an *afterall* which occurs in lower-level speech acts, and a *so* and a *well*. But clearly, these are not synonymous with the *afterall*, *so* and *well* that I have been talking about here.

3   Conceptual Non-Truth Conditional Meaning

The point here is that there *are* expressions which are non-truth conditional and contribute to 'higher-level' speech acts but which seem to have synonymous truth conditional counterparts in lower order acts. Consider for example, the sentence adverb in (1) and its synonymous counterpart in (23). Or the apposition marker in (6) and its synonymous counterpart in (24).

(1) *Confidentially*, she is going to leave.
(23) He spoke to her confidentially.
(6) [She wants some time alone] *In other words*, she's going to leave.
(24) She asked the student to put it in other words.

As Bach & Harnish (1979) have argued, the illocutionary adverbial in (1) does not contribute to the proposition expressed: the truth of (1) does not depend on whether the speaker is speaking confidentially. The same point can be made about the apposition marker in (6). On the other hand, as Wilson & Sperber (1993) have argued, the fact that *confidentially* in (1) is synonymous with *confidentially* in (23) would seem to suggest that the sentence adverbial and the VP adverbial encode the same concept. That is, if the adverb in (23) is to be analysed as as encoding a constituent of a propositional representation, then so should the sentence adverb in (1). The same point applies to the apposition marker in (6).

There is a further respect in which many sentence adverbials and so-called apposition markers contrast with the expressions I analysed as encoding procedural constraints. As (25) and (26) show, sentence adverbials can be semantically complex:

(25)   In total, absolute confidence, she's going to leave.
(26)   To put it in slightly different and perhaps more brutal terms, you're fired.

As Wilson and Sperber say, while it is not obvious what this compositionality would mean in procedural terms, it is not difficult to explain if illocutionary adverbials and apposition markers are analysed as encoding conceptual representations which undergo semantic interpretation rules in the regular way (Wilson & Sperber 1993:18).

If these expressions encode concepts which are not part of the truth conditional content of the utterances that contain them, then what are they part of?

Wilson and Sperber's answer is that although these expressions do not contribute to the proposition expressed by the utterance that contains them, they nevertheless contribute to its explicit content. This answer hinges on the argument that explicit content or explicature is not encoded by the semantic representation of an utterance, but is obtained by fleshing out or enriching a linguistically encoded semantic representation on the basis of contextual assumptions and the principle of relevance. These enrichment processes are not confined to the recovery of the proposition expressed, but also include the enrichment of a semantic representation to obtain *higher-level* explicatures in which the proposition expressed is embedded under a higher-level illocutionary or attitudinal predicate. For example, the speaker of (27) might have intended to communicate the higher-level descriptions in (28):

(27)   She's going to leave.

(28)   (a)   The speaker of (27) is telling the hearer that she is going to leave.
       (b)   The speaker of (27) is telling the hearer confidentially that she is going to leave.

Although these descriptions are obtained by enriching the semantic representation of (27), they are not part of the truth conditions for that utterance. This means that the linguistic form of an utterance not only contributes to the proposition expressed, but also to explicatures which, although they may be true or false in their own right, make no contribution to truth conditions. Thus although the adverbial *confidentially* in (1) does not contribute to the proposition expressed, it does contribute to a proposition that is explicitly communicated - that is (28b).

This analysis raises a number of questions, notably, how do we *explain* the non-truth conditionality of expressions like *confidentially* as they are used in (1)? In my recent work on apposition markers I have been exploring an idea which has also been applied by Ifantidou (1994) in her work on evidentials. The suggestion is that we take Wilson and Sperber's analysis even further and treat a parenthetical adverbial as contributing to a distinct discourse unit with its own truth conditions and relevance. Then the intuition that the parenthetical constituent does not contribute to the truth conditions of the utterance as a whole can be explained by the fact that it achieves relevance in a different way from the host utterance, namely in the way it comments on the interpretation of the host utterance.

This sort of analysis is supported by recent work in syntax (Haegeman 1988, Fabb 1990, Espinal 1991) which argues that parenthetical constructions are syntactically independent. Clearly, much more work needs to be done before we can accept what is really quite a radical departure from the standard view that utterances encodes a single logical form and expresses a single proposition. However, I would like to leave the questions raised by conceptual non-truth conditional meaning for another occasion and end this paper with the discussion of a phenomenon which, it seems, may provide further support for the argument that non-truth conditional meaning may be either procedural or conceptual.

4   Procedural Meaning and Fragmentary Utterances

My interest in this phenomenon derives from a comment made by a (non-linguist) colleague after he had produced the single word utterance in (29) in response to a secretary's account of the explanation a student had given for the non-submission of work:

(29)   Nevertheless.

His comment was, 'You can communicate a whole proposition with *nevertheless*'.

But can you? Perhaps what he had in mind here was that his audience could reasonably have been expected to recover a proposition which *nevertheless* introduces say (30).

(30)   She could have handed in some of the work.

This is not a proposition encoded by *nevertheless*. But nor is it a proposition expressed by a lower-order speech act. There has been no lower-order speech act. It might be suggested that although there has not been any actual lower order speech act, a hearer can interpret (29) as if there was. That is, she could interpret (29) as if the speaker had intended to produce the utterance in (31).

(31)   Neverthless she could have handed in some of the work.

If this is right, then the utterance in (29) is elliptical or incomplete in the same way as, for example, (19). However, I do not think that it is. (29) is complete as it stands.

This is not to say that the speaker did not expect the hearer to recover some proposition. The point is that this proposition is the one in (30). The secretary would have been equally justified in constructing any one of the assumptions in (32).

(32)   (a)   This student's behaviour does not justify bending the rules.
            (b)   This student's behaviour has not been good.
            (c)   There are other students who have experienced difficulties too.

This does not exhaust the range of assumptions that could have been constructed by the hearer of (29). However, clearly the range is constrained by the utterance of *nevertheless* insomuch as the actual assumption constructed by the hearer does not matter as long as it gives rise to the right sort of contextual effects. In other words, the speaker's intention is that hearer construct a proposition which gives rise to contextual effects consistent with the constraint encoded by *nevertheless*. Indeed, in some cases the speaker' intention may not even include the construction of a proposition. Consider, for example the utterances in (33) and (34).

(33)   It'll be a lot of work and it's a 12 hour plane journey. *Still*.

(34)   A: Has anyone explained the situation to you?
            B: *Well*.

Or consider those cases where a speaker's contribution to a conversation trails off and ends *anyway*, or the conversations that begin with *so*. In these cases it seems that the utterance of the discourse marker is simply intended to activate the kind of contextual effects which satisfy the constraint it encodes.

It may be argued that the phenomenon exhibited in (29) is not restricted to procedural non-truth conditional expressions. Speakers also produce single word utterances consisting of what I have analysed as conceptual non-truth conditional expressions. For example, the sentence adverbial *unfortunately* encodes a concept rather than a procedure, but the utterance in (35) seems to be as complete as the utterance of *nevertheless* in (29).

(35)   A: Have you got any homework?
            B: Unfortunately.

However, in contrast with (29), the hearer of (35) will interpret B's response as communicating a specific lower level explicature, namely, *I have got some homework*, as well as the higher-level explicature whose relevance lies in the information it gives about the speaker's attitude towards the lower-level explicature. In other words, these are two quite different phenomena, and the difference seems to lie in the difference between the two types of non-truth conditional meaning which linguistic expressions may encode.

Notes

1   In fact according to Grice's actual analyses *so*, the speaker is indicating that (9b) is an *explanation* for (9a). However, as Wilson & Sperber (1993) point out, this does not cover the full range of examples discussed in my earlier work (Blakemore 1987). In particular, it does not work for the discourse initial use of *so* in (i) which is uttered in a situation where the speaker has seen someone arrive home laden with shopping:
(i) So you've spent all your money.
Nor does it work in those cases (also discussed in Blakemore 1987) where the speaker produces (ii) in a situation in which she has failed to understand the relevance of another speaker's remark.
(ii) So?
However, my objection to Grice in this paper does not so much hinge on the actual content of the higher-order speech act as much as the fact that he analysed expressions like *so* in conceptual rather than procedural terms.

References

Bach, K. & R. Harnish: (1979): Linguistic Communication and Speech Acts. Cambridge, Mass.: The MIT Press.
Blakemore, D.L. (1987): Semantic Constraints on Relevance. Oxford: Blackwell.
Blakemore, D.L. (1988a): "*So* as a constraint on relevance". In: R. Kempson, ed.: Mental Representations: the interface between language and reality. Cambridge: Cambridge University Press, 183-196.
Blakemore, D.L. (1988b): "The organization of discourse". In: F. Newmeyer, ed.: Linguistics: The Cambridge Survey, vol 4. Cambridge: Cambridge University Press, 229-250.
Blakemore, D.L. (1992): Understanding Utterances. Oxford: Blackwell.
Blakemore, D.L. (forthcoming): "Are reformulation markers discourse markers?". To appear in: Journal of Linguistics.
Carston, R. (1988): "Implicature, explicature and truth theoretic semantics". In: R. Kempson, ed.: Mental Representations: the interface between language and reality. Cambridge: Cambridge University Press, 155-82.
Carston, R. (1993): "Conjunction, explanation and relevance". Lingua 90 (1/2), 27-48.
Carston, R. (forthcoming): "Quantity maxims and generalised implicature". To appear in: Lingua.
Dummett, M. (1973): Frege: Philosophy of Language. London: Duckworth.
Espinal, M. Teresa (1991): "The representation of disjunct constituents". Language 67 (4), 726-762.
Fabb, N. (1990): "The difference between English restrictive and non-restrictive relative clauses". Journal of Linguistics 26 (1), 57-78.
Fraser, B. (1990): "An approach to discourse markers". Journal of Pragmatics 14, 383-395.
Grice, H.P. (1989): Studies in the Way of Words. Cambridge, Mass.: Harvard University Press.
Haegeman, L. (1988): "Parenthetical adverbials: the radical orphanage approach". In: S. Chiba et al., eds.: Aspects of Modern English Linguistics: papers presented to Nasdano Uhagi on his 60th birthday. Tokyo: Kaitakushi, 232-254.
Hobbs, J. (1979): "Coherence and co-reference". Cognitive Sciences 3, 67-90.
Ifantidou, E. (1994): Evidentials and Relevance. University of London PhD thesis.
Karttunen, L. (1974): "On pragmatic and semantic aspects of meaning". Paper presented at the 11th Annual Philosophy Colloquium.

Karttunen, L. & S. Peters (1975): "Conventional implicature in Montague Grammar". Proceedings of the Annual Meeting of the Berkeley Linguistics Society 1, 266-278.
Knott, A. & R. Dale (1994): "Using a set of linguistic phenomena to motivate a set of coherence relations". Discourse Processes 18, 35-62.
Schiffrin, D. (1987): Discourse Markers. Cambridge: Cambridge University Press.
Sperber, D. & D. Wilson (1986): Relevance: Communication and cognition. Oxford: Blackwell.
Stalnaker, R. (1974): "Pragmatic presupposition". In: M. Munitz & P. Unger, eds.: Semantics and Philosophy: Studies in Contemporary Philosophy. New York: New York University Press, 197-213.
Wilson, D. & D. Sperber (1993): "Linguistic form and relevance". Lingua 90, 5-25.
Urmson, J. (1963): "Parenthetical verbs". In: C. Caton, ed.: Philosophy and Ordinary Language. Urbana, IL: University of Illinois Press, 220-240.

Enrichment and Loosening: Complementary Processes in Deriving the Proposition Expressed?[*]

Robyn Carston, London

1 Introduction

One important consequence of the relevance-theoretic view of cognition and communication is the following: we can think many thoughts that our language cannot encode, and we can communicate many thoughts that our utterances do not encode. Strictly speaking, virtually no sentence encodes a complete thought; certain processes of contextual filling-in are required before anything of a propositional nature emerges at all. However, that more basic point is not my primary concern in this short paper. The idea is that, even given such processes of propositional completion, a great many of our thoughts are of a much finer grain than that of the minimal propositions which result from these processes. It follows that there are many more concepts (construed as constituents of thoughts) than there are words in the language.

One way of trying to account for this would be to suggest that words are multiply ambiguous, many of them encoding a vast number of discrete senses. This is not, of course, the way a relevance-theoretic approach to communication would explain this fact. Most other inferential pragmatic approaches to communication and interpretation would not take the ambiguity line either. The relevance theory view (Sperber & Wilson 1986, 1995) is that our powerful inferential capabilities enable us to construct ad hoc concepts out of lexically encoded concepts during our on-line interpretation of utterances, on the hoof as it were. This process is both driven by and constrained by the inevitable considerations of processing effort and cognitive effects. The two main varieties of ad hoc concept construction that Dan Sperber and Deirdre Wilson have discussed in various lectures and seminars over the past decade are the 'narrowing' of a lexically encoded concept and its 'loosening' (leaving aside the echoic or quotational use of concepts for the time being). Other terms are sometimes used: narrowing is sometimes called enrichment or strengthening; loosening is sometimes called broadening or weakening. It is these processes which I want to consider here, particu-

---

[*] Many thanks to Deirdre Wilson whose communicated thoughts on these matters have, as always, given me many (positive) cognitive effects.

larly loosening or broadening, and their contribution, if any, to the proposition expressed by an utterance.

2   Enrichment

This term covers a variety of cases, some of which have been discussed extensively elsewhere, for instance:

(1)   (a) Everyone got drunk.
         (b) I've got nothing to wear to the party.
         (c) He handed her the scalpel and she made the incision.
         (d) The police hit the suspect and she had to go to hospital.
         (e) He begged her not to jump.

In the first two examples a domain for the quantifier to range over has to be contextually inferred, thereby narrowing down the interpretation. In the two conjunction examples, the encoded assumption that there is some connection or other between the events is further specified by the inference of a temporal relation in (1c) and a cause-consequence relation in (1d), these relations being supplied perhaps by highly accessible general knowledge schemas concerning relevant ways in which events connect up. Note that in (1c) the second conjunct is further narrowed by the obvious assumption that the incision was made with the scalpel mentioned in the first conjunct. Similarly in (1e), a further constituent may be supplied so that, in an appropriate context, this could be taken to communicate that he begged her not to jump off the ledge of a high building. I will be focusing on a slightly different type of enrichment in this paper and won't return to these examples (for detailed discussion of them, see Carston 1988, 1993; Récanati 1989, 1993; Wilson & Sperber 1993).

The examples of primary interest here are of the following sort:

(2)   (a) He wears rabbit.
         (b) I want to meet some bachelors.
         (c) Mary cut the cake.
         (d) She has a brain.
         (e) The cinema is some distance from the restaurant.
         (f) Something's happened.

What distinguishes these from the previous set is that, rather than adding a conceptual constituent, the enrichment targets a particular lexical item and strengthens the concept it encodes. For instance, in (2a) the noun 'rabbit', which encodes something like *rabbit stuff*, is narrowed to *rabbit fur/skin*. One possible narrowing of the *bachelor* concept in (2b) would take place in a context in which the speaker had made it clear that she wants to settle down and have children; then the denotation of the relevant *bachelor* concept would be a subset of the set of unmarried men. A crucial component of the narrowed concept would be 'eligible for marriage'. In the case of (2c), it is not any old severing of the fibres of the cake that would be communicated in most contexts but rather a particular mode of cutting; comparison with different objects of cutting makes this apparent, for instance *grass, hair, cloth, flesh*, etc. The last three examples have in common that their linguistically encoded content is a truism: all human beings have a brain, there is inevitably a measurable space between two locations, etc. Some pragmatic narrowing down is required, of the sort of brain she has in (2d), of the distance involved in (2e) and of the nature of the event in (2f).

In short, there is a subset relation between the extension of the concept actually communicated in these examples and the extension of the lexical concept from which it has been derived, shown schematically in (3), where L is the extension of the lexical concept and C' is the extension of the narrowed ad hoc concept, the relevant concept in each case.

(3)

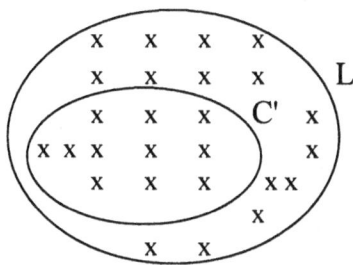

Now one of the features of relevance theory which distinguishes it quite sharply from standard Gricean theory is the view that these strengthenings, of both the types exemplified in (1) and (2), may contribute to the explicit level of communication, specifically to the propositional form of the utterance. On the Gricean approach they have the status of implicatures, communicated assumptions which are independent from, external to, the core proposition communicated by the utterance ("what is said", for Grice). Relevance theorists favour the former view because, in many instances at least, these appear to contribute to the truth-conditional content of the utterance, to what makes it true or false. Various arguments and tests have been put forward in support of this view (see Carston 1988; Récanati 1989, 1993; Wilson & Sperber 1993). For the purposes of this paper I am going to assume that it is correct, so that the proposition expressed (and communicated) by (2b) is as in (4), where *bachelor'* represents the new narrowed *bachelor* concept.

(4) S_x *wants at t_i to meet some bachelors'*

It is the interaction of this propositional form with a set of contextual assumptions that will give rise to contextual effects and some of those contextual assumptions will be derived from the encyclopedic entry of the narrowed concept, *bachelor'*, (for instance, that the people in question should be heterosexual, youngish, interested in marriage, etc). Finally, it should be emphasised that this narrowing is a local process; it doesn't necessarily follow that the proposition derived will always be logically stronger than the proposition before that strengthening took place, as is obvious in the case of narrowings within the scope of negation and certain quantifiers.

3   Loosening

The other, putatively opposite, process of loosening or broadening, is exemplified by the following, where the loosely used concept is the one encoded by the highlighted lexical item:

(5)   (a)   France is *hexagonal*.
       (b)   I love *bald* men.
       (c)   This steak is *raw*.
       (d)   Have you eaten my chocolate *heart*?
       (e)   Here's my new *flatmate*. [referring to a newly acquired cat]

This relaxing of a linguistically encoded meaning has been pretty much ignored outside the relevance-theoretic framework, though a general unease with any process of pragmatic loosening has been expressed. When discussing words which seem to have several related meanings, one stronger than the other, Grice (1978: 119) says:

> If one makes the further assumption that it is more generally feasible to *strengthen* one's meaning by achieving a superimposed implicature, than to *make a relaxed use* of an expression (and I don't know how this assumption would be justified), then Modified Occam's Razor would bring in its train the principle that one should suppose a word to have a less restrictive rather than a more restrictive meaning, where choice is possible. (my emphasis)

Atlas (1992), who works within a Gricean view of pragmatics, refers to this passage and says:

> The "strengthening" assumption can be justified by discovering that there is an intelligible inference that brings about the strengthening of a speaker's meaning - intelligible in the sense that such inferences can be formulated and rationalized - but no intelligible inference that brings about the relaxation of a speaker's meaning. Loose uses of words don't seem particularly rule-governed.

But, then, what about the examples in (5)? It seems pretty clear that we do not want the concepts encoded by the lexical items 'heart' and 'flatmate' to include in their extension confectionery in the one case, nonhumans in the other. The same holds for 'hexagonal', 'bald' and 'raw', though this might need more argument to convince everyone (not, however, Grice or Atlas, who keep their semantics as minimalist as possible). Loose use is a fact and has to be accounted for by an adequate pragmatic theory. With a few notable exceptions, neo-Griceans have tended to steer clear of it.[1]

The standard relevance theory account of loose talk, including metaphorical talk, has been around for some time (see Sperber & Wilson 1985/86), so I'll give just its bare outline here by way of reminder. The idea is that in some instances a speaker chooses to produce an utterance which is a less-than-literal (that is, loose) interpretation of the thought she intends to communicate. This will arise when she judges that communication of her thought is facilitated by such a non-literal utterance in that it makes that thought more accessible to the hearer than a literal one would. The process of interpreting loose uses is as follows: the hearer decodes the lexically encoded concept, thereby gaining access to certain logical and encyclopedic properties; he treats the utterance as a rough guide to what the speaker intends to communicate, and, in effect, sorts through the available properties, rejecting those that are not relevant in the particular context and accepting those that are, as reflections of the speaker's view. For instance, in the case of 'raw' in (5c), the definitional property of *not cooked* would be rejected while the encyclopedic property of, say, *difficult to eat*, when applied to meat, would be maintained. The idea is that the lexical concept *raw* is in a relation of 'non-identical resemblance' with the concept that figures in the speaker's thought regarding the state of the steak; that is, they share some logical and contextual implications. So also for a metaphorical statement such as 'Bill is a bulldozer', where the lexical concept *bulldozer* is used to represent the non-lexicalised concept that figures in the speaker's thought about Bill; it represents it by non-identical resemblance.

As is well known, the relevance theory account of metaphor is very different from the Gricean account - differences that I won't go into here - and considerably more explanatory. However, there is one respect in which it stays close to the Gricean account, at least in the existing published work, and that is that utterances involving metaphorical uses of words and, in fact, loose uses quite generally, do not communicate the proposition they express. The propositional form is not an explicature of the utterance but just a vehicle for the communication of a range of implicatures. The same is so for Grice. When he wants to maintain that "what is said" has, as part of its definition, that it must be meant by the speaker (in his technical sense of speaker meaning), he moves to a different term altogether in discussing metaphorical utterances. He writes of "what a speaker makes as if to say", precisely because the proposition literally expressed in a metaphorical case is not part of speaker meaning; only the implicatures of the utterance are meant (communicated, in relevance theory terms).

What I want to question here is the prevailing relevance theory adherence to this position. It is reflected in the upper part of the diagram which summarises the Sperber and Wilson view on the descriptive and interpretive dimensions of language use:

(6)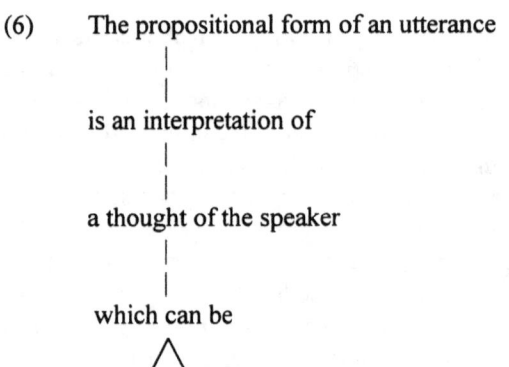

(Sperber & Wilson 1986, 1995: 232)

In this diagram the concept of "interpretation" (or interpretive resemblance) is intended to accommodate not only literal interpretations but also the cases where a concept in the thought the speaker intends to communicate departs in certain ways from a concept featuring in the proposition expressed by the utterance, that is, cases of loose use, including metaphor.

This then marks a clear asymmetry between the two pragmatic processes of enrichment and loosening. Cases of enrichment contribute to the propositional form of the utterance; the result of strengthening a lexical concept gets built in as a new ad hoc concept; enrichment is taken to be one of those pragmatic processes, along with reference assignment and disambiguation, that are involved in arriving at the proposition expressed. Loosening on the other hand has no such role; the lexical concept, which provides the point of departure for the loose use, stays in place in the propositional form of the utterance which simply resembles the one the speaker has in mind. My question is simple: why is there this asymmetry?

This question first arose for me when I heard a talk by Dan Sperber in 1989 (to appear in revised form in Sperber & Wilson forthcoming). There he discussed the narrowing and broadening of lexically encoded concepts as if they were symmetrical processes, the one adding material, the other subtracting it. In that talk he did not address the issue of why they do not both appear in the proposition expressed. If they are just two opposite processes of concept building, as they seem to be, strengthening vs. weakening, narrowing vs. broadening, i.e. a move away from strict literalness in both cases, albeit in opposite directions (above and below literalness), wouldn't we expect that either the results of both processes should figure in the proposition expressed by the utterance or that the results of neither should? This issue has now been in the air for a few years, discussed informally at our summer relevance seminars and with students at UCL working on metaphor. I think it is time to take a careful look at what the implications of moving to a symmetrical account would be. The merest beginnings will be made here.

4   Symmetrifying Enrichment and Loosening

There are two ways, in principle, of symmetrifying: bring narrowing into line with the existing account of loosening or bring loosening into line with the propositional boosting account of enrichment. I'll look at these in that order.

To bring narrowing into line with the established relevance theoretic account of loosening would entail not building a denser concept in the enrichment case, but using the lexical concept as a jumping off point to contextual effects, as it is for loose and metaphorical uses. That is, at the level of the proposition expressed the lexical concept would remain and the enrichment of that concept or its effects would emerge as implicatures. This would, of course, involve a move back in the direction of the Gricean concept of what is said. It would maintain the section of the diagram given in (6) and in fact extend the number of cases which would fall within the concept of non-literal interpretive resemblance: enrichment cases could be seen as a particular type of interpretive resemblance where the logical implications of the propositional form of the utterance would be a proper subset of those of the thought of the speaker.

This may be workable for lexical concepts with encyclopedic entries, such as *bachelor*, with its various bachelor prototypes, bundles of features comprising chunks or units within the overall encyclopedic entry. For example, in (2b) the lexical concept *bachelor* might give access to a bunch of prototypical properties of bachelors: youngish, heterosexual, free to marry, childless, etc, (along with the logical property *unmarried*), from which various implicatures regarding the sort of person the speaker wants to meet would follow. A relevance-driven sorting process, similar to that assumed in the loose use cases, would ensure that other possible bachelor prototypes, e.g. that of the fussy, old, misogynous type of bachelor, would be bypassed, as would the pope and various others who are technically bachelors but do not have the relevant properties.

However, there are a number of cases of enrichment for which this just won't work. While a range of implicatures can be easily derived from a lexical item used loosely, this is not so for at least some instances of enrichment. What a loose use entails is that, in effect, the original (lexical) concept makes available more information than you need, so you can simply disregard whatever does not contribute to relevance (cognitive effects), on the particular occasion. But, of course, the opposite is the case in many instances of narrowing/enrichment; here what the lexical concept makes available is often rather less than one needs to derive the intended effects. Examples (2e) and (2f) are such cases: nothing follows from these literal and trivial truths; the concepts of *some* and *something* simply do not give access to a rich set of specific assumptions from which the intended concept is built. These enrichments are effected in some other way, relying on contextual information from a wider range of sources, perhaps information from the perceptual environment.

Trying to treat these enrichment cases, where the lexical concept lacks anything much by way of an encyclopedic entry, as cases of interpretive resemblance would give a very odd result within relevance theory: the relevance of the utterance, its effects, would seem to derive from an interaction of contextual assumptions alone, with the proposition expressed playing no role. This is exemplified in (7), where it can be seen that the effects follow from the implicature (an implicated premise), which represents the strengthening of 'some distance', together with other accessible assumptions concerning such a situation:

(7) Proposition expressed: There is a distance between the cinema and the restaurant.
 Implicature: The distance between the cinema and the restaurant is longer than you may think.
 Effects: We shouldn't plan to walk from the restaurant to the cinema,
 We should call a taxi to get to the cinema, etc.

On the general account of contextual effects within relevance theory this is not possible: cognitive effects follow from an inferential interaction of the proposition expressed and contextual assumptions. I conclude that this tack, a partial retreat back to Grice, as it might be seen, is not a possible way of symmetrifying the treatment of narrowed and loosened ad hoc concepts within relevance theory.

So let's consider the opposite possibility: bringing loosening into line with narrowing. This involves building into the proposition expressed an ad hoc concept, which is a weakening of the encoded lexical concept. In parallel with the representation in (4) of the propositional form of an enrichment case, we'd have the following propositional form for (5c):

(8) [This steak]$_y$ is raw*.
 (where *raw** indicates a loosening of the lexical concept *raw*)

From this, as on the original account, would follow a bunch of implicatures, communicated with varying degrees of strength: the steak is insufficiently cooked, the steak is inedible, the speaker is very unhappy with the state of the steak, the speaker wants this steak replaced by another which has received more cooking, etc.

So let us suppose this is the version of the symmetry thesis we would opt for, if we went for one at all. I shall now list and briefly consider some possible objections to making this move; that is, to incorporating into the proposition expressed those ad hoc concepts which are loosenings, along with those that are strengthenings, of lexical concepts:

[1] Someone might object that one upshot of this view of things is that some word meanings (lexical concepts) are virtually never used literally; for instance, 'bald' (meaning *totally hairless*), `silent' (which would strictly speaking apply only to a soundproof chamber), 'hexagonal' (a property of a perfect abstract form not actually found in nature), etc. The objection would depend on the assumption that it is very implausible that words are not used literally at least some of the time. But this assumption is not very compelling; it seems quite clear that we simply do have concepts of geometrical perfection and that we use these as a point of departure in entertaining other concepts, that are approximations to them. That this might extend to quite a range of the concepts encoded in natural language should not be seen as troublesome but as a downright useful feature of language, given our undoubted capacity to recognise resemblances. Suppose one were in the business of designing a public representation system for human communicative purposes, given that the general cognitive capacities of the species were already in place: the ability to attribute complex mental states

(such as higher order beliefs and intentions) to conspecifics, the ability to draw inferences from newly impinging stimuli by placing them in a context of existing assumptions, and the ability to recognise conceptual and other resemblances from a range of points of view. I think a designer might well opt for a public representation system with quite minimal and even generally uninstantiated encodings (in the sense that little, if anything, in the actual world falls under the concept), given that these more fundamental abilities can be relied on to make the appropriate adjustments, with relative ease, in a number of directions. Perhaps then, more often than not, our communication is nonliteral in just this way.

[2] Here's a second, this time rather theory-internal, objection. If both strengthenings and broadenings are taken to contribute to the propositional form of the utterance, then won't the propositional form of the utterance always be identical to the propositional form of the thought of the speaker, so that the distinction caught in the diagram in (6) falls away. The question really concerns the concept of "interpretive resemblance", which is arguably one of the most constructive innovations of relevance theory. But there would be no diminishing of its importance as a result of the move being considered. Apart from its fundamental role in the account of irony and other cases involving the attribution/echo of a thought, the relation of interpretive resemblance would continue to be the key relation between lexical concepts and communicated concepts: the concepts in the logical form or semantic representation of an utterance would be in a relation of interpretive resemblance with those in the propositional forms of both the thought of the speaker and the utterance expressing that thought. The diagram would need to be adjusted and one of those adjustments might be as follows:

(9)   Logical form of the utterance
        (structured set of lexical concepts)
                |
                |
        is an interpretation of
                |
                |
        Propositional form of the utterance
        (structured string of concepts, many of which are enrichments or loosenings of the lexical concepts)

Of course, there may well be a disparity between the thought of the speaker and the propositional form derived by the hearer on the basis of his contextual resources and guided by his search for optimal relevance. So THE propositional form of the utterance is somewhat of an idealisation here, but so it was under the original conception (diagram (6)), where the propositional form admitted only ad hoc concepts which resulted from enrichment. This issue of the propositional form of, or proposition expressed by, an utterance is taken up again briefly in the final section.

[3] The third potential objection is related to the second: wouldn't we be slipping a maxim of literalness or truthfulness back into the picture? It seems that even in the case of meta-

phorical utterances we would be saying that the propositional form of the utterance is a literal interpretation of the thought the speaker intends to communicate. Statements such as the following, which have been quite central to the relevance theory picture, would seem to no longer carry much weight:

(10) [...] the hearer is not invariably entitled to expect a literal interpretation of the speaker's thought, nor is such an interpretation always necessary for successful communication to take place. A less-than-literal interpretation of the speaker's thought may be good enough; may indeed be better on some occasions than a strictly literal one. (Sperber & Wilson 1985/86: 158)

But this is very different from the concept of literalness or truthfulness at issue in the Gricean maxim, which concerned the relation between the linguistically encoded (or conventional) meaning and that which the speaker meant or communicated. On the proposed symmetrical treatment of loose use cases, it would indeed follow that the speaker always endorses the proposition her utterance expresses, but the point is that this proposition is now going to depart even more radically than before from the literal linguistic content in the logical form of the utterance, so that the first maxim of Quality "Do not *say* what you believe to be false" (my emphasis) is hopelessly inapplicable.

Of course, if we move to the Supermaxim of Quality: "Try to make *your contribution* one that is true" (my emphasis) where we take 'contribution' to include both the proposition expressed and the implicatures, then it would appear that cases of loose use and metaphor conform with this. I won't argue it here but in fact this simply follows from the presumption of optimal relevance (specifically from what constitutes a contextual effect) and no separate maxim or principle is needed (see Ifantidou 1994 and Wilson 1995).

Tangentially, it should be noted that the propositional form of the utterance will now always be communicated, hence an explicature; the only level in the whole process of utterance interpretation that is not communicated is the logical form. This seems just fine to me; there was always a kind of redundancy in the standard account of loose use and metaphor in that there were two representational levels (logical form and propositional form) that were mere tools or vehicles for getting at what was in fact communicated. There is a technical point to be attended to concerning the definition of an 'explicature' as a communicated assumption which is a *development* of a logical form of the utterance; the need to spell out what the possibilities are for developing a logical form would seem even more pressing if we could in effect knock out bits of encoded linguistic content, which is what this symmetry thesis entails.

[4] What of the concept of THE truth-conditional content of the utterance? First, it is not clear that we really want such a notion in our pragmatics at all, especially if, as relevance theorists tend to argue, the proper domain of a truth conditional semantic theory is thoughts/assumptions (or, at least, their propositional forms). However, suppose we did think there was good reason to maintain that concept, then wouldn't we be a bit alarmed that now an utterance of 'Bill is a bulldozer' could come out as true, provided Bill had certain properties that appear in the encyclopedic entry of the lexical concept *bulldozer* and which

are central to the new non-lexical concept *bulldozer** ? Surely, the one thing we do have in this area is relatively robust intuitions that 'Bill is a bulldozer' is false and 'Bill is not a bulldozer' is true (and these intuitions are to be explained by the presence of the literal encoded concept in the propositional form of the utterance). We would be having to turn these clear intuitions right around.

Well, just how robust are these intuitions and what is their source? We can, after all, agree or disagree with someone who utters 'Bill is a bulldozer', as in (11), or even say 'that's *true*' or 'that's *not true*':

(11)   A: Bill's a bulldozer (or: a bit of a bulldozer).
           B: He certainly is; let's not have him on the committee.
           C: He's not really a bulldozer; in fact he's quite insecure.

It could be that 'true' is being used loosely in such a response, that what we have is loose use all the way (first the predication of bulldozerhood and then the confirmation or denial of it). But I don't see any reason to suppose that; surely what is being denied by C at the explicit level is that the ad hoc concept *bulldozer**, formed from the loosely used lexical concept, applies to Bill. Examples of conditionals with loose or metaphorical uses of concepts in their antecedent point in the same direction:

(12)   (a)   If Bill is a bulldozer he'll be ideal on the committee.
           (b)   If Mick is a loose cannon we better keep him out of the negotiations.

It seems pretty clear that what is being communicated by (12a) is that if Bill is of a particular aggressive disposition, unmoved by the views of others, etc., he'll be ideal on the committee. If the arguments based on these various examples are right, the source of the original intuition that 'Bill's a bulldozer' is false might simply be the conceptual content of the logical form of the utterance rather than its propositional form (that is, our knowledge of word meaning).

It does not look as if there is anything in these various considerations to decisively deter us from symmetrifying the picture by building both sorts of ad hoc concepts into the proposition expressed. However, let's take a look at the process (or processES) of loosening a little more closely. In some lectures on this a year or two ago, Deirdre Wilson drew the diagram given above in (3) to illustrate the relation between a lexical concept and an enrichment of it: I interpret this as showing that the set of entities falling in the denotation of the lexical concept L contains as a proper subset the set of entities in the denotation of the strengthened ad hoc concept C'. One might think that if we are dealing in symmetrical processes then the corresponding diagram for loosening will look as in (13), where C* is the result of loosening the lexical concept. In fact it came out as in (14), where the picture is one of a kind of concept shift or transfer rather than a simple broadening, where the denotations of the lexical concept and the concept which results from the 'loosening' process merely intersect:

(13)
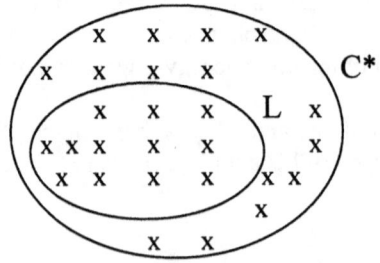

(14)
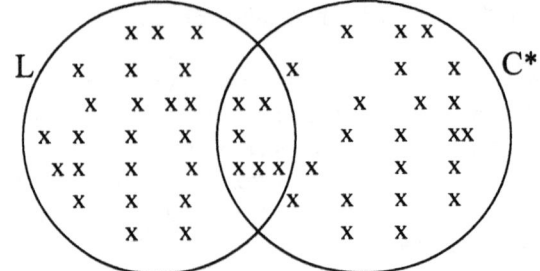

In fact, when we come to look at particular cases it looks as if there may be three subcases of loosening, only one of which seems to be the true counterpart or complement of enrichment:

(15) a.
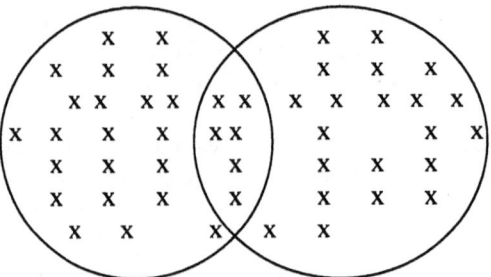

The room is *rectangular*,
The room was *silent*,
John's a real *bachelor*.

b.

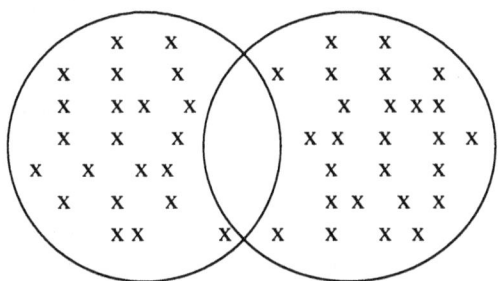

Where's my plastic *duck?*,
Bill is a *bulldozer*,
The fringed *curtains* of thine eyes advance.

c.

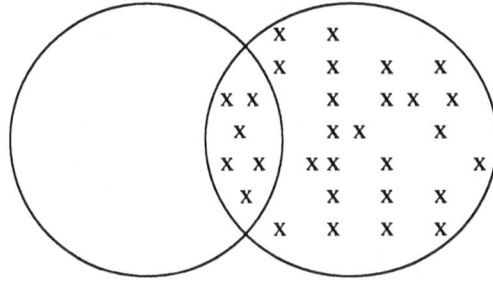

I love *bald* men,
I need a *silent* place to work,
The steak is *raw*.

Taking *rectangular* in (15a), for example: this is a loose use since the room in question might have all sorts of little irregularities that render it not strictly rectangular (i.e. not having four right angles). The extension of the loosened concept would, however, include some cases of strict rectangles while excluding others; it might, for instance, exclude those with two of their sides a mile long and the other two only a few inches long. Now consider (15b); the idea here is that there is actually no extensional overlap of the two concepts. Metaphors which involve sortal or categorial incorrectness, as in the examples in (15b), are candidates here. Among the properties of the lexical concept that are discarded are, crucially, logical or definitional ones. For instance, in the 'plastic duck' cases the property of belonging to a biological species is dropped. The picture in (15c) represents the case where the extension of the new loosened concept does in fact encompass the entire denotation of the original lexical concept, indicated here by the emptiness of the non-intersecting part of the lexical concept; this could and should be redrawn as the picture in (13). This is broadening in a strict sense, the symmetrical counterpart to the narrowing cases. For instance, the extension of the *bald** concept would include all the entities which fall within the extension of the lexical concept *bald*, i.e. all the hairless entities (assuming this is the right semantics for *bald²*) and a further group which depart to some degree or other from complete hairlessness but which are relevantly low on hair.

Setting aside the (15b) cases for a moment, let us consider the relation between (15a) and (15c). The sort of loose use exemplified in (15a) could be thought of as one that involves both broadening (as in (15c)) and narrowing; for instance, the concept *bachelor** might include married men who behave in a certain stereotypic bachelor-like way (individuals in the non-intersecting part of C*) and it might exclude some men who are in fact UNmarried but do not have the particular stereotypical bachelor properties (individuals in the non-intersecting part of L). Note that the concept *silent* occurs in examples given for both types of case; depending on the particularities of the context, the new ad hoc concept might be either a strict broadening, hence include in its extension all that the original lexical concept includes or might involve, in addition, some degree of narrowing (excluding perhaps unnatural, manmade instances of utterly noiseless spaces such as soundproof chambers). Doubtless, these two possibilities also arise in the loose use of other lexical concepts.

The fact that both processes might be required in forming a communicated ad hoc concept makes it look all the more likely that they both contribute to the proposition expressed. It would be very hard to find a principled reason for supposing that the result of narrowing the concept of *rectangular* in the example in (15a) figures at this level while its simultaneous widening is registered only at the level of implicature. It follows then that those cases of broadening which are the true counterpart to narrowing, that is, those in (15c), also contribute a new concept to the proposition expressed.

Briefly, let us reconsider the examples in (15b). On reflection, it is far from clear that this category of concept construction really arises. What it would require is not just the dropping of the logical or definitional properties of the lexical concept from which the ad hoc concept is derived but the inclusion of the negation of these properties among its own defining features. For instance, this view requires that a defining feature of *duck** would be 'not a living creature' and a defining feature of *bulldozer** would be 'not a manmade machine', etc. This is both unnecessary and counterintuitive; the relevant loosened concept of *duck** might as well include in its extension some biological ducks and some artefactual ducks, the common properties concerning physical appearance being all that the new concept has retained from the lexical concept *duck*. Of course, in the case of 'plastic duck' the modifier whittles down the set to exclude living creatures. If this is the right way to view these examples then they are just further instances of the type of concept construction in (15a); that is, they involve broadening (for instance, to include certain artificial ducks) and narrowing (for instance, to exclude members of the biological species of ducks which do not have a particular stereotypical appearance). As with the other cases given in (15a), on the symmetry view the new concepts so formed would contribute to the proposition expressed.

5   Categorial Falsehoods and Trivial Truths

It is often pointed out that positive metaphorical utterances such as (16) are category mistakes (sortally incorrect), clearly flouting Grice's first maxim of truthfulness. Their negative counterparts, as in (17), are naturally obvious truths, a point made long ago by Wilson & Sperber (1981) in their catalogue of the short-comings of Grice's account of metaphor and other tropes, the point being that there is no violation of any maxim of truthfulness.

(16) (a) Bill is a bulldozer.
      (b) Losing Jane is losing the sun.

(17) (a) Bill isn't a bulldozer.
      (b) Losing Jane isn't losing the sun.

Johannes Flieger has recently discussed some further examples of obvious falsehoods that he takes to be metaphorical; he calls them metaphorical negations, the idea being that a phrase consisting of a negated term is used metaphorically as a whole:

(18) (a) Ari isn't a lion; he's a pussycat.
           [where Ari is, in fact, a lion]
      (b) Englebert isn't a surgeon; he's a butcher.
           [where Englebert is a surgeon by profession]
      (c) Huckleberry isn't a butcher; he's a surgeon.
           [where Huckleberry is a butcher by profession]
      (d) Engelbert isn't a human being; he's a wild beast.
      (e) Huckleberry isn't a human being; he's a buddha.
      (these examples are all taken from Flieger 1996)

In each case the referent does in fact have the property (taken literally) that the speaker is denying he has and does not have the property (taken literally) that the speaker predicates of him in the next clause, and this is mutually manifest to speaker and hearer. These are very interesting examples in the context of a discussion of pragmatic processes of enrichment and loosening, because while Flieger sees these as cases of metaphor (hence of loosening, in relevance-theoretic terms) they can just as well be described as cases of negated enrichments. Take (18d) for instance: while Engelbert is in fact a member of the human species, what the speaker is denying is that he belongs to a narrower category which consists of (perhaps) thoughtful, compassionate, civilised human beings. It is unsurprising that such examples can be seen as either cases of metaphorical (loosely used) negatives or cases of negated strengthenings; it follows from the concept of negation, the complementarity of the two processes of enrichment and loosening, and their local nature.

From a processing point of view, I think the enrichment account looks more promising than the loosening account; it would require less effort to, as it were, dive into the encyclopedic entry for *human being*, pull out a positive stereotype and negate that than to form the concept *non-human-being* and then loosen that to include some actual human beings. In fact the latter would not give quite the right result since the vast category *non-human-being* would have to be drastically narrowed (to exclude tables, trees, trumpets, theories, etc., all of which are, after all, not human beings) in addition to being widened to include such humans as Engelbert. The local enrichment account meshes well with the widespread recognition that negations are more complex to process than their corresponding positives (negation being the *marked* member of the positive/negative opposition) and that the processing of a negative in some sense presupposes the availability of the corresponding positive (see Horn 1989: chapter 3).

What these examples bring home to me, then, is that we must surely go for an account which offers parity of treatment of enrichment and loosening as regards the ad hoc concepts they result in and their role in representations built by the hearer. A representation of the base explicature of (proposition expressed by) utterances of (18d) and (18e) would be something like the following:

(19)   (a)   *E. is not a human being'; he's a wild beast**
        (b)   *H. is not a human being"; he's a buddha**

where the double prime in (19b) is meant to indicate that the ad hoc concept in (19b) derived by a process of enriching the linguistically encoded concept *human being* is distinct from the ad hoc concept in (19a) also derived by a process of enriching that linguistic encoding.

We could go on from here and consider cases of obvious truths, whether positive or negative, where clearly the speaker is not intent on predicating of the referents a property that they are known by all concerned to have or denying that they have a property which it is well known they do not have:

(20)   (a)   Caroline is our princess.
        (b)   Uncle Bob is a sergeant-major.
        (c)   Tom is a human being (not a machine).
        (examples from Flieger 1996)

I repeat the examples in (17) for convenience since they are cases of negations which are obvious truths:

(21)   (a)   Bill isn't a bulldozer; (he's a juggernaut).[3]
        (b)   Losing Jane isn't losing the sun.

The idea with (20a) is that, while the Caroline in question is in fact a princess, the intention of the speaker does not concern her status in a royal family but rather such properties as her haughty, spoilt ways. The same goes, mutatis mutandis, for (20b). Are these cases of metaphorical loosening or of enrichment? Flieger sees them as all cases of metaphor, all having a 'figurative' feel. A bid for parity of treatment with the account above of (16) and (18) would suggest that while the examples in (21) are indeed negated metaphors (negations of ad hoc concepts constructed through loosening), the examples in (20) should be enrichments, so that the propositions expressed in each case are, respectively, that Caroline be-longs to a particular proper subset of the set of princesses, that Uncle Bob is a certain type of sergeant-major (perhaps the authoritarian, humourless, etc., stereotype), and that Tom has the frailties of human flesh. It seems to me that here it could go either way; the ad hoc *princess* concept formed from the lexical concept might or might not include the logical (definitional) property of the lexical concept (female member of royal house) and the same holds, mutatis mutandis, for the ad hoc *sergeant major* concept. Whether these are technically loosenings or enrichments hinges on whether or not logical (definitional) properties are dropped. The case for a symmetrical account of enrichment and loosening cases is further supported by these considerations. What matters here, at least from a communicative point of view, is that the relevant concept is constructed out of the logical and encyclopedic information which is made accessible by the encoded lexical concept; whether the construction process is strictly speaking a loosening or an enrichment does not seem consequential and certainly should not lead to two utterly different ways of treating the resultant concept.[4]

6 Economy of Effort and Enrichment / Loosening Symmetry

The considerations of the last two sections make quite a strong case, I think, for the appearance of ad hoc concepts in the proposition expressed, whether the process that the original lexical concept has undergone is one of strengthening/narrowing or weakening/widening, or a combination of both. But the question that comes to mind now is what is achieved by lodging the loosened ad hoc concept in the propositional form? Is this just symmetry for symmetry's sake?

At this point I'd like to turn to some recent work by Anna Papafragou (see in particular Papafragou 1995). Her main concern has been to give an account of metonymic expressions, as in (22a), which are standardly used referentially[5], but she also looks briefly at metaphorical expressions used referentially (as opposed to the predicational cases I've concentrated on so far), such as the one in (22b):

(22)   (a)   The burgundy hat left in a hurry.
       (b)   The wilting violet has finally left.

Here the description 'the wilting violet' is being used to refer to a particular woman, let's call her Jasmine Jones (JJ), known to both the speaker and the hearer. As Papafragou says, our account of the interpretation of this utterance has to address the fact that part of what is communicated at the explicit level is that the particular woman, JJ, has left, this being just an instance of reference assignment, which is one of the subtasks involved in arriving at the proposition expressed (on anyone's conception of the proposition expressed). She proposes for this sort of case, as for metonymic cases, that the hearer MUST construct an ad hoc concept from the encoded *wilting violet* concept in order to derive the referent Jasmine Jones; that is, reference assignment proceeds via this concept (of a certain sort of shy, retiring person, let us suppose) in whose extension JJ could be reasonably supposed to fall. Although Papafragou does not say so, I assume that the final propositional form of the utterance is something like (23), where the individuating (de re) concept of JJ and the loosened descriptive concept *wilting violet* both appear:[6]

(23)   JJ[wilting violet]* has finally left.

The ad hoc concept, like any concept in a referentially used definite description, gives easy access through its encyclopedic entry to contextual assumptions: JJ is shy, reticent, uncommunicative, delicate, sensitive, makes everyone feel uncomfortable, can't take robust treatment, etc. These interact with the proposition expressed, shown in (23), to give an array of effects: the speaker is relieved that JJ has gone, they can all relax now, they can tell bad jokes now, etc.

Interestingly, Papafragou does not extend this treatment, in which the propositional form registers the ad hoc concept, to cases of metaphorical predication, and her reason for this is that it is not necessary to do so. The classical relevance theory account of these cases works just fine: the propositional form with the literal encoded concept in it gives the hearer easy access to all the intended implications (implicatures), the derivation of which, after all, is what is required in order to arrive at the intended interpretation. Predication is a means of ascribing a range of properties to a referent and these can simply be read off the lexical concept without any intermediate step of setting up an ad hoc concept. The underlying principle here seems to be: make only those moves, set up only those representations, which are necessary in order to arrive at the intended interpretation. If you can get there without setting up new conceptual addresses/labels (which are generally going to be of an evanescent nature anyway) then don't set them up. This seems entirely in keeping with the principle of relevance according to which we expend as little processing effort as possible in deriving a satisfactory yield of effects.

Furthermore, as Deirdre Wilson has pointed out, there are cases of sustained metaphor where it seems to be not only not necessary but probably impossible to build ad hoc concepts into the proposition expressed:

(24)   (a)   Love is the lighthouse and the rescued mariners.
              (example from Oshar Davico)
        (b)   Life's but a walking shadow, a poor player that struts and frets his hour upon
              the stage, and then is heard no more; ...
              (*MacBeth* V, v, 24-26)

Building in ad hoc concepts at the explicit level looks equally problematic for the following examples which, while less poetic, involve whole sentences being used metaphorically:

(25)   (a)   The cracks are beginning to show.
        (b)   The lion is roaring again.
        (c)   The patient has yet to leave his sick-bed and take a few tottering steps in the
              sunshine.

The treatments of metonymy and metaphor are different in certain crucial ways; after all, there is not a relation of resemblance between the conceptual content of 'ham sandwich' and 'person who ordered the ham sandwich' or 'burgundy hat' and 'woman wearing the burgundy hat'. I won't look here at the interesting account of the particularities of metonymy that Papafragou gives, but focus instead on the respects in which the two phenomena behave the same. Consider the following pairs of examples, the (a) cases involving metonymy and the (b) cases metaphor. The two pairs differ in that the figuratively used expressions are referential in (26) and predicative in (27):

(26) (a) The pretty face just went out.
     (b) The pretty doll just went out.

(27) (a) Maria is a divine voice.
     (b) Maria is a nightingale.
     (examples from Papafragou 1995: 149)

In both the metonymic and the metaphoric referring expressions in (26) an ad hoc concept has to be constructed if the referent is to be located. Both involve kinds of interpretive use of concepts through which the speaker gives a new name to an individual enabling both reference assignment and, in many instances, particular cognitive effects. This is akin to nicknaming and other spontaneous dubbings, as in 'Nosey has just left' and 'Prince Charming is laying it on thick'.

In both the metonymic and the metaphoric predications in (27) it is not necessary to construct a new concept: the properties whose predication of Maria the speaker endorses can be accessed directly from stored information concerning divine voices and nightingales (the choice constrained, of course, by relevance considerations). An array of implicatures is thereby constructed and a fully propositional form at the explicit level need never be entertained. The classical relevance theory account of loose use and metaphor seems, after all, entirely satisfactory for these examples. However, another asymmetry, that between referring and predicating,[7] has to be taken into account. When it is, it seems that the classical story works well for the predicational cases while referring by means of a figurative use requires a process of constructing an ad hoc concept which enters into the proposition expressed.

Lastly, continuing to pursue symmetry in the accounts of the processes of enrichment and loosening, this "ad hoc concepts only when necessary" position has to be extended to the enrichment cases. Recall that in the discussion in section 4, it was pointed out that some enrichment cases COULD work the same way as the classic loosening account, e.g. the *bachelor* case with its rich encyclopedic entry which includes certain assumptions which cluster together to delimit a stereotype. So an utterance of 'John's a bachelor' in the context of a discussion of Mary's desire to get married could implicate that John is heterosexual, youngish, eligible for marriage, etc., without the setting up of a new address/label for the narrowed ad hoc concept *bachelor'*. Other cases of enrichment could NOT work this way; these are the linguistically encoded concepts that do not have much encyclopedic information attached, such as 'some distance' in (2e).

121

So there is a *third symmetry position* which deserves serious consideration: (a) SOME cases of enrichment and SOME cases of loosening have to be built into the propositional form of the utterance; a hearer/reader won't arrive at the intended interpretation if they are not; (b) other cases do not need to appear in the propositional form of the utterance, in that the intended interpretation can be derived without them (by an encyclopedic sorting process), and therefore they should not be. This way of viewing the matter gives processing effort primacy and meshes well with the quote in (10) in that (paraphrasing and modifying the final sentence) 'a non-literal interpretation of the speaker's thought may be better on some occasions than a strictly literal one', 'better' in the sense that, for those cases where it is possible (the (b) cases) the hearer derives the intended interpretation with less processing effort than it would take to first derive the propositional form of the speaker's thought and then derive the intended effects from that.[8]

Returning to the question at the beginning of this section, the idea that any departure from the lexically encoded concept requires the building in of the new communicated concept at the level of the proposition expressed might well be a case of symmetry for symmetry's case and so be poorly motivated. The third symmetry position, on the other hand, is grounded in fundamental facts about cognitive processing: we want effects, so we are prepared to expend effort to get them, but we want them as cheaply as we can get them, so we do just that work, build only those representations, that are necessary in order to achieve them.

7 Loose (but Rich) End

What I have been calling the proposition expressed throughout this paper is an explicitly communicated proposition which may have among its constituents non-lexicalised concepts which have been pragmatically constructed out of the concepts encoded in the logical form (or semantic representation) of the utterance. It is an explicature, in relevance theory terms; it is a base level explicature as it does not involve any embedding into assumption schemas such as 'the speaker believes that ...', 'the speaker says that ...' which give higher-level explicatures.

It should be clear that this is a very different entity from the one that certain philosophically oriented pragmatists refer to as 'the proposition strictly and literally expressed'. The proposition strictly and literally expressed is how many people, including Grice, I believe, characterise 'what is said' by an utterance; it is the minimal proposition that can be constructed from the semantic representation of the utterance, something which departs as little as possible from encoded content and yet which has a determinate truth-condition. It is usually assumed that fixing the referents of referring expressions and selecting among the senses of ambiguous linguistic expressions will be sufficient to transform the logical form into something minimally propositional. However, there are many uncertainties around, and reconstruals of, the concept of what is said: Wilson (1995) discusses an equivocation in Grice's own use of the term, turning on whether 'saying' does or does not entail meaning/communicating; Bach (1994a, 1994b) construes the concept so that it does not entail speaker meaning (communicating) and need not even be fully propositional (so as to accommodate phrasal utterances); on Récanati (1989, 1993)'s reconstrual it has become more or less equivalent to the concept of the proposition expressed that I have been advocating in this paper and it would help to reduce terminological confusion if he adopted another label.

Is there any role for a proposition literally and strictly expressed (a 'what is said') in the account of utterance interpretation that I have been setting out here? If there is, I am unable to see what it is. Language users' intuitions seem to discriminate quite readily between explicature and implicature and not between what is (strictly and literally) said and explicature (see Récanati 1989; Gibbs & Moise 1996). There is no evidence that they naturally (pretheoretically) pick out a level of minimal propositionality, though with the requisite (philosophical) training they can learn to do so. However, these intuition tests all used examples in which the explicatures concerned contain conceptual enrichments only; so far such tests have not been run on utterances involving loose use. My guess is that the results here would be less clearcut but not because there is an extra level of minimal propositionality. We have fairly strong intuitions about what the words of our language refer to so competent speakers of the language will generally agree, for example, that 'hexagonal' refers to the property of being 'six-sided', 'raw' is a property of things that have never been cooked, 'lion' refers to a certain biological species, etc. Asked whether it is true or false that France is hexagonal or whether John, who everyone agrees has behaved bravely and nobly, is a lion, some people (I predict) would say 'true' and some would say 'false'. I don't think this would be because they have different views on the shape of France or on John's character, but rather their responses would be grounded in intuitions coming from distinct sources; the 'true'-sayers would be considering the proposition they take the speaker to be expressing and endorsing, while the 'false'-sayers would be tapping their knowledge of linguistic meaning, the literal encoded conceptual content of the utterance. The split in responses would be caused by the inescapable fact that with loose use some element of the core linguistic meaning is lost, while with enrichment linguistic meaning is simply augmented so that when the enriched concept is true of a referent so is the unenriched lexical concept.

Intuitions aside, it is difficult to see what a level of minimal propositionality would be for, given linguistic meaning (logical form), on the one hand, and the basic explicature, on the other hand. More generally, a theory of utterance interpretation has to acknowledge two quite distinct sorts of things: (a) linguistic content, which is not communicated; it is not the sort of thing that can be communicated, but is rather a vehicle for communicating (some might say, a function from contexts to propositions), and (b) what is communicated, which is a set of assumptions with propositional forms.

The set of communicated assumptions can be partitioned into explicatures and implicatures, but this is not a distinction which is of great importance for a hearer, at least if it is viewed as a representational distinction which is supposed to have some impact on the way he views the set of communicated assumptions. It is really no more than a reflection of the undoubted fact that there are two ways of *deriving* communicated assumptions: (a) developing the linguistically encoded logical form (semantic representation) and (b) inferring whole new assumptions. What does play an important role in the final interpretation of the utterance is the strength with which individual assumptions in the set have been communicated; a hearer has to register the relative degree of backing the speaker gives to any derived assumption if he is to arrive at the intended interpretation.

Implicatures may be communicated relatively strongly or relatively weakly (see Sperber & Wilson 1986, 1995: chapter 4); a strongly communicated implicature is one whose particular propositional form is a member of the set I, the assumptions which fall within the speaker's communicative intention; a weakly communicated implicature is one whose particular propositional form does not fall in the set I but which is one of a range of possible propositional forms falling under a more abstract and general propositional schema that falls within the set I. As Grice originally pointed out, the implicatures of an utterance are often indeterminate. A speaker encourages exploration in a certain conceptual region but the hearer bears the main responsibility for the particular propositional forms within this region that he constructs. The metaphorical types of loose use typically give rise to a range of weakish implicatures; the more creative or unusual the metaphor the wider the range of possibilities and the weaker the speaker's endorsement of any specific implicated propositional form.

The strong/weak continuum has not generally been applied to explicatures[9] but if either of the symmetry positions considered above turns out to be correct, in which ad hoc concepts resulting from loosening of linguistic content contribute to the proposition expressed (basic explicature), the property of indeterminacy will have to be extended to explicatures as well. Just exactly what concept is the hearer of (16a) 'Bill is a bulldozer' expected to construct out of the lexical concept *bulldozer*? The construction process is constrained by the information stored in the individual hearer's encyclopedic entry for *bulldozer* and by his bid for an interpretation consistent with optimal relevance. But this leaves a degree of leeway so that the ad hoc concept actually constructed is to that degree the hearer's responsibility. The ad hoc concept intended in more creative cases is more indeterminate, leaves more to the hearer, and so the concept which he does build receives less endorsement from the speaker, is less strongly communicated. This is essentially parallel to the indeterminacy of implicatures. Explicatures are communicated with varying degrees of strength; a conceptual range is endorsed by the speaker without any specific concept in that range being given full endorsement. Different hearers construct different possible ad hoc concepts within this range, just as different hearers construct different implicatures within the propositional range endorsed by the speaker.

On the third symmetry position where the ad hoc concept is incorporated into the proposition expressed only if it is necessary for the derivation of effects there will be cases where there simply is no complete proposition expressed by the speaker or constructed by the
hearer. For instance, from the logical form of 'Bill is a bulldozer' or indeed of 'Bill is a bachelor' (that is, an enrichment case) a propositional schema with reference assigned may be formed:

(28) $Bill_x$ is [ ]

on the basis of which implicatures, endorsed to varying degrees by the speaker's use of the lexical item 'bulldozer' or 'bachelor', are derived by the hearer.

If this, as yet very roughly sketched, picture turns out to be viable it may require some further technical changes, for instance, to the way in which contextual/cognitive effects are defined. It would be premature to pursue that line here.

Notes

1. The exceptions are Bach (1994a, 1994b) and Récanati (1995), who both discuss a range of cases of non-literalness, within broadly Gricean frameworks. A comparison of their accounts with one another and with the relevance theory account remains to be done.
2. Reboul (1989) supports Sperber and Wilson in their advocacy of this precise semantics for the lexical concept *bald* and discusses the apparent paradox that arises as a result for phrases like 'very bald' and '... balder than ...' which would appear to have an anomalous linguistic meaning given the imposition of scalar modification on an absolute concept. I think the account in terms of ad hoc concepts resulting from a quite standard practice of using 'bald' loosely can explain these satisfactorily but I leave that for another time.
3. This example has an echoic feel to it and would be most natural in the context of a previous utterance of 'Bill is a bulldozer'; it looks like an example of what has been traditionally termed metalinguistic negation (Horn 1985, 1989) and more recently analysed in terms of the relevance-theoretic concept of echoic use (Carston 1996). As far as I know, examples of negated metaphors have not yet been discussed in this context.
4. Flieger outlines an account of metaphor understanding which involves a pragmatically driven process of choosing a particular property complex from a set of property complexes which form a semilattice structure, which itself is a representation of the set of properties made available by the original lexical concept. He proposes to run a model-theoretic semantics over the resulting representation, thereby capturing intuitions of metaphorical truth (and falsehood).
5. The essence of Papafragou's (1995) account of metonymy is that metonymic expressions involve the (implicit) echoic use of concepts and they are instances of naming (rather than direct referring). However, in Papafragou (1996), a revised and cut version of the previous paper, she recognises that echoic use is too narrow to cover all metonymies and instead employs the concept of interpretive (or loose) use of a concept, though the interpretive relation in the case of metonymy is not one of resemblance, as in the case of metaphor, but one of association (or accessibility, in relevance-theoretic terms), between elements of encyclopedic knowledge.
6. I follow here the relevance-theoretic position on definite descriptions developed by Rouchota (1992). She argues that both the referent of a referentially used definite description and the conceptual content of the description feature in the proposition expressed by the utterance and so affect the truth conditions of the utterance.
7. This has been long recognised by philosophers of language; see, for example, Strawson (1974).
8. Incorporating an ad hoc concept into the proposition expressed in such cases would in fact be an 'after the event' sort of move. It has been suggested to me (by Deirdre Wilson) that the ad hoc concept might be formed 'later' in this way, after the derivation of implicatures, when the hearer wants to store what was communicated in a manageable form. This does indeed seem likely in some instances, but it would not be a case of constructing an ad hoc concept in pursuit of an interpretation consistent with the second (communicative) principle of relevance. Rather, it would be a process which follows from the more general first principle of relevance alone, according to which all our cognitive activity, including memory organisation, is geared towards maximising relevance.

9   In fact the idea that the concept of weak communication might be extended to explicatures has been suggested before, by Gurkan Dogan (1992), as a result of his analyses of poems in which reference assignment indeterminacies were clearly intended by the author/speaker.

References

Atlas, J. (1992): "Why 'three' doesn't mean 3". Unpublished ms.
Bach, K. (1994a): "Semantic slack: What is said and more". In: S. Tsohatzidis, ed.: Foundations of Speech Act Theory: Philosophical and Linguistic Perspectives. London and New York: Routledge, 267-291.
Bach, K. (1994b): "Conversational impliciture". Mind and Language 9, 124-162.
Carston, R. (1988): "Implicature, explicature and truth-theoretic semantics". In: R. Kempson, ed.: Mental Representations: The Interface between Language and Reality. Cambridge: Cambridge University Press, 155-181. Reprinted in 1991 in: S. Davis, ed.: Pragmatics: A Reader. Oxford: Oxford University Press, 33-51.
Carston, R. (1990): "Quantity maxims and generalised implicature". UCL Working Papers in Linguistics 2, 1-31. Revised version in 1995 in Lingua 96, 213-244.
Carston, R. (1993): "Conjunction, explanation and relevance". Lingua 90, 27-48.
Carston, R. (1996): "Metalinguistic negation and echoic use". Journal of Pragmatics 25, 309-330.
Dogan, G. (1992): "The pragmatics of indeterminacy and indirectness of meaning: a relevance-theoretic approach to epigrams and graffiti in Turkish". PhD thesis, University of Manchester.
Flieger, J. (1996): "Metaphor and categorization". Seminar paper, Linguistics Dept., School of Oriental and African Studies, London.
Gibbs, R. & J. Moise (1997): "Pragmatics in understanding what is said". Cognition 62, 51-74.
Grice, H.P. (1978): Further notes on logic and conversation. Syntax and Semantics 9: Pragmatics. New York: Academic Press, 113-127.
Horn, L. (1985): "Metalinguistic negation and pragmatic ambiguity". Language 61, 121-74.
Horn, L. (1989): A Natural History of Negation. Cicago: University of Chicago Press.
Ifantidou, E. (1994): "Parentheticals and relevance". PhD thesis, University College London.
Papafragou, A. (1995): "Metonymy and relevance". UCL Working Papers in Linguistics 7, 141-175.
Papafragou, A. (1996): "Figurative language and the semantics/ pragmatics interface". Language and Literature.
Reboul, A. (1989): "Relevance and argumentation: how bald can you get?" Argumentation 3, 285-302.
Récanati, F. (1993): "Truth-conditional pragmatics". In: F. Récanati: Direct Reference: From Language to Thought. Oxford: Blackwell, 233-254.
Récanati, F. (1995): "The alleged priority of literal meaning". Cognitive Science 19, 207-232.
Rouchota, V. (1992): "On the referential/attributive distinction". Lingua 87, 137-167.
Sperber, D. (1989): "Concepts and fuzziness". Talk at the Relevance Theory Workshop, Essex.
Sperber, D. & D. Wilson, (1985/86): "Loose talk". Proceedings of the Aristotelian Society LXXXVI, 153-171.
Sperber, D. & D. Wilson, (1986): Relevance: Communication and Cognition. Oxford: Blackwell.
Sperber, D. & D. Wilson, (1995): Relevance: Communication and Cognition, Second Edition. Oxford: Blackwell.
Sperber, D. & D. Wilson, (forthcoming): Relevance and Meaning. Oxford: Blackwell.
Strawson, P. (1974): Subject and Predicate in Logic and Grammar. London: Methuen.
Wilson, D. (1993/94): Philosophy of Language lectures. Ms, University College London.

Wilson, D. (1995): "Is there a maxim of truthfulness?". UCL Working Papers in Linguistics 7, 197-212.
Wilson, D. & D. Sperber, (1981): "On Grice's theory of conversation". In: P. Werth, ed.: Conversation and Discourse. London: Croom Helm, 155-179.
Wilson, D. & D. Sperber, (1993): "Pragmatics and time". UCL Working Papers in Linguistics 5, 277-298.

Conversation and Norms

Steven Davis, Burnaby

Conversing is an activity involving two or more people that consists of a number of component acts.[1] These acts, minimally described, are linguistic acts, acts of uttering sentences or semi sentences. There is some dispute about how these acts should be described over and above describing them as utterance acts.[2] For the moment I shall call them speech acts. By using this term I do not want to be thought to be committed to any particular view about speech acts, but at this point only that the level of description necessary for giving an adequate account of conversing and other talk exchanges is over and above describing the subacts of these activities as utterance acts. Let us assume that we have a settled idea about what constitutes a speech act. Clearly, a series of speech acts by different speakers is not sufficient to constitute a conversation. If I say something and then Alice says something, but her saying what she says is not linked in the appropriate way to what I have said, she and I would not be said to be having a conversation.[3] Contrast this case with one in which I ask Alice what time it is and in answer to my question she tells me what she believes the time to be. In this example we would have a linked talk exchange in which two speech acts have been performed, my asking Alice a question and her answering me. The first speech act is linked to the second in that Alice's response[4] is in answer to my question.[5] H.P. Grice has played a leading role in characterizing conversation and thus the difference between these two exchanges. Grice's views are complicated by the fact that they have changed over time in light of criticisms offered to his theory. I shall take as my starting point the view of conversation that he offers in "Logic and Conversation," a section of his book, *Studies in the Way of Words*. Where appropriate, I shall supplement it by his emendations in, "Retrospective Epilogue." My main concern is not to give an exegesis of Grice's theory, but to use it as a way of approaching questions relating to normativity and the use of language.

On Grice's theory what characterizes the difference between the disconnected exchange and the linked exchange between Alice and me is that the second, but not the first is rational in that it is a cooperative goal directed activity. Both participants in the conversation, on Grice's view, have a "common purpose, or at least a mutually accepted direction." (Grice 1989: 26) The purpose or the direction of the conversation can arise in a variety of ways. I might begin a conversation by proposing that we should discuss the theory of direct reference, or the purpose might evolve during the conversation. It might be definite or quite vague, leaving a great deal of latitude about what can be said next in the conversation. At least, says Grice, the common purpose makes "some possible conversational moves [...] conversationally unsuitable." (Grice 1989: 26)

Grice claims that what makes certain moves conversationally suitable is that there is a general principle, the Cooperative Principle (CP), that the participants in the conversation

> [...] will be expected (ceteris paribus) to observe, namely: Make your contribution such as is required, at the stage at which it occurs, by the accepted purpose or direction of the talk exchange in which you are engaged. (Grice 1989: 26)

Related to the CP are more specific conversational maxims "the following of which will, in general, yield results in accordance with the Cooperative Principle." (Grice 1989: 26) The conversational maxims, then, are specifications of ways in which the CP can be fulfilled. Grice groups them into four categories: Quantity, Quality, Relation and Manner.

Quantity
Make your contribution as informative as is required (for the current purposes of the exchange).
Do not make your contribution more informative than is required. (Grice 1989: 26)

Quality
Supermaxim: Try to make your contribution one that is true.
  Do not say what you believe to be false.
  Do not say that for which you lack evidence. (Grice 1989: 27)

Relation
Be Relevant. (Grice 1989: 27)

Manner
Supermaxim: Be perspicuous.
  Avoid obscurity of expression.
  Avoid ambiguity.
  Be brief (avoid unnecessary prolixity).
  Be orderly. (Grice 1989: 27)

In the space that I have available I cannot discuss all the maxims. Rather, I shall concentrate my attention on the first maxim of Quality and make some passing remarks about the CP. My main purpose is to consider the CP and the maxims not as part of an explanatory theory of language use and understanding, but as apart of our normative practices governing the use of language.

Let us begin with the CP. Although many conversations are cooperative activities where the participants mutual agree on the purpose of the conversation, many conversations and other sorts of talk exchanges are not. Consider, for example, a police officer questioning a suspect, an attorney cross examining a hostile witness or a journalist interviewing a politician. What distinguishes these talk exchanges from most ordinary conversations is that they are or can be adversarial. The participants in the conversation do not have a cooperative purpose. The police officer wants to uncover evidence that would lead to the suspect's conviction, while the suspect wishes to hide any incriminating evidence that could lead to his being convicted; the attorney wants to discredit the hostile witness, while the witness wants to appear to the jury to be credible. As well, ordinary conversations in which the participants do not have any special socially determined role can be adversarial, for example, my colleague and I discussing our theories that we take to be mutually incompatible. She and I want to show why the other's theory is mistaken and why our own theory is correct. Our conversation does not have a mutually agreed on purpose that we cooperate to achieve; in fact our purposes' conflict. In the "Retrospective Epilogue," because of criticisms of this sort raised against the CP, Grice abandons it (Grice 1989: 369). I think, however, that he was too hasty in doing so. Even in an adversarial conversation the participants have a common goal, namely, that their linguistic interventions be understood (Sperber and Wilson 1995: 268). The goal is not one, however, for which there has to be mutual agreement. I believe that Grice's CP can be replaced by

> Make your contribution such as is required, at the stage at which it occurs, by the common purpose or direction of the talk exchange in which you are engaged.

I shall continue to call this the *CP*.

In stating the CP and the maxims, Grice assumed that conversation was a species of rational purposive behaviour, the goal of which is "a maximally effective exchange of information." (Grice 1989: 28) For Grice the assumption that conversations have this goal simplified his presentation of the CP and the maxims. He recognized that not all conversations have this purpose and that because of this, the maxims would have to be revised. There are several ways in which *exchange of information* can be applied to conversation. As Grice, himself, realized, the way in which he applies it to talk exchanges opens up his theory to the sorts of counter examples in the paragraph above.[6] I shall argue that there is another way in which *exchange of information* can be applied to conversations so that the participants in any kind of talk of exchange have as one of their goals the exchange of information. In my initial presentation of Grice's theory, however, I shall accept his way of applying *exchange of information* to conversations, but when I come to discuss the first maxim of Quality in more detail, I shall show how there is another way *exchange of information* can be applied to conversations and other talk exchanges that is related to their connection with understanding.

In Grice's theory the role of the CP and the maxims is to specify whether a conversational intervention is suitable or unsuitable in a conversation that has as its goal the exchange of information (Grice 1989: 26). For Grice a suitable move is one that furthers the common purpose of the conversation and an unsuitable move is one that does not. Thus, a suitable move is one a participant in a conversation ought to make and an unsuitable move is one he ought not to make, given the common goals of the participants in a conversation. Normative claims that specify what agents ought and ought not to do entail that there are standards that call for the agents to perform or not to perform certain actions.[7] A standard

[...] is not a proposition, but [...] it specifies that certain conditions are to be met by things of a certain category, perhaps under certain conditions, and [...] it is something to which things (the things in question) can conform or fail to conform and with which (if the thing in question is an agent) an agent can comply or fail to comply. (Copp 1995: 19)

Such standards can be expressed by the use of imperatives. Thus, a statement to the effect that an agent ought or ought not to perform an action entails that there is a standard that has a certain standing expressible by an imperative that calls for the agent to perform or not to perform the action. If the imperative were used, it would, then, express a standard that would call for the agent to act in a certain way and would be satisfied by the agent's performing or not performing an action that falls under the standard. We can take it, then, that in Grice's theory the CP and the maxims express standards that call for speakers to converse in a certain way.

Some standards are specific. If I say to Alice, *Close the door now*, the standard expressed by my use of the imperative is directed at a particular person to perform a particular kind of action with respect to a particular door at a particular time and place. Other standards are more general. They apply to any agent, perhaps one who meets certain conditions, for example, the standard expressed by a use of, *Be honest*. The standard that this imperative expresses applies to any person. To distinguish these different kinds of standards, let us call the former *particular* and the latter, *general*. I shall call general standards, *norms*. They specify that certain conditions are to be met by any agent. The CP and the maxims express norms directing any participant in a conversation about what kinds of interventions they should or should not make, given their conversational goals. The CP and the maxims have other features that make them general. Not only do they apply to any participant in a conversation, they do not specify the particular actions that a speaker must perform. Consider, for example, the supermaxim of Quality, *Try to make your contribution one that is true*. This applies to any participant in a conversation and does not tell him what he should try to say in particular, but only that *anything* he says should be something that is true.

One of Grice's motivations for introducing the CP and the maxims is to explain what he calls *conversational implicature*.[8] In a conversation a speaker can say *p* and imply, suggest or mean that *q*, to use Grice's technical term, implicate *q*. For Grice conversational implicatures are part of speaker meaning. Hence, in implicating something a speaker must have the intention that his audience recognize his intention to implicate. To use an example of Grice (1989: 32) suppose Alice is planning a trip to visit John and she asks me

(1)   Where does John live?

I reply

(2)   Somewhere in the South of France.

I have said something that is not as informative as required at this point in the conversation. Thus, it appears that I have violated the first maxim of Quality. On the assumption that I have not opted out of the CP and the maxims my answer can be understood as conforming to the CP and the maxims only by supposing that I implicated that I did not know where John lives.[9] Ostensibly, the purpose of our conversation is to exchange information (Grice 1989: 28). So I would only be trying to achieve the ends of the conversation by implicating something that you would take to be informative. The upshot is that even though my saying, 'Somewhere in France,' violates one of the maxims, my implicating that I do not know where John lives makes my contribution one that serves the purpose of the conversation, namely, an exchange of information. Thus, although my saying what I did violates one of the maxims, at the level of what I have implicated I have not violated the CP and the maxims (Grice 1989: 86).

One way of viewing the CP and the maxims is to take them to be part of a theory that is supposed to explain a speaker's implicative ability and his audience's capacity to understand what is implicated. A theory of this sort can be divided into two parts: a theory of competence and a theory of performance.[10] The former specifies the tacit knowledge that a speaker has which enables him to communicate that includes as a part the knowledge that enables him to implicate and to understand implication; the latter accounts for the on line processing involved in communication that will *a fortiori* account for the ways in which implicatures are produced and in which understanding of what is implicated is achieved. On this view of the CP and the maxims we can locate them as constituents of a speaker's communicative competence. A theory of implicature is part of a general theory of the human cognitive capacity to communicate. The adequacy of the theory is then to be judged by how well it accounts for these capacities. In particular the adequacy of the CP and the maxims is determined by how well they account for implicatures and their understanding.[11] As a consequence, what would substantiate our believing in the existence of the CP and the maxims as part of our communicative capacities is a well founded theory of our communicative capacities in which the CP and the maxims played an explanatory role.

There is, however, another way in which the CP and the maxims can be construed. They can be thought of as being specifications of norms that are involved in our normative practices. Viewed in this way they can be taken to express what we regard to be justified norms to which we ought to subscribe to further certain of our non-moral or moral ends. When the maxims are taken in this way, they are part of an account of our normative practices. They would be part of how we think that we ought to act. One way in which a moral theory is regarded is as a theory of our moral intuitions, perhaps under some idealized conditions. It would be, then, an account of our normative competence that would itself have normative import for how we ought to behaviour. We might view Rawl's theory of justice to be a theory of this sort. The way in which I shall consider the CP and the maxims is as part of a theory of our normative practices. If the CP and the maxims are regarded to be justified norms, to ask for their justification is not to ask for evidence for a theory in which they play an explanatory role. If the ends are non-moral, it is to ask for an account of how complying with the norms would effect those ends. To give such an account would involve us in a species of practical reasoning. If the ends are moral, the justification would have to show how observing the maxims furthered certain moral ends. This would mean that we would have to show how the norms expressed by the CP and the maxims fit into a general theory of morality. In either case if the norms were justified, we would have reasons to act in certain ways and reasons for subscribing to certain standards, rather than a theory that explained how in fact we act.

To regard the CP and the maxims as norms leaves it open as to whether they express practical or moral norms. I believe that Grice viewed them as practical norms that are part of an account of rational conversational activity.

> It is the rationality or irrationality of conversational conduct which I have been concerned to track down rather than any more general characterization of conversational adequacy. (Grice 1989: 369)

So on this view the CP and the maxims would be part of an account of how we ought to act in a conversation to be rational. I think that some of the maxims could be construed as practical norms, but I do not think that regarding the first maxim of Quality, *Don't say what you believe to be false,* in this way captures its full normative import. It is after all another way of expressing the moral norm, *Don't lie.* I shall first consider the CP and the maxims as practical norms, concentrating my attention on the first maxim of Quality. Second, I shall raise some considerations that suggest that the first maxim of Quality should be taken to be a moral norm.

On Grice's theory what is supposed to justify the norms that are expressed by the CP and the maxims is that following them has utility in achieving conversational goals. Performing an action that complies with the norms furthers the attainment, although does not provide a guarantee, of the conversational goals of the participants in a conversation. To see whether the standards that the CP and the maxims express can be justified in this way we must have a clear idea about the goals of conversational participants. For Grice the common goal of conversational participants is an exchange of information. (Grice 1989: 28). Let us consider the first maxim of Quality, *Do not say what you believe to be false,* with respect to this goal. In the "Retrospective Epilogue" Grice raises a question about whether this maxim is on a par with the others.

> The maxim of Quality [...] does not seem to be just one among a number of recipes for producing contributions; it seems rather to spell out the difference between something's being, and (strictly speaking) failing to be, any kind of contribution at all. False information is not an inferior kind of information; it just is not information. (Grice 1989: 371)

There are two ways in which *information* can be understood. First, a proposition, *p,* is information just in case it is true (Dretske 1981). Second, a proposition, *p,* is information just in case it is presented as being true, or it is believed to be true[12] (Sperber & Wilson 1995: 2). As we see from the quotation above, Grice opts for the first of these.[13] To illustrate what Grice has in mind let us return to the second of my exchanges with Alice. Suppose that both of us follow the CP and the maxims. I ask, 'What time is it?' and she replies, 'It is 5:00 p.m.' Suppose further that I have understood what she said and because I have no reason to mistrust her, I believe that it is 5:00 p.m. In asking my goal was to have Alice tell me what time it was; in answering Alice's goal was to tell me. We have, then, the common goal of an exchange of information from Alice to me. Despite her believing what she says to be true and having evidence for it (she looks at her normally accurate watch) what she says can still be mistaken. Obviously, believing that p and having evidence for p does not guarantee the truth of p. Let us suppose that Alice is mistaken about the time; it is 4:00 p.m. On Grice's construal of information, what I believe is not information. Consequently, there would not be an exchange of information and our conversation would not have reached its goal. According to Grice's theory, then, what justifies the first maxim of Quality? Suppose that in general Alice did not refrain from saying what she believed to be false. It would follow that there would be a greater possibility for what she said to be false. If what she said were false, it would be impossible for there to be any exchange of information between Alice and me, since what she would tell me, on Grice's view of information, would not be information. Hence, Alice's not saying what she believes to be false is not a means for an exchange of information; it is, rather, a precondition that increases the likelihood for such an exchange to be possible.

It is not clear, however, how Grice's views about the nature and the place of information in a conversation are to integrated into an account of our normative practices in conversing. Despite Alice's being mistaken, there is nothing amiss about the conversation. I asked Alice a question; she understood what I asked; she replied to my question, giving what she thought to be a correct answer; I have understood her reply and finally, because I have no reason not to trust her,[14] I believed what she said. There has been a transfer of something between Alice and me, even if it is not information, namely, the belief that it is 5:00 p.m. There is nothing irrational in any part of my conversation with Alice, even if she did not tell me the correct time. In an account of this linked conversation whether the proposition is true or false is irrelevant. In effect its truth or falsity is external to the conversation,[15] that is, neither the success of a conversation as a conversation, nor the rationality of the conversation is tied to the attainment of the Gricean goal of the conversation, namely, an exchange of information, where *information* is construed along Gricean lines. Suppose that we construe *information* in such a way that there is an exchange of information, even if what Alice says is false, as long as I believe what she says. We could say that the goal in the conversation is the transfer of belief and the norms expressed by the CP and the maxims would be justified just in case the actions governed by these norms would serve to achieve this goal. There are many conversations, however, in which the transfer of belief is not a goal, for example, the conversational chatter at cocktail parties. In such conversations the participants do not have as their goal getting others to believe anything. Often what is said is common knowledge among the participants. Moreover, although such conversations might not be very interesting, there is nothing irrational about them. Consequently, if the aim is to give an account of conversation as a rational activity, an exchange of information, construed in either of the ways above, cannot be the common goal of conversation.

There is, however, a role that the exchange of information plays in conversation, in Grice's sense of *information*. Alice and I have the following common goals: She understands what I say and I understand what she says. If these common goals are reached, then I understand what she said and she understands what I said. For this to be the case each of us must come to know what the other said. Consider what Alice said and my understanding of it. Alice uttered, 'It is 5:00 p.m.' and meant in uttering it to say that it is 5:00 p.m. For me to understand what she said, I must come to know that she said that it is 5:00 p.m. Alice, then, has the information, in Grice's sense of *information*, that in uttering, 'It is 5:00 p.m.' she said that it is 5:00 p.m., that is, she knows what she said. If I understand what she said, I come to have the information, again in Grice's sense of *information*, that in uttering 'It is 5:00 p.m.' she said that it is 5:00 p.m.[16] This does not exhaust the range of information that is exchanged in conversations that arises because the participants understand one another. To have a full account we should consider, as well, the understanding of what is conversationally implicated and pragmatically presupposed. Even without a full account we can say that in every case in which there is understanding in a conversation, there is an exchange of information. The exchange of information is information about what the speakers said, implicated and/or presupposed. Let us call what is said, implicated or presupposed *a speaker's linguistic intervention*. Consequently, if the participants in a conversation have the common goal of understanding each other's linguistic interventions, then they have the common goal of exchanging information. If the CP and the maxims, then, are practical norms, the compliance with these norms should play a role in effecting the common goal of understanding.

I would now like to consider the first maxim of Quality, *Do not say what you believe to be false*. To begin with we should notice that the maxim misses certain generalizations. First, a maxim of this sort should apply to what is conversationally implicated as well as what is said. Suppose that Alice and I consider one another to be friends. Fred tells me that she told him that I am a bit pompous. I know that she does not believe this. She was being ironic and Fred missed the irony. Perversely, I want to embarrass her and say in front of others

(3)   Fred tells me that you said that I am pompous. You're a fine friend.

She later says

(4)   Why did you let others think that we are not on good terms? You *know* that I am your friend.

Alice's remark is meant to criticize me for implicating what I do not believe to be true, namely, that she is not my friend. Second, the maxim should also apply to what is presupposed by a speech act. Suppose that I say

(5)   Have you stopped mistreating your students?

What I ask presupposes that you have been mistreating your students. If I do not believe that you have been mistreating your students, then I am open to criticism.

(6) Why did you say that? You know that I don't mistreat my students.

Third, the maxim is related to what Searle calls the sincerity condition of asserting (Searle 1969: 66-67). As Searle points out, there is a range of speech acts that have sincerity conditions.[17] This maxim, however, does not capture conversational interventions that are not instances of asserting. For example, if I congratulate Alice for having done something, my congratulations are sincere only if I am pleased about what she did. Finally, the maxim should apply not just to conversations and other talk exchanges, but to instances of saying or other speech acts that are not parts of conversations. If I cry out in a crowed theater, *There is a fire in the theater*, where doing so is not part of a conversation, or any other talk exchange, I should say what I believe to be true. Not to do so opens me up to very serious criticism. A more generalized norm that covers these cases is expressed by, *Don't be insincere in your linguistic interventions*.[18] Let us call this *the sincerity maxim*. A violation of the sincerity maxim occurs only if a linguistic intervention expresses an intentional state and the speaker fails to have the requisite intentional state.

I would now like to turn to a consideration of the relationship between understanding and the sincerity maxim. Let us return to my talk exchange with Alice. I utter, 'What time is it?' intending in so uttering to ask Alice what time it is. I also intend that she understand that I have asked what time it is and intend that she tell me what time it is. Let us call the first intention the *speech act intention*, the second the *uptake intention* and the third the *result intention*. The uptake intention and the speech act intention are related. The uptake intention is the intention that Alice recognize my speech act intention. Let us suppose further that my first intention is fulfilled, an intention the fulfillment of which does not depend on Alice. Thus, in uttering, 'What time is it?' I have asked Alice what time it is. The fulfillment of the other two intentions depends on Alice: Alice's understanding that I have asked what time it is and Alice's telling me what time it is. With both intentions I have the intention that Alice recognize my intentions. Alice would understand that in uttering, 'What time is it?' I have asked her what time it is, if she understands that I intend to ask her what time it is. Moreover, Alice would understand that I have this intention just in case she comes to know that I have this intention.

How does Alice come to know that I have this intention? She comes to know this by inferring it from what I have uttered, from other information in the context and from her background information.[19] We can say then that in uttering, 'What time is it?' I provide Alice with evidence that she uses in coming to know my speech act intention. Moreover, my very act of addressing Alice in uttering the sentence has as part of its content the presumption that my utterance is worth trying to understand (Sperber & Wilson 1995: 270-271). If this is part of the content of the act of addressing Alice, then the act expresses the belief that what has been uttered is worth trying to understand. In addition the act of uttering the sentence expresses my uptake intention. There are then two places where there can be violations of the sincerity maxim. The speaker might fail to have the belief that what he uttered is worth understanding or fail to have the intention that what he utters be understood. If either of these were the case, the speaker would violate the sincerity maxim.

To see that this is possible let us consider the following case. Suppose that there is a philosopher, let us call him D, who has constructed a theory that is dizzyingly complex. Moreover, D knows that his theory cannot be understood. He thinks that it is nonsense, but he wants his audience to be impressed by him and to take him to be a great philosopher. In addition, he wants his audience to think that he is modest. Hence, he does not want his audience to recognize that he intends them to be impressed and to take him to be a deep philosopher. D, then, does not have the intention that what he says be understood, since he believes that what he says cannot be understood and thus does not believe that it is worth understanding. Hence, he does not have an uptake intention with respect to what he says. Let us suppose further that D's deception is discovered by his acolytes. D would, then, be open to severe criticism in which appeals could be made to the sincerity maxim, a maxim that he violated.

It might be thought that my example above shows that not all linguistic interventions have as their goal understanding, for it appears that D has no such goal. It would seem to follow that the CP and the maxims cannot be viewed as practical norms. This conclusion is, perhaps, too hastily drawn. D has in fact three distinct uptake intentions. First, D's utterance acts carry with them the content that they are worth trying to understand, a content that they can carry, of course, even though it is false that they are worth trying to understand. Moreover, D intends that his audience believe that his utterances are worth trying to understand and he intends that his audience recognize this intention. If his audience did not take his utterances to be worth understanding, they would not pay attention to them. Hence, D would not be able in uttering what he does to get his audience to recognize his implication that he is a great philosopher. Second, although D might not intend that his audience understand what he says, since he believes that what he says is nonsense and so cannot be understood, he intends that his audience recognize his intention that he is saying something, rather than asking or requesting something. His uptake intention is an intention about his audience's understanding what speech act he intends to perform. This is not to suggest, however, that in every instance of a linguistic intervention a speaker performs a speech act, but only that if he performs a speech act, he intends that his audience recognize his intention to perform the speech act (Sperber & Wilson 1995: 247). Third, in advancing his philosophical theories D implies that he is a great philosopher and with respect to this D has an uptake intention. This case is complicated and there are a number of features that must be kept distinct. Although D intends to imply that he is a great philosopher, he does not intend that his audience recognize this intention. For if they did, it would undermine his intention that his audience thinks that he is modest. Thus, D does not have an uptake intention with respect to his intention to imply that he is a great philosopher, but he has one with respect to his implying that he is, that is, he intends that his audience understands that he is implying that he is a great philosopher, but that they take this to be unintended.[20]

I would now like to consider what kind of justification can be given for the sincerity maxim with respect to uptake intentions. Before taking this up I shall apply to talk exchanges the descriptive apparatus of the theory of rational choice. We are creatures who seek to fulfill a range of desires, preferences and goals. Let us call these our interests. Under one conception of rationality if other people's interests are not effected, an agent is rational if and only if he tries to maximize his own interests. Following David Gauthier, let us call this the *maximizing* conception of rationality.[21] Gauthier distinguishes this from what he calls the *universalizing* conception of rationality. On this conception of rationality an agent is rational if and only if he tries to maximize interests without consideration of whose interests they are. Hence, built into this conception of rationality is "the moral notion of impartiality" (Gauthier 1985: 6). My interest is in discovering just what kind of normative properties the sincerity maxim has. Consequently, I shall not make use of the universalizing conception of rationality in characterizing talk exchanges. This would build into the descriptive apparatus a moral notion, but I want to leave open whether the first maxim of Quality expresses a moral norm.

On my reworking of Grice's theory talk exchanges are goal directed activities where the common goal of such exchanges is understanding. In my talk exchange with Alice my goal is that she tells me what time it is. To achieve this I want her to understand that in uttering, 'What time is it?' I have asked her a question. To align this with the theory of rational choice instead of talking about goals we can talk about preferences. So in my connected talk exchange with Alice my preference is that she understand that I have asked her what time it is. There are a number of possible outcomes that my exchange with Alice could have. She could take me to be telling her what time it is; she could pay no attention to what I said, she could understand that I have asked her what time it is, etc. It is the latter state of affairs that I prefer more than any of the other state of affairs that are possible in this situation. Hence, I attach greater utility to this state of affairs than to the other state of affairs that are possible in the situation. Consequently, my utility is maximized if my preference is fulfilled. Thus, for me to be rational in this situation what I should try to do is to maximize my utility, that is, I should do what would bring about the state of affairs to which I attach the highest degree of utility, namely, Alice's understanding that I have asked her what time it is. To achieve this end, and thus, to maximize my preferences, I should choose among the actions available to me the action that has the greatest probability to achieve this end. Given my knowledge of our linguistic practices, information that I have about the situation and knowledge that I have about Alice, the action that has the highest probability to achieve that end is to utter, 'What time is it?' with the intention that she recognize my intention that she understand that I have asked her what time it is. Hence, what is rational for me to choose in this situation is to ask Alice what time it is. The question that I wish to consider is what role the compliance with the sincerity maxim plays in speakers reaching the goal of conversational exchanges.

There are different ways that norms can be justified with respect to intentionally goal directed activities of agents that are utility maximizers.[22] First, there are norms that are justified by the fact that the actions they call for are means for an agent to attain the goal he desires. Let us suppose that Alice wishes to go from Montreal to Toronto by the most direct route. I say

(7) If you want to get to Toronto in the most direct way possible, then you should go west on the 401.

The advice I give her implies a norm that is expressed by the following hypothetical imperative:

(8) Go west on the 401, if you to want to reach Toronto from Montreal by the most direct route.

Let us call the norm that this imperative expresses, *an instrumental norm*. What justifies the norm is that going west on the 401 leads from Montreal to Toronto, that the 401 is a well-maintained road and that it is the most direct road from Montreal to Toronto. Alice has a certain preference: to get from Montreal to Toronto by the most direct route and traveling west on the 401 from Montreal is a means to reach her goal. I shall call this kind of justification for a norm, *an instrumental justification*. We can say in general that a norm is an instrumental norm just in case for any agent who has a particular preference, performing actions that comply with the norm are a means for him to obtain the state of affairs that he prefers. The norm is justified for the agent, if in the situation to which the norm applies, the kind of action that it calls for, among the kinds of actions that the agent has the ability to perform, has the highest probability of obtaining for the agent the state of affairs that he prefers.

Second, some norms are justified, because compliance with them is a precondition for agents to be able to engage in certain goal directed actions and activities. Consider the following rule of the road, leaving aside that it is a law in Canada.

(9) You should drive on the right hand side of the road in Canada.

This entails that there is the norm expressed by

(10) Drive on the right hand side of the road in Canada.

Let us call this *a background norm*.[23] Its justification is that given the amount of traffic on the roads, how people drive, roads constructed, automobiles built, etc., general compliance with the norm would make it possible for people to reach the various goals that they have in using the roads. There is some arbitrariness about the rule of the road. A rule of the road that people should drive on the left hand side of the road would have equally served the purposes of the rule that was adopted in Canada. Given the conditions cited above and drivers diverse goals in using the roads, what is not arbitrary is that some rule be adopted that directs people to drive on the same side of the road. Hence, general compliance with the right hand driving rule of the road, including Alice's compliance, makes it possible for Alice to fulfill her desire to get to Toronto from Montreal by taking the 401, but general compliance is not a means for her to fulfill this desire. Rather it is what makes it possible for her to take the 401 west and get from Montreal to Toronto. Let us call this kind of justification, *a background justification*. A norm has this sort of justification just in case for an agent who desires to reach certain goals, general compliance with the norm by members of the agents' community makes it possible for the agent to be successful in achieving these goals by engaging in actions and activities that are a means for achieving the goals.

I would now like to consider what kind of justification can be given for the sincerity maxim with respect to uptake intentions. Let us return to D who violates the sincerity maxim and yet, whose uptake intentions are fulfilled. His audience takes him to be saying something, rather than asking something and they have grasped the implication that he is a great philosopher. His fulfilling his uptake intentions while also violating the sincerity maxim, however, depends upon there being general compliance with the maxim in the community of which D is a part. To see this let us consider how D fulfills his uptake intentions. He utters phrases and sentences like, 'I say that ... ,' 'I claim that ... ,' 'I maintain that ... ,' and a series of declarative sentences that are syntactically complex and filled with technical philosophical vocabulary that give his audience evidence for concluding that he is saying something and that there is an implication that he is a great philosopher. Moreover, he does not give the appearance of not complying with the sincerity maxim, that is, he does not give the appearance of being insincere in saying and implying what he does. Since the background assumption in most situations is to take people to be complying with the sincerity maxim, lack of evidence to the contrary would lead D's audience to believe that he is complying. Given this default assumption, presenting his theories and not appearing not to comply would do the trick in inducing in his audience this belief. To see that appearances are necessary suppose he did not appear to be sincere. His audience would, then, not have any interest in trying to understand what he says, for they would not believe that he believes what he says. Thus, this would defeat his uptake intentions. That D's uptake intentions are fulfilled and yet, he violates the sincerity maxim shows that the actions that the sincerity maxim calls for are not a means for D to fulfill his uptake intentions. Hence, the sincerity maxim with the respect to a speaker's preference to fulfill his uptake intentions is not an instrumental norm.

In fulfilling his uptake intentions we have seen that D relies on the default assumption that in normal situations people comply with the sincerity maxim. Hence, given D's uptake intentions, he has an interest in being part of a linguistic community in which there is the general expectation among members of the community that speakers, including D, subscribe to the sincerity maxim. Being in a community in which there is the general expectation of compliance makes it possible for D to fulfill his uptake intentions. To see this let us consider the situation from the point of view of his audience. If D's audience, that is, interpreters, did not assume that there was general compliance with the sincerity maxim, they would have no grounds for taking others, including D, to be speaking a language, since they would have no grounds for saying of anyone that they were performing linguistic interventions.[24]

To see this let us begin with speech acts and consider the inference the interpreter makes from D's uttering, 'I say that p,' to the conclusion that D says that p. Given D's utterance, information in the context and background information that the interpreter has, an interpreter can make a non-demonstrative inference to a conclusion about what speech act D is performing. To reach this conclusion the interpreter must attribute to D the intention to say that *p* and the intention that this intention is to be recognized. If the interpreter did not attribute to D these intentions, then he could not attribute to him the speech act of saying that *p*, since one cannot say that *p* without having these intentions. Suppose that the interpreter did not take D to be sincere. This would be to take D not to have these intentions and thus, not to be saying that *p*. Could the interpreter not attribute to D these intentions and still take him to be speaking a language? He could, if he attributed to him other speech act intentions. But this would involve a presumption of sincerity with respect to these speech act intentions. Does the interpreter have to attribute to the speaker some speech act intentions or other? There are uses of language in which a speaker utters something without performing any speech act (Sperber & Wilson 1995: 247). To use an example of Sperber and Wilson suppose that a speaker says

(11)   What monster would harm a sleeping child?

There are uses of this sentence in which a speaker is not asking a question, saying something or performing any other speech act, but is implicating something. What is required for the interpreter to have grounds for taking the speaker to be implicating something is that he attributes to the speaker in uttering this sentence the intention to be implicating something and the intention that this intention be recognized, since having such intentions is a necessary condition for someone to implicate something. Let us suppose that the interpreter did not take the speaker to be sincere, then he would not attribute to him these intentions and thus, would have no grounds for taking him to be implicating anything. To generalize the point, if the interpreter made no assumption of compliance with the sincerity maxim with respect to any of the speaker's utterances, he would have no grounds for attributing to the speaker the performance of any linguistic intervention. In this case the interpreter would have no grounds for taking D's utterance acts to be acts in which D is speaking a language. If the interpreter did not take D to be speaking a language, he would have no interest in trying to understand his linguistic interventions. Consequently, this would defeat D's preference that his uptake intentions be fulfilled. Hence, the sincerity maxim is a background maxim and its justification is a background justification. I have argued that an assumption on the part of interpreters that there is compliance with the sincerity maxim is necessary for there to be the possibility that a speaker's uptake intentions could be fulfilled. Let us now imagine general non-compliance. If this were the case, interpreters' assumption that there is compliance would be undermined. Thus, general compliance with the sincerity maxim makes it possible for speakers to use language to perform a variety of goal directed activities, including the goal of having their uptake intentions fulfilled.

 D has another interest in being in a community in which there is general compliance with the sincerity maxim. In many cases of verbal exchange what he wants to know is the way the world is. One of the main sources of D's information about the world is what others say.[25] To obtain information from others it helps to understand their linguistic interventions. Hence, D has an interest in others subscribing to the sincerity maxim. To put this simply he has an interest that others not lie to him, but what has not been shown, however, is that he has a corresponding interest that he not lie to them. We might take the best case scenario for D to be one in which he is an undetected liar, that is, an undetected defector from the sincerity maxim, and in which others not defect from the sincerity maxim. To be an undetected defector he might on occasion have to comply with the sincerity maxim, since it is very difficult and time consuming to be a constant consummate defector. What would enable him to fulfill his uptake intentions is that he not appear not to subscribe to the sincerity maxim and that there be general compliance with the maxim in his linguistic community. From D's point of view there is a quasi justification for the sincerity maxim. Others should comply with it and he should comply with it often enough so that he does not gain the reputation of being insincere. This does not give D a background justification for the maxim. The most that has been shown is that for D the following maxim is justified: *Don't be insincere in your linguistic interventions, unless it serves your interests to be insincere and you can get away with it.* To provide a background justification we would have to show that D does not have a reason to be a defector to maximize utility, that is, that he has a reason as a maximizer of utility to comply with the sincerity maxim, everything else being equal. To show this, I believe, we would have to consider D's preferences beyond his preferences to have his uptake intentions fulfilled. We would have to embed them in a more general theory that would take account of the range of D's considered preferences (Gauthier 1986: 23) and would show how such a theory could give a justification for the norm of sincerity. To do this would involve us in the construction of what Gauthier (1986: 6) has called a moral theory, a theory that does not presuppose any moral notions but tries to show how moral principles can arise out of considering individuals to be constrained maximizers. To do this goes well beyond Grice's project of regarding the first maxim of Quality, and the CP and the other maxims as well, to be a maxim of rationality governing linguistic interventions.

Even if a theory that attempts to develop moral theory as a part of the theory of rational choice could show why it is rational for D not to be a defector with respect to the maxim of Quality and thus why he should subscribe to the norm, it might not be enough. What more would be required for such a theory to be completely adequate is that it capture the distinctive moral features of the sincerity maxim. To lie to someone is not to treat him with respect. Moreover, a person who lies is not honourable. It is an open question whether a moral theory that is an extension of the theory of rational choice can account for these moral properties of the sincerity maxim, a question that I shall leave for another time.[26]

Notes

1 Talking to oneself is not a conversation, although I can have an imaginary conversation in my head with someone else. I shall leave these sorts of cases aside.
2 See Searle (1969) for one view and Sperber & Wilson (1995) for another about these acts.
3 There is a complication here. In a conversation there can be a change of subject so that what a person says is not linked in any with what is previously said. Such changes of subject can be part of a single conversation, although there is no link between the different parts of the conversation. In the case I am imagining here there is no on going conversation in which there is

a change of subject. Rather, someone says something and then some else says something, but without there being an intended connection between the two.

4   A minimal condition on the linking is that Alice understands what I have said or implicated and that her response is relevant to what I have said or implicated.

5   I do not think that we would regard my exchange with Alice to be a conversation, since it is much too brief. It appears that duration of a talk exchange is a condition for it to be a conversation. I shall, however, leave this consideration out of the discussion.

6   One might argue that the talk exchange between the policeman and the suspect, the politician and the journalist and the attorney and the witness are not conversations, but are, respectively, instances of interrogations, interviews and cross examinations and that Grice's theory does not apply to these cases. Hence, they are not counter examples to his theory. I think that such an argument would sell Grice's theory short. It would only have limited interest if it did not apply to these and other kinds of talk exchanges as well. In part Grice introduced the CP and the maxims to account for conversational implicature, a phenomenon that can arise in all these talk exchanges.

7   The account of the connection between normative claims and imperatives that express standards is drawn from Copp (1995: 9-36).

8   Grice's underlying motivation is philosophical. He wishes to show that there is no divergence in meaning between the connectives in first order logic and their ordinary language counterparts (Grice 1995: 24).

9   What a Gricean theory must provide to be a fully explicit theory are the necessary and sufficient conditions for a speaker in saying p to implicate that q and for an interpreter to understand that I have implicated that I do not know where John lives.

10 I am drawing on the distinction that Chomsky (1965) makes between theories of competence and performance.

11 One of the criticisms raised against Grice and those who have taken up his views is that there is no such theory (Sperber & Wilson 1995: 31-38). For the sake of the discussion I shall assume that it is possible to construct a fully articulated theory on Gricean lines.

12 This is only a rough approximation of the way in which Sperber and Wilson treat information in the first edition of *Relevance*, but it is good enough for my present purposes. It should be noted that in the second edition of *Relevance* Sperber & Wilson (1995: 263-266) revise their definition of relevance in terms of positive cognitive effects that is supposed to capture a cognizer's interest in the truth or falsity of his beliefs.

13 This is Grice's view about information in the "Retrospective Epilogue" (Grice 1989). I take it that it is not an emendation of his position, but a clarification of what he meant by 'information' in "Logic and Conversation" (Grice: 1967). Dretske and Grice's notion of *information* is much too crude for Grice's purpose. Suppose that Alice says that it is 5:00 p.m., but it is really one second past five. Strictly speaking, there has not been an exchange of information and my and Alice goal of exchanging information would not be reached. Alice's reply is, however, accurate enough for the matter at hand.

14 Sperber & Wilson (1995: 248) take it that the grounds for believing what someone says is trust. I think that this is too strong. There are no grounds to trust most people with whom we communicate where we believe what they say. Rather, we do not have any reason not to trust them.

15 Truth does play a role, however, in explaining why we have our communicative abilities. My aim in asking Alice what time it is, is not just to have a belief about what time it is, but to know what time it is, that is, to have a true belief. If our communicative abilities did not generally lead to true beliefs, there would not have been evolutionary reasons for us to have acquired them. To put this another way if our communicative abilities had led in general to

false beliefs, creatures with such abilities would have been selected out and would not have been our evolutionary ancestors. The question is how to build this into a theory of conversation and communication, a question that I shall not take up here (Sperber & Wilson 1995: 263-266).
16 It might be thought that this is what Grice had in mind and that my suggestion here does not differ from his views. I believe that Grice would regard someone's saying something false not to be a case in which what is said is information and hence, there could be no exchange of information.
17 Not all speech acts have sincerity conditions, greetings for example (Searle 1969: 67). See also Sperber & Wilson (1995: 246-247) for a discussion of sincerity conditions.
18 'Insincere' is not being used in its ordinary sense. It would be odd to say that Alice is insincere, if she tells me that it is 5:00 p.m. and does not believe what she says. The use of 'sincere' is meant to cover the conditions that fall under Searle's sincerity conditions.
19 See Sperber & Wilson (1995) for the details of an inferential theory of communication.
20 Since D does not intend that his audience recognize his intention to imply that he is a great philosopher, his implying is not a case of implicature.
21 The material about rational choice is from Gauthier (1985).
22 I have been guided in my discussion here by Copp (1995: 10).
23 The notion of background is not the same as Searle's (1995: 127-147).
24 See Davidson (1975) for a discussion of these issues.
25 I use 'say' here as short for 'speech acts and conversational implicatures.'
26 I would to thank David Copp, Jöelle Proust, Marcel Liberman, François Récanati, Dan Sperber, Roberto Casati, Elizabeth Pacherie and the other members of CREA for their help with this paper.

References

Chomsky, N. (1965): Aspects of the Theory of Syntax. Cambridge, Mass.: The MIT Press.
Copp, D. (1995): Morality, Normativity and Society. Oxford: Oxford University Press.
Davidson, D. (1975): "Thought and talk". In: Inquiries into Truth and Interpretation. Oxford: Oxford University Press, 155-170.
Dretske, F. (1981): Knowledge and the Flow of Information. Oxford: Blackwell.
Gauthier, D. (1986): Morals by Agreement. Oxford: Oxford University Press.
Grice, H.P. (1967): James Lectures: Logic and Conversation. (Unpublished).
Grice, H.P. (1975): "Logic and Conversation". In: J. Cole & P. Morgan, eds.: Syntax and Semantics. Vol. 3. New York: Academic Press, 41-58.
Grice, H.P. (1989): Studies in the Way of Words. Cambridge, Mass.: Harvard University Press.
Rawls, J. (1971): A Theory of Justice. Cambridge, Mass.: Harvard University Press.
Searle, J.R. (1969): Speech Acts. Cambridge: Cambridge University Press.
Searle, J.R. (1995): The Construction of Social Reality. New York: The Free Press.
Sperber, D. & D. Wilson (1995): Relevance. Communication and Cognition. Oxford: Blackwell.

Nicht-zentrale Sprechakte

Jörg Hagemann, Hamburg / Eckard Rolf, Münster

1   Vorbemerkung

Hinsichtlich solcher Ausdrücke wie 'mithin', 'folglich', 'aber' und 'des weiteren' vertritt Grice eine interessante These. Während zum Beispiel noch Searle & Vanderveken (1985: 2) solche Ausdrücke als syntaktische Realisationen von Wahrheitsfunktionen betrachten, deren Eigenschaften im Rahmen der Aussagenlogik zu untersuchen seien, besteht die semantische Funktion dieser und ähnlicher Ausdrücke nach Grice darin, daß mit ihnen *angezeigt*, aber nicht *gesagt* werden könne, daß zwischen den vom Sprecher thematisierten Inhalten bestimmte Beziehungen bestehen. Wenn jemand zum Beispiel den Satz (SI) 'Peter ist Philosoph und hat folglich Mut' äußert, dann ist, Grice zufolge, nicht davon auszugehen, daß "derjenige, der (SI) äußert, damit *gesagt* hat, daß die Tatsache, daß Peter Mut hat, daraus folgt, daß er Philosoph ist, auch wenn er durchaus gesagt haben mag, daß Peter Philosoph ist und daß er Mut hat." (Grice [1968]/1993: 90) Daß das eine (daß Peter Mut hat) aus dem anderen (daß Peter Philosoph ist) folgt, gehört nach Grice nicht zum Gesagten - und (folglich) nicht in den Bereich dessen, was von einer Wahrheitsbedingungen-Semantik erfaßt werden kann: Die zwischen den beiden Inhalten hergestellte Folgebeziehung wird durch den Gebrauch des Wortes 'folglich' lediglich *angezeigt*.

In dem erwähnten Zusammenhang spricht Grice übrigens von *nicht-zentralen Sprechakten* (vgl. ebd.: 91). Was für Entitäten könnten das sein? Was könnte es mit ihnen auf sich haben? Und wie sind sie in sprechakttheoretischer Hinsicht einzuschätzen?

Mit solchen Elementen wie 'folglich' oder 'mithin' wird also etwas angezeigt, und sie sind "verknüpft" (Grice [1968]/1993: 91) mit nicht-zentralen Sprechakten. Als 'zentral' müßten solche Sprechakte wie Behaupten, Auffordern, Versprechen etc. angesehen werden. Nicht-zentrale Sprechakte sind als den zentralen Sprechakten nachgeordnet zu betrachten bzw. können sie in ihrem Vollzug als von diesen abhängig erwiesen werden (vgl. ebd.). "So würde z. B. die Bedeutung von 'des weiteren' mit dem Sprechakt des Hinzufügens verknüpft, dessen Vollzug den Vollzug des einen oder anderen zentralen Sprechakts erforderte." (Ebd.)

Bach, der hinsichtlich der nicht-zentralen Sprechakte auch von Sprechakten zweiter Ordnung spricht (s. Bach 1994c: 16), nennt weitere Beispiele für solche Akte: den Akt der Vereinfachung ('simplifying'), den der Modifizierung ('qualifying'), den des Schließens ('concluding') (vgl. Bach 1994a: 149; 1994b: 277) und den Akt der Gegenüberstellung bzw. der Entgegensetzung ('contrasting') (s. Bach 1994c: 16).

Der Vollzug eines nicht-zentralen Sprechakts, das muß beachtet werden, sollte, Grice ([1968]/1993: 91) zufolge, nicht als ein Fall von *Sagen, daß* *p betrachtet werden. ('"*' ist ein *Platzhaltersymbol* für einen Modus-Indikator, im Unterschied zu spezifischen Modus-Indikatoren wie '⊢' (indikativisch bzw. assertorisch) oder '!' (imperativisch)." (Ebd.: 86))

Darüber hinaus muß beachtet werden, daß bei Grice hinsichtlich der Verwendung der von ihm ins Auge gefaßten Ausdrücke von *Sprech*akten, nicht von *illokutionären* Akten, die Rede ist. Es gibt unterschiedliche Arten von Sprechakten: neben dem illokutionären und dem perlokutionären Sprechakttyp gibt es z. B. auch den propositionalen Akt und den Äußerungsakt (vgl. Searle 1971: 38ff. und Searle & Vanderveken 1985: 8ff.). Zu dieser Gruppe der Sprechakt*arten* scheinen auch die nicht-zentralen Sprechakte gerechnet werden zu können.

Welche Ausdrücke gehören zu dem ins Auge gefaßten Ausdrucksinventar? Außer den eingangs erwähnten stehen solche Ausdrücke wie die folgenden unter dem Verdacht, die Eigenschaft, mit einem nicht-zentralen Sprechakt verknüpft zu sein, aufzuweisen: 'demgemäß', 'entsprechend', 'schließlich', 'immerhin', 'jedenfalls', 'wenigstens', 'obgleich', 'obwohl', 'wenn auch', 'dennoch', 'trotzdem', 'nichtsdestoweniger', 'sozusagen', 'gleichsam', 'außerdem', 'zudem', 'ferner', 'überdies', 'darüber hinaus', 'übrigens', 'letztendlich', 'kurzum', 'vor allen Dingen', 'auf jeden Fall', 'im Gegensatz zu', 'offen gestanden', 'gelinde gesagt', 'strenggenommen', 'wenn ich das so sagen darf', 'andererseits', 'zunächst', 'zu allererst' (vgl. Bach 1994a: 148; 1994b: 277).

Bach & Harnish bezeichnen Ausdrücke dieser Art generell als *illokutionäre Adverbiale*. Solche Ausdrücke werden Bach & Harnish (1979: 219) zufolge dazu gebraucht, die hinter einer Äußerung stehende illokutionäre Absicht zu kommentieren: Ausdrücke dieser Art dienen *nicht* dazu, den Hauptsatz des geäußerten Satzes zu modifizieren, sie leisten nicht einmal einen Beitrag zum lokutionären Akt, sie dienen dazu, die *Äußerung* des Hauptsatzes in der einen oder anderen Weise zu charakterisieren (s. ebd.: 220).

Drei Beispiele:

(1) Übrigens, ich kann meine Brille nicht wiederfinden.
(2) Andererseits, wer zögert, ist verloren.
(3) Wir haben des weiteren keinen Wein mehr.

Der in (1) vorkommende Ausdruck 'übrigens' zeigt den digressiven Charakter der auf ihn folgenden Äußerung an; 'andererseits' in (2) zeigt an, daß, was folgt, einem zuvor thematisierten Inhalt widerspricht; und der in (3) enthaltene Ausdruck 'des weiteren' zeigt an, daß, was mit dem Rest von (3) gesagt wird, eine Ergänzung zu etwas zuvor Gesagtem darstellt.

Das Konzept der nicht-zentralen Sprechakte hat bislang wenig Beachtung gefunden; es ist auch kaum ernst genommen worden. Ziel des vorliegenden Aufsatzes ist es, auf die nicht-zentralen Sprechakte und die mit ihnen einhergehenden Eigentümlichkeiten aufmerksam zu machen. Wie sich dabei herausstellen wird, sind es nicht nur vereinzelte Ausdrücke, die als nicht-zentrale Sprechakte beschrieben werden können; das Phänomen ist verbreiteter, als bisher angenommen worden ist - sofern es überhaupt wahrgenommen worden ist, was etwa bei Bach (1994a: 141ff.), Rolf (1994: 92, 171), Liedtke (1995: 42f.) oder Rolf (1997: 110f.) geschehen ist.

Wenn etwas, das übermittelt wird, nicht zum Gesagten gehört, ist es dann auch - oder erst recht - nicht zu dem zu rechnen, was behauptet wird? Kann man eine Behauptung aufstellen, ohne *etwas* zu behaupten?

Nach Austin geht der Vollzug eines lokutionären Aktes mit dem Vollzug eines illokutionären Aktes einher: "Einen lokutionären Akt vollziehen heißt im allgemeinen auch und eo ipso einen *illokutionären* Akt vollziehen" (ebd.: 114). Gilt auch das Umgekehrte? Setzt auch der Vollzug eines illokutionären Aktes den Vollzug eines lokutionären Aktes voraus?

Konzentrieren wir uns auf die folgenden beiden Aspekte: *etwas sagen* und *etwas behaupten, feststellen, mitteilen*. Angenommen, jemand sagt über jemand anderen

(4)   Er ist Engländer.

Was der Sprecher in einem solchen Fall *sagt*, ist, daß diejenige Person, auf die 'er' referiert, Engländer ist; was der Sprecher tut, ist, daß er seinem Gesprächspartner letzteres *mitteilt*.

(5)   Er ist tapfer.

Das, was mit (5) gesagt wird, ist, daß diejenige Person, auf die *er* referiert, tapfer ist; in illokutionärer Hinsicht liegt eine Behauptung vor. Was aber ist der Fall, wenn ein Satz wie (6) geäußert wird?

(6)   Er ist Engländer; er ist mithin tapfer.

Was sagt der Sprecher in diesem Fall? Er sagt, daß die Person, über die er spricht, Engländer ist. Letzteres teil er mit. Und er sagt, daß die fragliche Person tapfer ist. Das behauptet er. Behauptet der Sprecher auch, daß die Tapferkeit eine Konsequenz dessen ist, daß die betreffende Person Engländer ist? *Sagt* der Sprecher das? Oder deutet er es nur an, so daß es sich erschließen läßt? Wenn der Sprecher nicht *sagt*, daß zwischen der Tatsache, daß der Referent Engländer ist, und dem Umstand, daß er tapfer ist, ein Folgerungszusammenhang besteht, wenn er lediglich *andeutet*, daß ein solcher Folgerungszusammenhang besteht, dann scheint es nicht so zu sein, daß das Bestehen dieses Folge-rungszusammenhangs behauptet wird. Um einen illokutionären Akt - zu behaupten, daß der fragliche Folgerungszusammenhang besteht - vollziehen zu können, müßte der Sprecher, das wäre die Annahme, auch den entsprechenden lokutionären Akt vollziehen, das heißt, er müßte *sagen*, daß ein Folgerungszusammenhang besteht. Letzteres aber ist der von Grice vertretenen Position zufolge nicht der Fall.

Was spricht für die Annahme, daß in (6) der Folgerungszusammenhang lediglich angedeutet wird, daß aber nicht gesagt - und infolgedessen auch nicht behauptet - wird, daß er besteht? Es sind die folgenden wahrheitsfunktionalen Gründe. Jemand, der (6) äußert, sagt nichts Falsches, wenn der fragliche Folgerungszusammenhang *nicht* besteht: Für die Wahrheit des geäußerten Satzes ist es ohne Bedeutung, ob der Folgerungszusammenhang besteht oder nicht, letzteres bleibt ohne Auswirkung auf den Wahrheitswert von (6). Grice ([1975] / 1993: 248) spricht mit Bezug auf Sätze wie (6) von konventionalen Implikaturen; diese gehen mit der Verwendung solcher Ausdrücke wie 'mithin' einher. Grice vertritt die These, daß die semantische Funktion eines Ausdrucks wie 'mithin' darin besteht, "daß der betreffende Sprecher *anzeigen* (wenngleich auch nicht *sagen*) kann, daß eine gewisse Folgebeziehung vorliegt" (Grice [1968]/1993: 90). Wir haben es hier offenbar mit dem Phänomen zu tun, daß etwas zwar übermittelt, aber nicht gesagt wird. Und wird nichts gesagt, dann kann mit der Verwendung solcher Ausdrücke wie 'mithin' auch nicht eo ipso ein illokutionärer Akt verknüpft sein. Dann aber stellt sich die Frage, wie die betreffenden Ausdrücke, zumal sprechakttheoretisch, einzuschätzen sind.

Mit den nachfolgenden Bemerkungen wird folgendes versucht: Zunächst geht es um eine kurze Darstellung des Kontextes, in dem Grice die Idee der nicht-zentralen Sprechakte dargelegt hat. Der nächste Schritt wird darin bestehen zu klären, wie der Begriff des Sagens definiert sein muß, wenn er zur Unterscheidung der zentralen von den nicht-zentralen Sprechakte soll herangezogen werden können. Im darauffolgenden Abschnitt wird dargelegt, wie die Ausdrücke, die Grice mit dem Konzept der nicht-zentralen Sprechakte in den Griff zu bekommen versucht, in der Sprechakttheorie eingeschätzt worden sind (sie sind von Anfang an als problematisch eingestuft worden). Im Anschluß daran werden einige Beispiele nicht-zentraler Sprechakte diskutiert. Im letzten Abschnitt soll es darum gehen aufzuzeigen, daß und auf welche Weise Grices Konzept der nicht-zentralen Sprechakte in den Rahmen der Illokutionslogik hineingestellt werden kann.

2   Das Gricesche Programm

Die Gricesche Theorie der Konversations-Implikaturen beinhaltet eine ganz bestimmte Unterscheidung "innerhalb der Gesamtbedeutung einer Äußerung" (Grice [1968]/1993: 85): die "Unterscheidung zwischen dem, was der Sprecher *gesagt* [...], und dem, was er *impliziert*" (ebd.: 85f.) hat. Das, was der Sprecher impliziert hat, kann entweder *konventionell* oder *nicht-konventionell* sein: Im ersteren Fall impliziert der Sprecher, was er impliziert, "kraft der Bedeutung eines von ihm verwendeten Wortes bzw. einer von ihm gebrauchten Wendung" (ebd.: 86), im anderen Fall fällt "die Bestimmung der Implikatur nicht mehr unter die Bestimmung der konventionellen Bedeutung der verwendeten Wörter" (ebd.).

Aus der obigen Unterscheidung leitet Grice eine Unternehmung ab, die unterschiedliche Bedeutungsbegriffe miteinander verknüpfen soll. Die Verknüpfung, die ihm dabei vorschwebt, ist die zwischen dem Begriff der sogenannten Sprecher-Bedeutung auf der einen Seite und den Begriffen der Satz- bzw. Wortbedeutung auf der anderen. Dieses Unternehmen ist Teil eines umfassenderen Programms, das auf zweierlei abzielt: (a) auf eine Klärung des von Grice "favorisierten Sinns von 'sagen'" (ebd.) und (b) "auf eine Klärung der zwischen diesem 'sagen' und dem Begriff der konventionellen Bedeutung bestehenden Beziehung" (ebd.).

Das von Grice verfolgte Programm umfaßt insgesamt sechs Stufen; auf diesen Stufen werden Unterscheidungen getroffen, Begriffe zu klären versucht und Definitionen vorgeschlagen. Unterschieden wird beispielsweise zwischen der 'Situations-Bedeutung' und 'Satz-Bedeutung' (Stufe I); einer Klärung näher gebracht werden Begriffe wie der der 'angewandten zeitunabhängigen Bedeutung' (Stufe IV); und vorgeschlagen werden Definitia wie das folgende, das für die 'Situations-Bedeutung' gelten soll: "'Mit dem Äußern von x

[...] meinte S, daß *p'" (ebd.: 86). Für das Verständnis des dabei favorisierten Sinns von 'sagen' ist aufschlußreich, daß Grice sich darauf festlegt, "daß angewandte zeitunabhängige Bedeutung und Situations-Bedeutung koinzidieren können, d. h., daß sowohl zutreffen kann, daß (i) X, von S geäußert, u. a. '*p' bedeutet, als auch, daß (ii) S mit der Äußerung von X u. a. gemeint hat, daß *p." (Ebd.: 90) Grice beabsichtigt, den Ausdruck 'auf konventionelle Weise meinen, daß' so zu verwenden, "daß die Erfüllung der zwei eben erwähnten Bedingungen für die Wahrheit von 'S meinte auf konventionelle Weise, daß *p' hinreichend (und notwendig) ist - auch wenn sie für die Wahrheit von 'S sagte, daß *p' nicht hinreicht." (Ebd.) Es kann also durchaus vorkommen, daß von S gesagt werden kann, er habe das-und-das (auf konventionelle Weise) *gemeint*, ohne daß gleichzeitig behauptet werden könnte, S habe Entsprechendes auch *gesagt*. Es kann, mit anderen Worten, vorkommen, daß bestimmte Elemente einer Äußerung Bedeutungen übermitteln, die nicht Teil dessen sind, was gesagt wurde.

Was das Verhältnis zwischen dem Gesagten und dem konventionell Gemeinten betrifft, so lassen sich zwei Fälle unterscheiden: Im ersteren Fall ist "das von S mit einer Äußerung konventionell Gemeinte auch Teil des von S Gesagten" (ebd.), im anderen Fall enthält eine Äußerung und mithin das konventionell Gemeinte Elemente, "die *nicht* Teil des Gesagten sind." (Ebd.: 91)

In Anbetracht des Ziels, den von ihm favorisierten Sinn von 'sagen' herauszuarbeiten und die Beziehung zu klären, die "zwischen diesem 'sagen' und dem Begriff der konventionellen Bedeutung" (ebd.: 86) besteht, mag die von Grice eingeschlagene Analyserichtung zunächst etwas verwirren: Ausgangspunkt seines Programms zur Herleitung zeitunabhängiger Bedeutung ist das, was ein Sprecher *meint* - das zu erreichende Ziel besteht darin zu bestimmen, was er *sagt*. Eine grundlegende Voraussetzung, die dabei in Rechnung zu stellen ist, besteht in dem Primat der Sprecher-Bedeutung: Das, was ein Sprecher zu verstehen zu geben beabsichtigt, ist 'ursprünglicher' als das, was er sagt. Das bedeutet: Intendierte Bedeutungseffekte sind letztlich auf seiten des Sprechers, sie sind nicht im Bereich der Satz-Bedeutung zu lokalisieren. Grice ist offensichtlich der Überzeugung, "that utterer's meaning is analytically 'primary' or 'basic' " (Neale 1992: 551).

Wie sieht das Programm zur Herleitung der zeitunabhängigen Bedeutung im einzelnen aus?

An einer x-beliebigen Äußerung kann Grice ([1968]/1993: 86) zufolge zunächst unterschieden werden zwischen der Situations-Bedeutung und der Bedeutung, die ein Äußerungs-Typ X besitzt (= Stufe I).

Darauf aufbauend soll auf Stufe II (des insgesamt sechs Stufen umfassenden Programms) versucht werden, die Situations-Bedeutung - also das, was ein Sprecher mit seiner Äußerung in einer bestimmten Situation konkret meint - zu bestimmen.

Auch die Rede von der Bedeutung eines Äußerungs-Typs X erfordert eine nähere Bestimmung. Stufe III beinhaltet eine erste Ausdifferenzierung der Bedeutung eines Äußerungs-Typs X (i) in die Bedeutung, die X für den Sprecher hat (zeitunabhängige 'Idiolekt-Bedeutung'), und (ii) die Bedeutung, die X in einer bestimmten Sprache hat (zeitunabhängige 'sprachliche Bedeutung').

Da nicht auszuschließen ist, daß ein Äußerungs-Typ X mehrere zeitunabhängige Bedeutungen haben kann, ist es von Vorteil, auf wenigstens eine davon in eindeutiger Art und

Weise Bezug nehmen zu können: Bei Grice ist es die angewandte zeitunabhängige Bedeutung eines Äußerungs-Typs X, um deren Explikation es auf Stufe IV geht. Grice legt hier die Orientierung an einem Schema wie "X (Äußerungs-Typ) bedeutet *hier* '...'" (ebd.: 88) nahe. Für den Fall, daß die angewandte zeitunabhängige Bedeutung mit der auf Stufe II explizierten Situations-Bedeutung zusammenfällt, kann davon gesprochen werden, daß der Sprecher auf konventionelle Weise meinte, daß p (vgl. ebd.: 90).

Im Gegensatz zu dem auf konventionelle Weise Gemeinten geht es auf Stufe V um die Explikation des Gesagten. Der von Grice favorisierte Sinn von 'sagen' erweist sich dabei als sprechakttheoretisch bedingt: Das Gesagte ist an den Vollzug eines zentralen Sprechakts gebunden (vgl. ebd.: 90f.): Ein Sprecher hat mit dem Äußern von X *gesagt* (und nicht konventionell gemeint), daß p, wenn "X eine konventionelle Form enthält, deren Bedeutung derart ist, daß ihr Vorliegen in X anzeigt, daß der betreffende Sprecher" (ebd.: 91) einen zentralen Sprechakt vollzieht. Was aber hat man sich unter einer konventionellen Form vorzustellen? Es liegt nahe, hier die illokutionär relevanten Merkmale ins Spiel zu bringen, die dafür sorgen, daß ein Sprechakt, z. B. ein assertiver, auch als solcher erkannt wird. Zu nennen sind hier vor allem der Modus des Verbs, die Verbstellung, Adverbien, Partikeln, der spezielle propositionale Gehalt, die Intonation etc. (vgl. Vanderveken 1990: 9; Rolf 1997: 56ff.). Grices an der Sprechakttheorie ausgerichtete Begriffsbestimmung des von ihm favorisierten Sinns von 'sagen' erinnert stark an Austins Ausführungen zum lokutionären und illokutionären Akt. Grice scheint den Umstand, "daß ich immer, wenn ich etwas sage (bloße Ausrufe wie 'Verdammt!' und 'Au!' vielleicht ausgenommen), sowohl lokutionäre als auch illokutionäre Akte vollziehe" (Austin [1962]/1972: 150), im Auge zu haben, wenn er davon spricht, daß das Gesagte an den Vollzug eines zentralen Sprechakts gebunden ist.

Die Elemente, um die es hier geht - bei Grice geschieht das auf Stufe VI -, gehören zur konventionellen Bedeutung einer Äußerung, sie sind aber nicht Teil des Gesagten - für den Wahrheitswert des geäußerten Satzes sind sie nicht relevant. Insofern als sie nicht zum Gesagten gehören, sind sie auch nicht zu den konventionellen Formen zu rechnen, die indizieren, welcher zentrale Sprechakt vollzogen wird. Die Bedeutung dieser "problematischen Elemente" (Grice [1968]/1993: 91) sieht Grice, wie bereits gesagt, mit *nichtzentralen* Sprechakten verknüpft: Deren Vollzug ist abhängig vom Vollzug des einen oder anderen zentralen Sprechakts: Ein Ausdruck wie 'des weiteren' zum Beispiel, ist mit dem Sprechakt des Hinzufügens verknüpft. Mit Ausdrücken dieser Art kann ein Sprecher Bedeutungsaspekte ins Spiel bringen, die über das Gesagte hinausgehen: Die fraglichen Ausdrücke sind Träger konventionaler Implikaturen.

Grice bestimmt das Gesagte also im Hinblick auf den Vollzug des einen oder anderen zentralen Sprechakts, oder anders ausgedrückt, im Hinblick auf den illokutionären Aspekt einer Äußerung. Der propositionale Aspekt kommt dabei 'nur' in Form der Bezugnahme auf den Wahrheitswert zur Geltung. *Daß* das Gesagte an den Vollzug eines zentralen Sprechakts gebunden ist, ist unbestritten; der lokutionäre Aspekt kann jedoch nicht mit dem illokutionären gleichgesetzt werden. Es scheint vielmehr - das die These des folgenden Abschnitts - das *Sagen des zu Sagenden* zu sein, das in zentralen Sprechakten realisiert ist. Sollte sich diese Modifikation des Griceschen Begriffsapparats als zutreffend erweisen, muß neu darüber nachgedacht werden, worin die Realisierung nicht-zentraler Sprechakte besteht.

3 Das Gesagte und dessen Verwendung

Ähnlich wie jemand, der immer mal wieder auf ein vermeintliches Problem aufmerksam gemacht worden ist, räumt Grice letztendlich (fast möchte man sagen: um des lieben Friedens willen) ein, daß er "in einem gewissen favorisierten, in einem gewissen Maße meinetwegen auch künstlichen Sinne von 'sagen'" (Grice [1968]/1993: 85) spricht. Das Künstliche daran ist die Reduzierung dessen, wovon Grice behaupten möchte, ein Sprecher hätte es gesagt, auf die Satz-Bedeutung bzw. auf die für den Wahrheitswert des Satzes konstitutiven Elemente seiner Äußerung. Mit dieser eher abstrakten Propositionsbestimmung gibt sich Grice zufrieden; und im Hinblick auf das von ihm verfolgte Ziel, solche Phänomene wie Konversations-Implikaturen adäquat beschreiben zu können, scheint eine derart wahrheitsfunktional determinierte Satz-Bedeutung auch tatsächlich auszureichen: Der "bereitgestellte Apparat wird beliebigen Implikaturen gerecht" (Grice [1975]/1993: 247). Um nicht den Verdacht aufkommen zu lassen, er wäre sich der potentiellen Unterbestimmtheit des Gesagten (in dem von ihm anvisierten Sinne) nicht bewußt, macht Grice noch das folgende Zugeständnis: "Um jedoch ganz und gar zu bestimmen, was der Sprecher gesagt hat, müßte man (a) die Identität von x, (b) den Zeitpunkt der Äußerung und (c) die bei dieser Äußerungsgelegenheit vorliegende Bedeutung" (ebd.) mehrdeutiger Ausdrücke kennen. Das 'ganz und gar' bestimmte Gesagte, die konkrete Propositionsbestimmung, möchten wir hier als *Diktum* bezeichnen. Der Unterschied zwischen dem Gesagten (von jetzt an immer: im Griceschen Sinne) und dem Diktum läßt sich wie folgt auf den Begriff bringen: Für das Gesagte sind die Ausdrücke konstitutiv, die für den Wahrheitswert des geäußerten Satzes von Belang sind, für das Diktum spielt darüber hinaus die Berücksichtigung des wirklichen Äußerungskontextes (die damit einhergehende Referenzbestimmung indexikalischer Ausdrücke, die Ellipsenexplikation etc.) eine Rolle. Wie sich noch herausstellen wird, ist es durchaus sinnvoll, auf eine zum Ausdruck gebrachte Proposition so Bezug nehmen zu können, daß es einen Unterschied macht, ob vom Gesagten oder vom Diktum die Rede ist.

Betrachten wir zunächst den illokutionären Aspekt einer Äußerung. Der Umstand, daß Grice das Gesagte in einen engen Zusammenhang mit dem Vollzug eines zentralen Sprechakts stellt, ist im Hinblick auf die oben getroffene Unterscheidung zwischen dem Gesagten und dem Diktum erklärungsbedürftig. Daß jemand mit dem Äußern von X *gesagt* hat, daß p, wenn er einen zentralen Sprechakt vollzieht, läßt die Frage aufkommen, wie dann die konkrete Proposition, das Diktum, zum Ausdruck gebracht wird. Grice ([1975]/1993: 248) zufolge werden - im Hinblick auf die Gesamtbedeutung einer Äußerung - die Elemente, die nicht Teil des Gesagten sind, konventional impliziert, wobei diese Implikaturen mit dem Vollzug nicht-zentraler Sprechakte einhergehen. Die Illokution einer Äußerung scheint also aufteilbar zu sein: in den zentralen Sprechakt auf der einen Seite (an dessen Vollzug ist das Gesagte geknüpft); und in den nicht-zentralen Sprechakt auf der anderen Seite (dessen Vollzug konstituiert das konventional Implizierte).

An dieser Stelle ist es ratsam, sich zu vergegenwärtigen, was der Ausgangspunkt unserer Überlegung gewesen ist: Es ist der Umstand, daß der Sprecher mit seiner Äußerung etwas meint oder gemeint hat. Damit ein Sprecher überhaupt etwas zu verstehen geben kann, muß er auch eine entsprechende Absicht haben. Grice ([1969]/1993: 20) zufolge muß er (1) die Absicht haben, eine gewisse Reaktion beim Hörer hervorzurufen; er muß (2) die Absicht haben, daß der Hörer erkennt, daß der Sprecher (1) beabsichtigt; und er muß (3) die Absicht haben, daß die Erkenntnis der primären Absicht zumindest zum Teil einen Grund für den Hörer darstellt, die Reaktion, die der Sprecher bei ihm hervorzurufen beabsichtigt, zu zeigen. Ein wesentliches Merkmal der Absichtserkenntnis (= (2)) dürfte darin bestehen, daß der Hörer erkennt, welcher zentrale Sprechakt vollzogen worden ist - was durch die konventionelle Form des geäußerten Satzes angezeigt wird. Um aber der vom Sprecher intendierten Gesamtbedeutung der Äußerung auf die Spur zu kommen, um auch das Diktum zu verstehen, ist es notwendig, daß der Hörer erkennt, auf wen oder was referiert wird, welche Bedeutung mehrdeutige Ausdrücke in der konkreten Äußerungssituation haben - und nicht zuletzt: was konventional impliziert ist, das heißt welcher nicht-zentrale Sprechakt vollzogen worden ist.

Darüber hinaus besteht die Möglichkeit, daß der Sprecher etwas *konversational* impliziert. Grices Hinweis, der Träger einer Konversations-Implikatur sei "nicht das Gesagte, sondern nur das Sagen des Gesagten, bzw. das 'Es-mal-so-Sagen'" (Grice [1975]/1993: 265), spricht dafür, den Begriff des Gesagten, anders als Grice, vorrangig auf den Bedeutungsaspekt der jeweiligen Äußerung zu beschränken: Es ist nicht das Gesagte, das sich als Vollzug des einen oder anderen zentralen Sprechakts manifestiert, es ist das Sagen des zu Sagenden.

Bis hierhin ergibt sich folgendes Bild: Während das Gesagte in einen Zusammenhang mit den Wahrheitsbedingungen des geäußerten Satzes, mit dem Bedeutungsaspekt, zu bringen ist, läßt sich der illokutionäre Aspekt bestimmen als bestehend (a) aus dem Sagen des zu Sagenden, das in zentralen Sprechakten (die Träger konversationaler Implikaturen sein können) realisiert ist, und (b) der Verwendung spezieller Ausdrücke, die in nicht-zentralen Sprechakten (die Träger konventionaler Implikaturen sind) realisiert ist - wobei weder das Sagen des zu Sagenden noch die Verwendung spezieller Ausdrücke mit dem Gesagten selbst gleichzusetzen ist. Während mit dem Sagen des zu Sagenden eine Tatsache geschaffen wird (*daß* jemand etwas gesagt hat), wird mit der Verwendung spezieller Ausdrücke das Ergebnis eines Auswahlverfahrens präsentiert (und nicht nur einfach eine semantische Einheit bezeichnet). Dafür spricht insbesondere der Umstand, daß die entsprechenden Implikaturen der beiden Implikaturträger im Falle des Sagens des zu Sagenden nichtabtrennbar sind, im Falle der Verwendung spezieller Ausdrücke aber sind sie es (vgl. Rolf 1994: 122).

Bezogen auf die Absichtserkenntnis (= (2)) heißt das soviel wie: Um zum vollen Verständnis einer Äußerung zu gelangen, muß der Hörer (i) wissen, was gesagt wurde; er muß (ii) erkennen, welcher zentrale Sprechakt vollzogen wurde, um die mit dem Sagen des zu Sagenden möglicherweise einhergehenden konversationalen Implikaturen zu verstehen; und er muß (iii) erkennen, welche nicht-zentralen Sprechakte vollzogen wurden, um die damit einhergehenden konventionalen Implikaturen zu verstehen. Das heißt, daß zum vollen Verständnis des *Diktums* mehr gehört als zum Verständnis des Gesagten: Neben der Identität der Referenten, dem Zeitpunkt der Äußerung, der Bestimmung mehrdeutiger Ausdrücke etc. ist das mit dem Vollzug nicht-zentraler Sprechakte einhergehende konventional Implizierte dem Komplex vorauszusetzender Kenntnisse hinzuzufügen.

Hinsichtlich der Frage, ob Implikaturen generell als Sprechakte einzuschätzen sind, kommt Liedtke (1995: 43f.) zu einem negativen Ergebnis. Der Grund: Sprechakte, die keinen Äußerungsakt aufweisen, kann es nicht geben, oder anders ausgedrückt, dort, wo kein entsprechender lokutionärer Akt vollzogen wurde, liegt auch kein illokutionärer Akt vor. Liedtke beschließt seine Argumentation mit dem Hinweis darauf, daß es "keinen konventionellen Zusammenhang zwischen dem Geäußerten und der kommunikativen Interpretation, die wir ihm angedeihen lassen" (ebd.: 44), gibt - außer (man höre und staune) bei den konventionalen Implikaturen. Als Grund, warum die letzteren dennoch nicht als Sprechakte in Frage kommen, führt Liedtke die mangelnde Komplexität der Trägerausdrücke ins Feld.

Daß mit der Verwendung spezieller Ausdrücke (der hier thematisierten Art) Sprechakte vom Format eines *eigenständigen* assertiven, kommissiven, direktiven, deklarativen oder expressiven illokutionären Akts vollzogen werden, soll hier *nicht* behauptet werden. Mit dem Hinweis auf die vergleichsweise einfach strukturierten Trägerausdrücke, mit denen konventionale Implikaturen einhergehen, ist es jedoch auch nicht getan. Denn daß sich mit der Äußerung eines Satzes wie z. B. (6) ohne den Ausdruck 'mithin' ein andersartiger Bestand an illokutionären Akten manifestieren würde, davon ist, der Unscheinbarkeit des Ausdrucks 'mithin' zum Trotz, auszugehen. Nicht zentrale, sondern nicht-zentrale Sprechakte müssen in Sätzen wie (6) eine Rolle spielen, oder der Sinn der kommunikativen Handlung bliebe unverändert.

Ausdrücke wie 'mithin', 'des weiteren', 'aber', 'offen gesagt' etc. gehören einerseits nicht zum Gesagten, andererseits kann mit ihrer Verwendung aber auch nicht, wie im Falle konversationaler Implikaturen, etwas *anderes* gemeint sein. Da sie sich als Träger konversationaler Implikaturen nicht eignen, können sie weder einer der fünf Klassen illokutionärer Akte zugeordnet werden, noch konstituieren sie eine eigene zentrale Sprechaktklasse. Sie könnten aber nichtsdestotrotz ein illokutionäres Potential besitzen.

Das Problem, die Verwendung spezieller Ausdrücke der erwähnten Art sprechakttheoretisch in den Griff zu bekommen, hat Tradition: Die von Grice als problematische Elemente bezeichneten Ausdrücke bereiteten schon Austin (einiges) Kopfzerbrechen.

4 Der Überhang aus Austins tour de force

In Searles Einteilung der Sprechakte in die fünf Klassen der Assertiva, Kommissiva, Direktiva, Deklarativa und Expressiva ist eine der Klassen, die Austin ([1962]/1972: 165f.) ihrer illokutionären Rolle nach unterscheidet, nicht eingegangen: die Klasse der expositiven Sprechakte. Diejenigen Beispiele expositiver Sprechakte, die Austin ([1962]/1972: 178) für zentral hält (*feststellen, behaupten, leugnen, betonen, erläutern, antworten*), finden Unterschlupf bei Searles Assertiva. In Anbetracht dieser Beispiele kann man sich Searle (1992: 142) anschließen, der feststellt: "I do think that most of the actual acts of which the expositive verbs are true will turn out to have an assertive force". Doch Austins Liste für expositive Sprechakte ist länger. Sie umfaßt z. B. auch *anmerken, einflechten, einwenden, bestreiten, korrigieren, folgern, schließen, (mit etwas) anfangen, (als etwas) kennzeichnen, näher erläutern, weiter ausführen, (etwas so und so) ausdrücken, sich beziehen auf* u.v.m. - auch dies 'problematische Elemente', zumal deren illokutionäres Potential nicht von der

Hand zu weisen ist. Weder kann man sie unter den Tisch fallen lassen, noch lassen sie sich in ihrer Gesamtheit auf die Searleschen Sprechaktklassen verteilen.

Austin weist zunächst auf die Schwierigkeiten hin, die ihm gerade die Klasse der Expositiva bereitet. Mit ihrer Einteilung ist er unzufrieden, und zwar deshalb, "weil sie unglaublich zahlreich und wichtig sind, und weil sie einerseits zu den anderen Klassen zu gehören scheinen und andererseits in einer Weise einzigartig sind, die ich mir selbst noch nicht habe klarmachen können" (Austin [1962]/1972: 167). Ihre Einzigartigkeit zeigt sich unter anderem darin, daß sie vom Sprecher selbst getätigte Äußerungen zum Gegenstand haben können, daß sie Schlußfolgerungen beinhalten können, daß ein Sprecher mit ihnen Argumentationsstränge verknüpfen, auflösen oder kommentieren kann etc. Das Problem dabei ist, daß die in Form expositiver Äußerungen vollzogenen kommunikativen Handlungen mit den gängigen Sprechakten zwar kombinierbar, nicht aber gleichzusetzen sind. Austin zufolge machen Äußerungen, die dem expositiven Sprachgebrauch zuzurechnen sind, klar, "welchen Platz unsere Äußerungen in einer Unterhaltung oder Diskussion haben, wie wir unsere Worte gebrauchen; allgemein gesprochen, verdeutlichen sie" (ebd.). Expositive Äußerungen können also auch als eine Art Interpretationshilfe zu anderen Äußerungen aufgefaßt werden. Sie haben den Sinn, "klarzumachen, wie die Äußerungen zu nehmen sind, mit denen man seine Ansichten darlegt, seine Begründungen durchführt, die Bedeutung der eigenen Worte erklärt" (ebd.: 177).

Wie geht Searle mit diesem Überhang aus Austins tour de force um? Die zentralen Beispiele bringt er, wie gesagt, in der Klasse der assertiven illokutionären Akte unter. Den anderen Beispielen spricht er die illokutionäre Kraft ab: "I think that there are *no such things as* expositive illocutionary forces, because the verbs in question do not name a type of illocutionary force at all but another feature of a speech act, namely how it relates to the rest of the conversation" (Searle 1992: 142). Searle verbannt die Expositiva nicht aus dem Reich der Sprechakte, er schreibt ihnen allerdings eine andere Rolle zu: Sie benennen seines Erachtens ein anderes Merkmal eines Sprechakts als das der illokutionären Kraft, sie benennen die Beziehung, in der die Äußerungen, mit denen sie einhergehen, zum Rest des Gesprächsbeitrags stehen. Diese Rolle ist keine der illokutionären Rollen, auf die die Einteilung der Sprechakte in die fünf Klassen zurückzuführen ist. An dieser Stelle liegt es nahe, Grices Konzept der nicht-zentralen Sprechakte ins Spiel zu bringen. Unsere These lautet: Ein Teil der Beispiele für expositive Äußerungen sind als nicht-zentrale Sprechakte einzuschätzen (die vom Vollzug des einen oder anderen zentralen Sprechakts abhängig sind).

Searle veranschaulicht die Position, die er vertritt, am Beispiel des expositiven Verbs 'hinzufügen'. Daß etwas hinzugefügt wird, ist keine Beschreibung einer eigenständigen kommunikativen Handlung, da "just to say that something was 'added' does not tell me what sort of a speech act was performed at all" (ebd.). Des weiteren hebt er hervor: "a speech act could not be just a case of adding but must be some other type of speech act, as well" (ebd.). Diese Überlegungen können in einen unmittelbaren Zusammenhang mit Grices Ausführungen zu den nicht-zentralen Sprechakten gebracht werden: Eine Äußerung, in der beispielsweise ein Ausdruck wie 'des weiteren' verwendet wird, ist auch für Grice nicht einfach ein Sprechakt des Hinzufügens; es ist Grice zufolge vielmehr so, daß mit der Verwendung des Ausdrucks 'des weiteren' der nicht-zentrale Sprechakt des *Andeutens einer Hinzufügung* verknüpft ist. Die mit dem Vollzug eines nicht-zentralen Sprechakts einhergehende konventionale Implikatur besteht darin, daß *angezeigt* wird, daß der Sprecher eine nachfolgende Äußerung als Ergänzung zu einer vorangehenden Äußerung verstanden wissen will. Der Umstand, daß ein Ausdruck wie 'des weiteren' nicht an sich, sondern nur unter der Voraussetzung der Realisierung eines vorangehenden und eines nachfolgenden Sprechakts verwendet werden kann, zeigt die von Grice für nicht-zentrale Sprechakte geltend gemachte Abhängigkeit von dem Vollzug des einen oder anderen Sprechakts (in diesem Fall bezieht sich die Abhängigkeit sogar auf den Vollzug des einen *und* anderen Sprechakts).

Grices Vorschlag, neben den zentralen auch mit nicht-zentralen Sprechakten zu operieren, erweist sich gerade im Hinblick auf einen großen Teil der von Austin benannten Beispiele für expositive Äußerungen als praktikabel. Und auch Searles Ausführungen zum expositiven Überhang aus Austins tour de force stehen dem Konzept nicht-zentraler Sprechakte nicht entgegen.

Es ist nun an der Zeit, einige konkrete Beispiele aus dem Bereich expositiver Äußerungen zu diskutieren, Beispiele, in denen nicht-zentrale Sprechakte realisiert werden.

5   Nicht-zentrale Sprechakte

Zunächst das inzwischen bekannte Beispiel:

(6)   Er ist Engländer; er ist mithin tapfer.

Das Gesagte läßt sich unter Berücksichtigung der Wahrheitsbedingungen bestimmen. Wenn die Person, auf 'er' referiert, nicht Engländer, aber tapfer ist; wenn sie tapfer, aber nicht Engländer ist; oder wenn sie weder Engländer noch tapfer ist, dann ist die Äußerung von (6) falsch. Sie ist wahr, wenn die Person, auf die Bezug genommen wird, sowohl Engländer als auch tapfer ist - sie ist sogar dann wahr, wenn diese Person nicht deshalb tapfer ist, weil sie Engländer ist.

Die zentralen Sprechakte, die vollzogen werden, indem ein Sprecher (6) äußert, sind (a) eine Mitteilung und (b) eine Behauptung. Das Sagen des zu Sagenden manifestiert sich in der Mitteilung, daß die Person, auf die Bezug genommen wird, Engländer ist, und in der Behauptung, daß sie tapfer ist. Grice stellt heraus, was seiner Ansicht nach zum Sagen des zu Sagenden gehört und was nicht: "Während ich gesagt habe, er sei Engländer, und gesagt habe, er sei tapfer, möchte ich nicht sagen, ich hätte (im bevorzugten Sinn) *gesagt*, seine Tapferkeit folge daraus, daß er Engländer ist - obwohl ich dies sicherlich angedeutet und somit impliziert habe" (Grice [1975]/1993: 248). Mit der Verwendung des Ausdrucks 'mithin' wird ein nicht-zentraler Sprechakt vollzogen. Mit diesem geht eine konventionale Implikatur einher. Sie gehört nicht zum Gesagten, ist aber dennoch Teil der Gesamtbedeutung der Äußerung - und mithin für die Bestimmung des Diktums wesentlich: Die Verwendung des Ausdrucks 'mithin' ist mit dem nicht-zentralen Sprechakt der *Andeutung eines Folgerungszusammenhangs* verknüpft; das konventional Implizierte besteht darin, daß angezeigt wird, daß der Sprecher die Beziehung zwischen der Mitteilung und der Behauptung als Folgebeziehung verstanden wissen will. Hierin zeigt sich der expositive Charakter.

Ein weiteres Beispiel:

(7)   Sie war arm, aber ehrlich.

Die zentralen Sprechakte, die der Sprecher mit der Äußerung von (7) realisiert, sind die Mitteilung, daß die Person, auf die 'sie' referiert, arm gewesen ist, und die Behauptung, daß sie ehrlich gewesen ist. Der nicht-zentrale Sprechakt ist verbunden mit dem Ausdruck 'aber', die Verwendung des Ausdrucks 'aber' ist mit dem nicht-zentralen Sprechakt der *Andeutung eines Kontrastes* verknüpft. Zum Diktum gehört unter anderem das mit diesem nicht-zentralen Sprechakt einhergehende konventional Implizierte: Der Sprecher zeigt an, daß Armut und Ehrlichkeit für ihn einen Kontrast darstellen, er signalisiert seine Abneigung, arme Menschen für ehrlich zu halten (vgl. Rolf 1994: 122). Für die Auffassung, den Ausdruck 'aber', oder genauer, die Verwendung dieses Ausdrucks nicht als Bestandteil des Gesagten zu behandeln, sondern als Träger einer konventionalen Implikatur, für diese Auffassung spricht, neben dem wahrheitsfunktionalen Argument, auch der Umstand, daß die Implikatur abtrennbar ist: Sie verschwindet, wenn der Ausdruck 'aber' durch einen Ausdruck wie 'und' ersetzt wird, die konventionale Implikatur 'klebt', anders gesagt, an dem Ausdruck 'aber'. Ein Sprecher kann den Ausdruck *aber* nicht verwenden, ohne den Bedeutungseffekt - die Andeutung eines Kontrastes - ins Spiel zu bringen. Auch die These von der Abhängigkeit nicht-zentraler Sprechakte von dem Vollzug zentraler Sprechakte findet sich hier bestätigt: Die Verwendung des Ausdrucks 'aber' erfordert, daß der Sprecher auch sagt, *was* er im Kontrast *wozu* sieht; der Vollzug entsprechender zentraler Sprechakte ist notwendige Bedingung für die Verwendung dieses Ausdrucks.

Noch ein Beispiel:

(8)   Die Erde ist, grob gesagt, von einem Kraftfeld umgeben.

Zentraler Sprechakt ist die Behauptung, daß die Erde von einem Kraftfeld umgeben ist. Die Verwendung des Ausdrucks 'grob gesagt' realisiert den nicht-zentralen Sprechakt der *Andeutung eines Vorbehalts*. Das konventional Implizierte besteht darin, daß der Sprecher anzeigt, daß er für die von ihm aufgestellte Behauptung keine angemessenen Gründe anführen kann. Auch an diesem Beispiel zeigt sich die Abhängigkeit vom Vollzug eines zentralen Sprechakts: Nur zu sagen, daß etwas grob gesagt ist, reicht nicht aus, um zu bestimmen, welcher Sprechakt überhaupt vollzogen wurde. Der Beitrag, den die Verwendung des Ausdrucks 'grob gesagt' zum Diktum beisteuert, besteht, um es mit Austin zu sagen, darin, "klarzumachen, wie die Äußerungen zu nehmen sind, mit denen man seine Ansichten darlegt" (Austin [1962]/1972: 177) - in diesem Fall unter dem Vorbehalt, daß das, was der Sprecher behauptet, indem er sagt, was er sagt, von ihm nicht angemessen begründet werden kann.

Anstatt nun weitere Beispiele zu analysieren, möchten wir auf einen Zusammenhang aufmerksam machen, der einer weiteren Erhellung des Status nicht-zentraler Sprechakte förderlich sein könnte: Grices Konzept nicht-zentraler Sprechakte ist mit der Illokutionslogik von Searle und Vanderveken nicht nur kompatibel, es scheint sogar vollständig darin integrierbar zu sein.

6 Eine illokutionslogische Erklärung

Eine Äußerung wie

(7)   Sie war arm, aber ehrlich.

mag einem Vertreter der Sprechakttheorie erst auf den zweiten Blick Schwierigkeiten bereiten. Viel offensichtlicher verhält es sich da mit Äußerungen, die Ausdrücke enthalten wie 'ehrlich gesagt'; 'unglücklicherweise'; 'hurra'; 'ich bedaure, daß' etc. Daß die Verwendung solcher Ausdrücke Auswirkungen auf die illokutionäre Kraft der Äußerung hat, ist nicht von der Hand zu weisen. Ein Sprecher, der

(9)   Er ist tot

äußert, sagt, daß die Person, auf die 'er' referiert, tot ist. Und indem er das behauptet, ist er auf die damit zum Ausdruck gebrachte Aufrichtigkeitsbedingung - daß er glaubt, was er sagt - festgelegt. Mit einer Äußerung wie

(10)   Er ist - unglücklicherweise - tot

wird darüber hinaus eine weitere Aufrichtigkeitsbedingung zum Ausdruck gebracht. Der Sprecher glaubt nicht nur, was er sagt, er hält das im propositionalen Gehalt Repräsentierte auch für einen unglücklichen Umstand. Da jemand, sofern er aufrichtig ist, nur das für einen unglücklichen Umstand halten kann, wovon er auch glaubt, daß es wahr ist, besteht zwischen der Äußerung solcher Sätze wie (9) und (10) ein ganz bestimmtes Verhältnis: Ein Sprecher, der (10) äußert, legt sich auf den Vollzug von (9) fest. Im vorliegenden Fall heißt das: Wer beklagt, daß jemand tot ist, legt sich darauf fest zu behaupten, daß dieser Jemand wirklich tot ist. Allgemein gilt: Bei jeweils gleichbleibendem propositionalen Gehalt bewirkt die Verwendung zusätzlicher illokutionär relevanter Ausdrücke - von Ausdrücken, die sich modifizierend auf die illokutionäre Kraft auswirken -, daß die Äußerung - aufgrund der Bedeutung der Zusätze - keine grundsätzlich anderen, sondern 'nur' speziellere illokutionäre Akte realisiert.

Dies ist eines der wichtigeren Ergebnisse der illokutionslogischen Studien von Searle und Vanderveken. Ausgehend von der Zerlegbarkeit einer illokutionären Kraft in die sechs Komponenten illokutionärer Zweck, Durchsetzungsmodus des illokutionären Zwecks, Bedingungen des propositionalen Gehalts, vorbereitende Bedingungen, Aufrichtigkeitsbedingung und Stärkegrad der Aufrichtigkeitsbedingung formuliert Vanderveken sechs mögliche Operationen. Diese "consist in *restricting the mode of achievement* of the illocutionary point by imposing a new special mode, in increasing or decreasing the degree of strength of the sincerity conditions and in *adding new special propositional content, preparatory or sincerity conditions*" (Vanderveken 1990: 127f.). Auf dieser Grundlage gelangt er zu den fundamentalen "laws for illocutionary forces" (ebd.: 145ff.), von denen eines das oben beschriebene Verhältnis, in dem bestimmte Äußerungen zueinander stehen können, beinhaltet. Vanderveken zufolge ist davon auszugehen, "that an illocutionary force F_1 implies another force F_2 when all speech acts of the form $F_1(P)$ strongly commit the speaker to the corresponding acts of the form $F_2(P)$" (ebd.: 148).

So weit, so gut. Doch wie hat man sich den Zusammenhang vorzustellen, der zwischen Grices nicht-zentralen Sprechakten und Vandervekens speziellen illokutionären Akten besteht? Nach Grice werden mit der Verwendung spezieller Ausdrücke (der hier thematisierten Art) nicht-zentrale Sprechakte realisiert, mit denen konventionale Implikaturen einhergehen. Vanderveken zufolge läuft die Verwendung der entsprechenden speziellen Ausdrücke darauf hinaus, daß spezielle illokutionäre Akte vollzogen werden: Eine gegebene illokutionäre Kraft wird mit zusätzlichen Komponenten angereichert.

Diese beiden Konzepte weisen unübersehbare Übereinstimmungen auf. Erstens: Weder bei Grice noch bei Vanderveken ist die Verwendung der speziellen Ausdrücke dazu geeignet, einen Sprechaktklassenwechsel zu bewirken. Nicht-zentrale Sprechakte bzw. zusätzlich realisierte Komponenten der illokutionären Kraft können zwar als illokutionsmodifizierend bezeichnet werden, einen Wechsel der Illokutionsklasse aber bewirken sie nicht. Zweitens: Sowohl bei Grice als auch bei Vanderveken hat die Verwendung spezieller Ausdrücke zur Folge, daß der Sprecher *festgelegt* ist: Einerseits sind die mit nicht-zentralen Sprechakten einhergehenden konventionalen Implikaturen nicht annullierbar; andererseits legt der Vollzug eines speziellen illokutionären Akts den Sprecher auf den Vollzug des weniger speziellen Akts, der bis auf die zusätzlich realisierte Komponente mit diesem identisch ist, fest. Der Zusammenhang, der hier besteht, läßt sich wie folgt bestimmen: Nicht-zentrale Sprechakte sind an den Vollzug eines zentralen Sprechakts gebunden - und zwar an den Vollzug desjenigen illokutionären Akts, auf den sich der Sprecher festlegt mit der Äußerung, die einen speziellen Ausdruck enthält, der eine zusätzliche Komponente der illokutionären Kraft realisiert.

Sollte sich dieser Zusammenhang als zutreffend erweisen, müßte die Bestimmung des konventional Implizierten, das mit der Verwendung spezieller Ausdrücke einhergeht, auf die Beschreibung der Komponente hinauslaufen, durch deren Anreicherung aus einem einfachen illokutionären ein spezieller illokutionärer Akt wird - und umgekehrt. Nicht-zentrale Sprechakte könnten dann als mögliche Realisierungsformen einzelner Komponenten illokutionärer Kräfte identifiziert werden.

Ein Beispiel:

(6) (a) Er ist Engländer, und er ist tapfer.
 (b) Er ist Engländer; er ist mithin tapfer.

Ein Sprecher, der (6a) äußert, macht zwei Mitteilungen. Eine Äußerung wie (6b) setzt sich dagegen zusammen aus einer Mitteilung und einer Behauptung; zudem wird ein Folgerungszusammenhang angedeutet. Wer das Bestehen eines Folgerungszusammenhangs andeutet, behauptet das im propositionalen Gehalt der zweiten Äußerung Repräsentierte, mit einem durch die Verwendung des Ausdrucks 'mithin' - die den Vollzug eines nicht-zentralen Sprechakts darstellt, mit dem eine konventionale Implikatur einhergeht - angezeigten speziellen Durchsetzungsmodus: Es wird auf einen Grund für die Behauptung Bezug genommen. Auf die Realisierung dieser zusätzlichen Komponente ist zurückzuführen, daß in (6b) gegenüber (6a) eine speziellere illokutionäre Kraft am Werk ist.

Ein zweites Beispiel:

(7) (a) Sie war arm und ehrlich.
(b) Sie war arm, aber ehrlich.

Äußert ein Sprecher einen Satz wie (7a), dann macht er eine bloße Mitteilung (oder auch zwei). Ein Sprecher, der hingegen einen Satz wie (7b) äußert, macht eine *kontrastive Mitteilung*. Wer eine kontrastive Mitteilung macht, thematisiert die im propositionalen Gehalt repräsentierten Sachverhalte, wobei das mit der Verwendung des Ausdrucks 'aber' einhergehende konventional Implizierte dem entspricht, was aus dem einfachen illokutionären Akt einen speziellen illokutionären Akt macht: die zusätzliche Aufrichtigkeitsbedingung, daß der Sprecher glaubt, daß Armut und Ehrlichkeit in einem gewissen Kontrast zueinander stehen.

Ein drittes Beispiel:

(11) (a) Es geht dabei darum, daß an die Stelle des Verschuldungsprinzips das Zerrüttungsprinzip tritt.
(b) Kurz gesagt, geht es dabei darum, daß an die Stelle des Verschuldungsprinzips das Zerrüttungsprinzip tritt.

Mit einer Äußerung wie (11a) erklärt ein Sprecher, um was es bei dem thematisierten Ehescheidungsgesetz geht. Demgegenüber stellt die Äußerung von (11b) eine *pointierte Erklärung* dar. Ein Sprecher, der eine pointierte Erklärung macht, erklärt den im propositionalen Gehalt repräsentierten Sachverhalt mit einem speziellen Durchsetzungsmodus: Er zeigt mit der Verwendung des Ausdrucks 'kurz gesagt' an, daß eigentlich mehr gesagt werden müßte, um einer angemessenen Darstellung des thematisierten Sachverhalts gerecht zu werden bzw. um den assertiven Zweck durchzusetzen. Die Spezifik des illokutionären Akts, den ein Sprecher mit dem Äußern von (11b) vollzieht, ist also auf den speziellen Durchsetzungsmodus zurückzuführen, mit dessen Hilfe sich auch das konventional Implizierte bestimmen läßt, das mit dem nicht-zentralen Sprechakt, der mit der Verwendung des Ausdrucks 'kurz gesagt' verknüpft ist, einhergeht. (Zu weiteren Beispiele, insbesondere im Hinblick auf solche diktumscharakterisierenden Ausdrücke wie 'ehrlich gesagt', 'metaphorisch gesprochen', 'wie bereits gesagt' etc. siehe Hagemann (1997).)

Um es zusammenzufassen: Obwohl davon auszugehen ist, daß Grice "generally avoided the jargon of speech act theory and seemed rather unconcerned with its distinctions" (Bach 1994b: 271), ist sein Konzept der nicht-zentralen Sprechakte weder unmotiviert noch ein sprechakttheoretisches bzw. illokutionslogisches Unding. Wie sich herausgestellt hat, besteht zwischen den von Grice ins Feld geführten konventionalen Implikaturen, die mit nicht-zentralen Sprechakten einhergehen, und den von Searle und Vanderveken ins Auge gefaßten Komponenten illokutionärer Kräfte ein systematischer Zusammenhang: Nichtzentrale Sprechakte *sind* mögliche Realisierungsformen einzelner Komponenten der illokutionären Kraft. Die mit der Verwendung spezieller Ausdrücke (der erwähnten Art) einhergehenden konventionalen Implikaturen lassen sich unter Bezugnahme auf die 'Spezialisierung' des betreffenden illokutionären Akts systematisch beschreiben als Komponenten der illokutionären Kraft.

Literatur

Austin, J.L. ([1962]/1976): How to Do Things With Words. Second Edition. Oxford: Oxford University Press.- Übers.: Zur Theorie der Sprechakte. Stuttgart: Reclam (1972).
Bach, K. (1994a): "Conversational impliciture". Mind & Language 9, 124-162.
Bach, K. (1994b): "Semantic slack: what is said and more". In: S.L. Tsohatzidis, ed.: Foundations of speech act theory. Philosophical and linguistic perspectives. London: Routledge, 267-291.
Bach, K. (1994c): "Introduction". In: R. M. Harnish, ed.: Basic Topics in the Philosophy of Language. New York: Harvester, 3-20.
Bach, K. & R.M. Harnish (1979): Linguistic Communication and Speech Acts. Cambridge, Mass.: The MIT Press.
Grice, H.P (1968): "Utterer's Meaning, Sentence-Meaning, and Word-Meaning". Foundations of Language 4 , 1-18.- Übers.: "Sprecher-Bedeutung, Satz-Bedeutung und Wort-Bedeutung". In: G. Meggle, ed. (1993), 85-111.
Grice, H.P. (1969): "Utterer's Meaning and Intentions". The Philosophical Review 78, 147-177.- Übers.: "Sprecher-Bedeutung und Intentionen". In: G. Meggle, ed. (1993), 16-51.
Grice, H.P. (1975): "Logic and Conversation" In: P. Cole & J. Morgan, eds.: Syntax and Semantics. Vol. 3. New York: Academic Press, 41-58.- Übers.: "Logik und Konversation". In: G. Meggle, ed. (1993), 243-265.
Hagemann, J. (1997): Reflexiver Sprachgebrauch. Diktumscharakterisierung aus Gricescher Sicht. Opladen: Westdeutscher Verlag.
Liedtke, F. (1995): "Das Gesagte und das Nicht-Gesagte: Zur Definition von Implikaturen". In: F. Liedtke, ed.: Implikaturen. Grammatische und pragmatische Analysen. Tübingen: Niemeyer, 19-46.
Meggle, G., ed. (1993): Handlung, Kommunikation, Bedeutung. Frankfurt/Main: Suhrkamp.
Neale, S. (1992): "Paul Grice and the philosophy of language". Linguistics and Philosophy 15, 509-559.
Rolf, E. (1994): Sagen und Meinen. Paul Grices Theorie der Konversations-Implikaturen. Opladen: Westdeutscher Verlag.
Rolf, E. (1997): Illokutionäre Kräfte. Grundbegriffe der Illokutionslogik. Opladen: Westdeutscher Verlag.
Searle, J.R. (1971): Sprechakte. Ein sprachphilosophischer Essay. Frankfurt/Main: Suhrkamp.
Searle, J.R. (1992): "Conversation reconsidered". In: J.R. Searle, ed.: (On) Searle on conversation. Amsterdam: Benjamins, 137-147.
Searle, J.R. & D. Vanderveken (1985): Foundations of illocutionary logic. Cambridge: Cambridge University Press.
Vanderveken, D. (1990): Meaning and speech acts. Vol. 1: Principles of language use. Cambridge: Cambridge University Press.

Performatives and Standardization: A Progress Report

Robert M. Harnish, Tucson

1 The Problem of Performatives

The basic problem of performatives is to explain their 'performative force', the (often nonconstative) force marked by the performative element of the sentence, within the framework of a compositional semantics.[1] An account of performatives would be easy, were we to give up one or the other. If performative utterances were always just constative in their force, then the grammatical form of performative sentences could be straightforwardly declarative (or truth-valuable). On the other hand, if we ignore compositionality, then their performative force could be given by special conventions of force that attach to the performative element in (just) the performative sentence. But neither option is very attractive. Sentences (1a-c) really do seem to be used nonconstatively:

(1)   (a)   I (hereby) order you to leave.
        (b)   I (hereby) promise to pay you five dollars.
        (c)   I (hereby) declare this meeting adjourned.
        (d)   I ordered you to leave.

And these sentences seem to be semantically compositional - the meaning of the whole sentence is a function of the meaning of its constituents in other, non-performative, sentences and their grammatical relations, and the fact that they seem to be used to perform the act named by the performative verb (or noun etc.) that they contain. We will call this formulation of semantic compositionality, 'innocent compositionality', and it rolls together two separate principles: (i) *compositionality* the meaning of a complex expression is a function of the meaning of its constituents plus their (grammatical) relations, and (ii) *innocence* constituents contribute the same (range of) meanings to every expression that contains them. These principles can pull apart, as famously in Frege's analysis of indirect speech: indirect sense and reference, so long as they are construed as non-inherent, satisfy (i) but not (ii).[2] A grammar or truth definition that can treat the contribution of e.g. 'order' in (1a) the same as 'order' in (1d) will have at least two advantages. First, a compositional theory need not explain how such a word looses the (normal) compositional meaning it has in (1d) when it occurs in (1a). Second, a compositional theory will not make the prediction that each of these performative words, and the sentences they occur in, is ambiguous, and so it will not have to provide separate performative and non-performative clauses for each such verb in the language. Furthermore, we must solve the problem of performatives within the wider context of explaining how performatives work: how speakers are able to utter performative sentences with a (their) performative force, and hearers are able to understand what the speaker intends to communicate.

Recent work has clustered around one type of solution to the problem of performatives.[3] This solution has two parts, one answering to each source of tension in the problem. On the compositionality side the theory says that performative sentences are semantically compositionally declarative, and hence truth-valuable. On the force side the theory says that performative force is (pragmatically) indirect, and the result of a process or 'standardization'. Furthermore, this solution to the problem of performatives is presented within the context of a general theory of speech acts and linguistic communication. There are variations on this theme: Searle (1989) treats performatives as unambiguous and compositional, does not want to invoke special conventions of force, and wants to embed a solution to the problem of performatives within a more general theory of speech acts and communication. He criticizes Bach & Harnish (1979) and proposes an alternative 'declarational' theory. Bach & Harnish (1992) reply that (i) his arguments against the earlier theory are insufficient, and (ii) his alternative theory is defective. Recently Reimer (1995) has challenged Bach & Harnish (1992) and Harnish (1988) arguing that the notion of 'standardization' will not bear the burden we have placed on it. Bach (1995) attempts to defuse Reimer's criticism and defend the standardization thesis. But, it is not clear that the concept wasn't destroyed in order to be saved, or at least that will be part of my brief. To see this we must back up to a notion of indirection that seems to occupy common ground among the disputants. Which is not to say it has not gone unchallenged - see for instance Bertolet's (1994) interesting critique of the notion of indirect speech acts. Though this is not the place to discuss his worries in detail, they may reduce in part to a (terminological?) dispute over whether such events as expressing a desire, in uttering something, can constitute a directive *speech act* (see especially ibid.: 340).

2   Background

2.1   The Indirect SAS

Bach and Harnish (1979) argue for a conception of linguistic communication as cooperative problem solving, as a sort of invited inference to the best explanation. A speaker in a particular context against a background of mutual beliefs, utters a linguistic expression which has a certain meaning and as having that meaning with the intention that what the speaker wants to communicate be recognized in those circumstances by the hearer. One important pattern of inference relied upon by the hearer (and as anticipated by the speaker) can be schematized as follows. We will call this pattern the 'indirect SAS'.[4]

(2) *Indirect SAS*
L1. S is uttering e

Basis hearing S utter e

(a) e means ... and ___ in L

Basis knowledge of L

(b) S means ... by e, or S means ___ by e

(c) The supposition that S means ___ by e is contextually less appropriate, so

L2. S means ... by e

Basis L1, LP, MCBs

L3. S is saying that *(...p...)

Basis L2, LP, MCBs

L4. S, if speaking literally, is F*-ing that P

Basis L3, CP, MCBs

Either *(direct literal)*

L5. S could be F*-ing that P

Basis L4, MCBs

L6. S is F*-ing that P

Basis L5, PL

And possibly *(literally based indirect)*
L7'. S could not be merely F*-ing that P

Basis L6, MCBs

L8. There is some F-ing that Q connected in a way identifiable under the circumstances to F*-ing that P, such that in F*-ing that P, S could also be F-ing that Q

Basis L7', CP

163

L9. S is F*-ing that P and thereby F-ing that Q

Basis L8, MCBs

L6 records the (literal and) direct communicative act, and L9 records the (literally based) indirect communicative act.[5] Here the reader's attention should be drawn to L7', where it is required that the literal and direct act, F*-ing that P, would be contextually inappropriate if it were the speaker's sole contribution to the talk exchange at that point, and such contextual inappropriateness drives the hearer to search for another communicative act i.e. F-ing that Q.

Typical examples of such indirect inferences come from the class of indirect directives: the speaker utters "My mouth is parched" and intends to be indirectly requesting the hearer to give the speaker a drink. At step L7' the contextual/conversational inappropriateness of just mentioning that one's mouth is parched is what drives the hearer to search for an additional communicative intent that would make uttering "My mouth is parched" appropriate in the circumstances. This search terminates in the directive interpretation (see Bach & Harnish 1979: chapter 4).

2.2 Performatives and Indirection: Pattern 1

Bach & Harnish (1979: chapter 10.1) propose to analyze performative utterances as a type of indirect communicative act, thus securing the twin advantages of compositionality and performative force. The original inference pattern offered was:

(3) *Constative No Flouting*
1. S is uttering "I (hereby) order you to leave",
2. S is stating that S is ordering me to leave,
3. If S's statement is true, then S must be ordering me to leave,
4. If S is ordering me to leave, it must be S's utterance that constitutes the order (what else could it be?),
5. Presumably, he is speaking the truth, [conversational presumption]
6. Therefore, in stating that S is ordering me to leave S is ordering me to leave.

Notice: this does *not* conform to the SAS model of indirect directives - no maxim was flouted, and no contextual inappropriateness initiated the search for an indirect force. The inference in fact proceeds on the assumption that the maxims are being *obeyed* at the level of the direct act.[6]

Bach & Harnish (1992), in their reply to Searle, similarly suggest the following generalized version of the 1979 pattern of indirect inference for performatives, generalized in that it does not mention or require the utterance itself to be the vehicle of the performance:

(4) *Generalized Constative No flouting*
1. S is saying that S F-s that P ("I (hereby) order you to leave."),

2. S is stating that S is F-ing that P (ordering me to leave),
3. If S's statement is true, then S must be F-ing that P (ordering me to leave),
4. If S is ordering me to leave, it must be something, X, that S is doing that constitutes the order (default value: X = the utterance itself),
5. Presumably, S is speaking the truth, [conversational presumption: truthfulness]
6. Therefore, S is F-ing that P (ordering me to leave).

This version does contain, at line 2, a specification of the direct constative force of the utterance, but again it does *not* conform to the directive model of non-standardized indirect directives - no maxim has been flouted, and no contextual inappropriateness initiated the search for an indirect force.

2.3 Performatives and Indirection: Pattern 2

In order to construct an inference pattern that instantiates the original indirect SAS (see (2) again) we would require steps similar to the following (we leave inessentials out):

(5) *Generalized Constative Flouted*

L3
1. S is saying that S F-s that P ("I (hereby) order you to leave."),

L6
2. S is (literally and directly) stating that S is F-ing that P (ordering me to leave),

L7'
3. It would be contextually inappropriate for S to be just stating that S is ordering H to leave,

L8
4. If S's statement is true, then S must be F-ing that P (ordering me to leave),
5. Presumably, S is speaking the truth, [conversational presumption: truthfulness]

L9
6. Therefore, S is F-ing that P (ordering me to leave).

Notice that at step 2 a constative is mentioned, at step 3 it is recorded as contextually inappropriate, if it is the sole contribution, and nothing regarding the vehicle of the indirect act appears in the inference, just as no such reference appeared in the case of directives.

2.4 Standardization

As Searle (1975) emphasized, indirect directives, as well as other categories of communicative illocutionary acts, can grow, as he put it, "conventions of use that are not conventions of meaning". Bach and Harnish call these 'standardized uses'. Certain inferences can be shortened by precedent (and perhaps stipulation). In these cases Bach and Harnish said the illocutionary act had become standardized for this indirect use:

> T is *standardly* used to F in group G if and only if: (i) it is mutually believed in G that generally when a member of G utters T, his illocutionary intent is to F, and (ii) Generally when a member of G utters T in a context in which it would violate the conversational presumptions to utter T with merely its [direct] force, his illocutionary intent is to F. (Bach & Harnish 1979: 195)[7]

From this definition we can extract an important corollary that we will use shortly:

> *Corollary*: If T is standardized in G for F-ing, then if in just directly F*-ing S would violate a contextual appropriateness condition, then S is F-ing.

Typical examples of sentences that have become standardized for an indirect directive use are "Can you pass the salt" vs. "Do you have the ability to pass the salt". In these cases standardization knocks out step L8 of the SAS, the step requiring the H to find the indirect force of the utterance. So the inference for standardized indirect directives might be (we leave out inessentials; the line [1]-[5] in boldface are the main steps):

(6) *Standardized Indirection*
 [1] "Can you pass the salt?" (= e)

  L1. S is uttering e

  Basis hearing S utter e

  (a) e means ... and ___ in L

  Basis knowledge of L

  (b) S means ... by e, or S means ___ by e

  (c) The supposition that S means ___ by e is contextually less appropriate, so

  L2. S means ... by e

  Basis L1, LP, MCBs

L3. S is saying that *(...p...)

Basis L2, LP, MCBs

L4. S, if speaking literally, is F*-ing that P

Basis L3, CP, MCBs

[2] If speaking literally, S is directly asking H if H has the ability to pass the salt

Either (*direct literal*)

L5. S could be F*-ing that P

Basis L4, MCBs

L6. S is F*-ing that P

Basis L5, PL

And possibly (*literally based indirect*)

L7'. S could not be merely F*-ing that P

Basis L6, MCBs

[3] S could not be merely asking if H has the ability to pass the salt

Standardization of "Can you pass the salt?" T (= "Can you pass the salt?") is *standardly* used to request H to F (= pass the salt) in group G if and only if: (i) it is mutually believed in G that generally when a member of G utters T, his illocutionary intent is to F, and (ii) Generally when a member of G utters T *in a context in which it would violate the conversational presumptions to utter T with merely its [direct] force*, his illocutionary intent is to F (emphasis added).

[4] "Can you pass the salt?" is standardized for requesting H to pass the salt

L9. S is F*-ing that P and thereby F-ing that Q

Basis L6, L7' Standardization (corollary)

[5] S is (indirectly) requesting H to pass the salt

Notice that line L7' provides a premiss for the definition of standardization to apply to the argument. This happens via clause (ii) of the definition. Without it, standardization would not provide a premiss for the inference. Thus, in a straightforward sense, standardization short-circuits the SAS by *replacing L8* in the original indirect inference (2).

2.5 Two Patterns of Performative Standardization

Although Bach & Harnish (1979) discuss the standardization of performative inference, they never give a sample of such inferences. Neither do Bach & Harnish (1992). Harnish (1988) makes an attempt at such an inference pattern, but taking seriously the contextual inappropriateness in the analogy between performatives and indirect directives:

(7)   1. S has uttered "I (hereby) order you to leave",
      2. "I (hereby) order you ..." is standardly used to order,
      3. It would be contextually inappropriate for S just to be constating that S is ordering,
      4. So, S is ordering me to leave.

Notice that this inference is defective at step 3 because there is no step specifying the direct constative force of the utterance, and so the definition of standardization does not apply at step 2 - at least not on the model of indirect directives. To rectify this mistake we might revise and fill out the inference as follows:

(8)   *Generalized Constative Flouted*
      1. S has uttered "I (hereby) order you to leave",
      2. S is stating that S is ordering me to leave,
      3. "I (hereby) order you to leave" is standardly used to order,
      4. It would be contextually inappropriate for S just to be constating that S is ordering,
      5. So, S is ordering me to leave.

Line 5 now follows from the definition of standardization (see corollary) plus lines 2 and 4. Notice also that this *does* conform to the model of standardized directives - a maxim was flouted and contextual inappropriateness initiated the 'search' for an indirect force, which 'search' was short-circuited by standardization. We can put this in the pattern of the standardized indirect SAS:

(9)   *Standardized Generalized Constative Flouted*
      L3
      1. S is saying that S F-s that P ("I (hereby) order you to leave."),

      L6
      2. S is (literally and directly) stating that S is F-ing that P (ordering me to leave),

L7'
3. It would be contextually inappropriate for S to be just stating that S is ordering H to leave,

Standardization of "I (hereby) order you to leave" T (= "I (hereby) order you to leave") is *standardly* used to F (= order H to leave) in group G if and only if: (i) it is mutually believed in G that generally when a member of G utters T, his illocutionary intent is to F, and (ii) Generally when a member of G utters T in a context in which it would violate the conversational presumptions to utter T with merely its [direct] force, his illocutionary intent is to F.

L9
6. Therefore, S is F-ing that P (ordering me to leave).

Here we have a clear analogy with indirect directives, and the explicit use of standardization to short-circuit the inference - L8 of the original has been *replaced* with standardization.

2.6 Two Patterns of Standardization

We have been given two patterns of standardization in performative inference. The *first* pattern draws heavily on the analogy with indirect directives, and it finds a constative in the inference, which constative if the sole contribution to the talk exchange at that point would be contextually inappropriate, and so triggers the application of the definition of standardization. The *second* pattern is similar to Grice's example of implicatures that do not involve flouting a maxim, but rather conforming to the maxims. It does not find a constative in the inference which alone would be contextually inappropriate and so trigger the application of the definition of standardization. The stage is now set for the next round of controversy.

3 Current Issues

3.1 Constative Force and Standardization

Reimer (1995) is critical of what she calls the 'indirect theory of performatives (ITP)', and argues briefly for the alternative conventional theory of performatives (CTP). We will not be concerned here with the CTP. Her general strategy against the ITP is to argue that: [R1] there is no reason to suppose a performative utterance (PU) is constative, [R2] so, there is no reason to suppose the ITP is true. The Argument for [R1] seems to be an inference to the best explanation:

1. No amount of conscious reflection reveals that PUs are constative,
2. There is no reason to think we unconsciously process PUs as constative,

169

3. So, no amount of reflection conscious or unconscious would uncover the presence of a constative force in PUs,
4. The best explanation for 3 is that PUs are not constative,
5. So, PUs are not constative.[8]

Reimer's major task is to establish the first premiss, since H's recognition of S's communicative intent will probably have to be conscious. Her strategy in arguing for the first premiss is to argue against the analogy between *performatives* as standardized indirect acts and *directives* as standardized indirect acts, in that with the later, direct force is recoverable, but there are no clear examples of cases where direct force of a PU is (constative and) recoverable. Absent a general argument against introspectable direct constative force Reimer (ibid.: 666) takes one of the examples Bach & Harnish (1992) offer, and contests the intuitions by imagining a more elaborate scenario. Intuitions are not all that clear here and the analysis has various problems. Furthermore, as Bach (1995: ftnt. 5) notes, it is hard to have reliable intuitions in these cases against a background of standardization, because standardization specifies a belief state of the members of the group having the intuition. But other cases are available that are less easy to deal with (Harnish 1988). Suppose S is a Russian officer and plans to order H to the German front - which is so dangerous that all orders are required by the high command to be in writing. In signing H's order to the front S says "I hereby order you to the front". Here the utterance is both performative and descriptive, in that if S is actually signing a check for his wife's hat, what he says is false - and if S knows it, S is lying. So, the overall inference to the best explanation collapses if the explanandum is false, and it seems to be. And since claim [R1] is the primary support for claim [R2], [R2] is also yet to be established.

Bach (1995) attempts to defend ITP against Reimer's critique. He is concerned to argue: [B1] contra step 1 of the argument for [R2], i.e. that Reimer's case against PUs being constative is not good. And [B2] contra 2 of the same argument, that ITP doesn't require PU to be constative. Regarding [B1], we agree with almost all of the reservations Bach expresses regarding Reimer's case. He also advances an idea which if successful would help out ITP in two important ways, but which unfortunately needs elaboration if it is to succeed.

Here is the problem. Bach wants to argue that the reason why literal constative force is difficult to discern, as well as the reason why it is difficult to cancel (*I order you to leave, but I don't (order you to leave)) is that "the same belief is both expressed by the literal statement and implicated in the intention behind the performative act" (ibid.: 681). How is this supposed to work - how could this be an explanation? Here Bach mentions two principles, one general and one specific, though it appears that only the general one plays a role in the actual explanation:

General Principle (GP) intending to do something *involves* (but probably does not entail) believing that one is doing it (ibid.: 681).

This cannot be literally correct: I intend to ride my bike to school, but that does not involve in any way my believing that I am riding my bike to school. A simple revision:

General Principle (GP') doing something intentionally *involves* (but probably does not entail) believing that one is doing it.

The specific principle mentioned, but not actually used in the explanation is this:

Specific Principle (SP) the belief literally expressed in the use of a sentence of the form ' I V that S' is the belief that one is V-ing that S (ibid.: 680).

Analogously this also cannot be correct: sincere utterance of 'I ride my bike (daily)' does not express the belief that I am riding my bike (daily). (Worse for statives such as 'I know a little French': *I believe that I am knowing a little French). But disanalogously, it is not clear how to revise this principle, so it is perhaps fortunately not pressed into service.

Bach's explanation (ibid.: 680-681) of the above two difficulties (discernment, cancellability) involves the coincidence of expressed and involved beliefs - how? The idea seems to be that two chains of inference converge on this belief:

(A) 1. S utters 'I order you to leave',
    2. (Given ITP) S is literally and directly stating that S is ordering H to leave,
    3. Given 2, S is expressing the belief that S is ordering H to leave (assuming stating is expressing a belief).

(B) 1. S is intentionally ordering H to leave (indirect force),
    2. So, S believes S is ordering H to leave (GP').

Thus, the belief *expressed* in (A3) is identical to the belief *involved* in (B2). But how does this overlap or coincidence of belief explain the two phenomena it is supposed to account for?

Discernment Maybe the idea is that we don't see (A3) *because of* (B2) - that (B2) *masks* (A3). If this is supposed to be the explanation it will need some psychological justification (folk or scientific).

Non-Cancellability How does the explanation of non-cancellability in the form of 'I V that p, but I don't (V that p)' involve this coincidence of expressed and involved belief? (Some might say it is straightforwardly contradictory). A more likely candidate for a problem with ITP is what we might call the 'undeniability' of performatives, which contrast with ordinary indirect acts, such as directives in the following way: 'Could you pass the salt, but that's not a request, just a question' vs [?]'I (hereby) order you to leave, but that's not an order, just a statement'. The indirect force of the directive seems *deniable* in a way that the force of the performative does not. It would be nice to have an explanation of this, but I do not see one coming from coincidence of beliefs. So, though it would be useful for ITP if Bach's explanations worked, it appears that this account needs to be elaborated before these problems can be definitively put to rest.

The argument for [B2] involves the contextual inappropriateness of a sole constative force. According to Bach, this step (for instance, step 3 of inference (4)) "does not even appear in the original, fullblown inference supposedly abbreviated" (Bach: ftnt. 10) (the original being presumably the performative inference of Bach & Harnish (1979) recorded as inference (3) above). And it is true that explicit mention of contextual appropriateness of the constative force does not occur in that formulation. But explicit mention of contextual appropriateness is mentioned at step 5, in the appeal to the Presumption of Truth. Furthermore, and most importantly, Bach argues, *we don't need the contextual inappropriateness step* because with standardization we can, in eg. (4'), go directly from step 2 to step 4:

(4') 1. S has uttered "I (hereby) order you to leave",
      2. "I (hereby) order you ..." is standardly used to order,
      4. So, S is ordering me to leave.

Reimer (ibid.: ftnt. 6) worries that without step 3, there is no reason to call the inference indirect, and so no reason to call this an *indirect* theory of performatives. Bach (ibid.: 683) agrees that this "eliminates a characteristic feature of indirect speech acts", but goes on to claim (ibid.) that "it is precisely the absence of this step that distinguishes cases of standardized indirection." Bach adds that there is no need to rule out the constative explicitly.

As we have seen, this is controversial. Standardization should be viewed as short-circuiting the full inference by immediately providing a specification of the indirect act, given the contextual information that one is in the offing - it obviates at least some figuring out. Standardization should not be viewed as eliminating reference to a contextually inappropriate (constative) act. There are a couple of reasons for supposing that it should involve such reference. First, without such a reference, performatives are only indirect *historically*, in they way that dead metaphors ('foot of the mountain', 'neck of the bottle') are only nonliteral historically. Second, as we have already seen, given the way standardization was originally characterized in Bach & Harnish (1979), it is not clear how standardization could be used as a step in an inference when one of its conditions referring to such an act is not met, the condition requiring contextual inappropriateness.

Finally, Bach (ibid.: 683) argues against Reimer that "If her conclusion about performatives were correct [they are not indirect without contextual inappropriateness], it would generalize to other sorts of standardized indirect acts and rule out their possibility altogether [...] 'Why don't you leave?' would not count as [an] indirect request, but as [a] direct but nonliteral request. Yet they are indirect, even though they are standardized. So Reimer's conclusion rules out too much." This is puzzling. It was Reimer's strategy to argue that contra Bach and Harnish, there is a *disanalogy* between indirect directives and performatives in that with indirect directives the constative (or question) force can be recovered, but with performatives it cannot (we reviewed that argument in the previous section). So Reimer can claim that the conclusion does *not* generalize to indirect directives. She can adopt the short-circuited inference view of standardization for directives, but deny it for performatives.

3.2 The State of Play

So where are we? If we accept performatives as genuinely indirect and standardized, we have to acknowledge a constative basis, but then we face the introspection problem - although the constative force can become more apparent in cases where the vehicle is some collateral act (such as in the Russian soldier example). Seeing (simple) performatives as falling together with hedged ("I can recommend the Merlot") and embedded ("I would have to recommend the Merlot") performatives increases pressure to see them as normal compositional declarative sentences (see Bach & Harnish: 10.2, 10.3), but this is not definitive, because one who held that (simple) performatives were governed by conventions or rules that make explicit (rather than describe) the force of their utterance might try to extend such conventions or rules from the simple performative prefix ('I (hereby) VP-perf that P' and variations thereof) to hedged and embedded prefixes as well. However, the systematic assignment of such conventions or rules to large pieces of sentences could prove difficult to pull off non-compositionally (or even finitely). And if done compositionally, it might be difficult to keep such assigned conventions or rules from endowing the sentence with another meaning, in which case it would contradict not only ambiguity intuitions (Searle 1989) and evidence (Harnish 1989: 99ff.)), but would highlight the need to explain the consistency of non-performative continuations such as: "I might recommend the Merlot [but I might not]", or "I would have to recommend the Merlot [if asked, but not otherwise]". Furthermore, something needs to be said about the nature of these conventions or rules. If we bypass the constative step we avoid the introspection problem, but we do not have a case of standardized *indirect* speech acts, we will have only a theory which recognizes the historically indirect character of performatives. We will then need a detailed and explicit account of the connection between the utterance and the performative act that does not appeal to standardization (as defined) with its reference to a constative basis.

The upshot, then, is that all three theories have work to do: the standardized indirect theory of performative (SITP) still needs to solve the introspection problem, the conventional theory of performatives (CTP) still needs to solve the convention problem, and the pseudo-standardized indirect theory of performatives (PSITP) still need to solve the pseudo-standardization problem.[9] Or we need a very different kind of theory, but that is a story for another occasion.

Notes

1   We will use 'performative' as short for both a 'performative sentence' and the 'performative utterance' of a performative sentence. Context will make it clear when one, or both, is meant.
2   See Davidson (1968), Barwise & Perry (1983: chapter 8), and Crimmins (1992: chapter 1) for further discussion. Fodor & Pylyshyn (1988) in their extended discussion call compositional 'combinatorial' and they call innocence 'compositional'.
3   See Bach & Harnish (1979), Harnish (1988).
4   The annotations can be found in Bach & Harnish (1979: chapter 4), and are not essential for the purposes of this paper.

5   There are of course inference schemes for nonliteral direct and indirect acts, see Bach & Harnish (1979: chapter 4).
6   This is reminiscent of Grice's (1975) group A particularized conversational implicature where no maxim is flouted; for instance saying "There is a gas station around the corner" to someone who has announced they are out of gas. Such examples pose a problem for Grice's characterization of conversational implicature, though not for our notion of indirection, because Grice insists that such implicatures be capable of being worked out (even when arrived at intuitively) and such working out involves flouting a maxim at the level of what is said. Group A implicatures, which I discussed earlier under the label of 'direct implicatures' (Harnish 1976), seem to be forerunners of what has come to be called 'explicature' (Sperber & Wilson 1986; Carston 1988; Récanati 1989), or 'impliciture' (Bach 1994). In these cases the maxims of conversation, in conjunction with sentence meaning and context, are used fill out what is said: "There's a gas station [which is open now and is selling gas] around the corner." So Grice is not quite as guilty as is commonly thought of failing to see a category of information in communication between what is (explicitly) said and what is conversationally (via flouting) implicated.
7   Bach & Harnish (1979) originally had "literally determined" for "direct", but that is too strong because direct *nonliteral* acts can become standardized, as in the case of some figures of speech. What is important here is the directness of the base act, not its literality.
8   Reimer (1995: ftnt. 29) says that her central point against Bach and Harnish does not affect Searle's (1989) declarational theory of performatives, but it does, since her basic point is that PUs are not constative and Searle derives a constative act from a performative utterance - see the last few lines of Searle's communicative inference.
9   Bach (1995) does not elaborate.

References

Barwise, J. & J. Perry (1983): Situations and Attitudes. Cambridge, Mass.: The MIT Press.
Bach, K. & R. Harnish (1979): Linguistic Communication and Speech Acts. Cambridge, Mass.: The MIT Press.
Bach, K. (1994): "Conversational Impliciture". Mind and Language 9, 124-162.
Bach, K. (1995): "Standardization vs Conventionalization". Linguistics and Philosophy 18, 677-686.
Bertolet, R. (1994): "Are There Indirect Speech Acts?". In: S.L. Tsohatzidis, ed.: Foundations of Speech Act Theory. London: Routledge.
Carston, R. (1988): "Implicature, Explicature, and Truth-Theoretic Semantics". In: R. Kempson, ed.: Mental Representation: The Interface Between Language and Reality. Cambidge: Cambridge University Press. Reprinted in: S. Davis, ed. (1991): Pragmatics. Oxford: Oxford University Press.
Crimmins, M. (1992): Talk About Beliefs. Cambridge, Mass.: The MIT Press.
Davidson, D. (1968): "On Saying That". Synthese 19, 130-146.
Fodor, J. & Z. Pylyshyn (1988): "Connectionism and Cognitive Architecture". Cognition 28, 3-71.
Harnish, R. (1976): "Logical Form and Implicature". In: T. Bever et al., eds.: An Integrated Theory of Linguistic Descriptions. New York: Crowell. Reprinted in: S. Davis, ed. (1991): Pragmatics. Oxford: Oxford University Press.
Harnish, R. (1988): "Performatives are Default Reflexive Standardized Indirect Acts". Acta Linguistica Hungarica 38 (1-4), 83-106.
Récanati, F. (1989): "The Pragmatics of What is Said". Mind and Language 4, 295-329. Reprinted in: S. Davis, ed. (1991): Pragmatics. Oxford: Oxford University Press.

Reimer, M. (1995): "Performative Utterances: a Reply to Bach and Harnish". Linguistics and Philosophy 18, 655-675.
Searle, J.R. (1975): Indirect Speech Acts. In: P. Cole & J. Morgan, eds.: Syntax and Semantics, Vol. 3. New York: Academic Press.
Searle, J.R. (1989): "How Performatives Work". Linguistics and Philosophy 12, 535-558. Reprinted in: R. Harnish, ed. (1994): Basic Topics in the Philosophy of Language. Englewood Cliffs, NJ: Prentice Hall.
Sperber, D. & D. Wilson (1986). Relevance. Cambridge, Mass.: Harvard University Press.

Kategorien der Unterhaltsamkeit.
Grundlagen einer Theorie der Unterhaltung mit kritischem Rückgriff auf Grice

Josef Klein, Koblenz

1   Ein Theoriedefizit

Es ist erstaunlich, daß in einer Zeit, in der die Bedeutung von unterhaltungsorientierten Kommunikationsangeboten vor allem in den Massenmedien ebenso wie die Kritik an dieser Entwicklung unstreitig zunehmen, für die Analyse von Unterhaltungskommunikation bisher ein theoretischer Bezugsrahmen fehlt, der dem vergleichbar ist, was im Bereich der Informationskommunikation der Gricesche Entwurf darstellt. Grice buchstabiert das grundlegende "Kooperationsprinzip" in Form von Maximen aus, in denen sich

- Informativität
- Wahrheit
- Relevanz
- Klarheit

als grundlegende Kategorien manifestieren.[1]

Grice geht in seinem Entwurf zwar von Beispielen dialogischer Privatkommunikation aus. Da die Maximen für das Sprecherverhalten aber aus einer (tendenziell universellen) Rezipientenperspektive formuliert sind, ist die Gricesche Theorie auch in der Analyse und Kritik von Einwegkommunikation, z.B. von massenmedialer Kommunikation verwendbar. Dies hat für das Genre "Fernsehnachrichten" Straßner gezeigt,[2] und in rezeptionsanalytischen Untersuchungen von Zuschauerurteilen über das Kommunikationsverhalten von Politikern im Rahmen des Genres "Politische Fernsehdiskussion" in der zweiten Hälfte der 80er Jahre[3] konnte nachgewiesen werden, daß die Griceschen Kategorien mit leichten Genre-spezifischen Modifikationen und Erweiterungen bestimmend sind für die Ansprüche, die Zuschauer/-innen an diskutierende Politiker/-innen stellen.[4] Dies ist hier im Hinblick auf die Chance für einen sinnvollen Bezug auf Grice wichtig, weil dieser Beitrag sich auf Unterhaltungskommunikation im Sinne von 'entertainment' konzentriert, also auf einen Kommunikationstypus, der, anders als ein Gespräch mit wechselnder Rollenteilung zwischen den Teilnehmern, primär als Einwegkommunikation abläuft, bei der die Rollen festliegen: hier der Produzent des Unterhaltungsangebots, dort die Rezipienten mit weitgehender Beschränkung eventueller kommunikativer Aktivitäten auf Beifalls- oder Mißfallensäußerungen.

Wichtige Bestandteile einer Theorie sind die zentralen, den Gegenstandsbereich konzeptuell erfassenden und gliedernden Kategorien und die Klärung der Systematik der Verhältnisse dieser Kategorien zueinander. Hier soll versucht werden, die Kategorien der Unterhaltung nicht additiv zu den Kategorien der Informationskommunikation hinzuzustellen, sondern für beide ein gemeinsames theoretisches Fundament zu finden.

2 Vortheoretische Ansätze

"Unterhaltung" kann nicht unabhängig davon bestimmt werden, wodurch sich Rezipienten unterhalten fühlen. Daher ist es als heuristischer Einstieg methodisch sinnvoll, bei Begriffen anzusetzen, die als Bezeichnungen für Unterhaltungserleben und/oder für Unterhaltungsansprüche von Rezipienten akzeptiert und/oder formuliert werden. So hat Dehm in ihrer Studie zur Fernsehunterhaltung in einem Assoziationstest 309 durch Zufallsstichprobe ausgewählten Probanden 35 Adjektive vorgelegt und nach der Nähe zum Begriff 'Unterhaltung' bestimmen lassen. Dehm löst die Mehrdeutigkeit des Lexems "Unterhaltung" zunächst nicht auf. Sie zielt dabei sowohl auf primär mediale Unterhaltung im Sinne von "entertainment" als auch auf "soziale" Unterhaltung im Sinne von "talk", was sich übrigens auch in der Auswahl der Adjektive niederschlägt, die sie den Probanden vorlegt.[5] Dieselbe Liste wird den Probanden dann ein zweites Mal vorgelegt - diesmal sind die Adjektive auf ihre Nähe zu "Unterhaltungssendungen im Fernsehen" zu bestimmen.[6] Die Adjektive mit der jeweils größten Nähe und der jeweils größten Entfernung stimmen in beiden Zuordnungsdurchgängen zwar weitgehend überein. Doch wegen der linguistisch problematischen Vermischung zweier Bedeutungen von "Unterhaltung" im ersten Durchgang, ist das Ergebnis der zweiten Zuordnung für unseren Zweck interessanter. Die acht Adjektive, die der Rubrik "paßt gut zu 'Unter-haltungssendungen im Fernsehen'" am häufigsten zugeordnet wurden, sind:

- lustig
- leicht
- abwechslungsreich
- verständlich
- angenehm
- spannend
- interessant
- lebendig

Am häufigsten der Rubrik "paßt gar nicht zu 'Unterhaltungssendungen im Fernsehen'" wurden zugeordnet:

- kompliziert
- kraftvoll

- traurig
- ehrlich
- anspruchsvoll
- wertvoll
- wichtig
- eintönig[7]

Aufgrund ihrer Untersuchung kommt Dehm zu dem Ergebnis: "Als konstituierende Elemente von Unterhaltung schlechthin können *Spaß*, *Abwechslung* von der Tageshetze und - wenn auch nicht in so starkem Maße - *Genuß* sowie das Erhalten neuer *Informationen* gelten. Es handelt sich hier um Merkmale, die beide Unterhaltungsformen (soziale und mediale J.K.) haben, die diese miteinander verbindet und als Kern von Unterhaltung angesehen werden können.

Für *Fernseh*-Unterhaltung typischer sind neben der *Entspannung*, die dabei empfundene *Spannung*, daß man sich *nicht anstrengen* muß und auch daß *keine Forderungen* gestellt werden."[8]

Dehms Untersuchung ist eine wichtige heuristische Arbeit, aber noch keine Theorie. Abgesehen von einer - im Kontext der Gesamtuntersuchung am Rande bleibenden - Faktorenanalyse auf der Basis der Zuordnungshäufigkeiten[9] beschäftigt Dehm sich nicht damit, in welchem systematischen Verhältnis die Unterhaltungskategorien zueinander stehen. Die vorgegebenen Begriffe bleiben additiv, teilweise überlappen sie einander (z.B. "abwechslungsreich" und "lebendig") oder stehen auf unterschiedlichem Abstraktionsniveau (z.B. "gut" und "lustig"). Dazu kommt der methodische Mangel jeder Untersuchung, bei der Probanden lediglich aus einer geschlossenen Liste auswählen können: Es liegt die Gefahr nahe, daß relevante Kategorien außen vor bleiben. So ergaben sich in TV-Rezeptionsanalysen des Verfassers, in denen den Probanden keine kategorialen Vorgaben für ihre Beurteilung der Kommunikate gegeben wurden, folgende, im Vergleich zu Dehms Liste teilweise andere Kategorien, unter denen Unterhaltungssendungen vorrangig bewertet wurden (in alphabetischer Reihenfolge):[10]

- Abwechslung
- Amüsanz
- Erotik
- Interessantheit (insbes. im Sinne von Kuriosität oder Spektakularität)
- Spannung
- Sympathie

Auch die Kategorien der Informationskommunikation tauchen in den Zuschauerurteilen auf, allerdings in deutlich geringerem Maße als bei der Rezeption von Informationssendungen.

Auch dieser rezeptionsanalytisch ermittelte Katalog ist kein Kategoriensystem im Rahmen einer Theorie, und zwar aus folgenden Gründen:

1. Der Katalog ist additiv.
2. Die Theoriebildung darf sich nicht nur und nicht allzu eng an den Kategorien orientieren, die in Probandenurteilen artikuliert werden oder aus ihnen unmittelbar ableitbar sind. Denn bei allem heuristischen Wert, der Probandenurteilen zukommt, ist nicht auszuschließen, daß es relevante Kategorien gibt, die in Probandenäußerungen nicht (oder nur selten) thematisiert werden, weil sie z.B. so selbstverständlich sind, daß auf sie nicht expressis verbis Bezug genommen wird - es sind sozusagen konzeptuelle Ellipsen - oder auch, weil sie auf einem anderen Abstraktionsniveau zu formulieren sind als die alltagssprachlich geprägten Konzeptualisierungen der Probanden.
3. Es muß unterschieden werden zwischen Kategorien, die für Unterhaltung konstitutiv sind - wie die Griceschen Kategorien in ihrer Domäne[11] - und denjenigen Kategorien, die lediglich bestimmte, z.B. genrespezifische Ausprägungen von Unterhaltung sind. So steht die Kategorie sexuelle Stimulanz - von den Sendern meist euphemistisch als "Erotik" bezeichnet - im Zentrum von Unterhaltungsansprüchen an Soft-Pornos oder Entkleidungs-Shows, fehlt aber gänzlich in vielen anderen Unterhaltungsgenres.
4. Um für die Theorie nicht nur Beschreibungsadäquatheit, sondern auch Erklärungsadäquatheit beanspruchen zu können, ist es notwendig, die jeweiligen Hauptkategorien auf einer tieferen Ebene zu fundieren. Dies eröffnet u.U. auch die Möglichkeit der Verknüpfung mit anderen Theorien. In unserem Falle wäre eine Verknüpfung mit der Theorie der Informationskommunikation naheliegend.

Einen Versuch, die Kategorien der Unterhaltung in einen Theorierahmen einzuordnen, hat kürzlich Bosshart unternommen.[12]. Dabei bezieht er die "Assoziationen zum Begriff 'Unterhaltung'"[13] und die "konstituierende Elemente der Unterhaltung"[14] auf jeweils eines der "drei ineinander verflochtenen Teilsysteme" innerhalb des "hochkomplexen Humansystems": "physisches System", "psychisches System" und "soziales System".[15] Abgesehen von dieser - mit graphischen Mitteln symbolisierten - Zuordnung[16] bleibt das Verhältnis der angeführten Unterhaltungskategorien zueinander unbestimmt. Unter anthropologischen Gesichtspunkten mag Bossharts Ansatz interessant sein, eine kommunikationstheoretische Reflexion muß anders ansetzen. Das soll hier in Auseinandersetzung mit Grice geschehen.

3 Fundierung der Unterhaltungskategorien in Auseinandersetzung mit Grice

Grice erklärt lapidar, daß seine Maximen der Informativität, der Wahrheit, der Relevanz und der Klarheit "unter" die "in Anlehnung an Kant" so genannten Kategorien Quantität, Qualität, Relation und Modalität "fallen". Allerdings melden sich bei näherer Prüfung des Kontextes, in dem Kant diese Kategorien expliziert, Zweifel, ob diese "Anlehnung" an Kant den Status einer theoretischen Fundierung haben soll. Es handelt sich um die sog. "Urteilstafel", in der die Kategorien dazu dienen, die Urteile einzuteilen: der Quantität nach in allgemeine, besondere und einzelne, der Qualität nach in bejahende, verneinende und unendliche, der Relation nach in kategorische, hypothetische und disjunktive, der Modalität nach in problematische, assertorische und apodiktische Urteile.[17] Ein sachlogischer Zusammenhang der Griceschen Maximen mit Kants Kategorienkonzept ist nicht erkennbar. Das gilt vor allem für die Kategorien der Relation und der Modalität. Martinich hält es sogar für möglich, daß Grice' Kant-Bezug parodistisch gemeint sei.[18] Das bedeutet: Bei Grice ist das Fundierungsproblem offen.[19]

Im Folgenden wird dafür argumentiert,

1. daß die Griceschen Maximen bzw. die darin implizierten Kategorien Informativität, Wahrheit, Relevanz und Klarheit unter theoretischem Aspekt nicht in der Luft hängen, sondern daß sie in zentralen Faktoren der mentalen Verarbeitung von Kommunikationsangeboten fundiert sind,
2. daß diese Faktoren der mentalen Verarbeitung nicht nur die Basis für die Kategorien der Informationskommunikation, sondern ebenso das Fundament für die zentralen Kategorien der Unterhaltungskommunikation sind,[20]
3. daß sich von daher die bislang ungegliederte Vielzahl der Unterhaltungskategorien systematisieren und kommunikationstheoretisch verorten läßt.

Der Versuch, für Informations- und Unterhaltungskategorien eine gemeinsame Basis zu finden, stößt zunächst auf die Schwierigkeit, daß die Begriffe der Information und der Unterhaltung unterschiedlichen pragmatischen Ebenen angehören. "Information" ist ein Begriff der Illokutionsebene, "Unterhaltung" ein Begriff der Perlokutionsebene.

Die Kategorie "Information" impliziert den illokutionären Akt des INFORMIERENS: Wenn die sprechaktspezifischen Gelingensbedingungen erfüllt sind, u.a. die Voraussetzung, daß der Rezipient bisher keine Kenntnis von der Wahrheit des propositionalen Gehalts der Äußerung hatte, vollzieht man mit der Äußerung ein INFORMIEREN. Die anschließende Wirkung und/oder Reaktion des Rezipienten auf die Äußerung ist - anders als bei perlokutionären Akten - kein Identitätskriterium für die Handlung des INFORMIERENS. Ob man dagegen mit seinen Äußerungen Rezipienten UNTERHÄLT, das hängt von der Wirkung auf die Rezipienten ab. Wenn sie sich nicht unterhalten fühlen, dann hat man sie auch nicht UNTERHALTEN. Dann war die Handlung, die vollzogen wurde, ein mißlungenes UNTERHALTUNGSANGEBOT bzw. ein erfolgloser UNTERHALTUNGSVERSUCH. (Die Tatsache, daß die Wirkung auf die Rezipienten bzw. der Umgang der Rezipienten mit dem Kommunikat Identitätskriterium für UNTERHALTEN ist, hat im übrigen zur Folge, daß Rezipienten sich auch durch Kommunikate, die nicht als UNTERHALTUNGSVERSUCHE intendiert sind, UNTERHALTEN lassen können, z.B. durch die Polemik, in die politische Streithähne hineingeraten.)

Wie kann es angesichts dieses unterschiedlichen pragmatischen Status von INFORMIEREN und UNTERHALTEN gelingen, die Kategorien der Informationskommunikation und die Kategorien der Unterhaltungskommunikation in analoger Weise zu fundieren? Man muß sich verdeutlichen, daß die Griceschen Maximen *wirkungsbezogene Implikationen* besitzen. Grice formuliert sie zwar als Sprechermaximen - aber als Maximen für einen kooperativen Sprecher, d.h. einen Sprecher, der erwünschte bzw. zu vermeidende Wirkungen beim Gegenüber antizipativ berücksichtigt. Die Griceschen Maximen besitzen also ein *perlokutionäres Potential*. Wenn man dieses Potential herausarbeitet, wird gleichzeitig eine systematische Beziehung der Griceschen Maximen[21] zu zentralen Aspekten der mentalen Verarbeitung sichtbar:

Maximen der Informativität (M 1):
"1. Make your contribution as informative as is required (for the current purposes of the exchange).
2. Do not make your contribution more informative than is required."
M 1 bedeutet unter Wirkungsaspekten: Der Sprecher soll vermeiden, die vom Hörer bereitzustellende mentale Verarbeitungskapazität im Hinblick auf die *Informationsmenge* über- oder unterzubelasten.

Maximen der Wahrheit (M 2):
"1. Do not say what you believe to be false.
2. Do not say that for which you lack adequate evidence."
M 2 bedeutet unter Wirkungsaspekten: Der Sprecher soll nicht versuchen, den Hörer irrezuführen, und er soll versuchen, dem Gegenüber beweisbares Wissen zu vermitteln. Darin ist das hörerseitige *Ziel* des Informationsprozesses impliziert, über neues gesichertes Wissen zu verfügen.

Maxime der Relevanz (M 3):
"Be relevant."
M 3 bedeutet unter dem Aspekt der Wirkung: Der Sprecher soll sich mit seinen thematischen Selektionen an die Prioritäten halten, die die Gesprächsumstände verlangen, d.h. die als gemeinsame thematische *Focus-Prioritäten* für Sprecher u n d Hörer geboten sind.

Maximen der Klarheit (M 4):
"'Be perspicuous' - and various maxims such as:
    1. Avoid obscurity of expression.
    2. Avoid ambiguity.
    3. Be brief (avoid unnecessary prolixity).
    4. Be orderly."
M 4 bedeutet unter perlokutionärem Aspekt: Sprecher sollen vermeiden, die vom Rezipienten bereitzustellende kognitive Verarbeitungskapazität durch Mängel in der *Strukturierung der Information* überzubelasten.

So betrachtet, betreffen die Kategorien, die Grice in normativer Form als Maximen formuliert, die Eigenschaften des Kommunikats unter dem Aspekt zentraler Dimensionen des rezipientenseitigen mentalen Verarbeitungsprozesses:

– die Angemessenheit an das Prozess-Ziel (M 2),
– die Angemessenheit an die Focus-Präferenzen (M 3),

- die Angemessenheit an die Verarbeitungskapazität in quantitativer Hinsicht (M 1) und in struktureller Hinsicht (M 4).

Diese Dimensionen der mentalen Verarbeitung aber sind grundlegend für Kommunikationsangebote generell - auch für Unterhaltungsangebote. Nur diejenigen Kategorien der Unterhaltsamkeit, die sich unmittelbar auf diese Dimensionen der mentalen Verarbeitung beziehen lassen, sind grundlegende Kategorien und kommen als Pendants zu den kognitiv fundierten Kategorien der Informativität in Frage.

Meine These ist nun, daß sich bei Bezug auf die Dimensionen der mentalen Verarbeitung zwei Parallelreihen zwischen den grundlegenden Informationskategorien (I-Kategorien) und Unterhaltungskategorien (U-Kategorien) ergeben:

Dimension der mentalen Verarbeitung	*I-Kategorien*	*U-Kategorien*
Quantitative Angemessenheit an die Verarbeitungskapazität	Informativität	Abwechslung
Angemessenheit an das Verarbeitungsziel	Wahrheit	Unbeschwertheit
Angemessenheit an die Focus-Präferenz	Relevanz	Interessantheit
Angemessenheit an die strukturelle Verarbeitungskapazität	Klarheit	Eingängigkeit

Worin aber bestehen die zentralen Unterschiede, die uns zwingen, die Kategorien der Unterhaltsamkeit von vornherein lediglich als Pendants und nicht als letztlich identisch mit den Informationskategorien anzusetzen? Es sind im wesentlichen zwei Punkte:

1. Für die Verarbeitung von Kommunikationsangeboten als Unterhaltung spielt, anders als bei der Verarbeitung als Information, die emotionale Verarbeitung eine *konstitutive* Rolle - unbeschadet der Tatsache, daß Unterhaltungsangebote daneben in der Regel auch Gegenstand kognitiver Verarbeitungsprozesse sind (mit Ausnahme vielleicht mancher Arten von Musik).
2. Informationsbedürfnisse zielen auf die Gewinnung von Erkenntnis und von Wissen - unbeschadet der Tatsache, daß das Interesse an einer Erkenntnis oder an bestimmten Wissenstypen seinerseits durchaus emotionsmotiviert sein kann. Das Interesse an Un-

terhaltung zielt dagegen primär darauf, in einen angenehmen psychisch-physiologischen Zustand versetzt zu werden.[22]

Hier Erkenntnis und Wissen, dort ein Zustand als angenehm empfundener Unbeschwertheit - das hat Folgen in sämtlichen Dimensionen des Verarbeitungsprozesses. Die Unterschiedlichkeit im Ziel von Information und Unterhaltung - und damit in den Kategorien der zweiten Dimension, wenn man sich an der Griceschen Reihenfolge orientiert - ist wohl die zentrale Differenz. Erkenntnis und Wissen sind für den Einzelnen wie für die Gruppe in hohem Maße überlebensrelevant. Menschen suchen sie vor allem im Kontext dessen, was alltagssprachlich gern als "Ernst des Lebens" bezeichnet wird. Daher sind hier Fundiertheit der Information und Wahrhaftigkeit des Informierenden - bei Grice zusammengefaßt unter der Kategorie der *Wahrheit* - von zentraler Bedeutung. Das Unterhaltungsbedürfnis zielt demgegenüber auf Kommunikationsangebote, die den Ernst des Lebens geradezu ausblenden oder vergessen lassen. Für Unterhaltung ist *Unbeschwertheit* konstitutiv. Das gilt zumindest für prototypische Unterhaltung: Entweder sind die Themen harmlos - man denke an witzige Moderationen oder Game-Shows - oder, wo die Themen ernsthaft sind, z.B. Liebe und Leid in der Schmacht-Schnulze, oder gar Verbrechen, Tod und Grausamkeit in Krimi und Horrorfilm, da ist es die Fiktionalität der Produkte, die ihren Unernst verbürgt und so die Möglichkeit nahe legt, unbeschwert damit umzugehen. Der gemeinsame psychologische Nenner dafür ist das Verarbeitungsziel Entspannung. Entspannung ist ein Phänomen psychischer Ökonomie und setzt Spannung voraus. Wie sich in medienpsychologischen Experimenten gezeigt hat,[23] wird Entspannung als Ziel unter zwei Bedingungen angestrebt: Bei Langeweile werden vor allem Unterhaltungsangebote gesucht, in denen Spannung möglichst aktions- und abwechslungsreich aufgebaut wird - um dann am Ende die Entspannung des Happy-End oder heil überstandene Angstlust zu genießen. Vor dem Hintergrund stress- und konfliktreicher Lebensumstände werden dagegen eher Unterhaltungsangebote goutiert, die weniger durch Spannungsaufbau und Konflikte geprägt sind, sondern von vornherein angenehme Entspannungsgefühle vermitteln.

Die Differenz in den übrigen Kategorien sind eine Folge dieser Basis-Differenz zwischen den Zielen Wissen und Entspannung. Da sind einmal unterschiedliche Präferenzen bei der Focus-Wahl (Dimension 3): hier *Relevanz*, dort *Interessantheit*. Focus-Steuerung unter dem Vorzeichen von Wissenserwerb im Kontext von 'Ernst des Lebens' bedeutet Präferenz für Relevantes. Focus-Steuerung unter dem Vorzeichen von Entspannungsorientierung bedeutet Präferenz für Interessantes, Aufmerksamkeit-Erregendes, das nicht belastend wirkt.

Zum anderen wirkt sich die Basis-Differenz zwischen Wissensorientierung und Entspannungsorientierung auch bei den Eigenschaften aus, die im Hinblick auf die Verarbeitungskapazität beansprucht werden (Dimensionen 1 und 4): Die angemessene *Informationsmenge* (Dimension 1) wird in wissenorientierter Kommunikation bestimmt durch die - mit den Kommunikationsumständen durchaus wechselnde - Rezipienten-Disposition, für Informationen in höherem oder geringerem Maße empfänglich zu sein, sowie durch die Bereitschaft und die Fähigkeit, Informationen intensiver oder weniger intensiv mit vorhandenen Annahmen, Überzeugungen und Einstellungen zu verknüpfen und/oder in die verschiedenen Ebenen des Gedächtnisses zu transferieren. Demgegenüber ist bei Unterhaltungskommunikation die Verarbeitungsmenge weniger bestimmt durch kognitive Vernetzungsoperationen, die u.U. mit der Bereitschaft zu großen kognitiven Anstrengungen verbunden sein können, sondern durch die Aktivierung der Fähigkeit, den *Wechsel von* (mehr oder weniger großen) *Reizmengen* als angenehm wahrzunehmen, ohne sie tieferen Verarbeitungsebenen zuzuführen.

Und was die Kategorien in Dimension 4 betrifft, so gebietet die Priorität für die Verarbeitung von Informationsangeboten *Klarheit* im Sinne von Eindeutigkeit und systematischer Reihenfolge, damit die kognitive Kosten-Nutzen-Relation möglichst günstig ausfällt. Die Struktur von Unterhaltungsangeboten braucht dagegen nur *eingängig* zu sein. Denn hier geht es nicht um eine kognitive Kosten-Nutzen-Relation, sondern darum, den kognitiven Aufwand prinzipiell gering zu halten zugunsten des emotionalen Ertrags. Das bedeutet, daß ein Unterhaltungsangebot u.U. erhebliche chaotische Züge aufweisen darf, wenn es nur emotional reizvoll ist. Das Durcheinander stört dann nicht, wenn es gar nicht als Gegenstand für kognitive Verarbeitung empfunden wird. Man denke an Slapsticks oder an Büttenreden, wo ein Witz ohne plausiblen Zusammenhang an den anderen gereiht wird. Das Angebot darf nur keine Hindernisse für leichte emotionale Zugänglichkeit aufweisen.

Für die vier so gewonnenen grundlegenden Kategorien

- Abwechslung
- Unbeschwertheit
- Interessantheit
- Eingängigkeit

gilt, was auch für die grundlegenden Informationskategorien entsprechend gilt: Sie sind Ansprüche, die an *jedes* Unterhaltungsangebot gestellt sind - und insofern *konstitutiv*. Andere Kategorien der Unterhaltung, wie sie uns in den oben referierten prototheoretischen Arbeiten begegnet sind, gelten demgegenüber nur partiell: Nehmen wir Amüsanz. Ein Krimi muß nicht amüsant sein. Oder auch andere Kategorien: Eine Büttenrede braucht nicht spannend, eine Schnulze weder spannend noch amüsant, eine Game-Show nicht spektakulär und ein Slap-stick nicht erotisch animierend oder emotional stimulierend zu sein - aber keines darf langweilig, ernst, uninteressant oder schwer zugänglich sein, wenn es *unterhaltsam* sein soll.

Die meisten der gerade genannten nicht-konstitutiven Kategorien sind spezifische Ausprägungen der grundlegenden Kategorien. Oft liegt die Spezifik von Genres gerade darin, daß in ihnen Kategorien spezifischer Ausprägung dominieren - manchmal auch mit Anteil an mehr als einer der grundlegenden Kategorien.
So sind Action, Tempo und Überraschung, Vielfalt und Lebendigkeit Ausprägungen der Grundkategorie *Abwechslung*.

Amüsanz, Fiktionalität, Sympathie und Happy-End sind Ausprägungen der Grundkategorie *Unbeschwertheit*. Bei dieser Zuordnung sind vor allem Fiktionalität, Sympathie und Happy-End erläuterungsbedürftig: In Unterhaltungsangeboten mit den Themen Liebe, Tod, Grausamkeit (von der Seifenoper über den Krimi bis zum Horror-Film) ist es gerade deren Fiktionalität, die - anders als im Falle von Realität - für die Zuschauer die Chance verbürgt, sich damit nicht zu belasten. Sympathische Personen wirken nicht bedrohlich. Und wenn in Unterhaltungsangeboten das Happy-End zumindest für die wichtigsten sympathischen Figuren Standard ist, bedeutet das: Die Zuschauer können sich - zumindest am Ende - entspannt und unbeschwert fühlen.

In hohem Maße genrespezifisch sind die Ausprägungen der Grundkategorie *Interessantheit*, d.h. des Fesselns von Aufmerksamkeit: Amüsante Angebote, vor allem solche mit deutlicher Komik, sind interessant, insofern sie eine Art Provokation des Normalen darstellt - verbunden mit Unbeschwertheit. Spektakuläres ist interessant durch außergewöhnlich großes Ausmaß. Was spannend ist, ist interessant, insofern lange offen bleibt, wie eine erregende Angelegenheit ausgeht, vor allem ob sich die Waage zum Guten oder Schlechten neigt. Emotional Stimulierendes ist interessant, insofern es die Aufmerksamkeit in Form von Identifikation, Mitleiden oder Aggression in Anspruch nimmt. Erotisch Animierendes ist interessant, insofern es ein Mittel physisch-elementarer Aufmerksamkeitserregung darstellt. Horror-Angebote sind interessant, insofern sie eklatante Verstöße gegen die fundamentalen Werte Leben und Unversehrtheit darstellen und Aufmerksamkeit im Modus der Angstlust erregen.

Ausprägungen der Grundkategorie *Eingängigkeit* sind insbesondere Verständlichkeit (kognitiver Aspekt), Freundlichkeit/Sympathie (Beziehungsaspekt) und Konventionalität (Handlungsaspekt).

4 Unterhaltungsmaximen und Implikaturen

Auch die U-Kategorien generieren Implikaturen. So gut wie die I-Kategorien lassen sie sich in Maximen transformieren (*Mache deine Präsentation abwechslungsreich! Vermeide in deiner Präsentation moralisch oder emotional Belastendes! Präsentiere Interessantes! Gestalte deine Präsentation eingängig!*). Implikaturen entstehen vor allem dadurch, daß gegen Maximen ostentativ und eklatant ("blantently") verstoßen wird[24] - bei gleichzeitiger unbeeinträchtigter Geltung des Kooperationsprinzips ("Make your conversational contribution such as is required, at the stage at which it occurs, by the accepted purpose or direction of the talk echange in which you are engaged.")[25]

Grice hat das Prinzip der Implikatur im Bereich der Informationskommunikation expliziert. Unter analogen Bedingungen - a) das Kooperationsprinzip (mit Unterhaltung als "accepted purpose" der Kommunikation) bleibt gewahrt; b) es wird "blantently" gegen eine U-Maxime verstoßen - ergeben sich Implikaturen auch in der Unterhaltungskommunikation. So wie in informationsbezogenen Implikaturen der Schluß aus der Erkenntnis des Verstoßes gegen eine Maxime und der Kenntnis der jeweiligen Situationselemente eine Markierung und damit eine tendenzielle Verstärkung der Information bedeutet, so vermag der ostensive Verstoß gegen eine U-Maxime im geeignetem Kontext bei dafür empfänglichen Rezipienten erhebliche Unterhaltungseffekte zu erzielen. Das gilt für sämtliche U-Kategorien: So kann der ostentative Verstoß gegen die U-Maxime der *Abwechslung*, wie ihn bspw. der Kabarettist Rüdiger Hoffmann in Form übersteigender Langsamkeit, Redundanz und Monotonie präsentiert, außerordentlich unterhaltsam sein.

Die oben erwähnte Tatsache, daß Fiktionalität ermöglicht, auch ernste, im realen Leben belastende Themen wie Leid, Verbrechen und Tod als Unterhaltung zu behandeln, beruht auf einer Implikatur. Der thematische Verstoß gegen die Maxime der *Unbeschwertheit* wird 'geheilt' durch das Wissen um die Fiktionalität des Geschehens, das nicht zuletzt literarischen und massenmedialen Konventionen und der Ostensivität von Ankündigungen, Trailern u.ä. zu verdanken ist. Ein berühmtes Beispiel, wie todernst eine Präsentation genommen werden kann, wenn die Implikatur aufgrund fehlender Kontexthinweise auf Fiktionalität von Rezipienten nicht vollzogen wird, stellt Orson Wells' Hörspiel über eine Invasion von Außerirdischen dar, das in den 40er Jahren in New York bei Tausenden zu Panikreaktionen führte.

Auf dem implikativen Spiel mit eklatanten Verstößen gegen die U-Maxime der *Interssantheit* beruht zumindest zum großen Teil der Erfolg von Blödel-Kunst des Typs, den z.B. Helge Schneider mit Titeln wie "Katzenklo, Katzenklo macht die Katze froh" repräsentiert.

Dasselbe gilt für die Maxime der *Eingängigkeit* im Kontext von Clownerie oder Slap-Stick, wenn auf zunächst verwirrende Weise verkehrte, chaotische Welt präsentiert wird - oder auch wenn im Kabarett Karikaturen unverständlich redender Wissenschaftler vorgeführt werden.

5   U- und I-Kategorien in Texten

Auf der Ebene von Texten - oder weiter gefaßt: von semiotischen Produkten - mit Unterhaltungscharakter werden nicht allein die Grundkategorien der Unterhaltsamkeit und - in mehr oder weniger starker Profilierung - deren spezifische Ausprägungen realisiert, sondern auch Informationskategorien - allerdings in sekundärer Funktion. Am deutlichsten wird dies dann, wenn die Information (etwa über die Herz-Schmerz-Affäre eines gekrönten Hauptes) einzig der Unterhaltung dient. Auch in Informationskommunikation dürfen einige Qualitäten, die hier als Unterhaltungskategorien expliziert worden sind, - ohne dominant zu sein - nicht fehlen. Dies gilt vor allem, wenn die Verständlichkeit von Texten gefördert werden soll. Was Verständlichkeitsforscher als den verständlichkeitsfördernden Faktor 'Stimulanz' bezeichnen,[26] bedeutet großenteils die Realisierung von Abwechslung, Interessantheit (z.B. durch Kontrast oder Spannungsaufbau) oder Eingängigkeit (z.B. durch Anschaulichkeit oder Metaphorik). Wo die Dominanzverhältnisse nicht klar sind, spricht man heute in massenmedialen Kontexten von "Infotainment". Neu ist das Phänomen im Prinzip allerdings nicht. Die Reiseliteratur etwa kennt den Mix von I- und U-Kategorien seit Herodot.

Anmerkungen

1 Grice (1975). Zu den Maximen im einzelnen siehe unten S. 5f.
2 Straßner (1982: 49ff.).
3 Confrontainment-"Diskussionen" des Typs "Der heiße Stuhl" (RTL, Anfang 90er Jahre) gab es damals in deutschen Fernsehprogrammen noch nicht.
4 Klein (1988, 1989).
5 Dehm (1984: 132ff.).
6 Ebenda: 141ff.
7 a.a.O.: 143.
8 Ebenda: 189. Hervorhebungen von Dehm.
9 Ebenda: 134f.
10 Vgl. Klein (1996).
11 Vgl. Grice (1975: 49).
12 Bosshart (1994).
13 Als solche werden aufgeführt: *lustig, anregend, erfreulich, abwechslungsreich, kurzweilig, interessant, informativ, zwanglos, gesellig (Zugehörigkeit), lebendig, angenehm, sinnliche Lust*. Ebenda: 31.
14 Als solche werden aufgeführt: *Freude, Spaß, Spannung, Genuß, Entspannung, Abwechslung, neue Information, Entspannung (keine Forderungen)*. Ebenda: 32.
15 Ebenda: 28f.
16 Bosshart versinnbildlicht die Zuordnung mit Hilfe eines Schaubildes, in dem die "Teilsysteme" als drei Sektoren eines Kreises dargestellt sind. Die zugeordneten Unterhaltungsbegriffe sind außerhalb des Kreises angeordnet. Die Zuordnung wird jeweils durch einen Pfeil symbolisiert, der auf jeweils einen der drei Sektoren weist - in etlichen Fällen allerdings auf die Grenzlinie zwischen zwei Sektoren, so die "Assoziationen" *lustig, anregend* und *erfreulich* sowie die "konstituierenden Elemente" *Freude, Spaß, Spannung, Genuß, Entspannung* jeweils auf die Grenzlinie zwischen "psychischem" und "physischem System". Ebenda: 31f.
17 Vgl. Kant A (1781: 70) / B (1787: 95).
18 Martinich (1984: 21). (Nach Rolf (1994: 104)).
19 Dies verwundert nicht. Denn Grice gelang der große Wurf seines Maximen-Konzepts primär nicht in der Absicht, eine Theorie der Informationskommunikation zu entwerfen, sondern in der Absicht, ein Instrument zur Erklärung konversationeller Implikaturen zu entwickeln, die ihrerseits wiederum als Instrument der Erklärung der Bedeutungsunterschiede zwischen logischen Junktoren und Operatoren und deren Entsprechungen in der natürlichen Sprache dienen.
20 Wer sich an den Terminus "kognitive Verarbeitung" gewöhnt hat, wird den Ausdruck "mentale Verarbeitung" vielleicht verwunderlich finden. Der ist gewählt worden, weil bei der Verarbeitung von Unterhaltungsangeboten nicht nur der kognitive, sondern in hohem Maße auch der emotionale Bereich betroffen ist.
21 a.a.O.: 45f.
22 Vgl. Bosshart (1994: 38).
23 Vgl. Bryant & Zillmann (1984), auch Zillmann (1994: 45f.).
24 Vgl. Grice (1975: 49).
25 Ebenda: 45.
26 Vgl. Langer et al. (1974).

Literatur

Austin, J.L. (1962): How to do things with words. Oxford: Oxford University Press.

Bryant, J. & D. Zillmann (1984): "Using television to alleviate boredom and stress: Selective exposure as a function of induced excitational states". Journal of Broadcasting 28/1, 1-20.

Bosshart, L. (1994): "Überlegungen zu einer Theorie der Unterhaltung". In: L. Bosshart & W. Hoffmann-Riem, eds., 28-40.

Bosshart, L. & W. Hoffmann-Riem, eds. (1994): Medienlust und Mediennutz. Unterhaltung als öffentliche Kommunikation. Konstanz: UVK Medien.

Dehm, U. (1984): Fernseh-Unterhaltung. Zeitvertreib, Flucht oder Zwang. Eine sozialpsychologische Studie zum Fernsehleben. Mainz: v. Hase & Koehler.

Grice, H.P. (1975): "Logic and Conversation". In: P. Cole & J. Morgan, eds.: Syntax and Semantics. Vol. 3, New York/San Francisco/London: Academic Press, 41-58. (Original: Mimeo 1968).

Heringer, H.J. (1974): Praktische Semantik. Stuttgart: Klett.

Kant, I. (1781 = A / 1787 = B): Kritik der reinen Vernunft. Darmstadt: Wissenschaftliche Buchgesellschaft.

Klein, J. (1989): "Bewertungen des Diskussionsverhaltens von Spitzenpolitikern in Fernseh-Streitgesprächen durch Jung- und Erstwähler. Eine empirische Studie zur Ermittlung kommunikationsethischer Einstellungen". SuL 61, 79-87.

Klein, J. (1989): "Gesprächsregeln in fernsehtypischen Formen politischer Selbstdarstellung". In: W. Holly & P. Kühn & U. Püschel, eds.: Redeshows. Fernsehdiskussionen in der Diskussion. Tübingen: Niemeyer, 64-91.

Klein, J. (1996): "Unterhaltung und Information: Kategorien und Sprechhandlungsebenen. Medienlinguistische Aspekte von TV-Akzeptanzanalysen mit dem Evaluationsrecorder". In: E. Hess-Lüttich & W. Holly & U. Püschel, eds.: Textstrukturen im Medienwandel. Frankfurt/Main: Lang, 107-119.

Langer, J. & F. Schulz v. Thun & R. Tausch (1974): Verständlichkeit in Schule, Verwaltung, Politik und Wissenschaft. Basel: E. Reinhardt.

Levinson, S.C. (1983): Pragmatics. Cambridge: Cambridge University Press.

Martinich, A.P. (1984): Communication and Reference. Berlin: de Gruyter.

Rolf, E. (1994): Sagen und Meinen. Paul Grices Theorie der Konversations-Implikaturen. Opladen: Westdeutscher Verlag.

Straßner, E. (1982): Fernsehnachrichten. Eine Produktions-, Produkt- und Rezeptionsanalyse. Tübingen: Niemeyer.

Zillmann, D. (1994): "Über behagende Unterhaltung in unbehagender Medienkultur". In: L. Bosshart & W. Hoffmann-Riem, eds., 41-57.

Gesagt - getan: Über illokutionäre Indikatoren*

Frank Liedtke, Düsseldorf

Was fängt man als LinguistIn mit Sprechakten an? Diese Frage ist so alt wie die Sprechakttheorie (also nicht ganz so alt wie die Linguistik), und die Antworten darauf sind entsprechend vielfältig. In den letzten Jahren ist in der Linguistik ein Themenfeld in den Vordergrund getreten, das sich genau mit dieser Frage beschäftigt, also mit der Beziehung zwischen dem Gesagten (den geäußerten Sätzen) und dem, was man damit tut (den vollzogenen Sprechakten), und das unter dem Etikett "Grammatik-Pragmatik-Verhältnis" firmiert. Zu diesem Themenfeld zählen sehr unterschiedliche Ansätze: Zum einen die sprechakttheoretischen Arbeiten von Sadock (1974), Sadock & Zwicky (1985), Fraser (1987), Harnish (1995) - um nur ein paar zu nennen - ‚denen gemeinsam ist, daß sie die Frage der einzelsprachlichen Realisierung von Sprechakten angehen; dann die verschiedenen Ausprägungen der funktionalen Grammatiktheorie, die sich in letzter Zeit verstärkt der Untersuchung von Sprechakten und anderen pragmatischen Faktoren des Sprachgebrauchs widmen - u.a. Dik (1989), Givón (1984/1990: 1995), Engberg-Pedersen (1994); schließlich die im deutsch-skandinavischen Sprachraum entstandenen Arbeiten zum Satzmodus-Begriff, die auf eine Vermittlung grammatischer und pragmatischer Faktoren der Äußerungsbedeutung zielen (Meibauer 1987, Rosengren 1992/1993) sowie die Untersuchungen zu konversationellen und konventionellen Implikaturen (Rolf 1994, Liedtke 1995).

In den Diskussionen zum Grammatik-Pragmatik-Verhältnis ist ein Begriff nicht mehr wegzudenken, der trotz seines zentralen Stellenwerts eine eher beiläufige Aufmerksamkeit erfahren hat: der des illokutionären Indikators. Searle (1971) und einige andere Autoren haben ihn mehr oder weniger ausführlich diskutiert, jedoch ist er noch nie einer vertieften begrifflichen Analyse unterzogen worden. Ansätze dazu gibt es bei Ehrich & Saile (1972), Franck (1975), Sökeland (1980). Das Ziel dieses Beitrags ist es, einige Vorschläge für eine Explikation dieses Begriffs zu formulieren und so zu einer weiteren Ausbuchstabierung des Grammatik-Pragmatik-Verhältnisses im allgemeinen beizutragen.

---

* Dieser Beitrag ist die gekürzte Fassung eines Kapitels aus einer demnächst erscheinenden Monographie über Sprechakte und illokutionäre Indikatoren.

1 Wovon die Rede ist

Zu den Ausdrücken, die unter der Bezeichnung "illokutionäre Indikatoren" zusammengefaßt werden, zählen neben explizit performativen Formeln auch Modalverben und Satzadverbien, darüber hinaus die Wortfolge im Satz, der Modus des Hauptverbs, sowie die Intonation für mündliche und die Interpunktion für schriftliche Äußerungen. Die Aufgabe dieser Ausdruckstypen ist es, den Adressaten einer Äußerung sprachliche Hinweise zu geben, in welche Richtung sie bei der Zuschreibung eines bestimmten illokutionären Zwecks einer Äußerung zu gehen haben. So erfüllt *gefälligst* für einen Sprecher die Funktion, einen Satz wie

(1)   Du gehst ins Bett.

mit einem Indikator dafür auszustatten, daß es sich hier um eine eher kategorische Aufforderung handelt. Eine ähnliche Funktion haben Konstruktionen mit einem sprechaktbezeichnenden Verb in der ersten Person Singular, häufig unter Hinzufügung der Partikel hiermit, also die explizit performativen Formeln:

(2)   Ich fordere dich (hiermit) auf, daß du ins Bett gehst.

Es wird häufig die Meinung vertreten, daß solche illokutionsindizierenden Mittel nach einem minimalistischen Prinzip eingesetzt werden. Nur wenn die Umstände der Äußerung die illokutionäre Lesart nicht hinreichend festlegen, werden sie eingesetzt, um die verbleibende Unklarheit zu beseitigen. So werden explizit performative Formeln nur in entsprechend problematischen Kontexten eingesetzt, in denen die illokutionäre Kraft eines Sprechakts nicht erkannt wurde, oder in denen zwar die illokutionäre Kraft erkannt, aber nicht beherzigt wurde.

Allein schon um diese Auffassung diskutieren zu können, muß man sich Klarheit verschaffen über den jeweils vertretenen Begriff von *Illokutionsindikator*. Von der einen oder anderen Entscheidung hierüber hängt es unter anderem ab, ob es indikatorfreie Äußerungen überhaupt gibt, oder ob per definitionem jede Äußerung mit einer illokutionären Kraft einen oder mehrere Illokutionsindikatoren enthält. In einem ersten Schritt plädiere ich dafür, daß das Explikandum eine dreistellige Relation *Indizieren* darstellt, wobei als Argumente dieses Prädikats der Sprecher S, der Formtyp i und das Korrelat k (die indizierte Illokution) angenommen werden:

"S indiziert k mittels i" bzw. $I(s,k,i)$.

Hiervon ist eine zweite Relation zu unterscheiden, "Bedeuten", die lediglich zweistellig ist und als Argumente den Formtyp i und sein Denotat d enthält:

"i bedeutet d" bzw. $B(i,d)$.

Die Auffassung, daß *Indizieren* eine dreistellige Relation ist, der neben dem Indikator und dem Indikat auch der Sprecher angehört, berücksichtigt die Tatsache, daß Indikatoren ihre Funktion als Konstituenten eines Teilakts des illokutionären Aktes entfalten, der ja seinerseits als Handlungstyp auf einen Handlungsträger - hier den Sprecher - begrifflich angewiesen ist. Üblicherweise wird dies übersehen und die Explikation von *Indizieren* fälschlich der von *Bedeuten* angeglichen, indem die abkürzende Redeweise, Indikatoren würden eine Illokution anzeigen, für die ganze Wahrheit genommen wird; im Gegensatz dazu gilt hier, daß *Indizieren* und *Bedeuten* verschiedene *modi significandi* sind und sich der erstere gegenüber dem zweiten dadurch auszeichnet, daß er ein Personen-Prädikat enthält: demnach indizieren nicht Ausdrücke, sondern Sprecher mittels der Verwendung eines Ausdrucks.

Ein zweiter Punkt betrifft den Indikator i: In vielen Fällen kann i die ihm zugedachte Funktion nur erfüllen, wenn ihm (mindestens) ein Denotat d zukommt, wobei unter *Denotat* hier die konventionelle Bedeutung eines Ausdrucks verstanden wird.[1] Sprecher können Indikatoren nur verwenden, wenn diese ein Denotat haben - anders können Indikatoren ihre Funktion nicht erfüllen. Gleichwohl ist das, was der Sprecher mit dem Indikator indiziert, nicht das Denotat - dies wäre eine begriffliche Absurdität. Das Indizierende und das Indizierte müssen verschieden sein, was sich terminologisch zunächst darin widerspiegelt, daß wir das Indizierte als das *Korrelat* bezeichnen. Im Folgenden wird also die Rede davon sein, daß ein Sprecher einen Ausdruck mit dem zugehörigen Denotat dazu verwendet, um den illokutionären Zweck eines auszuführenden Sprechakts, das Korrelat, zu indizieren.

Soweit die terminologischen Festlegungen, die ein wenig deutlicher machen, wovon die Rede sein soll. Eine nähere Begründung und Explikation dieser Begrifflichkeit wird im Folgenden geleistet. Zunächst jedoch noch eine Warnung vor einem schön gelegenen Holzweg...

2 Der Zweck-Mittel-Fehlschluß

Die Hauptaufgabe des vorliegenden Beitrags wird die Klärung der Frage sein, von welcher Art die eingeführte Relation des Indizierens ist, also die Beziehung zwischen s, k und i. Klärungsbedürftig ist aber auch die Frage, welche Typen von Entitäten für k, das Korrelat, und i, den Indikator, jeweils einzusetzen sind. Mit der Einlassung, daß man für i eine Formkategorie und für k eine Funktionskategorie einzusetzen hat, ist solange nichts gewonnen, wie man die notorische Mehrdeutigkeit von *Form* und *Funktion* nicht aufhebt. Dies ist schon deswegen ratsam, weil so ein fataler Fehlschluß vermeidbar wird, den ich den *Zweck-Mittel-Fehlschluß* nennen möchte. Man könnte zum Beispiel sagen, für s sei i ein Mittel, um einen illokutionären Akt k auszuführen. Die Zweck-Mittel-Relation ist in diesem Fall jedoch eine falsche Metapher. Das Mittel - sprechakttheoretisch gesprochen: der Äußerungsakt oder ein Teil davon - wäre nämlich als sein Bestandteil im Zweck enthalten - dem illokutionären Akt. Eine in Termini der Zweck-Mittel-Relation gehaltene Redeweise in Bezug auf Teilhandlungen eines Sprechakts, die in einer indem-

Relation zueinander stehen, ist allerdings per definitionem ausgeschlossen. Searle ist zuzustimmen, wenn er schreibt:

> Es wäre falsch, anzunehmen, die Äußerungsakte und die propositionalen Akte stünden zu den illokutionären Akten in dem gleichen Verhältnis wie der Kauf einer Fahrkarte und das Besteigen des Zuges zu der Eisenbahnfahrt. Sie sind nicht Mittel zum Zweck; vielmehr verhalten sich Äußerungsakte zu propositionalen und illokutionären Akten wie z.B. das "X" auf einem Stimmzettel machen zum Wählen. (1971: 40 f.)

Ein *Äußerungsakt* wird zu einem *illokutionären Akt* aufgrund einer konstitutiven Regel oder anderer, vergleichbarer Faktoren, jedoch nicht aufgrund einer Zweck-Mittel-Relation. Es ist möglich, zwischen dem *illokutionären Akt* einerseits und dem *perlokutionären Akt* andererseits eine Zweck-Mittel-Relation zu etablieren. Perlokutionäre Akte sind nicht-konventionelle Folgen illokutionärer Akte, und so kann man sagen, daß Behauptungen aufgestellt werden (Mittel), um den oder die Adressaten davon zu überzeugen, daß etwas der Fall ist (Zweck) oder zumindest davon, daß der Sprecher glaubt, daß etwas der Fall ist; und es werden Aufforderungen geäußert (Mittel), um den oder die Adressaten zu einer Handlung zu veranlassen (Zweck). Es werden aber nicht Sätze geäußert ("Mittel"), um Behauptungen aufzustellen oder Aufforderungen an jemanden zu richten ("Zwecke"). Es scheint so zu sein, daß die Mittel-Zweck-Relation, bezieht man sie auf Handlungen, nur da anwendbar ist, wo der Zweck als *Folge* des Mittels aufgefaßt werden kann. Da dies für das Verhältnis von Äußerungsakt und illokutionärem Akt nicht zutrifft, ist diese Dichotomie hier auch nicht angemessen.

Heißt das, daß die Rede von Illokutionsindikatoren als "Mittel, die die illokutionäre Rolle anzeigen", obsolet ist? Sie ist in Ordnung, wenn man Indikatoren nicht als Mittel für den *Vollzug* eines illokutionären Aktes auffaßt, sondern als Mittel für die *Anzeige* einer illokutionären Kraft. Diese Unterscheidung ist subtil, aber entscheidend. An einem lebenspraktischen Beispiel kann man dies vielleicht besser zeigen: Nehmen wir an, ein Wanderer knickt im Wald einen Zweig ab, um den Folgenden zu zeigen, daß dies der richtige Weg ist. Man würde nicht sagen wollen, daß das *Abknicken* des Zweiges das Mittel ist, um den Folgenden mitzuteilen, daß hier der richtige Weg ist (Zweck). Mittel und Zweck haben hier nicht die nötige "Entfernung" voneinander - man würde eher sagen, daß das Abknicken des Zweiges das Mitteilen *ist*.

Daß damit die Rede vom illokutionären Zweck (illocutionary point or purpose) selbst mißverständlich ist, scheint Searle zu entgehen. Ich verwende diesen Begriff hier ebenfalls in Anlehnung an Searle, allerdings in strikter Weise bezogen auf den Zweck, den der illokutionäre Akt *hat* (und nicht auf den illokutionären Akt als Zweck des Äußerungs- und propositionalen Aktes). Der Zweck eines illokutionären Aktes wie BEHAUPTEN besteht also darin, einen Adressaten zu dem Glauben zu bringen, daß p, und nicht darin, eine Behauptung zu vollziehen. Diese Modifikation ergibt sich zwingend aus der Vermeidung des Zweck-Mittel-Fehlschlusses.

Für die sprechakttheoretische Begriffsbildung generell folgt daraus, daß man die beiden Ebenen a) Vollzug eines illokutionären Aktes und b) Indizierung einer bestimmten illokutionären Kraft unterscheiden muß. Searle berücksichtigt diesen Unterschied insofern, als er im zentralen Kapitel 3 von *Sprechakte* (1971) a) Bedingungen für den erfolgreichen Vollzug eines illokutionären Aktes (des Versprechens) und b) semantische Regeln für den Gebrauch von Mitteln, die als Indikatoren für die illokutionäre Kraft von Sprechakten dienen, gesondert aufführt - wobei die letzteren es sind, die als Einleitungsregeln, wesentliche Regeln etc. in die Geschichte eingegangen sind. Natürlich hängen a) und b) eng zusammen: die Chancen für den Erfolg eines illokutionären Aktes werden steigen, wenn für den Adressaten die illokutionäre Kraft zuverlässig indiziert ist. Andererseits nützt die sauberste Indizierung nichts, wenn nicht zentrale Bedingungen für den Vollzug des illokutionären Aktes erfüllt sind (darauf hat als erster Austin hingewiesen). Man indiziert dann etwas, was gar nicht stattfindet, weil wesentliche Voraussetzungen nicht erfüllt sind, so etwa in den berüchtigten Fällen, in denen der Koch die Trauungszeremonie vornimmt und nicht der Schiffskapitän. Nun kann man berechtigterweise die Frage stellen, ob man einen Sprechakt, den man gar nicht vollzieht, indizieren kann, oder ob das Indizieren nicht vielmehr an den Vollzug eines Sprechakts gebunden ist. Weiter kann man fragen, ob das Indizieren im letzteren Falle an das erfolgreiche Vollziehen oder nur an den ehrlichen Versuch, einen Sprechakt auszuführen, gebunden ist. Ich denke, man sollte von "indizieren" nur sprechen, wenn auch etwas "Indiziertes" vorhanden ist, so daß es nicht sinnvoll erscheint, Indikatoren für Sprechakte anzunehmen, die in einer Sprechergemeinschaft nicht (mehr) existieren. So kann man heutzutage keine Burg mehr zur Kapitulation auffordern, indem man äußert:

(3)   Hiermit fordere ich die Burg auf.

Dieser Sprechakt des Auffordems ist nicht mehr möglich, weshalb es nicht sinnvoll ist, dem Äußerer von (3) die Indizierung dieser speziellen Illokution zuzuschreiben.

Man sollte allerdings auf der anderen Seite nicht über's Ziel hinausschießen, indem man das Erfolgskriterium für den Akt des Indizierens an das Gelingenskriterium des indizierten Sprechakts bindet. Es genügt, wenn der Sprecher die indizierten Absichten hat - er muß nicht auch noch den beabsichtigten Sprechakt gelungenermaßen ausgeführt haben. Denn eine solche Bedingung würde zu dem Widerspruch führen, daß zum Beispiel die Aufforderung (2) als aufgestellt gelten müßte, damit man von Indizieren reden dürfte, wo doch das Indizieren selbst nur eine nicht-hinreichende Bedingung für das gelungene Auffordern ist. Erfolgreiches Indizieren ist nicht mit dem Erreichen des illokutionären Effekts zu identifizieren, denn es ist hierfür eine Voraussetzung.

3   Was sind illokutionäre Indikatoren?

Um diese Frage zu beantworten, sei noch einmal auf ihre Charakterisierung durch Searle zurückgegriffen, auf den dieser Terminus zurückgeht. Seiner Auffassung nach

> [...] lassen sich zwei (nicht notwendig getrennte) Elemente in der syntaktischen Struktur des Satzes unterscheiden, die wir den propositionalen Indikator und den

Indikator der illokutionären Rolle nennen wollen. Der Indikator der illokutionären Rolle zeigt an, wie die Proposition aufzufassen ist, oder, um es anders auszudrükken, welche illokutionäre Rolle der Äußerung zukommen soll, d.h., welchen illokutionären Akt der Sprecher vollzieht, indem er den Satz äußert. (1971: 49)

Nehmen wir also an, die Wortfolge in einem Satz sei eine der Eigenschaften, mit denen der Specher anzeigt, welchen illokutionären Akt er vollzieht, indem er diesen Satz äußert. Nehmen wir weiter an, ein Sprecher äußere einen Satz mit Spitzenstellung des finiten Verbs; da illokutionäre Indikatoren selten isoliert vorkommen, kommt eine ansteigende Intonationskontur hinzu. Man wird den Satz

(4)   Geht Monika heute ins Kino?

dann so analysieren, daß man Verberststellung und ansteigende Intonation als Indikatoren dafür nimmt, daß die Äußerung von (4) als Versuch gilt, vom Adressaten die Information zu bekommen, ob Monika heute ins Kino geht. Zum gelungenen Stellen einer Frage reicht es natürlich nicht aus, daß S diesen Satz äußert, sondern es müssen auch die von Searle aufgeführten Regeln für die Verwendung der Mittel, die die illokutionäre Rolle anzeigen sollen, korrekt befolgt sein.

Terminologisch nahegelegt ist schon, daß die *wesentliche Regel* zentral ist für den Gebrauch der Mittel, die die illokutionäre Kraft eines Sprechakts anzeigen. Die Beschreibung des Verhaltens, das dieser Regel folgt, ist logisch abhängig von ihrer Existenz. Searle faßt illokutionäre Indikatoren als Elemente auf, deren Aufgabe es ist, die Erfülltheit oder Nicht-Erfülltheit dieser Regel anzuzeigen. So spricht er einmal davon, daß "... eine Äußerung in einem gegebenen Zusammenhang die Erfüllung einer wesentlichen Bedingung anzeigen kann" (1971: 109); das, was angezeigt wird, ist also, daß die gemachte Äußerung als Versuch gilt, den Adressaten dazu zu bringen, A zu tun (Aufforderungen), oder als eine Versicherung des Inhalts gilt, daß p eine wirkliche Sachlage darstellt (Behaupten / Feststellen / Bestätigen), oder als Ausdruck der Dankbarkeit oder Anerkennung gilt (Danken) etc. Wir sehen also, daß Searle die Gelingenskriterien des Indizierens und des illokutionären Aktes miteinander identifiziert - eine Strategie, die in diesem Beitrag gerade nicht verfolgt wird. Andererseits ist der Begriff des Illokutionsindikators für Searle eng mit dem Begriff der konstitutiven Regel verwoben, woraus folgt, daß eine Äußerung dann keine illokutionären Indikatoren enthalten kann, wenn für sie keine konstitutive Regel formulierbar ist, die angibt, als was eine geäußerte Lautkette gelten soll. Es ist aber sehr wohl möglich, auf der Basis der konstitutiven Regel einen illokutionären Akt zu vollziehen, auch wenn der zugrundeliegende Satz keinen "expliziten" illokutionären Indikator enthält (s. Searle 1971: 109). So kann man mithilfe des Satzes

(5)   Könnten Sie das für mich tun?

eine Bitte an jemanden richten, obwohl (5) keine Indikatoren enthält, die dies anzeigen, sondern vielmehr Elemente, die eine Frage indizieren. Die hier angedeutete Konzeption eines "Konflikts" zwischen Illokutionsindikatoren und tatsächlicher illokutionärer Kraft wird in Searle (1982) dann zum Begriff des indirekten Sprechakts ausgearbeitet (s. hierzu auch Sökeland 1980).

Unabhängig davon, ob man den Begriff des Indikators an das Searlesche Erklärungsschema bindet oder nicht (im Verlaufe dieser Argumentation wird diese Bindung nicht vorgenommen), ist die Trennung von illokutionärem Indikator und dem, was er indiziert - also zwischen Indikator und Indikat - von größter Wichtigkeit, wenn man Kurzschlüsse der folgenden Art vermeiden will:

"Die Tatsache, daß S mit der Äußerung von (4) eine Frage stellt, ist darauf zurückzuführen, daß er einen V-1-Satz mit ansteigender Intonation verwendet."

Was ist an dieser Auffassung unzutreffend? Der Kardinalfehler liegt darin, daß die Rolle, die illokutionäre Indikatoren prinzipiell spielen können, heillos überschätzt wird. Es kann nicht auf die Indikatoren "zurückgeführt werden", daß eine Äußerung die-und-die Illokution hat; die Indikatoren zeigen vielmehr an, daß es bestimmte Faktoren gibt, auf die es zurückgeführt werden kann, daß die Äußerung die-und-die Illokution hat, und einer dieser Faktoren ist die kommunikative Intention des Sprechers. Auch an dieser Stelle müssen zwei Sachverhalte voneinander unterschieden werden, die eigentlich keinen Anlaß zur Verwechslung geben dürften. Es ist auf die spezifische grammatische Form der Äußerung zurückzuführen, daß der jeweilige Adressat diese Äußerung als Fragehandlung erkennt; diese Zuschreibung nimmt er aber nur vor, weil er hypothetisch unterstellt, daß der Sprecher damit seine kommunikative Intention zu erkennen gibt, eine bestimmte Information erlangen zu wollen, und dies ist das Entscheidende. Der Indikator zeigt, auf welche Sprecher-Intention eine bestimmte Äußerung zurückgeführt werden muß, und wenn diese einmal identifiziert ist, kann die Äußerung entsprechend pragmatisch interpretiert werden. Ohne diesen Rückgriff auf die Sprecher-Intention hängt jede Interpretation in der Luft, weil die zugrundeliegende sinngebende Instanz nicht in Betracht gezogen wurde. Es hat also seinen guten Grund, daß wir "Indizieren" als dreistelliges Prädikat mit dem Sprecher als einem Argument auffassen.

Wir sind damit einer Explikation des Indikatorbegriffs schon näher gekommen, doch reicht das Gesagte natürlich noch nicht aus. Im Zuge der begrifflichen Klärungsversuche wird bisweilen darauf hingewiesen, der Ausdruck "Indikator" sei ein Beispiel für wissenschaftliche Metaphern, weil er ursprünglich nicht für linguistische Untersuchungen geschaffen worden sei, sondern aus der Chemie komme. Ein typischer Anwendungsfall ist dort folgender: Indikatoren können dazu eingesetzt werden, um bestimmte chemische Eigenschaften von Flüssigkeiten herauszubekommen. So kann man zum Beispiel die H-Ionenkonzentration in einer Flüssigkeit dadurch ermitteln, daß man dieser eine Säure oder eine Base zusetzt und schaut, ob sie ihre Farbe verändert. Daß die zugesetzte Säure oder Base ihre Farbe verändert, ist ein Zeichen dafür, daß sie ihren Dissoziationsgrad verändert, und daß sie dies tut, ist wiederum die Folge einer bestimmten H-Ionenkonzentration in der zu analysierenden Flüssigkeit. Man kann also die Kette: Anstieg der H-Ionenkonzentration - Veränderung im Dissoziationsgrad der zugesetzten Säure oder Base - Farbveränderung - so auffassen, daß man sagt: die Säure oder Base ist ein Indikator dafür, ob sich die nicht-beobachtbare H-Ionenkonzentration in einer Flüssigkeit verändert oder nicht. Schlägt die Farbe um, tut sie's, verändert sich die Farbe nicht, bleibt sie konstant.

Eine wesentliche Eigenschaft dieses Bildspenders liegt darin, daß die Indikatorsäure oder -base nicht die H-Ionenkonzentration der zu analysierenden Flüssigkeit beeinflußt, sondern nur anzeigt. Sie macht etwas sichtbar, was dem Auge des Beobachters verborgen bleibt, aber dennoch und unabhängig davon abläuft. Ganz so verhält es sich mit illokutionären Indikatoren natürlich nicht: Illokutionäre Kräfte existieren nicht in der Welt, unabhängig davon, ob eine Äußerung vorliegt oder nicht, d.h. im Sprechakt kommen nicht ein Äußerungsakt und eine Illokution zusammen, sondern es wird ein Satz mit einer bestimmten illokutionären Kraft geäußert. Übertragbar allerdings ist, daß der Indikator nicht die Ursache für das ist, was er indiziert; genausowenig wie die zugesetzte Indikatorflüssigkeit die H-Ionenkonzentration der zu analysierenden Flüssigkeit beeinflußt (das würde sie als Indikator nachgerade disqualifizieren), sowenig beeinflußt ein Illokutionsindikator das, wofür er Anzeichen ist, nämlich die illokutionäre Kraft des Sprechakts. Andernfalls wäre er als Indikator nicht brauchbar.

Kehren wir der Chemie den Rücken und zu Monikas Kinobesuch zurück. Die Äußerung von (4) kann so beschrieben werden, daß man sagt: Indem S den Satz (4) mit den besagten illokutionsrelevanten Merkmalen äußert, vollzieht er den Sprechakt FRAGEN. Der Äußerungsakt als Träger der illokutionsindizierenden Elemente steht also in einer indem-Relation zum illokutionären Akt des Fragens. Der Indikator ist mithin in ganz spezifischer Weise in dem, was er indiziert, enthalten, er ist Element einer Teilhandlung des gesamten illokutionären Aktes. Wie man die Funktion des Indikators an diesem Punkt näher charakterisiert, ist letztlich eine Frage der Theoriewahl: In Searleschen Termini ausgedrückt indiziert die Äußerung von i (einem illokutionsindizierenden Element) die Erfüllung der für diesen Sprechakt einschlägigen wesentlichen Regel, das heißt sie indiziert: Die Äußerung von $s(i)$ (einem Satz, der i enthält) gilt als Versuch, vom Adressaten die Information zu erhalten, ob Monika ins Kino geht. $s(i)$ erfüllt also eine Zuordnungsfunktion, die eine geäußerte Lautkette einer bestimmten oder einer Menge von Illokutionen zuweist; es "sagt" dem Adressaten, daß diese spezifische Äußerung unter jene wesentliche Regel zu subsumieren ist. Die Tatsache, daß diese wesentliche Regel als Konvention in einer Einzelsprache vorkommt, bewirkt, daß die Äußerung als das gilt, was diese Regel angibt. Ist man der Auffassung, daß konstitutive Regeln der angegebenen Art nicht den Stellenwert besitzen, den sie (dem frühen) Searle zufolge in der sprachlichen Kommunikation einnehmen, dann muß man als Indikat eine andere Instanz wählen als die Erfülltheit der wesentlichen Regel. Der Rekurs auf sprecherseitige Einstellungen bietet sich hier als Alternative an, wobei man als Korrelat eines Indikators eine basale Sprecher-Einstellung wie *Glauben* oder *Beabsichtigen* anzunehmen hat, die zusammen mit einem propositionalen Gehalt den kommunikativen Sinn einer Äußerung ausmacht. Der wesentliche Punkt, auf den es hier zunächst ankommt, bleibt von der Explikationsstrategie jedoch unberührt: Auch sprecherseitige Einstellungen sind nicht auf die sprachlichen Strukturen zu reduzieren, mit deren Hilfe sie ausgedrückt werden, und nur erstere sind es, die einer Äußerung einen spezifischen kommunikativen Sinn verleihen.

Zusammenfassend kann man sagen, daß die Funktion des Indikators *i* gegenüber der zugrundeliegenden, für die illokutionäre Kraft verantwortlichen Instanz (wesentliche Regel, Sprechereinstellung) sekundär ist. Illokutionäre Indikatoren können ihre Funktion nur erfüllen, wenn die betreffenden Instanzen vorliegen, diese jedoch sind nicht auf die Tatsache angewiesen, daß ihr Vorliegen durch sprachliche oder sonstige Mittel indiziert wird.

Aus dem, was gesagt wurde, folgt, daß die Auffassung falsch ist, es läge am illokutionären Indikator selbst, daß eine Äußerung die illokutionäre Kraft hat, die der Indikator anzeigt. Indizieren ist etwas anderes als Konstituieren; eine Beschreibung dessen, was durch Regeln oder basale Einstellungen konstituiert wird, ist logisch abhängig von der Existenz dieser Regeln bzw. Einstellungen, eine Beschreibung dessen, was durch grammatische Elemente oder Strukturen indiziert wird, ist hingegen logisch unabhängig von dem, wodurch es indiziert wird. Anders gesagt: Ein Indikator der illokutionären Kraft zeigt an, daß der Äußerung bestimmte Faktoren unterliegen, dank derer der Sprechakt diese spezifische illokutionäre Kraft hat. Zu diesen Faktoren kann allerdings nicht der geäußerte Satz mit den in ihm enthaltenen Elementen zählen, denn der Satz indiziert sich schließlich nicht selbst.

Ich möchte an dieser Stelle einen Einspruch diskutieren, den M. Bierwisch in einem älteren Aufsatz (1979) erhebt. Seiner Auffassung nach gibt es eine Tendenz, zu viele Typen von Indikatoren anzunehmen, so daß eine möglichst restriktive Definition vonnöten ist, um diesen Begriff nicht zu entleeren. Bierwisch unterscheidet zwei Klassen von sprachlichen Mitteln, die "Kraft ihrer Bedeutung direkt mit kommunikativer Interaktion zu tun haben" (Bierwisch 1979: 134), nämlich

(a) sprachliche Mittel, deren Bedeutung Faktoren und Strukturen der sprachlichen Interaktion klassifiziert; (b) sprachliche Mittel, die Kraft ihrer Bedeutung Interaktionsstrukturen determinieren können. (Ebd.)

Zu den mit (b) gemeinten Mitteln zählt Bierwisch vor allem die Frage- und die Imperativsatzform als die "eigentlichen sprachlichen IFIDs" (ebd.); unter (a) fallen hauptsächlich sprechaktbezeichnende Verben in ihrer performativen Verwendung. Die Bedeutung eines Satzes, der ein performatives Verb enthält, kann nun spezifiziert werden, ohne daß dieses Verb als Illokutionsindikator interpretiert werden muß.
Ein Satz wie

(6)   Ich taufe Dich hiermit Auguste.

ist auf der Ebene der Äußerungsbedeutung nicht anders zu analysieren als ein Satz, der vom Schema für explizit performative Formeln abweicht (etwa: "Du taufst sie Auguste"). Insbesondere ist dieser Satz wie andere Deklarativsätze auch durch Wahrheitsbedingungen angemessen zu charakterisieren. Die spezifische Eigenschaft solcher Sätze, die es ihrem Äußerer erlaubt, den denotierten Sachverhalt durch die Äußerung herzustellen, ist nicht auf der Ebene ihrer Bedeutung, sondern auf der Ebene der Interaktionsstrukturen ("kommunikativer Sinn") zu explizieren.

Eine solche theoretische Arbeitsteilung erscheint prinzipiell plausibel, zumal Performativität nicht primär eine Eigenschaft von Sätzen, sondern von Satzäußerungen ist. Die Äußerungsebene wirkt jedoch auf die Ebene der sprachlichen Form insofern zurück, als es ja starke Restriktionen für performative Konstruktionen gibt, die für andere Deklarativsätze nicht gelten. Schon ein Wechsel von der ersten zur zweiten Person im angeführten Beispiel hat die Tilgung des Performativitäts-Effektes zur Folge, so daß bereits auf der Ebene der Äußerungsbedeutung spezifische Bedingungen gelten dafür, ob man eine bestimmte Art von Sprechakt überhaupt ausführen kann oder nicht. Wenn man nun eine nicht-deterministische Charakterisierung von illokutionären Indikatoren annimmt, dann kann man Sätze wie (6) als Träger eines solchen Indikators ansehen, denn mit ihnen klassifiziert der Sprecher nicht nur Faktoren und Strukturen der sprachlichen Interaktion, sondern er führt die solchermaßen klassifizierten Handlungen auch aus. Anders als das tokenreflexive

(7)   Ich lispele.

dessen Äußerung das Lispeln des Sprechers nicht verursacht, sondern unter Beweis stellt, produziert die Äußerung von (6) einen Zustand in der Welt, der vorher nicht bestanden hat. Aus diesem Grund sollte man performative Konstruktionen als vollwertige illokutionäre Indikatoren zulassen, und nicht nur als Mittel zu Klassifizierung von Faktoren sprachlicher Interaktion.

Akzeptiert man diese Position, dann kann man allerdings nicht mehr ohne weiteres die Zuschreibung von Wahrheitsbedingungen vornehmen, denn eine durch (6) vollzogene Äußerung wäre in ihrer performativen Lesart nicht mehr wahrheitswertfähig.[2] Ich schließe mich hier im wesentlichen der Auffassung Searles (1992) an, der performative Äußerungen als nicht-wahrheitswertfähige, in direkter Lesart als performativ zu interpretierende Äußerungen auffaßt. Bei allen Differenzen bleibt Bierwischs Mahnung zur Restriktion bestehen, und ich folge ihm insoweit, als man nicht zuviele Indikatortypen annehmen sollte, weil sonst die Gefahr der Entleerung des Indikatorbegriffs besteht: Wenn prinzipiell alles ein Indikator sein kann, dann kann man direkt auf den Begriff des Äußerungsaktes zurückgreifen und braucht keinen zweiten Ausdruck für diese Sprechaktebene.

Im folgenden soll nun ein Weg angegeben werden, wie man zu einer m.E. erfolgversprechenden Analyse des Stellenwerts von Indikatoren gelangen kann, wobei generell die Auffassung vertreten wird, daß das von den Indikatoren Angezeigte nichts ist, was in irgendeiner Weise - potentiell oder aktual - in der Bedeutung des geäußerten Satzes enthalten ist; gleichwohl wird unterstellt, daß die Bedeutung des Satzes und der darin enthaltenen Indikatoren eine entscheidende Rolle für seine Eignung als Korrelat eines illokutionären Aktes spielt. Ein Bild ist vielleicht geeignet, diese Funktion der Satzbedeutung zu verdeutlichen: So wenig, wie das (potentielle) Nägel-in-die-Wand-Treiben als Bestandteil des Werkzeugs Hammer aufzufassen ist (*Wo* ist es?), so sehr ist diese Funktion bestimmend für das, was einen Hammer ausmacht, ja konstituiert. Die Funktion ist die raison d'être des Werkzeugs, aber sie ist nicht sein Bestandteil.

4   Freges Einsicht und die Heterogenität von Wortverwendungen

In einem ersten Schritt hin zur Entwicklung eines tragbaren Indikatorbegriffs sei an eine Einsicht erinnert, die Frege in seiner Arbeit "Der Gedanke" formuliert hat, und die für die Diskussion des vorliegenden Themas äußerst relevant ist. Frege schreibt an einer Stelle:

> In der Form des Behauptungssatzes sprechen wir die Anerkennung der Wahrheit aus. Wir brauchen dazu das Wort "wahr" nicht. Und selbst, wenn wir es gebrauchen, liegt die eigentlich behauptende Kraft nicht in ihm, sondern in der Form des Behauptungssatzes, und wo diese ihre behauptende Kraft verliert, kann auch das Wort "wahr" sie nicht wieder herstellen. Das geschieht, wenn wir nicht im Ernste sprechen. (1918/1919, 1966: 36)

Die Anerkennung der Wahrheit eines Gedankens durch das Aussprechen eines Behauptungssatzes ist also in Folge dieser Bemerkung nicht das Resultat eines hinzugefügten "... ist wahr", sondern sie ist darauf zurückzuführen, daß die Kundgebung des Urteils mit behauptender Kraft, im Ernst oder aufrichtig vollzogen wurde. Wenn dies nicht gegeben ist, dann liegt trotz aller Anzeichen lediglich eine "Theaterbehauptung" vor (s. ebd.). Überträgt man diese frühe Einsicht auf das zur Diskussion stehende Verhältnis von illokutionsindizierenden Elementen und illokutionärer Kraft, so kommt man zu einer Position, die die Rolle dieser Elemente nicht darin sieht, Illokutionen zu determinieren, sondern darin, Anzeichen - Indikatoren eben - für Illokutionen zu sein; und dies ist eine weitaus bescheidenere Rolle, als üblicherweise angenommen wird. Das heißt, man muß versuchen, eine Explikation für illokutionäre Indikatoren zu formulieren, aus der nicht folgt, daß ihre Produktion oder Äußerung eine hinreichende Bedingung für die Ausführung eines Sprechakts ist.[3] Gelingt dies nicht, dann erhält man das empirisch falsche Ergebnis, daß jeder Sprecher sich mit der Äußerung eines Indikatoren enthaltenden Satzes zum Vollzug des entsprechenden Sprechakts zu bekennen hat. Dies wurde in solch naiver Fassung von keinem Sprechakttheoretiker je behauptet, doch gibt es eine durchgehende Tendenz, eine abgemilderte Version dieser Idee zu vertreten; so wird üblicherweise gesagt, daß im Normalfall eine Übereinstimmung von Indikatoren und "entsprechenden" illokutionären Akten festzustellen ist, die durch besondere Kontextbedingungen modifiziert werden kann.[4] Es liegt dabei völlig im Dunkeln, welche Kriterien dafür vorliegen, daß etwas ein "entprechender" Sprechakt ist und etwas anderes nicht; außerdem fehlen jegliche empirische Belege dafür, daß sich Sprecher in der Tat im Normalfall an die "entsprechende" Illokution halten, im Gegenteil scheint es eher Anzeichen dafür zu geben, daß sie es in vielen Situationen gerade nicht tun (s. hierzu Ervin-Tripp 1976; Gazdar 1981; Levinson 1983: 263 ff.). Da es also keinerlei Gründe dafür gibt, einen a priori geltenden Normalfall der "entsprechenden" Illokution anzunehmen, soll dies hier im weiteren Verlauf der Argumentation auch nicht mehr als selbstverständlich unterstellt werden. Es wird vielmehr von mehreren, gleichberechtigten Lesarten ausgegangen, die zunächst mit dem gleichen Normalitätsgrad der Äußerung eines Satzes zukommen können. Als Ergebnis von Konventionalisierungen sind besondere, naheliegende oder normale Zuordnungen natürlich möglich; diese haben ihren Ausgangspunkt allerdings nicht naturnotwendig in der wörtlichen Bedeutung des geäußerten Satzes, sondern sie können sich ebensogut auf eine nicht-wörtliche Lesart stützen. Obwohl ich diesen Punkt hier nur andeuten konnte, ist er doch zu wichtig, als daß man ihn ungenannt lassen dürfte.

Im folgenden seien einige Unterscheidungen eingeführt, die es gestatten, das hier skizzierte theoretische Anliegen terminologisch stringenter zu formulieren, wobei die erste hier vorgenommene Unterscheidung eher vorbereitenden Charakter für die zweite hat. Es soll die Auffassung vertreten werden, daß der Einflußgrad der Satzbedeutung auf die illokutionäre Lesart des mit seiner Äußerung vollzogenen Sprechakts keine feste Größe ist, sondern als Funktion des Verwendungsmodus illokutionärer Indikatoren anzusehen ist. Um deutlich zu machen, an welche Art von Unterscheidung hier gedacht ist, soll auf eine theoretische Differenzierung zurückgegriffen werden, die von einigen Sprachphilosophen zu einem anderen, jedoch verwandten Zweck eingeführt wurde.

K. Donnellan (1966) unterscheidet im Rahmen der Referenzsemantik zwei Verwendungsweisen von Kennzeichnungen, deren erste er referentielle und deren zweite er attributive Verwendung nennt. Die attributive Verwendung von Kennzeichnungen ist nur dann erfolgreich - d.h. ein sie enthaltender Satz hat nur dann Wahrheitsbedingungen - , wenn es einen Gegenstand gibt, der den verwendeten Ausdruck "erfüllt". Wenn wir angesichts eines völlig verwüsteten Zimmers behaupten:

(8)   Der Einbrecher war ein Choleriker.

dann hat (8) nur Wahrheitsbedingungen, wenn es einen Einbrecher gibt, andernfalls ist der mit (8) vollzogene Referenzakt nichtig, und die Äußerung weder wahr noch falsch.

Verwenden wir Kennzeichnungen hingegen referentiell, dann kommt es nicht darauf an, daß jede Komponente des Beschreibungsbündels auf den gemeinten Gegenstand oder die gemeinte Person zutrifft. Es kommt vielmehr darauf an, daß in der Situation klar wird, wer oder was gemeint ist, auch wenn das zur Referenz verwendete sprachliche Mittel defizient ist. Mit

(9)   Die Frau mit dem Rotwein im Glas ist die Schwester des Gastgebers.

kann man Widerspruch oder Zustimmung ernten, auch wenn im Glas nicht Rotwein, sondern Johannisbeersaft ist. Es beschädigt den Sprechakt nicht wesentlich, daß der Sprecher eine im strengen Sinne nicht zutreffende Kennzeichnung gewählt hat, eben weil es nicht darauf ankommt, auf der Basis dieser Kennzeichnung nach einer Frau mit Rotwein im Glas zu suchen; der in (9) enthaltene Referenzakt hat nur die Funktion einer Hilfestellung bei der Identifikation der gemeinten Person durch den Adresaten. Das sprachliche Mittel tritt hinter anderen Informationsquellen, die sich aus der Situation ergeben, zurück und kann deshalb auch in gewissen Grenzen unzutreffend sein. Dies gilt für attributive Verwendungen nicht: Hier ist der Zugang zur Welt (d.h. zum Referenzobjekt) allein durch die Sprache gegeben, und wenn das Sprachmittel defizient ist, dann ist auch die sprachliche Präsentation des Weltausschnitts wesentlich beeinträchtigt.

Erweitert man diese Idee so, daß sie auf illokutionäre Indikatoren angewendet werden kann, dann kommt man zu einem ähnlichen Ergebnis, was die Beziehung von Sprachmitteln zu den Äußerungsumständen betrifft. Es lassen sich so zwei basale Verwendungsweisen oder -modi sprachlicher Indikatoren unterscheiden: Im einen Fall ist das Sprachmittel ein Element der Kommunikationssituation, den andere Faktoren ebensogut oder besser erfüllen können - es kommt sprachlich nicht auf jede Einzelheit an; im anderen Fall steht und fällt die Interpretation mit den im Satz vorkommenden sprachlichen Elementen, und jede Abweichung und jeder Fehler wirkt sich auf das Ergebnis aus.

Den ersten Verwendungsmodus möchte ich den 'resultativen Modus' nennen. Er zeichnet sich dadurch aus, daß das Gelingen der Kommunikation weniger von den Eigenschaften des verwendeten Mittels abhängig ist als vielmehr von den Informationen, die der Adressat über den Sprecher und den Äußerungskontext hat oder bekommt. Die Stärke dieser Hintergrundinformationen als interpretationsrelevante Faktoren sorgt dafür, daß gewisse Defekte des Kommunikationsmittels durchaus toleriert werden bzw. nicht zum Mißverständnis führen, denn die Kenntnis des Kontextes wiegt dieses Defizit auf und darf es auch. Der resultative Verwendungsmodus ist kennzeichnend für informelle Situationen, in denen die Kommunikationsteilnehmer miteinander vertraut oder vertraulich sind, wie in familiärer Kommunikation, Gesprächen in der peer group, mit Arbeitskollegen, in Paarbeziehungen, im Beichtstuhl, oder in der Discothek. Der Erfolg von Äußerungen im Rahmen dieses Modus ist nicht abhängig von der Bedeutung der geäußerten Sätze, sondern von der Kenntnis der Biographie oder den Präferenzen des Spechers, von der Kenntnis der Situation und ihrer Geschichte, von "idiolektalen Bedeutungen" à la Grice und anderem. Resultativ heißt dieser Modus deshalb, weil die Eignung des verwendeten Indikators sich nach dem Resultat seiner Äußerung bemißt, und nicht nach Maßstäben für seine korrekte Form.

Der 'instrumentale Verwendungsmodus' ist demgegenüber dadurch ausgezeichnet, daß das Gelingen der Kommunikation mehr oder weniger vollständig von den Eigenschaften des Kommunikationsmittels abhängt. Dies kann daran liegen, daß die Informationsquellen, die der Kontext zur Verfügung stellt, so reduziert sind, daß das nichtsprachliche Hintergrund- oder Situationswissen des Adressaten wesentlich eingeschränkt ist - der vielzitierte Fall des anonymen Briefes, aber auch Autoreiserufe im Radio und anderes zählen dazu. Andere Gründe für das Vorliegen dieses Modus können darin liegen, daß Sprecher wie Adressat sich nicht auf diese Kontextinformationen verlassen wollen, weil sie nicht eindeutig bestimmbar sind. Gesetzesformulierungen, Verträge, polizeiliche Anordnungen und andere rechtlich relevante Texte oder Äußerungsformen sind hierfür charakteristisch. Liegt ein instrumentaler Verwendungsmodus vor, dann hat die situationsunabhängige Bedeutung der verwendeten sprachlichen Mittel einen großen Stellenwert. Die kleinste Abweichung oder der geringste Fehler kann eine Modifikation oder Beeinträchtigung des gesamten Sprechaktes zur Folge haben, und die Berufung darauf, daß es der Äußerer anders oder nicht so gemeint hat, nützt wenig.

Entsprechend stark ist auch der Einfluß der Satzbedeutung auf den illokutionären Zweck des in einem solchen Verwendungsmodus geäußerten Sprechakts. Die genannten illokutionsindizierenden Mittel - performative Formeln, Wortstellung, Adverbien u.a. - werden dafür sorgen, daß für die Interpretation des Sprechakts über die Bedeutung dieser

Mittel hinaus nicht viel Spielraum bleibt. Jedoch bleibt zu beachten, daß auch bei größtmöglicher Deckungsgleichheit der semantischen und der illokutionären Interpretation keine Identität beider Interpretationsebenen hergestellt ist - die Illokution wird nicht zur Satzbedeutung, nur weil letztere einen starken Einfluß auf die Interpretation der Äußerung hat.[5]

Äußerungen im resultativen Verwendungsmodus lassen der Wahl der illokutionsindizierenden Mittel einen großen Spielraum, und die Möglichkeiten, vom Vorliegen bestimmter sprachlicher Elemente auf die der Äußerung zukommende Illokution zu schließen, sind begrenzt. Entsprechend schwach ist der Einfluß der lexikalischen Elemente oder der strukturellen Eigenschaften des Satzes; wenn das Gerüst der zu kommunizierenden Botschaft steht, dann ist die Sprache von der Aufgabe genauerer Indizierung entlastet und übergibt diese an den Kontext - etwas verdinglicht ausgedrückt. Im resultativen Modus kann man eine Frage mit einem Deklarativsatz wie

(10)   Monika geht morgen ins Kino.

stellen und sich dabei darauf verlassen, daß der Adressat im Zuge der Interpretation von (10) sein Wissen über den Sprecher und die Sprechsituation anwendet, das zum Beispiel die Kenntnis umfaßt, der Sprecher wisse nicht, ob Monika morgen ins Kino geht. Ist diese Kenntnis nicht Teil des adressatenseitigen Wissens, kann es natürlich zu einem Mißverständnis kommen, das in diesem Fall in der irrtümlichen Zuschreibung einer assertiven Illokution besteht. Wenn der Sprecher jedoch gut kalkuliert hat, dann hat er hinreichende Hypothesen über die Situationskenntnis des Adressaten, und Mißverständnisse dieser Art werden nicht auftreten. Wie sicher oder unsicher eine solche Strategie auch ist - man kann es als Teil einer generellen Rationalitätsannahme auffassen, daß in dieser Weise mehrfach interpretierbare Äußerungen nur in einem resultativen Modus vorkommen werden. Im instrumentalen Modus wäre (10) inadäquat.

Der instrumentale Verwendungsmodus ist vermutlich der Typus, der zu der irrigen Auffassung geführt hat, Eigenschaften des Kommunikationsmittels könnten kommunikative Effekte "determinieren". Instrumentale Modi zeichnen sich durch eine größere Explizitheit des Kommunikationsmittels aus, da die Kommunizierenden sich nicht auf Nichtexplizites verlassen wollen oder können. Eine Vorladung, die wie

(11)   Kommen sie am Donnerstag doch mal beim Amtsgericht vorbei.

gehalten ist, wird nicht nur aus stilistischen Gründen als pragmatisch abweichend empfunden werden, sondern vor allem aus Gründen der mangelnden Explizitheit und der daraus resultierenden Möglichkeit für den Adressaten, ein Fernbleiben der unverbindlichen Form der Vorladung anzulasten. Es ist für eine Vorladung zwingend, daß die mit ihr verbundene Illokution eindeutig zum Ausdruck kommt, so daß sie nicht als *Ein*ladung oder Vor*schlag* fehlzudeuten ist. Aus genau diesem Grunde zeichnen sich Schriftstücke dieser und verwandter Art durch die Verwendung explizit performativer Formeln aus.

Durch die hier eingeführte Unterscheidung soll zweierlei gezeigt werden: Zunächst ist die Existenz des resultativen Verwendungsmodus Anlaß für eine Lockerung des Bezugs des indizierenden Mittels zu dem, was es indiziert, ein Bezug, der sich in gravierender Weise vom Bezug eines sprachlichen Ausdrucks zu dem, was dieser Ausdruck bedeutet, unterscheidet: Die Bedeutung eines Ausdrucks ist vollkommen unabhängig vom Verwendungsmodus seiner Äußerung. Zum anderen ist auch im instrumentalen Verwendungsmodus der enge Bezug des bedeutungsvollen Ausdrucks (Satzes) zu dem, was er indiziert, nicht Anlaß, *bedeuten* und *indizieren* miteinander zu verwechseln. Um diese Verwechslung nicht entstehen zu lassen, sei eine zweite terminologische Regelung eingeführt, die beides voneinander trennt.

5 Denotat und Korrelat

Nehmen wir der Einfachheit halber zunächst an, es ginge um einen besonderen Typ von illokutionären Indikatoren, der üblicherweise *performative Formel* genannt wird, also um Wendungen wie "Ich stelle fest ...", "Es wird angeordnet ...", "Sie sind gebeten ...". Ich habe das, was diese Ausdrücke bedeuten, ihr *Denotat genannt*, und das, was sie indizieren, ihr *Korrelat*. Die Angabe des Denotats der ersten Wendung lautet: Ein auf sich selbst referierender Sprecher prädiziert von sich, daß er etwas feststellt oder feststellen wird. Da es nur um die Angabe der sprachlich determinierten Bedeutung geht, wird nicht spezifiziert, um welchen Sprecher es sich handelt.

Die Angabe eines der Korrelate einer Äußerung der ersten Wendung lautet: S äußerte "Ich stelle fest ..." mit der M-Absicht, daß H denkt, daß S glaubt, daß p (nach Grice 1993: 93). Diese Explikation des Korrelats von "Ich stelle fest ..." läßt zwei Interpretationen zu, die entsprechend zwei verschiedene Korrelate implizieren: Bezieht man *p* auf den Teil des geäußerten Satzes, der hier durch drei Punkte wiedergeben wurde und der die Proposition des vollzogenen Sprechakts denotiert, dann liegt eine im klassischen Sinne performative Äußerung vor (H soll denken, daß *p*); bezieht man *p* auf den gesamten geäußerten Satz, dann liegt eine Behauptung vor, daß S etwas feststellt (H soll denken, daß S feststellt, daß *p*). Im zweiten Fall ist die Gesamtäußerung wahrheitswertfähig, im ersten nicht.

An diesem Beispiel wird schon deutlich, daß Denotat und Korrelat in der Tat zwei unterschiedliche Dimensionen sind. Wie aus der Diskussion über Performativität bekannt, läßt die Verwendung einer standardisierten Formel des angegebenen Typs dem Sprecher prinzipiell zwei Möglichkeiten: Er kann den durch das Verb denotierten Sprechakt vollziehen, oder er kann behaupten, ankündigen o.ä., daß er den denotierten Sprechakt vollzieht bzw. vollziehen wird. Der entscheidende Punkt ist, daß beide Möglichkeiten für den Sprecher bestehen, so daß man auf der Ebene des Korrelats eine andere Situation als auf der Ebene des Denotats hat.[6]

Die pragmatische Bifunktionalität hat keine semantische Mehrdeutigkeit der betreffenden Wendung zur Folge, die Äußerung ist nicht semantisch ambig, weil der Sprecher mit ihr unterschiedliche Sprechakte ausführen kann. Daraus folgt die Unabhängigkeit beider Ebenen voneinander, denn eine Variation des Korrelats der angegebenen Wendung hat keine entsprechende Variation des Denotats zur Folge. Der umgekehrte Fall gilt auch: Ob ich sage "Ich stelle fest ..." oder "Es wird festgestellt ..." - eine Variation des Denotats ist die Folge, - hat keinen Einfluß auf das Korrelat: beide Male kann eine Feststellung vollzogen werden, wobei allerdings anderweitige Unterschiede z.B. im Stil der Äußerung auftreten werden. Da also die Dimensionen des Denotats und des Korrelats insofern unabhängig voneinander sind, als sie separat variieren können, muß man annehmen, daß die Beziehung des Indikators, hier der Wendung "Ich stelle fest ...", zum Denotat und zum Korrelat jeweils unterschiedlich ist. Im folgenden seien einige Charakteristika dieses Unterschieds aufgewiesen - wobei die Beziehung des Indikators zu seinem Denotat und zu seinem Korrelat jeweils als unterschiedlicher *Signifikationsmodus* gekennzeichnet werden soll.

Der hauptsächliche Unterschied zwischen beiden Signifikationsmodi hängt damit zusammen, daß der Adressat auf unterschiedliche Weise Zugang zum jeweiligen Signifikat erhält. Welches Denotat einem Wort, einer Wendung oder einem ganzen Satz zukommt, kann der Adressat auf der Basis seines semantischen Wissens entscheiden, im Falle eines ganzen Satzes verbunden mit der Fähigkeit, die Satzbedeutung kompositionell aus der Bedeutung seiner Bestandteile zu ermitteln. Es wäre falsch zu sagen, daß der Adressat aus der Präsentation der Wendung "Ich stelle fest ..." schließt, daß diese Worte das-und-das bedeuten - er kennt ihre Bedeutung, das ist alles.

Die Rede von Schlußprozessen ist nur dann angemessen, wenn es darum geht, das Korrelat einer sprachlichen Äußerung zu ermitteln. Angenommen, das Korrelat lasse sich als eine spezifische Sprechereinstellung charakterisieren. Im Fall eines assertiven Sprechakts wäre dann die korrelierende Einstellung mit "S glaubt, daß p" wiederzugeben, im Falle eines direktiven Sprechakts mit "S wünscht, daß p" etc.[7] Man kann dann sagen, daß der Adressat das Korrelat erschließt, wobei die Kenntnis der Bedeutung der sprachlichen Mittel, also des Denotats, sowie die Kenntnis der Kontextbedingungen in die Prämissenmenge dieses Schlusses eingehen. Die Ausdrücke "Ich stelle fest ..." oder "Ich ordne an ..." *bedeuten* ja nicht "Der Sprecher glaubt, daß ..." oder "Der Sprecher wünscht, daß ...", sondern dieses Wissen ist Ergebnis einer adressatenseitigen Inferenz.

So wie es semantische Konventionen für Denotate gibt, so gibt es auch Konventionen, die das Verhältnis des geäußerten Ausdrucks zu seinem Korrelat regeln. Searle war der Meinung, daß diese Konventionen auf der Basis der konstitutiven Regeln ebenfalls semantischer Art seien - eben semantische Konventionen für den Gebrauch des illokutionsindizierenden Mittels. Ob das Korrelat wirklich als eine semantische Äußerungsdimension aufgefaßt werden sollte, erscheint zweifelhaft; aus dem eben Gesagten ergibt sich klar, daß man eine Inferenz der angedeuteten Art nicht als Bestandteil des semantischen Wissens auffassen sollte, und diese Auffassung wird hier auch weiterhin vertreten.

Die adressatenseitige Inferenz auf das Korrelat einer sprachlichen Äußerung ist für die Kommunikation deswegen relevant, weil die Zuschreibung einer Sprechereinstellung Auswirkungen hat auf die Zuordnung der Äußerung zu einer Klasse von illokutionären Akten. Der Stellenwert der Einstellung, die der einen Satz äußernden Person zugeschrieben wird, unterliegt in der sprechakttheoretischen Literatur unterschiedlichen Einschätzungen; einige Theoretiker sehen in ihr nur ein Klassifikationskriterium unter anderen, andere verwenden die Sprechereinstellung als einziges Kriterium. Auf jeden Fall muß man den Schritt von der zugeschriebenen Sprechereinstellung zum illokutionären Akt als eine weitere Inferenzleistung des Adressaten einordnen, in die dann wesentlich kontextuelle Faktoren als Prämissen eingehen.[8] Die Äußerung eines Deklarativsatzes mit zugehöriger epistemischer Sprechereinstellung ist nicht per se eine Feststellung; und auch die Äußerung von "Ich stelle fest ..." macht eine Äußerung nicht zu einer solchen, ohne daß minimale kontextuelle Bedingungen erfüllt sind. So muß die Person, die einen solchen gewichtigen Sprechakt ausführt, in gewisser Weise auch die Autorität dazu haben. Der Fußballfan in der Ostkurve kann nicht feststellen, daß der Ball im Aus war - das kann nur der Schiedrichter. Und wenn ein Kind einen Satz äußert, der mit "Ich stelle fest ..." beginnt, neigt man nicht zu harter Faktenüberprüfung. Das heißt, daß in diesen Fällen Bedingungen für den erfolgreichen Vollzug des Sprechakts erfüllt sein müssen, damit das Ziel des Sprechers erreicht wird - auf diese Bedingungen hingewiesen zu haben ist das Verdienst Searles. Daraus ergibt sich aber, daß der Adressat diese Bedingungen kennen, ihre Erfüllung erkennen und hieraus den Schluß ziehen muß, daß der Sprecher den Sprechakt des Feststellens ausgeführt hat.

Daß die Kenntnis des Denotats einer sprachlichen Äußerung und die Kenntnis ihres Korrelats in der Tat unterschiedlichen Teilsystemen der sprachlichen Kompetenz zuzuordnen sind, läßt sich auch an zwei Faktoren festmachen, die das Mißlingen eines Sprechakts betreffen.

Nehmen wir an, eine performative Formel werde als Illokutionsindikator in einem geäußerten Satz verwendet, der Sprecher habe aber die Einstellung, die er ausdrückt, nicht. Obwohl man schon darüber streiten kann, ob der Sprecher die Einstellung dann überhaupt noch "ausdrückt", soll hier über etwas anderes, allerdings Verwandtes nachgedacht werden. Die oben schon diskutierte Frage lautet in der hier eingeführten Terminologie: Ist die Eigenschaft eines sprachlichen Elements, Indikator der Illokution zu sein, an die Existenz eines Korrelats gebunden oder nicht?

Man kann vielleicht sagen, daß der prinzipielle Status von z.B. explizit performativen Formeln als Illokutionsindikatoren davon nicht unbedingt beeinträchtigt ist, daß Sprecher nicht aufrichtig sind und diese Indikatoren bisweilen benutzen, ohne daß sie die korrelierte Einstellung haben. Aktuell jedoch, in der spezifischen Situation, wird man das Fehlen des Korrelats diagnostizieren müssen, und infolgedessen indiziert der Indikator nur vermeintlich etwas, was der Sprecher aber gar nicht ausgebildet hat.

Der parallele Fall bei Denotaten verhält sich völlig anders. Nehmen wir an, jemand äußere "Ich stelle fest ..." in ironischer Absicht und ohne ein Anzeichen zu geben, für das Zutreffen seiner Feststellung auch einzustehen. Hat diese Situation zur Folge, daß man dem Sprecher nicht die entsprechende Einstellung und der Äußerung nicht das entsprechende Korrelat zusprechen kann, so bedeuten doch die verwendeten Ausdrücke das, was sie immer bedeuten. Die Tatsache, daß jemand ironisch, nicht-wörtlich oder nicht-ernsthaft spricht, hat keine Auswirkungen auf das Denotat des geäußerten Satzes. Die Wendung "Ich stelle fest ..." hat unabhängig von ihrer Verwendung dieselbe Bedeutung, ja der ironische Effekt lebt geradezu von der Bedeutungskonstanz. Wäre die Bedeutung der verwendeten Ausdrücke abhängig von ironischer oder nicht-wörtlicher Verwendung, dann wäre Ironie u.ä. nicht mehr möglich - es gäbe nur ernsthaften, wörtlichen Sprachgebrauch. Man kann also festhalten, daß Korrelate situationssensitiv sind insofern, als ihre Existenz von der aktuell ausgedrückten Sprechereinstellung abhängig ist, Denotate jedoch situationsunabhängig sind, weil sie nicht an das Vorhandensein sprecherseitiger Einstellungen gebunden sind.

Im Zusammenhang damit läßt sich ein zweiter Punkt festhalten, der nicht mit einer Abweichung seitens des Sprechers, sondern mit einem Fehler des Adressaten zusammenhängt. Beim sprachlichen Kommunizieren gibt es Fehlinterpretationen auf unterschiedlichen Äußerungsebenen. So kann der Adressat sowohl das Denotat wie auch das Korrelat falsch auffassen. Beide Fehlleistungen unterscheiden sich jedoch prinzipiell: Irrt sich der Adressat beim Erfassen des Korrelats, das heißt ordnet er einer Äußerung die falsche Sprechereinstellung zu, so kann das entweder daran liegen, daß er die Bedeutung der illokutionsindizierenden Wendung nicht kennt (Fehler im Denotat), oder, daß er zwar die Bedeutung kennt, aber die falschen Schlüsse aus der Tatsache zieht, daß der Sprecher diese Wendung gebraucht (Fehler im Korrelat). Beides sind Fehler unterschiedlicher Art. Den ersten Fehler kann man dadurch beheben, daß man die Vokabelkenntnis der Sprache, in der diese Wendung geäußert wurde, verbessert. Zur Vermeidung des Fehlers der zweiten Art wird diese Strategie nichts nützen. Was der Adressat falsch gemacht hat, ist nicht in der semantischen Komponente seiner sprachlichen Kompetenz anzusiedeln, sondern in der pragmatischen. Er hat einen Fehler gemacht, der die Zuordnung von sprachlichen Ausdrücken zu ausgedrückten Sprechereinstellungen betrifft, also einen Fehler im Korrelat. Beispielsweise kann der Adressat einer explizit performativen Äußerung irrtümlich nicht die performative, sondern die reportative Interpretation wählen, so daß er auf einen mit "Ich fordere dich auf ..." beginnenden Satz erwidern kann: "Gut, und was mache *ich* dann?" - er kann sich also verhalten, als ob der Sprecher und er selbst eine Szene einstudieren würden.

Beide Fehler, falsches Denotat bzw. falsches Korrelat, haben unterschiedliche Ursachen und müssen auf unterschiedliche Weise behoben werden. Ihr Zusammenwirken im Zuge des Sprechakt-Vollzugs läßt sich so beschreiben, daß der Sprecher dem Adressaten ein spezifisches Korrelat zu erkennen gibt, indem er einen Satz mit einem spezifischen Denotat äußert; die Entsprechung des auf diese Weise kommunizierten Korrelats ist mithin nicht der Satz als Lautkette, sondern eine syntaktisch spezifizierte Lautkette-mit-einem-Denotat. In den meisten Fällen ist die Voraussetzung für die Kommunikation eines Korrelats ein Satz-mit-Denotat, wenngleich auch Fälle auftreten, die als denotatfrei klassifiziert werden müssen: Sie sind dann gegeben, wenn parasprachliche Mittel gewählt werden, die keine Bedeutung im linguistischen Sinne besitzen, wie einige Interjektionen, Schulterzucken, Kopfschütteln, Schweigen (statt etwas zu sagen), sowie in den Fällen, in denen Eigennamen vokativ verwendet werden (Eigennamen haben kein Denotat, s. hierzu Kripke 1981).

Aus der Perspektive des Adressaten läßt sich der Kommunikationsvorgang so beschreiben, daß dieser auf der Basis der Audition einer Lautkette mit zugehörigem Denotat der Äußerung ein Korrelat zuschreibt, dessen Ermittlung je nach Situation mehr oder weniger vollständig auf der Kenntnis des Denotats beruht. Wie ist nun dieses Mehr-oder-Weniger genauer zu spezifizieren?

Hierzu soll auf die beiden in diesem Kapitel eingeführten Unterscheidungen - *instrumentaler vs. resultativer Verwendungsmodus* und *Denotat vs. Korrelat* zurückgegriffen werden, wodurch sich folgende Festlegung treffen läßt:

Der instrumentale und der resultative Verwendungsmodus lassen sich unterscheiden nach Maßgabe der spezifischen Funktion, die das Denotat einer sprachlichen Äußerung bei der Ermittlung des Korrelats durch den Adressaten spielen soll. Liegt ein instrumentaler Verwendungsmodus vor, dann soll der Adressat das Korrelat einer sprachlichen Äußerung im wesentlichen auf der Basis seines Denotat-Wissens erschließen; im resultativen Verwendungsmodus hingegen soll der Adressat das Korrelat auf der Basis kontextueller Informationen unter Zuhilfenahme seines Denotat-Wissens ermitteln. Das sprachliche Material darf im resultativen Verwendungsmodus so sparsam sein, daß das Denotat als Interpretationshilfe nur wenig explizite Informationen bietet; das Kontextwissen mitsamt der Kommunikationsgeschichte wird also einen hohen Stellenwert haben bei der Interpretation des Sprechakts und diesen Stellenwert auch haben dürfen.

6 Der linguistische Status von illokutionären Indikatoren

Es erscheint als Binsenwahrheit, daß die sprachlichen Mittel zur Indizierung einer Sprechakt-Illokution unterschiedlich explizit sein können. Man könnte diese Mannigfaltigkeit von Explizitheitsstufen dadurch aus der Analyse heraushalten, daß man sich auf den Laborfall beschränkt und maximale Explizitheit annimmt, in der nicht ganz unberechtigten Erwartung, daß die weniger expliziten Fälle ("Indirektheit") eine Klärung der expliziten Fälle voraussetzen. Das Problem, das eine solch elegante Vorgehensweise aufwirft, besteht allerdings darin, daß es unklar zu sein scheint, was maximale Explizitheit ist. An welchem Punkt kann man davon reden, daß - in der hier gewählten Terminologie - das Denotat den maximalen Grad an Informationen darüber enthält, welches Korrelat einer Äußerung zugewiesen werden muß, so daß die Präsentation eines Satzes in reduziertestem Kontext ausreicht, um das Korrelat bestimmen zu können? Gibt es Kriterien dafür, wann dieser Punkt erreicht ist?

Man könnte der Auffassung sein, daß maximale Explizitheit dann vorliegt, wenn das Korrelat der Äußerung von dieser selbst *benannt* wird, so daß es aus der Bedeutung der verwendeten Ausdrücke selbst hervorgeht, um welches Korrelat es geht. Dies ist offenkundig nicht der Fall, vielmehr ist eine solche Äußerung in der Regel pragmatisch abweichend, wie man an folgendem Beispiel sieht. Nehmen wir an, jemand formuliert den Satz

(12)   Sei morgen um 7 Uhr zur Stelle.

in der Absicht, möglichst explizit zu sein, folgendermaßen um:

(13)   Diese Äußerung gilt als Versuch, dich dazu zu bringen, morgen um 7 Uhr zur Stelle zu sein.

Eine Alternative ist dazu:

(14)   Ich beabsichtige, dich dazu zu bringen, morgen um 7 Uhr zur Stelle zu sein, und zwar aufgrund der Erkenntnis meiner Absicht.

Diese Beipiele zeigen, daß es eine Differenz geben muß zwischen dem Denotat und dem Korrelat einer sprachlichen Äußerung derart, daß das Denotat eines Satzes nicht das Korrelat seiner Äußerung enthalten darf. Ich fasse dies als ein weiteres Argument dafür auf, daß sich das Korrelat weder auf das Denotat reduzieren läßt noch durch das Denotat vollständig determiniert ist - anders läßt sich die pragmatische Inadäquatheit von (13)/ (14) nicht erklären.

Man könnte nun einwenden, daß die in (13)/(14) enthaltenen Ausdrücke jeweils Teil einer theoretischen Explikation eines Sprechakts sind, die für den aktuellen Sprachgebrauch nicht geeignet ist und deshalb auch nicht als Beispiel gewählt werden sollte. Dies mag sein, Beispiel (13)/(14) zeigt aber dennoch, daß es unabhängig von den näheren Gründen offenkundig Explizitheitsgrenzen sprachlicher Äußerungen gibt, die die besagte Differenz zwischen Denotat und Korrelat fordern. Betrachten wir eine näher an der Alltagssprache angesiedelte Version:

(15)   Ich wünsche, daß du morgen um 7 Uhr zur Stelle bist.

Auch hier liegt eine markierte Version vor, die wir nicht als die normale, übliche Art, eine Aufforderung zu vollziehen, empfinden. Die Äußerung von (15), mit der eine konstitutive Sprechereinstellung denotiert wird, macht einen konversationellen Schlußprozeß erforderlich, durch den vom Ausdruck der Einstellung auf die Illokution des Sprechakts geschlossen wird. Der Effekt, der durch eine solche Ausdrucksweise erzielt wird, ist der einer Intensivierung oder Verstärkung[9], mindestens aber wird hierdurch eine zwischen Sprecher und Adressat bestehende Hierarchie betont. Es liegt also nicht an der Formulierung, daß die aufgeführten Beispiele nicht als die üblichen, natürlichen Mittel des Vollzugs illokutionärer Akte angesehen werden können. Es liegt wohl daran, daß sie zuviel des Korrelats thematisieren.

Explizit performative Äußerungen sind schon aufgrund ihrer Bezeichnung gute Kandidaten für maximale Explizitheit, jedoch ist bekannt, daß auch sie nur in "problematischen" Kontexten eingesetzt werden.

(16)   Ich fordere dich auf, morgen um 7 Uhr zur Stelle zu sein.

Gemeinhin wird angenommen, daß (16) nur dann geäußert wird, wenn der Sprecher mit einem Widerstand des Adressaten, die Aufforderung zu erfüllen, rechnen muß. Auch hier liegt eine Verstärkung oder Intensivierung vor, die bestimmter kontextueller Bedingungen bedarf, um pragmatisch adäquat zu sein.

Hinzu kommt, daß der Adresssat in dem angenommenen reduzierten Kontext nicht zwischen der performativen und der reportativen Lesart unterscheiden kann. Er muß also wissen, daß der Sprecher ihn dazu auffordert, um sieben Uhr zur Stelle zu sein, und nicht über seinen Aufforderungsakt berichtet. Ist also

(12)   Sei morgen um 7 Uhr zur Stelle.

die maximal explizite Form des Vollzugs illokutionärer Akte? Vieles spricht dafür, zumal Satztypen und ihre Konstituenten, Wortstellung, Verbmodus u.a. als klassische Vertreter illokutionärer Indikatoren gelten. Andererseits gelten auch explizit performative Formeln als prototypische Indikatoren, so daß man diese beiden Formen als in einem Standardbereich von Explizitheit liegend ansehen sollte. Um einem Maßstab für einen sinnvollen Explizitheitsgrad näher zu kommen, sei hier vorgeschlagen, Explizitheit nicht unabhängig von pragmatischer Geeignetheit oder Adäquatheit zu definieren. Wer (13)/(14) äußert, sagt zwar Vieles, ist aber nicht maximal explizit, weil dieser Typ von Äußerung als pragmatisch inadäquat angesehen werden muß. Auch (15) ist nicht in diesem Sinne maximal explizit, nicht weil diese Äußerung inadäquat wäre, sondern weil es eines zusätzlichen Schlußprozesses zur Ermittlung des Korrelats bedarf. Am Beispiel eines kommissiven Sprechakts ist dies noch deutlicher zu sehen. Sagt jemand

(17)   Ich habe die Absicht, morgen um 7 Uhr zu Dir zu kommen.

dann ist hiermit weniger ein Versprechen vollzogen als vielmehr ein gewisser Unsicherheitsgrad ausgedrückt, der sich auf die Ankunft von S bezieht: Absichten können durchkreuzt werden. Somit ist (17) aber weniger explizit als

(18)   Ich verspreche, morgen um 7 Uhr zu Dir zu kommen.

Aus diesen Beobachtungen ergibt sich, daß die Kriterien für Explizitheit maximengesteuert sind. Genauer gesagt unterliegt die Wahl der Explizitheitsstufe der Griceschen Maxime der Quantität, die ja einerseits hinreichende Informativität, andererseits Vermeidung von Überinformativität fordert (s. Grice 1993: 249). Auf den vorliegenden Zusammenhang angewandt heißt dies, daß die Wahl des Illokutionsindikators dem Zweck der sprachlichen Äußerung angepaßt sein muß in dem Sinne, daß er nicht mehr als hinreichende Informationen über das mit der Äußerung verbundene Korrelat enthalten muß. Nach diesem Kriterium sind (14) und erst recht (13) überinformativ und scheiden deshalb als geeignete Explizitheitskandidaten aus.

Nach dem Kriterium der maximenadäquaten Explizitheit erweisen sich (12) und (16) als Äußerungen, die zur Indizierung des Korrelats die geeignetsten sind. Sie sind insbesondere geeignet, im instrumentalen Verwendungsmodus als illokutionäre Indikatoren bei reduziertem Kontext zu fungieren, so daß unterstellt werden kann, daß Adressaten bei der Präsentation dieser Äußerungen hinreichend über die illokutionäre Kraft informiert werden.

Nach diesen Bemerkungen zum Kriterium der geeigneten Explizitheit kommen wir nun zur Kernfrage dieses Beitrags, nämlich: wie illokutionäre Indikatoren zu definieren

sind. Ich möchte im Folgenden einen Vorschlag für eine solche Definition machen, der den genannten Gesichtspunkten soweit wie möglich Rechnung trägt:
Die Definition des Indikatorbegriffs lautet:

S indiziert k mit $i =_{\text{def.}}$
S intendiert mittels der Äußerung von ... i ... mit einem Denotat d einen propositionalen Einstellungstyp δ_k seitens A zu evozieren, indem er sich darauf verläßt, daß A auf der Basis seines Denotatwissens bezüglich ... i ... und seiner Kenntnis des resultierenden Verfahrens bezüglich $s(i)$ S's kommunikative Intention erkennt.

Da diese Definition nur für lexikalische Indikatoren (z.B. performative Formeln) gilt, muß sie bezüglich struktureller Indikatoren (Satztypen) modifiziert werden:

S indiziert k mit $s_a =_{\text{def.}}$
S intendiert mittels der Äußerung von s_a mit einem Denotat D einen propositionalen Einstellungstyp δ_k seitens A zu evozieren, indem er sich darauf verläßt, daß A auf der Basis des resultierenden Verfahrens und seines Denotatwissens bezüglich s_a S's Intention erkennt. [a bezeichnet Werte für zentrale Eigenschaften von Satztypen, als die gelten: 1 = Stirnsatz (V-1), 2 = Kernsatz (V-2) und 3 = Spannsatz (V-Letzt)).

Diese Definitionen müssen modifiziert werden für den Fall, daß S keine oder nicht primär eine Einstellung seitens A hervorzurufen intendiert, sondern das vollzieht, was man üblicherweise eine Deklaration nennt (Eröffnung, Beförderung, Verurteilung etc.). Hier muß man die Wendung *S intendiert ... einen Einstellungstyp zu evozieren* ersetzen durch *S intendiert ..., eine institutionelle Tatsache des Typs k zu konstituieren*. Diese optionale Modifikation gilt für beide Arten von Indikatoren, lexikalische wie strukturelle, und sie ist notwendig, weil sonst die Definitionen von illokutionären Indikatoren zu eng wären.

Diese für den instrumentalen Verwendungsmodus geltenden Definitionen sollen nun näher erläutert werden. Zunächst zur Definition lexikalischer Indikatoren:

i kennzeichnet den Indikator, der in diesem Falle ein Verb in der für Performativa geltenden Standardform mit seinen Ergänzungen sein kann (*Ich fordere Dich auf ...*), aber auch ein Modalverb (*Du sollst ...*) oder ein sogenannter modaler Infinitiv (*Du hast zu ...*). Der Satztyp ist in diesen Fällen immer gleich, er kann als Indikator zunächst ausgesondert werden. Die Punkte vor und nach i sollen andeuten, daß der Indikator in der Regel nicht isoliert stehen kann, sondern nur als Teil eines Satzes seine Funktion erfüllt. Obwohl die syntaktische Umgebung für den Indikatorstatus von i notwendig ist, gehört sie nicht zum illokutionären Indikator selbst.

Das Denotat d besteht in der lexikalischen Bedeutung des Indikators inklusive der in den morphologischen Merkmalen kodierten grammatischen Information. Die Wendung *Ich fordere Dich auf...* enthält zwei indexikalische Elemente mit Referenz auf den Sprecher und auf den Adressaten, und ein sprechaktbezeichnendes Verb mit entsprechender lexikalischer Bedeutung und den Merkmalen der 1.Ps.Sg.Präs.

Der propositionale Einstellungs*typ* δ_k ist vom propositionalen Einstellungs*gehalt* abgegrenzt. Diese Abgrenzung ist zentral, denn sie betrifft den Unterschied zwischen illokutionären und propositionalen Indikatoren. Einstellungstypen und somit Werte für k sind *Glauben, Beabsichtigen* etc., wobei nicht festgelegt ist, was der Gehalt des Glaubens oder der Absicht ist. Illokutionäre Indikatoren sind, obwohl sie in einer syntaktischen Umgebung vorkommen, per definitionem nur der Teil des geäußerten Satzes, der sich auf den Typ und nicht auf den Inhalt der zu evozierenden propositionalen Einstellung bezieht. Daher ist auch das Indizierte k nicht die gesamte Einstellung, sondern der Einstellungstyp oder, in Searles Terminologie, der psychologische Modus der Einstellung - soweit es sich um Nicht-Deklarationen handelt.

Das Denotatwissen von A ist eine Voraussetzung für den erfolgreichen Gebrauch des Indikators durch S. Läge adressatenseitige Kenntnis von d bzw. D nicht vor, so würde S i nicht einsetzen, denn dies widerspräche grundlegenden Rationalitätsanforderungen an das Sprachverhalten von S. i wäre ein ungeeignetes Mittel und sein Gebrauch daher nicht rational. Die vorliegende Festlegung macht noch einmal deutlich, wie das Verhältnis von Denotat und Korrelat zu sehen ist: Das Denotat-Wissen von A ist eine Voraussetzung dafür, daß A angesichts i auf das Vorliegen von k schließen kann. d bzw. D ist also eng bezogen auf i definiert, und beides ist die Grundlage für k.

Die Klausel, daß S sich auf A's Denotatwissen *verläßt*, ist schwächer als eine, die eine Sprecher-Intention hierzu fordert. Die schwächere Festlegung ist insofern realistischer, als eine diesbezügliche S-Intention kaum aufrechtzuerhalten ist: Woher soll der Sprecher die nötige Evidenz nehmen dafür, daß A keine anderen Quellen als sein Denotatwissen zu Hilfe nimmt, um i zu interpretieren - und vor allen Dingen, warum soll er dies ausschließen wollen? Es reicht, wenn S mit bestimmten adressatenseitigen Fähigkeiten rechnet und auf dieser Kalkulation sein Sprachverhalten aufbaut; eine *Intention*, die sich auf das aktuelle Motiv für die Reaktion des Adressaten richtet, ist unnötig.

Mit dieser Bemerkung möchte ich die Überlegungen zur Explikation des Begriffs illokutionärer Indikator abschließen. Ihr Sinn besteht darin, die notwendigen Faktoren und Bestimmungsgrößen für eine solche Explikation aufzuführen und zentrale Differenzierungen vorzunehmen. Wenn damit auch kein Vollständigkeitsanspruch erhoben werden kann, so ist doch der Kern einer Explikation aufgezeigt, der für einen weiteren Ausbau einer Theorie des Indikatorengebrauchs unerläßlich ist. Und vielleicht ist auch klarer geworden, was man als LinguistIn mit Sprechakten anfangen kann: Man hat meines Erachtens die Chance, zentrale Teilsysteme der kommunikativen Kompetenz in differenzierter Weise aufeinander zu beziehen und hieraus Schlüsse für das menschliche Sprachverhalten im allgemeinen zu ziehen, vor allem darüber, wie verbal miteinander Kommunizierende Gebrauch von schon vorliegenden oder konventionalisierten sprachlichen Formen zum Zwecke der Beeinflussung ihres Gegenübers machen. Dieser Mechanismus ist offensichtlich komplexer, als allgemein angenommen wird.

Anmerkungen

1 Die durch das Denotat bestimmte Referenz sei hier *Designat* genannt.
2 Eine wahrheitswertfähige "Behauptungs"-Lesart ist pragmatisch abweichend, denn der Adressat wäre ein Segelboot. Hieraus folgt, a] daß man (6) in diesem Kontext nur performativ interpretieren kann, und b] daß performative Äußerungen des Typs "Taufe" sich auf Objekte oder Personen beziehen können, die nicht die Adressaten der Äußerung sind. Vgl. die Taufe von Säuglingen mithilfe des gleichen Äußerungstyps. Ich nenne diesen Typ "rhetorische Anrede".
3 Alstons vielzitierter Begriff des Illokutionspotentials ist bis jetzt für linguistische Analysen nicht ausbuchstabiert (s. Alston 1964).
4 Dies entspricht, wie wir sahen, der von Searle vertretenen Auffassung indirekter Sprechakte. S. Searle 1982.
5 Eine verwandte Dichotomie führt G. Ungeheuer ein, indem er *kruziale* von *nicht-kruzialer* Kommunikation unterscheidet. Er differenziert somit Kommunikationstypen und nicht Verwendungsweisen von Äußerungen. Kruziale Kommunikation nennt er die "Sozialhandlungen, in denen das Sprechen, Mitteilen und Verstehen [...] weitgehend unabhängig von den sie umgebenden Tätigkeiten und Erfahrungen zu leisten ist" (Ungeheuer 1987: 321).
6 S. hierzu auch Searle (1989).
7 Zur Klassifikation von Sprechakten auf der Basis von Sprechereinstellungen s. Motsch & Pasch (1987).
8 Zur Explikation derartiger Inferenzen des Hörers s. Bach & Harnish (1979).
9 S. hierzu Lang (1983), Sellars (1966).

Literatur

Alston, W.P. (1964): Philosophy of Language. Englewood Cliffs: Prentice-Hall.
Bach, K. & R.M. Harnish (1979): Linguistic Communication and Speech Acts. Cambridge: The M.I.T. Press.
Bierwisch, M. (1979): "Wörtliche Bedeutung - eine pragmatische Gretchenfrage". In: G. Grewendorf, ed.: Sprechakttheorie und Semantik. Frankfurt/Main: Suhrkamp, 119-148.
Dik, S. (1989): The Theory of Functional Grammar. Part I: The Structure of the Clause. Dordrecht: Foris.
Donnellan, K. (1966): "Reference and Definite Descriptions". Philosophical Review 75, 281-304.
Ehrich, V. & G. Saile (1972): "Über nicht-direkte Sprechakte". In: D. Wunderlich, ed.: Linguistische Pragmatik. Frankfurt/Main: Athenäum, 255-287.
Engberg-Pedersen, E. u.a., eds. (1994): Function and Expression in Functional Grammar. Berlin/New York: de Gruyter.
Ervin-Tripp, S. (1976): "Is Sybil there? The structure of American English directives". Language in Society 5, 25-66.
Franck, D. (1975): "Zur Analyse indirekter Sprechakte". In: V. Ehrich & P. Finke, eds.: Beiträge zur Grammatik und Pragmatik. Kronberg: Scriptor, 219-231.
Fraser, B. (1985): "Pragmatic Formatives". In: J. Verschueren & M. Bertucelli-Papi, eds.: The Pragmatic Perspective. Selected Papers from the 1985 International Pragmatics Conference. Amsterdam: Benjamins, 179-194.
Frege, G. (1918/1919, 1966): "Der Gedanke". In: G. Frege: Logische Untersuchungen. Hg. v. G. Patzig. Göttingen: Vandenhoek, 30-53.

Gazdar, G. (1981): "Speech act assignment". In: A.K. Joshi u.a., eds.: Elements of Discourse Understanding. Cambridge: Cambridge University Press, 64-83.
Givón, T. (1984/1990): Syntax. A functional-typological introduction. Vol. I/II. Amsterdam: Benjamins.
Givón, T. (1995): Functionalism and Grammar. Amsterdam: Benjamins.
Harnish, R.M. (1995): "Mood, meaning, and speech acts". In: S.L. Tzohatzidis, ed.: Foundations of Speech Act Theory. London / New York: Routledge, 407-455.
Kripke, S. (1977): "Speaker's reference and semantic reference". In: P.A. French et al., eds.: Studies in the Philosophy of Language. Minneapolis, 255-276.
Kripke, S. (1981): Name und Notwendigkeit. Frankfurt/Main: Suhrkamp.
Lang, E. (1983): "Einstellungsausdrücke und ausgedrückte Einstellungen". In: R. Ruzicka & W. Motsch, eds.: Untersuchungen zur Semantik. Berlin: Akademie-Verlag, 305-341.
Liedtke, F., ed. (1995): Implikaturen. Grammatische und pragmatische Analysen. Tübingen: Niemeyer.
Meibauer, J., ed. (1987): Satzmodus zwischen Grammatik und Pragmatik. Tübingen: Niemeyer.
Motsch, W. & R. Pasch (1987): "Illokutive Handlungen". In: W. Motsch, ed.: Satz, Text, sprachliche Handlung. Berlin: Akademie-Verlag, 11-79.
Rolf, E. (1994): Sagen und Meinen. Paul Grices Theorie der Konversationsimplikaturen. Opladen: Westdeutscher Verlag.
Rosengren, I. (1992/1993): Satz und Illokution. Bd. I/II. Tübingen: Niemeyer.
Sadock, J.M. (1974): Toward a Linguistic Theory of Speech Acts. New York: Academic Press.
Sadock, J.M. & A.M. Zwicky (1985): "Speech act distinctions in syntax". In: T. Shopen, ed.: Language typology and syntactic description. Vol. I: Clause structure. Cambridge: Cambridge University Press, 155-196.
Searle, J.R. (1971): Sprechakte. Ein sprachphilosophischer Essay. Frankfurt/Main: Suhrkamp.
Searle, J.R. (1982): Indirekte Sprechakte. In: J.R. Searle: Ausdruck und Bedeutung. Untersuchungen zur Sprechakttheorie. Frankfurt/Main: Suhrkamp, 51-79.
Searle, J.R. (1989): "How performatives work". Linguistics and Philosophy 12, 535-558.
Sellars, W. (1966): Science, Perception, and Reality. London: Routledge & Kegan Paul.
Sökeland, W. (1980): Indirektheit von Sprechhandlungen. Eine linguistische Untersuchung. Tübingen: Niemeyer.
Ungeheuer, G. (1987): "Vor-Urteile über Sprechen, Mitteilen, Verstehen". In: G. Ungeheuer: Kommunikationstheoretische Schriften 1: Sprechen, Mitteilen, Verstehen. Hg. von J.G. Juchem. Aachen: Rader, 290-338.

Informatives and / or Directives?
(A New Start in Speech Act Classification)

Georg Meggle, Leipzig / Maria Ulkan, München

In order to avoid being thoroughly ad hoc, any classification has to be principled - which holds with classifying (types of) *illocutionary acts* in particular. As a theory of illocutionary acts is best seen to be a special branch of *action theory in general*, it seems to be clear where the relevant classification-principles have to come from. (i) It is a general theory of action, in terms of which (basic) illocutionary acts are to be explicated; and, in order to be reliable, (ii) the needed classification-principles have to be derived from (the *logical connections* existing between) these action-theoretic explications themselves. Now, although much lip-service has been paid to (i), until quite recently virtually nothing has been done about working it out systematically.[1] Consequently, the same holds true with the state of the art of task (ii). Thus, one has to make a new start.[2]

Of course, proceeding via the lines of (i) and (ii) cannot take the form of a broad attack seeking to conquer all the members of the huge 'class of illocutionary acts'[3] at one blow. Instead, we shall try to aim at what is taken by us to be the centre of the whole continent or - as the classification in question will be hierarchical in any case – perhaps more to the point, at what we think to be the highest peaks (or peak?) of the whole area Following Schiffer (1972), IV.2, we take it that (iii) informative and directive speech acts are the most general ones under which all the other communicative acts may be subsumed.[4] But, whereas Schiffer merely contends that the resulting system of *two classes* can't be further reduced, this is exactly the point to be called into question in this paper. (Notice, that in the following nothing depends on whether (iii) will in fact be accepted or not. The question of how informatives and directives are interrelated remains to be answered anyhow.)

1 Informal Characterization

Communicative acts are acts directed to other persons (addressees), produced with the *primary intention* of making the respective adressee either do something or acquire a certain propositional attitude. Communicative acts, when done with the primary intention that A is to *do* something, we call *directives* (short for 'directive communicative acts'), when done with the primary intention that A is to *believe* something, *informatives*.[5]

Primary intentions do not suffice to make an act a communicative one. But the essential further feature of communicative acts is not very hard to get at. It relates to how the speaker[6] *believes* he achieves his primary aim: In communicative acts the speaker believes he achieves his primary aim iff his act is understood by his audience A to be a communicative one done with the primary intention in question. Now, although this characterization is obviously circular, it gives us at least a *criterion of adequacy* for any non-circular explication. And it follows from it that, for an act to be a communicative one, the speaker S must not only intend A to recognize his primary intention, but also to recognize all the relevant communicative intentions, e.g., that A is to recognize S's primary intention, etc.

This first extremely rough characterization exploits Grice's (1957) definition of *utterer's meaning* which was shown in Schiffer (1972) not to fulfil our stated criterion of adequacy. Now, it should be clear that the problem of explicating communicative acts non-circularly is not a trivial one, and that some logical machinery has to be used in order to keep all the different things involved in reflexive intentions really distinct. In formal action-theoretic terms the explication problem was solved in *Grundbegriffe der Kommunikation* - in the following referred to as GBK. As in elucidating the conceptual connections between informatives and directives we need some part of this machinery, a simplified version of the *GBK*-explication will be presented in the next §.[7]

For his belief that A will recognize the relevant communicative intentions of his act S may have any reasons whatever. (Which is, of course, not to deny that in normal cases these reasons will be quite specific ones as including supposed common knowledge of linguistic and other conventions.) But, as none of these possible reasons is essentially connected with informatives and directives, there is no need to specify them at this stage. And, in fact, if our considerations are to be really general, they *should not* be specified either. (Doing this would already engage us in some kind of further sub-classification, which is another story - to be told elsewhere.)

2 Formal Explication

2.1 Preliminaries of Formal Explication

As communicative acts are a special kind of intentional acts, the latter term is to be explicated first. Writing $D(X,f)$ for 'At time t person X does (act of type) f', $B(X,p)$ for 'At t X (strongly) believes that p' and $W(X,p)$ for 'At t X wants that p', the relevant concept of intention can (restricting our considerations to situations of decision under certainty) easily be given as follows:[8]

D1: $I(X,f,p) := D(X,f) \& W(X,p) \& B(X, p \equiv D(X,f))$

   At t X does f with the intention to bring about p.

Clearly, in I(X,f,p) the proposition expressed by p has to be such that X believes it to be realized at time t', where t' is (usually immediately) following t. When talking about doings, beliefs and wants at t', we shall make this time-reference explicit by writing D',B' and W'.

Now, in order to get at the logical structure of our basic communicative acts (or act?), two further highly specific intention-concepts are needed. The first is the Gricean concept of an M-intention as used by him in the definiens of his (1957)-explication for *utterer's m*eaning, to be improved and made rnore precise as follows[9]- with K(X,p), for 'X knows that p', as short for B(X,p) & p, i.e.: X believes that p, and it is the case that p:

D2.1:   MI(X,Y,f,r) := I(X,f,D'(Y,r)) &
          B(X,D'(y,r) ≡ K'(Y,I(X,f,D'(y,r))))

> At t X does f with the M-intention that Y is, at t', to do r iff X does, at t, f with the (primary) intention to bring it about that, at t', Y is to do r, and S believes at t, that Y will, at t', do r if and only if S's primary intention will be recognized (known) by Y at t'.

For M-intentions with the primary aim that Y is to believe that p, we can stipulate correspondingly:

D2.2:   MI(X,Y,f,p) := I(X,f,B'(Y,p)) &
          B(X,B'(Y,p) ≡ K'(Y,I(X,f,B'(Y,p))))

> At t X does f with the M-intention that Y is, at t', to believe that p.

There is another concept, not contained in Grice's proposal, but necessary to make this very proposal adequate. It relates to the fact that in communication all the relevant communicative intentions must be intended by the speaker for his addressee to be quite out in the open. More generally defined (with ∀n as short for 'For all n'):

D3:   (a) $I_1(X,Y,f,p) := I(X,f,B'(Y,p))$

  (b) $I_{n+1}(X,Y,f,p) := I_1(X,Y,f,I_n(X,Y,f,p))$

  (c) $I^*(X,y,f,p) = \forall n I_n(X,Y,f,p)$

> That Y is to believe that p, is intended by X's doing of f in a way (intended by X) to be *absolutely out in the open* for Y.

(Note, that by I* (X,Y,f,p) it is not implied that X himself is believing that p.)

2.2 Informatives and Directives / Explications

Now, our criterion of adequacy for any definition of communicative acts can, for directives, be stated as follows. (The reader is asked to transform into the corresponding criterion for informatives by himself. The structures of both of these criteria may be compared with the structures of the definiens of D2.1 and D2.2.) That an act of type f produced by S at t is a directive communicative act with the primary intention that A is to do r, will be represented by the symbol $CA_d(S,A, f,r)$; correspondingly, we write $CA_i(S,A,f,p)$ for an informative primarily intending A to believe that p.[10]

(*) $\quad CA_d(S,A,f,r) \equiv I(S,f'D'(A,r))$ &
$\qquad B(S,D'(A,r) \equiv K'(H,CA_d(S,A,f,r)))$

As already proved in *GBK*, criterion (*) and its analogue for informatives are fulfilled by defining directives and informatives in the following way (thus proved to be adequate):[11]

D4.1: $\quad CA_d(S,A,f;r) := MI(S,A,f,r)$ &
$\qquad\qquad I^*(S,A,f,MI(S,A,f,r))$

D4.2: $\quad CA_i(S,A,f,p) := MI(S,A,f,p)$ &
$\qquad\qquad I^*(S,A,f,MI(S,A,f,p))$

So much for the *logical structure* of our two central communicative acts. As, in the end, they are defined exclusively by means of our three action theoretic concepts $D(X,f)$, $B(X,p)$ and $W(X,p)$ in application only to speaker S, it should be clear that neither $CA_d(S,A,f,r)$ nor $CA_i(S,A,f,p)$ entail anything about whether the respective communicative act is in fact understood by A, or anything about whether A really does or believes what he is primarily intended to do or to believe; i.e.: our communicatives are communicative acts in the wide sense of communication attempts - these attempts being successful (communicative acts in a stronger sense) or not. (Unfortunately, in what is usually taken to be a theory of speech acts this fundamental distinction between communicatives in a weak and in a strong sense is being systematically neglected.[12])

3 Logical Connections

A principled classification of communicative acts to be really worth its name has to be based on the logical structure of the acts to be classified. Now, having arrived at this structure for our two candidates, let's consider how these candidates are correlated. Then, the resulting logical connections will give us immediately the relevant classification principles which are to be discussed next.
Any directive is an informative, *too*, as shown by the following theorem:[13]

(1) $\quad CA_d(S,A,f,r) \supset CA_i(S,A,f,CA_d(S,A,f,r))$

And, although the sentence

(α) $p \supset q \, \delta \, CA_i(S,A,f,p) \supset CA_i(S,A,f,q)$, for any S and A

does not state a principle generally valid in communication-logic, it can be proved to be valid, when restricted to cases where (a) S believes that A will come to believe that q only via S's doing of f, and (b) S believes (a) to be, or to become, mutually known by himself and A.[14] Now, this condition being clearly fulfilled at least with respect both to I* (S,A,f, MI(S,A,f,r)) and MI(S,A,f,r) and I(S,f,D'(A,r)), at least the following principles can be derived from (1):

(2) $CA_d(S,A,f,r) \supset CA_i(S,A,f,I^*(S,A,f,MI(S,A,f,r)))$

(3) $CA_d(S,A,f,r) \supset CA_i(S,A,f,MI(S,A,f,r))$

and

(4) $CA_d(S,A,f,r) \supset CA_i(S,A,f,I(S,f,D'(A,r)))$.

Further, as may be proved by generalization for any of these principles (cf. note 9), it is analytically true that

(5) $CA_d(S,A,f) \supset CA_i(S,A,f)$

Any directive is an informative, *too*.

The reason why we are stressing the *too* should be obvious. That directives are informatives, too, is not to deny that there are important differences between them. By saying that an act f produced by S at t is a directive, we are implying that S's primary communicative intention is that A is to *do* something, by saying that the act in question is an informative, that S's primary communicative intention is that A is to *believe* something. But this essential difference is not being canceled by (5) and its more specific corollaries. Of none of the five theorems the converse holds without further qualification. Thus, to take just (4), it would be utterly false to regard a directive with the primary intention that A is to do r as being *the same* as an informative with the primary intention that A is to believe that S has this very intention - as proposed, e.g., by Armstrong (1971) and rightly rejected in Bennett (1976), § 41.[15] And the same verdict would have to be reached with respect to accepting the converse of the stronger theorems (1) to (3). (For a prima facie argument to the contrary drawing its apparent force from ordinary language usage see 5 below.)

Now, directives making up a special sort of the genus of informatives, the crucial question left to be answered is this: What feature has to be adjoined to informatives of the kind specified on the right side of our above theorems in order to get the respective directive expressed on their left side? As a first shot, one might try to start with (4) and adjoin to its right side I(S,f,D'(A,r)), thus getting

(β) $CA_d(S,A,f,r) \equiv CA_i(S,A,f,I(S,f'D'(A,r)))$ &
      $I(S,f,D'(A,r))$

The leading idea of this proposal consists in taking directives to be special kinds of informatives for which in producing them the speaker is *sincere*. (In general terms: In producing an informative act of kind $CA_i(S,A,f,p)$, S is sincere iff p is believed to be true by S himself.[16]) But, although this idea is absolutely correct, its realization in (β) is not the one needed to make (β) true. For its right side does not entail that (a) S believes that A will do r iff it is recognized by A that he is to do r - which is, as stated already by Grice (1957), a necessary condition for $CA_d(S,A,f,r)$. But substituting $MI(S,A,f,r)$ for $I(S,A,D'(A,r))$ wouldn't do either. For it is not entailed by the resulting new right side of (β) that S believes it to be known by A that (a) - which is a further necessary condition for $CA_d(S,A,f,r)$ following from our informal characterization of communicative acts in 1 (and, accordingly, derivable from our adequacy criterion (*) in 2.2.). Thus, we have to look for some stronger alternatives. To preclude having to enter into too much discussion, let us jump just to the right one. It follows already from our definitions D4.1 and D4.2 that[17]

(6) $CA_d(S,A,f,r) \equiv CA_i(S,A,f,MI(S,A,f,r))$ & $MI(S,A,f,r)$

Directives primarily intending that A is to do r *are* (analytically equivalent with) informatives primarily intending that A is to recognize that S M-intends A to do r, i.e., informatives primarily intending that A is to believe that $MI(S,A,f,r)$ and such that S is sincere.[18]

Thus, instead of defining in the beginning both informatives and directives, we might have started with informatives alone, directives then being defined as special (sincere) informatives in the form arrived at by (6). And this, as the converse procedure is not possible, this is enough to claim the primacy of informatives over directives to be fully justified. And thus, as we are accepting Schiffer's thesis (iii), stated in our introductory remarks, we may say that there is indeed just *one* peak which is the highest one in the wide area of communicative acts. Informatives constitute the only class under which *all* the other communicative acts can be subsumed. There is just one basic type of communicative acts.

The analogue of (6) holds for informatives as well:

(8) $CA_i(S,A,f,p) \equiv CA_i(S,A,f,MI(S,A,f,p))$ & $MI(S,A,f,p)$

Informatives primarily intending that A is to believe that p are (analytically equivalent with) informatives primarily intending that A is to recognize that S M-intends A to believe that p, i.e., informatives primarily intending that A is to believe that $MI(S,A,f,p)$ and such that S is sincere.

4 Beginning of Principled Classification

Taking (6) and (8) together, one can see that both $CA_d(S,A,f,r)$ and $CA_i(S,A,f,p)$ can be considered to be special cases of (sincere) informatives with the primary intention that A is to believe that S's doing of f is connected with some M-intention directed at A. Thus, starting with the idea that communicative acts are acts involving reflexive intentions, we obtain the general classification schema *figure 1*. ($P_{[\varphi,A]}$ is to stand for a sentence-schema containing "A" as referring to A and "φ" as expressing the quality φ of A, φ being either the quality of doing some action or the quality of believing something to be true.[19] Where the intention represented by $I(S,f,P'_{[\varphi, A]})$ is also a M-intention, we use the abbreviation $MI(S,f,P'_{[\varphi, A]})$ accordingly.[20])

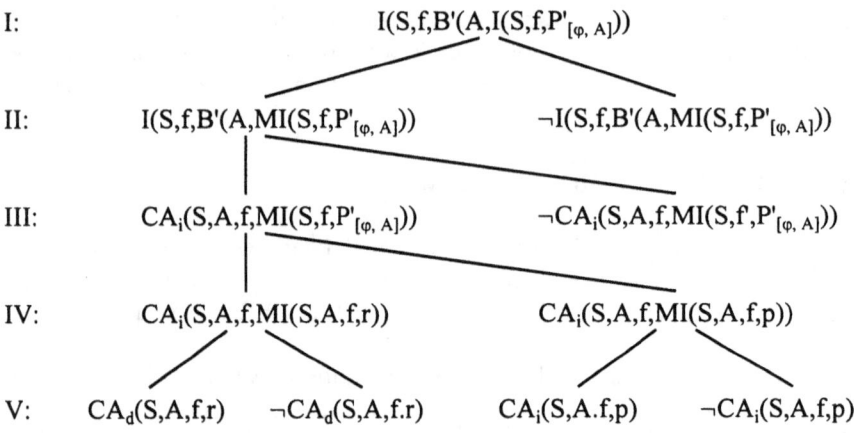

Figure 1

By step I and II communicative acts are imbedded into the frame of intentional acts of a particular kind; and after III the informatives of the represented kind is split up for some action or some belief of A, respectively. That step I is true, but also the right side of II, may be the case, if, for example, S does not believe that it is known by A that (a) S believes that $P'_{[\varphi, A]}$ will be true iff it is recognized by A that $I(S,f,P'_{[\varphi, A]})$. And that the left side of II is true, but also the right one of III, this may be the case, if, e.g., it is not believed by S that it is mutual knowledge between S and A that (a). (For an example, where $CA_i(S,A,f,MI(S,A,f,r))$, but not $CA_d(S,A, f,r)$, see 5.2 below.) Each entry on the left side of a branching entails the upper entry of which it is a branch; and each branching entry entails the alternative of its branches.

5 Informatives and Directives in Ordinary Language

Informatives and directives as defined in D4.1 and D4.2 are acts of a more abstract kind than ordinary language seems to be equipped with. Now, although the primary justification of these notions consists in their systematic fruitfulness, nevertheless it may be questioned whether we have got at the right notions for even the paradigm cases of ordinary informatives and directives to be able to be subsumed. The adequacy of starting with reflexive intentions of some kind already taken for granted, there are mainly two arguments by which our approach may be called into question; let us consider them separately.

5.1 The Informative / Directive Dichotomy

Ordinary language seems to contain the presupposition that a communicative act is either a directive or an informative, but never both - in clear opposition to our definitions by which, as already stated in 3 above, it follows that

(4) $CA_d(S,A,f,r) \supset CA_i(S,A,f,I(S,f,D'(A,r)))$

Now, although this does not mean (cf. 3) that directives are to be simply equated with informatives, our very thesis that directives are informatives, *too*, seems to be at variance with ordinary language, which, in Bennett's words, seeks to keep "the distinction between statements and injunctions [...] deep and secure" (ibid.: 135).

But this reliance on ordinary language does not make up a real objection to our more technical notions. As already noticed by Bennett himself (ibid.: 135), the informatives following from[21] $CA_d(S,A,f,r)$ are always such that they are about "a proposition about S's state of mind, which S seeks to communicate mainly or wholly because he thinks it is a means to achieving, through the Gricean mechanism [modified by us in D4.1 and D4.2], some other effect", in the case of $CA_d(S,A,f,r)$ this other effect being $D'(A,r)$. Now, when asked of what particular kind a particular communicative act is or, what on our general level would amount to the same, of what kind the primary communicative intention of the act in question is, it would be utterly misleading, if this question would be answered only with reference to one of the weaker communicative intentions, which are involved in the communicative act, too. In ordinary language the informative/directive distinction is exclusively connected with what the strongest communicative intentions of the action to be classified as such and such are. Not so in our more general approach. But as this approach may be brought in accordance with ordinary usage by means of the very distinction between stronger and weaker communicative intentions, nothing is lost. And that very much is to be gained by approaching communicative acts in our more general terms, seems to be clear enough. Finally it should be noticed that for $CA_d(S,A,f,r)$ and $CA_i(S,A,f,p)$, where p is *not* a proposition of the kind drawn attention to by Bennett, the distinction between these acts is as "deep and secure" as before. (In *figure*

1, both are represented at stage V; but both are to be subsumed under informatives of kind IV.)

5.2 Informatives and Directives in a Wider Sense

That our concepts of informatives and directives may also diverge from ordinary language usage in another respect was hinted at by Alston's (1964: 41) remark that for an act to be of illocutionary type T it need not be a *sincere* illocutionary act of type T. To borrow his example: Even if I know perfectly well that a certain door is already open, when saying to you 'Please open the door' I may nevertheless be said to be asking you to open the door, Thus, as asking you to do r does not imply that I do really intend you to do r, and asking someone to do something being clearly a special case of directives, it follows that directives don't generally involve the primary intention attributed to them by our definition D4.1. (And the same argument may be brought forward as far as informatives are concerned.)

As this intricate argument will be fully discussed elsewhere[22], let us just concentrate on its essential moral: Whereas in our approach sincerity of $CA_i(S,A,f,MI(S,A,f,r))$ or $CA_i(S,A,f,MI(S,A,f,p))$ is necessary for having a case of $CA_d(S,A,f,r)$ or $CA_i(S,A,f,p)$, respectively, this sincerity condition is not generally required in ordinary language according to which an act may be classified as a *directive°* (i.e., as a directive in the sense of ordinary language) or as an informative° iff S *intends his act to be taken to be a directive* or an informative (in our strict senses). Accordingly, explication of communicative acts in this wider sense is easy:

D5.1: $CA°_d(S,A,f,r) := I(S,f,B'(A,CA_d(S,A,f,r)))$
D5.2 $CA°_i(S,A,f,p) := I(S,f,B'(A,CA_i(S,A,f,p)))$

To give these directives° and informatives° their respective place in our *figure 1* classification is no problem at all, as the following two statements hold analytically:[23]

(9) $CA°_d(S,A,f,r) \equiv CA_i(S,A,f,MI(S,A,f,r))$
(10) $CA°_i(S,A,f,p) \equiv CA_i(S,A,f,MI(S,A,f,p))$

To conclude, informatives° and directives° are exactly the informatives of kind IV (of *figure 1*), under which our directives. and our $CA_i(S,A,f,p)$ informatives are to be subsumed, which is enough to prove that our general concept of informatives is being presupposed by *informatives°* and *directives°* in the same way as it was by our *directives*. Thus, this second reference to ordinary language, too, can by no means lead to a reasonable objection to the primacy of informatives.

Notes

1. The logic of illocutionary acts as given in Vanderveken (1991) is not formulated in action theoretical terms; therefore it is not an alternative to the approach sketched in this paper.
2. For a first sketch of the theoretical background used here, see Meggle (1997a).
3. As up to now there is no adequate explication of "illocutionary act" general enough to cover even such non-communicative acts as 'christening' (to take just one of Austin's speech-act favourites), this 'class' is not yet well-defined. It is exactly for this reason that we prefer to talk of communicative acts as characterized in 1 and 2 below.
4. In accepting Schiffer's (iii), we are opposing Searle's (1975) system of *five classes* of basic illocutionary acts; Searle's system criticised in Ballmer (1979) - but there not refuted, as shown in Ulkan (1992). In Schiffer, op.cit., our 'informatives' are called 'assertives'; but as with the latter term association with ordinary assertions might be unavoidable (by which our stressing of the more abstract nature of the type of communicative acts we have in mind would be cancelled), we prefer - in analogy to 'directives' - the more technical former one.
5. The very interesting questions of whether there are communicative acts with the primary intention that A is to *want* something (more general: that A is to acquire some preference), and, if affirmative, of whether their type, too, should be regarded as basic, belong to the many questions to be left unsettled here due to limitations of space. Proposals as to how this third type may be dubbed are welcome: meggle@rz.uni-leipzig.de.
6. Worth noting that 'speaker' is used here (as it is common practice in the literature) in the wide sense of 'communicator'. Thus, neither reference to phonetic nor even to auditive utterances is implied.
7. The main simplification consists in omitting a particular operator for conditionals, which already would have to come in to strengthen the equivalence contained in $B(X,p \equiv D(X,f))$, thus making D1 more adequate.
8. As we are treating all referring expressions occurring in the following intensional contexts as standard names, the problem of the distinction between de re vs. de dicto readings does not arise. For corresponding widenings see *GBK*, § 8. The logical principles regulating our use of the terms mentioned in the definiens of D1 as well as some principles connecting beliefs/wants ascribed to a particular person at different times are also mentioned or specified in *GBK*.
9. In Grice's own formulations the second condition of D2.1 contains 'S intends' instead of 'S believes'. But this is surely inadequate, as the truth of the embedded equivalence will not be brought about by S's doing of f. The further condition $I(S,f,B'(A,I(S,f,D'(A,r)))$ mentioned by Grice - of course, in ordinary language terms only - follows already from the definiens of D2.1; therefore, although in itself necessary, it need not be mentioned explicitly. With the help of the epistemic principle $B(X,p) \equiv B(X,B(X,p))$ and (**) $W(X,p) \equiv B(X,W(X,p))$ of note 17, the reader will be able to verify that the first condition of D2.1 (or D2.2) may be even reduced to $D(S,f)$, the other conditions of $I(S,f,D'(A,r))$ (or $I(S,f,B'(A, p))$) being entailed by $D(S,f)$ in conjunction with the respectiv second condition. The same holds with the conditions mentioned in (*) in 2.2 as well.
10. Of course, as the kind of primary intentions in question is already determined by referring to r (action) or p (proposition), respectively, the indices *d* and *i* in $CA_d(S,A,f,r)$ and $CA_i(S,A,f,p)$ are superfluous. But *not* so, when we are generalizing by abstracting from r and p, thus coming to $CA_d(S,A,f) := Vr(CA_d(S,A,f,r))$ and $CA_i(S,A,f) := Vp(CA_i(S,A,f,p))$.
11. (*) and its informative cognate correspond to the communicationlogical theorem TK.41 in *GBK*; for D4.1 and D4.2 cf. ibid., the theorems T.K42 and T.K42 1.

12 In the rare cases where *illocutionary act* is in fact tried to be explained, addressee's understanding ('uptake') is following Austin (1962) - already regarded to be a necessary condition. For further criticism of this and related paints see Meggle (*HTS*), I.4, and Ulkan (1992).
13 (1) and (5) correspond to the theorems T.K67.1 and T.K70 of *GBK*, proved in its appendix. The restriction needed for the soundness of (α) is formulated in T.K72 as presented and proved in Meggle (*HTS*), by means of which, in connection with (1), (2) to (4) can easily be shown to be valid.
14 For a precise statement of the conditions of mutual knowledge see Meggle (1993).
15 Bennett ibid.: 134: "The crucial objection is that [Armstrong's] account of injunction-meaning obliterates the distinction between S's telling A to do r and S's *merely* informing A that S favours A's doing r. It is no defence to say that one can tell someone to do r by informing him that one wants him to do r; that is not in dispute. My point is that one can seek *just* to inform someone that one favours his doing r, not aiming to tell or advise or request or recommend him to do r; but on Armstrong's account this is impossible, for if you tell the person that you favour [intend] his doing r then you have *ipso facto* fulfilled Armstrong's conditions for telling him to do r. In short, in Armstrong's account the whole essence of injunctions, as of statements, is informative." To make our position clear once more: It is - cf. (5) - in fact *part* of the essence of directives to be informative, too, but this is not their *whole* essence.
16 It is not entailed by $CA_i(S,A,f,p)$ that $B(S,p)$ is true. For the question why this entailment *should* not be generally allowed, see the intuitive discussion in *GBK*, 3.1.3. Nevertheless, in *normal* cases $B(S,p)$ will be true, too. But, intuitive reasons apart, there is a further theoretic advantage - not yet noted in *GBK*, but heavily enforcing its settlement of this problem - of $B(S,p)$ *not* being involved in $CA_i(S,A,f,p)$: Not taking this position would preclude any possibility of distinguishing between $CA_d(S,A,f,r)$ and the wider concept of directives mentioned in 5 below.
17 (6) is the theorem T.K78 listed and proved in Meggle (1984), where it is also shown that the right sides of (1), (2) and (3) are equivalent.
18 Strictly speaking, sincerity of $CA_i(S,A,f,MI(S,A,f,r))$ entails just $B(S,MI(S,A,f,r))$. But as it is generally true that
(**) $W(X,p) \equiv B(X,W(X,p))$,
it is also (cf. lemma L.15 of *GBK*) generally true that
(7) $MI(S,A,f,r) \equiv D(S,f) \wedge B(S,MI(S,A,f,r))$
And thus, as $D(S,f)$ is already entailed by $CA_i(S,A,f)$, sincerity of $CA_i(S,A,f,MI(S,A,f,r))$ entails $MI(S,A,f,r)$ as well.
19 See once more note 4.
20 Of course, $P'_{[\varphi,A]}$ is not allowed to be equivalent with a sentence not essentially containing "A" and "φ", as is the case, e.g., in $p \wedge (\varphi(A) \vee \neg\varphi(A))$.
21 Or, to put it alternatively in terms of *figure 1*: the informatives of which $CA_d(S,A,f,r)$ is a special case are such that ... .
22 In "Das sprechakttheoretische Unaufrichtigkeitsargument", forthcoming. Contact us by e-mail (see note 5 above) for further information.
23 (9) follows directly from the theorems T.K74 and T.K75 proved in Meggle (*HTS*); the general truth of (10) is to be shown easily by analogy.

References

Alston, W.A. (1964): Philosophy of Language. Englewood Cliffs, N.J: Prentice-Hall.
Armstrong, D.M. (1971): "Meaning and Communication". The Philosophical Review 80, 427-447.
Austin, J.L. (1962): How To Do Things With Words. Cambridge, Mass: Havard University Press.
Bach, K. & R.M. Harnish, (1979): Linguistic Communication and Speech Acts. Cambridge, Mass.: The MIT Press.
Ballmer, Th. (1979): "Probleme der Klassifikation von Sprechakten". In: G. Grewendorf, ed.: Sprechakttheorie und Semantik. Frankfurt/Main: Suhrkamp, 247-274.
Bennett, J. (1976): Linguistic Behaviour. Cambridge: Cambridge University Press.
Grice, H.P. (1957): "Meaning". The Philosophical Review 66, 377-388.
Meggle, G. (1981; 1997^2): Grundbegriffe der Kommunikation. Berlin: de Gruyter. (In the paper referred to by GBK)
Meggle, G.: HTS, Handlungstheoretische Semantik. Unpublished - but widely spread in at least five different versions by copies.
Meggle, G. (1993): "Gemeinsamer Glaube und Gemeinsames Wissen". In: W. Lenzen, ed.: Tractatus physico-philosophici. Osnabrücker Philosophische Schriften, 145-151. Reprinted in: Allgemeine Gesellschaft für Philosophie, ed.: Neue Realitäten - Herausforderung der Philosophie. Berlin, 761-767.
Meggle, G. & M. Ulkan: "Das sprechakttheoretische Unaufrichtigkeits-Argument". Forthcoming.
Meggle, G. (1997a): "Communicative Actions". In: G. Holmström-Hintikka & R. Tuomela, eds.: Contemporary Action Theory. Vol. II, The Philosophy and Logic of Social Action. Dordrecht: Reidel.
Searle, J.R. (1975): "A Taxonomy of Illocutionary Acts". In: K. Gunderson, ed.: Language, Mind and Knowledge. Minneapolis: University of Minnesota Press, 344-369.
Schiffer, S. (1972; 1988^2): Meaning. Oxford: Clarendon Press.

Modulare Pragmatik und die Maximen der Modalität[*]

Jörg Meibauer, Tübingen

1 Einleitung

Der Begriff der Modularität, so populär er auch seit den 80er Jahren ist, wird in der Sprachwissenschaft durchaus nicht einheitlich verstanden: Einige verstehen darunter ein methodisches Prinzip der wissenschaftlichen Entdeckung; einige den inneren Aufbau von Theorien in Form separater Komponenten, und einige ein inneres Organisationsprinzip des menschlichen Geistes oder Gehirns. Die letztgenannte Auffassung, wie sie in verschiedenen Schriften Chomskys und vor allem in Jerry Fodors "The modularity of mind" (Fodor 1983) vertreten wird, soll den folgenden Überlegungen zugrunde gelegt werden.

Seit Fodor (1983) hat es immer wieder Versuche gegeben, die Modularität oder Nicht-Modularität der Pragmatik nachzuweisen. Fodor selbst war in dieser Hinsicht nicht sehr ermutigend; das Studium zentraler kognitiver Prozesse, wie sie sich etwa im Aufstellen und Bestätigen wissenschaftlicher Hypothesen zeigen, lasse sich mit den heute gegebenen Mitteln kaum bewerkstelligen (Fodor 1983: 126). Und einiges spricht dafür, daß Pragmatik zentral mit dem Räsonnieren über Hypothesen befaßt ist. Das hat Pragmatiker aus verschiedenen Schulen jedoch nicht davon abgehalten, über die Sache zu spekulieren, wobei für die einen sicherlich die Aussicht einer kognitiven, mentalistischen Pragmatik eine Antriebskraft war, während für die anderen die Aussicht einer Pragmatik modulo Grammatik eher abschreckend war.

Wie zu erwarten, gibt es einerseits Modularisten wie etwa Harnish & Farmer (1984), Bach & Harnish (1979) und Kasher (1991a,b,c), andererseits Anti-Modularisten wie etwa Verschueren (1987) und Sperber & Wilson (1986, 1987). Ein detaillierter Vergleich dieser und weiterer Ansätze kann hier nicht erfolgen, zumal dies eine sorgfältige Analyse der verwendeten Modularitätsbegriffe erforderlich machen würde. Ich konzentriere mich auf die Ansätze von Asa Kasher sowie Dan Sperber und Deirdre Wilson, da beide Ansätze eine kognitiv-pragmatische Orientierung aufweisen und sich explizit auf die Annahmen von Fodor beziehen (vgl. Sinclair 1995).

Während beide Ansätze sich in der Gretchenfrage "Ist die Pragmatik modular oder nicht-modular?" radikal unterscheiden, besteht doch eine Übereinstimmung darin, daß der

---

[*] Die vorliegende Arbeit ist eine revidierte Fassung eines Vortrages, den ich auf dem Treffen des Netzwerks "Sprache und Pragmatik" in Rendsberg (2.-6.10.1995) gehalten habe (vgl. Meibauer 1996). Beatrice Primus und Eckard Rolf danke ich für ihre Verbesserungsvorschläge zu der früheren Version.

Apparat der Griceschen Implikaturen in den Bereich der zentralen Prozesse gehört. Über die Funktionsweise der zentralen Prozesse weiß man recht wenig; so ist weitgehend ungeklärt, welche Maximen, welche Prinzipien, welche Schlußprozesse, welche Implikaturentypen und welche Repräsentations- und Verarbeitungsformen man benötigt.

Diese Fragen sind in gewisser Weise am ernsthaftesten von Horn (1984) und Levinson (1987a) angegangen worden, die sich deutlich in die Gricesche Tradition stellen. Um die kognitiven Grundlagen ihrer Theoriebildung haben diese Autoren sich jedoch kaum bemüht. Man sollte daher einen Versuch machen, diese zwei theoretischen Stränge - Modularität einer "kognitiven" Pragmatik vis-à-vis theoretische und empirische Durchdringung des Griceschen Apparats - miteinander zu verknüpfen.

Ich versuche eine solche Verknüpfung am Beispiel der Modalitätsmaximen[1], die meines Erachtens nur in Teilbereichen gut untersucht sind, sich aber in auffälliger Weise von den anderen Maximen unterscheiden. Sowohl Horn als auch Levinson, obgleich beide Reduktionisten sind, halten an den Modalitätsmaximen fest: Horn deckt sie durch seine Q- und R-Prinzipien ab, Levinson nimmt ein eigenes M-Prinzip an. Ich argumentiere dagegen, daß man keine eigene Maximen der Modalität benötigt.

Ich gehe folgendermaßen vor: Zunächst skizziere ich, welchen Status der Gricesche Apparat bei Kasher und Sperber & Wilson hat (§2). Anschließend diskutiere ich die Reduktionsversuche von Horn (1984) und Levinson (1987a) (§3), unter besonderer Beachtung der Modalitätsmaximen. Ein eigener Reduktionsversuch bezüglich dieser Maximen schließt sich an (§4). Zuletzt diskutiere ich die Einordnung dieser Ergebnisse vor dem Hintergrund einer modularen Pragmatik (§5).

2   Zum modularen Status der Implikaturen

Modularen Charakter haben nach Fodor (1983) die *Inputsysteme* (dazu gehören auch Teile des perzeptuellen Systems und des Sprachverstehenssystems) und Teile des Outputsystems (dazu gehören auch Prozesse der motorischen Kontrolle und des Sprachproduktionssystems). Nicht-modularen Charakter haben dagegen, so wird vermutet, das Langzeitgedächtnis und alle Komponenten, die das Weltwissen betreffen. Neben den Inputsystemen gibt es noch die *zentralen Prozesse*, worunter allgemeine Denk- und Problemlöseprozesse zu verstehen sind. Auch diese werden als nicht-modular betrachtet.

Für Inputsysteme gelten nun die folgenden allgemeinen Eigenschaften, wobei man mit Garfield (1987) die ersten vier als Hauptkriterien, die letzten vier als Nebenkriterien betrachten kann:

(I) Sie sind *domänenspezifisch*. Das sprachliche System bezieht sich nur auf sprachliche Reize, das visuelle System bezieht sich nur auf visuelle Reize: das heißt, jedes Inputsystem hat seine eigene Domäne.

(II) Die Operationen der Inputsysteme sind *obligatorisch*. Das ist daran zu sehen, daß man keinen willentlichen Einfluß auf ihre Arbeit nehmen kann. Wenn man Geräusche mit einer sprachlichen Struktur wahrnimmt, dann versteht man - ob man das will oder nicht - unmittelbar ihre Bedeutung.

(III)   Inputsysteme sind *informationell eingekapselt*. Das heißt, sie lassen sich in ihrer Arbeit nicht durch Informationen aus anderen Modulen irritieren.
(IV)   Inputsysteme arbeiten *schnell*. Zum Beispiel kann man das Gehörte in Bruchteilen von Sekunden verarbeiten; denkt man jedoch über etwas nach, dauert das bedeutend länger. Dies läßt sich damit erklären, daß die dabei beteiligten zentralen Prozesse auf nicht-modulare Komponenten zurückgreifen.
(V)   Inputsysteme sind dadurch gekennzeichnet, daß andere Module *keinen Zugang zu den von ihnen erstellen Zwischenrepräsentationen* haben. Wenn sie solch einen Zugang hätten, würde die Schnelligkeit der Verarbeitung darunter leiden.
(VI)   Inputsysteme haben seichte *Outputs*. Damit ist gemeint, daß die Repräsentationen, die Inputsysteme erstellen, nicht besonders reichhaltig sind, weil Inputsysteme eben nicht wie die zentralen Prozesse auf Weltwissen zurückgreifen können.
(VII)   Inputsysteme sind im Gehirn *lokalisierbar*, sie haben ihren Sitz an bestimmten Stellen des Gehirns. Werden diese Stellen verletzt, dann zeigen sich Ausfallerscheinungen, die spezifisch für das entsprechende Inputsystem sind.
(VIII) Und schließlich weisen Inputsysteme charakteristische *Ausfallerscheinungen* auf, wenn sie durch Trauma oder Verletzung beschädigt werden.

Man kann sich nun fragen, ob Pragmatik ein Inputsystem ist. Das wird im allgemeinen mit Hinweis darauf abgelehnt, daß bei der Äußerungsinterpretation wechselseitige Hintergrundannahmen und Annahmen über Institutionen eine Rolle spielen und Inputsysteme dazu keinen Zugang haben (Kasher 1991a: 387; Wilson & Sperber 1991: 584f.).

Allerdings folgt daraus, daß Pragmatik kein Inputsystem im Fodorschen Sinne ist, nach Kasher noch nicht, daß Pragmatik nicht-modular ist. Lege man nämlich andere Kriterien für Modularität zugrunde, dann könne es sehr wohl pragmatische Module geben. Für Kasher ist ein System dann modular, wenn es domänenspezifisch (I), informationell eingekapselt (III), lokalisierbar (VII) ist, wenn es mit bestimmten Ausfallerscheinungen (breakdown patterns) assoziiert ist (VII) und es eine bestimmte Ontogenese aufweist (Kasher 1991b: 389; Sinclair 1995: 516).

Obligatorik (II), Schnelligkeit (IV), mangelnder Zugang zu Zwischenrepräsentationen (V) und seichter Output (VI) werden jedoch als Kriterien für Modulstatus in Frage gezogen, vgl. Kasher 1991a: 389, Fn. 9). Insgesamt sieht Kasher (1991a: 389f.) folgende pragmatische Module vor:[2]

(1) *Pragmatische Module nach Kasher (1991a)*[3]
   I. *Kernpragmatik* (core-pragmatics):
      Wissen über Basis-Sprechakttypen wie Behauptung, Befehl und Frage
   II. *Konversationspragmatik* (talk-in-interaction pragmatics):
      Wissen über Sprecherwechsel, Sequenzierung und Reparatur
   III. *Zentralpragmatik* (central pragmatics):
      Wissen über konversationelle Implikaturen, indirekte Sprechakte, Höflichkeit, Register und Stil

IV. *Schnittstellen-Pragmatik* (interface pragmatics): Pragmatisches Wissen, das die Integration sprachlicher Daten etwa mit Wahrnehmungsdaten erlaubt, z.B. bei indexikalischen Ausdrücken

Man kann dieser Aufstellung entnehmen, daß "Wissen über konversationelle Implikaturen" in die Zentralpragmatik gehört; der Begriff "Zentralpragmatik" ist offenbar in Anlehnung an die Fodorschen zentralen Prozesse geprägt worden. Zu fragen ist, warum der Implikaturenapparat nicht ein eigenes Modul bildet.

Erstens führt Kasher die Griceschen Maximen auf ein allgemeines Rationalitätsprinzip (etwa "größtmöglicher Nutzen bei kleinstmöglichem Aufwand") zurück (Kasher 1991c: 577f.). Solch ein Prinzip ist aber nicht domänenspezifisch, sondern eher charakteristisch für einen allgemeinen kognitiven Prozeß.

Zweitens haben konversationelle Implikaturen die Eigenschaft der Streichbarkeit. Aus diesem Grund ist es unplausibel, daß sie durch ein System mit obligatorischen Prozessen geschaffen werden. (Allerdings ist dies kein gutes Argument, da Kasher (1991a: 389) Obligatorik als modulkonstitutives Kriterium bezweifelt.)

Nimmt man drittens indirekte Sprechakte hinzu, die ja auch via Implikaturen analysiert worden sind, dann läßt sich argumentieren, daß sich die intendierte Bedeutung nicht durch ein informationell eingekapseltes System ableiten lasse, da Indirektheit Zugriff auf Sprecherannahmen voraussetzt.

Ob nun aber das Zentralpragmatik-Modul die notwendigen modularen Eigenschaften aufweist - das hieße ja unter anderem, daß der Apparat zur Ableitung konversationeller Implikaturen domänenspezifisch, informationell eingekapselt, lokalisierbar, assoziiert mit typischen Ausfallerscheinungen und ontogenetisch fixiert wäre - , wird nicht geklärt und ist daher wohl zunächst Spekulation.

Im Gegensatz zu Kasher lehnen Sperber und Wilson eine modulare Pragmatik ab. Pragmatik sei überhaupt kein "special purpose system" wie die Grammatik, sondern einfach der Interaktionsbereich von Grammatik, Logik und Gedächtnis (Wilson & Sperber 1991: 583). Pragmatik sei im wesentlichen eine Theorie über die kognitiven Prinzipien und Fähigkeiten der Äußerungsinterpretation. Bei der Äußerungsinterpretation handelt es sich nach Wilson und Sperber um einen *Dekodierungsprozeß* (bei dem das *Language input module* im Sinne von Fodor beteiligt ist - die Grammatik ist ein Teil davon), und einen *Schlußfolgerungsprozeß*, der in den Bereich der *zentralen kognitiven Systeme* fällt.

Die zentralen kognitiven Systeme enthalten ein deduktives System, Kurzzeit- und Langzeitgedächtnis und die kognitive Umgebung des Interpreten. In den Aufgabenbereich der zentralen kognitiven Systeme gehören so gut wie alle klassischen pragmatischen Phänomene: Anreicherung des expliziten Inhalts einer Äußerung, stilistische Effekte, Metapher, Ironie, Illokution (direkt und indirekt), eventuell Diskurskohärenz, auf jeden Fall aber Implikaturen (Sperber & Wilson 1986: 193-202).

Es ergeben sich also folgende Unterschiede: Während Kasher vier pragmatische Module identifiziert, jedoch den Fodorschen Modulbegriff modifiziert, lehnen Sperber und Wilson jegliche Modularität der Pragmatik ab. Es besteht aber Übereinstimmung zwischen Kasher, Sperber und Wilson darin, daß Implikaturen einen "zentralen" Status haben, nämlich als Teil der Zentralpragmatik bei Kasher und als Teil der zentralen kognitiven Systeme bei Sperber und Wilson.

Prinzipiell sollten Modularitätsannahmen empirisch, d.h. durch einschlägige psycholinguistische Testverfahren, überprüfbar sein. Ansätze zu einer experimentellen Pragmatik gibt es etwa bei Bayer (1991), Foldi (1987), Shapiro & Murphy (1993), Gibbs (1994), Harnish (1995). Wenn auch zu bedenken ist, daß psycholinguistische Kriterien weder einen privilegierten Zugang zu den kognitiven Prozessen bieten (vgl. Kasher 1991b: 568), noch in einem 1:1-Verhältnis zur linguistischen Modellbildung stehen müssen, so darf doch die Relevanz der experimentellen Pragmatik für die kognitive Pragmatik nicht unterschätzt werden.

Während psycholinguistische Ergebnisse in der Pragmatik eher mit Zögern aufgenommen werden, besteht doch eine gewisse Übereinstimmung darin, daß die Griceschen Maximen in kognitiver Hinsicht mit Informationsverarbeitung zu tun haben. Dies ist nicht nur die Überzeugung der Relevanztheoretiker Sperber und Wilson, die die Äußerungsinterpretation auf das Relevanzprinzip zurückführen (wobei Relevanz als Verhältnis von kontextuellen Effekten zu Verarbeitungsaufwand definiert wird), sondern erfreut sich recht breiter Akzeptanz. So bringt Horn die Maximen mit dem Zipfschen Gesetz in Verbindung, Kasher führt sie auf das Rationalitätsprinzip (größtmöglicher Effekt bei kleinstmöglichem Aufwand) zurück, und Levinson sieht ein Wechselspiel zwischen Minimierung und Anreicherung am Werk.

Vor diesem Hintergrund ist es legitim, die vor allem von Horn und Levinson vorangetriebenen Versuche einer Reduktion der Griceschen Maximen daraufhin zu überprüfen, was sie unter dem Gesichtspunkt der Informationsverarbeitung bzw. dem modularen oder nichtmodularen Status des Implikaturenapparats leisten.

3 Reduktion der Griceschen Maximen

Bevor ich auf die Reduktionsversuche von Horn und Levinson eingehe, seien hier die von Grice (1989a) vorgeschlagenen Maximen aufgeführt:

(2) *Die Griceschen Maximen (Grice 1989a)*
The Maxim of Quantity
1. Make your contribution as informative as is required (for the current purposes of the exchange).
2. Do not make your contribution more informative than is required.

The Maxim of Quality
Try to make your contribution one that is true.
1. Do not say what you believe to be false.
2. Do not say that for which you lack adequate evidence.

The Maxim of Relation
Be relevant.

The Maxim of Manner
Be perspicuous.
1. Avoid obscurity of expression.
2. Avoid ambiguity.
3. Be brief (avoid unnecessary prolixity).
4. Be orderly.

Wenn ich im folgenden von "der Modalitätsmaxime" spreche, beziehe ich mich auf den Maximentyp. Sonst differenziere ich zwischen der Obermaxime und den vier Untermaximen; meine ich sowohl die Obermaxime als auch die Untermaximen, rede ich von "den Modalitätsmaximen". Entsprechendes gilt für die anderen Maximen, falls notwendig.

Die wichtigsten reduktionistischen Ansätze liegen von Horn (1984) und Levinson (1987a) vor. Dieses Ansätze werden oft als "neugriceianisch" bezeichnet (z.B. Levinson 1987a), weil sie das Gricesche Programm über weite Strecken akzeptieren. Dagegen investieren Sperber & Wilson (1986) keine Mühe in die Verbesserung der Griceschen Implikaturentheorie, sondern schlagen - unter Benutzung und Umdeutung des Griceschen Relevanzbegriffs - eine alternative Theorie vor.

Horn (1984) geht von zwei Prinzipien aus, dem Q(uantitäts)-Prinzip und dem R(elations)-Prinzip.[4] (Die Qualitätsmaxime wird von seinem Reduktionsvorschlag nicht erfaßt.)

(3) *Q-Principle*
Make your contribution sufficient: Say as much as you can (given R).

(4) *R-Principle*
Make your contribution necessary: Say no more than you must (given Q).

Das Q-Prinzip entspricht der ersten Quantitätsmaxime und den ersten beiden Untermaximen der Modalitätsmaxime, und das R-Prinzip entspricht der zweiten Quantitätsmaxime, der Relationsmaxime, sowie der dritten und vierten Untermaxime der Modalitätsmaxime. Vgl. die folgende Tabelle:[5]

(5) *Horn (1984) vs. Grice (1989a)*

Q-Prinzip	Quantität I
	Modalität I, II
R-Prinzip	Quantität II
	Relation
	Modalität III, IV

Das Q-Prinzip zielt auf eine Maximierung des Inhalts ab und, damit einhergehend, auf die Wirkung, die auf den Hörer ausgeübt werden soll; das R-Prinzip zielt dagegen auf die Minimierung des Ausdrucks ab und, damit einhergehend, auf den Aufwand, den ein Sprecher betreiben muß (vgl. Rolf 1994: 249).

Das Q-Prinzip trägt typischerweise skalaren Implikaturen Rechnung. Zum Beispiel implikatiert *Es ist warm* dann *Es ist nicht heiß*, wenn man die Beachtung des Q-Prinzips unterstellt. Hätte die Sprecherin mehr sagen können, dann hätte sie es auch tun sollen. Das R-Prinzip kommt für alle Fälle auf, wo man sowenig sagt, wie nur irgend möglich. Zum Beispiel erlaubt die Bemerkung *Er hat sich nicht gerade nett benommen* die Implikatur *Er hat sich wie ein Flegel benommen*.

Der Gricesche Apparat läßt sich also auf ein Zusammenspiel des Q-Prinzips mit dem R-Prinzip zurückführen; dies drückt das Prinzip der pragmatischen Arbeitsteilung aus:[6]

(6) *The Division of Pragmatic Labour*
The use of a marked (relatively complex and/or prolix) expression when a corresponding unmarked (simpler, less 'effortful') alternative expression is available ends to be interpreted as conveying a marked message (one which the unmarked alternative would not or could not have conveyed).

Das R-Prinzip genießt normalerweise Vorrang gegenüber dem Q-Prinzip. Bestimmte Q-Implikaturen können nur dann entstehen, wenn das R-Prinzip nicht strikt beachtet worden ist.

Levinson (1987a: 73) hat nun Horn vorgeworfen, daß er zwei Dinge miteinander vermischt, nämlich Minimierung des Inhalts (Präferenz einer generellen Bedeutung gegenüber einer spezifischen Bedeutung) und Minimierung des Ausdrucks (Kürze oder Länge von Ausdrücken). Entsprechend sei auch die Aufteilung der Modalitätsmaximen auf die Weise wie in (5) unzulässig, da die Modalitätsmaxime grundsätzlich formorientiert sei, d.h. unter Minimierung des Ausdrucks falle.

Levinson (1987a) geht dagegen von drei Prinzipien aus, nämlich dem Q(uantitäts)-Prinzip, dem I(nformativitäts)-Prinzip und dem M(anner)-Prinzip. Diese haben einen sprecherbezogenen und einen hörerbezogenen Aspekt:[7]

(7) *Q-Principle*
  1. Speaker's maxim: "Make your contribution as informative as is required for the current purposes of the exchange". Specifically: don't provide a statement that is informationally weaker than your knowledge of the world allows, unless pro-viding a stronger statement would contravene the I-principle
  2. Recipient's corollary: Take it that the speaker made the strongest statement consistent with what he knows, and therefore that:
  (a) f the speaker asserted A(W), and <S, W> form a Horn scale, then one can infer K ⌐(A(S)) i.e. 'the speaker knows that the stronger statement would be false'
  (b) if the speaker asserted A(W) and A(W) fails to entail an embedded proposition q, which a stronger statement A(S) would entail, and S & W are 'about' the same semantic relations (form a contrast set), then one can infer:

~Kq, i.e. Pq, P ~q (i.e. The speaker doesn't know that q obtains, or equivalently, it is epistemically possible that q or that not-q obtains).

(8) *I-Principle*
1. *Speaker's maxim*: The Maxim of Minimization
"Say as little as necessary" i.e. produce the minimal linguistic clues sufficient to achieve your communicational ends, bearing Q in mind
2. *Recipient's corollary*: Enrichment Rule
"Amplify the informational content of the speaker's utterance, by finding a more specific interpretation, up to what you judge to be the speaker's m-intended[8] point"
Specifically
(a) Assume that stereotypical relations obtain between referents or events, unless (i) this is inconsistent with what is taken for granted, or (ii) the speaker has broken the maxim of Minimization, by choosing a prolix expression
(b) Assume the existence or actuality of what a sentence is 'about', if that is consistent with what is taken for granted
(c) Assume referential parsimony - avoid interpretations that multiply entities in the domain of reference; specifically, prefer co-referential readings of reduced NPs (pronouns or zeros).

Obgleich Levinson (1987a: 76) keinen Zweifel daran läßt, daß die Modalitätsmaxime nicht reduzierbar ist, läßt er die Sache insofern offen, als daß er für sie keine explizite Formulierung angibt. Eine vergleichsweise klare Formulierung des M-Prinzips findet sich jedoch in Levinson (1991: 110f.), wo es heißt: "It [the I-principle, J.M.] is balanced by a Manner Maxim or M-principle, which induces from the use of a prolix or marked expression an interpretation that is complementary to the one that would have been induced by the I-principle from the use of a semantically general expression (this is what Horn (1985)[sic!] calls the 'division of pragmatic labour')."

Ich folge hier der Rekonstruktion des Levinsonschen M-Prinzips bei Turner (1995: 70):[9]

(9) *M-Principle*
Speaker's maxim: Do not use a prolix, obscure or marked expression without reason.
Recipient's corollary: If the speaker used a prolix or marked expression, he or she did not mean the same as he or she would have had used the unmarked expression - specifically, he or she was trying to avoid the stereotypical associations and I-implicatures of the unmarked expression.

Damit ergibt sich der folgende Vergleich zwischen Levinson und Grice (Levinson 1987a: 78):

(10) Levinson (1987a) vs. Grice (1989a)

>   Q-Prinzip   Quantität I
>   I-Prinzip   Quantität II
>   M-Prinzip   Modalität

Das Q-Prinzip ist verantwortlich für alle skalaren und klausalen Implikaturen; es operiert auf Mengen von Kontrastelementen von der Art der sog. Horn-Skalen.[10] Hier ein Beispiel für eine skalare Implikatur: Sei eine Horn-Skala <immer$_S$, oft$_W$>, dann kann man aus der Äußerung *Ich habe* oft *resigniert* schließen *Ich habe* nicht immer *resigniert*. Die Assertion des schwächeren Ausdrucks (Index W) erlaubt die Implikatur, daß der stärkere Ausdruck (Index S) nicht gilt.

Das I-Prinzip funktioniert genau andersherum: Es erlaubt den Schluß von einem schwächeren Ausdruck auf die Gültigkeit des stärkeren Ausdrucks. Sei eine Menge <und dann$_S$, und$_W$> gegeben, dann kann aus *Nastassja drückte auf den Knopf und die Rakete ging los* geschlossen werden Nastassja drückte auf den Knopf und dann ging die Rakete los. Der Anwendungsbereich des I-Prinzips übersteigt diesen Typ asymmetrischer Koordination jedoch beträchtlich, und die Fälle, die damit erfaßt werden sollen, sind heterogen (vgl. Levinson 1987a: 65; 1987b: 403f.; Turner 1995: 70f.).[11]

Für die Ausformulierung des I-Prinzips ist der Begriff der *Minimierung* zentral. Ob aber die unterschiedenen Minimierungsbegriffe, nämlich Minimierung$_1$: "semantisch allgemeine Ausdrücke sind gegenüber semantisch spezifischen zu bevorzugen", und Minimierung$_2$, "kürzere Ausdrücke (mit weniger Einheiten der Sprachproduktion) sind gegenüber längeren zu bevorzugen" wirklich unter den Deckel des I-Prinzips gehören, ist nicht so klar (vgl. Levinson 1987a: 74).[12] Man beachte, daß Kürze des Ausdrucks bei Grice unter die Modalitätsmaxime (genauer, die dritte Untermaxime) fällt, und in der (rekonstruierten) Formulierung der Modalitätsmaxime bei Levinson nicht mehr vorkommt. Entsprechend wird der klassische Fall der asymmetrischen Koordination bei Levinson unter dem I-Prinzip behandelt, während man sonst die Modalitätsmaxime (genauer, die vierte Untermaxime) dafür veranschlagt (vgl. § 4.5).

Eine andere Schwierigkeit schafft der für das I-Prinzip zugrundegelegte Informativitätsbegriff, der wegen Präzisierungsproblemen weitgehend intuitiv bleibt (vgl. Levinson 1987a: 74). Dieser Begriff besagt, daß A informativer ist als B gdw. die Menge der Folgerungen aus B eine echte Teilmenge der Menge der Folgerungen aus A ist. Die Schwierigkeit mit dieser Definition ist jedoch, wie Levinson (1987a: 74) feststellt, daß dies nur eine notwendige, aber keine hinreichende Bedingung für Informativität ist. Zum Beispiel seien die spezifischeren Bedeutungen, die qua I-Prinzip entstehen, damit nicht zu erfassen.[13] Das M-Prinzip macht einerseits Anleihen bei Grices Modalitätsmaxime (das betrifft prolixity und obscurity), anderseits bei Horns Prinzip der pragmatischen Arbeitsteilung (vgl. [6]), dem der Begriff der Markiertheit entnommen ist. Levinson benötigt das M-Prinzip für zwei Zwecke: Erstens für die in Levinson (1987a: 70) so genannten "Q/M-Implikaturen", eine Gruppe von Implikaturen, die sich wesentlich auf die Kürze bzw. Weitschweifigkeit eines

Ausdrucks beziehen, und die Horn (1984) als Q-Implikaturen betrachtet hatte.[14] Zum Beispiel Q/M-implikatiert *emanuensis* 'male secretary', und *Larry caused the car to stop* Q/M-implikatiert 'Larry stopped the car in an unusual manner, e.g. by using the hand-brake'. Zweitens aber - und da spielt der Begriff der Markiertheit eine Rolle - benötigt es Levinson (1987a,b, 1991) für seine Anapherntheorie. Markierte Formen sollen nicht-stereotypische Interpretationen bewirken. Nimmt man nun eine Markiertheitsskala "Lexikalische NP ® Pronomen ® 0" an, so daß lexikalische NPs am markiertesten sind, dann kann mithilfe des M-Prinzips erklärt werden, daß lexikalische NPs nicht als koreferent interpretiert werden (falls an ihrer Stelle auch ein Pronomen hätte stehen können), vgl. *Maya$_i$ came early and the child.*$_{*i/j}$/*she began to play*.

Der Ansatz von Levinson ist von Ariel (1994) ausführlich kritisiert worden, wobei unter anderem argumentiert wird, (a) daß Koreferenz nicht unbedingt als unmarkiert gelten kann, und daß (b) Markiertheit nicht unbedingt mit mehr Inhalt oder Länge korrelieren muß. Ich kann hier auf diese Debatte nicht im Detail eingehen.

Auch Levinson sieht eine Reihenfolge der Anwendung der Prinzipien vor: Zunächst werden Q-Implikaturen erstellt, dann stereotypenbasierte spezifische I-Implikaturen; es sei denn, es gibt einen markiert/unmarkiert-Kontrast zweier verfügbarer Ausdrücke: in diesem Fall induziert der unmarkierte die normalen I-Implikaturen, der markierte die Q/M-Implikaturen (vgl. Levinson 1987b: 409).

Zusammenfassend kann man feststellen, daß sowohl Horn als auch Levinson dem Gehalt der Modalitätsmaxime Rechnung tragen. Horn reduziert sie, indem er die beiden ersten Untermaximen bei Grice dem Q-Prinzip zuordnet, die beiden letzten dem R-Prinzip. Levinson hält an einer separaten Modalitätsmaxime fest, zögert jedoch, eine explizite Formulierung vorzuschlagen. Der Aspekt der "Kürze eines Ausdrucks", der sonst für die Modalitätsmaxime typisch ist, wird jedoch bei Levinson dem I-Prinzip zugeordnet; dagegen spielt "Markiertheit", bei Horn als "complex/prolix" verstanden, bei Levinsons M-Prinzip eine wichtige - nicht zuletzt auf die Anaphernproblematik bezogene - Rolle.

4 Die Modalitätsmaximen: Ein Reduktionsversuch

Die Gricesche Modalitätsmaximen seien hier noch einmal wiedergegeben. Sie bestehen aus einer Obermaxime und vier Untermaximen, die den folgenden Wortlaut haben (ich zitiere das englische Original und gebe deutsche Übersetzungen in eckigen Klammern):

(11) *The Maxim of Manner [Modalitätsmaxime](Grice 1989a)*
  Be perspicuous. [Sei klar.]
  I. Avoid obscurity of expression. [Vermeide Dunkelheit des Ausdrucks.]
  II. Avoid ambiguity. [Vermeide Mehrdeutigkeit.]
  III. Be brief (avoid unnecessary prolixity). [Sei kurz (vermeide unnötige Weitschweifigkeit).]
  IV. Be orderly. [Der Reihe nach!]

Ironischerweise hat diese Maxime, wie Green (1989: 89) bemerkt hat, einen selbstvereitelnden Charakter. Die Ausdrücke *perspicuous* und *prolixity* sind unnötig obskur im Vergleich zu den Ausdrücken *clear* und *verbosity*; damit ist die Untermaxime I verletzt. Die Untermaxime III ist weder kurz - also verletzt sie sich selbst -, noch - wegen der Paraphrase in Klammern - deutlich, sie verletzt also Untermaxime I. Zudem steht die Untermaxime IV nicht in der richtigen Reihenfolge im Vergleich zu den anderen Untermaximen - sie sollte zuerst stehen, verletzt sich also selbst. Insgesamt ist also die Modalitätsmaxime weit entfernt davon, klar zu sein, verletzt also die Obermaxime.

Daß die Modalitätsmaxime einen speziellen Status genießt, zeigt ein Vergleich mit den Schwestern Quantität, Qualität und Relation. Während sich die letztgenannten Maximen nämlich auf den *Inhalt* von Äußerungen beziehen (also auf das, *was* gesagt wurde), bezieht sich die Modalitätsmaxime auf die *Form* von Äußerungen (also darauf, *wie* es gesagt wurde). Entsprechend gilt folgendes: Ändert man bezüglich der anderen Maximen den Wortlaut der Äußerung, die die Implikatur auslöst, behält aber die gleiche wörtliche Bedeutung bei, dann taucht die entsprechende Implikatur trotzdem auf. Bei der Maxime der Art und Weise ist das nicht so, weil Veränderung des Wortlauts der Äußerung ja zugleich eine veränderte Art der Präsentation des Inhalts bedeutet. Daher ist das Kriterium der Nicht-Abtrennbarkeit (nondetachability) nicht anwendbar.

Im folgenden soll die Berechtigung einer eigenen Modalitätsmaxime geprüft werden. Ich gehe zunächst kurz auf die Obermaxime ein und dann auf die vier Untermaximen. Betrachtet man den Bereich sprachlicher Phänomene, zu deren Erklärung die einzelnen Modalitätsmaximen herangezogen wurden, scheint es so, als seien nicht alle Untermaximen gleich wichtig. Die am meisten diskutierten Untermaximen sind die Maximen "Vermeide Dunkelheit des Ausdrucks!" und "Der Reihe nach!". Ich möchte zunächst zeigen, daß die beiden anderen Maximen strenggenommen überflüssig sind, und ich argumentiere dann, daß eine Ableitung der Maximen der Dunkelheitsvermeidung und der Beachtung der Reihenfolge aus unabhängig benötigten Prinzipien durchaus möglich erscheint.

4.1 Eine Bemerkung zur Obermaxime der Modalität

Das Verhältnis der Obermaxime der Modalität zu den vier Untermaximen kann einerseits so verstanden werden, daß die Obermaxime durch die vier Untermaximen expliziert wird. Dann wäre die Obermaxime nur Etikett für die vier Untermaximen. Sie kann aber auch so aufgefaßt werden, daß sie sozusagen die Richtschnur angibt, nach der die vier Untermaximen zu interpretieren sind.

Ein Indiz für das zuletzt genannte Verständnis könnte folgender Vorschlag zur Erweiterung der Modalitätsmaximen sein, den Grice (1989b: 273) in seinem Aufsatz über "Präsupposition und konversationelle Implikatur" gemacht hat:

> I would be inclined to suggest that we add to the Maxims of Manner which I originally proposed some maxim which would be, as it should be, vague: 'Frame whatever you say in the form most suitable for any reply that would be regarded as appropriate', or, 'Facilitate in your form of expression the appropriate reply'.

Obgleich dies als zusätzliche Modalitätsmaxime verstanden wurde, scheint mir, daß hier der Wesenskern der Modalitätsmaxime liegt: Eine Äußerung sollte so präsentiert werden, daß sie möglichst einfach zu verarbeiten ist; das erleichtert die kommunikative Kooperation. Ich denke, daß genau dies mit der Obermaxime "Sei klar!" gemeint ist. Eine kognitive, auf Informationsverarbeitung abzielende Deutung der Modalitätsmaxime ist also durchaus angebracht.

4.2 Die zweite Untermaxime der Modalität

Betrachten wir zunächst die zweite Untermaxime der Modalität, die besagt, daß absichtliche Mehrdeutigkeit vermieden werden soll. Nach Grice (1989a: 35) fallen entsprechende Beispiele in zwei Gruppen, mit Eindeutigkeit der Interpretation als Unterscheidungsmerkmal. Dazu betrachten wir die folgenden Originalbeispiele unter (12):

(12)   (a)   Never seek to tell thy love, *Love that never told can be*.
               1. 'Love that cannot be told'.
               2. 'Love that if told cannot continue to exist'.
    (b)   Peccavi.
               1. 'I have sinned.'
               2. 'I have Sind.'

In William Blake's Zeile "Never seek to tell thy love, Love that never told can be" sei keine deutliche Bevorzugung einer der möglichen Interpretationen festzustellen. Da *love* in *love that never told can be* sowohl 'Geliebte' oder 'Geliebter' als auch 'Liebe' heißen kann, ergeben sich für den kursivierten Satzteil in (12a) die Deutungen: Erstens 'love that cannot be told' und zweitens 'love that if told cannot continue to exist'.

Dagegen werde in der Äußerung *Peccavi* des britischen Generals, der die Provinz Sind eingenommen hat, die Deutung im Sinne von 'I have Sind' gegenüber der Übersetzung 'I have sinned' bevorzugt. Die letztgenannte Deutung sei zwar auch möglich, jedoch von speziellen Situationsumständen abhängig.

Man kann sich nun fragen, worin genau die Implikatur besteht und inwiefern zu ihrer ordnungsgemäßen Rekonstruktion gerade die zweite Untermaxime der Modalität benötigt wird. In bezug auf (12a) möchte ich argumentieren, daß hier gar keine Implikatur entsteht, weil die Doppeldeutigkeit durch die Metonymie von *love* entsteht. Diese braucht jedoch nicht eigens durch einen Rekonstruktionsprozeß abgeleitet zu werden (anders als möglicherweise Metapher und Ironie), sondern gehört zum lexikalisch-konzeptuellen Wissen.

Im Fall (12b) wird die Deutung 'I have sinned' als "straightforward interpretant" angesehen, die Deutung 'I have Sind' als "nonstraightforward interpretant". Nehmen wir an, daß letzteres eine Implikatur ist, dann muß diese via die Deutung 'I have sinned' (die wörtliche Übersetzung) zusammen mit der Hintergrundbedeutung (Feldzug in Spanien, Existenz der Provinz Sind, etc.) erstellt worden sein. Prüfen wir dazu einen möglichen Schlußprozeß. Zu beachten ist dabei, (a) daß es sich um einen (scheinbaren) Verstoß gegen die zweite Untermaxime der Modalität handeln soll, und (b) daß es gerade die Art der Formulierung der Äußerung ist, die Auslöser für die Implikatur ist (vgl. Grice 1989a: 39)

(13)   (a)   Der General hat *Peccavi* geäußert.
      (b)   Damit hat er anscheinend gegen das Kooperationsprinzip verstoßen. Es besteht aber kein Grund zu der Annahme, daß er aus der Konversation aussteigen will.
      (c)   Lat. *Peccavi* ist mit engl. *I have sinned* zu übersetzen.
      (d)   Ich habe keinen Grund zu der Annahme, daß der General *I have sinned* sagen wollte. Wenn er das hätte sagen wollen, hätte er es gleich auf englisch tun können.
      (e)   Es muß also einen besonderen Grund dafür geben, daß er gerade diese Formulierung gewählt hat.
      (f)   Engl. *I have sinned* wird genauso ausgesprochen wie *I have Sind* (phonologische Ambiguität). Damit hat der General gegen die zweite Untermaxime der Modalität verstoßen.
      (g)   Der General befindet sich gerade auf Kriegszug in Spanien. Dort gibt es eine Provinz namens Sind (Hintergrundwissen).
      (h)   Der General wollte mitteilen, daß er die Provinz Sind eingenommen hat.
      (i)   Der General weiß, daß ich fähig bin, (h) herauszuarbeiten.
      (j)   Er hat mich nicht daran gehindert. Also nehme ich (h) an.

Zunächst einmal ist zu bemerken, daß über den scheinbaren Verstoß gegen das Kooperationsprinzip hinaus auch die Maxime der Relevanz tangiert ist. Der Schritt (e) ist wichtig, um den Bezug zur Modalität herzustellen. In der Formbezogenheit unterscheidet sich ja gerade dieser Maximentyp von seinen Schwestern. Dagegen ist der Bezug auf die zweite Modalitätsmaxime in (13f) wenig überzeugend. Dies liegt daran, daß Ambiguität sonst im Sinne semantischer Ambiguität (wie in (12a)) verstanden wird, es sich hier aber nur um phonologische Ambiguität handelt. Auf diese kommt man aber nur über das Hintergrundwissen, daß die Provinz Sind in diesem Zusammenhang irgend eine Rolle spielen könnte. Die Äußerung *I have sinned* ist auf keinen Fall semantisch zweideutig. Hierin scheint ja gerade der Witz dieser Äußerung zu liegen, daß man als Hörer darauf kommen muß, diesen recht weit hergeholten Zusammenhang herzustellen.

    Die Beispiele (12a) und (12b) unterscheiden sich also nicht nur hinsichtlich der Eindeutigkeit der Interpretation, sondern vor allem hinsichtlich des Typs der Ambiguität. Diese ist im ersten Fall rein lexikalisch vermittelt, muß aber im zweiten Fall selbst erst erschlossen werden. Daher paßt auf beide Fälle das Kriterium der Vermeidung von Ambiguität nicht.

    Die diskutierten Beispiele sind insofern prekär, als daß sie - selbst für partikularisierte konversationelle Implikaturen - sehr spezielle Kontexte benötigen. Nun hat (12b) deutlich den Charakter eines Wortspiels oder Witzes, und dies scheinen auch die für die Alltagskonversation typischen Fälle zu sein. Während es aber kaum zu bestreiten ist, daß Ambiguität in Witzen und Wortspielen ausgenutzt wird, ist es doch fragwürdig, ausschließlich für diese Fälle eine eigene Untermaxime vorzusehen. Es läßt sich nämlich argumentieren, daß Witzemachen nicht mit dem normalerweise akzeptierten Gesprächszweck übereinstimmt, wie es das Kooperationsprinzip verlangt (vgl. Attardo 1993).

Darüber hinaus läßt sich argumentieren, daß beabsichtigte Ambiguität immer ein Fall von Unterinformativität ist. Der Sprecher hätte ja die exakte Lesart deutlich und unmißverständlich formulieren können, wenn er nur gewollt hätte. Unterläßt er dies, um Implikaturen Auftrieb zu geben, dann ist er weniger informativ als er hätte sein können. Also ist hier die Quantitätsmaxime tangiert.

Es ist eine Überlegung wert, ob man in Analogie zur zweiten Untermaxime der Modalität eine Maxime "*Vermeide Synonymie!*" aufstellen sollte. Maximen oder Prinzipien dieser Art sind unter anderem von Aronoff (1976), Kiparsky (1983) und Clark (1993) postuliert worden und dienen dazu, das morphologische Phänomen der Blockierung zu erklären (vgl. Briscoe, Copestake & Lascarides 1995, Werner 1995). Nach der Definition von Werner (1995: 43) wird unter Blockierung in der Regel verstanden, "daß eine (ansonsten produktive) Wortbildungsregel (WBR) auf einzelne Formen nicht angewendet werden kann, weil das Produkt dieser Regel bedeutungsgleich mit einem bereits existierenden (lexikalisierten) Wort wäre." Zum Beispiel sollte die Wortbildung *Flieger* im Sinne von 'Flugzeug' aufgrund einer Maxime oder eines Prinzips der Synonymievermeidung blockiert sein, weil das Wort *Flugzeug* bereits lexikalisiert ist. Dennoch kann man beobachten, daß der Ausdruck *Flieger* im Sinne von 'Flugzeug' gebraucht wird. Man kann das so erklären, daß der scheinbare Verstoß gegen die Maxime "Vermeide Synonymie!" zu einer Implikatur der Art berechtigt, daß Fliegen für den Sprecher nichts Besonderes ist, daß er dem Jet-Set angehört, etc. Während die Annahme durchaus plausibel ist, daß auch der absichtliche Verstoß gegen die Maxime der Synonymievermeidung Implikaturen auslösen kann, scheint es durchaus so, daß diese neue Information im Prinzip auch explizit hätte ausgedrückt werden können. Damit kommt aber wiederum die Maxime der Quantität ins Spiel. Der Sprecher hat einfach weniger gesagt, als er im Prinzip hätte sagen können.

Man hat es hier mit einem wichtigen Prozeß des semantischen Wandels zu tun. Das, was im Prinzip propositional ausdrückbar wäre, wird zunächst als Implikatur eines lexikalischen Trägers erschlossen, bevor es in einem Prozeß der Konventionalisierung konversationeller Implikaturen zu einem Bestandteil der wörtlichen Bedeutung eines Lexems wird (vgl. Meibauer 1995).

4.3 Die dritte Untermaxime der Modalität

Betrachten wir nun die dritte Untermaxime der Modalität, die besagt, daß man sich kurz fassen, d.h. unnötige Weitschweifigkeit vermeiden soll. Hier sollen drei Anwendungsbereiche dieser Maxime unterschieden werden: Diskursphänomene, Lexeme und syntaktische Konstruktionen. Das klassische Beispiel von Grice ist diskursbezogen; es besteht in der Bemerkung (14a) eines Konzertkritikers (Grice 1989a: 37):

(14) (a) Fräulein X brachte eine Reihe von Tönen hervor, die entfernte Ähnlichkeit mit der Melodie von "Home sweet home" aufwiesen.
 (b) Fräulein X sang "Home sweet home."

Wenn der Kritiker (14a) äußert - er hätte stattdessen ja auch (14b) wählen können -, drückt er sich nicht kurz und bündig aus, und er implikatiert daher, daß der Gesang von Fräulein X geradezu scheußlich war. Die mit (14a) verbundene Weitschweifigkeit ist unnötig im Vergleich mit der durch (14b) vermittelten Information.

Ein weiteres Beispiel ist in (15a) zu finden (vgl. Levinson 1983: 108):

(15) (a) Geh zur Tür, dreh den Griff in Uhrzeigerrichtung, bis es nicht mehr weitergeht, und dann ziehe den Griff langsam in deine Richtung.
 (b) Öffne die Tür.

Wenn eine Sprecherin (15a) anstelle von (15b) wählt, dann würde sie implikatieren, daß alle Teilhandlungen mit besonderer Aufmerksamkeit und Sorgfalt ausgeführt werden müssen.

Der springende Punkt ist hier, wie man nötige Weitschweifigkeit von unnötiger Weitschweifigkeit unterscheiden kann. Zur Feststellung unnötiger Weitschweifigkeit wird immer eine Vergleichsproposition benötigt, die das Gleiche ausdrückt. Da dies bei den besprochenen Beispielen nicht der Fall ist, bleibt nur die Annahme, daß die Weitschweifigkeit nötig war (nötig, damit bestimmte Implikaturen entstehen können), und damit kann es sich nicht mehr um einen Fall des Verstoßes gegen die dritte Untermaxime handeln.

Es ist also unklar, inwiefern der Begriff der unnötigen Weitschweifigkeit operationalisiert werden kann. Wenn es sich nur um den Informationsgehalt einer Äußerung handelt (etwa die Menge der Folgerungen aus einer Proposition), ist offensichtlich die Quantitätsmaxime einschlägig.[15]

Entsprechend ist denn auch die dritte Untermaxime der Modalität auch meist in bezug auf Paare von Lexemen bzw. Paare von einem Lexem und einer Phrase diskutiert worden.

Allerdings muß hier klar sein, was unter Kürze/Weitschweifigkeit genau zu verstehen ist. Horn (1984) hat in seinem Prinzip der pragmatischen Arbeitsteilung in (6) von markierten Ausdrücken gesprochen: diese seien "relativ komplex und/oder weitschweifig". Folgt man der Rekonstruktion des Levinsonschen M-Prinzips durch Turner (1995), dann denkt Levinson an "weitschweifige, obskure oder markierte" Ausdrücke. "Kürze" spielt aber auch bei Levinson (1987a) eine Rolle; Levinson möchte garantiert wissen, daß bei Implikaturen, die durch das I-Prinzip ausgelöst werden, die entsprechenden starken und schwachen Ausdrücke gleich lang sind, damit der kürzere Ausdruck nicht nur wegen Beachtung der Maxime der Kürze verwendet wird - daher die Formulierung in (8a ii).

Man hat nun argumentiert, daß es bei dem Gebot der Kürze anscheinend nicht auf den Informationsgehalt ankomme - denn dieser ist durch die Quantitätsmaxime bereits abgedeckt -, sondern diese Maxime eigentlich folgendes besage (vgl. Matsumoto 1995: 44): *"Wähle den kürzeren Ausdruck von zwei Ausdrücken, die ungefähr synonym sind."* Wenn jemand also einen längeren Ausdruck benutzt, da, wo er genausogut auch einen kürzeren hätte benutzen können, gibt er Implikaturen Auftrieb.

Nehmen wir an, man könne Kürze/Weitschweifigkeit über die Anzahl involvierter Beschreibungseinheiten wie Laut, Silbe, Morphem, Wort operationalisieren, und nehmen wir ferner an, daß es "ungefähr synonyme" Ausdrücke gibt; man kann dann das Problem anhand folgender Beispiele aufreißen (vgl. auch die Daten in Muthmann 1994):

(16) (a) female sibling - sister (vgl. Carston 1995)
 (b) im Vorfeld - vor (vgl. Meibauer 1995)
 (c) Holocaust - Holo (Schwäbisches Tagblatt, 22.5.95)
 (d) acquired immunity deficiency syndrome - AIDS
 (e) more big - bigger (vgl. Poser 1992: 120f.)

In diesem Sinne sind die unter (16) zuerst genannten Ausdrücke immer die längeren. Wenn jemand äußert *I have a female sibling* [vs. sister], dann implikatiert sie Carston (1995: 217) zufolge 'I don't have normal sisterly relations with her'. Was in diesem Fall eine Rolle spielt, ist aber nicht die Länge des Ausdrucks, sondern seine Ungewöhnlichkeit - genau wie etwa selten gebrauchte Fremdwörter zu Implikaturen einladen. In Äußerungen wie *Im Vorfeld [vs. vor] der Konferenz kam es zu Auseinandersetzungen* wird implikatiert, daß die Auseinandersetzungen eine gewisse zeitliche Ausdehnung hatten (vgl. Meibauer 1995). Auslöser für diese Implikatur ist aber nicht Länge oder Komplexität der komplexen Präposition und damit die dritte Untermaxime der Modalität, sondern die erste Quantitätsmaxime.

Die nächsten beiden Beispiele beziehen sich auf Wortbildungstypen. An (16c) kann man sehen, daß man auch durch kürzere Ausdrücke Implikaturen hervorbringen kann. So hat der NPD-Funktionär Günter Deckert in einer Gerichtsverhandlung das Wort *Holo* anstelle des Worts *Holocaust* benutzt, um sich "über die Ermordeten von Auschwitz lustig zu machen" (Schwäbisches Tagblatt, 22.5.95). Und anderseits muß nicht jede längere Formulierung zu besonderen Implikaturen Anlaß geben. Wenn man zum Beispiel in einem fachsprachlichen Kontext von *acquired immunity deficiency syndrome* redet statt von *AIDS*, brauchen damit keine besonderen Implikaturen verbunden zu sein. Schließlich kann man an dem Paar (16e) zeigen, daß der längere Ausdruck nicht unbedingt zu Implikaturen Anlaß geben muß; die Distribution auf syntaktische Kontexte ist unterschiedlich, und die Ausdrücke bedeuten nicht das Gleiche (vgl. Poser 1992).

Diese Beispiele zeigen, daß immer die Abweichung von den lexikalischen Konventionen und der Verwendungszusammenhang eine Rolle spielen. Länge oder Kürze des Ausdrucks per se - wie immer man das messen möchte - kann kein Kriterium sein, und wenn es auf den puren Informationsgehalt ankommt, ist die Maxime der Quantität einschlägig. Zu bedenken ist darüber hinaus, daß Beispiele exakter Synonymie äußerst rar sind, was den Vorschlag von Matsumoto von vornherein bedenklich macht.

Neben diesen diskurs- und lexembezogenen Anwendungen der Maxime gibt es noch eine Reihe von eher syntaktischen Phänomenen, die mit Kürze und/oder Weitschweifigkeit in Verbindung gebracht worden sind (vgl. Horn 1984: 23ff.). Vor allem sind hier die Interpretation von Anaphern und von lexikalischen Kausativkonstruktionen zu nennen.

Daß aber "Kürze" bei der Interpretation von Anaphern tatsächlich der entscheidende Begriff ist, und nicht geringer semantischer Gehalt, stereotypische Bedeutung, Markiertheit - alles Begriffe, die bei Levinson (1987a,b) unter Minimierung mitlaufen (oder gar alternativ: Zugänglichkeit), ist noch nicht ausgemacht (vgl. Ariel 1994). Und ebenso scheint es bei lexikalischen Kausativkonstruktionen (*John caused Mary to die* +> *John didn't kill Mary [directly or in a stereotypical way]*) nicht auf Kürze anzukommen, sondern eher auf stereotypische Bedeutung (vgl. Matsumoto 1994: 42). Da es hier primär um die Gricesche Fassung der Modalitätsmaxime geht, muß eine genauere Analyse der Levinsonschen

Theorie (insbesondere der Frage, ob er für seine Zwecke das M-Prinzip wirklich benötigt) unterbleiben.

4.4 Die erste Untermaxime der Modalität

Die erste Untermaxime der Modalität besagt, daß Dunkelheit des Ausdrucks vermieden werden soll. (Statt von Dunkelheit des Ausdrucks werde ich im folgenden auch von Obskurität sprechen.) Ein Beispiel für die absichtliche Verletzung dieser Untermaxime ist (17) (vgl. Levinson 1983: 104):

(17) A: Komm, wir kaufen den Kindern was!
     B: Gut, aber ich bin gegen E-I-S!

Die Eltern A und B unterhalten sich in Gegenwart ihrer Kinder, die generell scharf auf Eis sind. Durch die obskure Aussprache des Worts Eis hofft B, daß die Kinder nichts vom Gesprächsgegenstand mitkriegen und implikatiert zugleich gegenüber A, daß das Thema den Kindern nicht mitgeteilt werden soll.

Was eine dunkle Ausdrucksweise ist, ist jedoch alles andere als klar (vgl. auch Crystal 1990). Ganz allgemein müssen damit solche Ausdrucksweisen gemeint sein, die für den Adressaten aus verschiedenen Gründen unverständlich sein müssen. Eine Typologie der einschlägigen Fälle aufzustellen, ist hier nicht möglich. Dennoch möchte ich drei verschiedene Beispielgruppen unterscheiden: Erstens Beispiele mit absichtlicher Verletzung einer Sprachregel, zweitens Beispiele mit absichtlicher Verletzung von Sequenzierungsbedingungen, und drittens Beispiele mit Ignoranz bezüglich des Hintergrundwissens.

Ich gehe zunächst auf Fälle der *Verletzung einer Sprachregel* ein. Ein phonologisches Beispiel ist schon durch (17) gegeben, wo *E-I-S* buchstabiert statt in regulärer Weise ausgesprochen wird. In ähnlicher Weise implikatierend sind alle absichtlichen Abweichungen von der Standardlautung bzw. -schreibweise, sei es dialektale Aussprache bzw. Schreibweise anstelle der standardsprachlichen, falsche Rechtschreibung, der absichtliche Gebrauch fremdsprachlicher Prosodie oder der Nachahmung der typischen Aussprache anderer Sprecher. Ein Beispiel für standardsprachliche Abweichung ist (18a), eines für Abweichung von Rechtschreibregeln ist (18b):

(18) (a) "Ob nun der Mensch im Mittelpunkt der Politik steht oder mehr seine ganze *Famillje* oder gar die Humanität schlechthin - auf die Praxis kommt es an, nicht auf die Phrase." (ZEIT 8/8: 1)
     (b) Sätzer, Säzzer vs. Setzer; Volxküche vs. Volksküche

Als eine Abweichung von den gewöhnlichen Wortbildungsregeln kann man Wortkreuzungen betrachten. Wortkreuzungen sind nicht einfach zu interpretieren und zwingen den Interpreten, wie bei der Metapher, zu bestimmten Schlüssen bezüglich der neuen Bedeutung. In (19) finden sich einige Beispiele aus einer Glosse:

(19) Lektürium < Lektüre + Martyrium
Bestselleriesalat < Bestseller + Selleriesalat
Auto(r)gramm < Autor + Autogramm
hörkulische [Anstrengungen] < hör(en) + herkulisch
(Schwäbisches Tagblatt, 17.1.95)

Absichtliche Verletzungen semantischer oder lexikalischer Regeln der Sprache sind ein recht gewöhnlicher Fall. In dem folgenden Beispiel (20) redet der Kabarettist Helge Schneider über den Erfolg seiner letzten Tournee:

(20) Den größten Erfolg hatten wir in *Belgien*, ebenso allerdings auch in *Luxemburg* und besonders in den *Niederlanden*, vor allem eben in *Belgien* und in den gesamten *Benelux-Staaten*. In erster Linie aber in *Holland* und in den *Niederlanden*, etc.

(21) Köln, 20. Juni 2005: In alter Frische *rheumten* Mick Jagger und die Rolling Stones wieder einmal *ab*. (ZEIT 27/1995: 63)

Das ist vor allem deswegen obskur, weil die Synonymie von *Benelux-Staaten* und *Belgien, Niederlande, Luxemburg* sowie die Partonymie oder Synonymie von *Holland* und *Niederlande* nicht beachtet wird. Und ebenso ist die Verwendung des neugeprägten Verbs *abrheumen* im Text unter (21) obskur.

Absichtliche Verletzung syntaktischer Regeln ist zum Beispiel gegeben, wenn gegen Regeln der Kongruenz oder Kasusmarkierung verstoßen wird. Dies ist gut an den folgenden Beispielen zu beobachten (in [22] geht es um die französische Schriftstellerin Colette):

(22) Willy ließ Tausende von Fotos von sich drucken als "Claudines Papa" und schloß seine Frau jeden Tag vier Stunden ein, mit dem strengen Befehl, Fortsetzungen zu schreiben. Drei weitere Claudine-Romane erschienen, Autor: Willy. Nur ein paar hellsichtige Freunde durchschauten das perfide Spiel, ein Kritiker schrieb ironisch: '*Willy haben* ein großes Talent.' (ZEIT-magazin 45/1986: 64)

(23) Der Fußballspieler Lippens wird vom Schiedsrichter verwarnt mit den Worten: "Ich verwarne Ihnen." Darauf 'Ente' Lippens: "Ich danke Sie!" Lippens bekommt die gelbe Karte. (Groeben & Scheele 1984: 254)

Zusammenfassend kann man sagen, daß Obskurität durch den absichtlichen Verstoß gegen Sprachregeln entsteht, und daß Hörer durch deren Erkenntnis zur Ableitung von Implikaturen berechtigt sind.

Man könnte daraus schließen, daß die erste Untermaxime der Modalität vielleicht heißen sollte: "*Folge den Sprachregeln!*" Ich denke jedoch, daß eine solche Maxime insofern überflüssig ist, weil sie aus unabhängig benötigten Annahmen über normale Kommunikation ohnehin folgt. In jeder Sprachgemeinschaft gehen die Mitglieder nämlich von dem Glauben aus, daß die anderen Mitglieder die gleiche Sprache beherrschen, und in der Lage sind, das Gesagte zu identifizieren (vgl. *Linguistic Presumption* bei Bach & Harnish 1979:

9). Wenn Sprecher einer Sprachgemeinschaft die Sprache teilen, teilen sie auch die Regeln der Sprache. Die Identifikation des Gesagten ist nur möglich unter der Annahme, daß sich der Sprecher auch an die Regeln hält. Es ist daher klar, daß absichtlicher Verstoß gegen diese Regeln zu Implikaturen berechtigt.

Betrachten wir nun Fälle, in denen *Sequenzierungsbedingungen* verletzt werden. Es handelt sich besonders um Fälle der Wiederholung, wobei Fremd- und Selbstwiederholung zu unterscheiden sind. Natürlich sind nicht alle Arten von Wiederholungen als Verstöße gegen Sequenzierungsbedingungen zu werten. Es gibt jedoch recht klare Fälle, in denen die Wiederholung von Teilen einer Vorgängeräußerung des Hörers als Verletzung normaler Sequenzierungsgepflogenheiten aufgefaßt wird, vgl. ironisches Echo in (24), Rückfragen eines bestimmten Typs in (25), das bloße "Nachäffen" von Äußerungen in (26), Fälle metasprachlicher Negation wie in (27) (vgl. Meibauer 1987; Horn 1989: 362ff.; Aitchison 1994):

(24) A: Du bist besoffen. Ich rede kein Wort mehr mit dir.
      B: Oh ja *ich bin besoffen*, denn ich habe gestern zwei Kölsch getrunken.

(25) A: Die Stuttgarter haben wieder schlecht gespielt.
      B: *Die Stuttgarter haben schlecht gespielt?* Daß ich nicht lache!

(26) A: Mir ist so langweilig!
      B: *Mir ist so langweilig!*

(27) A: Dort kommen die DeBÜtanten.
      B: *Dort kommen nicht die DeBÜtanten*; dort kommen die DebüTANten.

Was alle diese Fälle gemeinsam haben, ist, daß in der B-Äußerung Material der A-Äußerung wiederholt wird und daß dabei das Kooperationsprinzip tangiert wird. Dies ist ein Indiz dafür, daß durch diese Äußerungen Implikaturen ausgelöst werden können.

Ein ähnlicher Effekt liegt bei zum Teil schon konventionellen Selbst-Wiederholungen eines bestimmten Typs vor. Auch diese verstoßen strenggenommen gegen die Bedingung, daß Äußerungen oder Äußerungsteile nicht wiederholt werden dürfen, und erwecken den Eindruck der Dunkelheit.

(28) Ich glaube, die haben den Platz gesucht *und gesucht* und nicht gefunden. Die haben das Ganze wohl unterschätzt. (Südwestpresse, 8.4.94)

(29) Seit 1702 liegt der Ritter Christian Friedrich von Kahlbutz in der Kirchengruft und will *und will* nicht vermodern - ein Schloßgespenst der ganz besonderen Art. (Südwestpresse, 3.12.94)

(Interessanterweise gibt es im Deutschen einige Adverbien wie *durch und durch, um und um, für und für*, bei denen die Wiederholung grammatikalisiert wurde.)

Es scheint so, als benötige man zur Erfassung dieser Fälle eine Maxime, die etwa heißen könnte: "*Vermeide die Wiederholung von Äußerungen oder Äußerungsteilen!*" Ob jedoch eine solche Maxime einen Platz unter den durch das Kooperationsprinzip kontrollierten Maximen einnehmen sollte, ist nicht ausgemacht. Erstens ist zu beachten, daß sämtliche Wiederholungs-Beispiele der zweiten Maxime der Quantität unterworfen sind, da Wiederholung intuitiv eine Art von Überinformation ist. Zweitens ist es wahrscheinlich, daß da, wo Wiederholung unangemessen ist, unabhängig motivierte Prinzipien der konversationellen Sequenzierung und Informationsverarbeitung dafür aufkommen müssen. Und drittens gilt, daß nicht jede Art von Wiederholung unangemessen ist, sondern daß es Typen der Wiederholung gibt, die die rasche Verarbeitung der Information unterstützen und erleichtern (vgl. Tannen 1989, Jucker 1994).

Ich komme nun zum dritten Fall, also zu Beispielen, in denen *Hintergrundwissen* des Hörers ignoriert wird. Typische Fälle sind Äußerungen, bei denen ein Eigenname verwendet wird, mit dem der Hörer nichts anfangen kann (vgl. Schegloff 1971; Matsumoto 1995: 40f.):

(30) A: Woher kommt Nastassja eigentlich?
      B: (a) Sie lebt in Kusterdingen.
          (b) Sie lebt in der Nähe von Stuttgart.

Die Antworten können obskur sein je nach dem Kenntnisstand des Hörers. Obskur ist die Antwort *in Kusterdingen* in (30a), wenn A sich überhaupt nicht im Stuttgarter Raum auskennt. Falls er sich aber in dieser Gegend auskennt, dann ist die Antwort *in der Nähe von Stuttgart* in (30b) obskur und berechtigt zur Implikatur, daß der Sprecher nicht genau weiß, an welchem Ort Nastassja lebt.

Bei näherer Betrachtung wird aber deutlich, daß es sich hier um Fälle von Unter- und Überinformativität handelt, die hier zur Dunkelheit des Ausdrucks beitragen. Nicht die Ausdrücke an sich sind ja dunkel, sondern sie sind es nur relativ zum Kenntisstand der Beteiligten. Damit ist aber wiederum die Quantitätsmaxime einschlägig.

Alles in allem scheint es recht schwer, Dunkelheit des Ausdrucks zu explizieren. Ich habe argumentiert, daß absichtliche Verstöße gegen Sprachregeln aus unabhängig benötigten Prinzipien für erfolgreiche Kommunikation abgeleitet werden können, und daß Verstöße gegen Sequenzierungsbedingungen und Ignoranz des Hintergrundwissens auf die Quantitätsmaxime zurückgeführt werden können.

4.5 Die vierte Untermaxime der Modalität

Die vierte Untermaxime der Modalität verlangt die richtige Reihenfolge. Diese Untermaxime wird im allgemeinen dazu benutzt, den notorischen Fällen asymmetrischer Koordination beizukommen. Neben den skalaren Implikaturen handelt es sich dabei um den Faktenbereich, der bisher am meisten linguistische Aufmerksamkeit auf sich gezogen hat (vgl. Cohen 1971; Schmerling 1975; Posner 1979; Bar-Lev-Palacas 1980; Hirschberg 1985;

Carston 1993, 1994, 1995; Lascarides & Oberlander 1993). Nicht zuletzt ist es gerade dieser Fall, mit dem Grice seine Argumentation in "Logic and Conversation" motiviert.

Es geht in dieser Debatte um die Bedeutung der koordinierenden Konjunktion *and/und*. Zunächst einmal gibt es symmetrische Koordination wie in (31):

(31) (a) In Köln war es heiß und in Stuttgart war es kalt.
 (b) In Stuttgart war es kalt und in Köln war es heiß.

Die Abfolge der Konjunkte hat hier keinerlei Einfluß auf die Gesamtbedeutung der Koordination. Anders verhält es sich jedoch bei Fällen der asymmetrischen Koordination:

(32) (a) Fritz heiratete und wurde Vater.
 (b) Fritz wurde Vater und heiratete.

Die Äußerung (32a) versteht man im allgemeinen so, daß Fritz erst heiratete und dann Vater wurde, während man die Äußerung (32b) so versteht, daß Fritz erst Vater wurde und dann heiratete. Die Anordnung der Konjunkte hat hier einen Einfluß auf die Gesamtbedeutung, da hier eine temporale Abfolge mitverstanden wird. Ebenso kann auch eine kausale Interpretation der Koordination vorgenommen werden.

Wenn man nicht die Bedeutungen der Konjunktion *und* vermehren möchte - also nicht 'und dann', 'und deswegen' usw. als weitere wörtliche Bedeutungen über die reine Verknüpfungsbedeutung hinaus -, dann kann die in (32) sichtbar werdende Asymmetrie der Interpretation unter Berufung auf die vierte Untermaxime der Modalität folgendermaßen erklärt werden. Da der Sprecher in solchen Koordinationsfällen die Maxime beachtet, Sachverhalte in der richtigen Reihenfolge anzuordnen, d.h. so wie sich in der Wirklichkeit zugetragen haben, ist der Hörer berechtigt, aus dieser Anordnung der Konjunkte etwas über deren temporale (und weitere) Relationen zu erschließen. Dies ist die klassische Position von Grice, die in Posner (1979) klar herausgearbeitet wird.

Wie erwähnt, beziehen sich Atlas & Levinson (1981) und Levinson (1987a) bei den von ihnen diskutierten Fällen asymmetrischer Koordination (alias 'conjunction buttressing') allerdings nicht auf die vierte Untermaxime der Art und Weise bzw. das M-Prinzip, sondern auf das I-Prinzip. Das I-Prinzip erlaubt den Schluß von einem schwächeren Ausdruck auf die Gültigkeit des stärkeren Ausdrucks. Sei eine Menge <und dann$_S$, und$_W$> gegeben, dann kann aus *Nastassja drückte auf den Knopf und die Rakete ging los* geschlossen werden *Nastassja drückte auf den Knopf* und *dann ging die Rakete los*. Der Nachteil dieses Ansatzes liegt darin, daß zwar nicht die Bedeutungen von und multipliziert werden, dafür aber entsprechend viele Skalen konstruiert werden müssen.

Wenn die Annahme der vierten Untermaxime der Modalität Sinn machen soll, dann sollte sie auch solchen Texten Rechnung tragen, wo Sachverhalte temporal oder kausal einzuordnen sind, ohne daß eine Verknüpfung mit und vorliegt. Ich unterscheide hier drei Beispieltypen:

(33) *hit/scream*-Fälle
   (a) $_p$He hit her. $_q$She screamed at him. (p→q; q→p)
   (b) $_q$She screamed at him. $_p$He hit her. (q→p; p→q)

Unabhängig von der Anordnung der Sätze ist jeweils eine Interpretation möglich, in der das Schreien auf das Schlagen folgt, und eine Interpretation, in der es ihm vorausgeht. In Anlehnung an den englischen Sprachgebrauch rede ich hier von Vorwärts- und Rückwärts-Interpretation.

(34) *stand up/greet*-Fälle
   (a) $_p$Max stood up. $_q$John greeted him. (p→q)
   (b) $_q$John greeted him. $_p$Max stood up. (q→p)

Hier ist die präferierte Interpretation die Vorwärtsinterpretation. Die Rückwärtsinterpretation ist nicht ausgeschlossen, ist aber "unreliable" im Sinne von Lascarides & Oberlander (1993: 6) - außer der Hörer weiß bereits aus dem Kontext, daß eine Rückwärtsinterpretation möglich ist.

(35) *push/fall*-Fälle
   (a) $_p$Max fell. $_q$John pushed him. (q→p)
   (b) $_q$John pushed him. $_p$Max fell. (q→p)

Im Fall (35a) ist die Rückwärtsinterpretation präferiert. Dies hängt offenbar mit unserem Weltwissen oder mentalem Skript zusammen, daß das Stoßen dem Fallen vorausgeht bzw. dieses verursacht, aber nicht umgekehrt. Ein vergleichbares Wissen existiert für den *stand up/greet*-Fall nicht. Auch bei (35a) ist natürlich im Prinzip auch eine Vorwärtsinterpretation denkbar.

Gegen die klassische Analyse von Grice sind vor allem zwei Argumente vorgebracht worden. Erstens sprechen Paare wie die folgenden dagegen, für die Erklärung der asymmetrischen Koordination die vierte Untermaxime der Modalität zu bemühen (Bsp. nach H. Clark, vgl. Gazdar (1979: 44, Fn. 9); Bar-Lev & Palacas 1980):

(36) (a) Max fell. John pushed him.
   (b) Max fell and John pushed him.

Während in (36a) der durch den zweiten Satz bezeichnete Sachverhalt als Grund für den durch den ersten Satz bezeichneten Sachverhalt gilt, ist eine solche Interpretation in (36b) nicht möglich; hier versteht man den Gesamtsatz immer so, daß der durch den zweiten Satz bezeichnete Sachverhalt auf den durch den ersten Satz bezeichneten Sachverhalt folgt. Dieser Effekt könne nichts mit der Anordnung der Sätze zu tun haben, da diese in beiden Fällen die gleiche sei.

Zweitens wecken Beispiele wie (37) den Verdacht, daß die Anordnung der Konjunkte entgegen der Griceschen Auffassung doch Einfluß auf die Wahrheitsbewertung hat (vgl. Cohen 1971; Levinson 1983: 35):

(37)   Es ist nicht wahr, daß Fritz Vater wurde und heiratete, er heiratete und wurde Vater.

Kempson (1988: 159f.) versucht dies relevanztheoretisch so zu erklären, daß die jeweiligen Propositionen - als sogenannte Explikatur - durch temporale Indizes angereichert werden. Was dann eine Rolle spielt, ist also nicht die Anordnung der Konjunkte per se, sondern deren Auffüllung mit den relevanten weiteren Informationen.

Es gibt nun eine Übereinstimmung darin, daß bei den Fällen (34)-(36) die Vorwärts- bzw. Rückwärtsinterpretation durch Weltwissen oder mentale Skripte gesteuert wird (Lascarides & Oberlander 1993; Carston 1995). Lascarides & Oberlander (1993) nehmen für die Erklärung des Falls (34a) ein 'Narration' genanntes Prinzip an, zur Erklärung von (35a) zusätzlich ein 'Causal Law' genanntes Prinzip. 'Narration' ist im Grunde eine Version der vierten Untermaxime der Modalität, während das 'Causal Law' nicht als ein Stereotyp über die Relation zwischen Stoßen und Fallen darstellt.

Das eigentliche Problem besteht darin, zu erklären, warum die asymmetrische Koordination nur Vorwärtsinterpretation zu erlauben scheint. Bar-Lev & Palacas (1980) postulieren folgendes Prinzip, das Rückwärtsinterpretationen in *und*-Koordinationen ausschließt:

(38)   *Semantic Command*
       The second conjunct (S") ist not prior to the first (S') (chronologically or causally).

Man beachte, daß dieses Prinzip nicht irgendwie eine Mehrdeutigkeit der Konjunktion beinhaltet; insofern ist es durchaus kompatibel mit dem Griceschen Ansatz. Es deckt die Fälle symmetrischer Koordination ab und läßt auch Raum für pragmatische Schlußverfahren, die auf Weltwissen oder mentale Skripte bezugnehmen, bezieht sich aber nicht auf eine Maxime vom Typ der vierten Untermaxime der Modalität. Was aber offenbleibt, ist der theoretische Status dieses Prinzips.

Carston (1993) argumentiert, daß ein solches Prinzip folgende Fälle nicht erklären könne:

(39)   If the old king has died of a heart attack and a republic has been formed, and the latter event has caused the former, then Tom will be upset.

(40)   A: Did Bill break the vase?
       B: Well, the vase broke and Bill dropped it.
       (Bsp. nach L. Horn)

Wenn (38) durchgängig Gültigkeit haben sollte, dann müßte (39) widersprüchlich wirken, und die präferierte Rückwärtsinterpretation in (40) ausgeschlossen sein. Allerdings kann man hier auch argumentieren, daß es sich bei (39) um einen Streichungskontext handelt, und daß bei (40) Weltwissen eine Rolle spielt, demzufolge das Fallenlassen eines Gegenstands typischerweise seinem Zerbrechen vorausgeht. Streichungen sind auch erwartbar, wenn man hier überhaupt noch von Implikaturen reden will. Problematisch ist dann hinsichtlich (38), von einer semantischen Bedingung auszugehen.

Daß auf der anderen Seite eine pragmatische Anreicherung einer Proposition Einfluß auf die Wahrheitsbedingungen haben kann, ist gerade eine Hauptüberzeugung der Anhänger der Relevanztheorie, die diesen Prozeß unter dem Stichwort der Explikatur diskutieren. Carstons (1993, 1995) eigene Analyse stützt sich weitgehend auf eine kognitive Deutung im Rahmen des Relevanzbegriffs, der sich auf den Verarbeitungsaufwand bezieht. *Und*-Konjunkte sind demzufolge eine einzige Verarbeitungseinheit und blockieren daher eine Analyse, in der das zweite Konjunkt als implizite Antwort auf das erste gedeutet werden kann (Carston 1995: 233). Wie allerdings die Beispiele (39), (40) analysiert werden können, bleibt offen. Vermutlich muß man hier auf eine pragmatische Anreicherung Bezug nehmen, eine Lösung, die sich auch für den Fall (37) anbietet.

Eine empirisch und theoretisch rundum befriedigende Lösung des Problems der asymmetrischen Koordination steht daher noch aus. Der Verdacht drängt sich jedoch auf, daß die vierte Untermaxime der Modalität zu ausschließlich an den zu erklärenden Fällen orientiert ist, als daß sie Anspruch auf Allgemeingültigkeit erheben könnte. Zwar haben Psycholinguisten wie Levelt (1989: 138) und Diskurslinguisten wie Brown & Yule (1983: 125ff.) anläßlich des Linearisierungsproblems auf den Umstand hingewiesen, daß bei bestimmten Textsorten wie Erzählungen oder Beschreibungen von Wohnräumen eine *ordo naturalis* präferiert wird, aber dies läßt sich nicht zuverlässig verallgemeinern oder aus anderen Prinzipien deduzieren; Levelt (1989: 139) weist in diesem Zusammenhang nur kurz auf Prinzipien der Gedächtnisorganisation und auf kulturspezifische Skripts hin. Wenn die vierte Untermaxime der Modalität aber ad hoc ist, sollte auch sie reduziert werden.

4.6 Resümee

Vor dem Hintergrund der Griceschen Konversationsmaximen habe ich die folgenden Reduktionsvorschläge gemacht. In bezug auf die erste Untermaxime der Modalität habe ich argumentiert, daß absichtliche Verstöße gegen Sprachregeln aus unabhängig benötigten Prinzipien für erfolreiche Kommunikation, wie etwa der *Linguistic Presumption* im Sinne von Bach & Harnish (1979) abgeleitet werden können, und daß Verstöße gegen Sequenzierungsbedingungen und Ignoranz des Hintergrundwissens auf die Quantitätsmaxime zurückgeführt werden können. In bezug auf die zweite Untermaxime der Modalität habe ich Fälle des Witzemachens als nicht durch das Kooperationsprinzip abgedeckt betrachtet; verbleibende Fälle absichtlicher Ambiguität werden als Verstoß gegen die Quantitätsmaxime gewertet. Letzteres gilt ebenfalls für die dritte Untermaxime der Modalität, bei der die Reduktion auf die Quantitätsmaxime - im Sinne des Informationsgehalts - naheliegt; Kürze per se scheint kein akzeptables Kriterium zu sein. Die vierte Untermaxime der Modalität wurde als ad hoc in bezug auf die zu erklärenden Fälle betrachtet. Während es noch nicht klar ist, wie das Rätsel der asymmetrischen Koordination gelöst werden kann, ist doch klar, daß es nicht allein durch die vierte Untermaxime der Modalität gelöst werden kann.

Die Methode der Untersuchung wurde durch die Diskussion einschlägiger Beispiele bestimmt; während dies in der pragmatischen Forschung das durchaus übliche Verfahren ist, kann man doch vermuten, daß längst nicht alle relevanten Fakten bekannt geschweige denn systematisiert sind. So ergibt sich etwa der Eindruck, daß einem großen Bereich sehr heterogener Fakten bei der ersten Untermaxime der Modalität, ein kleiner, aber recht robuster Bereich bei der vierten Untermaxime der Modalität entgegensteht. Bei allen Reduktionsversuchen ist zu bedenken, daß die empirische Basis oft sehr schmal ist.

Eine andere Schwierigkeit besteht in der Explikation des Begriffs der Informativität, wie er für die Quantitätsmaximen einschlägig ist. Einer der wenigen, der das klar gesehen hat, ist Levinson (1987a), der die Lösung des Problems aber als Desiderat betrachtet (vgl. §3). Bevor eine Reduktion wirklich als gelungen betrachtet werden kann, muß natürlich eine genaue Kontrolle möglich sein, ob die Maxime, die die neuen Lasten tragen soll, dazu auch tatsächlich in der Lage ist. Auch hier ist noch Präzisierungsarbeit zu leisten.

5 Diskussion

Wenn der Versuch, die Modalitätsmaxime zu reduzieren, erfolgreich wäre, spräche das gegen die Vorschläge von Horn (1984) und Levinson (1987a), die ja - jeder auf seine Weise - an der Modalitätsmaxime festhalten. Beide Ansätze haben sich in erster Linie auf die Quantitätsmaxime konzentriert und der Modalitätsmaxime eher eine unterstützende Funktion zugebilligt.

Die Frage, ob die bei der Auseinandersetzung mit der Griceschen Fassung der Modalitätsmaxime gewonnenen Argumente auf die Levinsonsche Fassung übertragbar wären, kann nur bei genauer Auseinandersetzung mit seinem Markiertheitsbegriff beantwortet werden, und das führt zwangsläufig zu einer Untersuchung des Minimierungskonzepts. Einige Probleme damit wurden schon angedeutet (vgl. Ariel 1994). Eine zentrale Frage scheint mir hier, ob markierte Interpretationen tatsächlich Implikaturen sind, oder nicht direkt mit einer stereotypischen Bedeutung oder mit Wortassoziationen verbunden sind. Eine Schwierigkeit ist ferner, daß dabei die Balance bzw. die Hierarchie zu den anderern Prinzipien zu beachten ist - ein Vergleich mit den Griceschen Maximen ist so erschwert, zumal Levinson auf Relation und Qualität nicht explizit eingeht.

Meine Hypothese, daß die Modalitätsmaxime reduzierbar ist, ist in Übereinstimmung mit der Meinung von Wilson & Sperber (1981), die allerdings keinen detaillierten Nachweis geboten haben, und dies auch nicht in Sperber & Wilson (1986) tun. Keinesfalls darf diese Übereinstimmung aber als eine Bestätigung ihres theoretischen Ansatzes verstanden werden, der in gewisser Hinsicht eher gegen Grice gerichtet ist. Ob ihre Reduktion der Griceschen Maximen auf den Aspekt der Relevanz gelungen ist, ist sehr umstritten. Wie Levinson (1987a, 76) argumentiert, läuft das Verständnis von Relevanz als Verhältnis von kontextuellen Effekten zum Verarbeitungsaufwand eigentlich auf eine Quantitätsmaxime heraus: der Komplex der kontextuellen Effekte, verstanden als maximale Information, entspricht Quantität I bei Grice und dem Q-Prinzip bei Levinson, Verarbeitungsaufwand entspricht teilweise Quantität II und dem I-Prinzip bei Levinson. Jedoch ist zu bedenken, daß Levinson dem kognitivistischen Ansatz von Sperber und Wilson generell skeptisch gegenübersteht; er selbst sieht sich eher in der rationalistischen Tradition (Levinson 1991: 109, Fn. 4). Trotz interessanter Kritikpunkte und Einzelbeobachtungen bringt auch die Verteidigung von Carston (1995) gegen die Levinsonsche Kritik nichts wesentlich Neues, weil die relevanztheoretischen Interpretationen der Fakten nicht zu einem vergleichbar widerlegungsfähigen Theoriegebäude führen, z.B. zu einer deutlichen Verortung des Konzepts der Explikatur. Diese Vagheit spiegelt sich in der wiederholten Kritik, der Levinsonsche Ansatz sei zu sehr dem generativen Paradigma verhaftet (Carston 1995: 219, 227, 241).

Überlegt man, welche Konsequenzen die Reduktion der Modalitätsmaxime für den Status des Implikaturenapparats in einer modularen Pragmatik hat (vgl. §2), lassen sich die folgenden Beobachtungen machen:

Zunächst wird der Maximenapparat "leichter" und sollte daher einfacher zu handhaben sein. Belassen wir mit den restlichen Maximen alles beim alten, dann ergibt sich immerhin, daß fünf von insgesamt elf Maximen wegfallen. Allerdings könnte es sich erweisen, daß diese Erleichterung des Maximenapparats durch die möglicherweise notwendig werdende Differenzierung der Quantitätsmaxime bzw. der Inanspruchnahme der *Linguistic Presumption* kompensiert wird. Bei der Kalkulation von Implikaturen kann es nicht mehr zu einer Kollision (clash) zwischen den Modalitätsmaximen und den anderen Maximen kommen; unter der Annahme, daß solch eine Kollision einen erhöhten Verarbeitungsaufwand erfordert, ist dies ein erwünschtes Ergebnis.

Vor allem aber sollten sich Konsequenzen hinsichtlich zweier Asymmetrien ergeben: der Form-Inhalts-Asymmetrie und der Verletzungs/Beachtungs-Asymmetrie. Wenn es zutrifft, daß die Modalitätsmaximen sich durch Formbezogenheit auszeichnen, dann sollte ihre Kalkulation den Zugriff auf formbezogene Repräsentationen des grammatischen Inputsystems erforderlich machen. Demgegenüber sind die anderen Maximen inhaltsorientiert, d.h. sie greifen auf semantische Repräsentationen (z.B. Wahrheitsbedingungen, logische Formen, 'Explikaturen') zurück. Ein Nutzen des skizzierten Reduktionsvorschlags könnte sein, daß ein uneinheitlicher Zugriff, der möglicherweise mit einem erhöhten Verarbeitungsaufwand verbunden wäre, vermieden wird. Darüber hinaus wäre auch eine Verallgemeinerung der Art, daß die Rekonstruktion von Implikaturen grundsätzlich auf semantischen Repräsentationen aufbaut, durchaus erstrebenswert.

Eine weitere, nicht sehr gut untersuchte Asymmetrie ist die Verletzungs/Beachtungs-Asymmetrie. Es ist auffällig, daß nur bei der vierten Untermaxime der Modalität eine Beachtung der Maxime veranschlagt wird, bei den anderen Untermaximen dagegen eine Verletzung. Eine Nullhypothese wäre, daß die scheinbare Verletzung einer Maxime einen höheren Verarbeitungsaufwand bedeutet als die Beachtung. Daß in Fällen der Beachtung aber eigens Kalkulationen erstellt werden, ist nicht sehr plausibel, denn das Normale und Erwartbare anzunehmen, sollte keiner eigenen Kalkulation bedürfen. In jedem Fall muß der Hörer aber eine Entscheidung treffen, ob ein Beachtungs- oder Verletzungsfall vorliegt. Wie die relevante Entscheidung getroffen wird, ist unklar, aber daß sie einen Einfluß auf den Verarbeitungsaufwand hat, scheint plausibel. Diese Schwierigkeit gilt natürlich genauso für die anderen Maximen, die Asymmetrie ist jedoch bei der Maxime der Modalität besonders gravierend. Ein weiterer Nutzen der Reduktion könnte sein, daß die damit verbundene Erhöhung des Verarbeitungsaufwands entfällt.

Direkte Evidenz für oder gegen den modularen Status des Implikaturenapparats kann aus einer solchen Reduktion, selbst wenn sie im Vergleich zu den Vorschlägen von Horn, Levinson und Sperber & Wilson als plausibel betrachtet werden sollte, jedoch nicht abgeleitet werden. Wenn man es für möglich hält, daß auch die Pragmatik modularen Charakter hat und Evidenz dafür sucht, müssen Reduktionsversuche wie die von Horn und Levinson als zu klassifikatorisch empfunden werden. Hier liegt sicher auch ein Grund für die verbreitete Akzeptanz der Relevanztheorie.

Zu fragen ist daher nach der kognitiven Realität des Griceschen Schlußprozesses. Man hat sich hier meist mit dem von Grice vorgegebenen Schema begnügt, ohne dieses so genau zu untersuchen wie den Maximenapparat. Folgt man aber den Auffassungen von Kasher, Sperber und Wilson, daß Implikaturen einen "zentralen" Status haben, dann müßte gerade aus der Eigenart dieses Schlußprozesses etwas über den modularen Status der Zentralpragmatik im Sinne von Kasher (die u.a. Wissen über konversationelle Implikaturen enthält) bzw. die nicht-modularen zentralen kognitiven Systeme bei Sperber & Wilson folgen.

Die kognitive Natur dieses Schlußprozesses ist umstritten. Zum einen ist unklar, in welchem Maße der Schlußprozeß formalen Charakter hat. Carston (1995: 224ff.) argumentiert gegen ein System des nicht-monotonen Schließens, wie es Levinson vorschwebt. Sie behauptet, daß die Relevanztheorie nicht-monotone Effekte durchaus mithilfe der monotonen Logik, in Zusammenarbeit mit anderen relevanztheoretischen Annahmen, erklären könne (ebd.: 237, Fn. 10). Auf der anderen Seite zeigt die nicht-monotone Logik von Lascarides & Oberlander (1993), daß rein pragmatische Prinzipien wie das Prinzip der 'Narration' durchaus in einer nicht-monotonen Logik implementierbar sind.

Zum anderen ist die kognitive Realität dieses Schlußprozesses im wesentlichen unbekannt. Einschlägig sind etwa die experimentellen Untersuchungen von Shapiro & Murphy (1993) zur Verarbeitung direkter und indirekter Sprechakte. Indirekte Sprechakte können nach Auffassung mancher Theoretiker mithilfe der Implikaturentheorie erfaßt werden (z.B. Searle 1975, Levinson 1983). Dabei ist eine Gemeinsamkeit des Searleschen Ansatzes zu indirekten Sprechakten einerseits und der Griceschen Auffassung zur Ableitung konversationeller Implikaturen anderseits, daß zuerst eine Repräsentation für die wörtliche Bedeutung erstellt wird und dann, darauf aufbauend, bzw. von dieser abweichend, eine Repräsentation für die nicht-wörtliche indirekte Bedeutung. Shapiro und Murphy kommen dagegen zu dem Ergebnis, daß (a) direkte und indirekte Bedeutungen parallel und nicht seriell erstellt werden, und daß (b) gleich eine einzige Bedeutung erstellt wird und nicht aus mehreren möglichen eine passende ausgewählt wird.

Unterstützt wird dieses Ergebnis auch von Récanati (1995), der eine Reihe von Argumenten gegen solche Modelle präsentiert, die davon ausgehen, daß eine wörtliche Interpretation bei der Sprachverarbeitung erstellt werden muß, bevor eine nichtwörtliche Interpretation erstellt werden kann. Dabei bezieht er sich nicht in erster Linie auf konversationelle Implikaturen, sondern auf Fälle abgeleiteter Interpretationen wie z.B. Metapher und Metonymie. Der Punkt ist, daß die in diesem Bereich benötigten Schlußprozesse nicht vollkommen verschieden sein dürften von den für klassische konversationelle Implikaturen benötigten. Récanati (1995: 214) verteidigt hier die Auffassung, daß solche nicht wörtlichen Interpretationen auf assoziative Art abgeleitet werden, nicht auf inferentielle Art; entsprechend stellt er den Begriff der kognitiven Zugänglichkeit (accessibility) gegenüber dem Begriff der Wörtlichkeit in den Vordergrund. Diese Ergebnisse und Argumente stellen die kognitive Realität des Griceschen Schlußschemas in Frage. Man muß diese Debatte abwarten, bevor man Genaueres über den modularen Status des Implikaturenapparats sagen kann. In der Zwischenzeit sind weitere Reduktionsbemühungen zumindest nützlich.

Anmerkungen

1 In Anlehnung an den Sprachgebrauch in der deutschen Übersetzung von Levinson (1983), und um Verwechselungen mit anderen Modalitätsbegriffen vorzubeugen, habe ich in Meibauer (1996) von der "Maxime der Art und Weise" gesprochen. Man beachte dazu, daß Grice (1989a: 27) von "manner" spricht, nicht etwa von "modality". Da sich der Terminus "Maxime der Modalität" in der deutschsprachigen Literatur durchzusetzen scheint, passe ich mich hier diesem Sprachgebrauch an.
2 Die von Harnish & Farmer (1984) gemachte Unterscheidung zwischen interner und externer Modularität bzw. Homogenität wird hier, soweit ich sehe, nicht beachtet.
3 Die erweiterte Kernpragmatik (Amplified Core Pragmatics) gehört nicht in diese Aufstellung, da sie zu den zentralen Prozessen gerechnet wird. Sie umfaßt weitere Sprechakttypen wie z.B. Gratulation oder Ernennung. Daß der Input der zentralen Prozesse prinzipiell der Output eines pragmatischen Moduls sein kann, wird zugelassen.
4 Relation und Relevanz wird oft äquivok gebraucht, vgl. auch Levinson (1987a: 67).
5 Die Qualitätsmaxime hält Horn für unreduzierbar, vgl. Horn (1989: 194) und Levinson (1987a: 75).
6 Zitiert nach Horn (1984: 22). In Horn (1989: 197) findet sich folgende Formulierung "*Given two coextensive expressions*, the briefer and/or more lexicalized form will tend to become associated through R-based implicature with some unmarked, stereotypical meaning, use, or situation, and the marked, more complex or prolix, less lexicalized expression tends to Q-implicate a marked message, one which the unmarked form could not or would not have conveyed." [Kursivierung von mir, J.M.]
7 Zitiert nach Levinson (1987a: 67f.). Kleinere Formulierungsunterschiede finden sich in der Darstellung bei Levinson (1987b: 401f.).
8 "m-intended" bezieht sich auf "meaning intention" im Sinne von Grice.
9 Man beachte, daß hier unter dem Punkt "Recipient's corollary" nicht mehr von einem obskuren Ausdruck die Rede ist.
10 Vgl. den Ausdruck *horn scale* in (7). Benannt sind diese Skalen nach Laurence R. Horn.
11 Die Zusammenstellung in Turner (1995: 65) - vgl. die dort gegebenen Beispiele - umfaßt (a) Conjunction buttressing, (b) Conditional perfection, (c) Bridging, (d) Inference to stereotype, (e) Mirror maxim, (f) Frame-based inferences, (g) Membership categorisation, (h) Preferred coreference, (i) Indirect Speech Acts und (j) Lexical narrowing.
12 Daß diese zwei Minimierungsbegriffe vermischt werden, kritisiert Ariel (1994: 20ff.). Es geht dabei unter anderem um die Frage, inwiefern Pronomen gegenüber lexikalischen Nominalphrasen semantisch allgemeiner und kürzer sind.
13 Natürlich ergibt sich das gleiche Problem auch schon für die klassische Fassung der Maxime der Quantität bei Grice.
14 Levinson ist hier in einer Zwickmühle: Einerseits wirft er Horn vor, daß dieser die Q/M-Implikaturen fälschlich zu den Q-Implikaturen rechnet, anderseits sieht Levinson eine deutliche Abhängigkeit dieser Implikaturen vom (Q-typischen) Informationsgehalt: "[...] since the unmarked expression of such a pair I-implicates a richer, stereotypical interpretation, the use of the marked member Q-implicates the negation of the richer interpretation." (Levinson 1987b: 409)
15 Vgl. den Vorschlag von Wilson & Sperber (1981: 173): "[...] given two utterances of different length which express the same propositions, it is always the shorter of the two that is appropriate."

Literatur

Aitchison, J. (1994): "'Say, Say It again Sam': The Treatment of Repetition in Linguistics". In: A. Fischer, ed.: Repetition. Tübingen: Narr, 15-34.
Ariel, M. (1994): "Interpreting anaphoric expressions: a cognitive versus a pragmatic approach". Journal of Linguistics 30, 3-42.
Aronoff, M. (1976): Word Formation in Generative Grammar. Cambridge, Mass.: The MIT Press.
Atlas, J..D. & S.C. Levinson (1981): "It-Clefts, Informativeness, and Logical Form: Radical Pragmatics (Revised Standard Version)." In: P. Cole, ed.: Radical Pragmatics. New York: Academic Press, 1-61.
Attardo, S. (1993): "Violation of conversational maxims and cooperation: The case of jokes". Journal of Pragmatics 19, 537-558.
Bach, K. & R.M. Harnish (1979): Linguistic Communication and Speech Acts. Cambridge, Mass.: The MIT Press.
Bar-Lev, Z. & A. Palacas (1980): "Semantic command over pragmatic priority". Lingua 51, 137-146.
Bayer, J. (1991): "German particles in a modular grammar: Neurolinguistic evidence". In: W. Abraham, ed.: Discourse Particles. Descriptive and theoretical investigations on the logical, syntactic and pragmatic properties of discourse particles in German. Amsterdam: Benjamins, 253-302.
Briscoe, T. & A. Copestake & A. Lascarides (1995): "Blocking". In: P. Saint-Dizier & E. Viegas, eds.: Computational lexical semantics. Cambridge: Cambridge University Press, 273-302.
Brown, G. & G. Yule (1983): Discourse Analysis. Cambridge: Cambridge University Press.
Carston, R. (1993): "Conjunction, explanation and relevance". Lingua 90, 27-48.
Carston, R. (1994): "Conjunction and pragmatic effects". In: R.E. Asher, ed.: The Encyclopedia of Language and Linguistics. Oxford: Pergamon Press, 692-698.
Carston, R. (1995): "Quantity maxims and generalised implicature". Lingua 96, 213-244.
Clark, E.V. (1993): The lexicon in acquisition. Cambridge: Cambridge University Press.
Cohen, J.L. (1971): "Some Remarks on Grice's Views about the Logical Particles of Natural Language". In: Y. Bar-Hillel, ed.: Pragmatics of Natural Languages. Dordrecht: Reidel, 50-68.
Crystal, D. (1990): "Linguistic Strangeness". In: M. Bridges, ed.: On strangeness. Tübingen: Narr, 13-24.
Fodor, J.A. (1983): The modularity of mind. Cambridge, Mass.: The MIT Press.
Foldi, N.S. (1987): "Appreciation of Pragmatic Interpretations of Indirect Commands: Comparison of Right and Left Hemisphere Brain-Damaged Patients". Brain and Language 31, 88-108.
Garfield, J.L. (1987): "Introduction: Carving the Mind at Its Joints". In: J.L. Garfield, ed.: Modularity in Knowledge Representation and Natural Language Understanding. Cambridge, Mass.: The MIT Press, 1-13.
Gazdar, G. (1979): Pragmatics. Implicature, Presupposition, and Logical Form. New York: Academic Press.
Gibbs, R.W., Jr. (1994): The poetics of mind. Figurative thought, language, and understanding. Cambridge: Cambridge University Press.
Green, G.M. (1989): Pragmatics and Natural Language Understanding. Hillsdale, N.J.: Erlbaum.
Grice, H.P. (1989a): "Logic and Conversation". In: H.P. Grice: Studies in the way of words. Cambridge, Mass.: Harvard University Press, 22-40.
Grice, H.P. (1989b): "Presupposition and Conversational Implicature". In: H.P. Grice: Studies in the way of words. Cambridge, Mass.: Harvard University Press, 269-282.
Groeben, N. & B. Scheele (1984): Produktion und Rezeption von Ironie. Bd. 1. Pragmalinguistische Beschreibung und psycholinguistische Beschreibungshypothesen. Tübingen: Narr.
Harnish, R.M. (1995): "Modularity and Speech Acts". Pragmatics & Cognition 3, 1-29.

Harnish, R.M. & A.K. Farmer (1984): "Pragmatics and the modularity of the linguistic system". Lingua 63, 255-277.

Hirschberg, J.B. (1985): A Theory of Scalar Implicature. PhD thesis. University of Pennsylvania. Ann Arbor: University Microfilms International.

Horn, L.R. (1984): "Toward a new taxonomy for pragmatic inference: Q-based and R-based implicature". In: D. Schiffrin, ed.: Georgetown University Round Table on Language and Linguistics 1984. Meaning, Form, and Use in Context: Linguistic Applications. Washington, D.C.: Georgetown University Press, 11-42.

Horn, L.R. (1989): A natural history of negation. Chicago: Chicago University Press.

Jucker, A.H. (1994): "Irrelevant Repetitions: A Challenge to Relevance Theory". In: A. Fischer, ed.: Repetition. Tübingen: Narr, 47-60.

Kasher, A. (1991a): "On the pragmatic modules: A lecture". Journal of Pragmatics 16, 381-397.

Kasher, A. (1991b): "Pragmatics and the modularity of the mind". In: St. Davis, ed.: Pragmatics. A Reader. Oxford: Oxford University Press, 567-582.

Kasher, A. (1991c): "Pragmatics and Chomsky's research program". In: A. Kasher, ed.: The Chomskyan turn. Oxford: Blackwell, 122-149.

Kempson, R.M. (1988): "Grammar and conversational principles". In: F.J. Newmeyer, ed.: Linguistics: The Cambridge Survey. Vol. II. Linguistic Theory: Extensions and Implications. Cambridge: Cambridge University Press, 139-163.

Kiparsky, P. (1983): "Word-Formation and the Lexicon". In: F. Ingeman, ed.: 1982 Mid-America Linguistics Conference Papers. Lawrence: University of Kansas, 3-29.

Lascarides, A. & J. Oberlander (1993): "Temporal coherence and defeasible knowledge". Theoretical Linguistics 19, 1-37.

Levelt, W.J.M. (1989): Speaking. From Intention to Articulation. Cambridge, Mass.: The MIT Press.

Levinson, S.C. (1983): Pragmatics. Cambridge: Cambridge University Press.

Levinson, S.C. (1987a): "Minimization and Conversational Inference". In: J. Verschueren & M. Bertucelli-Papi, eds.: The pragmatic perspective. Amsterdam: Benjamins, 61-129.

Levinson, S.C. (1987b): "Pragmatics and the grammar of anaphora: A partial pragmatic reduction of Binding and Control phenomena". Journal of Linguistics 23, 379-434.

Levinson, S.C. (1989): "A review of Relevance". Journal of Linguistics 25, 455-472.

Levinson, S.C. (1991): "Pragmatic reduction of the Binding Conditions revisited". Journal of Linguistics 27, 107-161.

Matsumoto, Y. (1995): "The conversational condition on Horn scales". Linguistics and Philosophy 18, 21-60.

Meibauer, J. (1987): "Zur Form und Funktion von Echofragen". In: I. Rosengren, ed.: Sprache und Pragmatik. Lunder Symposium 1986. Malmö: Almqvist & Wiksell, 335-356.

Meibauer, J. (1995): "Komplexe Präpositionen - Grammatikalisierung, Metapher, Implikaturen und division of pragmatic labour". In: F. Liedtke, ed.: Implikaturen: grammatische und pragmatische Analysen. Tübingen: Niemeyer, 47-74.

Meibauer, J. (1996): "Modulare Pragmatik und die Maxime der Art und Weise". Sprache und Pragmatik 38, 40-69.

Muthmann, G. (1994): Doppelformen in der deutschen Sprache der Gegenwart. Studie zu den Varianten in Aussprache, Schreibung, Wortbildung und Flexion. Tübingen: Niemeyer.

Poser, W. (1992): "Blocking of Phrasal Constructions by Lexical Items". In: I. Sag & A. Szabolsci, eds.: Lexical Matters. Stanford: CSLI, 111-130.

Posner, R. (1979): "Bedeutung und Gebrauch der Satzverknüpfer in den natürlichen Sprachen". In: G. Grewendorf, ed.: Sprechakttheorie und Semantik. Frankfurt/Main: Suhrkamp, 345-385.

Récanati, F. (1995): "The Alleged Priority of Literal Interpretation". Cognitive Science 19, 207-232.

Rolf, E. (1994): Sagen und Meinen. Paul Grices Theorie der Konversations-Implikaturen. Opladen: Westdeutscher Verlag.
Schegloff, E.A. (1971): "Notes on a conversational practice: Formulating place". In: D. Sudnow, ed.: Studies in Social Interaction. New York: Free Press, 71-119.
Schmerling, S.F. (1975): "Asymmetric conjunction and rules of conversation". In: P. Cole & J.L. Morgan, eds.: Syntax and Semantics 3. Speech Acts. New York: Academic Press, 211-231.
Searle, J.R. (1975): "Indirect Speech Acts". In: P. Cole & J.L. Morgan, eds.: Syntax and Semantics 3. Speech Acts. New York: Academic Press, 59-82.
Shapiro, A.M. & G.L. Murphy (1993): "Can You Answer a Question for Me? Processing Indirect Speech Acts". Journal of Memory and Language 32, 211-229.
Sinclair, M. (1995): "Fitting pragmatics into the mind: Some issues in mentalist pragmatics". Journal of pragmatics 23, 509-539.
Sperber, D. & D. Wilson (1986): Relevance. Communication and Cognition. Oxford: Blackwell.
Sperber, D. & D. Wilson (1987): "Précis of Relevance: Communication and Cognition". Behavioral and Brain Sciences 10, 697-710.
Tannen, D. (1989): Talking Voices: Repetition, Dialogue and Imagery in Conversational Discourse. Cambridge: Cambridge University Press.
Turner, K. (1995): "The principal principles of pragmatic inference: Co-operation". Language Teaching 28, 67-76.
Verschueren, J. (1987): Pragmatics as a Theory of Linguistic Adaption. IPRA Working Document 1. Antwerpen: International Pragmatics Association.
Werner, A. (1995): "Blockierungsphänomene in der Wortbildung". Papiere zur Linguistik 52, 43-65.
Wilson, D. & D. Sperber (1981): "On Grice's Theory of Conversation". In: P. Werth, ed.: Conversation and Discourse. New York: St. Martin's Press, 155-178.
Wilson, D. & D. Sperber (1991): "Pragmatics and Modularity". In: S. Davis, ed.: Pragmatics. A Reader. Oxford: Oxford University Press, 583-595.

Maximen in Interaktion:
Faktoren der Informativitätsverstärkung

Beatrice Primus, Stuttgart

1 Einleitung

1.1 Die Grundzüge des Ansatzes von Grice

Der vorliegende Beitrag[*] ordnet sich in die Tradition der Griceschen Theorie konversationeller Implikaturen ein. Aus diesem Grund werden zunächst die wichtigsten Begriffe und Annahmen dieses Ansatzes vorgestellt.

Die Grundlage der Konversationstheorie von Grice bildet das folgende Kooperationsprinzip (KP): "Mache deinen Gesprächsbeitrag jeweils so, wie es von dem akzeptierten Zweck oder der akzeptierten Richtung des Gesprächs, an dem du teilnimmst, gerade verlangt wird" (Grice 1979: 248). Nicht nur sprachliches, sondern auch nichtsprachliches Verhalten folgt dem KP. Man kann das KP daher auch als allgemeines Prinzip rationalen Verhaltens auffassen. Vier Gruppen von Maximen fallen unter das KP und präzisieren es (Grice 1979: 249f.):

Quantität:
Erste Submaxime: Mache deinen Beitrag so informativ wie (für die gegebenen Gesprächszwecke) nötig.
Zweite Submaxime: Mache deinen Beitrag nicht informativer als nötig.
Qualität:
Obermaxime: Versuche deinen Beitrag so zu machen, daß er wahr ist.
Erste Submaxime: Sage nichts, was du für falsch hältst.
Zweite Submaxime: Sage nichts, wofür dir angemessene Gründe fehlen.
Relation (auch: Relevanz):
Sei relevant.
Modalität:
Obermaxime: Sei klar.
Erste Submaxime: Vermeide Dunkelheit des Ausdrucks.
Zweite Submaxime: Vermeide Mehrdeutigkeit.

[*] Für wertvolle Hinweise zu einer früheren Fassung dieser Arbeit danke ich Joachim Jacobs und Thomas Becker.

Dritte Submaxime: Sei kurz (vermeide unnötige Weitschweifigkeit).
Vierte Submaxime: Der Reihe nach!

Die Maximen der Quantität, Relevanz und Qualität werden im Laufe dieses Beitrags eingehender diskutiert. Vorweg soll lediglich die Gricesche Auslegung des Relevanzbegriffs kurz erläutert werden. Eine Äußerung ohne signalisierten Themawechsel steht in der von der besagten Maxime geforderten Relation zum sprachlichen und außersprachlichen Kontext, wenn sie inhaltlich zu den vorhergehenden Äußerungen bzw. zur thematischen Vorgabe der Situation paßt (Grice 1979: 251). Dieser Relevanzbegriff unterscheidet sich vom weiteren Relevanzbegriff Sperbers und Wilsons (1986), vgl. auch Rolf (1994: 151f.).

Die wichtigste linguistische Funktion der Konversationsmaximen ist, daß unter der Annahme ihrer Befolgung auf der Basis des wörtlich Gesagten und der Äußerungssituation konversationelle Implikaturen entstehen können. Konversationelle Implikaturen sind aufhebbare, kontextabhängige Inferenzen, die im Normalfall die wörtliche Bedeutung anreichern. Eine konversationelle Implikatur wird oft auch als 'Andeutung' oder als das 'Gemeinte' bezeichnet.

Im Folgenden steht p für die wörtliche Bedeutung des Gesagten und q für die Implikatur, die auf der Basis von p, der Äußerungssituation von p und der Annahme der Befolgung einer oder mehrerer Maximen entsteht. Vereinfacht ausgedrückt werde ich auch von der Implikatur q von p sprechen. Eine wichtige Annahme des Ansatzes von Grice ist nun, daß der Adressat den Inhalt der Implikatur q ausrechnen kann, wenn er die im benutzten Sprachsystem verankerte wörtliche Bedeutung p sowie die Äußerungssituation kennt und davon ausgeht, daß es sich um ein rationales bzw. kooperatives Gespräch handelt. Das allgemeine Kalkulationsmuster für eine konversationelle Implikatur formuliert Grice (1979: 255) wie folgt:

(I) Er hat gesagt, daß p; es gibt keinen Grund anzunehmen, daß er die Maximen oder zumindest das KP nicht beachtet; er könnte sie nicht beachten, falls er nicht dächte, daß q; er weiß (und weiß, daß ich weiß, daß er weiß), daß ich feststellen kann, daß die Annahme, daß er glaubt, daß q, nötig ist; er hat nichts getan, um mich von der Annahme, daß q, abzuhalten; er will - oder hat zumindest nichts dagegen -, daß ich denke, daß q; und somit hat er impliziert, daß q.

Wichtig für unsere spätere Diskussion ist, daß Implikaturen sich dem Umstand verdanken, daß ihre Unterstellung für die Aufrechterhaltung der Annahme, daß das KP oder mindestens eine Maxime befolgt ist, notwendig ist. Damit ist garantiert, daß im Laufe eines rationalen Gesprächs das KP und die Konversationsmaximen immer befolgt werden, und zwar auf der Ebene der wörtlichen Bedeutung oder auf Implikaturebene.

Am Beispiel (1) kann dieser Kalkulationsmechanismus an der hier zur Diskussion stehenden ersten Quantitätsmaxime illustriert werden.

(1) (a) Sie: Wie viele Romane von Goethe hast du gelesen?
     (b) Er: Einen.

(c) +> Ich habe nicht alle Romane von Goethe gelesen
(d) +> Ich habe nur einen Roman von Goethe gelesen

In Anlehnung an Levinson (1990) werden konversationelle Implikaturen mit "+>" notiert. Die Antwort in (1b) löst unter der Annahme, daß der Sprecher so informativ wie nötig ist (d. h. unter der Annahme, daß er die erste Quantitätsmaxime befolgt), in einem Standardkontext wie dem in (1a) illustrierten die Implikatur in (1c) aus. Solche Implikaturen können typischerweise, wie in (1d) gezeigt, auch einen Inhalt aufweisen, der mit Hilfe der Fokuspartikel *nur* paraphrasiert werden kann (vgl. auch Levinson 1990: 109). Die Paraphrasemöglichkeit mit *nur* wird im Folgenden als heuristisches Kriterium für diesen Typ von Implikaturen herangezogen.

Der Kalkulationsmechanismus für eine derartige Implikatur befolgt das weiter oben zitierte allgemeine Schema: Er hat gesagt, daß er einen Roman von Goethe gelesen hat; es gibt keinen Grund anzunehmen, daß er sich nicht kooperativ verhält und insbesondere nicht so informativ wie nötig ist; er könnte nicht so informativ wie nötig sein, wenn er nicht dächte, daß er nicht alle Romane von Goethe gelesen hat (Begründung: wenn es der Fall wäre, daß er alle oder mehrere Romane von Goethe gelesen hat und er (1b) sagen würde, dann wäre er nicht so informativ wie nötig); er weiß (und weiß, daß sie weiß, daß er weiß), daß sie feststellen kann, daß die Annahme, daß er glaubt, daß er nicht alle Romane von Goethe gelesen hat, nötig ist; er hat nichts getan, um sie von der Annahme, daß er nicht alle Romane von Goethe gelesen hat, abzuhalten; er will - oder hat zumindest nichts dagegen -, daß sie denkt, daß er nicht alle Romane von Goethe gelesen hat. Das Kalkulationsschema besagt, daß eine Äußerung mit einer derartigen quantitätsbasierten Implikatur informativer ist als ohne Implikatur und daß erst die Implikatur die Äußerung so informativ wie nötig macht.

In den Abschnitten 2 und 3 dieser Arbeit werden Standardimplikaturen wie die in (1c, d) illustrierten zur Diskussion stehen. Bei solchen Implikaturen wird keine Maxime offensichtlich bzw. demonstrativ verletzt (vgl. Levinson 1990: 107). Der Inhalt eines bestimmten Typs von Standardimplikaturen der Quantität kann in den meisten Fällen mit Hilfe von *nur* paraphrasiert werden und kann seinerseits mittels eines spezifischeren Ableitungsmechanismus, der in den nächsten Abschnitten näher diskutiert wird, kalkuliert werden. Bei Implikaturen, die keine Standardimplikaturen sind, verletzt der Sprecher eine Maxime offensichtlich. Offensichtliche Verletzungen der ersten Quantitätsmaxime liegen z. B. bei notwendig oder offensichtlich wahren Aussagen vor, wie z. B. *Tue es oder laß es bleiben!* oder *Luise ist eben eine Frau*.

1.2 Thema und Zielsetzung der vorliegenden Arbeit

Der vorliegende Beitrag versucht einerseits zu zeigen, daß bestimmte Typen von Implikaturen konsequenter als in anderen Ansätzen auf der Basis des Griceschen Kalkulationsmusters für konversationelle Implikaturen rekonstruiert werden können. Er führt aber andererseits den Ansatz von Grice in zwei Hinsichten weiter.

Zum einen wird gezeigt, daß Implikaturen, die auf der Basis der ersten Quantitätsmaxime entstehen (sogenannte 'skalare' Implikaturen), unterschiedliche Eigenschaften aufweisen, je nachdem, ob sie durch Fokusinformation ausgelöst werden oder nicht. In diesem Punkt werden Ideen aufgegriffen und weiterentwickelt, die schon bei Fretheim (1992), Hirschberg (1991), Krifka (1995) oder van Kuppevelt (1996) zu finden sind. Der folgende Beitrag unterscheidet sich von diesen Ansätzen dadurch, daß die Fokussensitivität solcher Implikaturen zurückgeführt wird auf die Interaktion der ersten Quantitätsmaxime mit der Qualitätsmaxime und auf die Tatsache, daß die Qualitätsmaxime auf Bedeutungsrepräsentationen greift, die durch illokutive Operatoren angereichert und in Fokus-Hintergrund strukturiert sind.

Außerdem versuche ich zu zeigen, daß für die Rekonstruktion solcher Quantitätsimplikaturen nicht der Bezug auf Informativitätsskalen, sondern der Bezug auf Alternativen im fokustheoretischen Sinn von primärer Relevanz ist. M. a. W. ist es für das Entstehen von solchen Quantitätsimplikaturen nicht notwendig, daß die Menge aus assertiertem Element und kontextuell relevanten Alternativen nach dem Grad der Informativität skaliert ist. Der empirische Wert dieser Auffassung zeigt sich darin, daß Implikaturen, die als typische, unauffällige Quantitätsimplikaturen ausgewiesen werden können, aber in alternativen Ansätzen nur unter der Annahme eines hohen Kalkulationsaufwands oder mit Hilfe anderer Maximen rekonstruiert wurden, auf der Basis der alternativenbezogenen Auffassung der ersten Quantitätsmaxime auf eine einfache Weise erfaßt werden können.

Zu diesen Fällen sind auch Implikaturen zu rechnen, die unter der Bezeichnung Konditionalverstärkung (engl. *conditional perfection*, vgl. Geiss und Zwicky (1971)) in der einschlägigen Literatur besprochen wurden. Ein Beispiel liefert der Internationale Arbeitskreis für Orthographie in der amtlichen Vorlage für die Neuregelung der deutschen Rechtschreibung (1995: 23):

(2) Für kurzes [ε] schreibt man *ä* statt *e*, wenn es eine Grundform mit *a* gibt. [...] In wenigen Wörtern schreibt man ausnahmsweise *ä*. Dies betrifft Wörter wie: *ätzen, dämmern, Geländer, Lärm, März, Schärpe*. [...] In wenigen Wörtern schreibt man ausnahmsweise *e*. Dies betrifft Wörter wie: *Eltern* (trotz *alt); schwenken - schwanken*.

Während die zweite Gruppe von Beispielen die *wenn-dann*-Aussage der Regel tatsächlich falsifiziert, tut dies die erste Gruppe von Beispielen nicht bzw. nur unter der Interpretation als *genau-dann-wenn*-Aussage. Es ist offensichtlich, daß die Verfasser das eine sagen und etwas anderes meinen und das Gemeinte als Regel ansetzen. Dieses Beispiel zeigt auch, wie unauffällig und 'normal' pragmatische Konditionalverstärkungen sind.

Ein zweiter Aspekt, unter welchem der vorliegende Beitrag den Griceschen Ansatz weiterführt, ist, daß die erste Quantitätsmaxime in einer systematischen Beziehung zu den anderen Griceschen Maximen der Konversation gesetzt wird. In dieser Hinsicht entwickelt der folgende Beitrag Gedanken von Matsumoto (1995) weiter. Durch die Interaktion mit anderen konversationellen Maximen entstehen verschiedene Typen quantitätsbasierter Implikaturen, wobei sich darunter auch solche befinden, die in alternativen

Ansätzen auf andere für diesen Zweck eigens eingeführte Maximen zurückgeführt wurden.

Zwei verschiedene Typen von quantitätsbasierten Implikaturen zeigen (3b) und (3c):

(3)   (a) Ich empfehle Ihnen, dieses Buch zu kaufen.
     (b) +> Ich fordere Sie nicht auf, dieses Buch zu kaufen.
     (c) +> Ich fordere Sie auf, dieses Buch zu kaufen.

Während in der einschlägigen Literatur für solche Fälle zwei Maximen bzw. Submaximen herangezogen werden, werden sie im vorliegenden Ansatz als zwei verschiedene Typen der Informativitätsverstärkung auf der Grundlage der ersten Quantitätsmaxime und ihrer Interaktion mit anderen Maximen der Konversation erklärt.

Die vorliegende Arbeit gliedert sich wie folgt. Im 2. Abschnitt wird das Interpretationsschema für eine bestimmte Klasse von Quantitätsimplikaturen in alternativen skalenbasierten Ansätzen besprochen. Der 3. Abschnitt führt die wichtigsten Probleme vor, mit denen alternative Ansätze konfrontiert sind, und präsentiert den hier vorgestellten Lösungsvorschlag. Der 4. Abschnitt diskutiert weitere Typen der konversationellen Informativitätsverstärkung. Der 5. Abschnitt faßt die Ergebnisse dieser Untersuchung zusammen.

2   Informativitätsskalen

Von Informativitätsskalen und dementsprechend von skalaren Quantitätsimplikaturen wird insbesondere unter Bezugnahme auf die Arbeiten von Gazdar (1979), Horn (1984, 1989) und Hirschberg (1991) gesprochen. Diese Autoren zeigen, daß Standardimplikaturen der Quantität auf der Basis von Informativitätsskalen immer wieder nach demselben Schema interpretiert werden. Solche Skalen beziehen sich auf Wortfelder, deren Elemente nach Informativitätsgraden skaliert sind. In den Beispielen in (4)-(7) bilden die fett gedruckten Elemente in (a) und (b) solche Skalen, so daß die Aussagen in (a) informativer bzw. stärker sind als die Aussagen in (b):

(4)   (a) Max geht *immer* ins Kino.
     (b) Max geht *manchmal* ins Kino.
     (c) +> Max geht *nicht immer* ins Kino.

(5)   (a) Ich habe *meinen* Mann gesehen.
     (b) Ich habe *einen* Mann gesehen.
     (c) +> Ich habe *nicht meinen* Mann gesehen

(6)   (a) Es gibt zum Nachtisch Eis *und* Kaffee.
     (b) Es gibt zum Nachtisch Eis *oder* Kaffee.
     (c) +> Es gibt zum Nachtisch *nicht* beides, Eis *und* Kaffee.

(7) (a) Max wird *sicher* kommen.
    (b) Max wird *vielleicht* kommen.
    (c) +> Es ist *nicht sicher*, daß Max kommen wird.

Der Inhalt der Implikaturen in (c) erklärt sich folgendermaßen: Wenn jemand eine schwächere Aussage anstelle einer stärkeren Aussage macht, und dies mit einem guten Grund tut, dann darf der Adressat davon ausgehen, daß der Sprecher weiß, daß die stärkere Aussage nicht zutrifft (Gazdar 1979: 59). Hirschberg (1991: 79f.) schwächt Gazdars Vorschlag wie folgt ab: der Sprecher weiß nicht, ob die stärkere Aussage zutrifft, oder er weiß, daß die stärkere Aussage nicht zutrifft.

Weitere Skalen, die in der einschlägigen Literatur für die Rekonstruktion von Quantitätsimplikaturen herangezogen wurden, sind z. B. folgende:

(II) alle > mehrere > einige > ein   (vgl. Beispiel (1))
      überall > vielerorts > mancherorts
      müssen > können
      befehlen > erlauben
      wissen, daß p > glauben, daß p
      überglücklich > glücklich

Das Zeichen ">" symbolisiert 'ist informativer bzw. stärker als'.

Viele Skalen entstehen durch eine unilaterale semantische Implikation bzw. Folgerung zwischen den Aussagen, die entsprechend skalierte Elemente eines Wortfelds enthalten. In (4)-(7) z. B. folgen aus den Aussagen in (a) die Aussagen in (b). Es gibt jedoch auch Rangordnungen, die nicht auf der konventionellen Bedeutung der darin vorkommenden Ausdrücke beruhen und derartige Implikaturen auslösen können (vgl. Hirschberg 1991: 97f., Horn 1989: 233f., van Kuppevelt 1996: 423f.). Eine solche kontextuell gegebene Rangordnung illustriert (8) weiter unten, wo das Entstehen einer skalaren Implikatur dadurch motiviert ist, daß unter normalen Umständen die Handlung des Abschicken eines Briefes das Verfassen eines Inhalts voraussetzt.

Wie Krifka (1995: 223) und Matsumoto (1995: 25) zeigen, ist der Grund, eine schwächere Aussage anstelle einer stärkeren Aussage zu machen, bei den beiden Submaximen der Qualität zu suchen. Wenn der Sprecher weiß, daß die stärkere Aussage nicht zutrifft, würde er mit deren Assertion gegen die erste Qualitätsmaxime verstoßen ("Sage nichts, was du für falsch hältst"). Wenn der Sprecher nicht weiß, ob die stärkere Aussage zutrifft, würde er mit deren Assertion gegen die zweite Qualitätsmaxime verstoßen ("Sage nichts, wofür dir angemessene Gründe fehlen"). Für Matsumoto ist die zweifache Abhängigkeit skalarer Implikaturen von der ersten Quantitätsmaxime und der einen oder anderen Maxime der Qualität definitorisch. Vgl. (III):

(III) Quantitätsbasierte Standardimplikaturen des skalaren Typs und nur diese unterliegen der folgenden Bedingung:Die Assertion einer schwächeren Aussage W anstelle einer stärkeren Aussage S ist nur durch die erste Quantitätsmaxime und die

Qualitätsmaximen motiviert, letzteres dadurch, daß der Sprecher nicht weiß, ob die stärkere Aussage S zutrifft, oder weiß, daß sie nicht zutrifft.
(D. h.: die Wahl von W anstelle von S darf nicht dadurch motiviert sein, daß S andere in der Konversation operierende und die Informationswahl betreffende Maximen verletzt.)

(III) schließt Matsumoto zufolge aus, daß bei quantitätsbasierten Implikaturen die Wahl der stärkeren Aussage gegen die Relevanzmaxime, zweite Quantitätsmaxime oder Höflichkeitsmaximen verstößt. Ob die Modalitätsmaxime einschlägig ist, müßte eingehender untersucht werden. Für Matsumoto zählt sie nicht zu den informationsauswählenden Maximen. Wie diese Restriktion operiert, zeigen (8) und (9):

(8) A: Hast du den Brief abgeschickt?
    B: Ich habe ihn getippt. +> Ich habe ihn nicht abgeschickt

(9) A: Hast du den Brief handgeschrieben?
    B: Ich habe ihn getippt. #+> Ich habe ihn nicht abgeschickt

In (8) entsteht die angegebene skalare Implikatur nicht nur aufgrund der Tatsache, daß unter normalen Umständen die Handlung des Abschickens eines Briefes das Verfassen eines Inhalts voraussetzt, sondern auch aufgrund der Tatsache, daß die stärkere Alternative in den Kontext passen würde und somit im Griceschen Sinne relevant wäre. In (9), wo das Abschicken des Briefes eine irrelevante stärkere Alternative wäre, ist die entsprechende skalare Implikatur blockiert, was hier durch '#' angezeigt wird. (III) garantiert also im allgemeinen, daß W und S zueinander passende, diskursrelevante Alternativen sind.

Die Formulierung in (III) unterscheidet sich von Matsumotos Conversational Condition (1995: 25) im wesentlichen dadurch, daß sie auf quantitätsbasierte Implikaturen des skalaren Typs beschränkt ist. Wie weiter unten im Abschnitt 4 gezeigt wird, sind nicht alle quantitätsbasierten Standardimplikaturen durch die Interaktion mit den Qualitätsmaximen erklärbar. Andere Typen entstehen durch die Interaktion mit anderen Maximen.

Die Bezugnahme auf die Qualitätsmaximen bei der Rekonstruktion quantitätsbasierter Implikaturen hat zwei Konsequenzen. Zum einen wird klar, daß im Normalfall mehrere Maximen interagieren. Harnish (1976, zitiert nach 1991: 340) ist ein früher Vertreter dieser Auffassung. Er formuliert nämlich die erste Submaxime der Quantität unter Bezugnahme auf die Anforderungen der Maxime der Relevanz und Qualität: "Make the strongest relevant claim justifiable by your evidence". Zum anderen muß man davon ausgehen, daß skalare quantitätsbasierte Implikaturen auf Bedeutungsrepräsentationen greifen, die durch illokutive Operatoren angereichert sind. Dies liegt daran, daß die Maxime der Qualität in der Formulierung von Grice nur auf assertive bzw. Assertionen implizierende Sprechakte Anwendung findet und für andere Sprechakttypen dementsprechend zu modifizieren ist (vgl. Rolf 1994). Dieser Konsequenz trägt Krifka (1995) dadurch Rechnung, daß er für skalare Implikaturen Bedeutungsrepräsentationen ansetzt, die durch den illokutiven Operator ASSERT angereichert sind und in Fokus-Hintergrund strukturiert sind.

3 Skalenbezug vs. Alternativenbezug

3.1 Die Fokussensitivität von skalaren Quantitätsimplikaturen

Es gibt einen Zusammenhang zwischen Fokus-Hintergrund-Struktur und der Entstehung einer skalaren Quantitätsimplikatur, auf die u. a. Fretheim (1992), Hirschberg (1991), Krifka (1995) und van Kuppevelt (1996) aufmerksam gemacht haben. Die Beispiele (10) und (11) sind Übersetzungen aus van Kuppevelt (1996: 411):

(10) A: Wer hat vier Bücher gekauft?
B: HARRY hat vier Bücher gekauft. De facto hat er sieben gekauft.

(11) A: Wie viele Bücher hat er gekauft?
B: Er hat VIER Bücher gekauft. ??De facto hat er sieben gekauft.

Innerhalb des Abschnitts, der den Fokus der Assertion bildet, muß ein Hauptakzent liegen (vgl. Jacobs 1983, Uhmann 1991). Hier und im Folgenden werden Hauptakzente durch Großschreibung des gesamten akzenttragenden Wortes notiert.

Für van Kuppevelt ist die Antwort B in (10) akzeptabel und in (11) nicht, wobei dies seiner Meinung nach damit zusammenhängt, daß der Implikaturauslöser *vier* nur in (11) Fokusinformation ("comment") ist. Davon leitet van Kuppevelt die Annahme ab, daß skalare Implikaturen, die von einem Implikaturauslöser in Fokusposition abhängen, semantische Implikationen und somit wahrheitskonditional sind. Diese Annahme geht zu weit. Denn erstens wird der erste Teil der Antwort in (11) nicht falsch, wenn die skalare Implikatur ('er hat nicht mehr als vier Bücher gekauft') durch den zweiten Teil der Antwort korrigiert wird. Und zweitens gibt es Ausdrücke, die ohne Akzeptabilitätsminderung die Entstehung der Implikatur blockieren wie z. B. in *Soviel ich weiß, hat er vier Bücher gekauft*.

Die Widersprüchlichkeit der Antwort in (11) bzw. die Tatsache, daß die zur Diskussion stehende skalare Implikatur in (11) zwingender ist als in (10) kann auf der illokutiven Ebene besser erklärt werden. In (10) steht *Harry* im Fokus der Assertion und liefert neue Information. Vom assertiven Operator inhaltlich besonders betroffen ist nur der Fokusteil der Äußerung (vgl. Jacobs 1984: 29). Bezüglich dieser Fokusinformation verpflichtet sich der Sprecher in besonders hohem Maße - in Einklang mit den Maximen der Qualität - nur das zu assertieren, was er für wahr hält bzw. wofür er genügend Evidenz hat. Die Fortsetzung in (10) widerspricht nicht diesem Qualitätskriterium, da sie sich nicht auf die Fokusinformation bezieht. Ganz anders verhält es sich in (11), wo *vier* in Fokusposition steht. Die Fortsetzung in (11) widerspricht dem epistemischen Qualitätskriterium für skalare Implikaturen: der Sprecher weiß, daß seine Antwort auf die stärkere Alternative *sieben* nicht zutrifft oder er hat keine Evidenz für die Wahrheit der stärkeren Aussage. Die Fortsetzung in (11) versucht somit, nicht nur die Quantitätsimplikatur, sondern auch die Qualitätsimplikatur des ersten Teils der Antwort aufzuheben. Dadurch erklärt sich die größere Inakzeptabilität von (11) gegenüber (10).

Van Kuppevelt diskutiert auch die Frage, ob der erste Teil der Antwort in (10) die zur Diskussion stehende skalare Implikatur überhaupt auslösen kann. Seiner Meinung nach ist das nicht der Fall, so daß die illustrierte Fortsetzung keine Implikatur zu annullieren braucht. Diese Annahme van Kuppevelts ist schwer zu überprüfen, weil die Personen, die ich befragt habe, bezüglich der skalaren Implikatur in (10) sehr unsicher waren. Dagegen waren sich alle Befragten sicher, daß eine skalare Implikatur mit einem fokussierten Implikaturauslöser wie in (11) zwingender ist als eine mit einem nicht-fokussierten Implikaturauslöser. Die Unsicherheit der Befragten bei einem nicht-fokussierten Implikaturauslöser wie in (10) kann wie folgt erklärt werden: in (10) liefert der Sprecher keinen qualitätsbasierten Grund für die Wahl der assertierten Alternative *vier*, so daß der Adressat auf sich gestellt ist, wenn er eine skalare Implikatur ansetzt. In (11) liefert der Sprecher einen qualitätsbasierten Grund für die Implikatur: *vier* ist die stärkste Alternative, von der er weiß und wofür er Evidenz hat, daß sie die Aussage wahr macht.

Ich werde im Folgenden bei Implikaturen, die eine Antwort wie in (10) mutmaßlich auslösen können, von einfachen quantitätsbasierten Implikaturen sprechen. Demgegenüber werde ich Implikaturen wie in (11), die der Beschränkung in (III) unterliegen, als quantitäts- und qualitätsbasierte Implikaturen (kurz: qq-Implikaturen) auffassen.

Aus der Tatsache, daß qq-Implikaturen auf der illokutiven Ebene der Assertion anzusiedeln sind, ergibt sich automatisch die Konsequenz, daß sie mit Mengen von Alternativen zu tun haben. Das hängt damit zusammen, daß in Einklang mit der einschlägigen Forschung (vgl. Jacobs 1984, 1991 und Krifka 1995) angenommen werden muß, daß der Skopus des Assertionsoperators von einer Proposition gebildet wird, die in Fokus-Hintergrund strukturiert ist. Insbesondere ist die Annahme von Jacobs (1984: 29) wichtig, daß der Fokus der Assertion derjenige Teil ist, der vom assertiven Operator besonders betroffen ist.

(12c) illustriert eine in Fokus-Hintergrund strukturierte Bedeutungsrepräsentation, die (12b) z. B. im Kontext der Frage (12a) aufweist, in der Notation von Jacobs (1984: 33):

(12   (a)   Wer besucht Gerdas Schwester?
        (b)   PETER besucht Gerdas Schwester.
        (c)   ASS(λX^{NP}[X besucht Gerdas Schwester], Peter)

ASS ist der oberflächensyntaktisch unsichtbare assertive Illokutionsoperator, der auf eine in Fokus und Hintergrund strukturierte Proposition Anwendung findet. Die erste Argumentstelle dieses Operators beherbergt die Hintergrundinformation, die zweite Argumentstelle die Fokusinformation. Der Fokusteil entspricht einer durch Lambda-Operator gebundenen Variablen im ersten Argument, womit gewährleistet wird, daß Fokus und Hintergrund zueinander passen. Durch Lambda-Konversion kann eine in Fokus-Hintergrund strukturierte Bedeutungsrepräsentation in eine diesbezüglich unstrukturierte Repräsentation überführt werden.

Im Folgenden gehe ich vom relationalen Fokusbegriff bei Jacobs (1984, 1991) aus. Nach dieser Auffassung ist Fokus eine Relation zwischen einem Satzabschnitt X und einem nicht notwendigerweise sichtbaren Fokusoperator Z. Der nicht fokussierte Teil eines Satzes bzw. einer Äußerung ist der Hintergrund des Operators Z.

Diese Auffassung ermöglicht eine einheitliche Behandlung von Assertionsfokus (auch: Rhema, engl. comment) und Partikelfokus. Bei Assertionsfokus gibt es im Deutschen einen unsichtbaren Fokusoperator. Partikelfokus hat man im Beispiel *Nur PETER kam*. Parallel zu (12c) kann man die fokussierende Leistung der Gradpartikel *nur* wie in (13b) rekonstruieren, wobei dabei der zusätzliche Beitrag des Assertionsoperators vernachlässigt wird:

(13)   (a)   Nur PETER besucht Gerdas Schwester.
       (b)   NUR(λX^{NP}[X besucht Gerdas Schwester], Peter)

Der inhaltliche Beitrag einer Fokussierung wird spätestens seit Rooth (1985) als die Menge von Propositionen bestimmt, die man aus der normalen Bedeutung durch Einsetzung von Alternativen in die Fokusposition gewinnt. Diese Leistung der Fokussierung wird in Jacobs (1991: 576) wie folgt formuliert:

(IV)   In einem Satz S ist ein Abschnitt X Fokus und ein Abschnitt Y Hintergrund eines Elements Z genau dann, wenn X gegenüber Y hervorgehoben ist und diese Hervorhebung eine für das Wirken von Z relevante Beziehung zwischen X und inhaltlichen Alternativen zu X anzeigt, die unter Voraussetzung der Beibehaltung von Y gilt.

Die für Z spezifische inhaltliche Beziehung zwischen Fokus X und Alternativen zu X kann eine Quantifikation über Alternativen sein, wie beim Fokus von *nur*, oder eine Skalierung auf einer Bewertungsskala (z. B. Wahrscheinlichkeitsskala) wie bei *Sogar PETER kam*. Diese inhaltlichen Komponenten können auch gemeinsam auftreten. So werden z. B. bei der Fokussierung durch *sogar* Alternativen sowohl quantifiziert (es gibt mindestens eine Alternative zu Peter, die kam) als auch bewertet (alle anderen Alternativen haben einen geringeren Wahrscheinlichkeitswert bezüglich der Hintergrundinformation 'kam').

Es ist wichtig festzuhalten, daß mehrere Autoren (u. a. Fretheim 1992, Hirschberg 1991, van Kuppevelt 1996) zwar auf den Zusammenhang zwischen Fokus-Hintergrund-Struktur und skalaren Quantitätsimplikaturen hingewiesen haben, aber den Fokusbegriff nicht im Sinne eines Alternativenbezugs rekonstruiert haben. Hirschberg und van Kuppevelt fassen außerdem Fokus als das auf, was im Zentrum der Aufmerksamkeit steht, so daß auch Phänomene der Diskurskohärenz und Topikalität im Sinne von Satzgegenstand darunter fallen. Außerdem benützen sie den Fokusbegriff bzw. Topikbegriff um den Skalenbezug solcher Implikaturen zu präzisieren. Weiter unten wird jedoch gezeigt, daß Informativitätsskalen eine Folgeerscheinung des Alternativenbezugs darstellen, der den qq-Implikaturen zugrunde liegt. Zunächst sollen jedoch qq-Implikaturen besprochen werden, die bei negierten Aussagen entstehen.

In der Literatur zum Thema wurde wiederholt darauf hingewiesen, daß sich Informativitätsskalen bei Einbettung unter Negation oder anderen Funktoren umkehren. So ist *kein X* informativer als *nicht alle X*, *nie* informativer als *nicht immer* und *unmöglich* informativer als *nicht notwendig*. Unter der Annahme umgekehrt gerichteter Skalen, funktioniert das Ableitungsschema skalenbasierter Ansätze auch für negierte Aussagen prima facie recht gut. Vgl. (14):

(14) (a) Ich habe keinen Roman von Goethe gelesen (= Ich habe alle Romane von Goethe nicht gelesen).
 (b) Ich habe nicht ALLE Romane von Goethe gelesen.
 (c) +> aber einen

(14a) ist die informativste negative Aussage, (14b) ihre schwächere Alternative, deren Verwendung die Implikatur in (14c) auslöst. Nach dem skalenbasierten Ableitungsschema ergibt die äußere Negation der informativsten negativen Aussage, im Beispiel die äußere Negation von (14a), tatsächlich einen Inhalt, der bei Elimination der dualen Negation mit Hilfe des Existenzquantors wie in (14c) formuliert werden kann.

Das Problem für skalenbasierte Ansätze ist, daß die Implikatur (14c) vom Akzentmuster und der damit korrelierenden Fokus-Hintergrund-Struktur von (14b) abhängt. Die Negation in (14b) ist ein typischer in der einschlägigen Literatur immer wieder illustrierter Implikaturauslöser, weil sie aufgrund ihrer Stellung nur als Negation interpretiert werden kann, die einen Fokusakzent auf dem Implikaturauslöser *alle* verlangt.

In den Beispielen (15)-(17) hingegen weist die Position der Negation nicht eindeutig auf die fokussierende Interpretation hin. Nur der Akzent auf dem Implikaturauslöser und der Fragekontext garantieren diese Interpretation:

(15) Geht er oft ins Kino?
 Er geht nicht OFT ins Kino. +> aber manchmal/nur manchmal

(16) Ist es sicher, daß du kommst?
 Es ist nicht SICHER, daß ich komme. +> aber möglich/nur möglich

(17) Weißt du, ob er kommt?
 Ich WEISS nicht, ob er kommt. +> aber ich vermute es/ich vermute es nur

Auch diese Implikaturen können mit *nur* paraphrasiert werden. Diagnostisch für qq-Implikaturen bei negierten Aussagen ist die Möglichkeit der Versprachlichung mit dem Einleitewort *aber* (vgl. Jacobs 1991: 586).

Wichtig für die folgende Diskussion ist Jacobs' Beobachtung (1982, 1991), daß es eine fokussierende und eine nicht-fokussierende, d. h. neutrale Negation gibt. Eine fokussierende Negation mit Fokus auf X impliziert, daß die Ersetzung von X durch kontextuell passende Alternativen aus dem Sachverhalt einen machen würde, dessen Negation im jeweilgen Kontext nicht mehr angebracht wäre (Jacobs 1982: 28; Jacobs 1991:

575). So z. B. impliziert *Nicht PETER besucht Gerdas Schwester*, daß für mindestens eine andere Person die Negation des Sachverhalts nicht mehr angebracht wäre.

Eine fokussierende Negation kann kontrastierend oder nicht-kontrastierend sein (vgl. Jacobs 1982: 176f. und S. 292f.). In Jacobs (1991: 585f.) wird diese Unterscheidung als "replazive vs. nicht-replazive Negation" bezeichnet. Als Kriterium für eine kontrastierende Negation gilt nach Jacobs die Tatsache, daß ein Alternativenbezug mit Hilfe eines durch *sondern* eingeleiteten Zusatzes als notwendig empfunden wird: *Nicht PETER besucht Gerdas Schwester, sondern MARIA*. Ferner ist der Alternativenbezug konventionalisiert und Jacobs zufolge auf semantischer Ebene anzusiedeln.

Man könnte prima facie annehmen, daß die Implikaturen in (15)-(17) von einer kontrastierenden Negation im Sinne von Jacobs ausgelöst werden. Denn Negationen wie diese lassen auch eine Interpretation als kontrastierende Negation zu (vgl. Jacobs 1982: 294f.). Vgl. (18):

(18)   (a)   Er geht nicht OFT ins Kino, sondern IMMER.(vgl. (15))
        (b)   Ronald ist nicht Filmstar ODER Politiker, sondern BEIDES.
        (c)   Er hat nicht DREI Freunde, sondern VIER.

Eine kontrastierende Negation wie in (18) unterscheidet sich in mehreren Hinsichten von dem Zusammenspiel von Fokus und Negation, das für die Implikaturen in (14)-(17) verantwortlich ist: a) durch die Möglichkeit und Dringlichkeit, den Alternativenbezug durch einen mit *sondern* eingeleiteten Zusatz zu versprachlichen, b) dadurch, daß der Alternativenbezug konventionalisiert ist und nach Jacobs auf semantischer Ebene anzusiedeln ist, und schließlich c) durch die inhaltliche Auswahl der Alternative. Eine Alternative, die eine kontrastierende Negation mit den Merkmalen a) und b) impliziert, kann, wie (18) zeigt, auch mit einer stärkeren Alternative deckungsgleich sein. Dieser Inhalt kann nicht durch das skalare Ableitungsschema rekonstruiert werden.

Auf den unterschiedlichen Inhalt von Quantitätsimplikaturen bei Negation eines Skalenelements und dessen Abhängigkeit von der Akzentkontur auf dem Implikaturauslöser hat u. a. Hirschberg (1991: 49) aufmerksam gemacht. Der mit *aber* eingeleitete Implikaturtyp (z. B. *Er hat nicht DREI Freunde, aber ZWEI*), der auch in (14)-(17) illustriert wurde, wird bevorzugt durch eine Wurzelkontur (fallend-steigend √) auf dem Implikaturauslöser intonatorisch markiert. Der mit *sondern* eingeleitete Alternativenbezug (vgl. (18c)) wird normalerweise durch einen fallenden Akzent auf *drei* und einen anschließenden Anstieg auf *Freunde* markiert. Hirschberg übersieht aber den Zusammenhang zwischen den beiden Typen von Alternativenbezug und dem kontrastierenden vs. nicht-kontrastierenden Status der Negation. Erschwert wird der Zugang zu diesem Zusammenhang im Englischen dadurch, daß diese Sprache *sondern* und *aber* in den hier diskutierten Verwendungen lexikalisch nicht unterscheidet (vgl. Jacobs 1991: 586).

Es ist plausibel anzunehmen, daß in (14)-(17) unter der Annahme der angegebenen Implikaturen - im Gegensatz zu (18) - fokussierende nicht-kontrastierende Negationen vorliegen. Daß es sich um einen Negationsfokus und nicht um den Assertionsfokus (= Rhema) handelt, zeigt sich darin, daß der akzentuell hervorgehobene skalare Implikaturauslöser auch unmittelbar vorerwähnte Information sein kann. Dies verdeutlicht der in

(14)-(17) angegebene Fragekontext, der den Implikaturauslöser bereits enthält. Daß es sich um den Fokus einer nicht-kontrastierenden Negation handelt, darauf weist - wie bereits erwähnt - auch der Inhalt der Implikatur hin, der nicht mit einem *sondern*-Zusatz paraphrasiert wird, nicht-konventionalisiert ist und nach dem skalenbasierten Ableitungsschema rekonstruiert werden kann.

Vergleichen wir nun die Implikaturen einer fokussierenden nicht-kontrastierenden Negation mit den möglichen Implikaturen einer neutralen, d. h. nicht-fokussierenden Negation. Bei einer neutralen Negation können die besprochenen qq-Implikaturen nicht ausgelöst werden. Vgl. die neutrale Negation in (19), wo nur die Negation im Assertionsfokus steht und keine Alternative zu *Kino* impliziert wird, mit (20), wo sowohl *Kino* als auch die Negation hervorgehoben sind und zu Kino Alternativen konversationell impliziert werden, auf die die Hintergrundprädikation zutrifft:

(19)　Geht er ins Kino?
　　　Nein, er geht NICHT ins Kino.

(20)　Geht er ins Kino?
　　　Nein, ins KINO geht er NICHT.

Die in diesem Abschnitt gezeigte Fokussensitivität der qq-Implikaturen erklärt sich dadurch, daß solche Implikaturen von der Qualitätsmaxime abhängen, und diese operiert auf der Ebene der Bedeutungsrepräsentationen, die durch den assertiven illokutiven Operator und gegebenenfalls durch einen fokussierenden Negationsoperator angereichert und in Fokus-Hintergrund strukturiert sind.

3.2 Wortsemantische Bedeutungsinklusion

Die nun folgenden Abschnitte 3.2 - 3.5 befassen sich mit einer weiteren Annahme über qq-Implikaturen. Für das Entstehen solcher Implikaturen ist es nicht notwendig, daß die Menge, die aus assertiertem Element und kontextuell relevanten Alternativen besteht, nach dem Grad der Informativität skaliert ist. Für solche Implikaturen ist somit nicht der Bezug auf Informativitätsskalen, sondern der Bezug auf Alternativen im fokustheoretischen Sinn von primärer Relevanz.

Ein Problem für skalenbasierte Ansätze bieten wortsemantische Bedeutungsinklusionen. Sie entstehen innerhalb eines Wortfelds und können auf einfachste Weise mit Hilfe der unilateralen semantischen Implikation rekonstruiert werden. Insoweit stellen sie eine ideale Informativitätsskala dar. So z. B. impliziert auf semantischer Ebene *I have a Siamese* in der zur Diskussion stehenden Lesart unilateral *I have a cat*. Es ist aber nicht ohne weiteres der Fall, daß die Assertion der schwächere Aussage, nämlich *I have a cat*, die Negation der stärkeren Aussage als Standardimplikatur erzeugt: *I don't have a Siamese cat*.

Dieses Problem hängt zwar mit mehreren Tatsachen zusammen, aber allen ist gemeinsam, daß der Alternativenbezug bei wortsemantischen Bedeutungsinklusionen nicht ohne weiteres hergestellt werden kann (vgl. auch Becker 1996, in diesem Band).

Hirschberg (1991: 156f.) zeigt, daß skalare Implikaturen möglich sind, wenn der Unterbegriff zur Diskussion steht bzw. diskurssalient ist, wie im folgenden Beispiel:

(21)   A: Do you have a Siamese?
           B: I have a cat +> not a Siamese cat

Ein klarer Unterschied zu den anderen bisher diskutierten qq-Implikaturen besteht darin, daß die Antwort von B die Quantitätsmaxime offensichtlich verletzt, indem sie nicht die gewünschte Information liefert. Es handelt sich also nicht um eine Standardimplikatur.

Man kann festhalten, daß die klaren skalaren Informativitätsverhältnisse, an denen Unter- und Oberbegriff beteiligt sind, nicht ausreichen, um qq-Implikaturen auszulösen. Ausschlaggebend ist die Zugänglichkeit und Diskursrelevanz des Oberbegriffs als Alternative zum Unterbegriff (vgl. auch Matsumoto 1995: 28f.).

3.3   Kohyponyme

Ein anderes Problem für skalenbasierte Ansätze ist, daß qq-Implikaturen, die auf der Basis der Kohyponymrelation entstehen, in skalenbasierten Ansätzen nur unter einem recht hohen Aufwand rekonstruiert werden können. Vgl. das Beispiel in (22) aus Harnish (1991: 319):

(22)   Die Fahne ist weiß. +> Die Fahne ist nur weiß.

Die Menge von Kohyponymen, die für die Implikatur in (22) relevant ist, kann mittels einer Konjunktion von Kohyponymen im Gazdarschen Sinne skalar modelliert werden (vgl. Hirschberg 1991: 90 und van Kuppevelt 1996: 433). So kann man folgende Informativitätsskala annehmen: *Die Fahne ist weiß und rot und schwarz > Die Fahne ist weiß*. Auf der Basis dieser Skala kann die qq-Implikatur nach dem bekannten Ableitungsschema wie folgt rekonstruiert werden: +> *Es ist nicht der Fall, daß die Fahne rot und schwarz ist*.

Unplausibel ist bei dieser Lösung nicht nur der große Aufwand für die Rekonstruktion einer unauffälligen Implikatur, sondern auch die Tatsache, daß sie den Alternativenbezug von *nur* und somit den Inhalt der Implikatur nicht adäquat wiedergibt. Denn gerade Implikaturen wie die in (22) negieren im Normalfall nicht bestimmte stärkere Alternativen, sondern alle (bestimmten oder unbestimmten) Alternativen.

Ähnlich gelagert sind auch Implikaturen wie die in (23) illustrierte:

(23)   (a)   Welche Romane von Goethe hast du gelesen?
           (b)   Die Wahlverwandtschaften.
           (c)   +> nur die Wahlverwandtschaften

Auch hier ist es unplausibel anzunehmen, daß der Adressat von (23b) die Romane von Goethe nach ihrer Informativität skaliert oder mit Hilfe der Konjunktion aller bzw. einiger Romane von Goethe eine Quantitätsskala bildet. Am einfachsten und plausibelsten ist die Annahme, daß der Adressat über die ungeordnete Menge der alternativen Romane von Goethe allquantifiziert.

Man kann Implikaturen wie die in (22) und (23) zu erfassen versuchen, indem man die Skalenbedingung solcher Implikaturen wie bei Hirschberg erweitert (1991: 57): "they [scalar implicatures] involve inferences about utterances that reference - in Horn's terminology - not only the higher and lower values Horn and Harnish allow, but what I will term ALTERNATE values as well. Roughly speaking, these are values which are neither higher nor lower than one another but which share a common higher or lower value." Wichtig im Zusammenhang des hier verteidigten Alternativenbezugs ist, daß Hirschberg nicht-skalierte alternative Werte heranzieht. So geht sie davon aus, daß die Behauptung eines niedrigeren Skalenwerts ebenso wie die Behauptung eines alternativen Werts die skalare Implikatur erlaubt, daß der höhere bzw. der (oder ein) andere(r) Wert falsch oder dem Sprecher unbekannt ist (1991: 65).

Die Bezeichnung "alternativer Wert" sollte nicht darüber hinwegtäuschen, daß Hirschberg den Alternativenbezug nicht illokutiv- und fokustheoretisch modelliert und den Skalenbezug nicht als sekundäre Erscheinung skalarer Implikaturen, sondern als gleichberechtigte Bezugsmöglichkeit ansetzt. Damit kann es einem solchen Ansatz nicht gelingen, die weiter oben beobachtete Fokussensitivität von skalaren Implikaturen systematisch zu erfassen.

Die in diesem Abschnitt behandelten Fälle verdeutlichen, daß es für das Entstehen von qq-Implikaturen nicht notwendig ist, daß die Menge, die aus assertiertem Element und kontextuell relevanten Alternativen besteht, nach dem Grad der Informativität skaliert ist. Was notwendig ist, ist die Eröffnung einer Menge von diskursrelevanten Alternativen im fokustheoretischen Sinn.

3.4 Gegenläufige Quantitätsimplikaturen

Das letzte Problem skalenbasierter Ansätze, das hier besprochen werden soll, betrifft u. a. die bereits in der Einleitung genannte und illustrierte Konditionalverstärkung (vgl. (2) weiter oben) und die Informativitätsskala, an der Äußerungen mit der Fokuspartikel *nur* beteiligt sind. Unter der hier gegebenen Voraussetzung, daß eine konditionale Aussage (A → B) assertiert wird, entsteht die Stärkeskala (A ↔ B) > (A → B). Analog entsteht bei der Assertion von A die Skala *Nur* A > A. Unter dieser Voraussetzung folgt nämlich aus *Nur* A die einfache Aussage A (vgl. jedoch Horn 1996 für den Fall, daß diese Voraussetzung nicht erfüllt ist).

Entgegen der Prognose skalenbasierter Ansätze läuft die Implikatur bei diesen Skalen nicht auf die Negation der stärkeren Alternative hinaus, sondern auf deren Affirmation. Ein Beispiel für eine Konditionalverstärkung liefert neben (2) weiter oben der folgende unauffällige Dialog:

(24) (a) Sie: Wenn es regnet, gehe ich joggen.
(b) Er: Es regnet nicht, wieso gehst du joggen?
(c) +> nur wenn es regnet, gehe ich joggen

Seine Reaktion auf (24a) zeigt, daß er ihre Aussage im Sinne von (24c) interpretiert hat.

Die Konditionalverstärkung kann ebenfalls mit Hilfe der Fokuspartikel *nur*, wie in (24c) angegeben, paraphrasiert werden. Das erklärt sich wie folgt: durch die Assertion der Aussage A → B entsteht die Implikatur B → A (zusammen ergeben sie den Inhalt A ↔ B). Nun kann der Inhalt *Nur Regensituationen sind Joggingsituationen* (Nur A(x) ist B(x)) durch *Alle Joggingsituationen sind Regensituationen* (Für alle x: B(x) → A(x)) paraphrasiert werden (vgl. z. B. Horn 1996: 18).

Obwohl die Paraphrasemöglichkeit mit *nur* auf das Vorliegen einer unauffälligen qq-Implikatur hinweist, kann sie nur unter einem sehr hohen Kalkulationsaufwand mit Hilfe des skalaren Ableitungsschemas hergeleitet werden (vgl. Hirschberg 1991: 88f.). Die Aussage A → B ist äquivalent mit der Aussage ¬ A v B. Die Assertion von ¬ A v B erzeugt aufgrund der Skala (A ∧ B) > (A v B) die skalare Implikatur ¬(¬ A ∧ B). Dieser Inhalt ist äquivalent mit A v ¬ B, was wiederum äquivalent ist mit der gesuchten qq-Implikatur B → A.

Gegen einen solchen Kalkulationsaufwand spricht, daß die Konditionalverstärkung eine der unauffälligsten und häufigsten Implikaturen dieser Art ist. Die Paraphrasemöglichkeit mit *nur* erklärt dies auf natürliche Weise: Alle alternativen Bedingungen zur assertierten Bedingung werden negiert. Es handelt sich also um dieselbe einfache Operation, die auch bei den anderen hier diskutierten qq-Implikaturen Anwendung findet. Der Skalenbezug und das in der einschlägigen Literatur vorgeschlagene skalare Ableitungsschema steht also einer einfachen bzw. korrekten Lösung im Wege.

Bei dieser Rekonstruktion stellt sich außerdem die Frage, warum bei der Kalkulation der Implikatur die naheliegende Quantitätsskala (A ↔ B) > (A → B) nicht ausgenützt wird. Aufgrund dieser Skala müßte die qq-Implikatur auf ¬ (A ↔ B) hinauslaufen, was nicht der Fall ist. Matsumoto (1995: 44f.) bietet eine Erklärung für diese Tatsache, die hier nur kurz erwähnt werden soll. Nicht-monotone Ausdrücke, zu denen auch das Bikonditional zählt, qualifizieren sich nicht für Skalen, die qq-Implikaturen auslösen. Die Rekonstruktion des Inhalts der hier zur Diskussion stehenden qq-Implikatur bleibt jedoch auch bei Matsumoto unbefriedigend. Demnach ist eine Disjunktion von Antezedensbedingungen (A or A' or A" or ...) → B die gesuchte stärkere Alternative zu A → B, so daß die skalare Implikatur auf die Negation der Alternativen A' oder A" usf. hinausläuft. Unplausibel bei dieser Lösung ist die Tatsache, die schon im Zusammenhang der Kohyponyme im letzten Abschnitt erwähnt wurde. Der Alternativenbezug von *nur* und somit der Inhalt der Implikatur wird nicht adäquat wiedergegeben. Denn gerade solche unauffälligen qq-Implikaturen wie die in (22)-(24) illustrierten negieren im Normalfall nicht bestimmte Alternativen, sondern alle (bestimmten oder unbestimmten) Alternativen.

Genauso problematisch für skalenbasierte Ansätze ist die Stärkeskala *Nur A > A*. Wie bei der Konditionalverstärkung negiert die qq-Implikatur der schwächeren Aussage nicht die stärkere Alternative, sondern ist mit dieser deckungsgleich. Vgl. (25):

(25) (a) Wer ist gestern vorbeigekommen?
 (b) Peter.
 (c) +> nur Peter ist gestern vorbeigekommen

Man kann diese Implikatur in skalenbasierten Ansätzen nur durch einen sehr hohen und zu unplausiblen Ergebnissen führenden Kalkulationsaufwand rekonstruieren, der weiter oben für (22) im Zusammenhang der Kohyponyme vorgeführt und kritisiert wurde. Auch hier steht die Bezugnahme auf Informativitätsskalen der einfachsten Lösung im Weg.

Mit Hilfe der Negation und Allquantifikation über eine ungeordnete Menge von Alternativen hingegen kann man diese unauffällige qq-Implikatur viel einfacher erklären: für alle kontextuell relevanten Alternativen zu Peter wird die Hintergrundprädikation negiert ('alle anderen sind gestern nicht vorbeigekommen') und dieser Inhalt kann als *Nur Peter ist gestern vorbeigekommen* paraphrasiert werden. Daß sich der Inhalt der Implikatur in einigen Fällen mit der stärkeren Aussage deckt, statt sie zu negieren, ist in den Fällen (24) und (25) dadurch zu erklären, daß die Allquantifikation über die Menge der Alternativen und die Negation der Hintergrundprädikation genau die stärkere Alternative erzeugt. Das ist bei den in (II) illustrierten Skalen und in den Beispielen (4)-(7) weiter oben nicht der Fall.

Für die Konditionalverstärkung und andere qq-Implikaturen, die mit den skalaren Implikaturen in Konflikt zu geraten scheinen, haben Atlas & Levinson (1981), Levinson (1990) und Horn (1989) Lösungen vorgeschlagen, die auf andere Maximen rekurrieren. Levinsons Lösung geht von einem Informativitätsprinzip aus, "das uns in einigen Umständen erlaubt, in eine Äußerung mehr Information hineinzulesen, als wirklich enthalten ist, im Gegensatz zur Quantität, die (soweit der Sprecher weiß) nur die zusätzliche Inferenz zuläßt, daß keine stärkere Aussage gemacht werden konnte" (1990: 148). Das Informativitätsprinzip hat in einigen Fällen, zu denen (24) und (25) gehören, Vorrang gegenüber dem Quantitätsprinzip, in anderen Fällen unterliegt es dem Quantitätsprinzip, wie z. B. in den Beispielen (4)-(7) weiter oben.

Ein erstes Problem seines Lösungsvorschlags bespricht Levinson selbst (1990: 148f.). Es betrifft die noch nicht hinreichend geklärte Interaktion und Gewichtung der beiden Prinzipien.

Ein zweites Problem für Levinsons Vorschlag ist die Tatsache, daß eine Kalkulation gegenläufiger Quantitätsimplikaturen auf der Basis des Informativitätsprinzips nicht dem Griceschen Ableitungsschema (I) entspricht. Ganz im Gegenteil, man kann leicht nachweisen, daß die Informativitätsverhältnisse zwischen Assertion mit Implikatur und Assertion ohne Implikatur auf eine Ausbeutung der ersten Quantitätsmaxime hinweisen. Ohne Implikatur sind die Aussagen in (24) und (25) - genau wie in den Standardfällen (4)-(7) - weniger informativ als mit Implikatur. In allen Fällen führt die Implikatur zu einer Informativitätsverstärkung. Dies entspricht dem Ableitungsschema auf der Basis der ersten Quantitätsmaxime. Darauf weist auch die Paraphrasemöglichkeit aller Implikaturen dieser Art mit *nur* hin. Daß für die Implikaturen in (24) und (25) keine andere Maxime herangezogen werden braucht, demonstriert auch die Tatsache, daß ihr Inhalt nach dem Ableitungsschema skalarer Quantitätsimplikaturen auf der Basis der ersten

Quantitätsmaxime rekonstruiert werden kann, wenngleich dies mit einem erheblichen Paraphrasierungsaufwand verbunden ist.

Diskussionswürdig ist auch die Lösungsmöglichkeit auf der Basis der zweiten Quantitätsmaxime, die Horn für die Fälle anvisiert, die Levinson mit seinem Informativitätsprinzip zu erfassen versucht. Horn faßt die zweite Quantitätsmaxime mit der Relevanzmaxime unter dem folgenden R-Prinzip zusammen: Sag nicht mehr, als du mußt (Horn 1984: 13; 1989: 194). Was den Vorrang bzw. die Gewichtung der ersten Quantitätsmaxime (Horns Q-Prinzip) und des R-Prinzips betrifft, macht Horn die korrekte Beobachtung, daß Standardimplikaturen auf der Grundlage des R-Prinzips in der Regel durch soziale Normen (z. B. durch ein Höflichkeitsgebot) gesteuert sind oder aufgrund stereotyper Interpretationen entstehen (vgl. für eine eingehendere Diskussion Abschnitt 4 weiter unten). Den gewichtigeren Kritikpunkt an Levinsons Vorschlag kann jedoch auch Horn nicht umgehen. Die Informativitätsverhältnisse zwischen Assertion mit Implikatur und Assertion ohne Implikatur deuten in (24)-(25) auf eine Ausbeutung der ersten Quantitätsmaxime hin. Aufgrund der zweiten Quantitätsmaxime würde man erwarten, daß die Assertion ohne Implikatur informativer oder irrelevanter ist als die Assertion mit Implikatur. Das ist nicht der Fall.

3.5 Der Skalenbezug als Folgeerscheinung

Die skalenbezogenen Implikaturen im engeren Sinn entstehen dadurch, daß die Menge der Alternativen nach Informativitätsgraden skaliert sind. Beispiele solcher Skalen liefert (II) weiter oben, vgl. auch (4)-(7). Es stellt sich somit die Frage, wie die bei Kohyponymen oder bei der Konditionalverstärkung wirksame Allquantifikation über Alternativen bei skalierten Alternativen einzuschränken ist. Denn es steht fest, daß bei skalierten Alternativen nie schwächere Alternativen eingesetzt werden dürfen. M. a. W. ist die Allquantifikation in Richtung stärkerer Alternativen gerichtet (z. B. auf den in (II) angegebenen Skalen nach links).

Die gewünschte Restriktion liefert ein allgemeineres, in der einschlägigen Literatur mehrheitlich akzeptiertes Prinzip, das für alle Implikaturen mit Ausnahme von Implikaturen, die die Qualitätsmaximen offensichtlich verletzen (Metaphern u. ä.), greift. Angewandt auf Quantitätsimplikaturen kann man es wie in (V) formulieren:

(V) Quantitätsimplikaturen dürfen zur konventionellen Bedeutung des Assertierten nicht in Widerspruch stehen.

Man kann die Wirkung von (V) überprüfen, indem man versucht, die Hintergrundprädikation nach Einsetzen einer schwächeren Alternative zu negieren, und anschließend testet, ob dadurch ein Widerspruch zum Assertierten entsteht. So kann man z. B. mit *Ich habe viele Romane von Goethe gelesen* nicht konversationell implizieren, daß man keinen (= nicht einen) Roman von Goethe gelesen hat oder daß man nicht einmal zwei Romane von Goethe gelesen hat, weil solche Implikaturen dem Assertierten widersprechen. Entsprechendes gilt für negierte Aussagen. *Ich habe nicht VIELE Romane von*

Goethe gelesen steht - bei der Interpretation der Negation als nicht-kontrastierende fokussierende Negation, weil nur dieser Negationstyp Implikaturen nach dem hier diskutierten Ableitungsschema auslöst - in Widerspruch zu *ich habe alle Romane von Goethe gelesen*. Deswegen ist letzterer Sachverhalt keine mögliche qq-Implikatur der Assertion des ersten Sachverhalts.

(V) sagt auch korrekt voraus, daß die stärksten Skalenelemente keine qq-Implikaturen auslösen können. So z. B. kann die Äußerung *Es ist sicher, daß Peter kommt* (mit *sicher* als Implikaturauslöser) keine Quantitätsimplikatur der hier besprochenen Art erzeugen. Dies liegt daran, daß es nur schwächere Alternativen zum Implikaturauslöser gibt. Die Implikatur, daß für eine beliebige dieser schwächeren Alternativen die Hintergrundprädikation nicht gilt, führt in jedem Fall zu einem Widerspruch (vgl. *Es ist sicher, daß Peter kommt* mit *Es ist nicht möglich, daß Peter kommt*).

(V) ermöglicht es, den Bezug auf Skalen bei der Rekonstruktion von Quantitätsimplikaturen dieser Art völlig zu eliminieren. Daß die Allquantifikation bei skalierten Alternativen nur eine bestimmte Richtung betrifft, kann man durch die unabhängig motivierte allgemeine Einschränkung, deren Spezialfall (V) darstellt, besser erklären als durch eine Skalenbeschränkung, die für qq-Implikaturen eigens eingeführt werden muß. Aufgrund von (V) kann das Kalkulationsschema für qq-Implikaturen von (III) zu (III') wie folgt verändert werden:

(III') Quantitäts- und qualitätsbasierte Implikaturen (qq-Implikaturen):
Die Assertion einer Aussage A anstelle anderer beliebiger Aussagen $B_1, ..., B_n$ ist nur durch die erste Quantitätsmaxime und die Qualitätsmaximen motiviert, letzteres dadurch, daß der Sprecher nicht weiß, ob $B_1, ..., B_n$ zutreffen, oder weiß, daß $B_1, ..., B_n$ nicht zutreffen.
(D. h.: die Wahl von A anstelle von $B_1, ..., B_n$ darf nicht dadurch motiviert sein, daß $B_1, ..., B_n$ andere in der Konversation operierende und die Informationswahl betreffende Maximen verletzen.)

Daß A und $B_1, ..., B_n$ zueinander passende Alternativen sind, garantiert (III') dadurch, daß A und $B_1, ..., B_n$ gleichermaßen diskursrelevant sein müssen.

Die Fokussensitivität dieser Art von Implikaturen erklärt sich folgendermaßen: die Qualitätsmaxime in der Formulierung von Grice ist mit einigen Gelingensbedingungen assertiver Sprechakte deckungsgleich (vgl. Levinson 1990: S. 107); sie greift somit auf eine mit Hilfe eines assertiven Operators angereicherte und in Fokus-Hintergrund strukturierte Bedeutungsrepräsentation; vom assertiven Operator inhaltlich besonders betroffen ist nur der Fokusteil der Äußerung; damit ist garantiert, daß die epistemische Andeutung der Qualität, die in (III') erscheint, besonders den Fokusteil einer Äußerung betrifft.

(III') garantiert auch, daß eine qq-Implikatur der Informativitätsverstärkung dient. Wie der allgemeine Kalkulationsmechanismus von Grice in (I) weiter oben verlangt, ist die Assertion ohne Implikatur weniger informativ als die Assertion mit Implikatur. Salopp formuliert negiert die Zusatzinformation alle kontextuell relevanten (stärkeren) Alternativen.

Der hier postulierte Inhalt einer qq-Implikatur erklärt ohne weitere Zusatzannahme, daß solche Implikaturen in der Regel mit Hilfe von *nur* versprachlicht werden können. Ohne in die Details verschiedener Ansätze zur Behandlung des inhaltlichen Beitrags von *nur* eingehen zu wollen (vgl. Altmann 1976, Horn 1996, Jacobs 1983, König 1991), genügt es, die allgemein akzeptierte Annahme festzuhalten, daß es sich um eine Grad- bzw. Fokuspartikel handelt. Deren inhaltlicher Beitrag ist somit auf der Ebene der Fokus-Hintergrund-Struktur zu rekonstruieren. Außerdem besteht Einigkeit darüber, daß ihr inhaltlicher Beitrag in etwa dem hier rekonstruierten Inhalt von qq-Implikaturen entspricht. So z. B. impliziert die Aussage *Nur Peter kam*, daß für alle kontextuell relevanten Alternativen zu 'Peter', die Hintergrundprädikation 'kam' nicht gilt. Es gibt auch Unterschiede zwischen dem inhaltlichen Beitrag dieser Fokuspartikel und dem hier rekonstruierten Inhalt von qq-Implikaturen. Ein wichtiger Unterschied ist, daß der quantifizierende Alternativenbezug von *nur* zur konventionellen Bedeutung zu rechnen ist.

4 Andere Typen der Informativitätsverstärkung

4.1 Quantität und Höflichkeit

Der folgende 4. Abschnitt bespricht quantitätsbasierte Implikaturen, die in anderen Ansätzen nicht auf der Basis der ersten Quantitätsmaxime rekonstruiert wurden. Eine genaue Anwendung des allgemeinen Kalkulationsschemas von Grice in (I) weiter oben ergibt jedoch, daß es sich um Implikaturen auf der Basis der ersten Quantitätsmaxime handeln muß. Daß die in diesem Abschnitt diskutierten Implikaturen keine qq-Implikaturen sind, wird hier über die Interaktion der ersten Quantitätsmaxime mit anderen Maximen als die der Qualität erklärt.

Zunächst sollen Implikaturen besprochen werden, die durch Höflichkeitsmaximen motiviert werden. Daß der Gricesche Apparat um solche Maximen erweitert werden muß, da sie zur Auslösung von Implikaturen führen, darauf haben u. a. Brown & Levinson (1987), Leech (1983) und Levinson (1990) hingewiesen.

(VI) Quantitäts- und höflichkeitsbasierte Implikaturen (kurz qh-Implikaturen):
Die Assertion einer Aussage A anstelle anderer beliebiger Aussagen $B_1, ..., B_n$ ist nur durch die erste Quantitätsmaxime und die Höflichkeitsmaximen motiviert, letzteres dadurch, daß $B_1, ..., B_n$ mindestens eine Höflichkeitsmaxime verletzen würden.

(VI) besagt, daß die Wahl von A anstelle von $B_1, ..., B_n$ nicht dadurch motiviert sein darf, daß $B_1, ..., B_n$ andere in der Konversation operierende und die Informationswahl betreffende Maximen verletzen. Insbesondere verlangt (VI), daß bei einer solchen Implikatur nicht nur A, sondern auch die Alternative B die Qualitätsmaxime und Relevanzmaxime befolgt. Der Bezug auf die Informativitätsstärke von A und B ist überflüssig, da bei dieser Konstellation nur ein stärkeres impliziertes B die von der ersten Quantitätsmaxime geforderte Informativitätsverstärkung garantiert. In der Literatur

besprochene Höflichkeitsmaximen sind u. a. folgende: Bedränge niemanden! Tue oder sage niemandem etwas Unangenehmes! Sei freundlich! Gib nicht an!
Beispiele für Implikaturen dieses Typs bieten (26)-(30):

(26) Ich empfehle Ihnen, dieses Buch zu kaufen.
Ich rate Ihnen, diese Buch zu kaufen.
+> Ich fordere Sie auf, dieses Buch zu kaufen

(27) Ich verspreche dir eins: wenn du noch einmal frech wirst, wird das Taschengeld gestrichen.
+> ich drohe dir das Taschengeld zu streichen, wenn du noch einmal frech wirst.

(28) Ich bin etwas verärgert über diesen Vorschlag.
+> Ich bin sehr verärgert über diesen Vorschlag

(29) Rundfunknachricht am 13.11.1995. Die DB und das Bayerische Wirtschaftsministerium haben eine Info-Broschüre über die Lokalbahnen in Bayern herausgebracht und dabei Niederbayern nicht berücksichtigt. Die Reaktion in Niederbayern gegenüber der Presse:
In Niederbayern reagiert man mit Unverständnis.
+> In Niederbayern reagiert man mit Unzufriedenheit/Empörung

(30) Herr Vogts, welche Chancen räumen Sie unserer Nationalelf ein?
Es ist nicht ausgeschlossen, daß wir Europameister werden.
+> es ist sehr gut möglich, daß wir Europameister werden.

In allen Beispielen erfüllen in der intendierten Lesart sowohl das Assertierte als auch die illustrierte Implikatur die Maximen der Qualität und Relevanz. Außerdem gelten die angegebenen Implikaturen tatsächlich nur unter der Bedingung, daß der Sprecher höflich sein wollte und die angedeutete stärkere Alternative eine Höflichkeitsmaxime verletzt hätte. Für (26) könnte man "Bedränge niemanden!" heranziehen, für (27) "Tue oder sage niemandem etwas Unangenehmes!", für (28) und (29) "Sei freundlich!" und für (30) "Gib nicht an!". Die in (29) illustrierte Implikatur ist nur unter der zutreffenden Annahme plausibel, daß der niederbayerische Vertreter sehr regierungsfreundlich ist und vor der Presse keine unhöfliche Bemerkung machen möchte, die das Bayerische Wirtschaftsministerium betrifft.

Für Fälle wie in (26)-(30) bietet Horn eine Lösung auf der Basis der zweiten Quantitätsmaxime an. Horn faßt die zweite Quantitätsmaxime mit der Relevanzmaxime unter dem folgenden R-Prinzip zusammen: Sag nicht mehr, als du mußt (Horn 1984: 13). Ein ernstes Problem dieses Rekonstruktionsversuchs ist, daß solche Implikaturen das allgemeine Gricesche Ableitungsschema in (I) nicht zu befolgen scheinen. In keinem der Beispiele (26)-(30) ist die Assertion ohne Implikatur zu informativ oder irrelevant und erst mit Implikatur relevant bzw. nicht zu informativ. Vielmehr deutet die wortgetreue Anwendung des allgemeinen Ableitungsschemas darauf hin, daß solche Implikaturen auf der Basis der ersten Quantitätsmaxime entstehen. Die Assertion ohne Implikatur ist nämlich eher weniger informativ als mit Implikatur. Auch in solchen Fällen liefert die Implikatur eine Informationsverstärkung. In allen Beispielen in (26)-(30) ist die angedeutete Alternative auf einer semantischen oder pragmatischen Informativitätsskala stärker als die assertierte Alternative. Man muß allerdings Horn zugute halten, daß er auf die Wirkung der Höflichkeitsmaximen bei der Entstehung solcher Implikaturen hingewiesen hat (Horn 1984: 15f.).

Der Unterschied zwischen den qq-Implikaturen und den in (26)-(30) illustrierten qh-Implikaturen wird im vorliegenden Ansatz über die Interaktion mit den Qualitätsmaximen (vgl. (III) und (III')) bzw. Höflichkeitsmaximen (vgl. (VI)) erklärt.

4.2 Quantität und Relevanz

In diesem Abschnitt werden Standardimplikaturen besprochen, die durch die Interaktion der ersten Quantitätsmaxime mit der Relevanzmaxime motiviert sind. Vgl. (VII):

(VII) Quantitäts- und relevanzbasierte Implikaturen (kurz qr-Implikaturen): Die Assertion einer Aussage A anstelle anderer beliebiger Aussagen $B_1, ..., B_n$ ist nur durch die erste Quantitätsmaxime und die Relevanzmaxime motiviert, letzteres dadurch, daß $B_1, ..., B_n$ die Relevanzmaxime verletzen würden.

Beispiele für Implikaturen dieses Typs bietet (31):

(31) (a) Ich lese Zeitung.
           +> Ich lese Zeitung zur Äußerungszeit
      (b) Stell dir vor, ich lese gestern gerade Zeitung, als meine Schwester
           anruft, um mir zu sagen, daß ihr Kater gestorben ist.
           +> Ich lese Zeitung vor der Äußerungszeit
      (c) Morgen werde ich wieder Zeitung lesen.
           +> ich lese Zeitung nach der Äußerungszeit

(31) untermauert die neuere Auffassung, daß das Präsens im Deutschen semantisch keine bestimmte Zeitrelation denotiert (vgl. Vennemann 1987, Engel 1991). Das Präsens kann aufgrund von kontextuell gegebenen Zeitangaben wie *gestern* oder *morgen* in (31b) und (31c) mit Vergangenheitsbezug bzw. Zukunftsbezug interpretiert werden. Wenn keine bestimmte Zeitangabe kontextuell gegeben ist, wie in (31a), so ist der Zeitpunkt der Assertion (d. h. die Äußerungszeit) relevant. Dadurch entsteht der Gegenwartsbezug des Präsens in (31a). Die temporale Implikatur des Präsens ist somit durch die Relevanzmaxime motiviert, denn andere als die in (31) angegebenen Zeitrelationen würden ohne weitere Kontextannahmen die Relevanzmaxime verletzen. Daß die konversationell implizierten Zeitrelationen auch durch die erste Quantitätsmaxime determiniert sind, zeigt sich darin, daß sie informativer bzw. stärker sind als die assertierte unbestimmte Zeitrelation.

Auch weitere Fälle von relevanzdeterminierter Informativitätsverstärkung kann man analog erklären. Vgl. (32)-(36):

(32) Ich habe ein Buch verloren. +> Ich habe mein Buch verloren.

(33) Wir verbrachten unsere Ferien in Österreich. Wir gingen oft langlaufen.
+> Wir gingen in Österreich langlaufen.

(34) Ich habe ein neues Auto. Die Fenster lassen sich schwer öffnen.
+> Die Fenster des neuen Autos lassen sich schwer öffnen.

(35) Hans wurde von der Polizei angehalten. Er hatte etwas getrunken.
+> Hans hatte Alkohol getrunken.

(36) Er drehte den Schalter an, und der Motor sprang an.
Z. B. in einem Bericht über einen Handlungsablauf:
+> Er drehte den Schalter an, und dann sprang der Motor an
Z. B. wenn es, um die Frage geht, warum der Motor ansprang:
+> Er drehte den Schalter an, und deshalb sprang der Motor an

Beispiele wie die in (32)-(36) illustrierten wurden auch in alternativen Ansätzen auf der Basis der Relevanzmaxime bzw. des R-Prinzips von Horn erklärt (vgl. Levinson 1990, Horn 1984). Anders als in alternativen Ansätzen gehe ich aber davon aus, daß sie auch durch die erste Quantitätsmaxime motiviert sind.

Für solche Implikaturen schlägt Levinson eine Lösung vor, die von einem Informativitätsprinzip ausgeht, "das uns in einigen Umständen erlaubt, in eine Äußerung mehr Information hineinzulesen, als wirklich enthalten ist" (1990: 148). Dieses Informativitätsprinzip wurde weiter oben bereits diskutiert, da es Levinson auch für Konditionalverstärkungen beansprucht. Sowohl bei der Konditionalverstärkung als auch bei Implikaturen wie in (32)-(36) sind die Informativitätsverhältnisse derart, daß die Assertion ohne Implikatur weniger informativ ist als mit Implikatur. Solche Informativitätsverhältnisse deuten auf eine Ausbeutung der ersten Quantitätsmaxime hin. Die Annahme einer zusätzlichen Konversationsmaxime ist überflüssig.

5 Zusammenfassung und Ausblick

Eine wichtige Voraussetzung für die Ergebnisse des vorliegenden Beitrags ist die Annahme, daß Konversationsmaximen interagieren. Eines der Ziele der Untersuchung war zu zeigen, daß über die Interaktion verschiedener Maximen mit der ersten Maxime der Quantität verschiedene Typen von Standardimplikaturen der Quantität entstehen.

Im ersten Teil der Arbeit (Abschnitt 2 und 3) wurde die Interaktion der ersten Quantitätsmaxime mit den Qualitätsmaximen eingehender besprochen. Bei dieser Interaktion entstehen Quantitätsimplikaturen (qq-Implikaturen), die in der bisherigen Literatur als skalare Implikaturen rekonstruiert wurden. Aus der Interaktion mit den Qualitätsmaximen läßt sich zum einen der typische Inhalt solcher Implikaturen ableiten: der Sprecher weiß nicht, ob eine stärkere Alternative zutrifft, oder er weiß, daß sie nicht zutrifft. Zum anderen kann dadurch ihre Fokussensitivität erklärt werden. Wichtig für die Erklärung der Fokussensitivität solcher Implikaturen ist die Tatsache, daß die Qualitätsmaximen in der Formulierung von Grice mit einigen Gelingensbedingungen assertiver Sprechakte deckungsgleich sind. Die Qualitätsmaximen greifen somit auf eine mit Hilfe eines assertiven Operators angereicherte und in Fokus-Hintergrund strukturierte Bedeutungsrepräsentation des Gesagten. Entscheidend für die Fokussensitivität solcher Implikaturen ist nun, daß nur der Fokusteil der Äußerung vom assertiven Operator inhaltlich besonders betroffen ist. Damit ist garantiert, daß die epistemische Andeutung der Qualität, die jede 'skalare' Implikatur charakterisiert, besonders den Fokusteil einer Äußerung betrifft.

Unabhängig von diesen Annahmen ist ein weiteres Ergebnis der vorliegenden Arbeit zu bewerten. Für das Entstehen von qualitätsbasierten Quantitätsimplikaturen ist es nicht notwendig, daß die Menge der Alternativen nach dem Grad der Informativität skaliert ist. Für solche Implikaturen ist somit nicht der Bezug auf Informativitätsskalen, sondern der Bezug auf Alternativen im fokustheoretischen Sinn von primärer Relevanz. Im einfachsten Fall gilt für jede Alternative zum Assertierten, daß der Sprecher nicht weiß, ob sie zutrifft, oder daß er weiß, daß sie nicht zutrifft. Durch diese Annahme konnten die für andere Ansätze problematischen Implikaturen, an denen Kohyponyme und *wenn-dann* Aussagen beteiligt sind, sowie ihre Paraphrasierbarkeit mit Hilfe von *nur* erklärt werden. Daß bei skalierten Alternativen die qualitätsbasierte epistemische Implikatur nur stärkere Alternativen betrifft, ergibt sich aus der allgemeineren Restriktion, daß Implikaturen im allgemeinen und Quantitätsimplikaturen im besonderen nicht in Widerspruch stehen dürfen zur assertierten konventionellen Bedeutung. Bei skalierten Alternativen führt die Negation einer schwächeren Alternative zu einem Widerspruch, so daß nur stärkere Alternativen in semantischer Kompatibilität mit dem assertierten Inhalt per Implikatur negiert werden können.

Im zweiten Teil der Arbeit (Abschnitt 4) wurde das interaktionale Modell in Bezug auf das Zusammenwirken zwischen der ersten Quantitätsmaxime und den Höflichkeitsmaximen einerseits und zwischen der ersten Quantitätsmaxime und der Relevanzmaxime andererseits weiterverfolgt. Es ergaben sich unterschiedliche Typen von Standardimplikaturen, für die in alternativen Ansätzen ein Zusammenhang mit den Höflichkeitsmaximen oder der Relevanzmaxime bestätigt, ein Zusammenhang mit der ersten Quantitätsmaxime jedoch abgestritten wurde. Die wortgetreue Anwendung des allgemeinen Ableitungsschemas für konversationelle Implikaturen, das wir Grice verdanken, zeigt eindeutig, daß auch solche Implikaturen auf der Basis der ersten Quantitätsmaxime entstehen. Die Assertion ohne Implikatur ist nämlich auch in solchen Fällen weniger informativ als mit Implikatur. Allen in diesem Beitrag diskutierten Implikaturen ist gemeinsam, daß sie der Informationsverstärkung dienen.

Was in der vorliegenden Arbeit nicht geleistet werden konnte, ist, den Bezug zwischen der ersten Quantitätsmaxime und den Modalitätsmaximen zu diskutieren. Da die Existenz der Modalitätsmaximen (vgl. Meibauer 1996) und deren Zusammenwirken mit der Quantitätsmaxime umstritten ist (vgl. Matsumoto 1995) bedarf diese Fragestellung einer eigenen eingehenderen Untersuchung.

Aus metatheoretischer Perspektive zeigt der präsentierte Ansatz Merkmale, die neuere prinzipienbasierte Modelle charakterisieren: Datenrestriktionen werden, so weit wie möglich, über die Interaktion unabhängig motivierter allgemeiner Prinzipien ohne Rekurs auf spezifische, für den behandelten Datenbereich eigens eingeführte Regeln erfaßt.

Literatur

Altmann, H. (1976): Die Gradpartikeln im Deutschen. Tübingen: Niemeyer.
Atlas, D.J. & S.C. Levinson (1981): "*It*-clefts, informativeness and logical form". In: P. Cole, ed.: Radical pragmatics. New York: Academic Press, 1-61.
Becker, Th. (1996): "Was wir von Aristoteles über die Bedeutung deutscher Wörter lernen können: über konversationelle Implikaturen und Wortsemantik". In diesem Band.
Brown, P. & S.C. Levinson (1987): Politeness. Cambridge: Cambridge University Press.
Engel, U. (1991): Deutsche Grammatik. Heidelberg: Groos.
Fretheim, T. (1992): "The effect of intonation on a type of scalar implicature". Journal of Pragmatics 18, 1-30.
Gazdar, G. (1979): Pragmatics: implicature, presupposition and logical form. New York: Academic Press.
Geiss, M.L. & A.M. Zwicky (1971): "On invited inferences". Linguistic Inquiry 2, 561-566.
Grice, H.P. (1979): "Logik und Konversation". In: G. Meggle, ed.: Handlung, Kommunikation, Bedeutung. Frankfurt/Main: Suhrkamp, 243-265.
Harnish, R.M. (1991): "Logical form and implicature". In: S. Davis, ed.: Pragmatics. A reader. Oxford: Oxford University Press, 316-364 (Nachdruck aus: T. B. Bever et al., eds. (1976): An integrated theory of linguistic ability).
Hirschberg, J. (1991): A theory of scalar implicature. New York: Garland.
Horn, L.R. (1984): "Toward a new taxonomy for pragmatic inference: Q-based and R-based implicature". In: D. Schiffrin, ed.: Meaning, form, and use in context: Linguistic applications. Washington: Georgetown University Press, 11-42.
Horn, L.R. (1989): A natural history of negation. Chicago: University of Chicago Press.
Horn, L.R. (1996): "Exclusive company: *only* and the dynamics of vertical inference". Journal of Semantics 13, 1-40.
Internationaler Arbeitskreis für Orthographie, ed. (1995): Deutsche Rechtschreibung. Vorlage für die amtliche Regelung. Tübingen: Narr.
Jacobs, J. (1982): Syntax und Semantik der Negation im Deutschen. München: Fink.
Jacobs, J. (1983): Fokus und Skalen. Tübingen: Niemeyer.
Jacobs, J. (1984): "Funktionale Satzperspektive und Illokutionssemantik". Linguistische Berichte 91, 25-58.
Jacobs, J. (1991): "Negation". In: A.v. Stechow & D. Wunderlich, eds.: Semantik. Ein internationales Handbuch der zeitgenössischen Forschung. Berlin: de Gruyter, 560-596.
König, E. (1991): The meaning of focus particles: A comparative perspective. London: Routledge.
Krifka, M. (1995): "The semantics and pragmatics of polarity items". Linguistic Analysis 25, 209-257.
Leech, G. (1983): Principles of pragmatics. London: Longman.
Levinson, S.C. (1990): Pragmatik. Tübingen: Niemeyer.

Matsumoto, Y. (1995): "The conversational condition on Horn scales". Linguistics and Philosophy 18, 21-60.
Meibauer, J. (1996): "Modulare Pragmatik und die Maxime der Art und Weise". Sprache und Pragmatik 38, 40-69.
Rolf, E. (1994): Sagen und Meinen. Paul Grices Theorie der Konversations-Implikaturen. Opladen: Westdeutscher Verlag.
Rooth, M. (1985): Association with focus. PhD thesis. University of Massachusetts at Amherst.
Sperber, D. & D. Wilson (1986): Relevance. Communication and cognition. Oxford: Blackwell.
Uhmann, S. (1991): Fokusphonologie. Tübingen: Niemeyer.
Van Kuppevelt, J. (1996): "Inferring from topics. Scalar implicatures as topic-dependent inferences". Linguistics and Philosophy 19, 393-443.
Vennemann, T. (1987): "Tempora und Zeitrelationen im Standarddeutschen". Sprachwissenschaft 12, 234-249.

Liste der verwendeten Symbole

+>	konversationelle Implikatur
#	Blockade einer konversationellen Implikatur
→	*wenn-dann* (Konditional)
↔	*genau-dann-wenn* (Bikonditional)
∨	einschließendes *oder*
∧	*und*
¬	*nicht*
>	*informativer als*

Reduction and Contextualization in Pragmatics and Discourse Analysis

Anne Reboul / Jacques Moeschler, Geneva

1 Introduction

Discourse analysis is built on a premise:

(1) Syntax and semantics are not sufficient to account for linguistic interpretation because their domain is the sentence.

Discourse analysts draw a conclusion from that premise:

(2) To account for linguistic interpretation, it is necessary to have a unit larger than the sentence.

Discourse analysis has an obvious candidate for the status of larger unit: *discourse* (or *text* for the written language approaches). Yet it does not seem that discourse is in any way a well-defined entity and a unit which may be circumscribed through linguistic means. We will come back to that question in the next section.
    Given that there is no precise definition of discourse, it is hard to evaluate the validity of an approach which substitutes discourse to sentence as a unit of scientific investigation, but it should be remarked that discourse, if it is a *linguistic* unit (as is claimed by most discourse analysts), cannot easily account for indexicals, to name only one thing. What is more, it may be doubted whether the lack of a precise or acceptable definition of discourse is a matter of chance: in fact, we think that a definiton of discourse which would justify the investigation of discourse as a scientific endeavour is impossible.

2 The Difficulties of Defining Discourse

As a good number of linguistic and cognitive terms, *discourse* also belongs to everyday language, where it is ambiguous between the interpretation where it means a sequence of utterances produced by a single individual in a special circumstance (inaugural speech, etc.), an understanding where it means a sequence of utterances which limits are determined by the circumstances, a third understanding where it means the linguistic expression of a thought, and a last understanding where it means a mere chatting. None of these common sense interpretations can be used to circumscribe a scientific entity. What is more, it does not seem that discourse analysts have succeeded in circumscribing the notion of discourse in a satisfactory way, their description, based on an analogy with the relation between sentence and grammaticality, defining discourse on the basis of coherence. In other words, a discourse is defined as a *coherent* sequence of utterances in the same way as a sentence is defined as a *grammatical* sequence of words. Yet, the analogy with syntax is not straightforward as the sentence can be defined through grammaticality because grammaticality is described through the rules of syntax, whereas coherence does not seem to obey a finite number of precise rules. Indeed, coherence, a quality which is attributed to discourse and should be enough to define it, does not connect with determined linguistic markers such as those of cohesion:[1] it is easy to show that cohesion markers are independent of the intuitive judgment of coherence or non-coherence bearing on a given sequence of utterances. There are incoherent sequences of utterances with or without cohesion markers and coherent sequences of utterances with or without cohesion markers (see Blass (1985), Moeschler (1989), Reboul (to appear), Reboul & Moeschler (1995, 1996), among others). For instance, the discourse in (3) cannot be said to be coherent, and the adjunction of cohesion markers (indicated in bold for connectives, italics for discourse anaphora and Δ for ellipsis) does not solve the problem of coherence in (4):

(3)   John bought a cow. It is red-haired like a squirrel. It lives in the forest and hibernates during winter. It is very cold in this part of the world.

(4)   John bought a cow. **Indeed** *it* is red-haired like a squirrel. *It* lives in the forest and Δ hibernates during winter. **But** *it* is very cold in this part of the world.

In the same way, the lack of cohesion markers in (5) does not impede an interpretation (7), given the right context, such as (6):

(5)   We'll have guests tonight. Calderon was a great writer.

(6)   (a) Today is the anniversary of Calderon's birth.
      (b) The speaker is a fan of Calderon.

(7)   The speaker is organising a diner in hommage to Calderon.

Thus the coherence judgment is independent of the presence or absence of cohesion markers.

It should be added, before coming back to the possibility of defining discourse, that the notion of coherence does not have the advantages expected: it does not help interpret indexicals (as it applies exclusively at the linguistic level); it does not yield an interpretation of discourse anaphora and, most notably, of definite descriptions (mainly because definite descriptions do not always refer back to an already mentioned object)[2]; it does not help either to interpret evolving reference[3] anymore than it helps with tense or connectives. In other words, it seems that the notion of coherence is an intuitive and pretheoretical notion and that, far from being of any help to analyse anything whatsoever, a judgment of coherence itself needs to be explained through other factors.

Let us come back to the definiton of discourse: trying to define it through coherence does not seem highly efficient and recourse to linguistic markers yields circular or inadequate definitions. Thus, some discourse analysts (see Roulet et al. (1985) advanced the hypothesis that there are structures peculiar to discourse. Yet, it can be shown that one and the same discourse can receive two different structures or more, which leads to the thought that the structure is neither more nor less than the more or less formal representation of an interpretation: it is not an essential characteristic of a discourse, nor a help toward an interpretation (see Reboul & Moeschler 1985).

Discourse, despite the widespread use of the notion, still has to be defined in a precise way. Our ambition here is not to give a definition of discourse which would justify the use to which discourse analysis puts it. Rather, we think that one must say how discourse is interpreted and, with this objective in view, we define it as follows:

Def1 *Definition of discourse*
A discourse is a non-arbitrary sequence of utterances.[4]

This definition cannot be used to identify a unit yielding an analysis, but rather sequences of sentences in need of an analysis.

3   Reductionism

As long as we accept that the interpretation of discourses (under the above definition) must be accounted for, it could be asked in which way our proposal is different from that of discourse analysts. The answer is simple: we do not think that discourse has the necessary characteristics to be used as a minimal unit for any analysis whatever. Rather, the analysis of a given discourse must use other units of which none is the discourse concerned. In other words, we adopt an explicitly reductionist approach on discourse.

On our view, an explicitly reductionist position is a position which accounts for phenomena from scientifically relevant categories. A category is *scientifically relevant* only if it cannot be reduced to its elements and to the relations between these elements, i.e. when it is emergent in a specific sense or when it does not have any element. We distinguish between *emergent1* facts and *emergent2* facts:[5]

Def2 Definition of emergence1
A fact F is emergent1 iff:
(i)   F is composed of elements a, b, c ...
(ii)   F has some features which are not or not necessarily features of a, b, c ...
(iii) Some of the features of F can be deduced or computed from the features of a, b, c ... on the basis of their arrangement or composition.
(iv) Some other features of F are explained in terms of the causal interactions among a, b, c ...: those are causally emergent features.

Def3 Definition of emergence2
A fact F' is emergent2 iff:
(i) F' is emergent1.
(ii) F' has causal powers which cannot be explained by the causal interactions of a, b, c ...

According to us, a category is scientifically relevant if it is emergent2 and we think that discourse is not an emergent2 category, but an emergent1 category. To justify this position, we must do two things: on the one hand, we must show that discourse does not have causal properties which cannot be explained through the causal interactions between its elements; on the other hand, we must say what are the elements of discourse. We will begin by the second task.

If we come back to linguistics, each of the traditional domains in linguistics corresponds to a scientifically emergent category, either because this category is emergent2, or because it cannot be divided into smaller units. Thus, phonology has as its category the phoneme and the relations between phonemes and, at least from a linguistic point of view,[6] there are no smaller units of which the phoneme would be composed. Syntax and semantics have as a scientifically relevant category the morpheme which is a typical example of emergent2 fact: indeed, if, from a phonological perspective, the morpheme is composed of phonemes, neither the syntactic category it belongs to nor its meaning can be reduced to its phonemes or to the relations between these phonemes.[7] On the reverse, the sentence is an emergent1 fact, which can be reduced to the elements which compose it (the morphemes) and to the relations between these elements.[8] If we come back to the postulate of discourse analysis (1), it might be tempting to conclude that discourse is an emergent2 fact and thus a scientifically relevant category:

(1) Syntax and semantics are not sufficient to account for linguistic interpretation because of their domain, which is the sentence.

In a reductionist perspective, this postulate could be reformulated in the following way:

(1') (a) Discourse cannot be reduced to sentences which compose it and to the relations between these sentences because the sentence is not a scientifically relevant category.
 (b) Discourse cannot be reduced to morphemes because the morphemes which compose it and the relations between them are not sufficient toaccount for the causal properties of discourse.

Thus it would seem that discourse is an emergent2 fact and, in this sense, constitutes a scientifically relevant category.

Still, if discourse cannot be reduced to sentences or morphemes, this does not mean that it cannot be reduced to something else and, in this case, we rather naturally think of utterances. If the proposal to reduce discourse to utterance is to be meaningful, we must: a) define utterance; b) show that utterance is a scientifically relevant category; c) show that discourse can be reduced to the utterances which compose it and to the relations between these utterances.

In a highly unoriginal way, we adopt the following definition of utterance:

Def4 *Definition of utterance*
An utterance is the result of the specific production of a sentence.

We must still show that utterance does not reduce to sentence. To do this, it is enough to show that utterance interpretation requires non linguistic informations. This is of course the case for indexicals and it is sufficient to show that utterance is more than sentence and does obviously not reduce to morphemes[9]. Thus, the interpretation of (8):

(8)   I am here now.

as the occurrence of a sentence, will change depending on the speaker, time and place of production. All occurrences of sentence (8) will yield different interpretations for the deictics.

What is more, utterance interpretation cannot reduce only to the linguistic informations transmitted by the corresponding sentence, as is shown by the problem of discourse anaphora. It does not seem doubtful that utterance is both distinct from the sentence (i.e. does not reduce to it) and constitutes a scientifically relevant category. Thus, discourse might well not be a scientifically relevant category, despite (1'), in as much as it could be reduced to the utterances which make it. We will show that this is right below.

4   Reductionism and Contextualism

Showing that discourse is not a scientifically relevant category and that it can be reduced to utterances composing it and to the relations between utterances is a reductionist goal, which success goes paradoxically through contextualist considerations. Récanati (1994) describes the differences between contextualist and anti-contextualist approaches in the history of analytical philosophy and indicates, rightly, that the distinction between the one or the other of these approaches goes through the importance attributed to the distinction between formal language and natural language. If the sentences of a formal language have an interpretation fixed and independent of context, it is, to say the least, doubtful that it is the case for the sentences of a natural language which interpretation seems influenced by context. According to contextualism, this difference is very important, while anti-contextualists think that it can be resolved if the problem is seen from a certain level of abstraction. The thesis of the anti-contextualists is based on the following principle (Récanati 1994: 157):

(9)   For every statement which can be made using a context-sensitive sentence in a given context, there is an eternal sentence[10] that can be used to make the same statement in any context.

If anti-contextualists were right, it would have to be admitted that discourse can be reduced to morphemes and that there are no basic differences between sentence and utterance, i.e. that utterance interpretation is the same as the corresponding sentence interpretation. We have seen above that this is not the case and we will not discuss it any further. Récanati, in his paper (*ibid*.: 161), shows that Grice's anti-contextualist argument is not acceptable because it relies on a *petitio principii* by presupposing a principle, the *Parallelism Principle*, which is not acceptable for contextualists:

(10) *Parallelism Principle*
If a (syntactically complete) sentence can be used in different contexts to say different things (to express different propositions), then the explanation for this contextual variation of content is that the sentence has different linguistic meanings - is semantically ambiguous.

Obviously the alliance between the principle of parallelism and the principle of modified Occam's razor (which prohibits the multiplication of linguistic meanings) forbids that the same sentence can be used in different contexts with different interpretations. Yet, it should be noticed that the principle of parallelism supposes that utterance interpretation, reduced on this view to sentence interpretation, is entirely codic, that is that linguistic interpretation strictly speaking (syntax and semantics) is enough to utterance interpretation, which is highly doubtful. As Récanati says, a contextualist position does not commit one to attributing a basic ambiguity to sentences or morphemes: it is enough to postulate an under-determination in language and to consider that utterance interpretation is equivalent with sentence meaning. The sentence is thus not ambiguous, but under-determined. The proposition expressed does not depend exclusively, on this view, on linguistic meaning, but also depends on contextual elements. Note that this position, which Récanati names *Methodological Contextualism*, is exactly that which we have defended in the previous section: it is tantamount with considering that utterance is emergent2 relative to sentence.

Hence the paradox evoked above can be solved: to defend a reductionist position regarding discourse, one must adopt a contextualist position regarding utterance. We will now develop this position and show how the utterance is interpreted and how utterance interpretation is sufficient to account for discourse.

5 Contextualism and Utterance

Coming back to the anti-contextualist thesis in (9), note that, even if it were true, it has nothing to say about the function which the context does or does not play in utterance interpretation, mainly because it does not deal with utterance interpretation or even with sentence interpretation:

(9)   For every statement which can be made using a context-sensitive sentence in a given context, there is an eternal sentence that can be used to make the same statement in any context.

In this and the next sections, we will deal not with the existence or non-existence of eternal sentences but with utterance interpretation and the respective weight of linguistic and contextual data in this interpretation.

Taking a contextualist stance does not imply denying that linguistic data (lexicon, syntax, etc.) have a role in utterance interpretation. It merely means saying that these data are not sufficient and that they must be completed by non-linguistic interpretation processes, which can be called *contextual*. Utterance belongs to the domain of pragmatics rather to that of linguistics, i.e. to the domain of language use, rather than to that of language *simpliciter*. We thus adopt a pragmatic perspective, the post-gricean perspective which was developed by Sperber and Wilson in their book, *Relevance* (1995).

Relevance Theory is a pragmatic theory of a new kind, in as much as it is both cognitive (it lies in the chomskyan paradigm where the study of language is a part of cognitive science), truth-conditional and inferential. According to Sperber and Wilson, faithful to Fodor's modular theory (1983), pragmatics is the last step in utterance interpretation. It is a non-specific process which belongs to the central system and uses an inference device to interpret the utterance. The inference device has as its premises the data accessed through the input system specialised in the processing of linguistic data and the propositions in the context. These propositions come from different origins: the interpretation of preceeding utterances, encyclopaedic knowledge of the world, perception data coming from the physical environment where the communication occurs. They are selected on the basis of a principle, the *principle of relevance*, which says that every utterance carries the presumption of its own optimal relevance. Relevance is a function both of the cost of utterance processing (the less difficult to process the utterance, the more relevant it is) and of the effects produced by the utterance in a given context (the more effects produced by an utterance in a given context, the more relevant this utterance in this context). The effects concerned are of three kinds: changing the force with which a proposition is entertained; yielding new propositions or synthetic contextual implications, deduced from the utterance *and* the context; suppressing a proposition when a contradiction occurs. On this view, the propositions in the context have been chosen because they were the best able to yield an interpretation consistent with the principle of relevance. The principle of relevance also comes into play at the end of the interpretation process to stop it when an interpretation consistent with the principle of relevance has been attained.

Note that, though they are contextualist, Sperber and Wilson are nonetheless of the gricean family, especially in their view of what an utterance is: they insist on the importance of speaker's intentions in the communicative process and distinguish the speaker's informative intention (making manifest or more manifest to the hearer a set of assumptions) and the speaker's communicative intention (making mutually manifest that the speaker has this informative intention). Communication is successful when the speaker's communicative intention has been satisfied: through his utterance, he or she made manifest to his hearer the set of assumptions which was the object of his or her informative intention. We will here adopt this theory of utterance interpretation.

Thus, the reason why we say that utterances rather than sentences are emergent2 is that utterance interpretation is a central system process, going through an inferential device relative to a context, whereas sentence interpretation is an input system process which goes through purely linguistic devices and is not relative to a context.

6   Contextualism and Discourse

We still have to say how discourse is interpreted and to show that it is in fact reducible to the utterances of which it is made and to the relations between these utterances. It seems that discourse, like utterance, is interpreted *via* people's ability to mutually attribute to themselves and others beliefs, intentions, feelings, etc.: in other words, *via* what was called by Dennett (1987) the *intentional stance*. The intentional stance is both the ability and the tendency to attribute to others internal representations (beliefs, desires, intentions, etc.). It has the rather notable characteristic of being mandatory and to apply farther than other beings, to the most simple mechanical devices. As Dennett says: "[there is an] unavoidability of the intentional stance, with regard to oneself and one's fellow intelligent beings". This characteristic of the intentional stance partially explains the principle of relevance, that is the fact that each utterance conveys a guarantee of its own optimal relevance. As Sperber and Wilson say, the principle of relevance is not a constraint which the speaker should try to satisfy or to which he might disobey: it is a general principle of interpretation which applies in all circumstances.

If the intentional stance is one of the origins of the principle of relevance, it is clear that it applies at the level of discourse as much as at the level of utterance and this is also true of the principle of relevance. This means that if utterance interpretation aims to recover the informative intention of the speaker at a local level, it seems plausible that there are one or more intentions behind a discourse and that discourse interpretation aims to recover these intentions.[11] We will distinguish *local intentions* which have to do with utterance from *global intentions* which have to do with discourse. The problem, to justify that discourse can be reduced to utterances, is to show how global intentions can be recovered on the basis of local intentions (i.e. how discourse interpretation can be reduced to utterance interpretation).

How then can one go from local intentions to global intentions? It seems to us that a static analysis where local intentions accumulate to form a global intention which would be accessible only at the end of discourse and which would be equivalent with the set of local intentions would not be satisfying. We would rather propose a dynamic analysis of the interpretation process. According to us, in the same way as utterance interpretation is a dynamic process, discourse interpretation is also a dynamic process. Let us return to the intentional stance: it has as its object the intentions, etc. of other people. Its main interest is that it allows to predict the future behaviour and intentions of other people. In a good number of cases, it allows to choose appropriate reactions or to anticipate the behaviour of other people. In the case of linguistic communication, the same thing is true because the intentional stance is accompanied by the principle of relevance which reinforces its predictive power. At utterance level, this means that utterance interpretation also proceeds by anticipation. The hearer forms anticipatory hypotheses on what will be the end of the utterance based on its beginnig, and thus reduces, when these hypotheses are right, the processing cost. That this process occurs can be seen each time an individual begins a sentence which his or her hearer ends for him or her. On our view, discourse interpretation implies, as utterance interpretation, that anticipatory hypotheses are built on the basis of the interpretation of successive utterances and of the inferences which the hearer can draw from them about the speaker's global intentions.

The passage from local intentions to global intentions occurs here: as soon as the first utterance is produced by the speaker, the hearer builts a representation of the speaker's global intention (he wants to talk of this or that subject, etc.). This global intention is then modified with each new utterance, with three possibilities which, not surprisingly, are the same as those which occur in the context:

(i) A local intention can contradict one element of the global intention, in which case this element will be erased;

(ii) a local intention can change the force with which an element of the global intention is entertained, making it either more or less plausible;

(iii) a local intention can, in conjunction with the elements in the global intention, inferentially produce one or more new elements in the global intention.

Let us illustrate with the help of a short example the process of construction of anticipatory hypothesis which lead to the attribution of a global intention on the basis of local intentions:

(10) (a) My aunt was exceedingly pretty, and (b) when she looked at me she smiled admiringly. (c) Turning to my mother she said, 'You know, Minnie, Julius has the loveliest big brown eyes I've seen.'

(d) Until that moment I had never given my eyes a thought. Oh, I knew I was nearsighted, but it never occured to me that my eyes were anything out of the ordinary. (e) Conscious of my new-found charms, I lifted my eyebrows as high as I could and stared at her. She didn't look at me again but I continued to stare, hoping that if my eyes continued to bulge she would pay me another compliment. But no, she was busily gossiping with my mother and apparently had forgotten all about me. I kept walking up and down in front of her, hoping she would again say something flattering about my big brown eyes. [...]

(f) I finally realized that my case was hopeless and [...] I staggered from the room puzzled and feverish, (g) but happy at the first compliment I had ever received from a woman ... even if it was only a casual remark from an aunt.

(h) It wasn't until much later that I looked into a mirror - (i) and discovered that my eyes are gray. (G. Marx: *Memoirs of a mangy lover*)

Very roughly, (a) establishing the "exceeding prettiness" of Groucho's aunt, allows the reader to draw the conclusion that Groucho is attracted to her and ready to take whatever it is that she would say very seriously. (b) and (c) indicate what it was that she did say, i.e. the compliment in Groucho's eyes. Given all the conclusions that can be drawn from (a), (b) and (c), the reader is not surprised by the description of Groucho's state of mind and activities in (d) and (e). (f) and (g) reinforce all the previous conclusions on Groucho's happiness at being paid such a compliment by his pretty aunt. (h) and (i) come as a kind of counterpoint to all the preceeding, establishing that, no matter whether the aunt's compliment was or was not sincere, it was, anyway ill-founded: either she is color-blind or she did not pay him the attention that he had thought she had. One could sum the whole thing up by saying that, though all the local intentions attached to the previous utterances lead to the local intention attached to the last utterance (i), the global intention is not the simple accumulation of those local intentions: it is rather the intention to lead the reader to an array of conclusions about the failibility of women, the unability of men to understand that women may not mean what they say, etc., relying for strenght of these effects on the conclusion drawn previously on the state of mind of Groucho.

All of this leads to the thesis that the elements of the global intention have a propositional form and that, in one way or another, they are integrated to the context and correspond, in the context, to the information drawn from the interpretation of preceeding utterances or, rather, to some of them. This contextualist hypothesis on discourse interpretation and utterance interpretation allows a reductionist approach of discourse which reduces to utterances and to the relations between utterances which are established during the interpretation process. We would like now, as a conclusion, to say a few words about coherence.

7   Discourse and Coherence

As said above (see § 2), it seems extraordinarily difficult to define discourse and the most common endeavour to do so relies on the common sense notion of *coherence*. Yet it appears that coherence is not a more precise or more easily defined notion than is discourse and all the research trying to establish it on linguistic markers have clearly failed. Yet, just as there are discourses in the sense of definition Def1, there are judgments of coherence and these judgments, no matter how intuitive they are, must be integrated to a theory of discourse interpretation, that is it must account for them. It seems that there are two possible strategies: either new elements accounting for these coherence judgments must be added to the discourse theory outlined above, or elements already present in this theory can be used to account for these judgments, without adding anything to the theory. The first strategy would be a kind of justification for the idea that there is a notion of coherence at least partly independent from discourse, which might either be defined or taken as a primitive and which would itself allow the definition of discourse. The second strategy does not in any way ressuscitate the hope of a definition of discourse *via* coherence as, in a way, it dissolves coherence in utterance interpretation, without making it an independent principle or reality. Rather obviously, we will adopt the second strategy.

How are judgments of coherence formed? Do they depend on the properties of the discourse to which they are applied, independently of the interpretation of this discourse? It seems clear to us that coherence is not an intrinsic property of discourse and that coherence judgments depend both on the way discourse interpretation proceeded and on the richness or poverty of the global intention which the hearer (who is the source of the coherence judgment) has drawn from it. Just as relevance depends both on the processing cost and on the richness of effects, coherence is attributed to a discourse depending both on the difficulty encountered when constructing a global interpretation for this discourse and on the richness of this global intention. On this view, coherence, just as relevance, is a relative notion rather than an absolute notion and can bear degrees. We propose the following principle:

(16) Judgment of coherence
 (a) The more easy to construct the global intention of a given discourse is, the more coherent this discourse is.
 (b) The richer the global intention of a given discourse is, the more coherent this discourse is.

Yet, despite their apparent similarity, the notion of coherence and the notion of relevance are radically different. The first only applies at the end of the interpretation process and is not part of it, while the second is the main principle governing interpretation. Thus coherence is a static notion in as much as it only occurs at the end of the process, while relevance is a dynamic notion which guides the interpretation process. Note that, according to discourse analysts, the reverse formula should be true: *Relevance is a static notion in as much as it comes at the end of the process while coherence is a dynamic notion guiding the interpretation process.* What is wrong with such a formula? Obviously, the lack of a definition for coherence: if it is coherence which guides discourse interpretation, then, given the lack of a definition, discourse analysis makes the interpretation process opaque, and sees it, more or less, as a black box. On the reverse, relevance has a definition and, thus, the process of utterance interpretation and of discourse interpretation can be described and coherence can be defined as the product of interpretation rather than its moving principle or as an intrinsic and mysterious property of discourse.

8 Conclusion

Last, we would like to compare the two approaches, the one which we have criticised, discourse analysis, and the one which we defend, a theory of discourse interpretation which is both reductionist and contextualist in the theoretical framework of relevance theory. According to us, discourse analysts have never been able to give a satisfactory definition of discourse whether they tried to base such a definition on the notion of coherence or to define it *via* a structure which would be specific to it, in a teleological endeavour doomed to fail. What is more, discourse analysis fails to account for discourse interpretation, mainly because it bases this interpretation on the notion of coherence, failing to describe coherence and thus transforming the interpretation process into a mysterious process about which it seems difficult to say anything precise. On the reverse, we think that the unit which allows for the description of discourse interpretation is not discourse, but utterance and, in the perspective of relevance theory, we propose a contextualist theory of utterance interpretation and of discourse interpretation which offers an account of coherence. Under this definition, coherence is merely a result and is cut down to its true role, that is an epiphenomenon of the process of discourse interpretation.

Notes

1. It has long been thought in discourse analysis that the so-called *cohesion markers* (i.e. connectives, discourse anaphora, ellipsis) where what made a sequence of sentences coherent.
2. Definite descriptions at the beginning (first sentence) of novels, which are all perfectly understandable as is shown by the following examples, come to mind:
    (i) "The southbound train from Paris was the one we had always taken from time immemorial" (L. Durrell: *Monsieur or The Prince of Darkness*).
    (ii) "Between the silver ribbon of morning and the green glittering ribbon of sea, the boat touched Hardwich ..." (G.K. Chesterton: *Father Brown Stories*).
    (iii) "London, Michaelmas Term lately over, and the Lord Chancellor sitting in Lincoln's Inn Hall" (Ch. Dickens: *Bleak House*).
3. The expression *evolving reference* designates the phenomenon found in examples where an object is introduced under a description, and where then a sequence of actions which radically modify that object are described, though the object is still being refered to through the same description or through a third person pronoun (the standard example was given by Brown & Yule (1983): "Kill an active, plump chicken. Prepare it for the oven, cut it into four pieces and roast it with thyme for 1 hour"; on evolving reference, see Reboul (to appear)).
4. We will justify below the expression "non-arbitrary". By the way, it should be obvious that our ambition is not to give a definition of discourse which would allow it to be the unit of any domain in linguistics, as text linguistics and discourse analysts tried to. As will be seen in the next section, we do not think that discourse is a linguistic unit in the sense in which a phoneme or morpheme are linguistic units.
5. The form of this distinction is directly inspired by Searle (1992: 111f.). For a development, see Reboul & Moeschler (1995, 1996).
6. It is not the case in automatic speech recognition, but that is another problem...
7. Thus *radical reductionism* which would see no difficulty in reducing discourse, sentence or morpheme to phoneme and *moderate reductionism* which refuses this reduction without refusing to reduce the sentence to morphemes should not be confused.
8. It is the semantic hypothesis of compositionality.
9. Which means neither that the morphemes which compose a given utterance do not influence the interpretation of this utterance, nor that this interpretation can ignore syntactic and semantic analyses of the corresponding sentence. Simply, utterance interpretation is not equivalent with (= does not reduce to) syntactic and semantic analyses of sentence.
10. An eternal sentence is a sentence which interpretation is context-independent.
11. This does not mean that the hearer always attains the "right" intention, i.e. misunderstandings or errors are always possible.

References

Blass, R. (1985): "Cohesion, Coherence and Relevance". UCL, ms.
Brown, G. & G. Yule (1983): Discourse Analysis. Cambridge: Cambridge University Press.
Dennett, D.C. (1987): The Intentional Stance. Cambridge, Mass.: The MIT Press.
Fodor, J. (1983): The Modularity of Mind. Cambridge, Mass.: The MIT Press.
Moeschler, J. (1989): Modélisation du dialogue. Paris: Hermès.
Reboul, A. & J. Moeschler (1995): "Le dialogue n'est pas une catégorie naturelle scientifiquement pertinente". Cahier de Linguistique française 17, 229-248.
Reboul, A. & J. Moeschler (1996): "Faut-il continuer à faire de l'analyse de discours?". Hermes 16, 61-92.
Reboul, A. & J. Moeschler (forthcoming): Contre l'analyse de discours: la construction d'un sens commun. Paris: Armand Collin.
Reboul, A., ed. (forthcoming): Evolving Reference and Anaphora: Time and Objects. Amsterdam: Benjamins.
Récanati, F. (1994): "Contextualism and Anti-Contextualism in the Philosophy of Language". In: S.L. Tsohatzidis, ed.: Foundations of Speech Act Theory. London: Routledge, 156-166.
Roulet, E. et al. (1985): L'articulation du discours en français contemporain. Berne: Lang.
Searle, J.R. (1992): The Rediscovery of the Mind. Cambridge, Mass.: The MIT Press.
Sperber, D. & D. Wilson (1995): Relevance: Communication and Cognition. Oxford: Blackwell.

Der 'Gricesche Konversationszirkel'

Eckard Rolf, Münster

Um es vorwegzunehmen: So etwas wie den Griceschen Konversationszirkel gibt es nicht. Jedenfalls nicht in dem Sinne, der Levinson vorschwebt. Levinson selbst spricht übrigens nicht von einem 'Konversations'zirkel; in seinem (bisher nicht veröffentlichten) Manuskript mit dem Titel "Generalized Conversational Implicature and the Semantics/Pragmatics Interface (or how you can't do semantics without first doing pragmatics)" ist, auf S. 17ff., lediglich von "Grice's circle" die Rede.

Daß Grice Zirkularität vorgeworfen wird, geschieht nicht zum erstenmal. Einer der bekanntesten Vorwürfe dieser Art stammt von Max Black. Blacks Zirkularitätsdiagnose bezieht sich auf die Rolle, die Grice (im Kontext seiner Theorie der nicht-natürlichen Bedeutung) der Sprecherabsicht zuschreibt. Blacks Kritik gipfelt in der Feststellung, es sei nicht die Sprecherabsicht, die es einem Hörer erlaube, "die Bedeutung des Gesagten zu bestimmen, sondern umgekehrt: Die Entdeckung der Sprecherbedeutung ermöglicht es einem kompetenten Hörer, [...] auf die Sprecherabsicht zu schließen." (Black 1972-73/1993: 77). (Zu einer kritischen Auseinandersetzung mit diesem Zirkel-Vorwurf und mit verwandten Zirkularitäts-Vorwürfen s. Meggle 1990.) Um den von Levinson ins Auge gefaßten Zirkel von dem bei Black anvisierten zu unterscheiden - und um darauf hinzuweisen, daß der erstere Zirkel (nicht, wie der letztere, im Kontext der Theorie der nicht-natürlichen Bedeutung, sondern) im Kontext der Griceschen Konversationstheorie zu lokalisieren ist, bezeichne ich diesen als den Griceschen Konversationszirkel. Welcher Sachverhalt ist damit gemeint?

Levinson versucht darzulegen, daß, in einer Vielzahl von Fällen, in die Bestimmung der von einem Sprecher ausgedrückten Proposition Implikaturen eingehen. Da Grice nun aber die Bestimmung einer Konversations-Implikatur von einer vorherigen Bestimmung des Gesagten bzw. der zum Ausdruck gebrachten Proposition abhängig mache, entstehe der Eindruck, daß dem Gesagten nicht nur eine aktive, sondern auch eine passive Rolle zukomme, daß für das Gesagte beides zu gelten scheine: Implikaturen zu bestimmen und durch Implikaturen bestimmt zu werden.

Levinson versucht aufzuzeigen, daß der für die Gricesche Pragmatik-Konzeption charakteristische Folgerungsmechanismus Einfluß nimmt auf die Determination der ausgedrückten Proposition. Während die Pragmatik der Semantik nach Grices Ansicht eindeutig nachgeordnet ist, also *post*-semantisch operiert, müsse mit Blick auf die Determination der Proposition bestimmter Sätze angenommen werden, daß das Umgekehrte ebenfalls gelte: daß die Pragmatik auch *prä*-semantisch arbeite.

Levinson argumentiert unter Bezugnahme auf die skalaren Implikaturen, also diejenige Unterart der generalisierten Konversations-Implikaturen, die, vornehmlich durch Griceaner wie Harnish, Gazdar, Horn und Hirschberg erforscht, von allen Implikatur-Arten, zumindest in Linguisten-Kreisen, das bisher größte Interesse auf sich gezogen hat (vgl. auch Rolf 1994: 137ff.). Von skalaren Implikaturen kann im Hinblick auf eine Gruppe unterschiedlicher Ausdrucksarten gesprochen werden. Zu dieser Gruppe gehören bestimmte Konjunktionen, Numeralia, Quantorausdrücke und Modaladverbien ebenso wie bestimmte Verben und Adjektive. Hinsichtlich der entsprechenden Ausdrücke wird angenommen, daß sie auf Skalen angeordnet sind.

Alle beispielsweise beinhaltet *einige, vier* beinhaltet *drei, notwendig* beinhaltet *möglich, lieben* beinhaltet *mögen, ausgezeichnet* beinhaltet *gut, und* beinhaltet gewissermaßen *oder*. Ausdrücke, die weiter links auf einer Skala stehen sind in semantischer bzw. informationaler Hinsicht stärker als Ausdrücke, die weiter rechts auf derselben Skala stehen. Aus der Verwendung eines weiter rechts auf einer Skala stehenden, mithin schwächeren Ausdrucks kann in pragmatischer Hinsicht gefolgert werden, daß ein stärkerer, d. h. weiter links auf der Skala stehender Ausdruck nicht gebraucht werden kann. *Einige* impliziert konversationell *nicht alle, drei* impliziert nicht *vier, möglich* impliziert *nicht notwendig, mögen* impliziert *nicht lieben, gut* impliziert *nicht ausgezeichnet,* und *oder* impliziert nicht *und*. Implikaturen dieser Art werden als skalare Implikaturen bezeichnet.

Was Levinson nun zu zeigen versucht, ist, daß solche Implikaturen eine Rolle spielen bei der Determination der mit bestimmten Sätzen zum Ausdruck gebrachten Propositionen. Sowohl für die ersten beiden Griceschen Quantitätsmaximen als auch für die erste und die vierte der Griceschen Modalitätsmaximen legt Levinson dies anhand einer ganzen Reihe von Sätzen dar. Levinson tut das in Weiterverfolgung eines Programms, das vornehmlich von Carston, Kempson, Wilson und Blakemore, aber z. B. auch von Sperber und Récanati vorgestellt worden ist (s. auch Rolf 1994: 196ff.). Dabei ist unter der Bezeichnung 'Explikaturen' auf den Umstand hingewiesen worden, daß Propositionen, herkömmlicherweise als rein semantische Gebilde betrachtet, oftmals nur unter Anwendung pragmatischer Gesichtspunkte bestimmt werden können (vgl. Carston 1988).

1 Die auslösenden Spracherscheinungen

Es sind insgesamt (A) fünf Phänomenarten und (B) drei Satzkonstruktionstypen, mit Blick auf die Levinson (o. J.: 8f.) seine Behauptung illustriert, "that Gricean inferences are involved in determining WHAT proposition has been 'literally' expressed".

1.1 Die Phänomenarten

Daß eine wahrheits-konditionale Semantik zur Determination der mit bestimmten Sätzen zum Ausdruck gebrachten Propositionen nicht hinreicht, daß dazu vielmehr pragmatische Gesichtspunkte zu berücksichtigen sind, läßt sich anhand der folgenden Phänomenbereiche illustrieren: (i) der Disambiguierung, (ii) der Fixierung indexikalischer Parameter, (iii) der

Referenzidentifikation, (iv) der Ellipsen-Explikation und (v) der Generalitäts-Einschränkung.

Was die ersten drei dieser Phänomenbereiche anbelangt, so beruft sich Levinson (o. J.: 6, 8) übrigens auf eine Stelle aus Grices Artikel "Logic and Conversation", an der es mit Bezug auf den Satz 'Er kommt von dem Laster nicht los' heißt: Um "ganz und gar zu bestimmen, was der Sprecher gesagt hat, müßte man (a) die Identität von x [d. h. von Er], (b) den Zeitpunkt der Äußerung und (c) die bei dieser bestimmten Äußerungsgelegenheit vorliegende Bedeutung der Wendung 'von dem Laster nicht loskommen' [eine Entscheidung zwischen (1) [Laster = schlechter Charakterzug] und (2) [Laster = Beförderungsmittel]] kennen." (Grice 1975/1993: 247)

Bei Levinson werden bezüglich der einzelnen Phänomenbereiche jeweils mehrere Beispiele diskutiert. Da es hier zunächst nur darum geht, einen Eindruck von dem damit einhergehenden Problemkomplex zu vermitteln, beschränken wir uns bei der Anführung von Beispielen auf das nötigste.

(i) Disambiguierung

(1)   (a) Er ist als Hundeliebhaber nicht wählerisch;
       (b) Er liebt einige Katzen und Hunde.

Hinsichtlich des Satzes (b) ergeben sich zwei Strukturierungsmöglichkeiten. Der Skopus des Quantorausdrucks *einige* kann eng oder weit sein: Er kann sich auf *Katzen* oder auf *Katzen und Hunde* erstrecken. Im ersteren Fall ergibt sich - angesichts der ersten Griceschen Quantitätsmaxime ('Mache deinen Beitrag so informativ wie [...] nötig') und der durch sie induzierten generalisierten Konversations-Implikatur - die Lesart

(b') Er liebt einige-aber-nicht-alle Katzen und (sämtliche) Hunde.

In dem anderen Fall ergibt sich die Lesart

(b'') Er liebt einige-aber-nicht-alle Katzen und einige-aber-nicht-alle Hunde.

Anders als (b'), ist (b'') mit (1) (a) unverträglich. Infolgedessen muß (b''), mitsamt der ihr zugrundeliegenden syntaktischen Analyse von (b) (weiter Skopus des Quantorausdrucks einige), zurückgewiesen werden.

(ii) Fixierung indexikalischer Parameter

(2)   Das Treffen ist Donnerstag.

Wenn (2) an einem Mittwoch geäußert wird, dann Q1-impliziert diese Äußerung, daß das Treffen Donnerstag in einer Woche stattfindet. Wenn eine Wochentagsbezeichnung gebraucht wird dort, wo ein informativerer (und kürzerer) Ausdruck, morgen, vorhanden ist, dann wird impliziert 'nicht morgen'.

(iii) Referenzidentifizierung

(3)   Hans kam herein, und er setzte sich.

Aufgrund der zweiten Griceschen Quantitätsmaxime ('Mache deinen Beitrag nicht informativer als nötig') ist Referenzidentität zwischen *Hans* und *er* nahegelegt. Die Interpretation von *er* im Sinne von *Hans* erlaubt eine Maximierung des Informationsgehalts von (3).
    Daß auch Textualität-manifestierende Sätze vor dem Hintergrund Gricescher Maximen Konturen gewinnen, zeigt das folgende Beispiel:

(4)   (a)   Die Brücke brach zusammen.
      (b)   Das Holz war verfault.

Für die Kohärenz von (a) und (b) kann wiederum die zweite Quantitätsmaxime verantwortlich gemacht werden: Die Existenz dieser Maxime erlaubt es dem Hörer, einen Zusammenhang zwischen (a) und (b) anzunehmen.

(iv) Ellipsen-Explikation

(5)   S: Wer ist gekommen?
      H: Johannes (ist gekommen).

Das Ungesagte (ist gekommen) ist über die zweite Quantitätsmaxime lizensiert, das heißt, es kann in der Annahme, daß der Sprecher nur das Notwendigste gesagt hat, ergänzt werden.

(v) Generalitäts-Einschränkung

Der Satz

(6)   Er hat sich einen Finger verletzt.

wird, angesichts der Existenz des informativeren Wortes *Daumen*, vor dem Hintergrund der ersten Quantitätsmaxime so zu verstehen sein, daß es der Daumen nicht ist, der verletzt ist. *Finger* wird mithin in einem spezifischeren, den Daumen ausschließenden Sinn verstanden.
    In ähnlicher Weise, nun allerdings vor dem Hintergrund der zweiten Quantitätsmaxime, wird auch der Satz

(7)   Ich habe etwas getrunken.

in einem spezifischeren Sinne zu verstehen sein: im Sinne von 'Ich habe etwas Alkoholisches getrunken' (vgl. dazu auch Horn 1984).
    Sätze wie (6) und (7) werden sicherlich in der angegebenen spezifischen Weise verstanden, d. h. auf der Grundlage einer pragmatischen Spezifikation der in ihnen enthaltenen Prädikate, die in semantischer Hinsicht vergleichsweise generell sind. Ob auch die mit sol-

chen Sätzen zum Ausdruck gebrachten Propositionen pragmatisch determiniert werden, ist allerdings eine andere Frage.

1.2 Die Satzkonstruktionstypen

Die folgenden Satzkonstruktionsarten, Levinson (o. J.: 22ff.) bezeichnet sie als 'Einmischungs-Konstruktionen' ('intrusive constructions'), haben die Eigenschaft, daß ihre Wahrheitsbedingungen nicht nur von der jeweiligen *Bedeutung* ihrer Teile, sondern von den *Implikaturen* ihrer Teile abhängen.

(i) Komparativkonstruktionen

(8) Nach Hause zu fahren und drei Bier zu trinken ist besser als drei Bier zu trinken und nach Hause zu fahren.

Ein Satz wie dieser (er stammt übrigens von Wilson 1975) erscheint nur dann als sinnvoll, wenn das zweimalige Vorkommen der Konjunktion und im Sinne von 'und dann' verstanden wird. Würde *und* lediglich im Sinne einer bloßen Konnektivität der verknüpften Sachverhalte, also in dem Sinne, daß beides gilt (nach Hause zu fahren und drei Bier zu trinken bzw. drei Bier zu trinken und nach Hause zu fahren) verstanden, würde nicht klar, warum das eine besser sein sollte als das andere. Die spezifische Lesart von *und* ('und dann') kann als über die zweite Quantitätsmaxime vermittelt betrachtet werden.

(ii) Konditionale

(9) Wenn beide Mannschaften drei Tore erzielt haben, dann haben sie unentschieden gespielt.

Der Numeralausdruck *drei* muß hier im Sinne von 'drei und nicht mehr' bzw. 'drei und höchstens drei' verstanden werden. Eine solche Verstärkung des Sinns von *drei*, und damit des gesamten Antezedens von (9), kann als (skalare) Q1-Implikatur angesehen werden. Sie macht erneut deutlich, daß die Wahrheitsbedingungen des Ganzen, d. h. von (9), davon abhängen, daß eine Implikatur eines Teils (eines Teils des Antezedens) in Rechnung gestellt wird.

(iii) Metasprachliche Negationen

Es scheint Fälle zu geben, in denen, was negiert wird, eine Implikatur ist (vgl. insbes. Horn 1989). Letzteres könnte beispielsweise in solchen Sätzen wie den folgenden der Fall sein:

(10) Es ist nicht (nur) möglich, es ist (sogar) sicher.
(11) Helge hat nicht drei Kinder, er hat vier.
(12) Karin ist nicht glücklich, sie ist euphorisch.

Einem Satz wie (12) ist in der Regel eine Behauptung des Inhalts, daß Karin glücklich ist, vorangegangen. Wer (12) äußert, bringt zum Ausdruck, daß an der Vorgängeräußerung etwas (die Wahl des Prädikats) unzutreffend ist; (12) ist eine Richtigstellung (vgl. dazu auch Rolf 1997: 165f.): Das Vorkommen des Negationsausdrucks (*nicht*) ist metasprachlich insofern, als durch ihn die Angemessenheit bzw. die Behauptbarkeit der Vorgängeräußerung in Abrede gestellt wird. Warum aber wäre die Vorgängeräußerung unangemessen? Wegen ihrer skalaren Q1-Implikatur, der zufolge *glücklich nicht euphorisch* impliziert.

2 Problemlösungen

Die Phänomene des Bereichs (A) und die Satzkonstruktionstypen des Bereichs (B) werfen unterschiedliche Probleme auf. Wie hier dargelegt werden soll, kann man dem A-Problem mit Hilfe des Begriffs der Äußerungs-Implikatur begegnen (s. unten), das B-Problem könnte, wie Posner (1979) vorgeschlagen hat, im Sinne einer schrittweisen Berechnung gelöst werden.

2.1 Zum Satzkonstruktionstypen-Problem

Levinson (o. J.: 23) macht zur Verdeutlichung der von ihm bezogenen Position (daß sich die Pragmatik in die Determination der Wahrheitsbedingungen bestimmter Sätze einmischt) darauf aufmerksam, daß sein Ziel dem von Cohen verfolgten diametral entgegengesetzt sei. Cohens Absicht besteht in der Zurückweisung der sogenannten Konversationalistischen Hypothese zugunsten der sogenannten Semantischen Hypothese. Der Konversationalistischen Hypothese zufolge sind die 'Bedeutungsüberschüsse' von *und* in Fällen, in denen dieses Wort beispielsweise 'und dann' (oder 'und dort' etc.) bedeutet, auf Konversationsmaximen zurückzuführen; nach der Semantischen Hypothese hat *und* per se mehrere Bedeutungen, unter anderem 'und dann' sowie 'und dort'. (vgl. dazu auch Rolf 1994: 196ff.).

Angesichts des Gegensatzes der von Cohen und Levinson vertretenen Positionen verwundert es nicht, wenn letzterer sich für eine Auffassung einsetzt, die in den Augen des ersteren ein nahezu unüberwindliches Problem darzustellen scheint. Levinson versucht beispielsweise darzulegen, daß die im Antezedens eines Konditionalsatzes wie

(13) Wenn der alte König an einem Schlaganfall gestorben ist und die Republik ausgerufen worden ist, dann wird Tom völlig zufrieden sein.

enhaltene Konjunktion *und* aufgrund pragmatischer, sprich: Implikatur-bestimmter Einmischung im Sinne von 'und dann' verstanden wird; Cohen (1971/1993) hingegen führt (13) (dort = (9)!) als Gegenbeispiel zur Konversationalistischen Hypothese ins Feld. Cohen sagt:

> Es gibt [...] zumindest einen Typ von 'und'-Vorkommen, der von der Konversationalistischen Hypothese wohl kaum mehr erfaßt werden dürfte. Ich meine den Fall, wo 'und' im Vordersatz eines Konditionalsatzes vorkommt und die Wahrheit der mithilfe

dieses Konditionalsatzes gemachten Behauptung von der genauen Abfolge der durch dieses Vorkommnis von 'und' nahegelegten Ereignisabfolge abhängt. [...] Natürlich stünde es Grice offen, seine Theorie der Implikaturen so zu erweitern bzw. zu modifizieren, daß man mit der Behauptung eines Konditionalsatzes wie (9) [hier = (13)] normalerweise implizieren würde, daß die Wahrheit des ganzen Konditionalsatzes zum Teil von einer Bedingung der zeitlichen Abfolge abhängt, die kraft konversationeller Vorannahmen mit der Äußerung des Vordersatzes übermittelt wird. (Cohen 1971/ 1993: 405f.)

Letzteres scheint auch Levinson anzunehmen. Es wäre allerdings zu fragen, ob das *und*-Vorkommen, um das es hier geht, von der Konversationalistischen Hypothese wirklich nicht bzw. nur dann erfaßt werden könnte, wenn Grices Theorie der Konversations-Implikaturen erweitert oder modifiziert würde. Cohens Darstellung vermittelt, jedenfalls an dieser Stelle, den Eindruck, als habe die sogenannte Konversationalistische Hypothese nichts anderes zu ihrem Inhalt als die Identifikation der Bedeutungen solcher Ausdrücke wie *nicht*; *und*; *wenn, dann* und *oder* mit den formal-logischen Symbolen '¬', '∧', '⊃' und '∨'; der zweite Teil der Konversationalistischen Hypothese, der die spezielle Bedeutung der obigen Ausdrücke in speziellen Kontexten auf Konversations-Prinzipien zurückzuführen versucht, wird von Cohen in der obigen Aussage regelrecht unterschlagen. Denn daß das Antezedens von (9) bzw. (13) im Sinne einer zeitlichen Reihenfolge zu verstehen ist, wird seitens der Konversationalistischen Hypothese nicht geleugnet; es wird nur nicht - wie von seiten der Semantischen Hypothese angenommen - dem Vorkommen von *und* zugeschrieben.

Mit Bezug auf die oben erwähnte Reihenfolge-Interpretation des Vordersatzes von (9) (bzw. (13)) fährt Cohen fort, indem er sagt:

Dies dürfte aber kaum mit der von der Konversationalistischen Hypothese aufgestellten Behauptung konsistent sein, wonach 'wenn, dann' genau die gleiche wahrheitsfunktionale Bedeutung hat wie das formallogische Standardverknüpfungszeichen '⊃'. Denn wenn die Wahrheit von (9) [d. h. (13)] als ganzes nur eine Funktion der Wahrheitswerte des Vorder- und des Nachsatzes ist, und wenn 'und' rein wahrheitsfunktional ist, so daß der Wahrheitswert des Vordersatzes von (9) nur eine Funktion der Wahrheitswerte seiner konjunktiv verknüpften Konstituenten ist, so folgt, daß die Wahrheit von (9) in keiner Weise von irgendeiner Bedingung der zeitlichen Abfolge abhängt, die vermittels konversationeller Vorannahmen durch die Äußerung des Vordersatzes übermittelt wird. D. h. die Wahrheitsfunktionalität von 'und' könnte in solchen Fällen wie (9) nur um den Preis einer Aufgabe der Wahrheitsfunktionalität von 'wenn, dann' aufrechterhalten werden (sowie dadurch, daß in die Theorie der Implikaturen eine Reihe weiterer komplexer Bestimmungen aufgenommen würde). (Ebd.: 406)

Diese Stellungnahme ist in mehrfacher Hinsicht überraschend. Erstens müßte, angesichts der von Cohen (zu Beginn seiner Stellungnahme) ins Auge gefaßten Schwierigkeit einer gleichzeitigen Interpretation von *und* und *wenn, dann* im Sinne reiner Wahrheitsfunktionalität, die Erläuterung (am Ende dieser Stellungnahme) eigentlich umgekehrt lauten, nämlich so, daß die Wahrheitsfunktionalität von *wenn, dann* in solchen Fällen wie (9) nur um den

Preis einer Aufgabe der Wahrheitsfunktionalität von *und* aufrechtzuerhalten sei. Zweitens, die (im Mittelteil der Stellungnahme Cohens) gegebene Begründung ist tautologisch: Die Folgerung, von der dort gesprochen wird (daß die Wahrheit von (9) in keiner Weise von irgendeiner Bedingung der zeitlichen Abfolge abhängt), ist in dem zweiten der beiden vorangestellten Wenn-Sätze (der Begründung) bereits enthalten; denn dort wird vorausgesetzt, daß *und* 'rein wahrheitsfunktional ist, so daß der Wahrheitswert des Vordersatzes von (9) nur eine Funktion der Wahrheitswerte seiner konjunktiv verknüpften Konstituenten ist'.

Wie oben angedeutet, findet sich die bei Cohen aufgeworfene und bei Levinson wiederaufgegriffene Frage nach dem Verhältnis von Semantik und Pragmatik bei der Interpretation komplexer Sätze wie (13) samt der damit einhergehenden Problematik bereits bei Posner (1979) umrissen. Den Reihenfolge-Sinn von und in dem (dem Satz (13) entsprechenden) Satz 'Wenn Anna geheiratet hat und ein Kind bekommen hat, wird sich der Großvater freuen' (= (18)) als *Gesprächsandeutung* bezeichnend, stellt Posner fest:

> Gesprächsandeutungen der Teilsätze können [...] in gewissen Fällen für die Wahrheitsbewertung des Gesamtsatzes ausschlaggebend sein. In diesen Fällen kann man nicht mehr von einem rein wahrheitsfunktionalen Gebrauch der Satzverknüpfer sprechen. Die Erklärungsalternativen sind wie eine Zwickmühle:
> - Wer die Wahrheitsfunktionalität des 'und' retten möchte, indem er behauptet, daß der Vordersatz von (18) wahr ist, weil seine Teilsätze wahr sind, der opfert die Wahrheitsfunktionalität des 'wenn', denn er muß zugeben, daß der Nachsatz trotzdem falsch sein kann.
> - Wer die Wahrheitsfunktionalität des 'wenn' retten möchte, indem er behauptet, daß der Nachsatz von (18) nur dann falsch sein kann, wenn der Vordersatz falsch ist, der opfert die Wahrheitsfunktionalität des 'und', denn er muß zugeben, daß der Vordersatz falsch sein kann, obwohl seine Teilsätze wahr sind. (Posner 1979: 376)

Posner zufolge droht die Pointe einer durchgängig wahrheitsfunktionalen Behandlung aller einschlägigen Satzverknüpfer mit diesem Dilemma verloren zu gehen. Um zu verhindern, daß Ausdrücke dieser Art ungleich behandelt werden, zieht er folgendes in Erwägung:

> Eine Gleichbehandlung ist nur dann zu erreichen, wenn wir die These, daß in der natursprachlichen Kommunikation der Wahrheitswert des Gesamtsatzes eine Funktion der Wahrheitswerte der Teilsätze ist, in ihrer strengen Form fallen lassen. Sie ist nicht in dem Sinne aufrechtzuerhalten, daß in komplexen Satzgefügen der Wahrheitswert des Gesamtsatzes *direkt* aus den Wahrheitswerten der kleinsten Teilsätze errechenbar ist. Vielmehr müssen nach jedem wahrheitsfunktionalen Rechenschritt die anfallenden Gesprächsandeutungen modifizierend einbezogen werden. (Ebd.)

Dem diskutierten Problem versucht Posner also durch ein schrittweises Vorgehen zu begegnen. Wichtig dabei ist vor allem eins: Die Konversationalistische Hypothese darf auf keinen Fall so verstanden werden, als würde sie zum einen fordern, daß die als natürlichsprachliche Entsprechungen der aussagenlogischen Satzoperatoren interpretierten Konjunktionen auf die Bedeutung dieser Operatoren festgelegt seien, und gleichzeitig in Abrede stellen, daß die Konjunktionen in speziellen Kontexten spezielle Bedeutungen haben können. Letzteres wird gerade *nicht* geleugnet; es wird nur anders - und zwar außerhalb der Wortbedeutungen, soll heißen, vor dem Hintergrund der Konversationsmaximen - lokalisiert.

2.2   Zum Phänomenarten-Problem

Daß der K.u.K.-Zusammenhang, das Gricesche Kooperationsprinzip und die Griceschen Konversationsmaximen als bestandteil des sogenannten *Hintergrunds der Bedeutung* angesehen werden kann, dieser Umstand scheint bei Cohen und in der oben wiedergegebenen Argumentation von Levinson nicht hinreichend berücksichtigt zu werden. Searle hat in mehreren seiner Arbeiten darauf hingewiesen, daß die Wahrheitsbedingungen (bzw. andere Arten von Erfüllungsbedingungen) eines Satzes nur gegen einen Hintergrund von Annahmen und Praktiken determiniert werden können (vgl. Searle 1980: 231). Der Begriff der wörtlichen Bedeutung eines Satzes ist "kein kontextfreier Begriff; er hat nur relativ zu vorintentionalen Hintergrund-Annahmen und -Praktiken eine Anwendung." (Searle 1987: 185) "Ändern sich die Hintergrundannahmen, so auch die Wahrheitsbedingungen des Satzes" (Searle 1982: 147). Searle macht dabei geltend, daß sich solche Hintergrundannahmen "nicht als Teil des semantischen Gehalts des Satzes angeben lassen und auch nicht als Voraussetzungen für die Anwendbarkeit dieses semantischen Gehalts." (Ebd.: 148) Denn: "Wenn wir den Hintergrund als Teil des semantischen Gehalts darzustellen versuchten, so wüßten wir niemals, wo wir aufhören sollten; und jeder semantische Gehalt, den wir schaffen, wird noch mehr Hintergrund für sein Verständnis erforderlich machen." (Searle 1987: 188) Gerade darauf scheint hinauszulaufen, was von seiten der Semantischen Hypothese vorgeschlagen wird.

Bestandteil des Hintergrunds, kann der K.u.K.-Zusammenhang als etwas angesehen werden, worauf zurückgegriffen werden kann in Fällen, in denen das hilfreich ist. Auf den K.u.K.-Zusammenhang muß natürlich nicht immer Bezug genommen werden, wenn es gilt, eine Äußerung zu verstehen. Wie die folgenden Sätze zeigen, gibt es Vorkommen von und, die kein 'Aufrufen' des K.u.K.-Zusammenhangs erfordern, um ein Verständnis von und im Sinne von 'und dann', 'und dort' oder 'und währenddessen' etc. zu ermöglichen; solch ein Verständnis würde, wie in (14) und (15), entweder keine Rolle spielen oder, wie in (16), einfach nicht gegeben sein:

(14)   Helge hat das As ausgespielt und Werner die Zehn.
(15)   Werner hat die Zehn ausgespielt und Helge das As.
(16)   Helge ist Zahnarzt, und Werner ist Apotheker.

In all diesen Fällen zeigt das und lediglich an, daß die beiden thematisierten Sachverhalte zusammen gegeben sind.

Eine Bezugnahme auf den K.u.K.-Zusammenhang kann auch durch Explizitheit erübrigt werden, vgl.:

(17)   Anna hat ein Kind bekommen, und dann hat sie geheiratet.

Grice unterscheidet bekanntlich vier Arten der Nichterfüllung einer Maxime: (a) die undemonstrative Maximenverletzung, (b) die Außerkraftsetzung einer Maxime: den Ausstieg, (c) die Erfüllungskollision und (d) die flagrante Nichterfüllung: die Verhöhnung einer Maxime, den offenen Verstoß gegen eine Maxime (vgl. Grice 1975/1993: 253). Auch und gerade die zweite Art der Nichterfüllung einer Konversationsmaxime kann als Evidenz für deren Allgegenwart gewertet werden: Es gibt eine ganze Reihe von Redewendungen, die einen *Ausstieg* signalisieren und deren Existenz unter Bezugnahme auf den K.u.K.-Zusammenhang erklärt werden kann. Beispiele sind: *Ich muß das wahrscheinlich (jetzt) gar nicht sagen, aber ...* (2. Maxime der Quantität*); Ich bin mir nicht sicher, ob es wahr ist, aber ...* (1. Maxime der Qualität); *Ich weiß, es ist irrelevant, aber ...* (Maxime der Relation); *Ich muß dazu etwas weiter ausholen* (3. Maxime der Modalität) (s. Rolf 1994: 106f.). Außerdem gibt es eine relativ große Gruppe sogenannter redecharakterisierender Adverbiale, d. h. Ausdrücke wie *offen gesagt, grob gesagt* und *kurz gesagt*, die als Bezugnahmen auf Konversationsmaximen verstanden (vgl. ebd.: 170ff.; Hagemann 1997) und ebenfalls als Hinweise auf den Umstand angesehen werden können, daß diese Maximen faktisch in Rechnung gestellt werden.

Grice sagt im Hinblick auf Fälle, in denen eine konversationale Implikatur durch die Verhöhnung einer Maxime zustande kommt, die "Maxime sei ausgebeutet worden." (Ebd.: 254) Was aber tut jemand, der, im Unterschied zu einer Äußerung von (17), sagt:

(18)   Anna hat ein Kind bekommen, und sie hat geheiratet?

Eine Verhöhnung einer Konversationsmaxime stellt, was der Sprecher sagt, sicherlich nicht dar; genausowenig wie der Diskurs

(19)   Die Straßenbahn hielt. Der Schaffner stieg aus.

eine Verhöhnung einer Maxime darstellt. Was man allerdings feststellen kann, ist: daß der Sprecher in beiden Fällen, (18) und (19), nicht *mehr* sagt, als erforderlich ist. Das Verhalten des Sprechers steht, mit anderen Worten, in beiden Fällen in Übereinstimmung mit der zweiten Maxime der Quantität (nach der ein Sprecher seinen Beitrag nicht informativer als nötig machen soll). Wie ließe sich das Verhalten des Sprechers beschreiben? Da der Begriff der Ausbeutung für die Verhöhnung einer Maxime reserviert ist, könnte man angesichts solcher Äußerungen wie (18) und (19) davon sprechen, daß der Sprecher von der Existenz der zweiten Quantitätsmaxime *profitiert*: Der Sprecher ist in solchen Fällen ein - 'stiller' - *Nutznießer* der entsprechenden Maxime; er profitiert davon, daß der K.u.K.-Zusammenhang in Kraft ist. Der Sprecher mag sich darauf verlassen, daß der Adressat von sich aus - in der Annahme, daß die Maximen beachtet worden sind - in einem *erweiterten* Sinne versteht, was der Sprecher gesagt hat.

Es scheinen hier zwei grundsätzlich zu unterscheidende Implikatur-Arten vorzuliegen:
Fälle der ersteren Art - Fälle, in denen Maximenverhöhnungen vorliegen -, könnten als Sprecher-Implikaturen bezeichnet werden, Fälle der anderen Art - Fälle, in denen der Sprecher stiller Nutznießer des K.u.K.-Zusammenhangs ist -, könnten Äußerungs- oder vielleicht sogar Hörer-Implikaturen genannt werden (vgl. dazu auch Rolf 1994: 128ff.). Auße-

rungs-Implikaturen, das sind Folgerungen, die gezogen werden, damit nicht unterstellt werden muß, daß gegen eine Konversationsmaxime verstoßen worden sei. In diesem Sinne haben Äußerungs-Implikaturen das Moment der Kontrafaktizität. Äußerungs-Impliakturen führen zudem dazu, daß das jeweils Gesagte in einem umfassenden oder gar im vollen Sinne verstanden wird. Bei den Implikaturen, von denen Levinson behauptet, sie würden das Gesagte mitbestimmen, handelt es sich um Äußerungs-Implikaturen; das gilt jedenfalls für die Phänomene des Bereichs A.

Zumindest im Ansatz findet sich auch diese, im Grunde genommen Rezipienten-orientierte Einschätzung bereits bei Posner - selbst wenn dieser, die zur Debatte stehenden Erscheinungen (die speziellen Bedeutungen, die *und* annehmen kann) mit der Bezeichnung "Gesprächsandeutungen" (Posner 1979: 357) bzw. "conversational suggestions" (Posner 1980: 179) versehend, eine Sichtweise nahelegt, die immer noch etwas zu sehr eine spezielle Sprecher-Aktivität beinhaltet. Posner sagt:

> Die Konstruktion von Andeutungen ['suggestions'] entspricht dem Bestreben des Rezipienten, das Sprachverhalten des Kommunikationspartners als rationales Verhalten zu interpretieren. Wird ein Satz geäußert, dessen Bedeutung - wörtlich verstanden - kein Beitrag zum anerkannten Gesprächszweck ist, so fragt sich der Rezipient, ob der Sprecher etwas anderes meint, als was er - wörtlich verstanden - gesagt hat. (Posner 1979: 356)

Was gemeint gewesen sein könnte, versucht der Rezipient durch ein Räsonnement zu ermitteln, ein Räsonnement, von dem Posner (1979: 354) sagt, es laufe meist automatisch ab und bleibe "daher weitgehend unterhalb der Bewußtseinsschwelle".

Für den vorliegenden Diskussionszusammenhang von größter Wichtigkeit ist der *kontrafaktische* Charakter, den ein solches Räsonnement in den bei Posner erörterten Fällen hat. Eine *Verhöhnung* einer Konversationsmaxime, das ist zu beachten, liegt in diesen Fällen nämlich nicht vor. Posner stellt hinsichtlich des Räsonnements fest: "Damit das Räsonnement überhaupt in Gang kommt, ist es wichtig festzustellen, gegen welche Maxime rationalen Handelns die Äußerung verstoßen *hätte*, falls sie wörtlich verstanden *worden wäre*." (Ebd.: 356; Hervorhebung hinzugefügt)

Die Kontrafaktizität eines - (lediglich) auf seiten des Rezipienten imaginierten, in Wirklichkeit aber gar nicht vorgekommen - Verstoßes gegen eine Maxime ist bei Posner ein durchgängiges Merkmal der dem Rezipienten zugeschriebenen Zusammenhangs-Konstruktionen - der Konstruktionen, durch die der Rezipient den Sprecher gegen die Unterstellung, eine Maxime verhöhnt zu haben, in Schutz zu nehmen versucht. Solche Konstruktionen sind erforderlich, "wenn der Rezipient nicht annehmen will, daß der Sprecher gegen eine der Gesprächsmaximen verstößt." (Posner 1979: 369f.)

Kontrafaktisch, den Sprecher gegen die Unterstellung einer Maximenverhöhnung in Schutz nehmend, sind dann auch die Einzelfall-Beschreibungen, die Posner gibt. Solche Beschreibungen werden schon hinsichtlich solcher Sätze wie (20) bis (22) vorgenommen:

(20) Anna ist in der Küche, und (sie) bäckt Krapfen (... und dort/und da ...)
(21) Das Fenster war offen, und es zog (... und von dort/und daher ...)

(22)   Peter heiratete Anna, und sie bekam ein Kind (... und dann/und danach ...)
(vgl. ebd.: 365f.)

Das in diesen Sätzen vorkommende *und* kann in allen Fällen in einem spezifischen (dem in Klammern angegebenen) Sinn verstanden werden; dieser jeweilige Sinn läßt sich als Gesprächsandeutung rekonstruieren. In bezug auf (20) beispielsweise stellt Posner fest:

> Wer ausdrücklich darauf hinweist, daß Anna in der Küche ist, dann aber *ohne weitere Ortsangabe* sagt, daß sie Krapfen bäckt, macht sich der *Unterdrückung relevanter Information* schuldig, wenn er damit sagen will, daß die Krapfen an einem anderen Ort gebacken werden. Dies wäre ein Verstoß gegen [...] [die erste Maxime der Quantität]. Um ihn nicht annehmen zu müssen, interpretiert der Rezipient die Formulierung von [...] [(20)] als *Andeutung der Ortsgleichheit* (... und dort/und da ...). (Posner 1979: 371f.)

Nach dem gleichen Muster sind auch die anderen Charakterisierungen, die Posner gibt, gebildet. In bezug auf (22) beispielsweise heißt es:

> Wer zunächst berichtet, daß eine Frau heiratete und gleich danach ohne weitere Zeitangabe sagt, daß sie ein Kind bekam, macht sich *ungeordneter Berichterstattung* schuldig, wenn er damit sagen will, daß die Heirat erst nach der Geburt erfolgt ist. Das wäre ein Verstoß gegen [...] [die vierte Gricesche Modalitätsmaxime ('Der Reihe nach!')]. Um ihn nicht annehmen zu müssen, interpretiert der Rezipient die Formulierung von [...] [(22)] als *Andeutung einer gleichlaufenden Reihenfolge zwischen Bericht und Berichtetem* (... und dann/und danach ...). (Ebd.: 372)

Wem das in diesen Erklärungen vorkommende Wort 'Andeutung' als zu stark erscheint - vielleicht weil es etwas übertrieben ist, wenn man jemandem, der solche Sätze wie (20) bis (22) äußert, die Absicht unterstellt, er wolle damit über das von ihm Gesagte hinaus irgendetwas andeuten -, kann den Ausdruck 'als Andeutung' ersetzen durch 'im Sinne'. Die entsprechend modifizierten Formulierungen würden dem Umstand eher gerecht, daß es vorwiegend Aktivitäten des Rezipienten sind, von denen in den Erklärungen die Rede ist. Wirkliche Maximenverhöhnungen liegen im Falle von Äußerungen solcher Sätze wie (20) bis (22) nicht vor; die Interpretationen des Rezipienten erlauben es diesem, den Sprecher von dem (theoretisch möglichen) Verdacht einer Maximenverhöhnung freisprechen zu können.

Die bei Posner beschriebenen Fälle zeigen einen Rezipienten, der - eher mehr als weniger - von sich aus in Gricescher Hinsicht agiert: Es ist der Rezipient, der - an sich unauffällige - Äußerungen (wie (20) bis (22)) vor dem Hintergrund der Griceschen Maximen interpretiert, um nicht annehmen zu müssen, daß sich der Sprecher der Unterdrückung relevanter Information, ungeordneter Berichterstattung oder ähnlicher Vergehen schuldig gemacht hat - was der Sprecher im übrigen auch nur dann getan hätte, wenn er mit seiner jeweiligen Äußerung etwas hätte übermitteln wollen, was der - spezifischen - 'und dann'- etc. Interpretation, die der Rezipient zugunsten des Sprechers dessen Äußerung auferlegt, zuwiderlaufen würde.

Sollte es sich so, wie bei Posner geschildert, verhalten, dann ist davon auszugehen, daß der Gricesche Maximenkatalog allgegenwärtig ist, daß er selbst im Hinblick auf die harmloseste Äußerung in Rechnung zu stellen ist oder sogar gestellt wird. Das heißt, die Griceschen Konversationsmaximen werden nicht erst dann 'aufgerufen', wenn sie durch den Sprecher verhöhnt werden, sie bilden einen Hintergrund für prinzipiell jede Äußerung. Auch unauffällige oder unmarkierte Äußerungen scheinen in einem speziellen Sinn verstanden zu werden. Dieser jeweilige Sinn braucht aber nicht in die Bedeutung der geäußerten Ausdrücke hineinverlegt zu werden, wie von den Vertretern der Semantischen Hypothese vorgeschlagen; er braucht die sogenannte semantische Komponente nicht zu belasten, er ist über die Maximen zugänglich und kann unter Berufung auf diese in die jeweiligen Äußerungen hineingelesen werden.

In "Further Notes on Logic and Conversation" hat Grice noch einmal die von ihm vertretene Position bezüglich der Satzverknüpfer zu verdeutlichen versucht. Wer z. B. so etwas sagt wie:

(23)   Meine Frau ist in Oxford, oder sie ist in London.

bringt eine in epistemischer Hinsicht bestehende Unsicherheit zum Ausdruck oder, wie man auch sagen könnte, die Existenz nicht-wahrheitsfunktionaler Gründe dafür, daß er sich so geäußert hat, wie er es getan hat. Solche Gründe bzw. eine solche Unsicherheit möchte Grice nicht zu den Bedeutungsmerkmalen der Konjunktion *oder* rechnen; denn er ist der Meinung, daß die (von ihm entdeckten) Konversationsprinzipien es nicht zulassen würden, daß *oder* unter normalen Umständen ohne zumindest die Implikatur der Existenz nicht-wahrheitsfunktionaler Gründe verwendet würde (vgl. Grice 1989: 47). Sobald und insofern als Konversationsmaximen in Rechnung gestellt werden, ist die semantische Komponente entlastet. Und wenn es nicht der Sprecher ist, der durch die Verhöhnung einer Maxime auf diese aufmerksam macht, dann ist es der Hörer, der sie an die ihm gegenüber gemachten Äußerungen heranträgt, um möglichst viel Information aus ihnen herauszuholen.

Bliebe zu fragen: ob die semantische Komponente, wenn der Rezipient von sich aus bei der Interpretation von Äußerungen auf die Konversationsmaximen Bezug nimmt, in der Gefahr schwebt, von der (unter anderem durch die Maximen repräsentierten) pragmatischen Komponente 'überrumpelt' zu werden? Ist die vermeintliche Reinheit der semantischen Komponente gefährdet? Und ist, wenn letzteres sollte zu Recht zu befürchten sein, auch die von Grice favorisierte Erklärungsweise gefährdet? Daß Fragen wie diese mit 'Ja' zu beantworten sind, genau das ist es, was Levinson vorschwebt, wenn er von dem Griceschen Zirkel spricht (dem zufolge das Gesagte als eine der Vorbedingungen einer Konversations-Implikatur selbst durch solche Implikaturen determiniert sei).

Wie bereits angedeutet, beruft sich Levinson (o. J.: 6, 8) auf eine Stelle bei Grice, an der dieser sagt, daß eine vollständige Bestimmung des Gesagten (a) die Identität des Redegegenstands, (b) den Äußerungszeitpunkt und (c) die bei der Äußerungsgelegenheit vorliegende Bedeutung der geäußerten Phrase voraussetze. Bei dieser Berufung Levinsons auf Grice scheint es sich nun aber um einen typischen Fall von 'Aus-dem-Zusammenhang-Zitieren' zu handeln. Es hat zumindest den Anschein, als würde die Bemerkung von Grice, auf die sich Levinson bezieht, lediglich so etwas wie ein allgemeines Zugeständnis gegenüber feinkörnigen Propositionsbestimmungen sein. Um das überprüfen zu können, sei hier der Zusammenhang der Textstelle wiedergegeben, auf die sich Levinson beruft. (Die Stelle selbst ist in dem folgenden Zitat hervorgehoben.)

> Wie ich das Wort 'sagen' hier benutze, soll das, was jemand gesagt hat, in enger Beziehung zur konventionellen Bedeutung der von ihm geäußerten Worte (des geäußerten Satzes) stehen. Angenommen, jemand hat den Satz 'Er kommt von dem Laster nicht los' geäußert. Mit Kenntnis des Deutschen, aber ohne Kenntnis der Äußerungsumstände wüßte man - unter der Annahme, daß er gewöhnliches Deutsch und wörtlich gesprochen hat - etwas darüber, was der Sprecher gesagt hat. Man wüßte, daß er über eine bestimmte Person oder ein bestimmtes Tier männlichen Geschlechts x gesagt hat, daß zum Zeitpunkt der Äußerung (gleichgültig, wann das war) entweder (1) x unfähig war, sich selbst von einem schlechten Charakterzug zu befreien, oder (2) an einem Beförderungsmittel einer gewissen Art festhing (natürlich nur so in etwa dargestellt). *Um jedoch ganz und gar zu bestimmen, was der Sprecher gesagt hat, müßte man (a) die Identität von x, (b) den Zeitpunkt der Äußerung und (c) die bei dieser bestimmten Äußerungsgelegenheit vorliegende Bedeutung der Wendung 'von dem Laster nicht loskommen' [eine Entscheidung zwischen (1) und (2)] kennen.* Diese kurze Andeutung über meine Verwendung von 'sagen' läßt offen, ob jemand, der (heute) sagt 'Harold Wilson ist ein großer Mann', dasselbe gesagt hat wie einer, der (ebenfalls heute) sagt 'Der britische Premierminister ist ein großer Mann' - vorausgesetzt, beide wüßten, daß die beiden singulären Terme dieselbe Referenz haben. Wie die Entscheidung in dieser Frage aber auch immer ausfallen mag, der von mir sogleich bereitgestellte Apparat wird beliebigen Implikaturen gerecht werden können, für die es etwas ausmachen könnte, ob der eine - und nicht der andere - singuläre Term im geäußerten Satz vorkommt. Solche Implikaturen würden bloß zu verschiedenen Maximen in Beziehung stehen. (Grice 1975/1993: 246f.)

Grice, das ist die These, die hier - contra Levinson - vertreten werden soll, operiert bewußt mit einem eher vagen Begriff von 'sagen': Um in einer Implikatur-trächtigen Situation zu bestimmen, was der Sprecher gesagt hat, genügt es festzustellen, was über einen Gegenstand, welcher Art dieser auch sei, gesagt worden ist. Grice räumt zwar ein, daß zu einer genaueren oder umfassenden Bestimmung des Gesagten mehr gehört; er kann aber durchaus so verstanden werden, daß solch eine umfassende Bestimmung des Gesagten für die in Implikaturzusammenhängen relevanten Zwecke nicht erforderlich ist. Wie sonst wäre zu erklären, daß Grice, nachdem er eingeräumt hat, daß zu einer umfassenden Bestimmung des Gesagten mehr gehört (bzw. nachdem er aufgezählt hat, was seiner Ansicht nach alles dazu gehört), ausdrücklich darauf aufmerksam macht, daß die von ihm favorisierte Verwendung von 'sagen' offen lasse, ob mit den beiden Sätzen über Harold Wilson bzw. den britischen Premierminister dasselbe gesagt werde. Ob dasselbe gesagt wird, die Frage nach der Identität des Gesagten ist in Grices Augen offenbar mit dem Hinweis auf die Referenzidentität der Terme 'Harold Wilson' und 'Der britische Premierminister' noch nicht beantwortet. Und das

Gesagte, das in die Bestimmung dessen, was gegebenenfalls impliziert wurde, eingeht, muß selbst nicht umfassend bestimmt sein, um hinsichtlich der Bestimmung des Implizierten fungibel zu sein.

Daß es sich in der Tat so verhält, läßt sich anhand des folgenden, von Levinson (1983: 97) selbst vorgebrachten Beispiels illustrieren:

(24) S: Kannst du mir sagen, wie spät es ist?
      H: Nun, der Milchmann ist [gerade] gekommen.

Nach Levinsons zu dem Zirkelvorwurf führender Diagnose müßte S, um bestimmen zu können, was H gesagt hat, unter anderem die Identität des Referenten des Terms 'der Milchmann' kennen. Letzteres ist aber nicht notwendig: S kann verstehen, was H impliziert hat, ohne zu wissen, *wer* der Milchmann ist, den H erwähnt hat. Eine umfassende Bestimmung des Gesagten ist für die Ermittlung des Implizierten nicht erforderlich, es genügt, in einem vergleichsweise vagen Sinn zu wissen, was gesagt worden ist.

Auch wenn es die Zirkelfans enttäuscht und ihnen die Schadenfreude verdirbt - nach den vorangegangenen Bemerkungen muß festgestellt werden, daß Levinsons Zirkelvorwurf ungerechtfertigt ist. Die Fälle, die bei Levinson besprochen sind, vermitteln eine Ahnung von der Allgegenwart der Konversationsmaximen und der Möglichkeit des Rezipienten, vor deren Hintergrund möglichst viel in Äußerungen hineinzulesen; was sie *nicht* zeigen, ist, daß, was gesagt wurde, durch Implikaturen bestimmt werden muß, um zur Bestimmung der Implikaturen herangezogen werden zu können. Zu letzterem Behuf scheint eine vergleichsweise vage Bestimmung des Gesagten auszureichen. So jedenfalls scheint es Grice gemeint zu haben.

Literatur

Black, M. (1972-73/1993): "Bedeutung und Intention". In: G. Meggle, ed., 52-81.
Carston, R. (1988): "Implicature, Explicature, and Truth-Theoretic Semantics". In: R. Kempson, ed.: Mental Representations. The Interface between Language and Reality. Cambridge: Cambridge University Press, 155-181.
Cohen, L.J. (1971/1993): "Die logischen Partikel[n] der natürlichen Sprache. (Bemerkungen zu einer Hypothese von Grice)". In: G. Meggle, ed., 395-418.
Grice, H.P. (1975/1993): "Logik und Konversation". In: G. Meggle, ed., 243-265.
Grice, H.P. (1989): Studies in the Way of Words. Cambridge, Mass.: Harvard University Press.
Hagemann, J. (1997): Reflexiver Sprachgebrauch. Diktumscharakterisierung aus Gricescher Sicht. Opladen: Westdeutscher Verlag.
Horn, L.R. (1984): "Toward a New Taxonomy for Pragmatic Inference: Q-based and R-based Implicature". In: D. Schiffrin, ed. : Meaning, Form, and Use in Context: Linguistic Applications. Washington, D. C.: Georgetown University Press, 11-42.
Horn, L.R. (1989): A Natural History of Negation. Chicago: The University of Chicago Press.
Levinson, S.C. (1983): Pragmatics. Cambridge: Cambridge University Press.
Levinson, S.C. (o. J.): Generalized Conversational Implicature and the Semantics/Pragmatics Interface (or how you can't do semantics without first doing pragmatics). (Unveröffentlicht)

Meggle, G. (1990): "Intentionalistische Semantik. Ein paar grundsätzliche Mißverständnisse und Klärungen". In: Forum für Philosophie Bad Homburg, ed.: Intentionalität und Verstehen. Frankfurt/Main: Suhrkamp, 109-126.

Meggle, G., ed. (1993): Handlung, Kommunikation, Bedeutung. Frankfurt/Main: Suhrkamp.

Posner, R. (1979): "Bedeutung und Gebrauch der Satzverknüpfer in den natürlichen Sprachen". In: G. Grewendorf, ed.: Sprechakttheorie und Semantik. Frankfurt/Main: Suhrkamp, 345-385.- Übers.: "Semantics and Pragmatics of Sentence Connectives in Natural Language". In: J.R. Searle & F. Kiefer & M. Bierwisch, eds., 169-203.

Rolf, E. (1994): Sagen und Meinen. Paul Grices Theorie der Konversations-Implikaturen. Opladen: Westdeutscher Verlag.

Rolf, E. (1997): Illokutionäre Kräfte. Grundbegriffe der Illokutionslogik. Opladen: Westdeutscher Verlag.

Searle, J.R. (1980): "The Background of Meaning". In: J.R. Searle & F. Kiefer & M. Bierwisch, eds., 221-232.

Searle, J.R. (1982): "Wörtliche Bedeutung". In: J.R. Searle (1982): Ausdruck und Bedeutung. Untersuchungen zur Sprechakttheorie. Frankfurt/Main: Suhrkamp, 139-159.

Searle, J.R. (1987): Intentionalität. Eine Abhandlung zur Philosophie des Geistes. Frankfurt/Main: Suhrkamp.

Searle, J.R. & F. Kiefer & M. Bierwisch, eds. (1980): Speech Act Theory and Pragmatics. Dordrecht: Reidel.

Wilson, D. (1975): Presuppositions and Non-Truth-Conditional Semantics. New York: Academic Press.

Why Gricean Democracy Is Worse than Either Russellian or Strawsonian Monarchy

Savas L. Tsohatzidis, Thessaloniki

Triads of sentences like those below - that is, an affirmative subject-predicate sentence with a definite description in subject position, a negative subject-predicate sentence with the same definite description in subject position, and a sentence affirming that at least one entity of the sort denoted by the definite description exists - are well known for provoking incompatible reactions to the question whether classical two-valued logic provides an appropriate model for the representation of meaning in natural language:

(1)   The King of France is bald.
(2)   The King of France is not bald.
(3)   There is a King of France.

Strawson (1950) and Russell (1905) are classic expressions of conflicting answers to that question.

According to the Stawsonian analysis, these sentences clearly show that classical two-valued logic is not an appropriate metalanguage for natural language semantics. For, on Strawson's view, the falsity of (3) necessitates the falsity, if not the truth-valuelessness, not only of (1) but also of (2) - if there is no King of France, says Strawson, it cannot be true either that the King of France is bald, as (1) claims, or that the King of France is not bald, as (2) claims. But since (2) is the negation of (1), this means that classical two-valued logic cannot correctly represent that negation. For, on that logic, a sentence and its negation cannot be both true or both untrue - if the one is true, the other must be false, and conversely.

According to the Russellian analysis, however, there is no good reason to suppose that these sentences show that classical two-valued logic is an inappropriate metalanguage for natural language semantics. For, on Russell's view, the falsity of (3), though necessitating the falsity of (1), does not necessitate the falsity of (2) - if there is no King of France, says Russell, it cannot, of course, be true that the King of France is bald, as (1) claims, but it *is* true that the King of France is not bald, as (2) claims. Thus, (2), which is the negation of (1), does have a truth value opposite to that of (1), which is exactly what classical two-valued logic would lead us to expect, if it was assumed to provide an appropriate means for representing natural language negation.

The clash between the Strawsonian and the Russellian position in this dispute is a clash between a desire to respect certain intuitive demands and a desire to respect certain ideological demands. Strawson's view has the merit of respecting the intuitive demand that something must be recognized to be radically wrong with both (1) and (2) when the truth of (3) is not granted. But since the thing that, in such a case, is wrong with both (1) and (2) is, according to Strawson, that these sentences become either false or truth-valueless, his view cannot accommodate the ideological demand of respecting the authority of classical two-valued logic as a metalanguage for natural language semantics. Russell's view, on the other hand, has the merit of respecting precisely that ideological demand. However, it respects it only by refusing to respect the intuitive demand of recognizing that there is something radically wrong with both (1) and (2) when the truth of (3) is not granted. Given the character of this clash, it is not surprising that debates on the matter have tended to be inconclusive: if one is inclined to value one's intuitions on particular cases higher than any overall ideology, one is unlikely to be convinced by Russell; if one is determined to value one's overall ideology higher than any intuitions about particular cases, one is unlikely to be convinced by Strawson; and since values are things to which people tend to stick rather obstinately, Russellians and Strawsonians tend to form irreconcilable groups in this area.

In his characteristically eirenic way, Grice (1981) has proposed that a satisfactory compromise between the Strawsonian and the Russellian position is possible - a compromise that, if acceptable, would vindicate his own general theory of linguistic interpretation as well. Grice's basic idea is, in effect, that an uttered sentence's perceived significance is the joint result of two computations: a semantic computation that yields, notably, the sentence's *implications* (that is, those propositions whose untruth would render the sentence itself untrue), and a pragmatic computation that yields, notably, the sentence's conversational *implicatures* (that is, those propositions whose untruth would render the sentence itself not strictly speaking untrue, but nevertheless highly misleading). Armed with the implication-implicature distinction (and, more generally, with the semantics-pragmatics distinction), Grice then suggests that the Russell-Strawson dispute over the proper analysis of triads of sentences like those considered above can be resolved in a way that gives at least partial satisfaction to both interested parties.

According to Grice, the proper interpretation of both (1) and (2) does crucially involve the assumption that the proposition expressed in (3) is true rather than false. However, the level on which that assumption operates in the interpretation of (1) is not *of the same kind* as the level on which it operates in the interpretation of (2). In particular, the assumption that (3) is true is part of the semantic computation of (1), and (3) must consequently be described as an ordinary *implication* of (1): if it is not true that there is a King of France, it can certainly not be true that the King of France is bald, as (1) claims. However, the assumption that (3) is true is, according to Grice, not part of the semantic but rather part of the pragmatic computation of (2), and (3) must consequently be described not as an implication but rather as a conversational *implicature* of (2): if it not true that there is a King of France, Grice suggests, it is highly misleading, though not strictly speaking untrue, to claim, as (2) does, that the King of France is not bald. Given, then, that a satisfactory account of linguistic interpretation must pay equal attention to the semantic and to the pragmatic computations that such interpretation involves, the Russellian and the Strawsonian approaches, once properly interpreted, should be regarded as offering complementary rather than competing insights: What Russell was really investigating were the semantic effects of the falsity of (3) on the interpretation of (1) and (2); failing, however, to recognize that a proposition's falsity can have not only semantic but also pragmatic effects, he concluded that it is only (1) and not (2) that becomes in any way inappropriate when the truth of (3) is not granted. What Strawson was really investigating were the pragmatic effects of the falsity of (3) on the interpretation of (1) and (2); failing, however, to recognize that pragmatic and semantic effects are not of the same kind, he concluded that it is in exactly the same way that (1) and (2) become inappropriate when the truth of (3) is not granted. If, on the other hand, both the existence and, especially, the *distinctness* of semantic and pragmatic computations in linguistic interpretation is acknowledged, we can reconcile the Russellian and the Strawsonian accounts by retaining the former as an account of the semantics and the latter as an account of the pragmatics of the linguistic materials involved.

As Grice was well aware, many persons would be unlikely to be impressed by any of this, unless they were given some reasons for believing that the distinction between implications and conversational implicatures (and, hence, between semantics and pragmatics) can be shown to have some reliable linguistic reflexes, both in general and in the particular kind of case on which the Russell-Strawson debate is centered. If, given a sentence y and an assumption x that the utterance of the sentence communicates, two people strongly disagree as to whether (a) or (b) is the case,

(a)   assumption x is necessary for the truth and not merely for the non-misleadingness of sentence y

(b)   assumption x is necessary merely for the non-misleadingness and not for the truth of sentence y

then you can hardly hope to resolve the dispute between them just by loudly telling them that (a) is the case, or just by loudly telling them that (b) is the case. Instead, you must describe some dispositional, and intersubjectively ascertainable, property that the sentence x should reasonably be expected to manifest *if* (a) was indeed the case, you must describe another dispositional, and intersubjectively ascertainable, property that the sentence x should reasonably be expected to manifest *if* (b) was indeed the case, and, having tested whether the sentence x actually manifests the one or the other of these properties, you can then advise the disputants that it would be reasonable, given the test's results, to end the dispute by concluding that (a) is indeed the case, or, alternatively, that it would be reasonable, given the test's results, to end the dispute by concluding that (b) is indeed the case. Grice, accordingly, has tried to make the invocation of the distinction between semantic implications and pragmatic implicatures respectable by devising a test of the sort just described; and it is on the basis of the application of that test to the kind of data involved in the Russell-Strawson dispute that he has supposed that the dispute can be resolved to the partial satisfaction of both interested parties.

In its general (and ideal) form, this test, which is known as the "cancellability" test, says, in effect, the following:

(A) an assumption x is a semantic implication of a sentence y (that is, it is necessary for the truth and not merely for the non-misleadingness of sentence y) just in case it is *non-cancellable* (that is, just in case it is impossible for the sentence y to be acceptably conjoined with the denial of some formulation of x)

(B) an assumption x is a pragmatic implicature of sentence y (that is, it is necessary merely for the non-misleadingness and not for the truth of sentence y) just in case it is *cancellable* (that is, just in case it is possible for the sentence y to be acceptably conjoined with the denial of some formulation of x)

And a particular application of this test, Grice claims, does show that his proposed resolution of the Russell-Strawson dispute is indeed well motivated. The resolution's central claim, it will be recalled, is that the assumption about the existence of the entity denoted by a definite description is a semantic *implication* of affirmative subject-predicate sentences where the definite description occupies subject position, whereas it is a pragmatic *implicature* of negative subject-predicate sentences where the definite description occupies subject position. And, applied to the thesis, the test would claim that, if the thesis is true, then the conjunction of the denial of the existence assumption with the affirmative sentences should be unacceptable, whereas the conjunction of the denial of the existence assumption with the negative sentences would be acceptable. But this, Grice contends, is exactly what happens: when the affirmative sentences are conjoined with the denial of sentences expressing the relevant existence assumptions, the results are invariably unacceptable, as in (4) below, whereas when the negative sentences are conjoined with the denial of sentences expressing the relevant existence assumptions the results are invariably acceptable, as in (5) below:

(4) * The King of France is bald, but he doesn't exist.
(5) The King of France is not bald, since he doesn't exist.

The test, therefore, certifies that the existence assumption is a semantic implication of the affirmative sentences whereas it is only a pragmatic implicature of the negative sentences - which is precisely what Grice's resolution scheme was assuming, by construing Russell's analysis as a contribution to the semantics and Strawson's analysis as a contribution to the pragmatics of the sentences concerned.

It would be no exaggeration to say that Grice's approach is *the* dominant contemporary approach to the Russell-Strawson dispute on definite descriptions (which is not to deny, of course, that several variations within that approach are possible, including the one - whose examination would not be relevant for present purposes -, that tries to make finer distinctions between the kind of pragmatically conveyed propositions that are supposedly associated with definite descriptions and the kind of pragmatically conveyed propositions that are associated with more traditional instances of the phenomenon of conversational implicature). And it would also be no exaggeration to say that the cancellability test is *the* test to which everyone appeals when he or she is being asked to justify analytical decisions taken in the name of the supposed distinction between semantic and pragmatic aspects of linguistic interpretation. I believe, however, that Grice's proposed resolution of the Russell-Strawson debate is clearly unsuccessful. And I also believe that the reason for its failure is that, initial appearances notwithstanding, the cancellability test can be shown, by being applied to a rich variety of data relevant to the Russell-Strawson dispute, to be clearly unreliable as a means of giving determinate content to the supposed distinction between semantic and pragmatic aspect of linguistic interpretation. What I offer in what follows, then, is neither a novel way of resolving the Russell-Strawson dispute (if that dispute can ever be solved), nor a novel way of giving sense to the semantics-pragmatics distinction (assuming that that distinction is, in some sense, worth saving). My more limited (but, if attainable, presumably not unimportant) aim is to show, first, that the dominant, Gricean, resolution of the dispute is not really a resolution at all, and secondly, that the dominant way of justifying the semantics-pragmatics distinction, on which the supposed resolution was based, is deeply unsatisfactory, especially (but not exclusively) in so far as the treatment of theoretically crucial cases is concerned.

The justification of the proposed resolution of the Russell-Strawson dispute in terms of the implication-implicature distinction derives, Grice claims, from the results of the cancellability test. And this must be taken to mean that, according to Grice, all conjunctions of the form "The x F-s, but there are no such things as x-s" (or of relevant variants of this form, such as "The x F-s, but it is not the case that an x exists") and all conjunctions of the form "The x doesn't F, since there are no such things as x-s" (or of relevant variants of this form, such as "The x doesn't F, since it is not the case that an x exists") instantiate *only* the acceptability pattern shown in (i),

(i)   *The x F-s, but it is not the case that an x exists.
         The x doesn't F, since it is not the case that an x exists.

and not any of the other logically possible acceptability patterns shown in (ii) - (iv):

(ii)   The x F-s, but it is not the case that an x exists.
         *The x doesn't F, since it is not the case that an x exists.

(iii)   The x F-s , but it is not the case that an x exists.
         The x doesn't F, since it is not the case that an x exists.

(iv)   *The x F-s , but it is not the case that an x exists.
         *The x doesn't F, since it is not the case that an x exists.

It is, in fact, the instantiation of the acceptability pattern shown in (i) and not of any of the other logically possible ones that would show that the existence-assumption is (because of its non-cancellability) a semantic implication of affirmative sentences with definite descriptions in subject position and (because of its cancellability) a pragmatic implicature of negative sentences with definite descriptions in subject position. If, instead, the conjunctions followed the pattern shown in (ii), this would imply, contrary to Grice's claims, that the existence assumption is a semantic implication of the *negative* sentences and a pragmatic implicature of the *affirmative* ones; if the conjunctions followed the pattern shown in (iii), this would imply, contrary to Grice's claims, that the existence assumption is a pragmatic implicature (rather than a semantic implication) of *both* the affirmative and the negative sentences; and if the conjunctions followed the pattern in (iv), this would imply, contrary to Grice's claims, that the existence assumption is a semantic implication (rather than a pragmatic implicature) of *both* the affirmative and the negative sentences.

The obvious question to be asked, then, is whether all relevant conjunctions instantiate (like (4) and (5) above) the pattern shown in (i), or whether there are relevant conjunctions that instantiate any of the other logically possible acceptability patterns. And the answer to that question is that, unfortunately for Grice, *all the other logically possible patterns* are also instantiated.

Consider, to begin with, the following pairs of sentences:

(6)   (a) The King of France is a creature of your imagination, but he doesn't really exist.
       (b) *The King of France is not a creature of your imagination, since he doesn't really exist.

(7)   (a) The golden mountain is just a human invention, but it doesn't really exist.
       (b) *The golden mountain is not just a human invention, since it doesn't really exist.

(8)   (a) The Loch Ness monster is merely a fairy tale subject, but it doesn't really exist.
       (b) *The Loch Ness monster is not merely a fairy tale subject, since it doesn't really exist.

Since the (a)-members of these pairs are clearly acceptable and the (b)-members clearly unacceptable, each pair is an instance of the pattern shown in (ii), and must therefore be interpreted by the cancellability test as showing that the existence assumption is a semantic implication of the *negative* sentences where a definite description occupies subject position, whereas it is only a pragmatic implicature of the *affirmative* sentences where a definite description occupies subject position. And this, of course, is the exact opposite of Grice's claim that the existence assumption is semantically associated with the affirmative sentences and only pragmatically associated with negative ones. (It is worth noting here that it would be unwise to try to avoid these counterexamples by claiming that, because of a necessary connection between the concept of inexistence, on the one hand, and the concepts of imagination, invention and fiction, on the other, the affirmative sentences above are 'covertly' negative whereas the negative ones are 'covertly' affirmative, and that, therefore, the acceptabilities and unaccepabilities observed in the examples 'really' instantiate the pattern shown in (i), which conforms to Grice's predictions. The main problem with this suggestion is that none of the alleged necessary connections does in fact obtain. That an entity has become the subject of a fairy tale does not necessarily mean that that entity never existed (the fact that there may be fairy tales where Alexander the Great plays a prominent part, for example, does not necessarily mean that Alexander the Great has never existed). That something is a human invention does not necessarily mean that that thing does not exist (the standard meter and the dollar are merely human inventions, of course, but this seems hardly a reason for claiming that neither of these things exists). And that an object or a state of affairs is imagined does not necessarily mean that it is not actual (you may, for example, be imagining that someone is writing love letters to you, and it may be the case that, unbeknownst to you, that person is actually writing love letters to you at the very moment at which you are imagining him doing so). But if there are no necessary connections between the concept of inexistence, on the one hand, and the concepts of imagination, invention, and fiction, on the other, it cannot be supposed either that the affirmative sentences above are 'covertly' negative or the negative sentences above are 'covertly' affirmative. And if that supposition cannot be maintained, the only acceptability pattern that the examples must be acknowledged to instantiate is, as claimed, the one shown in (ii), which obviously contradicts Grice's predictions.) Even more readily available, however, are examples that show that, contrary again to Gricean expectations, the remaining two logically possible patterns, (iii) and (iv), are also instantiated.

As far as the pattern shown in (iii) is concerned, the following pairs of sentences should suffice:

(9) (a) The King of France causes much perplexity to philosophers, but (fortunately for us) he doesn't really exist.
 (b) The King of France doesn't cause much perplexity to philosophers, since (fortunately for us) he doesn't really exist.

(10) (a) The golden mountain has inspired many poets, but it doesn't really exist.
 (b) The golden mountain has not inspired many poets, since it doesn't really exist.

(11) (a) The monster of Loch Ness causes fear to these people, but it doesn't really exist.
 (b) The monster of Loch Ness doesn't cause fear to these people, since it doesn't really exist.

Since both the (a)-members and the (b)-members of these pairs are fully acceptable, each pair is clearly an instance of the acceptability pattern shown in (iii). The cancellability test, therefore, must interpret them as showing that, contrary to Grice's claim, the existence assumption is merely a pragmatic implicature, rather than a semantic implication, of *both* the affirmative and the negative sentences where a definite description occupies subject position. (The question why not only the second but also the first member of each of the above pairs is acceptable, even though all contemporary speakers would presumably deny the metaphysical thesis that non-existent things can really have any causal powers, is, of course, an independent question, and one whose answer cannot, obviously, be allowed to have any bearing on the operation of the test: the test was certainly not supposed to check which metaphysical beliefs about causation are correct and which incorrect, but which sentences are linguistically proper and which improper; and what it shows in this particular application is what should be expected anyway, namely, that the acceptablility or otherwise of a sentence is not necessarily dependent of the correctness or otherwise of the metaphysical beliefs expressed in that sentence.)

As far as the pattern shown in (iv) is concerned, the following pairs of sentences should suffice:

(12) (a) *The King of France is as friendly to me now as he was when I first met him, but he never existed.
 (b) *The King of France isn't as friendly to me now as he was when I first met him, since he never existed.

(13) (a) *The golden mountain is as impressive now as it was when I first climbed it, but it never existed.
 (b) *The golden mountain is not as impressive now as it was when I first climbed it, since it never existed.

(14) (a) *The monster of Loch Ness is as angry now as it was when it first attacked me, but it never existed.
 (b) *The monster of Loch Ness is not as angry now as it was when it first attacked me, since it never existed.

(15) (a) *The King of France / The golden mountain / The monster of Loch Ness is much older than you have just said, but he / it doesn't exist.
 (b) *The King of France / The golden mountain / The monster of Loch Ness isn't much older than you have just said, since he / it doesn't exist.

(16) (a) *The King of France / The golden mountain / The monster of Loch Ness is far from where you are standing right now, but he / it doesn't exist.
 (b) *The King of France / The golden mountain / The monster of Loch Ness isn't far from where you are standing right now, since he / it doesn't exist.

Since both the (a)-members and the (b)-members of these pairs are clearly unacceptable, each pair is an instance of the acceptability pattern shown in (iv). The cancellability test must, therefore, interpret them as showing that, contrary to Grice's claim, the existence assumption is a semantic implication, rather than a mere pragmatic implicature, of *both* the affirmative and the negative sentences where a definite description occupies subject position.

In short, the cancellability test, when supplied with a sufficient amount of the kind of data that it has been called to process, will deliver the following successive verdicts: that the existence assumption is semantically associated only with the affirmative sentences and pragmatically associated with the negative ones; that it is semantically associated only with the negative sentences and pragmatically associated with the affirmative ones; that it is semantically associated with both and pragmatically associated with neither; and that it is pragmatically associated with both and semantically associated with neither. The net result is, of course, that, if the question as to the semantic or pragmatic status of the existence assumption with respect to affirmative and negative sentences featuring definite descriptions in subject position is supposed to be - as it is clearly supposed by Grice to be - a question that admits of *generally* valid answers (that is, of answers that are valid for all affirmative and for all negative sentences of the specified kind), then the cancellability test simply cannot supply *any* coherent answer to that question. Until, therefore, supporters of the Gricean program either abandon the question itself as a fundamentally misconceived question or devise a much better test in order to justify (rather than just proclaim) their preferred answer to it, the conclusion that one would be entitled to draw is twofold: first, that there is, at present, no good reason for supposing that the Russell-Strawson dispute has been satisfactorily resolved by the Gricean appeal to the semantics-pragmatics distinction as this distinction is supposedly justified by the cancellability test; and second, that, to the extent that it is precisely the cancellability test that has been appealed to in order to support Gricean solutions to many other disputes of comparable importance and generality, the ultimate viability of these solutions is open to serious doubt.

We have been assuming thus far that, if all the conjunctions relevant to evaluating Grice's claim were found to instantiate the acceptability pattern shown in (i) and not any of the other logically possible ones, then Grice would he entitled to place on the results of the cancellability test the theoretical weight that he does place. It is now time to question that assumption - to show, that is, that even if the only pattern instantiated by the conjunctions were the one in (i), any inferences from this fact to the existence or non-existence of implicational relations between their conjuncts would be unwarranted.

Suppose, in fact, that all relevant conjunctions instantiated exclusively the acceptability pattern shown in (i). And consider, among those that do instantiate it, the ones appearing in the following pairs:

(17) (a) *The link between them is broken, but they never had a link.
      (b) The link between them is not broken, since they never had a link.

(18) (a) *The building's back door is locked, but the building has no back door.
      (b) The building's back door is not locked, since the building has no back door.

(19) (a) *The solution proposed in my book is flawed, but my book proposes no solution.
      (b) The solution proposed in my book is not flawed, since my book proposes no solution.

Now, according to Grice, the acceptability of the (b)-members of these pairs shows that the existence assumptions denied in the second conjuncts are not semantic implications of the first conjuncts. But since a non-implication of a sentence S cannot possibly become an implication of a *logically equivalent* sentence S', we should expect the (b)-members of each pair to remain acceptable if we replaced their first conjuncts with alternative but logically equivalent first conjuncts. And since most people - and especially Griceans, who are well known for their minimalism - would be quite unwilling to say that "unbroken" means anything other than "not broken", or that "unlocked" means anything other than "not locked", or that "flawless" means anything other than "not flawed", we should expect the (b)-members of each pair to remain acceptable if we replaced their first conjuncts with the suggested logically equivalent conjuncts - if, that is, we replaced "The link between them is not broken" with "The link between them is unbroken", "The building's back door is not locked" with "The building's back door is unlocked", and "The solution proposed in my book is not flawed" with "The solution proposed in my book is flawless". What we obtain when we proceed to these replacements, however, are the following three sentences, which, in sharp contrast to their respective logical equivalents (17b), (18b) and (19b), are definitely unacceptable:

(20) *The link between them is unbroken, since they never had a link.
(21) *The building's back door is unlocked, since the building has no back door.
(22) *The solution proposed in my book is flawless, since my book proposes no solution.

We must, therefore, either deny the obvious logical equivalencies between "unbroken" and "not broken", "unlocked" and "not locked", and "flawless" and "not flawed", or abandon the idea that the acceptabilities or unacceptabilities revealed by the cancellability test reliably indicate the existence or non-existence of implicational relations. And since the first option is clearly unacceptable - no one, presumably, would wish to deny that, for example, arguments like those in (21), (22) and (23) below are entirely valid - ,

(23) If their link is broken, they don't talk to each other. They talk to each other. Therefore, their link is unbroken.

(24) If the door is locked, he is not in. He is in. Therefore, the door is unlocked.

(25) If his reasoning is flawed, the red light is on. The red light is not on. Therefore, his reasoning is flawless.

the only remaining option is to abandon the idea that what the cancellability test reveals has anything to do with what it was intended to reveal, namely, systematic correspondences between the acceptability or unacceptability of certain compound sentences and the existence or non-existence of implicational relations between their parts.

What, if anything, the cancellability test really reveals, given that it does not reveal what it was expected to, is not a question that I intend to pursue here. But a possible suggestion would be that it reveals not propositional but *illocutionary* compatibilities and incompatibilities between sentences joined by a conjunction (that is, compatibilities or incompatibilities between the *acts* that fall under the illocutionary force potential of those sentences rather between their truth conditions). It is, in fact, well known that conjunctions can function either as propositional or as illocutionary connectives, and it is obvious that the particular conjunction appearing in the sorts of contexts invoked by Grice does have a well established use as an illocutionary connective, which is clearly responsible for many acceptability contrasts. Consider, for example, the following pairs of sentences:

(26) (a) There is a Chinese restaurant around the corner, since you are interested in Chinese food.
(b) ?There is a Chinese restaurant around the corner, since you are not interested in Chinese food.

(27) (a) It is stupid to start taking a pet care course, since you have no pets.
(b) ?It is stupid to start taking a pet care course, since you have pets.

(28) (a) I am not interested in bookcases, since I don't have books.
(b) ?I am not interested in bookcases, since I have books.

There is clearly a contrast in acceptability between the (a)-members and the (b)-members of these pairs, but this contrast has certainly nothing to do with the existence or non-existence of implicational relations between the sentences joined by the conjunction: in fact, none of these sentences entails or is entailed by any of the others. What makes the (a)-members acceptable and the (b)-members unacceptable, nevertheless, is that, in the (a)-cases, the illocutionary act performed by the utterance of the second conjunct offers an appropriate justification for the illocutionary act performed by the utterance of the first, whereas in the (b)-cases, the performance of the illocutionary act normally associated with the utterance of the second conjunct would not offer an appropriate justification for the performance of the illocutionary act normally associated with the utterance of the first. It might be the case, therefore, that whatever systematic contrasts the cancellability test reveals are indications of the illocutionary compatibility or incompatibility between sentences joined by certain conjunctions. What is certainly not the case, however, is that they are indications of the existence or non-existence of relations of implication between them.

To summarize, then, there are two fundamental respects in which the Gricean appeal to cancellability as a means of resolving the Russell-Strawson dispute is inadequate. Even if we assumed that the test is a reliable indicator of the supposed semantics-pragmatic division, we should recognize that its application to the data that would be relevant for settling that particular dispute could not coherently settle it, since the relevant data do not behave *uniformly* with respect to the test. And even if we assumed that the data do behave uniformly with respect to the test, we should recognize that their doing so would still fail to settle the dispute, since, on closer inspection, the test turns out not to be a reliable indicator of the supposed semantics-pragmatics division. We are further justified, then, in reiterating the double conclusion that the Gricean way of appealing to the supposed semantics-pragmatics distinction is certainly useless in resolving the Russell-Strawson dispute, and very probably equally useless in resolving any other disputes of comparable importance and generality. Russell and Strawson (as well as other pairs of theorists assuming analogous roles in analogous disputes) may have been both wrong, but their monolithic positions had at least the merit of making clearly visible the limitations of each other's views. On the contrary, the unbounded euphoria that prevails whenever the Gricean approach to a problem announces that no one is strictly speaking wrong and everyone is in some sense right, seems to be a sure way of masking the problems, and so of making their solution not just difficult to find but virtually impossible to seek.

References

Grice, P.H. (1981): "Presupposition and conversational implicature". In: P. Cole, ed.: Radical Pragmatics. New York: Academic Press, 183-198.
Russell, B. (1905): "On denoting". Mind 14, 479-499.
Strawson, P.F. (1950): "On referring". Mind 59, 320-344.

Formal Pragmatics of Non Literal Meaning[*]

Daniel Vanderveken, Québec

In the past decades, there has been much progress in the formal Semantics of ordinary language. Logicians, linguists and philosophers have extensively used logical formalisms in order to interpret directly or after translation important fragments of actual natural languages. They have thereby contributed to the foundations of the theory of sentence meaning. In formal Semantics, speaker meaning is reduced to sentence meaning: one assumes that speakers only mean what they say. Thus, formal semantics is a theory of literal meaning. However, in ordinary conversations, the speaker's meaning is often different from the sentence meaning. First, the primary illocutionary act that the speaker attempts to perform is different from the literal speech act expressed by the uttered sentence in the cases of metaphor, irony and indirect speech acts. Whenever the speaker indirectly requests the hearer to pass the salt by asking "Can you pass the salt?", the primary speech act of the utterance is the indirect request and not the literal question about the hearer's abilities. Second, the speaker means to perform secondary non literal illocutionary acts in the cases of conversational implicatures. By saying "If you are nice, I will give you something" the speaker can imply conversationally that he will not give anything to the hearer if he is not nice. In such a case, he makes a secondary non literal assertion in addition to the primary conditional promise. The speaker's capacity to make and understand non literal speech acts is clearly part of his linguistic competence. But it exceeds the capacity of understanding the sentence meaning.

The study of non literal speech acts and conversational implicatures is part of the task of pragmatics. It deals with questions such as these: (1) How does a speaker succeed in getting the hearer to understand that what he means is different from what the sentence that he uses means? (2) Once the hearer has understood this, how does he succeed in identifying the intended non literal speech acts?

Until the present, there has been little progress in the development of a formal pragmatics. Grice (1975) later joined by Searle (1979), Bach and Harnish, Récanati, Dascal and others made important remarks on non literal speaker meaning by exploring the idea that language use is governed by *conversational maxims* (like "Speak the truth!", "Be sincere!") which the speaker can exploit in order to get the hearer to understand what he means. Sperber and Wilson have studied the maxim of relevance. But these current analyses of speaker

---

[*] I am grateful to Steven Davis, François Lepage, Kenneth Mac Queen, Claude Panaccio, John Searle and Dietmar Zaefferer for helpful comments on a first draft of this paper.

meaning are informal, partial and heuristic. They lack precise theoretical content. The main purpose of this work is to use illocutionary logic in order to contribute to the foundations of a formal pragmatics capable of building up the speakers' ability to make and understand non literal utterances.

According to Grice, hearers understand the speaker's intention to perform non literal illocutionary acts by making inferences from the hypothesis of respect of conversational maxims. Given the logical framework of speech act theory, Searle (1975) and I (1990) have reformulated as follows his inferential approach: A speaker who means to perform non literal speech acts in a context of utterance intends that the hearer understand him by relying: 1) on the hearer's knowledge of the meaning of the sentence that he uses; 2) on his ability to understand the conditions of success, non defective performance and satisfaction of the literal speech act; and 3) to recognize certain facts of the conversational background on which he wants to draw his attention; and finally 4) on the hearer's capacity to make inferences on the basis of the hypothesis that the speaker respects conversational maxims. In this view, in order to understand the primary non literal speech act of an utterance, the hearer must first identify the literal speech act and understand that the speaker cannot mean simply to perform that literal speech act if he respects the conversational maxims. Thus, in our tripartition of semiotics, *pragmatics* conceived as the theory of speaker's meaning must add to *semantics* conceived as the theory of sentence meaning *a theory of conversational maxims* and *an analysis of* relevant facts of *the conversational background* of utterances.

I will first make a few basic remarks on sentence meaning and illocutionary acts. Next, I will explicate the conversational maxims of quality and quantity. I will also analyze how hearers use and exploit conversational maxims in order to infer non literal speaker meaning. Furthermore, I will proceed to the formal analysis of irony, indirect speech acts and conversational implicatures. I will show how formal pragmatics can construct these non literal illocutionary acts. Finally, I will explain why these non literal speech acts are always cancellable but non detachable.

1   Formal Semantics, Sentence Meaning and Illocutionary Acts

As Frege and Russell pointed out, in uttering sentences speakers refer to objects and predicate of them properties or relations. They thereby express propositions which are true or false depending on how things are in the actual world. To understand a proposition is mainly to understand under which conditions it is true. So, in order to analyze the logical form of propositions, we must elaborate a theory of truth. However, most formally oriented philosophers of language from Carnap to Montague have tended to consider that the main purpose of language is to serve to describe the world. For that reason, most contributions to formal semantics have been limited to the analysis of expressions such as proper names, predicates, quantifiers, truth and modal connectives whose meaning contributes to the determination of truth conditions.

However, the primary units of meaning in the use and comprehension of natural languages are not isolated propositions but complete speech acts of the type called by Austin *illocutionary acts*. Elementary illocutionary acts are of the form F(P): they consist of a propositional content P together with an *illocutionary force* F. Some examples of these are assertions, questions, orders, promises and declarations. Whenever a speaker expresses a proposition in a meaningful utterance, he always attempts to perform an illocutionary act. This attempted performance is part of what he *means* and intend to *communicate* to his audience in the context of his utterance. Consequently, meaning, communication and illocutionary acts are logically related in the semantic structure of language. It is not possible to express a proposition in the use of language without attempting to perform an illocutionary act. Thus every complete elementary sentence contains an *illocutionary force marker*. Common examples of illocutionary force markers are verbal mood, sentence type and punctuation signs. Thus, declarative sentences serve to make assertions and interrogative sentences serve to ask questions. Imperative sentences serve to make linguistic attempts to get the hearer to do something. Performative sentences serve to make declarations and exclamatory sentences serve to express the speaker's mental states.

As is the case for other human actions, attempts to perform illocutionary acts can succeed or fail. In order to make an assertion or promise, we must succeed in expressing what we want to assert or promise. Moreover, the context must be appropriate for the performance of the intended illocutionary act. As Searle and I pointed out (1985), we can define the conditions of success of elementary illocutionary acts from the components of their force and their propositional content. Thus a speaker succeeds in performing an illocutionary act of the form F(P) in a context of utterance if and only if 1) he achieves in that context the *illocutionary point* of force F on proposition P with the proper *mode of achievement* of F, and P satisfies the *propositional content conditions* of F, moreover 2) he also presupposes the propositions determined by the *preparatory conditions* of F(P) and 3) he expresses with the required *degree of strength* of F the psychological states determined by the *sincerity conditions* of F(P). For example, a speaker makes a promise in a context of utterance if and only if 1) the point of his utterance is to commit himself to doing something (illocutionary point and propositional content condition); 2) he puts himself under an obligation (mode of achievement); 3) he also presupposes that he is capable of doing what he promises and that it is good for the hearer (preparatory conditions); and finally 5) he expresses with a strong degree of strength an intention to do it (sincerity conditions). Now a speaker can presuppose a proposition which is false or express a psychological state which he does not have. So we distinguish in illocutionary logic between a successful and a non defective performance of an illocutionary act. An illocutionary act is non defective if and only if it is successfully performed and its preparatory and sincerity conditions obtain. Thus a promise is non defective if and only if it is successful and moreover the speaker is capable of keeping it and intends to keep it. On this account, all non defective illocutionary acts are successful, but the converse is not true.

In performing illocutionary acts speakers relate propositions to the world with the intention of achieving a success of fit between words and things from a certain direction of fit. Thus successful illocutionary acts are satisfied under certain conditions. For example, an assertion is satisfied if and only if it is true. A promise is satisfied if and only if it is kept. Even when they are non defective, successful illocutionary acts can still fail to be satisfied. Non defective promises can be violated. In order that a successful elementary illocutionary act be satisfied, it is not enough that its propositional content be true and fit the world. The success of fit between words and things must be achieved from the direction of fit of its force. Thus a request is granted if and only if the hearer carryies out the requested action in order to comply with the request. The satisfaction of elementary illocutionary acts is then a function of the truth of their propositional content and of the direction of fit of their illocutionary force. So the notion of satisfaction is both an extension and a generalization of the notion of truth.

The success and satisfaction conditions of illocutionary acts are not reducible to the truth conditions of their propositional contents. So formal semantics must do more than to further develop the theory of truth for propositions. It must also elaborate an integrated theory of success and satisfaction for illocutionary acts. As I have shown (1990-91), a general semantics of success, satisfaction and truth can analyze expressions like illocutionary force markers and performative verbs whose meaning serves to determine the illocutionary forces of utterances. Thanks to illocutionary logic, formal semantics can interpret sentences of all types that express speech acts with any possible force. It can also analyze practical as well as theoretical valid inferences that speakers are able to make by virtue of linguistic competence.

However, in spite of its generality, the new semantics of success and satisfaction remains a theory of literal meaning. It uniquely tends to construct that part of linguistic competence which consists in the speaker's ability to perform and understand literal illocutionary acts. By hypothesis, the *literal speech act* of the context of an utterance is always taken to be the *primary speech act*. So when an utterance is successful in a semantic interpretation, it is by way of performing the literal speech act that the speaker performs all other illocutionary acts in the context of that utterance. However, each natural language contains illocutionarily inconsistent sentences such as "I am not myself today" expressing self defeating illocutionary acts that speakers cannot even intend to perform. So speakers using such sentences never mean what they say. They have to mean non literally something else. Furthermore, an adequate theory of speaker meaning must account for non literal performances of illocutionary acts like indirect speech acts and irony where the literal speech act is neither the strongest nor the primary speech act of the utterance.

2 Conversational Maxims

Non literal speech acts have two important properties. First, they are *contextually cancellable:* speakers could use the same sentences in other possible contexts of utterance (with different backgrounds) without having the intention of performing these non literal speech acts. Thus an utterance of the sentence "Can you pass the salt?" can be just a question about the hearer's capacity to pass the salt. Suppose the speaker wants to test the movement abilities of the hearer. Non literal illocutionary acts can even be explicitly cancelled. Second, non literal speech acts are also in general *not detachable*: if the speaker had uttered another sentence expressing the same literal illocutionary act in the same context, he would also have meant to perform them.

From a theoretical point of view, these two properties of non literal speech acts are important for formal pragmatics: First, if non literal speech acts are cancellable, certain conditions must be necessary in order that a speaker can speak non literally in a context. When these conditions are not fulfilled in the conversational background, the speaker's meaning can only be literal. Furthermore, if non literal speech acts are not detachable, certain conditions relative to the form of the literal illocutionary act and the conversational background must be sufficient in order that a speaker speak non literally in the context of an utterance. When these conditions are fulfilled in the conversational background, the speaker's meaning cannot be entirely literal. The first objective of pragmatics is to state these necessary and sufficient conditions for non literal meaning.

2.1 Grice's Logic of Conversation

On Grice's account, any conversation is governed by a general principle of cooperation. Speakers must respect certain *conversational maxims* if they want to pursue with success a conversation without being liable to mislead. According to Grice, it is not without reasons that speakers respect conversational maxims in conversations. It is rational to respect these maxims.

Grice distinguishes different types of conversational maxims under Kant's categories of quality, quantity, manner and relation.

> *Maxims of quality*:
> "Speak the truth!"
> "Do not say anything you believe to be false!"
> "Have evidence for what you say!"
>
> *Maxims of quantity*:
> "Be as informative as is required (for the current purposes of the exchange)!"
> "Do not be more informative than required!"
>
> *A maxim of manner*:
> "Be perspicuous!"
> "Avoid obscurity of expression!"
> "Avoid ambiguity!"
> "Be brief!"
> "Be orderly!"
>
> *A maxim of relation*:
> "Be relevant!"

Unfortunately, Grice's conversational maxims are too vague. Their formulation lacks precise theoretical content. Moreover, Grice tends to consider the exchange of information as the sole aim of conversation. So his maxims only apply to assertive utterances. Unlike Kant, Grice does not provide any justification of his system of maxims.

2.2 A Generalization of the Maxims of Quality and of Quantity

As I have pointed out, illocutionary logic enables pragmatics to explicate the two fundamental maxims of quality and quantity.

The maxim of quality
From a logical point of view, an illocutionary act is of perfect quality if and only if it is entirely felicitous in Austin's (1956) sense, that is to say successful, non defective and satisfied. Thus, the maxim of quality turns out to be a general principle of speech act theory: Let the illocutionary act that you mean to perform be felicitous in the context of your utterance! There is an inductive definition of the conditions of success, non defective performance and satisfaction of speech acts in illocutionary logic. So the new principle is both an explication and a generalization of the maxim of quality. The new maxim holds for all types of utterances and not just for assertive utterances. Thus there is the following *sub-maxim of quality for commands*: Let your command be a successful attempt to get the hearer to do something! Let it be a command that you want him to obey and that he will eventually obey! Similarly, there is the following *sub-maxim of quality for assertions*: Let your assertion represent how the things to which you refer are in the world. Let it be an assertion supported by evidence, sincere and true! On this account, Grice's formulation of the maxim of quality is just the particular case for assertions.

In order to respect the maxim of quality, speakers must select appropriately the force as well as the propositional content of the attempted illocutionary act. Suppose that you want to direct someone to give you something. Do not command him if you are not in a position of authority over him. (Such a directive force would be inappropriate. For your speech act would be defective.) You should rather make a request if all depends on the hearer's good will. Moreover, do not ask something that the hearer would not or could not do. (An exaggerated request would turn out to be unsatisfied.)

As Grice remarks, speakers can "quietly and unostentatiously violate a maxim" like the maxim of quality without meaning eo ipso to perform a non literal primary speech act. We can lie and make promises that we do not intend to keep. In such cases, the speaker does not want that the hearer be aware of the violation of the maxim. If so, the speaker will be liable to mislead. Nearly all cases of blatant violation of the maxim of quality are what Grice calls "exploitations" of that maxim. When the background of the utterance is such that the literal act is obviously unfelicitous, given the conversational background, the speaker most often does not mean at all to perform the literal illocutionary act. He rather means to perform another primary illocutionary act whose felicity conditions are compatible with the context. So there is only an apparent violation of the maxim of quality in such contexts of utterance. Suppose that a speaker says "John is sober" in a context where the person to which he refers is staggering and obviously dead drunk. That speaker is exploiting the maxim of quality. He relies on the fact that his literal assertion is obviously false in order to assert ironically the opposite of what he says. And his ironical speech act is felicitous. So he repects the maxim in that context. Deliberate cases of violation of the maxim of quality without any reason are extremely rare. Most often speakers behave this way when they want to stop participating to the conversation.

The maxim of quantity
Each illocutionary act is a natural kind of use of language which can serve to achieve linguistic purposes in the course of conversations. From a logical point of view, an illocutionary act is of perfect quantity in the context of an utterance if and only if it is *as strong as required* to achieve the current linguistic purposes of the speaker in that context. Given their logical forms, certain speech acts are *stronger* than others, in the sense that they have more felicity conditions. Thus a supplication to a hearer that he spare the life of all children is stronger than a simple request that he save the life of people. Stronger speech acts serve to achieve stronger linguistic purposes. A speaker who would like to supplicate the hearer to save the life of all children but who simply requested that he save the life of persons, would perform a speech act too weak to achieve his purpose.

On the basis of these considerations, the maxim of quantity turns out to be: Let your speech act be as strong as required (i.e. neither too strong nor too weak) to achieve your current linguistic purposes in the context of each utterance! As the relation of being a stronger illocutionary act is rigorously defined in illocutionary logic, the new principle is both an explication and a generalization of the maxim of quantity. It can be applied to all types of meaningful utterances. Thus there is the special *sub-maxim of quantity for directives*: "Let your directive be as strong as required!" As one might expect, Grice's formulation of the maxim of quantity is just the special case for assertive utterances which aim to be informative. The maxim of quantity imposes conditions on the force as well as on the propositional content of attempted illocutionary acts. Thus your directive should not be too strong. If you just want to ask someone a glass of red wine, do not implore him (your directive force would be stronger than needed). And do not ask more than what you want. (Do not ask for a whole bottle of red wine (if you just want a glass). On the other hand, your directive should not be too weak. If you want to invoke your position of authority over the hearer, do not only tell him to do it (your directive force would be too weak). But give him a command. Furthermore, if you want him to give you red wine, do not only tell him to give you wine (you would not require enough).

As Grice notices, the speaker may be faced with a clash between two maxims. He may be unable to respect fully at the same time the maxims of quality and quantity. For example, you might really want to ask for a whole bottle of wine but refrain from making such a request (Violation of the maxim of quantity) because it would not be granted (Maxim of quality).

The conversational maxims of quality and quantity concern the logical forms of illocutionary acts. They are not relative to a particular human culture as Keenan and others have argued. On the contrary, these two maxims are *pragmatic universals of language use*. As Grice thought, they follow from the hypothesis that speakers are rational in the use of language. An illocutionary act is a means to achieving linguistic ends. Now just as rational agents should decide to use the best effective available means in each situation, rational speakers should attempt to perform in each context illocutionary acts which can be felicitous. So it is reasonable to respect the maxim of quality. Moreover, as Kasher (1982) pointed out, rational agents should respect a principle of the effective means. This is a principle of practical reason. So rational speakers should also attempt to perform in each context an illocutionary act which serves fully and most effectively their linguistic purposes. A speaker who would attempt to perform a weaker or stronger illocutionary act would not act most effectively to attain his ends. Consequently, it is also reasonable to respect the maxim of quantity.

2.3 Modes of Inference of Speaker Meaning

Grice did not attempt to analyze formally the nature of inferences that hearers make in order to understand what speakers mean. However, as I will show, we can reformulate and attempt to formalize the Gricean inferential approach within speech act theory. In my view, there are two main ways in which a speaker can get the hearer to infer what he means on the basis of the assumption that he respects the conversational maxims. These two ways are what I call hereafter the *exploitation* and *use* of a maxim.

The exploitation of a maxim
My notion of exploitation of a maxim is related to Grice's notion. But it is more general. A speaker *exploits a conversational* maxim if and only if certain facts of the conversational background to which he wants to attract the hearer's attention are such that he intends that the hearer recognize the following data: (1) The speaker would not respect the conversational maxim if the primary speech act were the literal speech act; but (2) he is able to respect the maxim without violating another maxim (there is no clash); moreover, (3) he wants to cooperate and contribute to the conversation, so (4) he intends to perform non literally another primary illocutionary act and finally, (5) the speaker also intends that the hearer believes that they both have a mutual knowledge of all this.

Now, in the case of an *exploitation of the maxim of quality*, the speaker intends that the hearer recognize that there are in the conversational background certain facts which are incompatible with felicity conditions of the literal speech act. Moreover the speaker also wants that the recognition of his intention be part of mutual background knowledge. Whenever the hearer recognizes this, he understands that the speaker does not mean to perform the literal illocutionary act but another primary illocutionary act with felicity conditions different from those which are violated in the conversational background. Furthermore, he identifies these other non literal conditions by drawing them from facts of the conversational background that the speaker intends him to recognize. Suppose that someone tells you "I promise that you will regret all this" with the intention of drawing your attention to the fact that he is committing himself to doing something which is not good for you. That speaker would be exploiting the maxim of quality. For he obviously does not presuppose the literal preparatory condition that a promise is good for the hearer. So his literal promise is unsuccessful and defective. Moreover, that speaker presupposes a non literal preparatory condition which is the opposite of the literal one which is violated. The future action represented is, on the contrary, bad for the hearer. So you should understand that he means to threaten you ironically. For such a threat differs from the literal promise by virtue of the fact that it has the opposite preparatory condition that the action represented is bad for the hearer. In the case of *exploitation of the maxim of quantity*, the speaker intends that the hearer recognize that the literal speech act is not as strong as required to achieve his current linguistic purposes in the context of the utterance. Thus a speaker who says "That painting is not bad!" exploits the maxim of quantity to make an *understatement* when it is part of background knowledge that he is obviously very impressed by the painting which is very good. In such a context, the hearer concludes that the speaker means to make indirectly a stronger assertion than the literal one.

As I said earlier, in the case of exploitation of a maxim, there is only an apparent violation of that maxim. The speaker blatantly fails to fulfill the maxim in saying what he says. He obviously would not respect the maxim if he were primarily meaning to perform the literal illocutionary act. But the speaker wants that the hearer recognize all this. Moreover some of the facts that prevent the speaker from meaning what he says are mental states - intentions, desires, beliefs - that the speaker has or expresses in the context of utterance. These commit him to perform another primary speech act compatible with the background. So the speaker respects the maxim (at least it is not obvious that he violates it) in attempting to perform that primary act.

The use of a maxim

A speaker *uses a conversational maxim* if and only if he intends the hearer to recognize that, given the existence of certain facts of the conversational background, he respects that maxim in performing the primary speech act only if a secondary non literal illocutionary act is felicitous. Moreover the speaker also intends that the hearer believe this to be mutually known. So he means to perform that secondary illocutionary act.

Whenever a speaker uses the maxim of quality, he intends the hearer to recognize certain facts of the conversational background and to get him to make an inference on the basis of the assumption of existence of these facts and of the hypothesis that the primary illocutionary act of his utterance is successful, non defective and satisfied. From the premises of that inference, the hearer draws the conclusion that a secondary non literal illocutionary act determined by the relevant facts of the background is also performed in the context of the utterance. For example, when the information that gay men do not have girlfriends is part of the background knowledge, a speaker who answers the question "Does Jones have a girlfriend?" by saying "He is gay", is using the maxim of quality. He means to answer that Jones has no girlfriend.

On the other hand, whenever a speaker uses the maxim of quantity, he intends that the hearer make an inference on the basis of the hypothesis that the primary speech act performed in the context of the utterance is actually as strong as required to achieve his current linguistic purposes. Usually the conversational background is such that the speaker means to perform that primary act instead of other stronger speech acts that were also relevant at that moment in the conversation. Thus the hearer comes to the conclusion that the speaker does not intend to perform these stronger illocutionary acts because, given the background, they would be unfelicitous in that context. Thus, a speaker who answers the question "Where is Paul?" by saying "He is in France or in Belgium" is using the sub-maxim of quantity "Be as informative as required!" when he wants to attract the hearer's attention to the fact that he did not answer "Paul is in France" or "Paul is in Belgium". If so, he can mean secondarily that he lacks evidence for making any one of these two stronger assertions.

As in the case of literal speech acts, non literal attempts at performance of illocutionary acts can be misunderstood. The speaker can wrongly believe that the hearer is aware of the facts of the conversational background on which he relies in order to exploit or use a conversational maxim. In such cases, the hearer does not understand fully the speaker's meaning. He can even fail to recognize the speaker's intention to perform a non literal speech act. Sometimes, the hearer wonders whether the speaker relies on a certain relevant fact of the conversational background whose nature could commit him to exploit or use a maxim. In such cases, he can reply by asking a question. The speaker's answer will serve determine *a posteriori* how to interpret the previous utterance.

3   Irony, Indirect Speech Acts and Conversational Implicatures

I conjecture first that a speaker means to perform a primary non literal speech act when he exploits conversational maxims and second that he implies something conversationally when he uses such maxims in the context of his utterance. As I will show in my next book on *Discourse*, important figures of non literal meaning such as irony, indirect speech acts and conversational implicatures can be explicated in this conception of pragmatics. Illocutionary logic enables speech act theory to construct the speaker's meaning from the sentence meaning, conversational maxims and background. Contrary to what Sperber and Wilson and others believe, there is a normal form of derivations of speaker meaning in the cases of irony and indirect speech acts. So we can compute the primary ironical or indirect speech act from the literal speech act, the relevant facts of the conversational background and the respect of the two conversational maxims of quality and quantity.

3.1   Irony

As I have explained earlier (1990), irony is an extreme case of exploitation of the maxim of quality. In making an ironic utterance, the speaker always exploits the maxim of quality by relying on facts of the conversational background whose existence commit him not to intend to perform the literal illocutionary act. In the case of irony, it is not only part of background mutual knowledge that certain literal felicity conditions are violated, but also that the speaker intends to perform a non literal illocutionary act with opposite conditions. Many felicity conditions of illocutionary acts are logically related. So the speaker's irony is often directed to several components of the literal illocutionary force and to the propositional content. When it is part of background mutual knowledge that the literal propositional content is false, it is in general also part of background knowledge that the speaker does not intend to achieve the literal illocutionary point on the literal propositional content and that he does not possess expressed psychological states. Suppose that a speaker ironically critizes the hearer by saying "I praise you for that" in a context where what the hearer has done is obviously not good. The speaker's irony concerns both the achievement of the literal illocutionary point and the literal propositional content. He does not intend to assert that what the hearer has done is good. On the contrary, he intends to assert that it is bad. Moreover, the speaker's irony also concerns a literal sincerity condition. He does not approve but disapproves of the hearer.

In this approach, we can analyze irony as follows: *The primary illocutionary act that the speaker intends to perform 'ironically' only differs from the literal speech act by the fact that it has instead of literal conditions obviously violated in the background the opposites of these conditions whenever such a non literal illocutionary act is performable in the context. Otherwise, the ironic illocutionary act is just the denegation of the literal speech act.* (Some conditions of success e.g. the achievement of the illocutionary point have no opposites. So when the speaker's irony concerns the literal illocutionary point, the speaker means to denegate the performance of the literal speech act.)

This analysis of irony explains why in the case of irony the speaker's meaning is always in opposition to the meaning of the sentence that is used. By definition, the primary speech act of an ironic utterance is incompatible with the literal speech act: both cannot be simultaneously performed. My analysis explicates the very notion of opposition which is part of the standard definition of irony. It also accounts for the two different kinds of irony in language use namely: 1) Irony as to the illocutionary force and 2) irony as to the propositional content of the literal speech act. (Most analysts have neglected until now the first kind of irony.) So my analysis enables me to present a reasoned classification of all the different possible elementary kinds of irony.

(i)   *Irony as to the achievement of the literal illocutionary point*
      By saying "Yes, I agree to give you all that!", the speaker ironically refuses to give what he says when it is part of background knowledge that he has no intention at all of committing himself to giving anything.

(ii) *Irony as to the literal mode of achievement*
      By saying "Please, get out immediately", the speaker ironically tells the hearer to leave in a context where he does not give him any option of refusal.

(iii) *Irony as to a literal preparatory condition*
      By saying "I promise that you will regret it", the speaker can ironically threaten the hearer as I have explained earlier.

(iv) *Irony as to a literal sincerity condition*
      By saying "I praise you for that", a speaker ironically criticizes the hearer when he obviously disapproves what he has done.

(v)   *Irony as to the propositional content*
      By saying "It was a splendid feat!" the speaker ironically asserts the opposite of what he says when it is part of background knowledge that the event was a terrible defeat.

As I said earlier, there is an effective method of decision for constructing the primary ironic illocutionary act. In the simple cases, we proceed in the following way in order to infer what the speaker ironically means:

(1)   We identify from our background knowledge the various literal felicity conditions to which the speaker's irony is directed.

(2)   These felicity conditions are by definition determined from components of the literal illocutionary force or of the literal propositional content (Speech act theory).
(3)   The ironic speech act is obtained from the literal speech act by replacing such literal components by their opposites when such opposite complements exist and the obtained non literal illocutionary act is performable. Otherwise, the ironic speech act is the illocutionary denegation of the literal speech act.

3.2   Indirect Speech Acts

So called indirect speech acts are performed indirectly by way of performing the literal illocutionary act. In my account, speech acts are cases of exploitation of the maxim of quantity indirect. A speaker means to perform indirectly a speech act by way of performing the literal illocutionary act if and only if he exploits the maxim of quantity by intending to draw the hearer's attention to the fact that certain conditions of non defective performance other than those of the literal illocutionary act are fulfilled in the conversational background. In such contexts, the speaker intends that the hearer recognize that the literal speech act is not strong enough to achieve all his current linguistic purposes. The speaker respects the maxim of quantity in attempting to perform indirectly another illocutionary act. For that indirect speech act serves to achieve all his other non literal purposes.

In the simplest cases of exploitation of the maxim of quantity, all the non literal conditions of non defective performance to which the speaker intends to draw the hearer's attention are relative to the literal propositional content. In such cases, the indirect and literal speech acts have the same propositional content. So the speaker's indirection is only directed to the illocutionary force. Thus we can make an indirect promise by saying "I will help you" in a context where we intend that the hearer recognize that we want to commit ourselves to doing something which is good for him. When the indirect speech act has a non literal propositional content, some of its non literal felicity conditions are conditions of satisfaction of the literal speech act. The speaker can assert that these conditions obtain and exploit the maxim of quantity by relying on the fact that his literal assertion is true given the conservational background. He can also ask the hearer whether these conditions obtain and exploit the maxim of quantity by relying on the fact that his literal question has or at least could have a positive answer given the conversational background. So we can indirectly offer and sometimes also promise help by way of saying "I could help you", "Can I help you?", "Would you like me to help you?" (preparatory conditions), "I intend to help you", "Don't you see that I intend to help you?" (sincerity conditions), "I should help you", "Should I help you?" (mode of achievement). In these idiomatic uses, the propositional content of the indirect speech act is part of the literal propositional content. But it is not always the case. So we can indirectly invite the hearer to a date by saying "Are you free tonight?".

In my approach we can analyze as follows indirect speech acts. When all the non literal conditions of non defective performance to which the speaker wants to draw the hearer's attention are relative to a single proposition P on which the speaker intends to achieve a certain illocutionary point, *the indirect speech act is the weakest elementary illocutionary act* with that propositional content P *having all these non literal conditions as well as the literal conditions* of non defective performance relative to P (if there are any).

As we will see, there always exists exactly one such non literal indirect illocutionary act. For a speaker exploiting the maxim of quantity can only rely on the existence of finitely many different facts of the conversational background. Otherwise, there would be no possible derivation of what he means. So there are only finitely many conditions of non defective performance to which the speaker intends to draw the hearer's attention. Each of them is determined by a particular literal or non literal component of illocutionary force. Moreover the force of the intended indirect speech act has all and only these components. It is obtained by adding to the primitive force with the intended illocutionary point all other components. In performing the indirect speech act, the speaker respects the maxim of quantity. For that indirect speech act is as strong as required to achieve all his other non literal linguistic purposes in the context of his utterance. Suppose that a speaker tells you "I intend to help you" with the intention of drawing your attention to the fact that he is committing himself to helping you (non literal commissive illocutionary point and non literal propositional content) so undertaking an obligation (non literal mode of achievement). Suppose that he obviously can and intend to help you and that his help is good for you (non literal preparatory and sincerity conditions). That speaker has made an indirect promise to you. And his non literal promise is the weakest commissive illocutionary act whose conditions of non defective performance are obviously fulfilled in the conversational background. For the indirect force of promise has all the non literal components (illocutionary point, mode of achievement, preparatory and sincerity conditions) which determine the conditions which are fulfilled in the conversational background.

My analysis of indirect speech acts explains why speaker meaning is always an extension of sentence meaning in the case of indirect speech acts. Contrary to what is the case for other non literal speech acts, the speaker cannot intend to perform an indirect speech act without also intending to perform the literal speech act. For both are required to achieve all his literal and non literal purposes in the context of utterance. My account of indirect speech acts supports Searle (1992) against Dascal, Holdcroft and others who deny the intended performance of the literal speech act. It also explicates the very notion of extension which is part of Searle's analysis. Notice that the hearer can always reply to the indirect speech act by way of replying to the literal speech act. Consider an indirect invitation made by way of asking "Can you come?" The hearer can accept (or refuse) that indirect invitation by answering "Yes" (or "No") to the literal question. It is part of the art of a good speaker to request indirectly what he wants by way of performing the right literal speech act.

Of course, the indirect speech act is always more important than the literal one. It is indeed the primary speech act of utterance. When a speaker indirectly invites the hearer by asking a question, he wants much more an answer to his invitation than to his literal question. The literal speech act is only a means to performing the indirect speech act. Hence, the word "indirect" in indirect speech acts. Using the terminology of philosophy of action, we can say that there is always a generation relation holding between the literal and the indirect illocutionary acts. The first is generating and the second is generated. From a logical point of view, the primacy of the indirect speech act over the literal speech act is shown in the fact that whenever the first is felicitous the second is *eo ipso* satisfied. Thus whenever the hearer accepts the previous indirect invitation he gives a positive implicit answer to the literal question.

The indirect speech act that the speaker means to perform can be categorical or conditional. So we can indirectly promise or offer help by way of saying "I could help you", "Can I help you?", "Do you want me to help you?". An indirect offer is an indirect promise which is conditional on the hearer's acceptance. Whenever all the non literal felicity conditions on which the speaker relies are fulfilled in the conversational background, the intended indirect speech act is categorical. But, when some of them depend on the hearer's reply, the indirect speech act is rather conditional. So we only intend to indirectly offer help when we are not sure that the hearer is willing any help. In that case, we are obliged to help the hearer only if he accepts our indirect offer.

Third, my analysis of indirect speech acts accounts for all the different kinds of indirection in language use. As I have shown, the speaker's indirection can be directed to the force and to the propositional content. Furthermore, indirect speech acts can be performed by way of performing literal speech acts with any illocutionary force and not only by way of assertions. My explication in terms of exploitation of the maxim of quantity is general enough to cover all cases. So I can make a reasoned classification of many possible kinds of indirect speech acts.

(i) *The indirect speech act has the literal propositional content.*
By saying "Please, help me!" a speaker indirectly supplicates the hearer to help him in a context where he is obviously very humble in his request (he kneels down before someone in power) and expresses a high intensity of desire.

(ii) *The literal propositional content is that the illocutionary point of the indirect speech act is achieved on a proposition.*
By saying "I am trying to get you to leave", a speaker can make an indirect attempt to get the hearer to leave.

(iii) *The literal propositional content represents a mode of achievement of illocutionary point of the indirect speech act.*
By saying "I have witnessed all this", a speaker can indirectly testify.

(iv) *The literal propositional content is that a preparatory condition of the indirect speech act obtains.*
By saying "You should absolutely stop smoking" a speaker can indirectly urge the hearer.

(v) *The literal propositional content represents a sincerity condition of the indirect speech act.*
By saying "I am not at all satisfied with your work", a speaker can indirectly complain.

(vi) *The illocutionary force of the indirect speech act has a stronger degree of strength.*
By saying "Reimburse me!", a speaker can make an indirect requirement when it is part of background knowledge that he strongly wants to be reimbursed.

(vii) *The indirect speech act has more preparatory conditions than the literal speech act.*
By saying " Do your home work!" a father can indirectly advize his child when he presupposes that it is very good for him or her.

(viii) *The indirect speech act has more sincerity conditions.*
By saying "I have won against all of them!" a speaker is indirectly boasting when he is obviously very proud of his victory.
(ix) *The indirect speech act has a non literal illocutionary point which is achieved on the literal propositional content.*
By saying imperatively "You will arrive on time" a speaker indirectly tells the hearer to arrive on time in a context where he does not give him any option of refusal.

As in the case of irony, there is an effective method for constructing the indirect speech act. In the simplest cases of exploitation of the maxim of quantity, we proceed as follows in order to infer the indirect speech act:

(1) First, we identify from our background knowledge the proposition P which is the propositional content of all non literal conditions of success and of non defective performance to which the speaker intends to draw the hearer's attention.
(2) If there is an exploitation of the maxim of quantity, the speaker intends to achieve an illocutionary point on the proposition P. For the achievement of an illocutionary point is an essential feature of the performance of speech acts.
(3) The indirect speech act of the utterance is the illocutionary act F(P) whose force F is obtained by adding to the primitive force with that illocutionary point all literal and non literal force components which determine the previous conditions of non defective performance relative to P.
(4) When the speaker intends to draw the hearer's attention to the facts that he achieves several illocutionary points on several propositions, the indirect speech act is the conjunction of all the indirect illocutionary acts which can be obtained in the same way.
(5) As I said earlier, such indirect speech acts are categorical when all their felicity conditions are obviously fulfilled in the conversational background of the utterance. Otherwise, they are conditional on the hearer's acceptance of these conditions.

I will analyze in detail the normal form of derivations that we make in order to understand ironic and indirect speech acts in my next book on *Discourse*. Of course the speaker and the hearer do not go consciously through all the steps of such derivations of non literal speech acts any more than they go consciously through all the steps of the construction of the literal speech acts. However, the existence of such derivations and their generation by effective methods enables pragmatics to explain the creative abilities that speakers have in making and understanding non literal utterances.

3.3 Why Non Literal Speech Acts Are not Detachable but Cancellable

The exploitations of the maxims of quality and quantity are generated by a conflict between facts of the conversational background and the hypothesis that the literal speech act is felicitous or as strong as needed in the context of the utterance. Thus, these exploitations occur if and only if it is part of the background that some felicity conditions of the literal speech act are violated or that the literal speech act is not as strong as required to achieve all the linguistic purposes of the speaker. Such exploitations are totally independent of the form of the sentence which is used by the speaker to express the literal speech act. This is why these non literal speech acts are not detachable. Nevertheless they are in general cancellable. For a speaker cannot attempt to perform such non literal acts in a context of utterance where the conversational background is not in conflict with the hypothesis that the literal speech act is felicitous or as strong as required.

Most sentences of natural languages can be used in possible contexts of utterance without any exploitation of the maxims of quality or quantity. But some sentences are exceptions to that rule. As I said earlier, speakers can never mean to perform the self defeating speech acts expressed by illocutionarily inconsistent sentences such as "I am not myself today". The reason for this is that these sentences express speech acts whose felicity conditions are *a priori* known to be violated. Consequently, the converse of Searle's Principle of Expressibility is false in Pragmatics. It is not true that there exists for every sentence at least one possible context of utterance of that sentence where the speaker's meaning would be identical with the meaning of that sentence. The speaker is always obliged to exploit the maxim of quality when he utters certain sentences.

3.4 Conversational Implicatures of Quality and Quantity

The content of a conversational implicature of quantity is that a non literal speech act that is stronger than the primary illocutionary act of the utterance is not felicitous. When the speaker implies conversationally that he does not perform an illocutionary act, he means to perform non literally the illocutionary denegation of that act. For example, a speaker who answers the question "Do you swear that?" by saying only "I believe it but I am not sure" usually conversationally implies that he does not want to swear and thereby non literally performs an illocutionary denegation. When the speaker implicates conversationally that a non literal illocutionary act is not satisfied, he means in general to deny non literally the propositional content of that act. For example, a speaker who answers the question "Is John's work excellent?" by saying only "It is satisfactory!" often conversationally implies and thereby asserts non literally that John's work is not excellent. Similarly, by implying conversationally that a non literal speech act would be defective, the speaker non literally denies a preparatory or sincerity condition of that act.

The content of a conversational implicature of quality is that a certain non literal speech act is felicitous in the context of the utterance. So a speaker who answers the question "Does Julius have a girlfriend?!" by saying "He is gay" can thereby non literally assert that Julius has no girlfriend.

3.5 There Are Different Ways of Performing Non Literal Speech Acts

First, a speaker can non literally perform a speech act by exploiting one or several conversational maxims as in the cases of indirect speech acts, metaphor or irony. The non literal speech act performed by way of exploiting a conversational maxim in an utterance is the primary speech act of that utterance and by way of performing it, the speaker also performs many other non literal speech acts (with weaker conditions of success). Thus a speaker who indirectly promises help by way of asserting literally that he will help also non literally commits himself to helping. Second, a speaker can also non literally perform one or several secondary illocutionary acts by using the conversational maxims in a context of utterance. But, in that case, these non literal speech acts do not have weaker conditions of success than the primary (literal or non literal) speech act of the utterance. Indeed, certain facts of the speaker and hearer's mutual knowledge of the conversational background which are relatively independent of the hypothesis that the speaker respects the maxims, must always be added to that hypothesis in order that there be a derivation of a conversational implicature. In a context where such facts are not part of the conversational background, the speaker can perform the same primary speech act without making any conversational implicature. For example, the assertion that Julius is gay does not strongly commit the speaker to the assertion that he has no girlfriend. That conversational implicature is cancellable. Indeed, there are conversational backgrounds where gay people are bisexual.

A speaker can both exploit and use conversational maxims in a context of utterance. In this case, he means to perform in addition to a primary non literal speech act another secondary non literal speech act. Thus by saying "I will not do it on that occasion" a speaker can exploit the maxim of quantity in order to commit himself indirectly to refraining from a certain course of action. He can also use the same maxim in order to assert secondarily (by conversational implicature) that he will carry out that action at another moment. (Suppose that he relies on the fact that he has said "on that occasion"). It is important to make a clear distinction between the primary non literal speech act that the speaker performs by exploiting maxims and the secondary non literal speech acts that he performs by using maxims. Contrary to what Grice wrongly assumes, ironical and indirect speech acts are not particular cases of conversational implicatures. Conversational implicatures are always secondary non literal speech acts.

There is an order in the comprehension of speaker meaning in Pragmatics. In order to understand what a speaker means, we must determine first the literal speech act, next (in case the speaker exploits a maxim) the primary non literal speech act and third (in case he is also using a maxim) the conversational implicatures.

References

Austin, J.L. (1962): How to Do Things with Words. Oxford: Clarendon Press.
Bach, K. & R. Harnish (1979): Linguistic Communication and Speech Acts. Cambridge: The MIT Press.
Dascal, M. (1990): "On the Pragmatic Structure of Conversation". In: J.R. Searle et al., eds. (1990), 35-56.

Grice, H.P. (1975): "Logic and Conversation". In: P. Cole & J.L. Morgan, eds.: Syntax and Semantics. Vol. 3, Speech acts. New York: Academic Press, 41-58.
Kasher, A. (1982): "Gricean Inference Revisited". Philosophica 29, III, 25-44.
Montague, R. (1974): Formal Philosophy. New Haven: Yale University Press.
Searle, J.R. (1979): Expression and Meaning. Cambridge: Cambridge University Press.
Searle, J.R. & D. Vanderveken (1985): Foundations of Illocutionary Logic. Cambridge: Cambridge University Press.
Searle, J.R. et al., eds. (1990): (On) Searle on Conversation. Amsterdam: Benjamins.
Sperber D. & D. Wilson (1986): Relevance. Cambridge: Harvard University Press.
Vanderveken, D. (1991): "Non Literal Speech Acts and Conversational Maxims". In: E. Lepore & R. Van Gulick, eds.: John Searle and his Critics. Oxford: Blackwell, 371-384.
Vanderveken, D. (1990-1991): Meaning and Speech Acts. Vol. 1, Principles of Language Use. Vol. 2, Formal Semantics of Success and Satisfaction. Cambridge: Cambridge University Press.
Wittgenstein, L. (1968): Philosophical Investigations. Oxford: Blackwell.

Mitarbeiter dieses Sonderheftes

Tanja Autenrieth
Rheinlandstraße 24
72070 Tübingen
Germany

Kent Bach
San Francisco State University
Department of Philosophy
San Francisco, California 94132
USA

Thomas Becker
Universität München
Institut für Deutsche Philologie
Schellingstraße 3
80799 München
Germany

Diane Blakemore
University of Southampton
School of Modern Languages
Linguistics
Highfield
Southampton
S017 1BJ
United Kingdom

Robyn Carston
Department of Phonetics and Linguistics
University College London
Gower Street
London
WC1E 6BT
United Kingdom

Steven Davis
Philosophy Department
Simon Frazer University
Burnaby, BC.
Canada V5A 1S6

Jörg Hagemann
Universität Hamburg
Germanistisches Seminar
Von-Melle-Park 6
20146 Hamburg
Germany

Robert M. Harnish
Department of Philosophy
Department of Linguistics
University of Arizona
Tucson, Arizona 85721
USA

Josef Klein
Universität Koblenz-Landau
Institut für Germanistik
Rheinau 1
56075 Koblenz
Germany

Frank Liedtke
Heinrich-Heine-Universität Düsseldorf
Germanistisches Seminar
Universitätsstraße 1, Gebäude 23.21
40225 Düsseldorf
Germany

Georg Meggle
Universität Leipzig
Institut für Philosophie
Augustusplatz 9
04109 Leipzig
Germany

Jörg Meibauer
Universität Tübingen
Deutsches Seminar
Wilhelmstraße 50
72074 Tübingen
Germany

Jacques Moeschler / Anne Reboul
La Cure, le Bourg
71250 Sainte-Cécile
France

Beatrice Primus
Universität Stuttgart
Institut für Linguistik
Keplerstraße 17
70174 Stuttgart
Germany

Anne Reboul (s. Jacques Moeschler)

Eckard Rolf
Westfälische Wilhelms-Universität
Institut für Deutsche Philologie I
Johannisstraße 1-4
48143 Münster
Germany

Savas L. Tsohatzidis
Department of Linguistics
Aristotle University of Thessaloniki
Thessaloniki
Greece

Maria Ulkan
Hedwigstraße 17
80636 München
Germany

Daniel Vanderveken
Université du Québec à Trois-Rivières
Department of Philosophy
C.P. 500, Trois-Rivières, Québec,
Canada G9A 5H7

Aus dem Programm Sprachwissenschaft

Eckard Rolf
Illokutionäre Kräfte
Grundbegriffe der Illokutionslogik
1997. 257 S. Kart. DM 49,80
ISBN 3-531-12921-X
Obwohl als DIE Weiterentwicklung der Sprechakttheorie anzusehen, ist die Illokutionslogik auch in Kreisen sprechakttheoretisch interessierter Linguisten und Philosophen bislang nicht gebührend beachtet worden. Um diesem Tatbestand zu begegnen, widmet sich diese Monographie, unter weitgehender Ausblendung rezeptionserschwerender Formalisierungen, denjenigen Aspekten und Problemen der Illokutionslogik, die für an der Sprechakttheorie interessierte Lehrende und Studierende relevant sind.

Eckard Rolf
Sagen und Meinen
Paul Grices Theorie der Konversations-Implikaturen
1994. 269 S. Kart. DM 52,–
ISBN 3-531-12640-7
Die durch den nichtwörtlichen Sprachgebrauch etablierte Indirektheit unserer Kommunikation kann mit Hilfe der von Paul Grice entwickelten Theorie der Konversations-Implikaturen in einer allgemeinen, auf Gesprächs"regeln" Bezug nehmenden Weise erklärt werden. Der von ihm aufgestellte Katalog der Konversationsmaximen erfaßt jedoch nur eine bestimmte Art von Sprachgebrauch: den informationalen. Um auch dem nichtinformationalen Sprachgebrauch gerecht werden zu können, muß der Maximenkatalog erweitert werden. Wie eine solche Erweiterung auszusehen hat, das wird im Zusammenhang einer Darstellung aufgezeigt, die den Weg von der sogenannten nicht-natürlichen Bedeutung bis zur Theorie der Konversations-Implikaturen nachzeichnet.

Ellen Brandner / Gisella Ferraresi (Eds.)
**Language Change
and Generative Grammar**
1996. 292 pp. (Linguistische Berichte, Sonderheft 7/95-96) Softc. DM 80,–
ISBN 3-531-12857-4
In recent years, generative grammar has paid increasing attention to diachronic aspects of syntax, also because the Principles and Parameters approach makes rather strong predictions with respect to language change and possible variation. The V/2 phenomenon found in Germanic and in (old) Romance languages is discussed in several articles from various perspectives. Other contributions cover, among other things, the genitive in Old and Middle High German and morphological Case reduction and its consequences for word order.

Änderungen vorbehalten.
Stand: November 1997

WESTDEUTSCHER VERLAG
Abraham-Lincoln-Str. 46 · 65189 Wiesbaden
Fax (06 11) 78 78 - 400

GPSR Compliance

The European Union's (EU) General Product Safety Regulation (GPSR) is a set of rules that requires consumer products to be safe and our obligations to ensure this.

If you have any concerns about our products, you can contact us on

ProductSafety@springernature.com

In case Publisher is established outside the EU, the EU authorized representative is:

Springer Nature Customer Service Center GmbH
Europaplatz 3
69115 Heidelberg, Germany